sentameNTs™

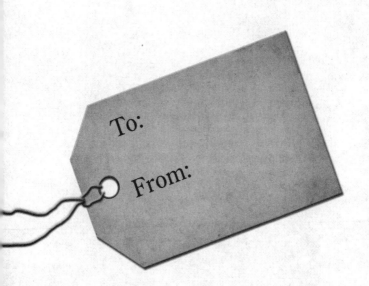

To:

From:

GOD'S WORD® Translation

sentaMeNTs™

New Testament

GOD'S WORD Translation

GREEN KEY BOOKS
Holiday, Florida

© 2007 by Green Key Books.

GOD'S WORD® Translation
© 1995 by God's Word to the Nations.
All rights reserved.

For permission questions or policy information, please write to God's Word to the Nations, PO Box 400, Orange Park, FL 32067. You may also contact them through their web site: www.godsword.org.

"How to Know Jesus Christ" and "Knowing and Sharing Your Story" taken from *Growing Faith* © 2006 by the Luis Palau Association. Used by permission.

Cover images used under license from Shutterstock, Inc.

Published by:
Green Key Books
2514 Aloha Place
Holiday, FL 34691

Printed in the United States of America.

07 08 09 10 11 / 10 9 8 7 6 5 4 3 2 1

Contents

1. God's Plan—Peace and Life

God loves you and wants you to fully experience the peace and life that only he can give.

The Bible says, "God loved the world this way: He gave his only Son so that everyone who believes in him will not die but will have eternal life" (John 3:16).

2. Humanity's Problem—Separation

Being at peace with God is not automatic because human beings by nature are separated from God.

The Bible says, "Because all people have sinned, they have fallen short of God's glory" (Romans 3:23). Romans 6:23 adds: "The payment for sin is death, but the gift that God freely gives is everlasting life found in Christ Jesus our Lord." Humanity has tried to bridge this separation in many ways...without success.

3. God's Remedy—the Cross

God's love bridges the gap of separation between God and humanity. When Jesus Christ died on the cross and rose from the grave, he paid the penalty for our sins.

In the Bible, Jesus Christ says, "I am the way, the truth, and the life. No one goes to the Father except through me" (John 14:6).

4. Our Response—Receive Jesus Christ

God invites us to respond to his love by crossing the bridge through trusting Jesus Christ. This means accepting Christ's death on the cross as payment for our personal sins and receiving him as our Savior and Lord.

The Bible says, "He gave the right to become God's children to everyone who believed in him [Christ]" (John 1:12).

The invitation is to:

Repent (turn from your sins), by faith receive Jesus Christ into your heart and life, and follow him in obedience as the Lord of your life.

What to pray:

God, I know I am a sinner. Right now I repent and turn from my sins. I believe Jesus Christ died for my sins, rose from the grave, and is alive forever. I open the door of my heart and life, receiving Jesus Christ as my Savior. I want to follow him as Lord of my life. Thank you for saving me. Amen.

Believing in Jesus Christ means more than agreeing with what the Bible says about him. Believing in Jesus is choosing to trust only him for eternal life. Good deeds and religious works won't get you into heaven—only Jesus can forgive your sins and give you eternal life.

Briefly describe how you received Jesus Christ as your Savior and how you know for certain that you have eternal life. _____

_____

_____

Now think about what made you realize you need Jesus Christ in your life. What was your life like without him? _____

_____

_____

How is God now changing your life through Jesus Christ? _____

_____

_____

These questions are the pieces that make up your story—your testimony. Learn to share it in sixty seconds or less. You never know when and where someone will need to hear it.

> But dedicate your lives to Christ as Lord. Always be ready to defend your confidence [in God] when anyone asks you to explain it. However, make your defense with gentleness and respect. Keep your conscience clear. Then those who treat the good Christian life you live with contempt will feel ashamed that they have ridiculed you. (1 Peter 3:15–16)

The New Testament

MATTHEW

The Family Line of Jesus Christ

1 ¹ This is the list of ancestors of Jesus Christ, descendant of David and Abraham.

² **Abraham** was the father of Isaac,
  Isaac the father of Jacob,
  Jacob the father of Judah and his brothers.

³ **Judah** and **Tamar** were the father and mother of Perez and Zerah.
  Perez was the father of Hezron,
  Hezron the father of Ram,

⁴ **Ram** the father of Amminadab,
  Amminadab the father of Nahshon,
  Nahshon the father of Salmon.

⁵ **Salmon** and **Rahab** were the father and mother of Boaz.
  Boaz and **Ruth** were the father and mother of Obed.
  Obed was the father of Jesse,

⁶ **Jesse** the father of King David.
  David and **Uriah's wife** ˻Bathsheba˼ were the father and mother of Solomon.

⁷ **Solomon** was the father of Rehoboam,
  Rehoboam the father of Abijah,
  Abijah the father of Asa,

⁸ **Asa** the father of Jehoshaphat,
  Jehoshaphat the father of Joram,
  Joram the father of Uzziah,

⁹ **Uzziah** the father of Jotham,
  Jotham the father of Ahaz,

Ahaz the father of Hezekiah,
10   **Hezekiah** the father of Manasseh,
     Manasseh the father of Amon,
     Amon the father of Josiah.
11   **Josiah** was the father of **Jechoniah** and his brothers.
       They lived at the time when the people were exiled to
         Babylon.

12 After the exile to Babylon,

     Jechoniah became the father of Shealtiel.
     Shealtiel was the father of Zerubbabel,
13   **Zerubbabel** the father of Abiud,
     Abiud the father of Eliakim,
     Eliakim the father of Azor,
14   **Azor** the father of Zadok,
     Zadok the father of Achim,
     Achim the father of Eliud,
15   **Eliud** the father of Eleazar,
     Eleazar the father of Matthan,
     Matthan the father of Jacob.
16   **Jacob** was the father of **Joseph,** who was the husband of
         Mary.
       Mary was the mother of **Jesus,** who is called Christ.

17 So there were

     14 generations from Abraham to David,
     14 generations from David until the exile to Babylon,
     14 generations from the exile until the Messiah.

The Virgin Birth of Jesus

18 The birth of Jesus Christ took place in this way. His mother
Mary had been promised to Joseph in marriage. But before they
were married, Mary realized that she was pregnant by the Holy
Spirit. 19 Her husband Joseph was an honorable man and did not
want to disgrace her publicly. So he decided to break the marriage
agreement with her secretly.

[20] Joseph had this in mind when an angel of the Lord appeared to him in a dream. The angel said to him, "Joseph, descendant of David, don't be afraid to take Mary as your wife. She is pregnant by the Holy Spirit. [21] She will give birth to a son, and you will name him Jesus [He Saves], because he will save his people from their sins." [22] All this happened so that what the Lord had spoken through the prophet came true: [23] "The virgin will become pregnant and give birth to a son, and they will name him Immanuel," which means "God is with us."

[24] When Joseph woke up, he did what the angel of the Lord had commanded him to do. He took Mary to be his wife. [25] He did not have marital relations with her before she gave birth to a son. Joseph named the child Jesus.

The Wise Men Visit

2 [1] Jesus was born in Bethlehem in Judea when Herod was king. After Jesus' birth wise men[a] from the east arrived in Jerusalem. [2] They asked, "Where is the one who was born to be the king of the Jews? We saw his star rising and have come to worship him."

[3] When King Herod and all Jerusalem heard about this, they became disturbed. [4] He called together all the chief priests and scribes and tried to find out from them where the Messiah was supposed to be born.

[5] They told him, "In Bethlehem in Judea. The prophet wrote about this:

[6]   Bethlehem in the land of Judah,
            you are by no means least among the leaders of Judah.
        A leader will come from you.
            He will shepherd my people Israel."

[7] Then Herod secretly called the wise men and found out from them exactly when the star had appeared. [8] As he sent them to

---

[a] 2:1 Or "astrologers."

Bethlehem, he said, "Go and search carefully for the child. When you have found him, report to me so that I may go and worship him too."

[9] After they had heard the king, they started out. The star they had seen rising led them until it stopped over the place where the child was. [10] They were overwhelmed with joy to see the star. [11] When they entered the house, they saw the child with his mother Mary. So they bowed down and worshiped him. Then they opened their treasure chests and offered him gifts of gold, frankincense, and myrrh.[b]

[12] God warned them in a dream not to go back to Herod. So they left for their country by another road.

The Escape to Egypt

[13] After they had left, an angel of the Lord appeared to Joseph in a dream. The angel said to him, "Get up, take the child and his mother, and flee to Egypt. Stay there until I tell you, because Herod intends to search for the child and kill him."

[14] Joseph got up, took the child and his mother, and left for Egypt that night. [15] He stayed there until Herod died. What the Lord had spoken through the prophet came true: "I have called my son out of Egypt."

[16] When Herod saw that the wise men had tricked him, he became furious. He sent soldiers to kill all the boys two years old and younger in or near Bethlehem. This matched the exact time he had learned from the wise men. [17] Then the words spoken through the prophet Jeremiah came true:

[18]   "A sound was heard in Ramah,
             the sound of crying in bitter grief.
         Rachel was crying for her children.
           She refused to be comforted
             because they were dead."

From Egypt to Nazareth

[19] After Herod was dead, an angel of the Lord appeared in a dream to Joseph in Egypt. [20] The angel said to him, "Get up, take

---

[b] 2:11 Myrrh is a fragrant resin used for perfumes, embalming, and deodorizers.

the child and his mother, and go to Israel. Those who tried to kill the child are dead."

²¹ Joseph got up, took the child and his mother, and went to Israel. ²² But when he heard that Archelaus had succeeded his father Herod as king of Judea, Joseph was afraid to go there. Warned in a dream, he left for Galilee ²³ and made his home in a city called Nazareth. So what the prophets had said came true: "He will be called a Nazarene."

John Prepares the Way—Mark 1:1–8; Luke 3:1–18; John 1:19–28

3 ¹ Later, John the Baptizer appeared in the desert of Judea. His message was, ² "Turn to God and change the way you think and act, because the kingdom of heaven is near." ³ Isaiah the prophet spoke about this man when he said,

> "A voice cries out in the desert:
> 'Prepare the way for the Lord!
> Make his paths straight!' "

⁴ John wore clothes made from camel's hair and had a leather belt around his waist. His diet consisted of locusts and wild honey. ⁵ Jerusalem, all Judea, and the whole Jordan Valley went to him. ⁶ As they confessed their sins, he baptized them in the Jordan River. ⁷ But when he saw many Pharisees and Sadducees coming to be baptized, he said to them, "You poisonous snakes! Who showed you how to flee from God's coming anger? ⁸ Do those things that prove you have turned to God and have changed the way you think and act. ⁹ Don't think you can say, 'Abraham is our ancestor.' I can guarantee that God can raise up descendants for Abraham from these stones. ¹⁰ The ax is now ready to cut the roots of the trees. Any tree that doesn't produce good fruit will be cut down and thrown into a fire. ¹¹ I baptize you with water so that you will change the way you think and act. But the one who comes after me is more powerful than I. I am not worthy to remove his sandals. He will baptize you with the Holy Spirit and fire. ¹² His winnowing*ᵃ* shovel is in his hand,

---

ᵃ 3:12 Winnowing is the process of separating husks from grain.

and he will clean up his threshing floor.[b] He will gather his wheat into a barn, but he will burn the husks in a fire that can never be put out."

John Baptizes Jesus—Mark 1:9–11; Luke 3:21–22

[13] Then Jesus appeared. He came from Galilee to the Jordan River to be baptized by John. [14] But John tried to stop him and said, "I need to be baptized by you. Why are you coming to me?"

[15] Jesus answered him, "This is the way it has to be now. This is the proper way to do everything that God requires of us."

Then John gave in to him. [16] After Jesus was baptized, he immediately came up from the water. Suddenly, the heavens were opened, and he saw the Spirit of God coming down as a dove to him. [17] Then a voice from heaven said, "This is my Son, whom I love—my Son with whom I am pleased."

The Temptation of Jesus—Mark 1:12–13; Luke 4:1–13

4 [1] Then the Spirit led Jesus into the desert to be tempted by the devil. [2] Jesus did not eat anything for 40 days and 40 nights. At the end of that time, he was hungry.

[3] The tempter came to him and said, "If you are the Son of God, tell these stones to become loaves of bread."

[4] Jesus answered, "Scripture says, 'A person cannot live on bread alone but on every word that God speaks.' "

[5] Then the devil took him into the holy city and had him stand on the highest part of the temple. [6] He said to Jesus, "If you are the Son of God, jump! Scripture says, 'He will put his angels in charge of you. They will carry you in their hands so that you never hit your foot against a rock.' "

[7] Jesus said to him, "Again, Scripture says, 'Never tempt the Lord your God.' "[a]

[8] Once more the devil took him to a very high mountain and showed him all the kingdoms in the world and their glory. [9] The

---

[b] 3:12 A threshing floor is an outdoor area where grain is separated from its husks.
[a] 4:7 Or "Never put the Lord your God to any test."

devil said to him, "I will give you all this if you will bow down and worship me."

¹⁰ Jesus said to him, "Go away, Satan! Scripture says, 'Worship the Lord your God and serve only him.' "

¹¹ Then the devil left him, and angels came to take care of him.

A Light Has Risen

¹² When Jesus heard that John had been put in prison, he went back to Galilee. ¹³ He left Nazareth and made his home in Capernaum on the shores of the Sea of Galilee. This was in the region of Zebulun and Naphtali. ¹⁴ So what the prophet Isaiah had said came true:

¹⁵   "Land of Zebulun and land of Naphtali,
           on the way to the sea,
               across the Jordan River,
                   Galilee, where foreigners live!
¹⁶   The people who lived in darkness
           have seen a bright light.
       A light has risen
           for those who live in a land overshadowed by death."

¹⁷ From then on, Jesus began to tell people, "Turn to God and change the way you think and act, because the kingdom of heaven is near!"

Calling of the First Disciples—Mark 1:16–20; Luke 5:1–11

¹⁸ As he was walking along the Sea of Galilee, he saw two brothers, Simon (called Peter) and Andrew. They were throwing a net into the sea because they were fishermen. ¹⁹ Jesus said to them, "Come, follow me! I will teach you how to catch people instead of fish." ²⁰ They immediately left their nets and followed him.

²¹ As Jesus went on, he saw two other brothers, James and John, the sons of Zebedee. They were in a boat with their father Zebedee preparing their nets to go fishing. He called them, ²² and they immediately left the boat and their father and followed Jesus.

Spreading the Good News in Galilee—Mark 1:35–39; Luke 4:42–44

²³ Jesus went all over Galilee. He taught in the synagogues and spread the Good News of the kingdom. He also cured every disease and sickness among the people.

²⁴ The news about Jesus spread throughout Syria. People brought him everyone who was sick, those who suffered from any kind of disease or pain. They also brought epileptics, those who were paralyzed, and people possessed by demons, and he cured them all. ²⁵ Large crowds followed him. They came from Galilee, the Ten Cities,ᵇ Jerusalem, Judea, and from across the Jordan River.

The Sermon on a Mountain:
The Beatitudes

5 ¹ When Jesus saw the crowds, he went up a mountain and sat down. His disciples came to him, ² and he began to teach them:

³   "Blessed are those who recognize they are spiritually
            helpless.
         The kingdom of heaven belongs to them.
⁴   Blessed are those who mourn.
         They will be comforted.
⁵   Blessed are those who are gentle.
         They will inherit the earth.
⁶   Blessed are those who hunger and thirst for God's
            approval.
         They will be satisfied.
⁷   Blessed are those who show mercy.
         They will be treated mercifully.
⁸   Blessed are those whose thoughts are pure.
         They will see God.
⁹   Blessed are those who make peace.
         They will be called God's children.
¹⁰   Blessed are those who are persecuted for doing what God
            approves of.

ᵇ 4:25 A federation of ten Greek city states east and west of the Jordan River.

The kingdom of heaven belongs to them.

11 "Blessed are you when people insult you,
persecute you,
lie, and say all kinds of evil things about you because
of me.
12 Rejoice and be glad because you have a great reward in
heaven!
The prophets who lived before you were persecuted in
these ways.

God's People Make a Difference in the World—
Mark 4:21–23; Luke 11:33

13 "You are salt for the earth. But if salt loses its taste, how will
it be made salty again? It is no longer good for anything except to
be thrown out and trampled on by people.

14 "You are light for the world. A city cannot be hidden when it is
located on a hill. **15** No one lights a lamp and puts it under a basket.
Instead, everyone who lights a lamp puts it on a lamp stand. Then
its light shines on everyone in the house. **16** In the same way let
your light shine in front of people. Then they will see the good that
you do and praise your Father in heaven.

Jesus Fulfills the Old Testament Scriptures

17 "Don't ever think that I came to set aside Moses' Teachings
or the Prophets. I didn't come to set them aside but to make them
come true. **18** I can guarantee this truth: Until the earth and the
heavens disappear, neither a period nor a comma will disappear
from Moses' Teachings before everything has come true. **19** So
whoever sets aside any command that seems unimportant and
teaches others to do the same will be unimportant in the kingdom
of heaven. But whoever does and teaches what the commands say
will be called great in the kingdom of heaven. **20** I can guarantee
that unless you live a life that has God's approval and do it more
faithfully than the scribes and Pharisees, you will never enter the
kingdom of heaven.

Jesus Talks About Anger

²¹ "You have heard that it was said to your ancestors, 'Never murder. Whoever murders will answer for it in court.' ²² But I can guarantee that whoever is angry with another believer[a] will answer for it in court. Whoever calls another believer an insulting name will answer for it in the highest court. Whoever calls another believer a fool will answer for it in hellfire.

²³ "So if you are offering your gift at the altar and remember there that another believer has something against you, ²⁴ leave your gift at the altar. First go away and make peace with that person. Then come back and offer your gift.

²⁵ "Make peace quickly with your opponent while you are on the way to court with him. Otherwise, he will hand you over to the judge. Then the judge will hand you over to an officer, who will throw you into prison. ²⁶ I can guarantee this truth: You will never get out until you pay every penny of your fine.

About Sexual Sin

²⁷ "You have heard that it was said, 'Never commit adultery.' ²⁸ But I can guarantee that whoever looks with lust at a woman has already committed adultery in his heart.

²⁹ "So if your right eye causes you to sin, tear it out and throw it away. It is better for you to lose a part of your body than to have all of it thrown into hell. ³⁰ And if your right hand leads you to sin, cut it off and throw it away. It is better for you to lose a part of your body than to have all of it go into hell.

³¹ "It has also been said, 'Whoever divorces his wife must give her a written notice.' ³² But I can guarantee that any man who divorces his wife for any reason other than unfaithfulness makes her look as though she has committed adultery. Whoever marries a woman divorced in this way makes himself look as though he has committed adultery.

---

a 5:22 Some manuscripts and translations add "without a cause."

About Oaths

33 "You have heard that it was said to your ancestors, 'Never break your oath, but give to the Lord what you swore in an oath to give him.' **34** But I tell you don't swear an oath at all. Don't swear an oath by heaven, which is God's throne, **35** or by the earth, which is his footstool, or by Jerusalem, which is the city of the great King. **36** And don't swear an oath by your head. After all, you cannot make one hair black or white. **37** Simply say yes or no. Anything more than that comes from the evil one.

Love Your Enemies—Luke 6:27–36

38 "You have heard that it was said, 'An eye for an eye and a tooth for a tooth.' **39** But I tell you not to oppose an evil person. If someone slaps you on your right cheek, turn your other cheek to him as well. **40** If someone wants to sue you in order to take your shirt, let him have your coat too. **41** If someone forces you to go one mile, go two miles with him. **42** Give to everyone who asks you for something. Don't turn anyone away who wants to borrow something from you.

43 "You have heard that it was said, 'Love your neighbor, and hate your enemy.' **44** But I tell you this: Love your enemies, and pray for those who persecute you. **45** In this way you show that you are children of your Father in heaven. He makes his sun rise on people whether they are good or evil. He lets rain fall on them whether they are just or unjust. **46** If you love those who love you, do you deserve a reward? Even the tax collectors do that! **47** Are you doing anything remarkable if you welcome only your friends? Everyone does that! **48** That is why you must be perfect as your Father in heaven is perfect.

The Sermon on a Mountain Continues:
Don't Do Good Works to Be Praised by People

6 **1** "Be careful not to do your good works in public in order to attract attention. If you do, your Father in heaven will not reward you. ² So when you give to the poor, don't announce it with trumpet fanfare. This is what hypocrites do in the synagogues and on the streets in order to be praised by people. I can guarantee this truth: That will be their only reward. ³ When you give to the poor, don't let your left hand know what your right hand is doing. ⁴ Give your contributions privately. Your Father sees what you do in private. He will reward you.

The Lord's Prayer—Luke 11:1–4

⁵ "When you pray, don't be like hypocrites. They like to stand in synagogues and on street corners to pray so that everyone can see them. I can guarantee this truth: That will be their only reward. ⁶ When you pray, go to your room and close the door. Pray privately to your Father who is with you. Your Father sees what you do in private. He will reward you.

⁷ "When you pray, don't ramble like heathens who think they'll be heard if they talk a lot. ⁸ Don't be like them. Your Father knows what you need before you ask him.

⁹ "This is how you should pray:

> Our Father in heaven,
>   let your name be kept holy.
> 10 Let your kingdom come.
>   Let your will be done on earth
>   as it is done in heaven.
> 11 Give us our daily bread today.
> 12 Forgive us as we forgive others.
> 13 Don't allow us to be tempted.
>   Instead, rescue us from the evil one.ᵃ

¹⁴ "If you forgive the failures of others, your heavenly Father will also forgive you. ¹⁵ But if you don't forgive others, your Father will not forgive your failures.

ᵃ 6:13 Or "rescue us from evil."

Fasting

16 "When you fast, stop looking sad like hypocrites. They put on sad faces to make it obvious that they're fasting. I can guarantee this truth: That will be their only reward. 17 When you fast, wash your face and comb your hair. 18 Then your fasting won't be obvious. Instead, it will be obvious to your Father who is with you in private. Your Father sees what you do in private. He will reward you.

True Riches

19 "Stop storing up treasures for yourselves on earth, where moths and rust destroy and thieves break in and steal. 20 Instead, store up treasures for yourselves in heaven, where moths and rust don't destroy and thieves don't break in and steal. 21 Your heart will be where your treasure is.

22 "The eye is the lamp of the body. So if your eye is unclouded, your whole body will be full of light. 23 But if your eye is evil, your whole body will be full of darkness. If the light in you is darkness, how dark it will be!

24 "No one can serve two masters. He will hate the first master and love the second, or he will be devoted to the first and despise the second. You cannot serve God and wealth.

Stop Worrying—Luke 12:22–34

25 "So I tell you to stop worrying about what you will eat, drink, or wear. Isn't life more than food and the body more than clothes?

26 "Look at the birds. They don't plant, harvest, or gather the harvest into barns. Yet, your heavenly Father feeds them. Aren't you worth more than they?

27 "Can any of you add a single hour to your life by worrying?

28 "And why worry about clothes? Notice how the flowers grow in the field. They never work or spin yarn for clothes. 29 But I say that not even Solomon in all his majesty was dressed like one of these flowers. 30 That's the way God clothes the grass in the field. Today it's alive, and tomorrow it's thrown into an incinerator. So how much more will he clothe you people who have so little faith?

31 "Don't ever worry and say, 'What are we going to eat?' or 'What are we going to drink?' or 'What are we going to wear?' **32** Everyone is concerned about these things, and your heavenly Father certainly knows you need all of them. **33** But first, be concerned about his kingdom and what has his approval. Then all these things will be provided for you.

34 "So don't ever worry about tomorrow. After all, tomorrow will worry about itself. Each day has enough trouble of its own.

The Sermon on a Mountain Continues: Stop Judging—Luke 6:37–42

7 **1** "Stop judging so that you will not be judged. **2** Otherwise, you will be judged by the same standard you use to judge others. The standards you use for others will be applied to you. **3** So why do you see the piece of sawdust in another believer's eye and not notice the wooden beam in your own eye? **4** How can you say to another believer, 'Let me take the piece of sawdust out of your eye,' when you have a beam in your own eye? **5** You hypocrite! First remove the beam from your own eye. Then you will see clearly to remove the piece of sawdust from another believer's eye.

Don't Throw Pearls to Pigs

6 "Don't give what is holy to dogs or throw your pearls to pigs. Otherwise, they will trample them and then tear you to pieces.

The Power of Prayer—Luke 11:5–13

7 "Ask, and you will receive. Search, and you will find. Knock, and the door will be opened for you. **8** Everyone who asks will receive. The one who searches will find, and for the one who knocks, the door will be opened.

9 "If your child asks you for bread, would any of you give him a stone? **10** Or if your child asks for a fish, would you give him a snake? **11** Even though you're evil, you know how to give good gifts to your children. So how much more will your Father in heaven give good things to those who ask him?

The Golden Rule—Luke 6:31

[12] "Always do for other people everything you want them to do for you. That is ˌthe meaning ofˌ Moses' Teachings and the Prophets.

The Narrow Gate

[13] "Enter through the narrow gate because the gate and road that lead to destruction are wide. Many enter through the wide gate. [14] But the narrow gate and the road that lead to life are full of trouble. Only a few people find the narrow gate.

False Prophets—Luke 6:43–45

[15] "Beware of false prophets. They come to you disguised as sheep, but in their hearts they are vicious wolves. [16] You will know them by what they produce.

"People don't pick grapes from thornbushes or figs from thistles, do they? [17] In the same way every good tree produces good fruit, but a rotten tree produces bad fruit. [18] A good tree cannot produce bad fruit, and a rotten tree cannot produce good fruit. [19] Any tree that fails to produce good fruit is cut down and thrown into a fire. [20] So you will know them by what they produce.

[21] "Not everyone who says to me, 'Lord, Lord!' will enter the kingdom of heaven, but only the person who does what my Father in heaven wants. [22] Many will say to me on that day, 'Lord, Lord, didn't we prophesy in your name? Didn't we force out demons and do many miracles by the power and authority of your name?' [23] Then I will tell them publicly, 'I've never known you. Get away from me, you evil people.'

Build on the Rock—Luke 6:47–49

[24] "Therefore, everyone who hears what I say and obeys it will be like a wise person who built a house on rock. [25] Rain poured, and floods came. Winds blew and beat against that house. But it did not collapse, because its foundation was on rock.

[26] "Everyone who hears what I say but doesn't obey it will be like a foolish person who built a house on sand. [27] Rain poured, and

floods came. Winds blew and struck that house. It collapsed, and the result was a total disaster."

²⁸ When Jesus finished this speech, the crowds were amazed at his teachings. ²⁹ Unlike their scribes, he taught them with authority.

Jesus Cures a Man With a Skin Disease—
Mark 1:40–45; Luke 5:12–16

8 ¹ When Jesus came down from the mountain, large crowds followed him.

² A man with a serious skin disease came and bowed down in front of him. The man said to Jesus, "Sir, if you're willing, you can make me clean."*ᵃ*

³ Jesus reached out, touched him, and said, "I'm willing. So be clean!" Immediately, his skin disease went away, and he was clean.

⁴ Jesus said to him, "Don't tell anyone about this! Instead, show yourself to the priest. Then offer the sacrifice Moses commanded as proof to people that you are clean."

A Believing Army Officer—*Luke 7:1–10*

⁵ When Jesus went to Capernaum, a Roman army officer came to beg him for help. ⁶ The officer said, "Sir, my servant is lying at home paralyzed and in terrible pain."

⁷ Jesus said to him, "I'll come to heal him."

⁸ The officer responded, "Sir, I don't deserve to have you come into my house. But just give a command, and my servant will be healed. ⁹ As you know, I'm in a chain of command and have soldiers at my command. I tell one of them, 'Go!' and he goes, and another, 'Come!' and he comes. I tell my servant, 'Do this!' and he does it."

¹⁰ Jesus was amazed when he heard this. He said to those who were following him, "I can guarantee this truth: I haven't found faith as great as this in anyone in Israel. ¹¹ I can guarantee that many will come from all over the world. They will eat with Abraham, Isaac, and Jacob in the kingdom of heaven. ¹² The

---

ᵃ 8:2 "Clean" refers to anything that Moses' Teachings say is presentable to God.

citizens of that kingdom will be thrown outside into the darkness. People will cry and be in extreme pain there.

¹³ Jesus told the officer, "Go! What you believed will be done for you." And at that moment the servant was healed.

Jesus Cures Peter's Mother-in-Law and Many Others—
Mark 1:29–34; Luke 4:38–41

¹⁴ When Jesus went to Peter's house, he saw Peter's mother-in-law in bed with a fever. ¹⁵ Jesus touched her hand, and the fever went away. So she got up and prepared a meal for him.

¹⁶ In the evening the people brought him many who were possessed by demons. He forced the ˎevilˎ spirits out of people with a command and cured everyone who was sick. ¹⁷ So what the prophet Isaiah had said came true: "He took away our weaknesses and removed our diseases."

¹⁸ Now, when Jesus saw a crowd around him, he ordered ˎhis disciplesˎ to cross to the other side of the Sea of Galilee.

What It Takes to Be a Disciple—Luke 9:57–62

¹⁹ A scribe came to him and said, "Teacher, I'll follow you wherever you go."

²⁰ Jesus told him, "Foxes have holes, and birds have nests, but the Son of Man has nowhere to sleep."

²¹ Another disciple said to him, "Sir, first let me go to bury my father."

²² But Jesus told him, "Follow me, and let the dead bury their own dead."

Jesus Calms the Sea—Mark 4:35–41; Luke 8:22–25

²³ Jesus' disciples went with him as he left in a boat. ²⁴ Suddenly, a severe storm came across the sea. The waves were covering the boat. Yet, Jesus was sleeping.

²⁵ So they woke him up, saying, "Lord! Save us! We're going to die!"

[26] Jesus said to them, "Why do you cowards have so little faith?" Then he got up, gave an order to the wind and the sea, and the sea became very calm.

[27] The men were amazed and asked, "What kind of man is this? Even the wind and the sea obey him!"

Jesus Cures Two Demon-Possessed Men—
Mark 5:1–20; Luke 8:26–39

[28] When he arrived in the territory of the Gadarenes on the other side ˻of the Sea of Galilee˼, two men met him. They were possessed by demons and had come out of the tombs. No one could travel along that road because the men were so dangerous.

[29] They shouted, "Why are you bothering us now, Son of God? Did you come here to torture us before it is time?"

[30] A large herd of pigs was feeding in the distance. [31] The demons begged Jesus, "If you're going to force us out, send us into that herd of pigs."

[32] Jesus said to them, "Go!" The demons came out and went into the pigs. Suddenly, the whole herd rushed down the cliff into the sea and died in the water. [33] Those who took care of the pigs ran into the city. There they reported everything, especially about the men possessed by demons.

[34] Everyone from the city went to meet Jesus. When they saw him, they begged him to leave their territory.

Jesus Forgives Sins—Mark 2:1–12; Luke 5:17–26

9 [1] Jesus got into a boat, crossed the sea, and came to his own city. [2] Some people brought him a paralyzed man on a stretcher.

When Jesus saw their faith, he said to the man, "Cheer up, friend! Your sins are forgiven."

[3] Then some of the scribes thought, "He's dishonoring God."

[4] Jesus knew what they were thinking. He asked them, "Why are you thinking evil things? [5] Is it easier to say, 'Your sins are for-

given,' or to say, 'Get up and walk'? ⁶ I want you to know that the Son of Man has authority on earth to forgive sins." Then he said to the paralyzed man, "Get up, pick up your stretcher, and go home."

⁷ So the man got up and went home. ⁸ When the crowd saw this, they were filled with awe and praised God for giving such authority to humans.

Jesus Chooses Matthew to Be a Disciple—
Mark 2:13–17; Luke 5:27–32

⁹ When Jesus was leaving that place, he saw a man sitting in a tax office. The man's name was Matthew. Jesus said to him, "Follow me!" So Matthew got up and followed him.

¹⁰ Later Jesus was having dinner at Matthew's house. Many tax collectors and sinners came to eat with Jesus and his disciples. ¹¹ The Pharisees saw this and asked his disciples, "Why does your teacher eat with tax collectors and sinners?"

¹² When Jesus heard that, he said, "Healthy people don't need a doctor; those who are sick do. ¹³ Learn what this means: 'I want mercy, not sacrifices.' I've come to call sinners, not people who think they have God's approval."

Jesus Is Questioned About Fasting—Mark 2:18–22; Luke 5:33–39

¹⁴ Then John's disciples came to Jesus. They said, "Why do we and the Pharisees fast often but your disciples never do?"

¹⁵ Jesus replied, "Can wedding guests be sad while the groom is still with them? The time will come when the groom will be taken away from them. Then they will fast.

¹⁶ "No one patches an old coat with a new piece of cloth that will shrink. When the patch shrinks, it will rip away from the coat, and the tear will become worse. ¹⁷ Nor do people pour new wine into old wineskins. If they do, the skins burst, the wine runs out, and the skins are ruined. Rather, people pour new wine into fresh skins, and both are saved."

A Synagogue Leader's Daughter and the Woman With Chronic Bleeding—Mark 5:21–43; Luke 8:40–56

¹⁸ A ˌsynagogueˌ leader came to Jesus while he was talking to John's disciples. He bowed down in front of Jesus and said, "My daughter just died. Come, lay your hand on her, and she will live."

¹⁹ Jesus and his disciples got up and followed the man.

²⁰ Then a woman came up behind Jesus and touched the edge of his clothes. She had been suffering from chronic bleeding for twelve years. ²¹ She thought, "If I only touch his clothes, I'll get well."

²² When Jesus turned and saw her he said, "Cheer up, daughter! Your faith has made you well." At that very moment the woman became well.

²³ Jesus came to the ˌsynagogueˌ leader's house. He saw flute players and a noisy crowd. ²⁴ He said to them, "Leave! The girl is not dead. She's sleeping." But they laughed at him.

²⁵ When the crowd had been put outside, Jesus went in, took her hand, and the girl came back to life.

²⁶ The news about this spread throughout that region.

Jesus Heals Two Blind Men

²⁷ When Jesus left that place, two blind men followed him. They shouted, "Have mercy on us, Son of David."

²⁸ Jesus went into a house, and the blind men followed him. He said to them, "Do you believe that I can do this?"

"Yes, Lord," they answered.

²⁹ He touched their eyes and said, "What you have believed will be done for you!" ³⁰ Then they could see.

He warned them, "Don't let anyone know about this!" ³¹ But they went out and spread the news about him throughout that region.

Jesus Forces a Demon out of a Man Who Couldn't Talk

³² As they were leaving, some people brought a man to Jesus. The man was unable to talk because he was possessed by a demon. ³³ But as soon as the demon was forced out, the man began to speak.

The crowds were amazed and said, "We have never seen anything like this in Israel!"

34 But the Pharisees said, "He forces demons out of people with the help of the ruler of demons."

Jesus' Compassion for People

35 Jesus went to all the towns and villages. He taught in the synagogues and spread the Good News of the kingdom. He also cured every disease and sickness.

36 When he saw the crowds, he felt sorry for them. They were troubled and helpless like sheep without a shepherd. **37** Then he said to his disciples, "The harvest is large, but the workers are few. **38** So ask the Lord who gives this harvest to send workers to harvest his crops."

Jesus Appoints Twelve Apostles—Mark 3:13–19; Luke 6:12–16

10 **1** Jesus called his twelve disciples and gave them authority to force evil spirits out of people and to cure every disease and sickness.

2 These are the names of the twelve apostles: first and foremost, Simon (who is called Peter) and his brother Andrew; James and his brother John, the sons of Zebedee; **3** Philip and Bartholomew; Thomas and Matthew the tax collector; James (son of Alphaeus), and Thaddaeus; **4** Simon the Zealot and Judas Iscariot, who later betrayed Jesus.

Jesus Sends Out the Twelve—Mark 6:7–13; Luke 9:1–6

5 Jesus sent these twelve out with the following instructions: "Don't go among people who are not Jewish or into any Samaritan city. **6** Instead, go to the lost sheep of the nation of Israel. **7** As you go, spread this message: 'The kingdom of heaven is near.' **8** Cure the sick, bring the dead back to life, cleanse those with skin diseases, and force demons out of people. Give these things without charging, since you received them without paying.

[9] "Don't take any gold, silver, or even copper coins in your pockets. [10] Don't take a traveling bag for the trip, a change of clothes, sandals, or a walking stick. After all, the worker deserves to have his needs met.

[11] "When you go into a city or village, look for people who will listen to you there. Stay with them until you leave ˻that place˼. [12] When you go into a house, greet the family. [13] If it is a family that listens to you, allow your greeting to stand. But if it is not receptive, take back your greeting. [14] If anyone doesn't welcome you or listen to what you say, leave that house or city, and shake its dust off your feet. [15] I can guarantee this truth: Judgment day will be better for Sodom and Gomorrah than for that city.

[16] "I'm sending you out like sheep among wolves. So be as cunning as snakes but as innocent as doves. [17] Watch out for people who will hand you over to the Jewish courts and whip you in their synagogues. [18] Because of me you will even be brought in front of governors and kings to testify to them and to everyone in the world. [19] When they hand you over ˻to the authorities˼, don't worry about what to say or how to say it. When the time comes, you will be given what to say. [20] Indeed, you're not the ones who will be speaking. The Spirit of your Father will be speaking through you.

[21] "Brother will hand over brother to death; a father will hand over his child. Children will rebel against their parents and kill them. [22] Everyone will hate you because you are committed to me. But the person who patiently endures to the end will be saved. [23] So when they persecute you in one city, flee to another. I can guarantee this truth: Before you have gone through every city in Israel, the Son of Man will come.

[24] "A student is not better than his teacher. Nor is a slave better than his owner. [25] It is enough for a student to become like his teacher and a slave like his owner. If they have called the owner of the house Beelzebul,[a] they will certainly call the family members the same name. [26] So don't be afraid of them. Nothing has been

---

[a] 10:25 *Beelzebul* is another name for the devil. See Matthew 12:24.

covered that will not be exposed. Whatever is secret will be made known. [27] Tell in the daylight what I say to you in the dark. Shout from the housetops what you hear whispered. [28] Don't be afraid of those who kill the body but cannot kill the soul. Instead, fear the one who can destroy both body and soul in hell.

[29] "Aren't two sparrows sold for a penny? Not one of them will fall to the ground without your Father's permission. [30] Every hair on your head has been counted. [31] Don't be afraid! You are worth more than many sparrows.

[32] "So I will acknowledge in front of my Father in heaven that person who acknowledges me in front of others. [33] But I will tell my Father in heaven that I don't know the person who tells others that he doesn't know me.

[34] "Don't think that I came to bring peace to earth. I didn't come to bring peace but conflict. [35] I came to turn a man against his father, a daughter against her mother, a daughter-in-law against her mother-in-law. [36] A person's enemies will be the members of his own family.

[37] "The person who loves his father or mother more than me does not deserve to be my disciple. The person who loves a son or daughter more than me does not deserve to be my disciple. [38] Whoever doesn't take up his cross and follow me doesn't deserve to be my disciple. [39] The person who tries to preserve his life will lose it, but the person who loses his life for me will preserve it.

[40] "The person who welcomes you welcomes me, and the person who welcomes me welcomes the one who sent me. [41] The person who welcomes a prophet as a prophet will receive a prophet's reward. The person who welcomes a righteous person as a righteous person will receive a righteous person's reward. [42] I can guarantee this truth: Whoever gives any of my humble followers a cup of cold water because that person is my disciple will certainly never lose his reward."

11 [1] After Jesus finished giving his twelve disciples these instructions, he moved on from there to teach his message in their cities.

John Sends Two Disciples—Luke 7:18–23

² When John was in prison, he heard about the things Christ had done. So he sent his disciples ³ to ask Jesus, "Are you the one who is coming, or should we look for someone else?"

⁴ Jesus answered John's disciples, "Go back, and tell John what you hear and see: ⁵ Blind people see again, lame people are walking, those with skin diseases are made clean, deaf people hear again, dead people are brought back to life, and poor people hear the Good News. ⁶ Whoever doesn't lose his faith in me is indeed blessed."

Jesus Speaks About John—Luke 7:24–35

⁷ As they were leaving, Jesus spoke to the crowds about John. "What did you go into the desert to see? Tall grass swaying in the wind? ⁸ Really, what did you go to see? A man dressed in fine clothes? Those who wear fine clothes are in royal palaces.

⁹ "Really, what did you go to see? A prophet? Let me tell you that he is far more than a prophet. ¹⁰ John is the one about whom Scripture says,

'I'm sending my messenger ahead of you
to prepare the way in front of you.'

¹¹ "I can guarantee this truth: Of all the people ever born, no one is greater than John the Baptizer. Yet, the least important person in the kingdom of heaven is greater than John. ¹² From the time of John the Baptizer until now, the kingdom of heaven has been forcefully advancing, and forceful people have been seizing it. ¹³ All the Prophets and Moses' Teachings prophesied up to the time of John. ¹⁴ If you are willing to accept their message, John is the Elijah who was to come. ¹⁵ Let the person who has ears listen!

¹⁶ "How can I describe the people who are living now? They are like children who sit in the marketplaces and shout to other children,

¹⁷   'We played music for you,
            but you didn't dance.

We sang a funeral song,
        but you didn't show any sadness.'

18 "John came neither eating nor drinking, and people say, 'There's a demon in him!' **19** The Son of Man came eating and drinking, and people say, 'Look at him! He's a glutton and a drunk, a friend of tax collectors and sinners!'

"Yet, wisdom is proved right by its actions."

Jesus Warns Chorazin, Bethsaida, and Capernaum

20 Then Jesus denounced the cities where he had worked most of his miracles because they had not changed the way they thought and acted. **21** "How horrible it will be for you, Chorazin! How horrible it will be for you, Bethsaida! If the miracles worked in you had been worked in Tyre and Sidon, they would have changed the way they thought and acted long ago in sackcloth and ashes. **22** I can guarantee that judgment day will be better for Tyre and Sidon than for you. **23** And you, Capernaum, will you be lifted to heaven? No, you will go down to hell! If the miracles that had been worked in you had been worked in Sodom, it would still be there today. **24** I can guarantee that judgment day will be better for Sodom than for you."

Jesus Praises the Father and Invites Disciples to Come to Him

25 At that time Jesus said, "I praise you, Father, Lord of heaven and earth, for hiding these things from wise and intelligent people and revealing them to little children. **26** Yes, Father, this is what pleased you.

27 "My Father has turned everything over to me. Only the Father knows the Son. And no one knows the Father except the Son and those to whom the Son is willing to reveal him.

28 "Come to me, all who are tired from carrying heavy loads, and I will give you rest. **29** Place my yoke[a] over your shoulders,

---

[a] 11:29 A yoke is a wooden bar placed over the necks of work animals so that they can pull plows or carts.

and learn from me, because I am gentle and humble. Then you will find rest for yourselves [30] because my yoke is easy and my burden is light."

Jesus Has Authority Over the Day of Worship—
Mark 2:23–28; Luke 6:1–5

12 [1] Then on a day of worship Jesus walked through the grain fields. His disciples were hungry and began to pick the heads of grain to eat.

[2] When the Pharisees saw this, they said to him, "Look! Your disciples are doing something that is not right to do on the day of worship."

[3] Jesus asked them, "Haven't you read what David did when he and his men were hungry? [4] Haven't you read how he went into the house of God and ate[a] the bread of the presence? He and his men had no right to eat those loaves. Only the priests have that right. [5] Or haven't you read in Moses' Teachings that on the day of worship the priests in the temple do things they shouldn't on the day of worship yet remain innocent? [6] I can guarantee that something[b] greater than the temple is here. [7] If you had known what 'I want mercy, not sacrifices' means, you would not have condemned innocent people.

[8] "The Son of Man has authority over the day of worship."

Jesus Heals on the Day of Worship—Mark 3:1–6; Luke 6:6–11

[9] Jesus moved on from there and went into a synagogue. [10] A man with a paralyzed hand was there. The people asked Jesus whether it was right to heal on a day of worship so that they could accuse him of doing something wrong.

[11] Jesus said to them, "Suppose one of you has a sheep. If it falls into a pit on a day of worship, wouldn't you take hold of it and lift it out? [12] Certainly, a human is more valuable than a sheep! So it is right to do good on the day of worship."

---

[a] 12:4 Some manuscripts and translations read "they ate."   [b] 12:6 Some manuscripts and translations read "someone."

¹³ Then he said to the man, "Hold out your hand." The man held it out, and it became normal again, as healthy as the other.

¹⁴ The Pharisees left and plotted to kill Jesus. ¹⁵ He knew about this, so he left that place.

Jesus Is God's Servant

Many people followed him, and he cured all of them. ¹⁶ He also ordered them not to tell people who he was. ¹⁷ So what the prophet Isaiah had said came true:

¹⁸   "Here is my servant
     whom I have chosen,
      whom I love,
        and in whom I delight.
  I will put my Spirit on him,
    and he will announce justice to the nations.
¹⁹   He will not quarrel or shout,
    and no one will hear his voice in the streets.
²⁰   He will not break off a damaged cattail.
    He will not even put out a smoking wick
      until he has made justice victorious.
²¹   The nations will have hope because of him."

Jesus Is Accused of Working With Beelzebul—
Mark 3:20–30; Luke 11:14–23

²² Then some people brought Jesus a man possessed by a demon. The demon made the man blind and unable to talk. Jesus cured him so that he could talk and see.

²³ The crowds were all amazed and said, "Can this man be the Son of David?" ²⁴ When the Pharisees heard this, they said, "This man can force demons out of people only with the help of Beelzebul, the ruler of demons."

²⁵ Since Jesus knew what they were thinking, he said to them, "Every kingdom divided against itself is ruined. And every city or household divided against itself will not last. ²⁶ If Satan forces Satan out, he is divided against himself. How, then, can his kingdom last?

²⁷ If I force demons out of people with the help of Beelzebul, who helps your followers force them out? That's why they will be your judges. ²⁸ But if I force demons out with the help of God's Spirit, then the kingdom of God has come to you. ²⁹ How can anyone go into a strong man's house and steal his property? First he must tie up the strong man. Then he can go through his house and steal his property.

³⁰ "Whoever isn't with me is against me. Whoever doesn't gather with me scatters. ³¹ So I can guarantee that people will be forgiven for any sin or cursing. However, cursing the Spirit will not be forgiven. ³² Whoever speaks a word against the Son of Man will be forgiven. But whoever speaks against the Holy Spirit will not be forgiven in this world or the next.

³³ "Make a tree good, and then its fruit will be good. Or make a tree rotten, and then its fruit will be rotten. A person can recognize a tree by its fruit. ³⁴ You poisonous snakes! How can you evil people say anything good? Your mouth says what comes from inside you. ³⁵ Good people do the good things that are in them. But evil people do the evil things that are in them.

³⁶ "I can guarantee that on judgment day people will have to give an account of every careless word they say. ³⁷ By your words you will be declared innocent, or by your words you will be declared guilty."

The Sign of Jonah—Luke 11:29–32, 24–26

³⁸ Then some scribes and Pharisees said, "Teacher, we want you to show us a miraculous sign."

³⁹ He responded, "The people of an evil and unfaithful era look for a miraculous sign. But the only sign they will get is the sign of the prophet Jonah. ⁴⁰ Just as Jonah was in the belly of a huge fish for three days and three nights, so the Son of Man will be in the heart of the earth for three days and three nights. ⁴¹ The men of Nineveh will stand up with you at the time of judgment and will condemn you, because they turned to God and changed the way they thought and acted when Jonah spoke his message. But look, someone greater than Jonah is here! ⁴² The queen from the south will stand up at

the time of judgment with you. She will condemn you, because she came from the ends of the earth to hear Solomon's wisdom. But look, someone greater than Solomon is here!

⁴³ "When an evil spirit comes out of a person, it goes through dry places looking for a place to rest. But it doesn't find any. ⁴⁴ Then it says, 'I'll go back to the home I left.' When it arrives, it finds the house unoccupied, swept clean, and in order. ⁴⁵ Then it goes and brings along seven other spirits more evil than itself. They enter and take up permanent residence there. In the end the condition of that person is worse than it was before. That is what will happen to the evil people of this day."

The True Family of Jesus—Mark 3:31–35; Luke 8:19–21

⁴⁶ While Jesus was still talking to the crowds, his mother and brothers were standing outside. They wanted to talk to him. ⁴⁷ Someone told him, "Your mother and your brothers are standing outside. They want to talk to you."

⁴⁸ He replied to the man speaking to him, "Who is my mother, and who are my brothers?" ⁴⁹ Pointing with his hand at his disciples, he said, "Look, here are my mother and my brothers. ⁵⁰ Whoever does what my Father in heaven wants is my brother and sister and mother."

A Story About a Farmer—Mark 4:1–20; Luke 8:4–15

13 ¹ That same day Jesus left the house and sat down by the Sea of Galilee. ² The crowd that gathered around him was so large that he got into a boat. He sat in the boat while the entire crowd stood on the shore. ³ Then he used stories as illustrations to tell them many things.

He said, "Listen! A farmer went to plant seed. ⁴ Some seeds were planted along the road, and birds came and devoured them. ⁵ Other seeds were planted on rocky ground, where there was little soil. The plants sprouted quickly because the soil wasn't deep. ⁶ But when the sun came up, they were scorched. They withered because their roots weren't deep enough. ⁷ Other seeds were planted among thornbushes, and the thornbushes grew up and choked them. **8** But other seeds were planted on good ground and produced grain. They produced one hundred, sixty, or thirty times as much as was planted. **9** Let the person who has ears listen!"

10 The disciples asked him, "Why do you use stories as illustrations when you speak to people?"

11 Jesus answered, "Knowledge about the mysteries of the kingdom of heaven has been given to you. But it has not been given to the crowd. **12** Those who understand ˌthese mysteriesˌ will be given ˌmore knowledgeˌ, and they will excel ˌin understanding themˌ. However, some people don't understand ˌthese mysteriesˌ. Even what they understand will be taken away from them. **13** This is why I speak to them this way. They see, but they're blind. They hear, but they don't listen. They don't even try to understand. **14** So they make Isaiah's prophecy come true:

'You will hear clearly but never understand.
You will see clearly but never comprehend.
15   These people have become close-minded
            and hard of hearing.
            They have shut their eyes
               so that their eyes never see.
            Their ears never hear.
            Their minds never understand.
            And they never return to me for healing!'

16 "Blessed are your eyes because they see and your ears because they hear. **17** I can guarantee this truth: Many prophets and many of God's people longed to see what you see but didn't see it, to hear what you hear but didn't hear it.

18 "Listen to what the story about the farmer means. **19** Someone hears the word about the kingdom but doesn't understand it. The evil one comes at once and snatches away what was planted in him. This is what the seed planted along the road illustrates. **20** The seed planted on rocky ground ˌis the person whoˌ hears the word and accepts it at once with joy. **21** Since he doesn't have any root,

he lasts only a little while. When suffering or persecution comes
along because of the word, he immediately falls ⌞from faith⌟. 22
The seed planted among thornbushes ⌞is another person who⌟
hears the word. But the worries of life and the deceitful pleasures
of riches choke the word so that it can't produce anything. 23 But
the seed planted on good ground ⌞is the person who⌟ hears and
understands the word. This type produces crops. They produce
one hundred, sixty, or thirty times as much as was planted."

A Story About Weeds in the Wheat

24 Jesus used another illustration. He said, "The kingdom of
heaven is like a man who planted good seed in his field. 25 But
while people were asleep, his enemy planted weeds in the wheat
field and went away. 26 When the wheat came up and formed ker-
nels, weeds appeared.

27 "The owner's workers came to him and asked, 'Sir, didn't you
plant good seed in your field? Where did the weeds come from?'

28 "He told them, 'An enemy did this.'

"His workers asked him, 'Do you want us to pull out the
weeds?'

29 "He replied, 'No. If you pull out the weeds, you may pull out the
wheat with them. 30 Let both grow together until the harvest. When
the grain is cut, I will tell the workers to gather the weeds first and
tie them in bundles to be burned. But I'll have them bring the wheat
into my barn.' "

Stories About a Mustard Seed and Yeast—Mark 4:30–34; Luke 13:18–21

31 Jesus used another illustration. He said, "The kingdom of
heaven is like a mustard seed that someone planted in a field. 32 It's
one of the smallest seeds. However, when it has grown, it is taller
than the garden plants. It becomes a tree that is large enough for
birds to nest in its branches."

33 He used another illustration. "The kingdom of heaven is like
yeast that a woman mixed into a large amount of flour until the
yeast worked its way through all the dough."

³⁴ Jesus used illustrations to tell the crowds all these things. He did not tell them anything without illustrating it with a story. ³⁵ So what the prophet had said came true:

> "I will open my mouth to illustrate points.
> I will tell what has been hidden since the world was made."

The Meaning of the Weeds in the Wheat

³⁶ When Jesus had sent the people away, he went into the house. His disciples came to him and said, "Explain what the illustration of the weeds in the field means."

³⁷ He answered, "The one who plants the good seeds is the Son of Man. ³⁸ The field is the world. The good seeds are those who belong to the kingdom. The weeds are those who belong to the evil one. ³⁹ The enemy who planted them is the devil. The harvest is the end of the world. The workers are angels. ⁴⁰ Just as weeds are gathered and burned, so it will be at the end of time. ⁴¹ The Son of Man will send his angels. They will gather everything in his kingdom that causes people to sin and everyone who does evil. ⁴² The angels will throw them into a blazing furnace. People will cry and be in extreme pain there. ⁴³ Then the people who have God's approval will shine like the sun in their Father's kingdom. Let the person who has ears listen!

Stories About a Treasure, a Merchant, and a Net

⁴⁴ "The kingdom of heaven is like a treasure buried in a field. When a man discovered it, he buried it again. He was so delighted with it that he went away, sold everything he had, and bought that field.

⁴⁵ "Also, the kingdom of heaven is like a merchant who was searching for fine pearls. ⁴⁶ When he found a valuable pearl, he went away, sold everything he had, and bought it.

⁴⁷ "Also, the kingdom of heaven is like a net that was thrown into the sea. It gathered all kinds of fish. ⁴⁸ When it was full, they pulled it to the shore. Then they sat down, gathered the good fish

into containers, and threw the bad ones away. ⁴⁹ The same thing will happen at the end of time. The angels will go out and separate the evil people from people who have God's approval. ⁵⁰ Then the angels will throw the evil people into a blazing furnace. They will cry and be in extreme pain there.

⁵¹ "Have you understood all of this?"

"Yes," they answered.

⁵² So Jesus said to them, "That is why every scribe who has become a disciple of the kingdom of heaven is like a home owner. He brings new and old things out of his treasure chest."

⁵³ When Jesus had finished these illustrations, he left that place.

Nazareth Rejects Jesus—Mark 6:1–6; Luke 4:14–30

⁵⁴ Jesus went to his hometown and taught the people in the synagogue in a way that amazed them. People were asking, "Where did this man get this wisdom and the power to do these miracles? ⁵⁵ Isn't this the carpenter's son? Isn't his mother's name Mary? Aren't his brothers' names James, Joseph, Simon, and Judas? ⁵⁶ And aren't all his sisters here with us? Where, then, did this man get all this?" ⁵⁷ So they took offense at him.

But Jesus said to them, "The only place a prophet isn't honored is in his hometown and in his own house."

⁵⁸ He didn't work many miracles there because of their lack of faith.

Recalling John's Death—Mark 6:14–29; Luke 9:7–9

14 ¹ At that time Herod, ruler of Galilee, heard the news about Jesus. ² He said to his officials, "This is John the Baptizer! He has come back to life. That's why he has the power to perform these miracles."

³ Herod had arrested John, tied him up, and put him in prison. Herod did this for Herodias, the wife of his brother Philip. ⁴ John had been telling Herod, "It's not right for you to be married to her." ⁵ So Herod wanted to kill John. However, he was afraid of the people because they thought John was a prophet.

⁶ When Herod celebrated his birthday, Herodias' daughter danced for his guests. Herod was so delighted with her that ⁷ he swore he would give her anything she wanted.

⁸ Urged by her mother, she said, "Give me the head of John the Baptizer on a platter."

⁹ The king regretted his promise. But because of his oath and his guests, he ordered that her wish be granted. ¹⁰ He had John's head cut off in prison. ¹¹ So the head was brought on a platter and given to the girl, who took it to her mother.

¹² John's disciples came for the body and buried it. Then they went to tell Jesus.

Jesus Feeds More Than Five Thousand—
Mark 6:30–44; Luke 9:10–17; John 6:1–14

¹³ When Jesus heard about John, he left in a boat and went to a place where he could be alone. The crowds heard about this and followed him on foot from the cities. ¹⁴ When Jesus got out of the boat, he saw a large crowd. He felt sorry for them and cured their sick people.

¹⁵ In the evening the disciples came to him. They said, "No one lives around here, and it's already late. Send the crowds to the villages to buy food for themselves."

¹⁶ Jesus said to them, "They don't need to go away. You give them something to eat."

¹⁷ They told him, "All we have here are five loaves of bread and two fish."

¹⁸ Jesus said, "Bring them to me."

¹⁹ Then he ordered the people to sit down on the grass. After he took the five loaves and the two fish, he looked up to heaven and blessed the food. He broke the loaves apart, gave them to the disciples, and they gave them to the people. ²⁰ All of them ate as much as they wanted. When they picked up the leftover pieces, they filled twelve baskets.

²¹ About five thousand men had eaten. (This number does not include the women and children who had eaten.)

Jesus Walks on the Sea—Mark 6:45–56; John 6:15–21

²² Jesus quickly made his disciples get into a boat and cross to the other side ahead of him while he sent the people away. ²³ After sending the people away, he went up a mountain to pray by himself. When evening came, he was there alone.

²⁴ The boat, now hundreds of yards from shore, was being thrown around by the waves because it was going against the wind.

²⁵ Between three and six o'clock in the morning, he came to them. He was walking on the sea. ²⁶ When the disciples saw him walking on the sea, they were terrified. They said, "It's a ghost!" and began to scream because they were afraid.

²⁷ Immediately, Jesus said, "Calm down! It's me. Don't be afraid!" ²⁸ Peter answered, "Lord, if it is you, order me to come to you on the water."

²⁹ Jesus said, "Come!" So Peter got out of the boat and walked on the water toward Jesus. ³⁰ But when he noticed how strong the wind was, he became afraid and started to sink. He shouted, "Lord, save me!"

³¹ Immediately, Jesus reached out, caught hold of him, and said, "You have so little faith! Why did you doubt?"

³² When they got into the boat, the wind stopped blowing. ³³ The men in the boat bowed down in front of Jesus and said, "You are truly the Son of God."

³⁴ They crossed the sea and landed at Gennesaret. ³⁵ The men there recognized Jesus and sent messengers all around the countryside. The people brought him everyone who was sick. ³⁶ They begged him to let them touch just the edge of his clothes. Everyone who touched his clothes was made well.

Jesus Challenges the Pharisees' Traditions—Mark 7:1–23

15 ¹ Then some Pharisees and scribes came from Jerusalem to Jesus. They asked, ² "Why do your disciples break the traditions of our ancestors? They do not wash their hands before they eat."

³ He answered them, "Why do you break the commandment of God because of your traditions? ⁴ For example, God said, 'Honor

your father and your mother' and 'Whoever curses father or mother must be put to death.' [5] But you say that whoever tells his father or mother, 'I have given to God whatever support you might have received from me,' [6] does not have to honor his father. Because of your traditions you have destroyed the authority of God's word. [7] You hypocrites! Isaiah was right when he prophesied about you:

[8] 'These people honor me with their lips,
    but their hearts are far from me.
[9] Their worship of me is pointless,
    because their teachings are rules made by humans.' "

[10] Then he called the crowd and said to them, "Listen and try to understand! [11] What goes into a person's mouth doesn't make him unclean.[a] It's what comes out of the mouth that makes a person unclean."

[12] Then the disciples came and said to him, "Do you realize that when the Pharisees heard your statement they were offended?"

[13] He answered, "Any plant that my heavenly Father did not plant will be uprooted. [14] Leave them alone! They are blind leaders. When one blind person leads another, both will fall into the same pit."

[15] Peter said to him, "Explain this illustration to us."

[16] Jesus said, "Don't you understand yet? [17] Don't you know that whatever goes into the mouth goes into the stomach and then into a toilet? [18] But whatever goes out of the mouth comes from within, and that's what makes a person unclean. [19] Evil thoughts, murder, adultery, ˏotherˎ sexual sins, stealing, lying, and cursing come from within. [20] These are the things that make a person unclean. But eating without washing one's hands doesn't make a person unclean."

The Faith of a Canaanite Woman—Mark 7:24–30

[21] Jesus left that place and went to the region of Tyre and Sidon.

[22] A Canaanite woman from that territory came ˏto himˎ and began to shout, "Have mercy on me, Lord, Son of David! My daughter is tormented by a demon."

---

[a] 15:11 "Unclean" refers to anything that Moses' Teachings say is not presentable to God.

²³ But he did not answer her at all. Then his disciples came to him and urged him, "Send her away. She keeps shouting behind us."

²⁴ Jesus responded, "I was sent only to the lost sheep of the nation of Israel."

²⁵ She came to him, bowed down, and said, "Lord, help me!"

²⁶ Jesus replied, "It's not right to take the children's food and throw it to the dogs."

²⁷ She said, "You're right, Lord. But even the dogs eat scraps that fall from their masters' tables."

²⁸ Then Jesus answered her, "Woman, you have strong faith! What you wanted will be done for you." At that moment her daughter was cured.

²⁹ Jesus moved on from there and went along the Sea of Galilee. Then he went up a mountain and sat there.

³⁰ A large crowd came to him, bringing with them the lame, blind, disabled, those unable to talk, and many others. They laid them at his feet, and he cured them. ³¹ The crowd was amazed to see mute people talking, the disabled cured, the lame walking, and the blind seeing. So they praised the God of Israel.

Jesus Feeds More Than Four Thousand—Mark 8:1–10

³² Jesus called his disciples and said, "I feel sorry for the people. They have been with me three days now and have nothing to eat. I don't want to send them away hungry, or they may become exhausted on their way home."

³³ His disciples asked him, "Where could we get enough bread to feed such a crowd in this place where no one lives?"

³⁴ Jesus asked them, "How many loaves of bread do you have?"

They answered, "Seven, and a few small fish."

³⁵ He ordered the crowd to sit down on the ground. ³⁶ He took the seven loaves and the fish and gave thanks to God. Then he broke the bread and gave it to the disciples, and they gave the bread and fish to the people.

³⁷ All of them ate as much as they wanted. The disciples picked up the leftover pieces and filled seven large baskets. ³⁸ Four thou-

sand men had eaten. (This number does not include the women and children who had eaten.)

39 After he sent the people on their way, Jesus stepped into the boat and came to the territory of Magadan.

The Pharisees Ask For a Sign From Heaven—Mark 8:11–13a

16 **1** The Pharisees and Sadducees came to test Jesus. So they asked him to show them a miraculous sign from heaven.

2 He responded to them, "In the evening you say that the weather will be fine because the sky is red. **3** And in the morning you say that there will be a storm today because the sky is red and overcast. You can forecast the weather by judging the appearance of the sky, but you cannot interpret the signs of the times.

4 "Evil and unfaithful people look for a miraculous sign. But the only sign they will be given is that of Jonah."

Then he left them standing there and went away.

The Yeast of the Pharisees—Mark 8:13b–21

5 The disciples had forgotten to take any bread along when they went to the other side of the Sea of Galilee.

6 Jesus said to them, "Be careful! Watch out for the yeast of the Pharisees and Sadducees!"

7 The disciples had been discussing among themselves that they had not taken any bread along.

8 Jesus knew about their conversation and asked, "Why are you discussing among yourselves that you don't have any bread? You have so little faith! **9** Don't you understand yet? Don't you remember the five loaves for the five thousand and how many baskets you filled? **10** Don't you remember the seven loaves for the four thousand and how many large baskets you filled? **11** Why don't you understand that I wasn't talking to you about bread? Watch out for the yeast of the Pharisees and Sadducees!"

12 Then they understood that he didn't say to watch out for the yeast in bread, but to watch out for the teachings of the Pharisees and Sadducees.

Peter Declares His Belief About Jesus—Mark 8:27–30; Luke 9:18–21

¹³ When Jesus came to the region of Caesarea Philippi, he asked his disciples, "Who do people say the Son of Man is?"

¹⁴ They answered, "Some say you are John the Baptizer, others Elijah, still others Jeremiah or one of the prophets."

¹⁵ He asked them, "But who do you say I am?"

¹⁶ Simon Peter answered, "You are the Messiah, the Son of the living God!"

¹⁷ Jesus replied, "Simon, son of Jonah, you are blessed! No human revealed this to you, but my Father in heaven revealed it to you. ¹⁸ You are Peter, and I can guarantee that on this rock[a] I will build my church. And the gates of hell will not overpower it. ¹⁹ I will give you the keys of the kingdom of heaven. Whatever you imprison, God will imprison. And whatever you set free, God will set free."

²⁰ Then he strictly ordered the disciples not to tell anyone that he was the Messiah.

*Jesus Foretells That He Will Die and Come Back to Life—
Mark 8:31–33; Luke 9:22*

²¹ From that time on Jesus began to inform his disciples that he had to go to Jerusalem. There he would have to suffer a lot because of the leaders, chief priests, and scribes. He would be killed, but on the third day he would be brought back to life.

²² Peter took him aside and objected to this. He said, "Heaven forbid, Lord! This must never happen to you!"

²³ But Jesus turned and said to Peter, "Get out of my way, Satan! You are tempting me to sin. You aren't thinking the way God thinks but the way humans think."

What It Means to Follow Jesus—Mark 8:34–9:1; Luke 9:23–27

²⁴ Then Jesus said to his disciples, "Those who want to come with me must say no to the things they want, pick up their crosses, and follow me. ²⁵ Those who want to save their lives will lose them.

---

a 16:18 In Greek there is a play on words between *petros* (Peter or pebble) and *petra* (rock).

But those who lose their lives for me will find them. ²⁶ What good will it do for people to win the whole world and lose their lives? Or what will a person give in exchange for life? ²⁷ The Son of Man will come with his angels in his Father's glory. Then he will pay back each person based on what that person has done. ²⁸ I can guarantee this truth: Some people who are standing here will not die until they see the Son of Man coming in his kingdom."

Moses and Elijah Appear With Jesus—Mark 9:2–13; Luke 9:28–36

17 ¹ After six days Jesus took Peter, James, and John (the brother of James) and led them up a high mountain where they could be alone.

² Jesus' appearance changed in front of them. His face became as bright as the sun and his clothes as white as light. ³ Suddenly, Moses and Elijah appeared to them and were talking with Jesus.

⁴ Peter said to Jesus, "Lord, it's good that we're here. If you want, I'll put up three tents here—one for you, one for Moses, and one for Elijah."

⁵ He was still speaking when a bright cloud overshadowed them. Then a voice came out of the cloud and said, "This is my Son, whom I love and with whom I am pleased. Listen to him!"

⁶ The disciples were terrified when they heard this and fell facedown on the ground. ⁷ But Jesus touched them and said, "Get up, and don't be afraid!" ⁸ As they raised their heads, they saw no one but Jesus.

⁹ On their way down the mountain, Jesus ordered them, "Don't tell anyone what you have seen. Wait until the Son of Man has been brought back to life."

¹⁰ So the disciples asked him, "Why do the scribes say that Elijah must come first?"

¹¹ Jesus answered, "Elijah is coming and will put everything in order again. ¹² Actually, I can guarantee that Elijah has already come. Yet, people treated him as they pleased because they didn't recognize him. In the same way they're going to make the Son of Man suffer."

¹³ Then the disciples understood that he was talking about John the Baptizer.

Jesus Cures a Demon-Possessed Boy—Mark 9:14–29; Luke 9:37–43a

¹⁴ When they came to a crowd, a man came up to Jesus, knelt in front of him, ¹⁵ and said, "Sir, have mercy on my son. He suffers from seizures. Often he falls into fire or water. ¹⁶ I brought him to your disciples, but they couldn't cure him."

¹⁷ Jesus replied, "You unbelieving and corrupt generation! How long must I be with you? How long must I put up with you? Bring him here to me!"

¹⁸ Jesus ordered the demon to come out of the boy. At that moment the boy was cured.

¹⁹ Then the disciples came to Jesus privately and asked, "Why couldn't we force the demon out of the boy?"

²⁰ He told them, "Because you have so little faith. I can guarantee this truth: If your faith is the size of a mustard seed, you can say to this mountain, 'Move from here to there,' and it will move. Nothing will be impossible for you."ᵃ

Jesus Again Foretells That He Will Die and Come Back to Life— Mark 9:30–32; Luke 9:43b–45

²² While they were traveling together in Galilee, Jesus told them, "The Son of Man will be betrayed and handed over to people. ²³ They will kill him, but on the third day he will be brought back to life." Then the disciples became very sad.

Paying the Temple Tax

²⁴ When they came to Capernaum, the collectors of the temple tax came to Peter. They asked him, "Doesn't your teacher pay the temple tax?"

²⁵ "Certainly," he answered.

ᵃ 17:20 Some manuscripts and translations add verse 21: "However, this kind ⌊of demon⌋ goes away only by prayer and fasting."

Peter went into the house. Before he could speak, Jesus asked him, "What do you think, Simon? From whom do the kings of the world collect fees or taxes? Is it from their family members or from other people?"

²⁶ "From other people," Peter answered.

Jesus said to him, "Then the family members are exempt. ²⁷ However, so that we don't create a scandal, go to the sea and throw in a hook. Take the first fish that you catch. Open its mouth, and you will find a coin. Give that coin to them for you and me."

Greatness in the Kingdom—Mark 9:33–37; Luke 9:46–48

18 ¹ At that time the disciples came to Jesus and asked, "Who is greatest in the kingdom of heaven?"

² He called a little child and had him stand among them. ³ Then he said to them, "I can guarantee this truth: Unless you change and become like little children, you will never enter the kingdom of heaven. ⁴ Whoever becomes like this little child is the greatest in the kingdom of heaven. ⁵ And whoever welcomes a child like this in my name welcomes me.

Causing Others to Lose Faith—Mark 9:42–50; Luke 17:1–4

⁶ "These little ones believe in me. It would be best for the person who causes one of them to lose faith to be drowned in the sea with a large stone hung around his neck. ⁷ How horrible it will be for the world because it causes people to lose their faith. Situations that cause people to lose their faith will arise. How horrible it will be for the person who causes someone to lose his faith!

⁸ "If your hand or your foot causes you to lose your faith, cut it off and throw it away. It is better for you to enter life disabled or injured than to have two hands or two feet and be thrown into everlasting fire. ⁹ If your eye causes you to lose your faith, tear it out and throw it away. It is better for you to enter life with one eye than to have two eyes and be thrown into hellfire.

¹⁰ "Be careful not to despise these little ones. I can guarantee that their angels in heaven always see the face of my Father, who is in heaven.ᵃ

The Lost Sheep—Luke 15:1–7

¹² "What do you think? Suppose a man has 100 sheep and one of them strays. Won't he leave the 99 sheep in the hills to look for the one that has strayed? ¹³ I can guarantee this truth: If he finds it, he is happier about it than about the 99 that have not strayed. ¹⁴ In the same way, your Father in heaven does not want one of these little ones to be lost.

Dealing With Believers When They Do Wrong

¹⁵ "If a believer does something wrong,ᵇ go, confront him when the two of you are alone. If he listens to you, you have won back that believer. ¹⁶ But if he does not listen, take one or two others with you so that every accusation may be verified by two or three witnesses. ¹⁷ If he ignores these witnesses, tell it to the community of believers. If he also ignores the community, deal with him as you would a heathen or a tax collector. ¹⁸ I can guarantee this truth: Whatever you imprison, God will imprison. And whatever you set free, God will set free.

¹⁹ "I can guarantee again that if two of you agree on anything here on earth, my Father in heaven will accept it. ²⁰ Where two or three have come together in my name, I am there among them."

Personally Forgiving Others

²¹ Then Peter came to Jesus and asked him, "Lord, how often do I have to forgive a believer who wrongs me? Seven times?"

²² Jesus answered him, "I tell you, not just seven times, but seventy times seven.

²³ "That is why the kingdom of heaven is like a king who wanted to settle accounts with his servants. ²⁴ When he began to do this,

---

ᵃ 18:10 Some manuscripts and translations add verse 11: "The Son of Man came to save the lost."   ᵇ 18:15 Some manuscripts and translations add "against you."

a servant who owed him millions of dollars was brought to him. [25] Because he could not pay off the debt, the master ordered him, his wife, his children, and all that he had to be sold to pay off the account. [26] Then the servant fell at his master's feet and said, 'Be patient with me, and I will repay everything!'

[27] "The master felt sorry for his servant, freed him, and canceled his debt. [28] But when that servant went away, he found a servant who owed him hundreds of dollars. He grabbed the servant he found and began to choke him. 'Pay what you owe!' he said.

[29] "Then that other servant fell at his feet and begged him, 'Be patient with me, and I will repay you.' [30] But he refused. Instead, he turned away and had that servant put into prison until he would repay what he owed.

[31] "The other servants who worked with him saw what had happened and felt very sad. They told their master the whole story.

[32] "Then his master sent for him and said to him, 'You evil servant! I canceled your entire debt, because you begged me. [33] Shouldn't you have treated the other servant as mercifully as I treated you?'

[34] "His master was so angry that he handed him over to the torturers until he would repay everything that he owed. [35] That is what my Father in heaven will do to you if each of you does not sincerely forgive other believers."

A Discussion About Divorce and Celibacy—Mark 10:1–12

19 [1] When Jesus finished speaking, he left Galilee and traveled along the other side of the Jordan River to the territory of Judea. [2] Large crowds followed him, and he healed them there.

[3] Some Pharisees came to test him. They asked, "Can a man divorce his wife for any reason?"

[4] Jesus answered, "Haven't you read that the Creator made them male and female in the beginning [5] and that he said, 'That's why a man will leave his father and mother and will remain united with his wife, and the two will be one'? [6] So they are no longer two but one. Therefore, don't let anyone separate what God has joined together."

⁷ The Pharisees asked him, "Why, then, did Moses order a man to give his wife a written notice to divorce her?"

⁸ Jesus answered them, "Moses allowed you to divorce your wives because you're heartless. It was never this way in the beginning. ⁹ I can guarantee that whoever divorces his wife for any reason other than her unfaithfulness is committing adultery if he marries another woman."

¹⁰ The disciples said to him, "If that is the only reason a man can use to divorce his wife, it's better not to get married."

¹¹ He answered them, "Not everyone can do what you suggest. Only those who have that gift can. ¹² For example, some men are celibate because they were born that way. Others are celibate because they were castrated. Still others have decided to be celibate because of the kingdom of heaven. If anyone can do what you've suggested, then he should do it."

Jesus Blesses Children—Mark 10:13–16; Luke 18:15–17

¹³ Then some people brought little children to Jesus to have him bless them and pray for them. But the disciples told the people not to do that.

¹⁴ Jesus said, "Don't stop children from coming to me! Children like these are part of the kingdom of God." ¹⁵ After Jesus blessed them, he went away from there.

Eternal Life in the Kingdom—Mark 10:17–31; Luke 18:18–30

¹⁶ Then a man came to Jesus and said, "Teacher, what good deed should I do to gain eternal life?"

¹⁷ Jesus said to him, "Why do you ask me about what is good? There is only one who is good. If you want to enter into life, obey the commandments."

¹⁸ "Which commandments?" the man asked.

Jesus said, "Never murder. Never commit adultery. Never steal. Never give false testimony. ¹⁹ Honor your father and mother. Love your neighbor as you love yourself."

²⁰ The young man replied, "I have obeyed all these commandments. What else do I need to do?"

²¹ Jesus said to him, "If you want to be perfect, sell what you own. Give the money to the poor, and you will have treasure in heaven. Then follow me!"

²² When the young man heard this, he went away sad because he owned a lot of property.

²³ Jesus said to his disciples, "I can guarantee this truth: It will be hard for a rich person to enter the kingdom of heaven. ²⁴ I can guarantee again that it is easier for a camel to go through the eye of a needle than for a rich person to enter the kingdom of God."

²⁵ He amazed his disciples more than ever when they heard this. "Then who can be saved?" they asked.

²⁶ Jesus looked at them and said, "It is impossible for people ˌto save themselvesˌ, but everything is possible for God."

²⁷ Then Peter replied to him, "Look, we've given up everything to follow you. What will we get out of it?"

²⁸ Jesus said to them, "I can guarantee this truth: When the Son of Man sits on his glorious throne in the world to come, you, my followers, will also sit on twelve thrones, judging the twelve tribes of Israel. ²⁹ And everyone who gave up homes, brothers or sisters, father, mother, children, or fields because of my name will receive a hundred times more and will inherit eternal life. ³⁰ However, many who are first will be last, and many who are last will be first.

A Story About Vineyard Workers

20 ¹ "The kingdom of heaven is like a landowner who went out at daybreak to hire workers for his vineyard. ² After agreeing to pay the workers the usual day's wages, he sent them to work in his vineyard. ³ About 9 a.m. he saw others standing in the market-place without work. ⁴ He said to them, 'Work in my vineyard, and I'll give you whatever is right.' So they went.

⁵ "He went out again about noon and 3 p.m. and did the same thing. ⁶ About 5 p.m. he went out and found some others standing around. He said to them, 'Why are you standing here all day long without work?'

⁷ " 'No one has hired us,' they answered him.

"He said to them, 'Work in my vineyard.'

⁸ "When evening came, the owner of the vineyard told the supervisor, 'Call the workers, and give them their wages. Start with the last, and end with the first.'

⁹ "Those who started working about 5 p.m. came, and each received a day's wages. ¹⁰ When those who had been hired first came, they expected to receive more. But each of them received a day's wages. ¹¹ Although they took it, they began to protest to the owner. ¹² They said, 'These last workers have worked only one hour. Yet, you've treated us all the same, even though we worked hard all day under a blazing sun.'

¹³ "The owner said to one of them, 'Friend, I'm not treating you unfairly. Didn't you agree with me on a day's wages? ¹⁴ Take your money and go! I want to give this last worker as much as I gave you. ¹⁵ Can't I do what I want with my own money? Or do you resent my generosity towards others?'

¹⁶ "In this way the last will be first, and the first will be last."

For the Third Time Jesus Foretells That He Will Die and Come Back to Life—Mark 10:32–34; Luke 18:31–34

¹⁷ When Jesus was on his way to Jerusalem, he took the twelve apostles aside and said to them privately, ¹⁸ "We're going to Jerusalem. There the Son of Man will be betrayed to the chief priests and scribes. They will condemn him to death ¹⁹ and hand him over to foreigners. They will make fun of him, whip him, and crucify him. But on the third day he will be brought back to life."

A Mother Makes a Request—Mark 10:35–45

²⁰ Then the mother of Zebedee's sons came to Jesus with her two sons. She bowed down in front of him to ask him for a favor.

²¹ "What do you want?" he asked her.

She said to him, "Promise that one of my sons will sit at your right and the other at your left in your kingdom."

²² Jesus replied, "You don't realize what you're asking. Can you drink the cup that I'm going to drink?"

"We can," they told him.

²³ Jesus said to them, "You will drink my cup. But I don't have the authority to grant you a seat at my right or left. My Father has already prepared these positions for certain people."

²⁴ When the other ten apostles heard about this, they were irritated with the two brothers. ²⁵ Jesus called the apostles and said, "You know that the rulers of nations have absolute power over people and their officials have absolute authority over people. ²⁶ But that's not the way it's going to be among you. Whoever wants to become great among you will be your servant. ²⁷ Whoever wants to be most important among you will be your slave. ²⁸ It's the same way with the Son of Man. He didn't come so that others could serve him. He came to serve and to give his life as a ransom for many people."

Jesus Gives Two Blind Men Their Sight—
Mark 10:46–52; Luke 18:35–43

²⁹ As they were leaving Jericho, a large crowd followed Jesus. ³⁰ Two blind men were sitting by the road. When they heard that Jesus was passing by, they shouted, "Lord, Son of David, have mercy on us!"

³¹ The crowd told them to be quiet. But they shouted even louder, "Lord, Son of David, have mercy on us!"

³² Jesus stopped and called them. "What do you want me to do for you?" he asked.

³³ They told him, "Lord, we want you to give us our eyesight back."

³⁴ Jesus felt sorry for them, so he touched their eyes. Their sight was restored at once, and they followed him.

The King Comes to Jerusalem—
Mark 11:1–11; Luke 19:29–44; John 12:12–19

21 ¹ When they came near Jerusalem and had reached Bethphage on the Mount of Olives, Jesus sent two disciples ahead of him. ² He said to them, "Go into the village ahead of you.

You will find a donkey tied there and a colt with it. Untie them, and bring them to me. ³ If anyone says anything to you, tell him that the Lord needs them. That person will send them at once."

⁴ This happened so that what the prophet had said came true:

⁵   "Tell the people of Zion,
         'Your king is coming to you.
             He's gentle,
                 riding on a donkey,
                     on a colt, a young pack animal.' "

⁶ The disciples did as Jesus had directed them. ⁷ They brought the donkey and the colt and put their coats on them for Jesus to sit on. ⁸ Most of the people spread their coats on the road. Others cut branches from the trees and spread them on the road. ⁹ The crowd that went ahead of him and that followed him was shouting,

"Hosanna to the Son of David!
    Blessed is the one who comes in the name of the Lord!
Hosanna in the highest heaven!"

¹⁰ When Jesus came into Jerusalem, the whole city was in an uproar. People were asking, "Who is this?"

¹¹ The crowd answered, "This is the prophet Jesus from Nazareth in Galilee."

Jesus Throws Out the Moneychangers—
Mark 11:15–19; Luke 19:45–48

¹² Jesus went into the temple courtyard and threw out everyone who was buying and selling there. He overturned the moneychangers' tables and the chairs of those who sold pigeons. ¹³ He told them, "Scripture says, 'My house will be called a house of prayer,' but you're turning it into a gathering place for thieves!"

¹⁴ Blind and lame people came to him in the temple courtyard, and he healed them.

¹⁵ When the chief priests and the scribes saw the amazing miracles he performed and the children shouting in the temple

courtyard, "Hosanna to the Son of David!" they were irritated. [16] They said to him, "Do you hear what these children are saying?"

Jesus replied, "Yes, I do. Have you never read, 'From the mouths of little children and infants, you have created praise'?"

[17] He left them and went out of the city to Bethany and spent the night there.

Jesus Curses the Fig Tree—Mark 11:12–14, 20–25

[18] In the morning, as Jesus returned to the city, he became hungry. [19] When he saw a fig tree by the road, he went up to the tree and found nothing on it but leaves. He said to the tree, "May fruit never grow on you again!" At once the fig tree dried up.

[20] The disciples were surprised to see this. They asked, "How did the fig tree dry up so quickly?"

[21] Jesus answered them, "I can guarantee this truth: If you have faith and do not doubt, you will be able to do what I did to the fig tree. You could also say to this mountain, 'Be uprooted and thrown into the sea,' and it will happen. [22] Have faith that you will receive whatever you ask for in prayer."

Jesus' Authority Challenged—Mark 11:27–33; Luke 20:1–8

[23] Then Jesus went into the temple courtyard and began to teach. The chief priests and the leaders of the people came to him. They asked, "What gives you the right to do these things? Who told you that you could do this?"

[24] Jesus answered them, "I, too, have a question for you. If you answer it for me, I'll tell you why I have the right to do these things. [25] Did John's right to baptize come from heaven or from humans?"

They discussed this among themselves. They said, "If we say, 'from heaven,' he will ask us, 'Then why didn't you believe him?' [26] But if we say, 'from humans,' we're afraid of what the crowd might do. All those people think of John as a prophet." [27] So they answered Jesus, "We don't know."

Jesus told them, "Then I won't tell you why I have the right to do these things.

A Story About Two Sons

28 "What do you think about this? A man had two sons. He went to the first and said, 'Son, go to work in the vineyard today.'

29 "His son replied, 'I don't want to!' But later he changed his mind and went.

30 "The father went to the other son and told him the same thing. He replied, 'I will, sir,' but he didn't go.

31 "Which of the two sons did what the father wanted?"

"The first," they answered.

Jesus said to them, "I can guarantee this truth: Tax collectors and prostitutes are going into the kingdom of God ahead of you. **32** John came to you and showed you the way that God wants you to live, but you didn't believe him. The tax collectors and prostitutes believed him. But even after you had seen that, you didn't change your minds and believe him.

A Story About a Vineyard—Mark 12:1–12; Luke 20:9–19

33 "Listen to another illustration. A landowner planted a vineyard. He put a wall around it, made a winepress, and built a watchtower. Then he leased it to vineyard workers and went on a trip.

34 "When the grapes were getting ripe, he sent his servants to the workers to collect his share of the produce. **35** The workers took his servants and beat one, killed another, and stoned a third to death. **36** So the landowner sent more servants. But the workers treated them the same way.

37 "Finally, he sent his son to them. He thought, 'They will respect my son.'

38 "When the workers saw his son, they said to one another, 'This is the heir. Let's kill him and get his inheritance.' **39** So they grabbed him, threw him out of the vineyard, and killed him.

40 "Now, when the owner of the vineyard comes, what will he do to those workers?"

41 They answered, "He will destroy those evil people. Then he will lease the vineyard to other workers who will give him his share of the produce when it is ready."

[42] Jesus asked them, "Have you never read in the Scriptures:

'The stone that the builders rejected
     has become the cornerstone.
The Lord is responsible for this,
     and it is amazing for us to see'?

[43] That is why I can guarantee that the kingdom of God will be taken away from you and given to a people who will produce what God wants. [44] Anyone who falls on this stone will be broken. If the stone falls on anyone, it will crush that person."[a]

[45] When the chief priests and the Pharisees heard his illustrations, they knew that he was talking about them. [46] They wanted to arrest him but were afraid of the crowds, who thought he was a prophet.

A Story About a Wedding Reception

22 [1] Again Jesus used stories as illustrations when he spoke to them. He said, [2] "The kingdom of heaven is like a king who planned a wedding for his son. [3] He sent his servants to those who had been invited to the wedding, but they refused to come. [4] He sent other servants to tell the people who had been invited, 'I've prepared dinner. My bulls and fattened calves have been butchered. Everything is ready. Come to the wedding!'

[5] "But they paid no attention and went away. Some went to work in their own fields, and others went to their businesses. [6] The rest grabbed the king's servants, mistreated them, and then killed them.

[7] "The king became angry. He sent his soldiers, killed those murderers, and burned their city.

[8] "Then the king said to his servants, 'The wedding is ready, but those who were invited don't deserve the honor. [9] Go where the roads leave the city. Invite everyone you find to the wedding.' [10] The servants went into the streets and brought in all the good people and all the evil people they found. And the wedding hall was filled with guests.

---

[a] 21:44 Some manuscripts and translations omit this verse.

[11] "When the king came to see the guests, he saw a person who was not dressed in the wedding clothes ⌐provided for the guests⌐. [12] He said to him, 'Friend, how did you get in here without proper wedding clothes?'

"The man had nothing to say. [13] Then the king told his servants, 'Tie his hands and feet, and throw him outside into the darkness. People will cry and be in extreme pain there.'

[14] "Therefore, many are invited, but few of those are chosen to stay."

A Question About Taxes—Mark 12:13–17; Luke 20:20–26

[15] Then the Pharisees went away and planned to trap Jesus into saying the wrong thing. [16] They sent their disciples to him along with Herod's followers. They said to him, "Teacher, we know that you tell the truth and that you teach the truth about the way of God. You don't favor individuals because of who they are. [17] So tell us what you think. Is it right to pay taxes to the emperor or not?"

[18] Jesus recognized their evil plan, so he asked, "Why do you test me, you hypocrites? [19] Show me a coin used to pay taxes."

They brought him a coin. [20] He said to them, "Whose face and name is this?"

[21] They replied, "The emperor's."

Then he said to them, "Very well, give the emperor what belongs to the emperor, and give God what belongs to God."

[22] They were surprised to hear this. Then they left him alone and went away.

The Dead Come Back to Life—Mark 12:18–27; Luke 20:27–40

[23] On that day some Sadducees, who say that people will never come back to life, came to Jesus. They asked him, [24] "Teacher, Moses said, 'If a man dies childless, his brother should marry his widow and have children for his brother.' [25] There were seven brothers among us. The first married and died. Since he had no children, he left his widow to his brother. [26] The second brother also died, as well as the third, and the rest of the seven brothers. [27] At last the

woman died. [28] Now, when the dead come back to life, whose wife will she be? All seven brothers had been married to her."

[29] Jesus answered, "You're mistaken because you don't know the Scriptures or God's power. [30] When people come back to life, they don't marry. Rather, they are like the angels in heaven. [31] Haven't you read what God told you about the dead coming back to life? He said, [32] 'I am the God of Abraham, Isaac, and Jacob.' He's not the God of the dead but of the living."

[33] He amazed the crowds who heard his teaching.

Love God and Your Neighbor—Mark 12:28–34

[34] When the Pharisees heard that Jesus had silenced the Sadducees, they gathered together. [35] One of them, an expert in Moses' Teachings, tested Jesus by asking, [36] "Teacher, which commandment is the greatest in Moses' Teachings?"

[37] Jesus answered him, " 'Love the Lord your God with all your heart, with all your soul, and with all your mind.' [38] This is the greatest and most important commandment. [39] The second is like it: 'Love your neighbor as you love yourself.' [40] All of Moses' Teachings and the Prophets depend on these two commandments."

How Can David's Son Be David's Lord?— Mark 12:35–37a; Luke 20:41–44

[41] While the Pharisees were still gathered, Jesus asked them, [42] "What do you think about the Messiah? Whose son is he?"

They answered him, "David's."

[43] He said to them, "Then how can David, guided by the Spirit, call him Lord? David says,

[44]   'The Lord said to my Lord,
        "Take the highest position in heaven
            until I put your enemies under your control." '

[45] If David calls him Lord, how can he be his son?"

[46] No one could answer him, and from that time on no one dared to ask him another question.

Jesus Disapproves of the Example Set By Scribes and Pharisees—
Mark 12:37b–40; Luke 20:45–47

23 ¹ Then Jesus said to the crowds and to his disciples, ² "The scribes and the Pharisees teach with Moses' authority. ³ So be careful to do everything they tell you. But don't follow their example, because they don't practice what they preach. ⁴ They make loads that are hard to carry and lay them on the shoulders of the people. However, they are not willing to lift a finger to move them.

⁵ "They do everything to attract people's attention. They make their headbands large and the tassels on their shawls long. ⁶ They love the place of honor at dinners and the front seats in synagogues. ⁷ They love to be greeted in the marketplaces and to have people call them Rabbi. ⁸ But don't make others call you Rabbi, because you have only one teacher, and you are all followers. ⁹ And don't call anyone on earth your father, because you have only one Father, and he is in heaven. ¹⁰ Don't make others call you a leader, because you have only one leader, the Messiah. ¹¹ The person who is greatest among you will be your servant. ¹² Whoever honors himself will be humbled, and whoever humbles himself will be honored.

The Hypocrisy of the Scribes and Pharisees

¹³ "How horrible it will be for you, scribes and Pharisees! You hypocrites! You lock people out of the kingdom of heaven. You don't enter it yourselves, and you don't permit others to enter when they try.[a]

¹⁵ "How horrible it will be for you, scribes and Pharisees! You hypocrites! You cross land and sea to recruit a single follower, and when you do, you make that person twice as fit for hell as you are.

¹⁶ "How horrible it will be for you, you blind guides! You say, 'To swear an oath by the temple doesn't mean a thing. But to swear an oath by the gold in the temple means a person must keep his oath.'

---

[a] 23:13 Some manuscripts and translations add verse 14: "How horrible it will be for you, scribes and Pharisees! You hypocrites! You rob widows by taking their houses and then say long prayers to make yourselves look good. You will receive a most severe punishment." (See Mark 12:40 and Luke 20:47.)

[17] You blind fools! What is more important, the gold or the temple that made the gold holy? [18] Again you say, 'To swear an oath by the altar doesn't mean a thing. But to swear an oath by the gift on the altar means a person must keep his oath.' [19] You blind men! What is more important, the gift or the altar that makes the gift holy? [20] To swear an oath by the altar is to swear by it and by everything on it. [21] To swear an oath by the temple is to swear by it and by the one who lives there. [22] And to swear an oath by heaven is to swear by God's throne and the one who sits on it.

[23] "How horrible it will be for you, scribes and Pharisees! You hypocrites! You give ˌGodˌ one-tenth of your mint, dill, and cumin. But you have neglected justice, mercy, and faithfulness. These are the most important things in Moses' Teachings. You should have done these things without neglecting the others. [24] You blind guides! You strain gnats ˌout of your wineˌ, but you swallow camels.

[25] "How horrible it will be for you, scribes and Pharisees! You hypocrites! You clean the outside of cups and dishes. But inside they are full of greed and uncontrolled desires. [26] You blind Pharisees! First clean the inside of the cups and dishes so that the outside may also be clean.

[27] "How horrible it will be for you, scribes and Pharisees! You hypocrites! You are like whitewashed graves that look beautiful on the outside but inside are full of dead people's bones and every kind of impurity. [28] So on the outside you look as though you have God's approval, but inside you are full of hypocrisy and lawlessness.

[29] "How horrible it will be for you, scribes and Pharisees! You hypocrites! You build tombs for the prophets and decorate the monuments of those who had God's approval. [30] Then you say, 'If we had lived at the time of our ancestors, we would not have helped to murder the prophets.' [31] So you testify against yourselves that you are the descendants of those who murdered the prophets. [32] Go ahead, finish what your ancestors started!

[33] "You snakes! You poisonous snakes! How can you escape being condemned to hell? [34] I'm sending you prophets, wise men, and teachers of the Scriptures. You will kill and crucify some of

them. Others you will whip in your synagogues and persecute from city to city. [35] As a result, you will be held accountable for all the innocent blood of those murdered on earth, from the murder of righteous Abel to that of Zechariah, son of Barachiah, whom you murdered between the temple and the altar. [36] I can guarantee this truth: The people living now will be held accountable for all these things.

[37] "Jerusalem, Jerusalem, you kill the prophets and stone to death those sent to you! How often I wanted to gather your children together the way a hen gathers her chicks under her wings! But you were not willing! [38] Your house will be abandoned, deserted. [39] I can guarantee that you will not see me again until you say, 'Blessed is the one who comes in the name of the Lord!'"

Jesus Teaches His Disciples on the Mount of Olives—
Mark 13:1–31; Luke 21:5–33

24 [1] As Jesus left the temple courtyard and was walking away, his disciples came to him. They proudly pointed out to him the temple buildings. [2] Jesus said to them, "You see all these buildings, don't you? I can guarantee this truth: Not one of these stones will be left on top of another. Each one will be torn down."

[3] As Jesus was sitting on the Mount of Olives, his disciples came to him privately and said, "Tell us, when will this happen? What will be the sign that you are coming again, and when will the world come to an end?"

[4] Jesus answered them, "Be careful not to let anyone deceive you. [5] Many will come using my name. They will say, 'I am the Messiah,' and they will deceive many people.

[6] "You will hear of wars and rumors of wars. Don't be alarmed! These things must happen, but they don't mean that the end has come. [7] Nation will fight against nation and kingdom against kingdom. There will be famines and earthquakes in various places. [8] All of these are only the beginning pains ˻of the end˼.

[9] "Then they will hand you over to those who will torture and kill you. All nations will hate you because you are committed to

me. ¹⁰ Then many will lose faith. They will betray and hate each other. ¹¹ Many false prophets will appear and deceive many people. ¹² And because there will be more and more lawlessness, most people's love will grow cold. ¹³ But the person who endures to the end will be saved.

¹⁴ "This Good News about the kingdom will be spread throughout the world as a testimony to all nations. Then the end will come.

¹⁵ "The prophet Daniel said that the disgusting thing that will cause destruction will stand in the holy place. When you see this (let the reader take note), ¹⁶ those of you in Judea should flee to the mountains. ¹⁷ Those who are on the roof should not come down to get anything out of their houses. ¹⁸ Those who are in the field should not turn back to get their coats.

¹⁹ "How horrible it will be for the women who are pregnant or who are nursing babies in those days. ²⁰ Pray that it will not be winter or a day of worship when you flee. ²¹ There will be a lot of misery at that time, a kind of misery that has not happened from the beginning of the world until now and will certainly never happen again. ²² If God does not reduce the number of those days, no one will be saved. But those days will be reduced because of those whom God has chosen.

²³ "At that time don't believe anyone who tells you, 'Here is the Messiah!' or 'There he is!' ²⁴ False messiahs and false prophets will appear. They will work spectacular, miraculous signs and do wonderful things to deceive, if possible, even those whom God has chosen. ²⁵ Listen! I've told you this before it happens. ²⁶ So if someone tells you, 'He's in the desert!' don't go out ˏlooking for himˏ. And don't believe anyone who says, 'He's in a secret place!' ²⁷ The Son of Man will come again just as lightning flashes from east to west. ²⁸ Vultures will gather wherever there is a dead body.

²⁹ "Immediately after the misery of those days, the sun will turn dark, the moon will not give light, the stars will fall from the sky, and the powers of the universe will be shaken.

³⁰ "Then the sign of the Son of Man will appear in the sky. All the people on earth will cry in agony when they see the Son of Man com-

ing on the clouds in the sky with power and great glory. [31] He will send out his angels with a loud trumpet call, and from every direction under the sky, they will gather those whom God has chosen.

[32] "Learn from the story of the fig tree. When its branch becomes tender and it sprouts leaves, you know that summer is near. [33] In the same way, when you see all these things, you know that he is near, at the door.

[34] "I can guarantee this truth: This generation will not disappear until all these things take place. [35] The earth and the heavens will disappear, but my words will never disappear.

No One Knows When the Son of Man Will Return

[36] "No one knows when that day or hour will come. Even the angels in heaven and the Son don't know. Only the Father knows.

[37] "When the Son of Man comes again, it will be exactly like the days of Noah. [38] In the days before the flood, people were eating, drinking, and getting married until the day that Noah went into the ship. [39] They were not aware of what was happening until the flood came and swept all of them away. That is how it will be when the Son of Man comes again.

[40] "At that time two men will be working in the field. One will be taken, and the other one will be left. [41] Two women will be working at a mill. One will be taken, and the other one will be left.

[42] "Therefore, be alert, because you don't know on what day your Lord will return. [43] You realize that if a homeowner had known at what time of the night a thief was coming, he would have stayed awake. He would not have let the thief break into his house. [44] Therefore, you, too, must be ready because the Son of Man will return when you least expect him.

[45] "Who, then, is the faithful and wise servant? The master will put that person in charge of giving the other servants their food at the right time. [46] That servant will be blessed if his master finds him doing this job when he comes. [47] I can guarantee this truth: He will put that servant in charge of all his property. [48] On the other hand, that servant, if he is wicked, may think that it will be

a long time before his master comes. ⁴⁹ The servant may begin to beat the other servants and eat and drink with the drunks. ⁵⁰ His master will return unexpectedly. ⁵¹ Then his master will severely punish him and assign him a place with the hypocrites. People will cry and be in extreme pain there.

A Story About Ten Bridesmaids

25 ¹ "When the end comes, the kingdom of heaven will be like ten bridesmaids. They took their oil lamps and went to meet the groom. ² Five of them were foolish, and five were wise. ³ The foolish bridesmaids took their lamps, but they didn't take any extra oil. ⁴ The wise bridesmaids, however, took along extra oil for their lamps. ⁵ Since the groom was late, all the bridesmaids became drowsy and fell asleep.

⁶ "At midnight someone shouted, 'The groom is here! Come to meet him!' ⁷ Then all the bridesmaids woke up and got their lamps ready.

⁸ "The foolish ones said to the wise ones, 'Give us some of your oil. Our lamps are going out.'

⁹ "But the wise bridesmaids replied, 'We can't do that. There won't be enough for both of us. Go! Find someone to sell you some oil.'

¹⁰ "While they were buying oil, the groom arrived. The bridesmaids who were ready went with him into the wedding hall, and the door was shut.

¹¹ "Later the other bridesmaids arrived and said, 'Sir, sir, open the door for us!'

¹² "But he answered them, 'I don't even know who you are!'

¹³ "So stay awake, because you don't know the day or the hour.

A Story About Three Servants

¹⁴ "The kingdom of heaven is like a man going on a trip. He called his servants and entrusted some money to them. ¹⁵ He gave one man ten thousand dollars, another four thousand dollars, and another two thousand dollars. Each was given money based on his ability. Then the man went on his trip.

¹⁶ "The one who received ten thousand dollars invested the money at once and doubled his money. ¹⁷ The one who had four thousand dollars did the same and also doubled his money. ¹⁸ But the one who received two thousand dollars went off, dug a hole in the ground, and hid his master's money.

¹⁹ "After a long time the master of those servants returned and settled accounts with them. ²⁰ The one who received ten thousand dollars brought the additional ten thousand. He said, 'Sir, you gave me ten thousand dollars. I've doubled the amount.'

²¹ "His master replied, 'Good job! You're a good and faithful servant! You proved that you could be trusted with a small amount. I will put you in charge of a large amount. Come and share your master's happiness.'

²² "The one who received four thousand dollars came and said, 'Sir, you gave me four thousand dollars. I've doubled the amount.'

²³ "His master replied, 'Good job! You're a good and faithful servant! You proved that you could be trusted with a small amount. I will put you in charge of a large amount. Come and share your master's happiness.'

²⁴ "Then the one who received two thousand dollars came and said, 'Sir, I knew that you are a hard person to please. You harvest where you haven't planted and gather where you haven't scattered any seeds. ²⁵ I was afraid. So I hid your two thousand dollars in the ground. Here's your money!'

²⁶ "His master responded, 'You evil and lazy servant! If you knew that I harvest where I haven't planted and gather where I haven't scattered, ²⁷ then you should have invested my money with the bankers. When I returned, I would have received my money back with interest. ²⁸ Take the two thousand dollars away from him! Give it to the one who has the ten thousand! ²⁹ To all who have, more will be given, and they will have more than enough. But everything will be taken away from those who don't have much. ³⁰ Throw this useless servant outside into the darkness. People will cry and be in extreme pain there.'

Jesus Will Judge the World

[31] "When the Son of Man comes in his glory and all his angels are with him, he will sit on his glorious throne. [32] The people of every nation will be gathered in front of him. He will separate them as a shepherd separates the sheep from the goats. [33] He will put the sheep on his right but the goats on his left.

[34] "Then the king will say to those on his right, 'Come, my Father has blessed you! Inherit the kingdom prepared for you from the creation of the world. [35] I was hungry, and you gave me something to eat. I was thirsty, and you gave me something to drink. I was a stranger, and you took me into your home. [36] I needed clothes, and you gave me something to wear. I was sick, and you took care of me. I was in prison, and you visited me.'

[37] "Then the people who have God's approval will reply to him, 'Lord, when did we see you hungry and feed you or see you thirsty and give you something to drink? [38] When did we see you as a stranger and take you into our homes or see you in need of clothes and give you something to wear? [39] When did we see you sick or in prison and visit you?'

[40] "The king will answer them, 'I can guarantee this truth: Whatever you did for one of my brothers or sisters, no matter how unimportant ˛they seemed˳, you did for me.'

[41] "Then the king will say to those on his left, 'Get away from me! God has cursed you! Go into everlasting fire that was prepared for the devil and his angels! [42] I was hungry, and you gave me nothing to eat. I was thirsty, and you gave me nothing to drink. [43] I was a stranger, and you didn't take me into your homes. I needed clothes, and you didn't give me anything to wear. I was sick and in prison, and you didn't take care of me.'

[44] "They, too, will ask, 'Lord, when did we see you hungry or thirsty or as a stranger or in need of clothes or sick or in prison and didn't help you?'

[45] "He will answer them, 'I can guarantee this truth: Whatever you failed to do for one of my brothers or sisters, no matter how unimportant ˛they seemed˳, you failed to do for me.'

⁴⁶ "These people will go away into eternal punishment, but those with God's approval will go into eternal life."

The Plot to Kill Jesus—Mark 14:1–2; Luke 22:1–6; John 11:45–57

26 ¹ When Jesus finished saying all these things, he told his disciples, ² "You know that the Passover will take place in two days. At that time the Son of Man will be handed over to be crucified."

³ Then the chief priests and the leaders of the people gathered in the palace of the chief priest Caiaphas. ⁴ They made plans to arrest Jesus in an underhanded way and to kill him. ⁵ But they said, "We shouldn't arrest him during the festival, or else there may be a riot among the people."

A Woman Prepares Jesus' Body for the Tomb— Mark 14:3–9; John 12:1–8

⁶ Jesus was in Bethany in the home of Simon, a man who had suffered from a skin disease. ⁷ While Jesus was sitting there, a woman went to him with a bottle of very expensive perfume and poured it on his head.

⁸ The disciples were irritated when they saw this. They asked, "Why did she waste it like this? ⁹ It could have been sold for a high price, and the money could have been given to the poor."

¹⁰ Since Jesus knew what was going on, he said to them, "Why are you bothering this woman? She has done a beautiful thing for me. ¹¹ You will always have the poor with you, but you will not always have me with you. ¹² She poured this perfume on my body before it is placed in a tomb. ¹³ I can guarantee this truth: Wherever this Good News is spoken in the world, what she has done will also be told in memory of her."

Judas Plans to Betray Jesus—Mark 14:10–11; Luke 22:3–6

¹⁴ Then one of the twelve apostles, the one named Judas Iscariot, went to the chief priests. ¹⁵ He asked, "What will you pay me if I hand him over to you?"

They offered him 30 silver coins. [16] From then on, he looked for a chance to betray Jesus.

Preparations for the Passover—Mark 14:12–17; Luke 22:7–17

[17] On the first day of the Festival of Unleavened Bread, the disciples went to Jesus. They asked, "Where do you want us to prepare the Passover meal for you?"

[18] He said, "Go to a certain man in the city, and tell him that the teacher says, 'My time is near. I will celebrate the Passover with my disciples at your house.'"

[19] The disciples did as Jesus had directed them and prepared the Passover.

[20] When evening came, Jesus was at the table with the twelve apostles.

Jesus Knows Who Will Betray Him— Mark 14:18–21; Luke 22:21–23; John 13:21–30

[21] While they were eating, he said, "I can guarantee this truth: One of you is going to betray me."

[22] Feeling deeply hurt, they asked him one by one, "You don't mean me, do you, Lord?"

[23] Jesus answered, "Someone who has dipped his hand into the bowl with me will betray me. [24] The Son of Man is going to die as the Scriptures say he will. But how horrible it will be for that person who betrays the Son of Man. It would have been better for that person if he had never been born."

[25] Then Judas, who betrayed him, asked, "You don't mean me, do you, Rabbi?"

"Yes, I do," Jesus replied.

The Lord's Supper—Mark 14:22–26; Luke 22:19–20

[26] While they were eating, Jesus took bread and blessed it. He broke the bread, gave it to his disciples, and said, "Take this, and eat it. This is my body."

[27] Then he took a cup and spoke a prayer of thanksgiving. He gave it to them and said, "Drink from it, all of you. [28] This is my

blood, the blood of the promise.[a] It is poured out for many people so that sins are forgiven.

29 "I can guarantee that I won't drink this wine again until that day when I drink new wine with you in my Father's kingdom."

30 After they sang a hymn, they went to the Mount of Olives.

Jesus Predicts Peter's Denial—
Mark 14:27–31; Luke 22:31–34; John 13:36–38

31 Then Jesus said to them, "All of you will abandon me tonight. Scripture says,

> 'I will strike the shepherd,
>   and the sheep in the flock will be scattered.'

32 "But after I am brought back to life, I will go to Galilee ahead of you."

33 Peter said to him, "Even if everyone else abandons you, I never will."

34 Jesus replied to Peter, "I can guarantee this truth: Before a rooster crows tonight, you will say three times that you don't know me."

35 Peter told him, "Even if I have to die with you, I'll never say that I don't know you!" All the other disciples said the same thing.

Jesus Prays in the Garden of Gethsemane—
Mark 14:32–42; Luke 22:39–46

36 Then Jesus went with the disciples to a place called Gethsemane. He said to them, "Stay here while I go over there and pray."

37 He took Peter and Zebedee's two sons with him. He was beginning to feel deep anguish. 38 Then he said to them, "My anguish is so great that I feel as if I'm dying. Wait here, and stay awake with me."

39 After walking a little farther, he quickly bowed with his face to the ground and prayed, "Father, if it's possible, let this cup of

---

a 26:28 Or "testament," or "covenant."

suffering, be taken away from me. But let your will be done rather than mine."

40 When he went back to the disciples, he found them asleep. He said to Peter, "Couldn't you stay awake with me for one hour? **41** Stay awake, and pray that you won't be tempted. You want to do what's right, but you're weak."

42 Then he went away a second time and prayed, "Father, if this cup cannot be taken away unless I drink it, let your will be done."

43 He found them asleep again because they couldn't keep their eyes open.

44 After leaving them again, he went away and prayed the same prayer a third time. **45** Then he came back to the disciples and said to them, "You might as well sleep now. The time is near for the Son of Man to be handed over to sinners. **46** Get up! Let's go! The one who is betraying me is near."

Jesus Is Arrested—Mark 14:43–52; Luke 22:47–54a; John 18:1–14

47 Just then, while Jesus was still speaking, Judas, one of the twelve apostles, arrived. A large crowd carrying swords and clubs was with him. They were from the chief priests and leaders of the people. **48** Now, the traitor had given them a signal. He said, "The one I kiss is the man you want. Arrest him!"

49 Then Judas quickly stepped up to Jesus and said, "Hello, Rabbi!" and kissed him.

50 Jesus said to him, "Friend, why are you here?"

Then some men came forward, took hold of Jesus, and arrested him. **51** Suddenly, one of the men with Jesus pulled out his sword and cut off the ear of the chief priest's servant. **52** Then Jesus said to him, "Put your sword away! All who use a sword will be killed by a sword. **53** Don't you think that I could call on my Father to send more than twelve legions of angels to help me now? **54** How, then, are the Scriptures to be fulfilled that say this must happen?"

55 At that time Jesus said to the crowd, "Have you come out with swords and clubs to arrest me as if I were a criminal? I used to sit teaching in the temple courtyard every day. But you didn't arrest me then. ⁵⁶ All of this has happened so that what the prophets have written would come true."

Then all the disciples abandoned him and ran away.

The Trial in Front of the Jewish Council—
Mark 14:53–65; Luke 22:63–71

⁵⁷ Those who had arrested Jesus took him to Caiaphas, the chief priest, where the scribes and the leaders had gathered together. ⁵⁸ Peter followed at a distance until he came to the chief priest's courtyard. He went inside and sat with the guards to see how this would turn out.

⁵⁹ The chief priests and the whole council were searching for false testimony to use against Jesus in order to execute him. ⁶⁰ But they did not find any, although many came forward with false testimony. At last two men came forward. ⁶¹ They stated, "This man said, 'I can tear down God's temple and rebuild it in three days.' "

⁶² The chief priest stood up and said to Jesus, "Don't you have any answer to what these men testify against you?"

⁶³ But Jesus was silent.

Then the chief priest said to him, "Swear an oath in front of the living God and tell us, are you the Messiah, the Son of God?"

⁶⁴ Jesus answered him, "Yes, I am. But I can guarantee that from now on you will see the Son of Man in the highest position in heaven. He will be coming on the clouds of heaven."

⁶⁵ Then the chief priest tore his robes in horror and said, "He has dishonored God! Why do we need any more witnesses? You've just heard him dishonor God! ⁶⁶ What's your verdict?"

They answered, "He deserves the death penalty!"

⁶⁷ Then they spit in his face, hit him with their fists, and some of them slapped him. ⁶⁸ They said, "You Christ, if you're a prophet, tell us who hit you."

Peter Denies Jesus—
Mark 14:66–72; Luke 22:54b–62; John 18:15–18, 25–27

⁶⁹ Peter was sitting in the courtyard. A female servant came to him and said, "You, too, were with Jesus the Galilean."

[70] But Peter denied it in front of them all by saying, "I don't know what you're talking about."

[71] As he went to the entrance, another female servant saw him. She told those who were there, "This man was with Jesus from Nazareth."

[72] Again Peter denied it and swore with an oath, "I don't know the man!"

[73] After a little while the men standing there approached Peter and said, "It's obvious you're also one of them. Your accent gives you away!"

[74] Then Peter began to curse and swear with an oath, "I don't know the man!" Just then a rooster crowed. [75] Peter remembered what Jesus had said: "Before a rooster crows, you will say three times that you don't know me." Then Peter went outside and cried bitterly.

The Death of Judas

27 [1] Early in the morning all the chief priests and the leaders of the people decided to execute Jesus. [2] They tied him up, led him away, and handed him over to Pilate, the governor.

[3] Then Judas, who had betrayed Jesus, regretted what had happened when he saw that Jesus was condemned. He brought the 30 silver coins back to the chief priests and leaders. [4] He said, "I've sinned by betraying an innocent man."

They replied, "What do we care? That's your problem."

[5] So he threw the money into the temple, went away, and hanged himself.

[6] The chief priests took the money and said, "It's not right to put it into the temple treasury, because it's blood money." [7] So they decided to use it to buy a potter's field for the burial of strangers. [8] That's why that field has been called the Field of Blood ever since. [9] Then what the prophet Jeremiah had said came true, "They took the 30 silver coins, the price the people of Israel had placed on him, [10] and used the coins to buy a potter's field, as the Lord had directed me."

Pilate Questions Jesus—Mark 15:1–5; Luke 23:1–4; John 18:28–38

¹¹ Jesus stood in front of the governor, ⌊Pilate⌋. The governor asked him, "Are you the king of the Jews?"

"Yes, I am," Jesus answered.

¹² While the chief priests and leaders were accusing him, he said nothing. ¹³ Then Pilate asked him, "Don't you hear how many charges they're bringing against you?"

¹⁴ But Jesus said absolutely nothing to him in reply, so the governor was very surprised.

The Crowd Rejects Jesus—Mark 15:6–15; Luke 23:18–25; John 18:39, 40

¹⁵ At every Passover festival the governor would free one prisoner whom the crowd wanted. ¹⁶ At that time there was a well-known prisoner by the name of Barabbas. ¹⁷ So when the people gathered, Pilate asked them, "Which man do you want me to free for you? Do you want me to free Barabbas or Jesus, who is called Christ?" ¹⁸ Pilate knew that they had handed Jesus over to him because they were jealous.

¹⁹ While Pilate was judging the case, his wife sent him a message. It said, "Leave that innocent man alone. I've been very upset today because of a dream I had about him."

²⁰ But the chief priests and leaders persuaded the crowd to ask for the release of Barabbas and the execution of Jesus.

²¹ The governor asked them, "Which of the two do you want me to free for you?"

They said, "Barabbas."

²² Pilate asked them, "Then what should I do with Jesus, who is called Christ?"

"He should be crucified!" they all said.

²³ Pilate asked, "Why? What has he done wrong?"

But they began to shout loudly, "He should be crucified!"

²⁴ Pilate saw that he was not getting anywhere. Instead, a riot was breaking out. So Pilate took some water and washed his hands in front of the crowd. He said, "I won't be guilty of killing this man. Do what you want!"

²⁵ All the people answered, "The responsibility for killing him will rest on us and our children."

²⁶ Then Pilate freed Barabbas for the people. But he had Jesus whipped and handed over to be crucified.

The Soldiers Make Fun of Jesus—Mark 15:16–19; John 19:1–3

²⁷ Then the governor's soldiers took Jesus into the palace and gathered the whole troop around him. ²⁸ They took off his clothes and put a bright red cape on him. ²⁹ They twisted some thorns into a crown, placed it on his head, and put a stick in his right hand. They knelt in front of him and made fun of him by saying, "Long live the king of the Jews!" ³⁰ After they had spit on him, they took the stick and kept hitting him on the head with it.

The Crucifixion—Mark 15:20–32; Luke 23:33–38; John 19:16b–24

³¹ After the soldiers finished making fun of Jesus, they took off the cape and put his own clothes back on him. Then they led him away to crucify him.

³² On the way they found a man named Simon. He was from the city of Cyrene. The soldiers forced him to carry Jesus' cross.

³³ They came to a place called Golgotha (which means "the place of the skull"). ³⁴ They gave him a drink of wine mixed with a drug called gall. When he tasted it, he refused to drink it. ³⁵ After they had crucified him, they divided his clothes among themselves by throwing dice. ³⁶ Then they sat there and kept watch over him. ³⁷ They placed a written accusation above his head. It read, "This is Jesus, the king of the Jews."

³⁸ At that time they crucified two criminals with him, one on his right and the other on his left.

³⁹ Those who passed by insulted him. They shook their heads ⁴⁰ and said, "You were going to tear down God's temple and build it again in three days. Save yourself! If you're the Son of God, come down from the cross." ⁴¹ The chief priests together with the scribes and the leaders made fun of him in the same way. They said, ⁴² "He saved others, but he can't save himself. So he's Israel's king! Let

him come down from the cross now, and we'll believe him. [43] He trusted God. Let God rescue him now if he wants. After all, this man said, 'I am the Son of God.' " [44] Even the criminals crucified with him were insulting him the same way.

Jesus Dies on the Cross—
Mark 15:33–41; Luke 23:44–49; John 19:28–30

[45] At noon darkness came over the whole land until three in the afternoon. [46] About three o'clock Jesus cried out in a loud voice, "Eli, Eli, lema sabachthani?" which means, "My God, my God, why have you abandoned me?" [47] When some of the people standing there heard him say that, they said, "He's calling Elijah." [48] One of the men ran at once, took a sponge, and soaked it in some vinegar. Then he put it on a stick and offered Jesus a drink. [49] The others said, "Leave him alone! Let's see if Elijah comes to save him."

[50] Then Jesus loudly cried out once again and gave up his life.

[51] Suddenly, the curtain in the temple was split in two from top to bottom. The earth shook, and the rocks were split open. [52] The tombs were opened, and the bodies of many holy people who had died came back to life. [53] They came out of the tombs after he had come back to life, and they went into the holy city where they appeared to many people.

[54] An army officer and those watching Jesus with him saw the earthquake and the other things happening. They were terrified and said, "Certainly, this was the Son of God!"

[55] Many women were there watching from a distance. They had followed Jesus from Galilee and had always supported him. [56] Among them were Mary from Magdala, Mary (the mother of James and Joseph), and the mother of Zebedee's sons.

Jesus Is Buried—*Mark 15:42–47; Luke 23:50–56; John 19:38–42*

[57] In the evening a rich man named Joseph arrived. He was from the city of Arimathea and had become a disciple of Jesus. [58] He went to Pilate and asked for the body of Jesus. Pilate ordered that it be given to him.

⁵⁹ Joseph took the body and wrapped it in a clean linen cloth.
⁶⁰ Then he laid it in his own new tomb, which had been cut in a
rock. After rolling a large stone against the door of the tomb, he
went away. ⁶¹ Mary from Magdala and the other Mary were sitting
there, facing the tomb.

The Chief Priests and Pharisees Secure Jesus' Tomb

⁶² The next day, which was the day of worship, the chief priests
and Pharisees gathered together and went to Pilate. ⁶³ They said,
"Sir, we remember how that deceiver said while he was still alive,
'After three days I will be brought back to life.' ⁶⁴ Therefore, give
the order to make the tomb secure until the third day. Otherwise,
his disciples may steal him and say to the people, 'He has been
brought back to life.' Then the last deception will be worse than
the first."

⁶⁵ Pilate told them, "You have the soldiers you want for guard
duty. Go and make the tomb as secure as you know how."

⁶⁶ So they went to secure the tomb. They placed a seal on the
stone and posted the soldiers on guard duty.

Jesus Comes Back to Life—Mark 16:1–8; Luke 24:1–12; John 20:1–10

28 ¹ After the day of worship, as the sun rose Sunday morning,
Mary from Magdala and the other Mary went to look at the
tomb.

² Suddenly, there was a powerful earthquake. An angel of the
Lord had come down from heaven, rolled the stone away, and was
sitting on it. ³ He was as bright as lightning, and his clothes were
as white as snow. ⁴ The guards were so deathly afraid of him that
they shook.

⁵ The angel said to the women, "Don't be afraid! I know you're
looking for Jesus, who was crucified. ⁶ He's not here. He has been
brought back to life as he said. Come, see the place where he was
lying. ⁷ Then go quickly, and tell his disciples that he has been
brought back to life. He's going ahead of them into Galilee. There
they will see him. Take note that I have told you."

[8] They hurried away from the tomb with fear and great joy and ran to tell his disciples.

[9] Suddenly, Jesus met them and greeted them. They went up to him, bowed down to worship him, and took hold of his feet.

[10] Then Jesus said to them, "Don't be afraid! Go, tell my followers to go to Galilee. There they will see me."

The Guards Report to the Chief Priests

[11] While the women were on their way, some of the guards went into the city. They told the chief priests everything that had happened.

[12] The chief priests gathered together with the leaders and agreed on a plan. They gave the soldiers a large amount of money [13] and told them to say that Jesus' disciples had come at night and had stolen his body while they were sleeping. [14] They added, "If the governor hears about it, we'll take care of it, and you'll have nothing to worry about."

[15] The soldiers took the money and did as they were told. Their story has been spread among the Jewish people to this day.

Jesus Gives Instructions to the Disciples

[16] The eleven disciples went to the mountain in Galilee where Jesus had told them to go. [17] When they saw him, they bowed down in worship, though some had doubts.

[18] When Jesus came near, he spoke to them. He said, "All authority in heaven and on earth has been given to me. [19] So wherever you go, make disciples of all nations: Baptize them in the name of the Father, and of the Son, and of the Holy Spirit. [20] Teach them to do everything I have commanded you.

"And remember that I am always with you until the end of time."

MARK

John Prepares the Way—Matthew 3:1–12; Luke 3:1–18

1 ¹ This is the beginning of the Good News about Jesus Christ, the Son of God.

² The prophet Isaiah wrote,

> "I am sending my messenger ahead of you
> to prepare the way for you."

³ "A voice cries out in the desert:
> 'Prepare the way for the Lord!
> Make his paths straight!' "

⁴ John the Baptizer was in the desert telling people about a baptism of repentance*ᵃ* for the forgiveness of sins. ⁵ All Judea and all the people of Jerusalem went to him. As they confessed their sins, he baptized them in the Jordan River.

⁶ John was dressed in clothes made from camel's hair. He wore a leather belt around his waist and ate locusts and wild honey.

⁷ He announced, "The one who comes after me is more powerful than I. I am not worthy to bend down and untie his sandal straps. ⁸ I have baptized you with water, but he will baptize you with the Holy Spirit."

John Baptizes Jesus—Matthew 3:13–17; Luke 3:21–22

⁹ At that time Jesus came from Nazareth in Galilee and was baptized by John in the Jordan River. ¹⁰ As Jesus came out of the water,

---

ᵃ 1:4 "Repentance" is turning to God with a complete change in the way a person thinks and acts.

he saw heaven split open and the Spirit coming down to him as a dove. [11] A voice from heaven said, "You are my Son, whom I love. I am pleased with you."

Satan Tempts Jesus—*Matthew 4:1–11; Luke 4:1–13*

[12] At once the Spirit brought him into the desert, [13] where he was tempted by Satan for 40 days. He was there with the wild animals, and the angels took care of him.

Calling of the First Disciples— *Matthew 4:18–22; Luke 5:1–11*

[14] After John had been put in prison, Jesus went to Galilee and told people the Good News of God. [15] He said, "The time has come, and the kingdom of God is near. Change the way you think and act, and believe the Good News."

[16] As he was going along the Sea of Galilee, he saw Simon and his brother Andrew. They were throwing a net into the sea because they were fishermen. [17] Jesus said to them, "Come, follow me! I will teach you how to catch people instead of fish." [18] They immediately left their nets and followed him.

[19] As Jesus went on a little farther, he saw James and John, the sons of Zebedee. They were in a boat preparing their nets ˎto go fishingˏ. [20] He immediately called them, and they left their father Zebedee and the hired men in the boat and followed Jesus.

Jesus Forces an Evil Spirit out of a Man—*Luke 4:31–37*

[21] Then they went to Capernaum. On the next day of worship, Jesus went into the synagogue and began to teach. [22] The people were amazed at his teachings. Unlike their scribes, he taught them with authority.

[23] At that time there was a man in the synagogue who was controlled by an evil spirit. He shouted, [24] "What do you want with us, Jesus from Nazareth? Have you come to destroy us? I know who you are—the Holy One of God!"

²⁵ Jesus ordered the spirit, "Keep quiet, and come out of him!" ²⁶ The evil spirit threw the man into convulsions and came out of him with a loud shriek.

²⁷ Everyone was stunned. They said to each other, "What is this? This is a new teaching that has authority behind it! He gives orders to evil spirits, and they obey him."

²⁸ The news about him spread quickly throughout the surrounding region of Galilee.

Jesus Cures Simon's Mother-in-Law and Many Others—
Matthew 8:14–18; Luke 4:38–41

²⁹ After they left the synagogue, they went directly to the house of Simon and Andrew. James and John went with them. ³⁰ Simon's mother-in-law was in bed with a fever. The first thing they did was to tell Jesus about her. ³¹ Jesus went to her, took her hand, and helped her get up. The fever went away, and she prepared a meal for them.

³² In the evening, when the sun had set, people brought to him everyone who was sick and those possessed by demons. ³³ The whole city had gathered at his door. ³⁴ He cured many who were sick with various diseases and forced many demons out of people. However, he would not allow the demons to speak. After all, they knew who he was.

Spreading the Good News in Galilee—
Matthew 4:23–25; Luke 4:42–44

³⁵ In the morning, long before sunrise, Jesus went to a place where he could be alone to pray. ³⁶ Simon and his friends searched for him. ³⁷ When they found him, they told him, "Everyone is looking for you."

³⁸ Jesus said to them, "Let's go somewhere else, to the small towns that are nearby. I have to spread ⌊the Good News⌋ in them also. This is why I have come."

³⁹ So he went to spread ⌊the Good News⌋ in the synagogues all over Galilee, and he forced demons out of people.

Jesus Cures a Man With a Skin Disease—Matthew 8:1–4; Luke 5:12–14

⁴⁰ Then a man with a serious skin disease came to him. The man fell to his knees and begged Jesus, "If you're willing, you can make me clean."ᵇ

⁴¹ Jesus felt sorry for him, reached out, touched him, and said, "I'm willing. So be clean!"

⁴² Immediately, his skin disease went away, and he was clean.

⁴³ Jesus sent him away at once and warned him, ⁴⁴ "Don't tell anyone about this! Instead, show yourself to the priest. Then offer the sacrifices which Moses commanded as proof to people that you are clean."

⁴⁵ When the man left, he began to talk freely. He spread his story so widely that Jesus could no longer enter any city openly. Instead, he stayed in places where he could be alone. But people still kept coming to him from everywhere.

Jesus Forgives Sins—Matthew 9:1–8; Luke 5:17–26

2 ¹ Several days later Jesus came back to Capernaum. The report went out that he was home. ² Many people had gathered. There was no room left, even in front of the door. Jesus was speaking ₗGod's₎ word to them.

³ Four men came to him carrying a paralyzed man. ⁴ Since they could not bring him to Jesus because of the crowd, they made an opening in the roof over the place where Jesus was. Then they lowered the cot on which the paralyzed man was lying.

⁵ When Jesus saw their faith, he said to the man, "Friend, your sins are forgiven."

⁶ Some scribes were sitting there. They thought, ⁷ "Why does he talk this way? He's dishonoring God. Who besides God can forgive sins?"

⁸ At once, Jesus knew inwardly what they were thinking. He asked them, "Why do you have these thoughts? ⁹ Is it easier to say to this paralyzed man, 'Your sins are forgiven,' or to say, 'Get up,

---

ᵇ 1:40 "Clean" refers to anything that Moses' Teachings say is presentable to God.

pick up your cot, and walk'? [10] I want you to know that the Son of Man has authority on earth to forgive sins." Then he said to the paralyzed man, [11] "I'm telling you to get up, pick up your cot, and go home!"

[12] The man got up, immediately picked up his cot, and walked away while everyone watched. Everyone was amazed and praised God, saying, "We have never seen anything like this."

Jesus Chooses Levi [Matthew] to Be a Disciple— Matthew 9:9–13; Luke 5:27–32

[13] Jesus went to the seashore again. Large crowds came to him, and he taught them.

[14] When Jesus was leaving, he saw Levi, son of Alphaeus, sitting in a tax office. Jesus said to him, "Follow me!" So Levi got up and followed him.

[15] Later Jesus was having dinner at Levi's house. Many tax collectors and sinners who were followers of Jesus were eating with him and his disciples. [16] When the scribes who were Pharisees saw him eating with sinners and tax collectors, they asked his disciples, "Why does he eat with tax collectors and sinners?"

[17] When Jesus heard that, he said to them, "Healthy people don't need a doctor; those who are sick do. I've come to call sinners, not people who think they have God's approval."

Jesus Is Questioned About Fasting—Matthew 9:14–17; Luke 5:33–39

[18] John's disciples and the Pharisees were fasting. Some people came to Jesus and said to him, "Why do John's disciples and the Pharisees' disciples fast, but your disciples don't?"

[19] Jesus replied, "Can wedding guests fast while the groom is still with them? As long as they have the groom with them, they cannot fast. [20] But the time will come when the groom will be taken away from them. Then they will fast.

[21] "No one patches an old coat with a new piece of cloth that will shrink. Otherwise, the new patch will shrink and rip away some of the old cloth, and the tear will become worse. [22] People don't pour

new wine into old wineskins. If they do, the wine will make the skins burst, and both the wine and the skins will be ruined. Rather, new wine is to be poured into fresh skins."

Jesus Has Authority Over the Day of Worship—
Matthew 12:1–8; Luke 6:1–5

²³ Once on a day of worship Jesus was going through the grainfields. As the disciples walked along, they began to pick the heads of grain.

²⁴ The Pharisees asked him, "Look! Why are your disciples doing something that is not permitted on the day of worship?"

²⁵ Jesus asked them, "Haven't you ever read what David did when he and his men were in need and were hungry? ²⁶ Haven't you ever read how he went into the house of God when Abiathar was chief priest and ate the bread of the presence? He had no right to eat those loaves. Only the priests have that right. Haven't you ever read how he also gave some of it to his men?"

²⁷ Then he added, "The day of worship was made for people, not people for the day of worship. ²⁸ For this reason the Son of Man has authority over the day of worship."

Jesus Heals on the Day of Worship—Matthew 12:9–15a; Luke 6:6–11

3 ¹ Jesus went into a synagogue again. A man who had a paralyzed hand was there. ² The people were watching Jesus closely. They wanted to see whether he would heal the man on the day of worship so that they could accuse him of doing something wrong.

³ So he told the man with the paralyzed hand, "Stand in the center ˻of the synagogue˼." ⁴ Then he asked them, "Is it right to do good or to do evil on the day of worship, to give a person back his health or to let him die?"

But they were silent. ⁵ Jesus was angry as he looked around at them. He was deeply hurt because their minds were closed. Then he told the man, "Hold out your hand." The man held it out, and his hand became normal again.

⁶ The Pharisees left, and with Herod's followers they immediately plotted to kill Jesus.

Many People Are Cured—Luke 6:17–19

⁷ Jesus left with his disciples for the Sea of Galilee. A large crowd from Galilee, Judea, ⁸ Jerusalem, Idumea, and from across the Jordan River, and from around Tyre and Sidon followed him. They came to him because they had heard about everything he was doing. ⁹ Jesus told his disciples to have a boat ready so that the crowd would not crush him. ¹⁰ He had cured so many that everyone with a disease rushed up to him in order to touch him. ¹¹ Whenever people with evil spirits saw him, they would fall down in front of him and shout, "You are the Son of God!" ¹² He gave them orders not to tell people who he was.

Jesus Appoints Twelve Apostles—Matthew 10:1–4; Luke 6:13–16

¹³ Jesus went up a mountain, called those whom he wanted, and they came to him. ¹⁴ He appointed twelve whom he called apostles.ᵃ They were to accompany him and to be sent out by him to spread ˌthe Good Newsˌ. ¹⁵ They also had the authority to force demons out of people.

¹⁶ He appointed these twelve: Simon (whom Jesus named Peter), ¹⁷ James and his brother John (Zebedee's sons whom Jesus named Boanerges, which means "Thunderbolts"), ¹⁸ Andrew, Philip, Bartholomew, Matthew, Thomas, James (son of Alphaeus), Thaddaeus, Simon the Zealot, ¹⁹ and Judas Iscariot (who later betrayed Jesus).

Jesus Is Accused of Working With Beelzebul—
Matthew 12:22–32; Luke 11:14–23

²⁰ Then Jesus went home. Another crowd gathered so that Jesus and his disciples could not even eat. ²¹ When his family heard about it, they went to get him. They said, "He's out of his mind!"

ᵃ 3:14 Some manuscripts and translations omit "whom he called apostles."

²² The scribes who had come from Jerusalem said, "Beelzebul is in him," and "He forces demons out of people with the help of the ruler of demons."

²³ Jesus called them together and used this illustration: "How can Satan force out Satan? ²⁴ If a kingdom is divided against itself, that kingdom cannot last. ²⁵ And if a household is divided against itself, that household will not last. ²⁶ So if Satan rebels against himself and is divided, he cannot last. That will be the end of him.

²⁷ "No one can go into a strong man's house and steal his property. First he must tie up the strong man. Then he can go through the strong man's house and steal his property.

²⁸ "I can guarantee this truth: People will be forgiven for any sin or curse. ²⁹ But whoever curses the Holy Spirit will never be forgiven. He is guilty of an everlasting sin." ³⁰ Jesus said this because the scribes had said that he had an evil spirit.

The True Family of Jesus—Matthew 12:46–50; Luke 8:19–21

³¹ Then his mother and his brothers arrived. They stood outside and sent someone to ask him to come out. ³² The crowd sitting around Jesus told him, "Your mother and your brothers are outside looking for you."

³³ He replied to them, "Who is my mother, and who are my brothers?" ³⁴ Then looking at those who sat in a circle around him, he said, "Look, here are my mother and my brothers. ³⁵ Whoever does what God wants is my brother and sister and mother."

A Story About a Farmer—Matthew 13:1–23; Luke 8:4–15

4 ¹ Jesus began to teach again by the Sea of Galilee. A very large crowd gathered around him, so he got into a boat and sat in it. The boat was in the water while the entire crowd lined the shore. ² He used stories as illustrations to teach them many things.

While he was teaching them, he said, ³ "Listen! A farmer went to plant seed. ⁴ Some seeds were planted along the road, and birds came and devoured them. ⁵ Other seeds were planted on rocky ground, where there wasn't much soil. The plants sprouted quickly because the soil wasn't deep. ⁶ When the sun came up, they were scorched. They didn't have any roots, so they withered. ⁷ Other seeds were planted among thornbushes. The thornbushes grew up and choked them, and they didn't produce anything. ⁸ But other seeds were planted on good ground, sprouted, and produced thirty, sixty, or one hundred times as much as was planted." ⁹ He added, "Let the person who has ears listen!"

¹⁰ When he was alone with his followers and the twelve apostles, they asked him about the stories.

¹¹ Jesus replied to them, "The mystery about the kingdom of God has been given ˌdirectlyˌ to you. To those on the outside, it is given in stories:

¹² 'They see clearly but don't perceive.
They hear clearly but don't understand.
They never return to me
and are never forgiven.' "

¹³ Jesus asked them, "Don't you understand this story? How, then, will you understand any of the stories I use as illustrations?

¹⁴ "The farmer plants the word. ¹⁵ Some people are like seeds that were planted along the road. Whenever they hear the word, Satan comes at once and takes away the word that was planted in them. ¹⁶ Other people are like seeds that were planted on rocky ground. Whenever they hear the word, they accept it at once with joy. ¹⁷ But they don't develop any roots. They last for a short time. When suffering or persecution comes along because of the word, they immediately fall ˌfrom faithˌ. ¹⁸ Other people are like seeds planted among thornbushes. They hear the word, ¹⁹ but the worries of life, the deceitful pleasures of riches, and the desires for other things take over. They choke the word so that it can't produce anything. ²⁰ Others are like seeds planted on good ground. They hear the word, accept it, and produce crops—thirty, sixty, or one hundred times as much as was planted."

A Story About a Lamp

21 Jesus said to them, "Does anyone bring a lamp into a room to put it under a basket or under a bed? Isn't it put on a lamp stand? **22** There is nothing hidden that will not be revealed. There is nothing kept secret that will not come to light. **23** Let the person who has ears listen!"

24 He went on to say, "Pay attention to what you're listening to! ˌKnowledgeˌ will be measured out to you by the measure ˌof attentionˌ you give. This is the way knowledge increases. **25** Those who understand ˌthese mysteriesˌ will be given ˌmore knowledgeˌ. However, some people don't understand ˌthese mysteriesˌ. Even what they understand will be taken away from them."

A Story About Seeds That Grow

26 Jesus said, "The kingdom of God is like a man who scatters seeds on the ground. **27** He sleeps at night and is awake during the day. The seeds sprout and grow, although the man doesn't know how. **28** The ground produces grain by itself. First the green blade appears, then the head, then the head full of grain. **29** As soon as the grain is ready, he cuts it with a sickle, because harvest time has come."

A Story About a Mustard Seed—
Matthew 13:31–32; Luke 13:18–19

30 Jesus asked, "How can we show what the kingdom of God is like? To what can we compare it? **31** It's like a mustard seed planted in the ground. The mustard seed is one of the smallest seeds on earth. **32** However, when planted, it comes up and becomes taller than all the garden plants. It grows such large branches that birds can nest in its shade."

33 Jesus spoke ˌGod'sˌ word to them using many illustrations like these. In this way people could understand what he taught. **34** He did not speak to them without using an illustration. But when he was alone with his disciples, he explained everything to them.

Jesus Calms the Sea—*Matthew 8:23–27; Luke 8:22–25*

35 That evening, Jesus said to his disciples, "Let's cross to the other side."

36 Leaving the crowd, they took Jesus along in a boat just as he was. Other boats were with him.

37 A violent windstorm came up. The waves were breaking into the boat so that it was quickly filling up. **38** But he was sleeping on a cushion in the back of the boat.

So they woke him up and said to him, "Teacher, don't you care that we're going to die?"

39 Then he got up, ordered the wind to stop, and said to the sea, "Be still, absolutely still!" The wind stopped blowing, and the sea became very calm.

40 He asked them, "Why are you such cowards? Don't you have any faith yet?"

41 They were overcome with fear and asked each other, "Who is this man? Even the wind and the sea obey him!"

Jesus Cures a Demon-Possessed Man—
Matthew 8:28–34; Luke 8:26–39

5 **1** They arrived in the territory of the Gerasenes on the other side of the Sea of Galilee. **2** As Jesus stepped out of the boat, a man came out of the tombs and met him. The man was controlled by an evil spirit **3** and lived among the tombs. No one could restrain him any longer, not even with a chain. **4** He had often been chained hand and foot. However, he snapped the chains off his hands and broke the chains from his feet. No one could control him. **5** Night and day he was among the tombs and on the mountainsides screaming and cutting himself with stones.

6 The man saw Jesus at a distance. So he ran ͺto Jesusͺ, bowed down in front of him, **7** and shouted, "Why are you bothering me now, Jesus, Son of the Most High God? Swear to God that you won't torture me." **8** He shouted this because Jesus said, "You evil spirit, come out of the man."

9 Jesus asked him, "What is your name?"

He told Jesus, "My name is Legion [Six Thousand], because there are many of us." [10] He begged Jesus not to send them out of the territory.

[11] A large herd of pigs was feeding on a mountainside nearby. [12] The demons begged him, "Send us into the pigs! Let us enter them!"

[13] Jesus let them do this. The evil spirits came out of the man and went into the pigs. The herd of about two thousand pigs rushed down the cliff into the sea and drowned.

[14] Those who took care of the pigs ran away. In the city and countryside they reported everything that had happened. So the people came to see what had happened. [15] They came to Jesus and saw the man who had been possessed by the legion of demons. The man was sitting there dressed and in his right mind. The people were frightened. [16] Those who saw this told what had happened to the demon-possessed man and the pigs. [17] Then the people began to beg Jesus to leave their territory.

[18] As Jesus stepped into the boat, the man who had been demon-possessed begged him, "Let me stay with you." [19] But Jesus would not allow it. Instead, he told the man, "Go home to your family, and tell them how much the Lord has done for you and how merciful he has been to you."

[20] So the man left. He began to tell how much Jesus had done for him in the Ten Cities.[a] Everyone was amazed.

Jairus' Daughter and a Woman With Chronic Bleeding—
Matthew 9:18–26; Luke 8:40–56

[21] Jesus again crossed to the other side of the Sea of Galilee in a boat. A large crowd gathered around him by the seashore.

[22] A synagogue leader named Jairus also arrived. When he saw Jesus, he quickly bowed down in front of him. [23] He begged Jesus, "My little daughter is dying. Come, lay your hands on her so that she may get well and live."

---

[a] 5:20 A federation of ten Greek city states east and west of the Jordan River.

²⁴ Jesus went with the man. A huge crowd followed Jesus and pressed him on every side.

²⁵ In the crowd was a woman who had been suffering from chronic bleeding for twelve years. ²⁶ Although she had been under the care of many doctors and had spent all her money, she had not been helped at all. Actually, she had become worse. ²⁷ Since she had heard about Jesus, she came from behind in the crowd and touched his clothes. ²⁸ She said, "If I can just touch his clothes, I'll get well." ²⁹ Her bleeding stopped immediately. She felt cured from her illness.

³⁰ At that moment Jesus felt power had gone out of him. He turned around in the crowd and asked, "Who touched my clothes?"

³¹ His disciples said to him, "How can you ask, 'Who touched me,' when you see the crowd pressing you on all sides?"

³² But he kept looking around to see the woman who had done this. ³³ The woman trembled with fear. She knew what had happened to her. So she quickly bowed in front of him and told him the whole truth.

³⁴ Jesus told her, "Daughter, your faith has made you well. Go in peace! Be cured from your illness."

³⁵ While Jesus was still speaking to her, some people came from the synagogue leader's home. They told the synagogue leader, "Your daughter has died. Why bother the teacher anymore?"

³⁶ When Jesus overheard what they said, he told the synagogue leader, "Don't be afraid! Just believe."

³⁷ Jesus allowed no one to go with him except Peter and the two brothers James and John. ³⁸ When they came to the home of the synagogue leader, Jesus saw a noisy crowd there. People were crying and sobbing loudly. ³⁹ When he came into the house, he asked them, "Why are you making so much noise and crying? The child isn't dead. She's just sleeping."

⁴⁰ They laughed at him. So he made all of them go outside. Then he took the child's father, mother, and his three disciples and went

to the child. **41** Jesus took the child's hand and said to her, "Talitha, koum!" which means, "Little girl, I'm telling you to get up!"

42 The girl got up at once and started to walk. (She was twelve years old.) They were astonished.

43 Jesus ordered them not to let anyone know about this. He also told them to give the little girl something to eat.

Nazareth Rejects Jesus—Matthew 13:54–58; Luke 4:14–30

6 **1** Jesus left that place and went to his hometown. His disciples followed him. **2** When the day of worship came, he began to teach in the synagogue. He amazed many who heard him. They asked, "Where did this man get these ideas? Who gave him this kind of wisdom and the ability to do such great miracles? **3** Isn't this the carpenter, the son of Mary, and the brother of James, Joseph, Judas, and Simon? Aren't his sisters here with us?" So they took offense at him.

4 But Jesus told them, "The only place a prophet isn't honored is in his hometown, among his relatives, and in his own house." **5** He couldn't work any miracles there except to lay his hands on a few sick people and cure them. **6** Their unbelief amazed him.

Jesus Sends Out the Twelve—
Matthew 10:5–42; Luke 9:1–6

Then Jesus went around to the villages and taught.

7 He called the twelve apostles, sent them out two by two, and gave them authority over evil spirits. **8** He instructed them to take nothing along on the trip except a walking stick. They were not to take any food, a traveling bag, or money in their pockets. **9** They could wear sandals but could not take along a change of clothes.

10 He told them, "Whenever you go into a home, stay there until you're ready to leave that place. **11** Wherever people don't welcome you or listen to you, leave and shake the dust from your feet as a warning to them."

12 So the apostles went and told people that they should turn to God and change the way they think and act. **13** They also forced

many demons out of people and poured oil on many who were
sick to cure them.

Recalling John's Death—Matthew 14:1–12; Luke 9:7–9

¹⁴ King Herod heard about Jesus, because Jesus' name had
become well-known. Some people were saying, "John the Baptizer
has come back to life. That's why he has the power to perform
these miracles." ¹⁵ Others said, "He is Elijah." Still others said, "He
is a prophet like one of the other prophets." ¹⁶ But when Herod
heard about it, he said, "I had John's head cut off, and he has come
back to life!"

¹⁷ Herod had sent men who had arrested John, tied him up,
and put him in prison. Herod did that for Herodias, whom he had
married. (She used to be his brother Philip's wife.) ¹⁸ John had
been telling Herod, "It's not right for you to be married to your
brother's wife."

¹⁹ So Herodias held a grudge against John and wanted to kill
him. But she wasn't allowed to do it ²⁰ because Herod was afraid
of John. Herod knew that John was a fair and holy man, so he
protected him. When he listened to John, he would become very
disturbed, and yet he liked to listen to him.

²¹ An opportunity finally came on Herod's birthday. Herod gave
a dinner for his top officials, army officers, and the most important
people of Galilee. ²² His daughter, that is, Herodias' daughter, came
in and danced. Herod and his guests were delighted with her. The
king told the girl, "Ask me for anything you want, and I'll give it
to you." ²³ He swore an oath to her: "I'll give you anything you ask
for, up to half of my kingdom."

²⁴ So she went out and asked her mother, "What should I ask for?"

Her mother said, "Ask for the head of John the Baptizer."

²⁵ So the girl hurried back to the king with her request. She
said, "I want you to give me the head of John the Baptizer on a
platter at once."

²⁶ The king deeply regretted his promise. But because of his
oath and his guests, he didn't want to refuse her. ²⁷ Immediately, the

king sent a guard and ordered him to bring John's head. The guard cut off John's head in prison. [28] Then he brought the head on a platter and gave it to the girl, and the girl gave it to her mother.

[29] When John's disciples heard about this, they came for his body and laid it in a tomb.

Jesus Feeds Five Thousand—
Matthew 14:13–21; Luke 9:10–17; John 6:1–14

[30] The apostles gathered around Jesus. They reported to him everything they had done and taught. [31] So he said to them, "Let's go to a place where we can be alone to rest for a while." Many people were coming and going, and Jesus and the apostles didn't even have a chance to eat.

[32] So they went away in a boat to a place where they could be alone. [33] But many people saw them leave and recognized them. The people ran from all the cities and arrived ahead of them. [34] When Jesus got out of the boat, he saw a large crowd and felt sorry for them. They were like sheep without a shepherd. So he spent a lot of time teaching them.

[35] When it was late, his disciples came to him. They said, "No one lives around here, and it's already late. [36] Send the people to the closest farms and villages to buy themselves something to eat."

[37] Jesus replied, "You give them something to eat."

They said to him, "Should we go and spend about a year's wages on bread to feed them?"

[38] He said to them, "How many loaves do you have? Go and see."

When they found out, they told him, "Five loaves of bread and two fish."

[39] Then he ordered all of them to sit down in groups on the green grass. [40] They sat down in groups of hundreds and fifties.

[41] After he took the five loaves and the two fish, he looked up to heaven and blessed the food. He broke the loaves apart and kept giving them to the disciples to give to the people. He also gave pieces of the two fish to everyone. [42] All of them ate as much as they wanted. [43] When they picked up the leftover pieces, they filled

twelve baskets with bread and fish. **44** There were 5,000 men who had eaten the bread.

Jesus Walks on the Sea—Matthew 14:22–36; John 6:15–21

45 Jesus quickly made his disciples get into a boat and cross to Bethsaida ahead of him while he sent the people away. **46** After saying goodbye to them, he went up a mountain to pray. **47** When evening came, the boat was in the middle of the sea, and he was alone on the land.

48 Jesus saw that they were in a lot of trouble as they rowed, because they were going against the wind. Between three and six o'clock in the morning, he came to them. He was walking on the sea. He wanted to pass by them. **49** When they saw him walking on the sea, they thought, "It's a ghost!" and they began to scream. **50** All of them saw him and were terrified.

Immediately, he said, "Calm down! It's me. Don't be afraid!" **51** He got into the boat with them, and the wind stopped blowing. The disciples were astounded. **52** (They didn't understand what had happened with the loaves of bread. Instead, their minds were closed.)

53 They crossed the sea, came to shore at Gennesaret, and anchored there.

54 As soon as they stepped out of the boat, the people recognized Jesus. **55** They ran all over the countryside and began to carry the sick on cots to any place where they heard he was. **56** Whenever he would go into villages, cities, or farms, people would put their sick in the marketplaces. They begged him to let them touch the edge of his clothes. Everyone who touched his clothes was made well.

Jesus Challenges the Pharisees' Traditions—Matthew 15:1–20

7 **1** The Pharisees and some scribes who had come from Jerusalem gathered around Jesus. **2** They saw that some of his disciples were unclean*a* because they ate without washing their hands.

---

a 7:2 "Unclean" refers to anything that Moses' Teachings say is not presentable to God.

³ (The Pharisees, like all other Jewish people, don't eat unless they have properly washed their hands. They follow the traditions of their ancestors. ⁴ When they come from the marketplace, they don't eat unless they have washed first. They have been taught to follow many other rules. For example, they must also wash their cups, jars, brass pots, and dinner tables.ᵇ)

⁵ The Pharisees and the scribes asked Jesus, "Why don't your disciples follow the traditions taught by our ancestors? They are unclean because they don't wash their hands before they eat!"

⁶ Jesus told them, "Isaiah was right when he prophesied about you hypocrites in Scripture:

'These people honor me with their lips,
    but their hearts are far from me.
⁷   Their worship of me is pointless,
    because their teachings are rules made by humans.'

⁸ "You abandon the commandments of God to follow human traditions." ⁹ He added, "You have no trouble rejecting the commandments of God in order to keep your own traditions! ¹⁰ For example, Moses said, 'Honor your father and your mother' and 'Whoever curses father or mother must be put to death.' ¹¹ But you say, 'If a person tells his father or mother that whatever he might have used to help them is *corban* (that is, an offering to God), ¹² he no longer has to do anything for his father or mother.' ¹³ Because of your traditions you have destroyed the authority of God's word. And you do many other things like that."

¹⁴ Then he called the crowd again and said to them, "Listen to me, all of you, and try to understand! ¹⁵ Nothing that goes into a person from the outside can make him unclean. It's what comes out of a person that makes him unclean. ¹⁶ Let the person who has ears listen!"ᶜ

¹⁷ When he had left the people and gone home, his disciples asked him about this illustration.

ᵇ 7:4 Some manuscripts and translations omit "and dinner tables."   ᶜ 7:16 Some manuscripts and translations omit this verse.

¹⁸ Jesus said to them, "Don't you understand? Don't you know that whatever goes into a person from the outside can't make him unclean? ¹⁹ It doesn't go into his thoughts but into his stomach and then into a toilet." (By saying this, Jesus declared all foods acceptable.) ²⁰ He continued, "It's what comes out of a person that makes him unclean. ²¹ Evil thoughts, sexual sins, stealing, murder, ²² adultery, greed, wickedness, cheating, shameless lust, envy, cursing, arrogance, and foolishness come from within a person. ²³ All these evils come from within and make a person unclean."

The Faith of a Greek Woman—Matthew 15:21–31

²⁴ Jesus left that place and went to the territory of Tyre. He didn't want anyone to know that he was staying in a house there. However, it couldn't be kept a secret.

²⁵ A woman whose little daughter had an evil spirit heard about Jesus. She went to him and bowed down. ²⁶ The woman happened to be Greek, born in Phoenicia in Syria. She asked him to force the demon out of her daughter.

²⁷ Jesus said to her, "First, let the children eat all they want. It's not right to take the children's food and throw it to the dogs."

²⁸ She answered him, "Lord, even the dogs under the table eat some of the children's scraps."

²⁹ Jesus said to her, "Because you have said this, go! The demon has left your daughter."

³⁰ The woman went home and found the little child lying on her bed, and the demon was gone.

Jesus Cures a Deaf Man

³¹ Jesus then left the neighborhood of Tyre. He went through Sidon and the territory of the Ten Cities*d* to the Sea of Galilee.

³² Some people brought to him a man who was deaf and who also had a speech defect. They begged Jesus to lay his hand on him. ³³ Jesus took him away from the crowd to be alone with

---

d 7:31 A federation of ten Greek city states east and west of the Jordan River.

him. He put his fingers into the man's ears, and after spitting, he touched the man's tongue. [34] Then he looked up to heaven, sighed, and said to the man, "Ephphatha!" which means, "Be opened!" [35] At once the man could hear and talk normally.

[36] Jesus ordered the people not to tell anyone. But the more he ordered them, the more they spread the news. [37] Jesus completely amazed the people. They said, "He has done everything well. He makes the deaf hear and the mute talk."

Jesus Feeds Four Thousand—Matthew 15:32–39

8 [1] About that time there was once again a large crowd with nothing to eat. Jesus called his disciples and said to them, [2] "I feel sorry for the people. They have been with me three days now and have nothing to eat. [3] If I send them home before they've eaten, they will become exhausted on the road. Some of them have come a long distance."

[4] His disciples asked him, "Where could anyone get enough bread to feed these people in this place where no one lives?"

[5] Jesus asked them, "How many loaves of bread do you have?" They answered, "Seven."

[6] He ordered the crowd to sit down on the ground. He took the seven loaves and gave thanks to God. Then he broke the bread and gave it to his disciples to serve to the people. [7] They also had a few small fish. He blessed them and said that the fish should also be served to the people. [8] The people ate as much as they wanted. The disciples picked up the leftover pieces and filled seven large baskets. [9] About four thousand people were there. Then he sent the people on their way.

[10] After that, Jesus and his disciples got into a boat and went into the region of Dalmanutha.

The Pharisees Ask For a Sign From Heaven—Matthew 16:1–4

[11] The Pharisees went to Jesus and began to argue with him. They tested him by demanding that he perform a miraculous sign from heaven.

¹² With a deep sigh he asked, "Why do these people demand a sign? I can guarantee this truth: If these people are given a sign, it will be far different than what they want!"

¹³ Then he left them there.

The Yeast of the Pharisees—Matthew 16:5–12

He got into a boat again and crossed to the other side of the Sea of Galilee. ¹⁴ The disciples had forgotten to take any bread along and had only one loaf with them in the boat.

¹⁵ Jesus warned them, "Be careful! Watch out for the yeast of the Pharisees and the yeast of Herod!"

¹⁶ They had been discussing with one another that they didn't have any bread.

¹⁷ Jesus knew what they were saying and asked them, "Why are you discussing the fact that you don't have any bread? Don't you understand yet? Don't you catch on? Are your minds closed? ¹⁸ Are you blind and deaf? Don't you remember? ¹⁹ When I broke the five loaves for the five thousand, how many baskets did you fill with leftover pieces?"

They told him, "Twelve."

²⁰ "When I broke the seven loaves for the four thousand, how many large baskets did you fill with leftover pieces?"

They answered him, "Seven."

²¹ He asked them, "Don't you catch on yet?"

Jesus Gives Sight to a Blind Man

²² As they came to Bethsaida, some people brought a blind man to Jesus. They begged Jesus to touch him. ²³ Jesus took the blind man's hand and led him out of the village. He spit into the man's eyes and placed his hands on him. Jesus asked him, "Can you see anything?"

²⁴ The man looked up and said, "I see people. They look like trees walking around."

²⁵ Then Jesus placed his hands on the man's eyes a second time, and the man saw clearly. His sight was normal again. He could see

everything clearly even at a distance. [26] Jesus told him when he sent him home, "Don't go into the village."

Peter Declares His Belief About Jesus—
Matthew 16:13–20; Luke 9:18–21

[27] Then Jesus and his disciples went to the villages around Caesarea Philippi. On the way he asked his disciples, "Who do people say I am?"

[28] They answered him, "Some say you are John the Baptizer, others Elijah, still others one of the prophets."

[29] He asked them, "But who do you say I am?"

Peter answered him, "You are the Messiah!"

[30] He ordered them not to tell anyone about him.

Jesus Foretells That He Will Die and Come Back to Life—
Matthew 16:21–23; Luke 9:22

[31] Then he began to teach them that the Son of Man would have to suffer a lot. He taught them that he would be rejected by the leaders, the chief priests, and the scribes. He would be killed, but after three days he would come back to life. [32] He told them very clearly what he meant.

Peter took him aside and objected to this. [33] Jesus turned, looked at his disciples, and objected to what Peter said. Jesus said, "Get out of my way, Satan! You aren't thinking the way God thinks but the way humans think."

What It Means to Follow Jesus—Matthew 16:24–28; Luke 9:23–27

[34] Then Jesus called the crowd to himself along with his disciples. He said to them, "Those who want to follow me must say no to the things they want, pick up their crosses, and follow me. [35] Those who want to save their lives will lose them. But those who lose their lives for me and for the Good News will save them. [36] What good does it do for people to win the whole world yet lose their lives? [37] Or what should a person give in exchange for life? [38] If people are ashamed of me and what I say in this unfaithful and

sinful generation, the Son of Man will be ashamed of those people
when he comes with the holy angels in his Father's glory."

9 ¹ He said to them, "I can guarantee this truth: Some people
who are standing here will not die until they see the kingdom
of God arrive with power."

Moses and Elijah Appear With Jesus—Matthew 17:1–8; Luke 9:28–36

² After six days Jesus took only Peter, James, and John and led
them up a high mountain where they could be alone.

Jesus' appearance changed in front of them. ³ His clothes
became dazzling white, whiter than anyone on earth could bleach
them. ⁴ Then Elijah and Moses appeared to them and were talking
with Jesus.

⁵ Peter said to Jesus, "Rabbi, it's good that we're here. Let's put up
three tents—one for you, one for Moses, and one for Elijah." ⁶ (Peter
didn't know how to respond. He and the others were terrified.)

⁷ Then a cloud overshadowed them. A voice came out of the
cloud and said, "This is my Son, whom I love. Listen to him!"

⁸ Suddenly, as they looked around, they saw no one with them
but Jesus.

⁹ On their way down the mountain, Jesus ordered them not to tell
anyone what they had seen. They were to wait until the Son of Man
had come back to life. ¹⁰ They kept in mind what he said but argued
among themselves what he meant by "come back to life." ¹¹ So they
asked him, "Don't the scribes say that Elijah must come first?"

¹² Jesus said to them, "Elijah is coming first and will put everything in order again. But in what sense was it written that the Son
of Man must suffer a lot and be treated shamefully? ¹³ Indeed, I can
guarantee that Elijah has come. Yet, people treated him as they
pleased, as Scripture says about him."

Jesus Cures a Demon-Possessed Boy—
Matthew 17:14–20; Luke 9:37–43a

¹⁴ When they came to the other disciples, they saw a large
crowd around them. Some scribes were arguing with them. ¹⁵ All

the people were very surprised to see Jesus and ran to welcome him.

¹⁶ Jesus asked the scribes, "What are you arguing about with them?"

¹⁷ A man in the crowd answered, "Teacher, I brought you my son. He is possessed by a spirit that won't let him talk. ¹⁸ Whenever the spirit brings on a seizure, it throws him to the ground. Then he foams at the mouth, grinds his teeth, and becomes exhausted. I asked your disciples to force the spirit out, but they didn't have the power to do it."

¹⁹ Jesus said to them, "You unbelieving generation! How long must I be with you? How long must I put up with you? Bring him to me!"

²⁰ They brought the boy to him. As soon as the spirit saw Jesus, it threw the boy into convulsions. He fell on the ground, rolled around, and foamed at the mouth.

²¹ Jesus asked his father, "How long has he been like this?"

The father replied, "He has been this way since he was a child. ²² The demon has often thrown him into fire or into water to destroy him. If it's possible for you, put yourself in our place, and help us!"

²³ Jesus said to him, "As far as possibilities go, everything is possible for the person who believes."

²⁴ The child's father cried out at once, "I believe! Help my lack of faith."

²⁵ When Jesus saw that a crowd was running to the scene, he gave an order to the evil spirit. He said, "You spirit that won't let him talk, I command you to come out of him and never enter him again."

²⁶ The evil spirit screamed, shook the child violently, and came out. The boy looked as if he were dead, and everyone said, "He's dead!"

²⁷ Jesus took his hand and helped him to stand up.

²⁸ When Jesus went into a house, his disciples asked him privately, "Why couldn't we force the spirit out of the boy?"

[29] He told them, "This kind of spirit can be forced out only by prayer."[a]

Jesus Again Foretells That He Will Die and Come Back to Life—
Matthew 17:22–23; Luke 9:43b–45

[30] They left that place and were passing through Galilee. Jesus did not want anyone to know where he was [31] because he was teaching his disciples. He taught them, "The Son of Man will be betrayed and handed over to people. They will kill him, but on the third day he will come back to life."

[32] The disciples didn't understand what he meant and were afraid to ask him.

Greatness in the Kingdom—*Matthew 18:1–5; Luke 9:46–48*

[33] Then they came to Capernaum. While Jesus was at home, he asked the disciples, "What were you arguing about on the road?" [34] They were silent. On the road they had argued about who was the greatest.

[35] He sat down and called the twelve apostles. He told them, "Whoever wants to be the most important person must take the last place and be a servant to everyone else." [36] Then he took a little child and had him stand among them. He put his arms around the child and said to them, [37] "Whoever welcomes a child like this in my name welcomes me. Whoever welcomes me welcomes not me but the one who sent me."

Using the Name of Jesus—*Luke 9:49–50*

[38] John said to Jesus, "Teacher, we saw someone forcing demons out of a person by using the power and authority of your name. We tried to stop him because he was not one of us."

[39] Jesus said, "Don't stop him! No one who works a miracle in my name can turn around and speak evil of me. [40] Whoever isn't against us is for us. [41] I can guarantee this truth: Whoever gives you a cup of

---

[a] 9:29 Some manuscripts and translations add "and fasting."

water to drink because you belong to Christ will certainly not lose his reward."

Causing Others to Lose Faith—*Matthew 18:6–10; Luke 17:1–4*

⁴² "These little ones believe in me. It would be best for the person who causes one of them to lose faith to be thrown into the sea with a large stone hung around his neck.

⁴³ "So if your hand causes you to lose your faith, cut it off! It is better for you to enter life disabled than to have two hands and go to hell, to the fire that cannot be put out.ᵇ ⁴⁵ If your foot causes you to lose your faith, cut it off! It is better for you to enter life lame than to have two feet and be thrown into hell. ⁴⁷ If your eye causes you to lose your faith, tear it out! It is better for you to enter the kingdom of God with one eye than to have two eyes and be thrown into hell. ⁴⁸ In hell worms that eat the body never die, and the fire is never put out. ⁴⁹ Everyone will be salted with fire. ⁵⁰ Salt is good. But if salt loses its taste, how will you restore its flavor? Have salt within you, and live in peace with one another."

A Discussion About Divorce—*Matthew 19:1–12*

10 ¹ Jesus left there and went into the territory of Judea along the other side of the Jordan River. Crowds gathered around him again, and he taught them as he usually did.

² Some Pharisees came to test him. They asked, "Can a husband divorce his wife?"

³ Jesus answered them, "What command did Moses give you?"

⁴ They said, "Moses allowed a man to give his wife a written notice to divorce her."

⁵ Jesus said to them, "He wrote this command for you because you're heartless. ⁶ But God made them male and female in the beginning, at creation. ⁷ That's why a man will leave his father and mother and will remain united with his wife, ⁸ and the two will

---

ᵇ 9:43 Some manuscripts and translations add verses 44 and 46, which both say: "In hell worms that eat the body never die, and the fire is never put out."

be one. So they are no longer two but one. ⁹ Therefore, don't let anyone separate what God has joined together."

¹⁰ When they were in a house, the disciples asked him about this. ¹¹ He answered them, "Whoever divorces his wife and marries another woman is committing adultery. ¹² If a wife divorces her husband and marries another man, she is committing adultery."

Jesus Blesses Children—Matthew 19:13–15; Luke 18:15–17

¹³ Some people brought little children to Jesus to have him hold them. But the disciples told the people not to do that.

¹⁴ When Jesus saw this, he became irritated. He told them, "Don't stop the children from coming to me. Children like these are part of the kingdom of God. ¹⁵ I can guarantee this truth: Whoever doesn't receive the kingdom of God as a little child receives it will never enter it."

¹⁶ Jesus put his arms around the children and blessed them by placing his hands on them.

Eternal Life in the Kingdom—Matthew 19:16–30; Luke 18:18–30

¹⁷ As Jesus was coming out to the road, a man came running to him and knelt in front of him. He asked Jesus, "Good Teacher, what should I do to inherit eternal life?"

¹⁸ Jesus said to him, "Why do you call me good? No one is good except God alone. ¹⁹ You know the commandments: Never murder. Never commit adultery. Never steal. Never give false testimony. Never cheat. Honor your father and mother."

²⁰ The man replied, "Teacher, I've obeyed all these commandments since I was a boy."

²¹ Jesus looked at him and loved him. He told him, "You're still missing one thing. Sell everything you have. Give the money to the poor, and you will have treasure in heaven. Then follow me!"

²² When the man heard that, he looked unhappy and went away sad, because he owned a lot of property.

²³ Jesus looked around and said to his disciples, "How hard it will be for rich people to enter the kingdom of God!"

²⁴ The disciples were stunned by his words. But Jesus said to them again, "Children, how hard it is to enter the kingdom of God! ²⁵ It is easier for a camel to go through the eye of a needle than for a rich person to enter the kingdom of God."

²⁶ This amazed his disciples more than ever. They asked each other, "Who, then, can be saved?"

²⁷ Jesus looked at them and said, "It's impossible for people ˏto save themselvesˏ, but it's not impossible for God to save them. Everything is possible for God."

²⁸ Then Peter spoke up, "We've given up everything to follow you."

²⁹ Jesus said, "I can guarantee this truth: Anyone who gave up his home, brothers, sisters, mother, father, children, or fields because of me and the Good News ³⁰ will certainly receive a hundred times as much here in this life. They will certainly receive homes, brothers, sisters, mothers, children and fields, along with persecutions. But in the world to come they will receive eternal life. ³¹ But many who are first will be last, and the last will be first."

For the Third Time Jesus Foretells That He Will Die and Come Back to Life—Matthew 20:17–19; Luke 18:31–34

³² Jesus and his disciples were on their way to Jerusalem. Jesus was walking ahead of them. His disciples were shocked ˏthat he was going to Jerusalemˏ. The others who followed were afraid. Once again he took the twelve apostles aside. He began to tell them what was going to happen to him. ³³ "We're going to Jerusalem. There the Son of Man will be betrayed to the chief priests and the scribes. They will condemn him to death and hand him over to foreigners. ³⁴ They will make fun of him, spit on him, whip him, and kill him. But after three days he will come back to life."

James and John Make a Request—Matthew 20:20–28

³⁵ James and John, sons of Zebedee, went to Jesus. They said to him, "Teacher, we want you to do us a favor."

³⁶ "What do you want me to do for you?" he asked them.

³⁷ They said to him, "Let one of us sit at your right and the other at your left in your glory."

³⁸ Jesus said, "You don't realize what you're asking. Can you drink the cup that I'm going to drink? Can you be baptized with the baptism that I'm going to receive?"

³⁹ "We can," they told him.

Jesus told them, "You will drink the cup that I'm going to drink. You will be baptized with the baptism that I'm going to receive. ⁴⁰ But I don't have the authority to grant you a seat at my right or left. Those positions have already been prepared for certain people."

⁴¹ When the other ten apostles heard about it, they were irritated with James and John. ⁴² Jesus called the apostles and said, "You know that the acknowledged rulers of nations have absolute power over people and their officials have absolute authority over people. ⁴³ But that's not the way it's going to be among you. Whoever wants to become great among you will be your servant. ⁴⁴ Whoever wants to be most important among you will be a slave for everyone. ⁴⁵ It's the same way with the Son of Man. He didn't come so that others could serve him. He came to serve and to give his life as a ransom for many people."

Jesus Gives Sight to Bartimaeus—Matthew 20:29–34; Luke 18:35–43

⁴⁶ Then they came to Jericho. As Jesus, his disciples, and many people were leaving Jericho, a blind beggar named Bartimaeus, son of Timaeus, was sitting by the road. ⁴⁷ When he heard that Jesus from Nazareth ˌwas passing byˌ, he began to shout, "Jesus, Son of David, have mercy on me!"

⁴⁸ The people told him to be quiet. But he shouted even louder, "Son of David, have mercy on me!"

⁴⁹ Jesus stopped and said, "Call him!" They called the blind man and told him, "Cheer up! Get up! He's calling you." ⁵⁰ The blind man threw off his coat, jumped up, and went to Jesus.

⁵¹ Jesus asked him, "What do you want me to do for you?"

The blind man said, "Teacher, I want to see again."

⁵² Jesus told him, "Go, your faith has made you well."

At once he could see again, and he followed Jesus on the road.

The King Comes to Jerusalem—
Matthew 21:1–11; Luke 19:29–44; John 12:12–19

11 ¹ When they came near Jerusalem, to Bethphage and Bethany, at the Mount of Olives, Jesus sent two of his disciples ahead of him. ² He said to them, "Go into the village ahead of you. As you enter it, you will find a young donkey tied there. No one has ever sat on it. Untie it, and bring it. ³ If anyone asks you what you are doing, say that the Lord needs it. That person will send it here at once."

⁴ The disciples found the young donkey in the street. It was tied to the door of a house. As they were untying it, ⁵ some men standing there asked them, "Why are you untying that donkey?" ⁶ The disciples answered them as Jesus had told them. So the men let them go.

⁷ They brought the donkey to Jesus, put their coats on it, and he sat on it. ⁸ Many spread their coats on the road. Others cut leafy branches in the fields and spread them on the road. ⁹ Those who went ahead and those who followed him were shouting,

> "Hosanna!
> Blessed is the one who comes in the name
>   of the Lord!
> ¹⁰   Blessed is our ancestor David's kingdom
>   that is coming!
> Hosanna in the highest heaven!"

¹¹ Jesus came into Jerusalem and went into the temple courtyard, where he looked around at everything. Since it was already late, he went out with the twelve apostles to Bethany.

Jesus Curses the Fig Tree—Matthew 21:18–19

¹² The next day, when they left Bethany, Jesus became hungry. ¹³ In the distance he saw a fig tree with leaves. He went to see if

he could find any figs on it. When he came to it, he found nothing but leaves because it wasn't the season for figs. ¹⁴ Then he said to the tree, "No one will ever eat fruit from you again!" His disciples heard this.

Jesus Throws Out the Moneychangers—
Matthew 21:12–17; Luke 19:45–48

¹⁵ When they came to Jerusalem, Jesus went into the temple courtyard and began to throw out those who were buying and selling there. He overturned the moneychangers' tables and the chairs of those who sold pigeons. ¹⁶ He would not let anyone carry anything across the temple courtyard.

¹⁷ Then he taught them by saying, "Scripture says, 'My house will be called a house of prayer for all nations,' but you have turned it into a gathering place for thieves."

¹⁸ When the chief priests and scribes heard him, they looked for a way to kill him. They were afraid of him because he amazed all the crowds with his teaching.

¹⁹ (Every evening Jesus and his disciples would leave the city.)

The Fig Tree Dries Up—*Matthew 21:20–22*

²⁰ While Jesus and his disciples were walking early in the morning, they saw that the fig tree had dried up. ²¹ Peter remembered ˍwhat Jesus had saidˌ, so he said to Jesus, "Rabbi, look! The fig tree you cursed has dried up."

²² Jesus said to them, "Have faith in God! ²³ I can guarantee this truth: This is what will be done for someone who doesn't doubt but believes what he says will happen: He can say to this mountain, 'Be uprooted and thrown into the sea,' and it will be done for him. ²⁴ That's why I tell you to have faith that you have already received whatever you pray for, and it will be yours. ²⁵ Whenever you pray, forgive anything you have against anyone. Then your Father in heaven will forgive your failures."[a]

---

[a] 11:25 Some manuscripts and translations add verse 26: "But if you don't forgive, your Father in heaven will not forgive your failures."

Jesus' Authority Challenged—Matthew 21:23–27; Luke 20:1–8

²⁷ Jesus and his disciples returned to Jerusalem. As he was walking in the temple courtyard, the chief priests, the scribes, and the leaders came to him. ²⁸ They asked him, "What gives you the right to do these things? Who told you that you could do this?"

²⁹ Jesus said to them, "I'll ask you a question. Answer me, and then I'll tell you why I have the right to do these things. ³⁰ Did John's right to baptize come from heaven or from humans? Answer me!"

³¹ They discussed this among themselves. They said, "If we say, 'from heaven,' he will ask, 'Then why didn't you believe him?' ³² But if we say, 'from humans,' ⌞then what will happen⌟?" They were afraid of the people. All the people thought of John as a true prophet. ³³ So they answered Jesus, "We don't know."

Jesus told them, "Then I won't tell you why I have the right to do these things."

A Story About a Vineyard—
Matthew 21:33–46; Luke 20:9–19

12 ¹ Then, using this illustration, Jesus spoke to them. He said, "A man planted a vineyard. He put a wall around it, made a vat for the winepress, and built a watchtower. Then he leased it to vineyard workers and went on a trip.

² "At the right time he sent a servant to the workers to collect from them a share of the grapes from the vineyard. ³ The workers took the servant, beat him, and sent him back with nothing. ⁴ So the man sent another servant to them. They hit the servant on the head and treated him shamefully. ⁵ The man sent another, and they killed that servant. Then he sent many other servants. Some of these they beat, and others they killed.

⁶ "He had one more person to send. That person was his son, whom he loved. Finally, he sent his son to them. He thought, 'They will respect my son.'

7 "But those workers said to one another, 'This is the heir. Let's kill him, and the inheritance will be ours.' 8 So they took him, killed him, and threw him out of the vineyard.

9 "What will the owner of the vineyard do? He will come and destroy the workers and give the vineyard to others. 10 Have you never read the Scripture passage:

> 'The stone that the builders rejected
>   has become the cornerstone.
> 11   The Lord has done this,
>   and it is amazing for us to see'?"

12 They wanted to arrest him but were afraid of the crowd. They knew that he had directed this illustration at them. So they left him alone and went away.

A Question About Taxes—
Matthew 22:15–22; Luke 20:20–26

13 The leaders sent some of the Pharisees and some of Herod's followers to Jesus. They wanted to trap him into saying the wrong thing. 14 When they came to him, they said, "Teacher, we know that you tell the truth. You don't favor individuals because of who they are. Rather, you teach the way of God truthfully. Is it right to pay taxes to the emperor or not? Should we pay taxes or not?"

15 Jesus recognized their hypocrisy, so he asked them, "Why do you test me? Bring me a coin so that I can look at it."

16 They brought a coin. He said to them, "Whose face and name is this?"

They told him, "The emperor's."

17 Jesus said to them, "Give the emperor what belongs to the emperor, and give God what belongs to God."

They were surprised at his reply.

The Dead Come Back to Life—Matthew 22:23–33; Luke 20:27–40

18 Some Sadducees, who say that people will never come back to life, came to Jesus. They asked him, 19 "Teacher, Moses wrote

for us, 'If a man dies and leaves a wife but no child, his brother should marry his widow and have children for his brother.' [20] There were seven brothers. The first got married and died without having children. [21] The second married her and died without having children. So did the third. [22] None of the seven brothers had any children. Last of all, the woman died. [23] When the dead come back to life, whose wife will she be? The seven brothers had married her."

[24] Jesus said to them, "Aren't you mistaken because you don't know the Scriptures or God's power? [25] When the dead come back to life, they don't marry. Rather, they are like the angels in heaven. [26] Haven't you read in the book of Moses that the dead come back to life? It's in the passage about the bush, where God said, 'I am the God of Abraham, Isaac, and Jacob.' [27] He's not the God of the dead but of the living. You're badly mistaken!"

Love God and Your Neighbor—Matthew 22:34–40

[28] One of the scribes went to Jesus during the argument with the Sadducees. He saw how well Jesus answered them, so he asked him, "Which commandment is the most important of them all?"

[29] Jesus answered, "The most important is, 'Listen, Israel, the Lord our God is the only Lord. [30] So love the Lord your God with all your heart, with all your soul, with all your mind, and with all your strength.' [31] The second most important commandment is this: 'Love your neighbor as you love yourself.' No other commandment is greater than these."

[32] The scribe said to Jesus, "Teacher, that was well said! You've told the truth that there is only one God and no other besides him! [33] To love him with all your heart, with all your understanding, with all your strength, and to love your neighbor as you love yourself is more important than all the burnt offerings and sacrifices."

[34] When Jesus heard how wisely the man answered, he told the man, "You're not too far from the kingdom of God."

After that, no one dared to ask him another question.

How Can David's Son Be David's Lord?—
Matthew 22:41–46; Luke 20:41–44

35 While Jesus was teaching in the temple courtyard, he asked, "How can the scribes say that the Messiah is David's son? **36** David, guided by the Holy Spirit, said,

> 'The Lord said to my Lord:
>> "Take the highest position in heaven
>>> until I put your enemies under your control.' "

37 David calls him Lord. So how can he be his son?"

Jesus Disapproves of the Example Set by Scribes—
Matthew 23:1–12; Luke 20:45–47

The large crowd enjoyed listening to him. **38** As he taught, he said, "Watch out for the scribes! They like to walk around in long robes, to be greeted in the marketplaces, **39** and to have the front seats in synagogues and the places of honor at dinners. **40** They rob widows by taking their houses and then say long prayers to make themselves look good. The scribes will receive the most severe punishment."

A Widow's Contribution—Luke 21:1–4

41 As Jesus sat facing the temple offering box, he watched how ˎmuchˌ money people put into it. Many rich people put in large amounts. **42** A poor widow dropped in two small coins, worth less than a cent.

43 He called his disciples and said to them, "I can guarantee this truth: This poor widow has given more than all the others. **44** All of them have given what they could spare. But she, in her poverty, has given everything she had to live on."

Jesus Teaches Disciples on the Mount of Olives—
Matthew 24:1–35; Luke 21:5–33

13 **1** As Jesus was going out of the temple courtyard, one of his disciples said to him, "Teacher, look at these huge stones and these beautiful buildings!"

² Jesus said to him, "Do you see these large buildings? Not one of these stones will be left on top of another. Each one will be torn down."

³ As Jesus was sitting on the Mount of Olives facing the temple buildings, Peter, James, John, and Andrew asked him privately, ⁴ "Tell us, when will this happen? What will be the sign when all this will come to an end?"

⁵ Jesus answered them, "Be careful not to let anyone deceive you. ⁶ Many will come using my name. They will say, 'I am he,' and they will deceive many people.

⁷ "When you hear of wars and rumors of wars, don't be alarmed! These things must happen, but they don't mean that the end has come. ⁸ Nation will fight against nation and kingdom against kingdom. There will be earthquakes and famines in various places. These are only the beginning pains ⌐of the end⌐.

⁹ "Be on your guard! People will hand you over to the Jewish courts and whip you in their synagogues. You will stand in front of governors and kings to testify to them because of me. ¹⁰ But first, the Good News must be spread to all nations. ¹¹ When they take you away to hand you over to the authorities, don't worry ahead of time about what you will say. Instead, say whatever is given to you to say when the time comes. Indeed, you are not the one who will be speaking, but the Holy Spirit will.

¹² "Brother will hand over brother to death; a father will hand over his child. Children will rebel against their parents and kill them. ¹³ Everyone will hate you because you are committed to me. But the person who endures to the end will be saved.

¹⁴ "When you see the disgusting thing that will cause destruction standing where it should not (let the reader take note), those of you in Judea should flee to the mountains. ¹⁵ Those who are on the roof should not come down to get anything out of their houses. ¹⁶ Those who are in the field should not turn back to get their coats.

¹⁷ "How horrible it will be for the women who are pregnant or who are nursing babies in those days. ¹⁸ Pray that it will not be in winter. ¹⁹ It will be a time of misery that has not happened from the beginning of God's creation until now, and will certainly never happen again. ²⁰ If the Lord does not reduce that time, no one will be saved. But those days will be reduced because of those whom God has chosen.

²¹ "At that time don't believe anyone who tells you, 'Here is the Messiah!' or 'There he is!' ²² False messiahs and false prophets will appear. They will work miraculous signs and do wonderful things to deceive, if possible, those whom God has chosen. ²³ Be on your guard! I have told you everything before it happens.

²⁴ "Now, after the misery of those days, the sun will turn dark, the moon will not give light, ²⁵ the stars will fall from the sky, and the powers of the universe will be shaken.

²⁶ "Then people will see the Son of Man coming in clouds with great power and glory. ²⁷ He will send out his angels, and from every direction under the sky, they will gather those whom God has chosen.

²⁸ "Learn from the story of the fig tree. When its branch becomes tender and it sprouts leaves, you know summer is near. ²⁹ In the same way, when you see these things happen, you know that he is near, at the door.

³⁰ "I can guarantee this truth: This generation will not disappear until all these things take place. ³¹ The earth and the heavens will disappear, but my words will never disappear.

No One Knows When the Earth and the Heavens Will Disappear

³² "No one knows when that day or hour will come. Even the angels in heaven and the Son don't know. Only the Father knows. ³³ Be careful! Watch! You don't know the exact time. ³⁴ It is like a man who went on a trip. As he left home, he put his servants in charge. He assigned work to each one and ordered the guard to be alert. ³⁵ Therefore, be alert, because you don't know when the

owner of the house will return. It could be in the evening or at midnight or at dawn or in the morning. [36] Make sure he doesn't come suddenly and find you asleep. [37] I'm telling everyone what I'm telling you: 'Be alert!' "

The Plot to Kill Jesus—
Matthew 26:1–5; Luke 22:1–2; John 11:45–57

14 [1] It was two days before the Passover and the Festival of Unleavened Bread. The chief priests and the scribes were looking for some underhanded way to arrest Jesus and to kill him. [2] However, they said, "We shouldn't arrest him during the festival, or else there will be a riot among the people."

A Woman Prepares Jesus' Body for the Tomb—
Matthew 26:6–13; John 12:1–8

[3] Jesus was in Bethany at the home of Simon, a man who had suffered from a skin disease. While Jesus was sitting there, a woman went to him. She had a bottle of very expensive perfume made from pure nard. She opened the bottle and poured the perfume on his head.

[4] Some who were there were irritated and said to one another, "Why was the perfume wasted like this? [5] This perfume could have been sold for a high price, and the money could have been given to the poor." So they said some very unkind things to her.

[6] Jesus said, "Leave her alone! Why are you bothering her? She has done a beautiful thing for me. [7] You will always have the poor with you and can help them whenever you want. But you will not always have me with you. [8] She did what she could. She came to pour perfume on my body before it is placed in a tomb. [9] I can guarantee this truth: Wherever the Good News is spoken in the world, what she has done will also be told in memory of her."

Judas Plans to Betray Jesus—*Matthew 26:14–16; Luke 22:3–6*

[10] Judas Iscariot, one of the twelve apostles, went to the chief priests to betray Jesus. [11] They were pleased to hear what Judas

had to say and promised to give him money. So he kept looking for a chance to betray Jesus.

Preparations for the Passover—
Matthew 26:17–20; Luke 22:7–17

[12] Killing the Passover lamb was customary on the first day of the Festival of Unleavened Bread. The disciples asked Jesus, "Where do you want us to prepare the Passover meal for you?"

[13] He sent two of his disciples and told them, "Go into the city. You will meet a man carrying a jug of water. Follow him. [14] When he goes into a house, tell the owner that the teacher asks, 'Where is my room where I can eat the Passover meal with my disciples?' [15] He will take you upstairs and show you a large room. The room will be completely furnished. Get everything ready for us there."

[16] The disciples left. They went into the city and found everything as Jesus had told them. So they prepared the Passover.

[17] When evening came, Jesus arrived with the twelve apostles.

Jesus Knows Who Will Betray Him—
Matthew 26:21–25; Luke 22:21–23; John 13:21–30

[18] While they were at the table eating, Jesus said, "I can guarantee this truth: One of you is going to betray me, one who is eating with me!"

[19] Feeling hurt, they asked him one by one, "You don't mean me, do you?"

[20] He said to them, "It's one of you twelve, someone dipping his hand into the bowl with me. [21] The Son of Man is going to die as the Scriptures say he will. But how horrible it will be for that person who betrays the Son of Man! It would have been better for that person if he had never been born."

The Lord's Supper—
Matthew 26:26–30; Luke 22:19–20

[22] While they were eating, Jesus took bread and blessed it. He broke the bread, gave it to them, and said, "Take this. This is my body."

²³ Then he took a cup, spoke a prayer of thanksgiving, and gave the cup to them. They all drank from it. ²⁴ He said to them, "This is my blood, the blood of the promise.ᵃ It is poured out for many people.

²⁵ "I can guarantee this truth: I won't drink this wine again until that day when I drink new wine in the kingdom of God."

²⁶ After they sang a hymn, they went to the Mount of Olives.

Jesus Predicts Peter's Denial—
Matthew 26:31–35; Luke 22:31–34; John 13:36–38

²⁷ Then Jesus said to them, "All of you will abandon me. Scripture says,

'I will strike the shepherd,
        and the sheep will be scattered.'

²⁸ "But after I am brought back to life, I will go to Galilee ahead of you."

²⁹ Peter said to him, "Even if everyone else abandons you, I won't."

³⁰ Jesus said to Peter, "I can guarantee this truth: Tonight, before a rooster crows twice, you will say three times that you don't know me."

³¹ But Peter said very strongly, "Even if I have to die with you, I will never say that I don't know you." All the other disciples said the same thing.

Jesus Prays in the Garden of Gethsemane—
Matthew 26:36–46; Luke 22:39–46

³² Then they came to a place called Gethsemane. He said to his disciples, "Stay here while I pray."

³³ He took Peter, James, and John with him and began to feel distressed and anguished. ³⁴ He said to them, "My anguish is so great that I feel as if I'm dying. Wait here, and stay awake."

ᵃ 14:24 Or "testament," or "covenant."

³⁵ After walking a little farther, he fell to the ground and prayed that if it were possible he might not have to suffer what was ahead of him. ³⁶ He said, "Abba!ᵇ Father! You can do anything. Take this cup ˎof suffering ˏ away from me. But let your will be done rather than mine."

³⁷ He went back and found them asleep. He said to Peter, "Simon, are you sleeping? Couldn't you stay awake for one hour? ³⁸ Stay awake, and pray that you won't be tempted. You want to do what's right, but you're weak."

³⁹ He went away again and prayed the same prayer as before. ⁴⁰ He found them asleep because they couldn't keep their eyes open. They didn't even know what they should say to him.

⁴¹ He came back a third time and said to them, "You might as well sleep now. It's all over.ᶜ The time has come for the Son of Man to be handed over to sinners. ⁴² Get up! Let's go! The one who is betraying me is near."

Jesus Is Arrested—Matthew 26:47–56; Luke 22:47–54a; John 18:1–14

⁴³ Just then, while Jesus was still speaking, Judas, one of the twelve apostles, arrived. A crowd carrying swords and clubs was with him. They were from the chief priests, scribes, and leaders of the people. ⁴⁴ Now, the traitor had given them a signal. He said, "The one I kiss is the man you want. Arrest him, and guard him closely as you take him away."

⁴⁵ Then Judas quickly stepped up to Jesus and said, "Rabbi!" and kissed him.

⁴⁶ Some men took hold of Jesus and arrested him. ⁴⁷ One of those standing there pulled out his sword and cut off the ear of the chief priest's servant.

⁴⁸ Jesus asked them, "Have you come out with swords and clubs to arrest me as if I were a criminal? ⁴⁹ I used to teach in the temple courtyard every day. But you didn't arrest me then. But what the Scriptures say must come true."

ᵇ 14:36 *Abba* is Aramaic for "father."   ᶜ 14:41 Greek meaning uncertain.

⁵⁰ Then all the disciples abandoned him and ran away.

⁵¹ A certain young man was following Jesus. He had nothing on but a linen sheet. They tried to arrest him, ⁵² but he left the linen sheet behind and ran away naked.

The Trial in Front of the Jewish Council—
Matthew 26:57–68; Luke 22:63–71

⁵³ The men took Jesus to the chief priest. All the chief priests, leaders, and scribes had gathered together. ⁵⁴ Peter followed him at a distance and went into the chief priest's courtyard. He sat with the guards and warmed himself facing the glow of a fire.

⁵⁵ The chief priests and the whole Jewish council were searching for some testimony against Jesus in order to execute him. But they couldn't find any. ⁵⁶ Many gave false testimony against him, but their statements did not agree.

⁵⁷ Then some men stood up and gave false testimony against him. They said, ⁵⁸ "We heard him say, 'I'll tear down this temple made by humans, and in three days I'll build another temple, one not made by human hands.' " ⁵⁹ But their testimony did not agree even on this point.

⁶⁰ So the chief priest stood up in the center and asked Jesus, "Don't you have any answer to what these men testify against you?"

⁶¹ But he was silent.

The chief priest asked him again, "Are you the Messiah, the Son of the Blessed One?"

⁶² Jesus answered, "Yes, I am, and you will see the Son of Man in the highest position in heaven. He will be coming with the clouds of heaven."

⁶³ The chief priest tore his clothes in horror and said, "Why do we need any more witnesses? ⁶⁴ You've heard him dishonor God! What's your verdict?"

All of them condemned him with the death sentence. ⁶⁵ Some of them began to spit on him. They covered his face and hit him with their fists. They said to him, "Prophesy!" Even the guards took him and slapped him.

Peter Denies Jesus—
Matthew 26:69–75; Luke 22:54b–62; John 18:15–18, 25–27

⁶⁶ Peter was in the courtyard. One of the chief priest's female servants ⁶⁷ saw Peter warming himself. She looked at him and said, "You, too, were with Jesus from Nazareth!"

⁶⁸ But Peter denied it by saying, "I don't know him, and I don't understand what you're talking about."

He went to the entrance. Then a rooster crowed.*ᵈ*

⁶⁹ The servant saw him. Once again she said to those who were standing around, "This man is one of them!" ⁷⁰ Peter again denied it.

After a little while the men standing there said to Peter again, "It's obvious you're one of them. You're a Galilean!"

⁷¹ Then Peter began to curse and swear with an oath, "I don't know this man you're talking about!" ⁷² Just then a rooster crowed a second time. Peter remembered that Jesus said to him, "Before a rooster crows twice, you will say three times that you don't know me." Then Peter began to cry very hard.

Pilate Questions Jesus—*Matthew 27:11–14; Luke 23:1–4; John 18:28–38*

15 ¹ Early in the morning the chief priests immediately came to a decision with the leaders and the scribes. The whole Jewish council decided to tie Jesus up, lead him away, and hand him over to Pilate.

² Pilate asked him, "Are you the king of the Jews?"

"Yes, I am," Jesus answered him.

³ The chief priests were accusing him of many things.

⁴ So Pilate asked him again, "Don't you have any answer? Look how many accusations they're bringing against you!"

⁵ But Jesus no longer answered anything, so Pilate was surprised.

ᵈ 14:68 Some manuscripts and translations omit this sentence.

The Crowd Rejects Jesus—
Matthew 27:15–26; Luke 23:18–25; John 18:39–40

⁶ At every Passover festival, Pilate would free one prisoner whom the people asked for. ⁷ There was a man named Barabbas in prison. He was with some rebels who had committed murder during a riot. ⁸ The crowd asked Pilate to do for them what he always did. ⁹ Pilate answered them, "Do you want me to free the king of the Jews for you?" ¹⁰ Pilate knew that the chief priests had handed Jesus over to him because they were jealous.

¹¹ The chief priests stirred up the crowd so that Pilate would free Barabbas for them instead.

¹² So Pilate again asked them, "Then what should I do with the king of the Jews?"

¹³ "Crucify him!" they shouted back.

¹⁴ Pilate said to them, "Why? What has he done wrong?"

But they shouted even louder, "Crucify him!"

¹⁵ Pilate wanted to satisfy the people, so he freed Barabbas for them. But he had Jesus whipped and handed over to be crucified.

The Soldiers Make Fun of Jesus—Matthew 27:27–30; John 19:1–3

¹⁶ The soldiers led Jesus into the courtyard of the palace and called together the whole troop. ¹⁷ They dressed him in purple, twisted some thorns into a crown, and placed it on his head. ¹⁸ Then they began to greet him, "Long live the king of the Jews!" ¹⁹ They kept hitting him on the head with a stick, spitting on him, and kneeling in front of him with false humility.

The Crucifixion—
Matthew 27:31–44; Luke 23:33–38; John 19:16b–24

²⁰ After the soldiers finished making fun of Jesus, they took off the purple cape and put his own clothes back on him. Then they led him out to crucify him. ²¹ A man named Simon from the city of Cyrene was coming ‚into Jerusalem‚ from his home in the country. He was the father of Alexander and Rufus. As he was about to pass by, the soldiers forced him to carry Jesus' cross.

²² They took Jesus to Golgotha (which means "the place of the skull"). ²³ They tried to give him wine mixed with a drug called myrrh, but he wouldn't take it. ²⁴ Next they crucified him. Then they divided his clothes among themselves by throwing dice to see what each one would get. ²⁵ It was nine in the morning when they crucified him. ²⁶ There was a written notice of the accusation against him. It read, "The king of the Jews."

²⁷ They crucified two criminals with him, one on his right and the other on his left.ᵃ

²⁹ Those who passed by insulted him. They shook their heads and said, "What a joke! You were going to tear down God's temple and build it again in three days. ³⁰ Come down from the cross, and save yourself!" ³¹ The chief priests and the scribes made fun of him among themselves in the same way. They said, "He saved others, but he can't save himself. ³² Let the Messiah, the king of Israel, come down from the cross now so that we may see and believe." Even those who were crucified with him were insulting him.

Jesus Dies on the Cross—
Matthew 27:45–56; Luke 23:44–49; John 19:28–30

³³ At noon darkness came over the whole land until three in the afternoon. ³⁴ At three o'clock Jesus cried out in a loud voice, "Eloi, Eloi, lema sabachthani?" which means, "My God, my God, why have you abandoned me?"

³⁵ When some of the people standing there heard him say that, they said, "Listen! He's calling Elijah." ³⁶ Someone ran and soaked a sponge in vinegar. Then he put it on a stick and offered Jesus a drink. The man said, "Let's see if Elijah comes to take him down."

³⁷ Then Jesus cried out in a loud voice and died. ³⁸ The curtain in the temple was split in two from top to bottom.

³⁹ When the officer who stood facing Jesus saw how he gave up his spirit, he said, "Certainly, this man was the Son of God!"

ᵃ 15:27 Some manuscripts and translations add verse 28: "And what the Scriptures said came true: 'He was counted with criminals.' "

40 Some women were watching from a distance. Among them were Mary from Magdala, Mary (the mother of young James and Joseph), and Salome. **41** They had followed him and supported him while he was in Galilee. Many other women who had come to Jerusalem with him were there too.

Jesus Is Buried—
Matthew 27:57–61; Luke 23:50–56; John 19:38–42

42 It was Friday evening, before the day of worship, **43** when Joseph arrived. He was from the city of Arimathea and was an important member of the Jewish council. He, too, was waiting for the kingdom of God. Joseph boldly went to Pilate's quarters to ask for the body of Jesus.

44 Pilate wondered if Jesus had already died. So he summoned the officer to ask him if Jesus was, in fact, dead. **45** When the officer had assured him that Jesus was dead, Pilate let Joseph have the corpse.

46 Joseph had purchased some linen cloth. He took the body down from the cross and wrapped it in the cloth. Then he laid the body in a tomb, which had been cut out of rock, and he rolled a stone against the door of the tomb. **47** Mary from Magdala and Mary (the mother of Joses) watched where Jesus was laid.

Jesus Comes Back to Life—
Matthew 28:1–10; Luke 24:1–12; John 20:1–10

16 **1** When the day of worship was over, Mary from Magdala, Mary (the mother of James), and Salome bought spices to go and anoint Jesus.

2 On Sunday they were going to the tomb very early when the sun had just come up. **3** They said to one another, "Who will roll away the stone for us from the entrance to the tomb?" **4** When they looked up, they saw that the stone had been rolled away. It was a very large stone. **5** As they went into the tomb, they saw a young man. He was dressed in a white robe and sat on the right side. They were panic-stricken.

⁶ The young man said to them, "Don't panic! You're looking for Jesus from Nazareth, who was crucified. He has been brought back to life. He's not here. Look at the place where they laid him. ⁷ Go and tell his disciples and Peter that he's going ahead of them to Galilee. There they will see him, just as he told them."

⁸ They went out of the tomb and ran away. Shock and trembling had overwhelmed them. They didn't say a thing to anyone, because they were afraid.ᵃ

Jesus Appears to His Followers

⁹ After Jesus came back to life early on Sunday, he appeared first to Mary from Magdala, from whom he had forced out seven demons. ¹⁰ She went and told his friends, who were grieving and crying. ¹¹ They didn't believe her when they heard that he was alive and that she had seen him.

¹² Later Jesus appeared to two disciples as they were walking to their home in the country. He did not look as he usually did. ¹³ They went back and told the others, who did not believe them either. ¹⁴ Still later Jesus appeared to the eleven apostles while they were eating. He put them to shame for their unbelief and because they were too stubborn to believe those who had seen him alive.

¹⁵ Then Jesus said to them, "So wherever you go in the world, tell everyone the Good News. ¹⁶ Whoever believes and is baptized will be saved, but whoever does not believe will be condemned.

¹⁷ "These are the miraculous signs that will accompany believers: They will use the power and authority of my name to force demons out of people. They will speak new languages. ¹⁸ They will pick up snakes, and if they drink any deadly poison, it will not hurt them. They will place their hands on the sick and cure them."

¹⁹ After talking with the apostles, the Lord was taken to heaven, where God gave him the highest position.

ᵃ 16:8 Some manuscripts and translations end Mark here; some add verses 9–20.

[20] The disciples spread ⌞the Good News⌟ everywhere. The Lord worked with them. He confirmed his word by the miraculous signs that accompanied it.

LUKE

Luke Writes to Theophilus

1 ¹ Many have attempted to write about what had taken place among us. ² They received their information from those who had been eyewitnesses and servants of God's word from the beginning, and they passed it on to us. ³ I, too, have followed everything closely from the beginning. So I thought it would be a good idea to write an orderly account for Your Excellency, Theophilus. ⁴ In this way you will know that what you've been told is true.

The Angel Gabriel Appears to Zechariah

⁵ When Herod was king of Judea, there was a priest named Zechariah, who belonged to the division of priests named after Abijah. Zechariah's wife Elizabeth was a descendant of Aaron. ⁶ Zechariah and Elizabeth had God's approval. They followed all the Lord's commands and regulations perfectly. ⁷ Yet, they never had any children because Elizabeth couldn't become pregnant. Both of them were too old to have children.

⁸ Zechariah was on duty with his division of priests. As he served in God's presence, ⁹ he was chosen by priestly custom to go into the Lord's temple to burn incense. ¹⁰ All the people were praying outside while he was burning incense.

¹¹ Then, to the right of the incense altar, an angel of the Lord appeared to him. ¹² Zechariah was troubled and overcome with fear.

¹³ The angel said to him, "Don't be afraid, Zechariah! God has heard your prayer. Your wife Elizabeth will have a son, and you will name him John. ¹⁴ He will be your pride and joy, and many people will be glad that he was born. ¹⁵ As far as the Lord is concerned, he will be a great man. He will never drink wine or any other liquor.

He will be filled with the Holy Spirit even before he is born. ¹⁶ He will bring many people in Israel back to the Lord their God. ¹⁷ He will go ahead of the Lord with the spirit and power that Elijah had. He will change parents' attitudes toward their children. He will change disobedient people so that they will accept the wisdom of those who have God's approval. In this way he will prepare the people for their Lord."

¹⁸ Zechariah said to the angel, "What proof is there for this? I'm an old man, and my wife is beyond her childbearing years."

¹⁹ The angel answered him, "I'm Gabriel! I stand in God's presence. God sent me to tell you this good news. ²⁰ But because you didn't believe what I said, you will be unable to talk until the day this happens. Everything will come true at the right time."

²¹ Meanwhile, the people were waiting for Zechariah. They were amazed that he was staying in the temple so long. ²² When he did come out, he was unable to speak to them. So they realized that he had seen a vision in the temple. He motioned to them but remained unable to talk.

²³ When the days of his service were over, he went home. ²⁴ Later, his wife Elizabeth became pregnant and didn't go out in public for five months. She said, ²⁵ "The Lord has done this for me now. He has removed my public disgrace."

The Angel Gabriel Comes to Mary

²⁶ Six months after Elizabeth had become pregnant, God sent the angel Gabriel to Nazareth, a city in Galilee. ²⁷ The angel went to a virgin promised in marriage to a descendant of David named Joseph. The virgin's name was Mary.

²⁸ When the angel entered her home, he greeted her and said, "You are favored by the Lord! The Lord is with you."

²⁹ She was startled by what the angel said and tried to figure out what this greeting meant.

³⁰ The angel told her,

"Don't be afraid, Mary. You have found favor*a* with God.
³¹   You will become pregnant, give birth to a son,

---

a 1:30 Or "grace."

and name him Jesus.
³² He will be a great man
and will be called the Son of the Most High.
The Lord God will give him
the throne of his ancestor David.
³³ Your son will be king of Jacob's people forever,
and his kingdom will never end."

³⁴ Mary asked the angel, "How can this be? I've never had sexual intercourse."

³⁵ The angel answered her, "The Holy Spirit will come to you, and the power of the Most High will overshadow you. Therefore, the holy child developing inside you will be called the Son of God.

³⁶ "Elizabeth, your relative, is six months pregnant with a son in her old age. People said she couldn't have a child. ³⁷ But nothing is impossible for God."

³⁸ Mary answered, "I am the Lord's servant. Let everything you've said happen to me."

Then the angel left her.

Mary Visits Elizabeth

³⁹ Soon afterward, Mary hurried to a city in the mountain region of Judah. ⁴⁰ She entered Zechariah's home and greeted Elizabeth.

⁴¹ When Elizabeth heard the greeting, she felt the baby kick. Elizabeth was filled with the Holy Spirit. ⁴² She said in a loud voice, "You are the most blessed of all women, and blessed is the child that you will have. ⁴³ I feel blessed that the mother of my Lord is visiting me. ⁴⁴ As soon as I heard your greeting, I felt the baby jump for joy. ⁴⁵ You are blessed for believing that the Lord would keep his promise to you."

Mary Praises God

⁴⁶ Mary said,

"My soul praises the Lord's greatness!
⁴⁷ My spirit finds its joy in God, my Savior,

⁴⁸   because he has looked favorably on me, his humble servant.

   "From now on, all people will call me blessed
⁴⁹   because the Almighty has done great things to me.
         His name is holy.
⁵⁰   For those who fear him,
             his mercy lasts throughout every generation.

⁵¹ "He displayed his mighty power.
     He scattered those who think too highly of themselves.
⁵²   He pulled strong rulers from their thrones.
         He honored humble people.
⁵³   He fed hungry people with good food.
             He sent rich people away with nothing.

⁵⁴ "He remembered to help his servant Israel forever.
⁵⁵   This is the promise he made to our ancestors,
       to Abraham and his descendants."

⁵⁶ Mary stayed with Elizabeth about three months and then
went back home.

John Is Born

⁵⁷ When the time came for Elizabeth to have her child, she gave
birth to a son. ⁵⁸ Her neighbors and relatives heard that the Lord
had been very kind to her, and they shared her joy.

⁵⁹ When the child was eight days old, they went ˻to the temple˼
to circumcise him. They were going to name him Zechariah after
his father. ⁶⁰ But his mother spoke up, "Absolutely not! His name
will be John."

⁶¹ Their friends said to her, "But you don't have any relatives
with that name."

⁶² So they motioned to the baby's father to see what he wanted
to name the child. ⁶³ Zechariah asked for a writing tablet and wrote,
"His name is John." Everyone was amazed.

⁶⁴ Suddenly, Zechariah was able to speak, and he began to
praise God.

⁶⁵ All their neighbors were filled with awe. Throughout the mountain region of Judea, people talked about everything that had happened. ⁶⁶ Everyone who heard about it seriously thought it over and asked, "What does the future hold for this child?" It was clear that the Lord was with him.

⁶⁷ His father Zechariah was filled with the Holy Spirit and prophesied,

> ⁶⁸ "Praise the Lord God of Israel!
> > He has come to take care of his people
> > and to set them free.
> ⁶⁹ He has raised up a mighty Savior for us
> > in the family of his servant David.
> ⁷⁰ He made this promise through his holy prophets long ago.
> ⁷¹ He promised to save us from our enemies
> > and from the power of all who hate us.
> ⁷² He has shown his mercy to our ancestors
> > and remembered his holy promise,ᵇ
> > > the oath that he swore to our ancestor Abraham.
> ⁷³
> ⁷⁴ He promised to rescue us from our enemies' power
> > so that we could serve him without fear
> ⁷⁵ > > by being holy and honorable as long as we live.
>
> ⁷⁶ "You, child, will be called a prophet of the Most High.
> > You will go ahead of the Lord to prepare his way.
> ⁷⁷ You will make his people know that they can be saved
> > through the forgiveness of their sins.
> ⁷⁸ > A new day will dawn on us from above
> > > because our God is loving and merciful.
> ⁷⁹ He will give light to those who live in the dark
> > and in death's shadow.
> > He will guide us into the way of peace."

⁸⁰ The child John grew and became spiritually strong. He lived in the desert until the day he appeared to the people of Israel.

ᵇ 1:72 Or "covenant."

Jesus Is Born

2 ¹At that time the Emperor Augustus ordered a census of the Roman Empire. ²This was the first census taken while Quirinius was governor of Syria. ³All the people went to register in the cities where their ancestors had lived.

⁴So Joseph went from Nazareth, a city in Galilee, to a Judean city called Bethlehem. Joseph, a descendant of King David, went to Bethlehem because David had been born there. ⁵Joseph went there to register with Mary. She had been promised to him in marriage and was pregnant.

⁶While they were in Bethlehem, the time came for Mary to have her child. ⁷She gave birth to her firstborn son. She wrapped him in strips of cloth and laid him in a manger because there wasn't any room for them in the inn.

Angels Announce the Birth of Jesus

⁸Shepherds were in the fields near Bethlehem. They were taking turns watching their flock during the night. ⁹An angel from the Lord suddenly appeared to them. The glory of the Lord filled the area with light, and they were terrified. ¹⁰The angel said to them, "Don't be afraid! I have good news for you, a message that will fill everyone with joy. ¹¹Today your Savior, Christ the Lord, was born in David's city. ¹²This is how you will recognize him: You will find an infant wrapped in strips of cloth and lying in a manger."

¹³Suddenly, a large army of angels appeared with the angel. They were praising God by saying,

¹⁴   "Glory to God in the highest heaven,
        and on earth peace to those who have his good will!"

¹⁵The angels left them and went back to heaven. The shepherds said to each other, "Let's go to Bethlehem and see what the Lord has told us about."

¹⁶They went quickly and found Mary and Joseph with the baby, who was lying in a manger. ¹⁷When they saw the child, they repeated

what they had been told about him. [18] Everyone who heard the shepherds' story was amazed.

[19] Mary treasured all these things in her heart and always thought about them.

[20] As the shepherds returned to their flock, they glorified and praised God for everything they had seen and heard. Everything happened the way the angel had told them.

Jesus' Parents Obey Moses' Teachings

[21] Eight days after his birth, the child was circumcised and named Jesus. This was the name the angel had given him before his mother became pregnant.

[22] After the days required by Moses' Teachings to make a mother clean[a] had passed, Joseph and Mary went to Jerusalem. They took Jesus to present him to the Lord. [23] They did exactly what was written in the Lord's Teachings: "Every firstborn boy is to be set apart as holy to the Lord." [24] They also offered a sacrifice as required by the Lord's Teachings: "a pair of mourning doves or two young pigeons."

Simeon's Prophecy

[25] A man named Simeon was in Jerusalem. He lived an honorable and devout life. He was waiting for the one who would comfort Israel. The Holy Spirit was with Simeon [26] and had told him that he wouldn't die until he had seen the Messiah, whom the Lord would send.

[27] Moved by the Spirit, Simeon went into the temple courtyard. Mary and Joseph were bringing the child Jesus into the courtyard at the same time. They brought him so that they could do for him what Moses' Teachings required. [28] Then Simeon took the child in his arms and praised God by saying,

[29]　　"Now, Lord, you are allowing your servant to leave in peace
　　　　　as you promised.
[30]　　My eyes have seen your salvation,

---

[a] 2:22 "Clean" refers to anything that Moses' Teachings say is presentable to God.

³¹ which you have prepared for all people to see.

³² He is a light that will reveal ˌsalvationˌ to the nations and bring glory to your people Israel."

³³ Jesus' father and mother were amazed at what was said about him. ³⁴ Then Simeon blessed them and said to Mary, his mother, "This child is the reason that many people in Israel will be condemned and many others will be saved. He will be a sign that will expose ³⁵ the thoughts of those who reject him. And a sword will pierce your heart."

Anna's Prophecy

³⁶ Anna, a prophet, was also there. She was a descendant of Phanuel from the tribe of Asher. She was now very old. Her husband had died seven years after they were married, ³⁷ and she had been a widow for 84 years. Anna never left the temple courtyard but worshiped day and night by fasting and praying. ³⁸ At that moment she came up to Mary and Joseph and began to thank God. She spoke about Jesus to all who were waiting for Jerusalem to be set free.

³⁹ After doing everything the Lord's Teachings required, Joseph and Mary returned to their hometown of Nazareth in Galilee. ⁴⁰ The child grew and became strong. He was filled with wisdom, and God's favor^b was with him.

Mary and Joseph Find Jesus With the Teachers in the Temple Courtyard

⁴¹ Every year Jesus' parents would go to Jerusalem for the Passover festival. ⁴² When he was 12 years old, they went as usual.

⁴³ When the festival was over, they left for home. The boy Jesus stayed behind in Jerusalem, but his parents didn't know it. ⁴⁴ They thought that he was with the others who were traveling with them. After traveling for a day, they started to look for him among their relatives and friends. ⁴⁵ When they didn't find him, they went back to Jerusalem to look for him.

^b 2:40 Or "grace."

⁴⁶ Three days later, they found him in the temple courtyard. He was sitting among the teachers, listening to them, and asking them questions. ⁴⁷ His understanding and his answers stunned everyone who heard him.

⁴⁸ When his parents saw him, they were shocked. His mother asked him, "Son, why have you done this to us? Your father and I have been worried sick looking for you!"

⁴⁹ Jesus said to them, "Why were you looking for me? Didn't you realize that I had to be in my Father's house?" ⁵⁰ But they didn't understand what he meant.

⁵¹ Then he returned with them to Nazareth and was obedient to them.

His mother treasured all these things in her heart. ⁵² Jesus grew in wisdom and maturity. He gained favor from God and people.

John Prepares the Way—*Matthew 3:1–12; Mark 1:1–8; John 1:19–28*

3 ¹ It was the fifteenth year in the reign of the Emperor Tiberius. Pontius Pilate was governor of Judea. Herod ruled Galilee, and his brother Philip ruled Iturea and Trachonitis. Lysanias was the ruler of Abilene. ² It was at the time when Annas and Caiaphas were chief priests that God spoke to John, son of Zechariah, in the desert. ³ John traveled throughout the region around the Jordan River. He told people about a baptism of repentance[a] for the forgiveness of sins. ⁴ As the prophet Isaiah wrote in his book,

"A voice cries out in the desert:
  'Prepare the way for the Lord!
  Make his paths straight!
5   Every valley will be filled.
      Every mountain and hill will be leveled.
        The crooked ways will be made straight.
        The rough roads will be made smooth.
6   All people will see the salvation that God gives.' "

---

[a] 3:3 Repentance is turning to God with a complete change in the way a person thinks and acts.

[7] Crowds of people were coming to be baptized by John. He would say to them, "You poisonous snakes! Who showed you how to flee from God's coming anger? [8] Do those things that prove that you have turned to God and have changed the way you think and act. Don't say, 'Abraham is our ancestor.' I guarantee that God can raise up descendants for Abraham from these stones. [9] The ax is now ready to cut the roots of the trees. Any tree that doesn't produce good fruit will be cut down and thrown into a fire."

[10] The crowds asked him, "What should we do?"

[11] He answered them, "Whoever has two shirts should share with the person who doesn't have any. Whoever has food should share it too."

[12] Some tax collectors came to be baptized. They asked him, "Teacher, what should we do?"

[13] He told them, "Don't collect more money than you are ordered to collect."

[14] Some soldiers asked him, "And what should we do?"

He told them, "Be satisfied with your pay, and never use threats or blackmail to get money from anyone."

[15] People's hopes were rising as they all wondered whether John was the Messiah. [16] John replied to all of them, "I baptize you with water. But the one who is more powerful than I is coming. I am not worthy to untie his sandal straps. He will baptize you with the Holy Spirit and fire. [17] His winnowing[b] shovel is in his hand to clean up his threshing floor.[c] He will gather the wheat into his barn, but he will burn the husks in a fire that can never be put out."

[18] With many other encouraging words, he told the Good News to the people.

[19] John spoke out against the ruler Herod because Herod had married his own sister-in-law, Herodias. He also spoke out against Herod for all the evil things he had done. [20] So Herod added one more evil to all the others; he locked John in prison.

---

[b] 3:17 Winnowing is the process of separating husks from grain.   [c] 3:17 A threshing floor is an outdoor area where grain is separated from its husks.

The Baptism of Jesus—Matthew 3:13–17; Mark 1:9–11

²¹ When all the people were baptized, Jesus, too, was baptized. While he was praying, heaven opened, ²² and the Holy Spirit came down to him in the form of a dove. A voice from heaven said, "You are my Son, whom I love. I am pleased with you."

²³ Jesus was about 30 years old when he began ˏhis ministryˏ.

The Ancestors of Jesus

Jesus, so people thought, was the son of Joseph, son of Eli, ²⁴ son of Matthat, son of Levi, son of Melchi, son of Jannai, son of Joseph, ²⁵ son of Mattathias, son of Amos, son of Nahum, son of Esli, son of Naggai, ²⁶ son of Maath, son of Mattathias, son of Semein, son of Josech, son of Joda, ²⁷ son of Joanan, son of Rhesa, son of Zerubbabel, son of Shealtiel, son of Neri, ²⁸ son of Melchi, son of Addi, son of Cosam, son of Elmadam, son of Er, ²⁹ son of Joshua, son of Eliezer, son of Jorim, son of Matthat, son of Levi, ³⁰ son of Simeon, son of Judah, son of Joseph, son of Jonam, son of Eliakim, ³¹ son of Melea, son of Menna, son of Mattatha, son of Nathan, son of David, ³² son of Jesse, son of Obed, son of Boaz, son of Salmon, son of Nahshon, ³³ son of Amminadab, son of Admin, son of Arni, son of Hezron, son of Perez, son of Judah, ³⁴ son of Jacob, son of Isaac, son of Abraham, son of Terah, son of Nahor, ³⁵ son of Serug, son of Reu, son of Peleg, son of Eber, son of Shelah, ³⁶ son of Cainan, son of Arphaxad, son of Shem, son of Noah, son of Lamech, ³⁷ son of Methuselah, son of Enoch, son of Jared, son of Mahalaleel, son of Cainan, ³⁸ son of Enos, son of Seth, son of Adam, son of God.

The Devil Tempts Jesus—Matthew 4:1–11; Mark 1:12–13

4 ¹ Jesus was filled with the Holy Spirit as he left the Jordan River. The Spirit led him while he was in the desert, ² where he was tempted by the devil for 40 days. During those days Jesus ate nothing, so when they were over, he was hungry.

³ The devil said to him, "If you are the Son of God, tell this stone to become a loaf of bread."

⁴ Jesus answered him, "Scripture says, 'A person cannot live on bread alone.' "ᵃ

⁵ The devil took him to a high place and showed him all the kingdoms of the world in an instant. ⁶ The devil said to him, "I will give you all the power and glory of these kingdoms. All of it has been given to me, and I give it to anyone I please. ⁷ So if you will worship me, all this will be yours."

⁸ Jesus answered him, "Scripture says, 'Worship the Lord your God and serve only him.' "

⁹ Then the devil took him into Jerusalem and had him stand on the highest part of the temple. He said to Jesus, "If you are the Son of God, jump from here! ¹⁰ Scripture says, 'He will put his angels in charge of you to watch over you carefully. ¹¹ They will carry you in their hands so that you never hit your foot against a rock.' "

¹² Jesus answered him, "It has been said, 'Never tempt the Lord your God.' "ᵇ

¹³ After the devil had finished tempting Jesus in every possible way, the devil left him until another time.

Nazareth Rejects Jesus—Matthew 13:54–58; Mark 6:1–6

¹⁴ Jesus returned to Galilee. The power of the Spirit was with him, and the news about him spread throughout the surrounding country. ¹⁵ He taught in the synagogues, and everyone praised him.

¹⁶ Then Jesus came to Nazareth, where he had been brought up. As usual he went into the synagogue on the day of worship. He stood up to read the lesson. ¹⁷ The attendant gave him the book of the prophet Isaiah. He opened it and found the place where it read:

¹⁸   "The Spirit of the Lord is with me.
        He has anointed me
            to tell the Good News to the poor.
        He has sent meᶜ

ᵃ 4:4 Some manuscripts and translations add "but on every word of God."
ᵇ 4:12 Or "Never put the Lord your God to any test."   ᶜ 4:18 Some manuscripts and translations add "to heal those who are brokenhearted."

to announce forgiveness to the prisoners of sin
and the restoring of sight to the blind,
to forgive those who have been shattered by sin,
¹⁹   to announce the year of the Lord's favor."

²⁰ Jesus closed the book, gave it back to the attendant, and sat down. Everyone in the synagogue watched him closely. ²¹ Then he said to them, "This passage came true today when you heard me read it."

²² All the people spoke well of him. They were amazed to hear the gracious words flowing from his lips. They said, "Isn't this Joseph's son?"

²³ So he said to them, "You'll probably quote this proverb to me, 'Doctor, cure yourself!' and then say to me, 'Do all the things in your hometown that we've heard you've done in Capernaum.' " ²⁴ Then Jesus added, "I can guarantee this truth: A prophet isn't accepted in his hometown.

²⁵ "I can guarantee this truth: There were many widows in Israel in Elijah's time. It had not rained for three-and-a-half years, and the famine was severe everywhere in the country. ²⁶ But God didn't send Elijah to anyone except a widow at Zarephath in the territory of Sidon. ²⁷ There were also many people with skin diseases in Israel in the prophet Elisha's time. But God cured no one except Naaman from Syria."

²⁸ Everyone in the synagogue became furious when they heard this. ²⁹ Their city was built on a hill with a cliff. So they got up, forced Jesus out of the city, and led him to the cliff. They intended to throw him off of it. ³⁰ But Jesus walked right by them and went away.

Jesus Forces an Evil Spirit out of a Man—Mark 1:21–28

³¹ Jesus went to Capernaum, a city in Galilee, and taught them on a day of worship. ³² The people were amazed at his teachings because he spoke with authority.

³³ In the synagogue was a man possessed by a spirit, an evil demon. He shouted very loudly, ³⁴ "Oh, no! What do you want with

us, Jesus from Nazareth? Have you come to destroy us? I know who you are—the Holy One of God!"

³⁵ Jesus ordered the spirit, "Keep quiet, and come out of him!" The demon threw the man down in the middle of the synagogue and came out without hurting him.

³⁶ Everyone was stunned. They said to one another, "What kind of command is this? With authority and power he gives orders to evil spirits, and they come out."

³⁷ So news about him spread to every place throughout the surrounding region.

Jesus Cures Simon's Mother-in-Law and Many Others—
Matthew 8:14–18; Mark 1:29–34

³⁸ Jesus left the synagogue and went to Simon's house. Simon's mother-in-law was sick with a high fever. They asked Jesus to help her. ³⁹ He bent over her, ordered the fever to leave, and it went away. She got up immediately and prepared a meal for them.

⁴⁰ When the sun was setting, everyone who had friends suffering from various diseases brought them to him. He placed his hands on each of them and cured them. ⁴¹ Demons came out of many people, shouting, "You are the Son of God!" But Jesus ordered them not to speak. After all, they knew he was the Messiah.

Spreading the Good News—Matthew 4:23–25; Mark 1:35–39

⁴² In the morning he went to a place where he could be alone. The crowds searched for him. When they came to him, they tried to keep him from leaving. ⁴³ But he said to them, "I have to tell the Good News about the kingdom of God in other cities also. That's what I was sent to do."

⁴⁴ So he spread his message in the synagogues of Judea.^d

Calling of the First Disciples—Matthew 4:18–22; Mark 1:14–20

5 ¹ One day Jesus was standing by the Sea of Galilee. The people crowded around him as they listened to God's word. ² Jesus

^d 4:44 Some manuscripts read "in the synagogues of Galilee."

saw two boats on the shore. The fishermen had stepped out of them and were washing their nets. ³ So Jesus got into the boat that belonged to Simon and asked him to push off a little from the shore. Then Jesus sat down and taught the crowd from the boat.

⁴ When he finished speaking, he told Simon, "Take the boat into deep water, and lower your nets to catch some fish."

⁵ Simon answered, "Teacher, we worked hard all night and caught nothing. But if you say so, I'll lower the nets."

⁶ After the men had done this, they caught such a large number of fish that their nets began to tear. ⁷ So they signaled to their partners in the other boat to come and help them. Their partners came and filled both boats until the boats nearly sank.

⁸ When Simon Peter saw this, he knelt in front of Jesus and said, "Leave me, Lord! I'm a sinful person!" ⁹ Simon and everyone who was with him was amazed to see the large number of fish they had caught. ¹⁰ James and John, who were Zebedee's sons and Simon's partners, were also amazed.

Jesus told Simon, "Don't be afraid. From now on you will catch people instead of fish."

¹¹ Simon and his partners brought the boats to shore, left everything, and followed Jesus.

Jesus Cures a Man With a Skin Disease—
Matthew 8:1–4; Mark 1:40–44

¹² One day Jesus was in a city where there was a man covered with a serious skin disease. When the man saw Jesus, he bowed with his face to the ground. He begged Jesus, "Sir, if you want to, you can make me clean."ᵃ

¹³ Jesus reached out, touched him, and said, "I want to. So be clean!" Immediately, his skin disease went away.

¹⁴ Jesus ordered him, "Don't tell anyone. Instead, show yourself to the priest. Then offer the sacrifice as Moses commanded as proof to people that you are clean."

ᵃ 5:12 "Clean" refers to anything that Moses' Teachings say is presentable to God.

¹⁵ The news about Jesus spread even more. Large crowds gathered to hear him and have their diseases cured. ¹⁶ But he would go away to places where he could be alone for prayer.

Jesus Forgives Sins—Matthew 9:1–8; Mark 2:1–12

¹⁷ One day when Jesus was teaching, some Pharisees and experts in Moses' Teachings were present. They had come from every village in Galilee and Judea and from Jerusalem. Jesus had the power of the Lord to heal.

¹⁸ Some men brought a paralyzed man on a stretcher. They tried to take him into the house and put him in front of Jesus. ¹⁹ But they could not find a way to get him into the house because of the crowd. So they went up on the roof. They made an opening in the tiles and let the man down on his stretcher among the people. (They lowered him in front of Jesus.)

²⁰ When Jesus saw their faith, he said, "Sir, your sins are forgiven." ²¹ The scribes and the Pharisees thought, "Who is this man? He's dishonoring God! Who besides God can forgive sins?"

²² Jesus knew what they were thinking. So he said to them, "What are you thinking? ²³ Is it easier to say, 'Your sins are forgiven,' or to say, 'Get up and walk'? ²⁴ I want you to know that the Son of Man has authority on earth to forgive sins." Then he said to the paralyzed man, "Get up, pick up your stretcher, and go home."

²⁵ The man immediately stood up in front of them and picked up the stretcher he had been lying on. Praising God, he went home.

²⁶ Everyone was amazed and praised God. They were filled with awe and said, "We've seen things today we can hardly believe!"

Jesus Chooses Levi [Matthew] to Be a Disciple—
Matthew 9:9–13; Mark 2:13–17

²⁷ After that, Jesus left. He saw a tax collector named Levi sitting in a tax office. Jesus said to him, "Follow me!" ²⁸ So Levi got up, left everything, and followed him.

²⁹ Levi held a large reception at his home for Jesus. A huge crowd of tax collectors and others were eating with them.

[30] The Pharisees and their scribes complained to Jesus' disciples. They asked, "Why do you eat and drink with tax collectors and sinners?"

[31] Jesus answered them, "Healthy people don't need a doctor; those who are sick do. [32] I've come to call sinners to change the way they think and act, not to call people who think they have God's approval."

Jesus Is Questioned About Fasting—Matthew 9:14–17; Mark 2:18–22

[33] They said to him, "John's disciples frequently fast and say prayers, and so do the disciples of the Pharisees. But your disciples eat and drink."

[34] Jesus asked them, "Can you force wedding guests to fast while the groom is still with them? [35] The time will come when the groom will be taken away from them. At that time they will fast."

[36] He also used these illustrations: "No one tears a piece of cloth from a new coat to patch an old coat. Otherwise, the new cloth will tear the old. Besides, the patch from the new will not match the old. [37] People don't pour new wine into old wineskins. If they do, the new wine will make the skins burst. The wine will run out, and the skins will be ruined. [38] Rather, new wine is to be poured into fresh skins.

[39] "No one who has been drinking old wine wants new wine. He says, 'The old wine is better!' "

Jesus Has Authority Over the Day of Worship—
Matthew 12:1–8; Mark 2:23–28

6 [1] Once, on a day of worship, Jesus was walking through some grainfields. His disciples were picking the heads of grain, removing the husks, and eating the grain.

[2] Some of the Pharisees asked, "Why are your disciples doing something that is not right to do on the day of worship?"

[3] Jesus answered them, "Haven't you read what David did when he and his men were hungry? [4] Haven't you read how he went into the house of God, ate the bread of the presence, and gave some

of it to the men who were with him? He had no right to eat those loaves. Only the priests have that right."

⁵ Then he added, "The Son of Man has authority over the day of worship."

Jesus Heals on the Day of Worship—Matthew 12:9–15a; Mark 3:1–6

⁶ On another day of worship, Jesus went into a synagogue to teach. A man whose right hand was paralyzed was there. ⁷ The scribes and the Pharisees were watching Jesus closely. They wanted to see whether he would heal the man on the day of worship so that they could find a way to accuse him of doing something wrong.

⁸ But Jesus knew what they were thinking. So he told the man with the paralyzed hand, "Get up, and stand in the center ⌊of the synagogue⌋!" The man got up and stood there. ⁹ Then Jesus said to them, "I ask you—what is the right thing to do on a day of worship: to do good or evil, to give a person his health or to destroy it?" ¹⁰ He looked around at all of them and then said to the man, "Hold out your hand." The man did so, and his hand became normal again.

¹¹ The scribes and Pharisees were furious and began to discuss with each other what they could do to Jesus.

Jesus Appoints Twelve Apostles—Matthew 10:1–4; Mark 3:13–19

¹² At that time Jesus went to a mountain to pray. He spent the whole night in prayer to God.

¹³ When it was day, he called his disciples. He chose twelve of them and called them apostles. ¹⁴ They were Simon (whom Jesus named Peter) and Simon's brother Andrew, James, John, Philip, Bartholomew, ¹⁵ Matthew, Thomas, James (son of Alphaeus), Simon (who was called the Zealot), ¹⁶ Judas (son of James), and Judas Iscariot (who became a traitor).

Many People Are Cured—Mark 3:7–12

¹⁷ Jesus came down from the mountain with them and stood on a level place. A large crowd of his disciples and many other people

were there. They had come from all over Judea, Jerusalem, and
the seacoast of Tyre and Sidon. [18] They wanted to hear him and be
cured of their diseases. Those who were tormented by evil spirits
were cured. [19] The entire crowd was trying to touch him because
power was coming from him and curing all of them.

Jesus Teaches His Disciples

[20] Jesus looked at his disciples and said,

"Blessed are those who are poor.
The kingdom of God is theirs.
[21]   Blessed are those who are hungry.
They will be satisfied.
Blessed are those who are crying.
They will laugh.
[22]   Blessed are you when people hate you, avoid you,
insult you, and slander you
because you are committed to the Son of Man.
[23]   Rejoice then, and be very happy!
You have a great reward in heaven.
That's the way their ancestors treated
the prophets.

[24]   "But how horrible it will be for those who are rich.
They have had their comfort.
[25]   How horrible it will be for those who are well-fed.
They will be hungry.
How horrible it will be for those who are laughing.
They will mourn and cry.
[26]   How horrible it will be for you
when everyone says nice things about you.
That's the way their ancestors treated
the false prophets.

Love Your Enemies—*Matthew 5:38–48*

²⁷ "But I tell everyone who is listening: Love your enemies. Be kind to those who hate you. ²⁸ Bless those who curse you. Pray for those who insult you. ²⁹ If someone strikes you on the cheek, offer the other cheek as well. If someone takes your coat, don't stop him from taking your shirt. ³⁰ Give to everyone who asks you for something. If someone takes what is yours, don't insist on getting it back.

³¹ "Do for other people everything you want them to do for you.

³² "If you love those who love you, do you deserve any thanks for that? Even sinners love those who love them. ³³ If you help those who help you, do you deserve any thanks for that? Sinners do that too. ³⁴ If you lend anything to those from whom you expect to get something back, do you deserve any thanks for that? Sinners also lend to sinners to get back what they lend. ³⁵ Rather, love your enemies, help them, and lend to them without expecting to get anything back. Then you will have a great reward. You will be the children of the Most High God. After all, he is kind to unthankful and evil people. ³⁶ Be merciful as your Father is merciful.

Stop Judging—*Matthew 7:1–5*

³⁷ "Stop judging, and you will never be judged. Stop condemning, and you will never be condemned. Forgive, and you will be forgiven. ³⁸ Give, and you will receive. A large quantity, pressed together, shaken down, and running over will be put into your pocket. The standards you use for others will be applied to you."

³⁹ Jesus also gave them this illustration: "Can one blind person lead another? Won't both fall into the same pit? ⁴⁰ A student is no better than his teacher. But everyone who is well-trained will be like his teacher.

⁴¹ "Why do you see the piece of sawdust in another believer's eye and not notice the wooden beam in your own eye? ⁴² How can you say to another believer, 'Friend, let me take the piece of saw-

dust out of your eye,' when you don't see the beam in your own eye? You hypocrite! First remove the beam from your own eye. Then you will see clearly to remove the piece of sawdust from another believer's eye.

Evil People—*Matthew 7:15–23*

⁴³ "A good tree doesn't produce rotten fruit, and a rotten tree doesn't produce good fruit. ⁴⁴ Each tree is known by its fruit. You don't pick figs from thorny plants or grapes from a thornbush. ⁴⁵ Good people do the good that is in them. But evil people do the evil that is in them. The things people say come from inside them.

Build on the Rock—*Matthew 7:24–29*

⁴⁶ "Why do you call me Lord but don't do what I tell you?

⁴⁷ "I will show you what everyone who comes to me, hears what I say, and obeys it is like. ⁴⁸ He is like a person who dug down to bedrock to lay the foundation of his home. When a flood came, the floodwaters pushed against that house. But the house couldn't be washed away because it had a good foundation. ⁴⁹ The person who hears ˻what I say˼ but doesn't obey it is like someone who built a house on the ground without any foundation. The floodwaters pushed against it, and that house quickly collapsed and was destroyed."

A Believing Army Officer—*Matthew 8:5–13*

7 ¹ When Jesus had finished everything he wanted to say to the people, he went to Capernaum. ² There a Roman army officer's valuable slave was sick and near death. ³ The officer had heard about Jesus and sent some Jewish leaders to him. They were to ask Jesus to come and save the servant's life. ⁴ They came to Jesus and begged, "He deserves your help. ⁵ He loves our people and built our synagogue at his own expense."

⁶ Jesus went with them. He was not far from the house when the officer sent friends to tell Jesus, "Sir, don't bother. I don't deserve to have you come into my house. ⁷ That's why I didn't come to you.

But just give a command, and let my servant be cured. ⁸ As you know, I'm in a chain of command and have soldiers at my command. I tell one of them, 'Go!' and he goes, and another, 'Come!' and he comes. I tell my servant, 'Do this!' and he does it."

⁹ Jesus was amazed at the officer when he heard these words. He turned to the crowd following him and said, "I can guarantee that I haven't found faith as great as this in Israel."

¹⁰ When the men who had been sent returned to the house, they found the servant healthy again.

Jesus Brings a Widow's Son Back to Life

¹¹ Soon afterward, Jesus went to a city called Nain. His disciples and a large crowd went with him. ¹² As he came near the entrance to the city, he met a funeral procession. The dead man was a widow's only child. A large crowd from the city was with her.

¹³ When the Lord saw her, he felt sorry for her. He said to her, "Don't cry."

¹⁴ He went up to the open coffin, took hold of it, and the men who were carrying it stopped. He said, "Young man, I'm telling you to come back to life!" ¹⁵ The dead man sat up and began to talk, and Jesus gave him back to his mother.

¹⁶ Everyone was struck with fear and praised God. They said, "A great prophet has appeared among us," and "God has taken care of his people." ¹⁷ This news about Jesus spread throughout Judea and the surrounding region.

John Sends Two Disciples—*Matthew 11:2–6*

¹⁸ John's disciples told him about all these things. Then John called two of his disciples ¹⁹ and sent them to ask the Lord, "Are you the one who is coming, or should we look for someone else?"

²⁰ The men came to Jesus and said, "John the Baptizer sent us to ask you, 'Are you the one who is coming, or should we look for someone else?' "

²¹ At that time Jesus was curing many people who had diseases, sicknesses, and evil spirits. Also, he was giving back sight to many who were blind.

²² Jesus answered John's disciples, "Go back, and tell John what you have seen and heard: Blind people see again, lame people are walking, those with skin diseases are made clean,ᵃ deaf people hear again, dead people are brought back to life, and poor people hear the Good News. ²³ Whoever doesn't lose his faith in me is indeed blessed."

Jesus Speaks About John—Matthew 11:7–19

²⁴ When John's messengers had left, Jesus spoke to the crowds about John. "What did you go into the desert to see? Tall grass swaying in the wind? ²⁵ Really, what did you go to see? A man dressed in fine clothes? Those who wear splendid clothes and live in luxury are in royal palaces. ²⁶ Really, what did you go to see? A prophet? Let me tell you that he is far more than a prophet. ²⁷ John is the one about whom Scripture says,

'I am sending my messenger ahead of you
        to prepare the way in front of you.'

²⁸ I can guarantee that of all the people ever born, no one is greater than John. Yet, the least important person in the kingdom of God is greater than John.

²⁹ "All the people, including tax collectors, heard John. They admitted that God was right by letting John baptize them. ³⁰ But the Pharisees and the experts in Moses' Teachings rejected God's plan for them. They refused to be baptized.

³¹ "How can I describe the people who are living now? What are they like? ³² They are like children who sit in the marketplace and shout to each other,

'We played music for you,
        but you didn't dance.
We sang a funeral song,
        but you didn't cry.'

ᵃ 7:22 "Clean" refers to anything that Moses' Teachings say is presentable to God.

³³ John the Baptizer has come neither eating bread nor drinking wine, and you say, 'There's a demon in him!' ³⁴ The Son of Man has come eating and drinking, and you say, 'Look at him! He's a glutton and a drunk, a friend of tax collectors and sinners!'

³⁵ "Yet, wisdom is proved right by all its results."

A Sinful Woman Receives Forgiveness

³⁶ One of the Pharisees invited Jesus to eat with him. Jesus went to the Pharisee's house and was eating at the table.

³⁷ A woman who lived a sinful life in that city found out that Jesus was eating at the Pharisee's house. So she took a bottle of perfume ³⁸ and knelt at his feet. She was crying and washed his feet with her tears. Then she dried his feet with her hair, kissed them over and over again, and poured the perfume on them.

³⁹ The Pharisee who had invited Jesus saw this and thought, "If this man really were a prophet, he would know what sort of woman is touching him. She's a sinner."

⁴⁰ Jesus spoke up, "Simon, I have something to say to you."

Simon replied, "Teacher, you're free to speak."

⁴¹ ˻So Jesus said,˼ "Two men owed a moneylender some money. One owed him five hundred silver coins, and the other owed him fifty. ⁴² When they couldn't pay it back, he was kind enough to cancel their debts. Now, who do you think will love him the most?"

⁴³ Simon answered, "I suppose the one who had the largest debt canceled."

Jesus said to him, "You're right!" ⁴⁴ Then, turning to the woman, he said to Simon, "You see this woman, don't you? I came into your house. You didn't wash my feet. But she has washed my feet with her tears and dried them with her hair. ⁴⁵ You didn't give me a kiss. But ever since I came in, she has not stopped kissing my feet. ⁴⁶ You didn't put any olive oil on my head. But she has poured perfume on my feet. ⁴⁷ That's why I'm telling you that her many sins have been forgiven. Her great love proves that. But whoever receives little forgiveness loves very little."

⁴⁸ Then Jesus said to her, "Your sins have been forgiven." ⁴⁹ The other guests thought, "Who is this man who even forgives sins?"

⁵⁰ Jesus said to the woman, "Your faith has saved you. Go in peace!"

Women Who Supported Jesus

8 ¹ After this, Jesus traveled from one city and village to another. He spread the Good News about God's kingdom. The twelve apostles were with him. ² Also, some women were with him. They had been cured from evil spirits and various illnesses. These women were Mary, also called Magdalene, from whom seven demons had gone out; ³ Joanna, whose husband Chusa was Herod's administrator; Susanna; and many other women. They provided financial support for Jesus and his disciples.

A Story About a Farmer—Matthew 13:1–23; Mark 4:1–20

⁴ When a large crowd had gathered and people had come to Jesus from every city, he used this story as an illustration: ⁵ "A farmer went to plant his seeds. Some seeds were planted along the road, were trampled, and were devoured by birds. ⁶ Others were planted on rocky soil. When the plants came up, they withered because they had no moisture. ⁷ Others were planted among thornbushes. The thornbushes grew up with them and choked them. ⁸ Others were planted on good ground. When they came up, they produced a hundred times as much as was planted."

After he had said this, he called out, "Let the person who has ears listen!"

⁹ His disciples asked him what this story meant. ¹⁰ Jesus answered, "Knowledge about the mysteries of the kingdom of God has been given ⌊directly⌋ to you. But it is given to others in stories. When they look, they don't see, and when they hear, they don't understand.

¹¹ "This is what the story illustrates: The seed is God's word. ¹² Some people are like seeds that were planted along the road. They hear the word, but then the devil comes. He takes the word away

from them so that they don't believe and become saved. ¹³ Some people are like seeds on rocky soil. They welcome the word with joy whenever they hear it, but they don't develop any roots. They believe for a while, but when their faith is tested, they abandon it. ¹⁴ The seeds that were planted among thornbushes are people who hear the word, but as life goes on the worries, riches, and pleasures of life choke them. So they don't produce anything good. ¹⁵ The seeds that were planted on good ground are people who also hear the word. But they keep it in their good and honest hearts and produce what is good despite what life may bring.

¹⁶ "No one lights a lamp and hides it under a bowl or puts it under a bed. Instead, everyone who lights a lamp puts it on a lamp stand so that those who come in will see the light. ¹⁷ There is nothing hidden that will not be revealed. There is nothing kept secret that will not come to light.

¹⁸ "So pay attention to how you listen! Those who understand ˌthese mysteriesˌ will be given ˌmore knowledgeˌ. However, some people don't understand ˌthese mysteriesˌ. Even what they think they understand will be taken away from them."

The True Family of Jesus—Matthew 12:46–50; Mark 3:31–35

¹⁹ His mother and his brothers came to see him. But they couldn't meet with him because of the crowd. ²⁰ Someone told Jesus, "Your mother and your brothers are standing outside. They want to see you." ²¹ He answered them, "My mother and my brothers are those who hear and do what God's word says."

Jesus Calms the Sea—Matthew 8:23–27; Mark 4:35–41

²² One day Jesus and his disciples got into a boat. He said to them, "Let's cross to the other side of the lake." So they started out. ²³ As they were sailing along, Jesus fell asleep.

A violent storm came across the lake. The boat was taking on water, and they were in danger. ²⁴ They went to him, woke him up, and said, "Master! Master! We're going to die!"

Then he got up and ordered the wind and the waves to stop. The wind stopped, and the sea became calm. [25] He asked them, "Where is your faith?"

Frightened and amazed, they asked each other, "Who is this man? He gives orders to the wind and the water, and they obey him!"

Jesus Cures a Demon-Possessed Man—
Matthew 8:28–34; Mark 5:1–20

[26] They landed in the region of the Gerasenes across from Galilee. [27] When Jesus stepped out on the shore, a certain man from the city met him. The man was possessed by demons and had not worn clothes for a long time. He would not stay in a house but lived in the tombs. [28] When he saw Jesus, he shouted, fell in front of him, and said in a loud voice, "Why are you bothering me, Jesus, Son of the Most High God? I beg you not to torture me!" [29] Jesus ordered the evil spirit to come out of the man. (The evil spirit had controlled the man for a long time. People had kept him under guard. He was chained hand and foot. But he would break the chains. Then the demon would force him to go into the desert.)

[30] Jesus asked him, "What is your name?"

He answered, "Legion [Six Thousand]." (Many demons had entered him.) [31] The demons begged Jesus not to order them to go into the bottomless pit.

[32] A large herd of pigs was feeding on a mountainside. The demons begged Jesus to let them enter those pigs. So he let them do this. [33] The demons came out of the man and went into the pigs. Then the herd rushed down the cliff into the lake and drowned.

[34] When those who had taken care of the pigs saw what had happened, they ran away. They reported everything in the city and countryside. [35] The people went to see what had happened. They came to Jesus and found the man from whom the demons had gone out. Dressed and in his right mind, he was sitting at Jesus' feet. The people were frightened. [36] Those who had seen this told the people how Jesus had restored the demon-possessed man to health.

³⁷ Then all the people from the surrounding region of the Gerasenes asked Jesus to leave because they were terrified.

Jesus got into a boat and started back. ³⁸ The man from whom the demons had gone out begged him, "Let me go with you."

But Jesus sent the man away and told him, ³⁹ "Go home to your family, and tell them how much God has done for you." So the man left. He went through the whole city and told people how much Jesus had done for him.

Jairus' Daughter and a Woman With Chronic Bleeding— Matthew 9:18–26; Mark 5:21–43

⁴⁰ When Jesus came back, a crowd welcomed him. Everyone was expecting him.

⁴¹ A man named Jairus, a synagogue leader, arrived and quickly bowed down in front of Jesus. He begged Jesus to come to his home. ⁴² His only daughter, who was about twelve years old, was dying. As Jesus went, the people were crowding around him.

⁴³ A woman who had been suffering from chronic bleeding for twelve years was in the crowd. No one could cure her. ⁴⁴ She came up behind Jesus, touched the edge of his clothes, and her bleeding stopped at once.

⁴⁵ Jesus asked, "Who touched me?"

After everyone denied touching him, Peter said, "Teacher, the people are crowding you and pressing against you."

⁴⁶ Jesus said, "Someone touched me. I know power has gone out of me."

⁴⁷ The woman saw that she couldn't hide. Trembling, she quickly bowed in front of him. There, in front of all the people, she told why she touched him and how she was cured at once.

⁴⁸ Jesus told her, "Daughter, your faith has made you well. Go in peace!"

⁴⁹ While Jesus was still speaking to her, someone came from the synagogue leader's home. He said, "Your daughter is dead. Don't bother the teacher anymore."

⁵⁰ When Jesus heard this, he told the synagogue leader, "Don't be afraid! Just believe, and she will get well."

⁵¹ Jesus went into the house. He allowed no one to go with him except Peter, John, James, and the child's parents. ⁵² Everyone was crying and showing how sad they were. Jesus said, "Don't cry! She's not dead. She's just sleeping."

⁵³ They laughed at him because they knew she was dead. ⁵⁴ But Jesus took her hand and called out, "Child, get up!" ⁵⁵ She came back to life and got up at once. He ordered her parents to give her something to eat. ⁵⁶ They were amazed. Jesus ordered them not to tell anyone what had happened.

Jesus Sends Out the Twelve—Matthew 10:5–42; Mark 6:7–13

9 ¹ Jesus called the twelve apostles together and gave them power and authority over every demon and power and authority to cure diseases. ² He sent them to spread the message about the kingdom of God and to cure the sick.

³ He told them, "Don't take anything along on the trip. Don't take a walking stick, traveling bag, any food, money, or a change of clothes. ⁴ When you go into a home, stay there until you're ready to leave. ⁵ If people don't welcome you, leave that city, and shake its dust off your feet as a warning to them."

⁶ The apostles went from village to village, told the Good News, and cured the sick everywhere.

Rumors About Jesus—Matthew 14:1–12; Mark 6:14–29

⁷ Herod the ruler heard about everything that was happening. He didn't know what to make of it. Some people were saying that John had come back to life. ⁸ Others said that Elijah had appeared, and still others said that one of the prophets from long ago had come back to life.

⁹ Herod said, "I had John's head cut off. Who is this person I'm hearing so much about?" So Herod wanted to see Jesus.

Jesus Feeds Five Thousand—
Matthew 14:13–21; Mark 6:30–44; John 6:1–14

10 The apostles came back and told Jesus everything they had done. He took them with him to a city called Bethsaida so that they could be alone. **11** But the crowds found out about this and followed him. He welcomed them, talked to them about the kingdom of God, and cured those who were sick.

12 Toward the end of the day, the twelve apostles came to him. They said to him, "Send the crowd to the closest villages and farms so that they can find some food and a place to stay. No one lives around here."

13 Jesus replied, "You give them something to eat."

They said to him, "We have five loaves of bread and two fish. Unless we go to buy food for all these people, that's all we have." **14** (There were about five thousand men.)

Then he told his disciples, "Have them sit in groups of about fifty." **15** So they did this.

16 Then he took the five loaves and the two fish, looked up to heaven, and blessed the food. He broke the loaves apart and kept giving them to the disciples to give to the crowd. **17** All of them ate as much as they wanted. When they picked up the leftover pieces, they filled twelve baskets.

Peter Declares His Belief About Jesus—
Matthew 16:13–20; Mark 8:27–30

18 Once when Jesus was praying privately and his disciples were with him, he asked them, "Who do people say I am?"

19 They answered, "Some say you are John the Baptizer, others Elijah, and still others say that one of the prophets from long ago has come back to life."

20 He asked them, "But who do you say I am?"

Peter answered, "You are the Messiah, whom God has sent."

21 He ordered them not to tell this to anyone.

Jesus Foretells That He Will Die and Come Back to Life—
Matthew 16:21–23; Mark 8:31–33

²² Jesus said that the Son of Man would have to suffer a lot. He would be rejected by the leaders, the chief priests, and the scribes. He would be killed, but on the third day he would come back to life.

What It Means to Follow Jesus—*Matthew 16:24–28; Mark 8:34–9:1*

²³ He said to all of them, "Those who want to come with me must say no to the things they want, pick up their crosses every day, and follow me. ²⁴ Those who want to save their lives will lose them. But those who lose their lives for me will save them. ²⁵ What good does it do for people to win the whole world but lose their lives by destroying them? ²⁶ If people are ashamed of me and what I say, the Son of Man will be ashamed of those people when he comes in the glory that he shares with the Father and the holy angels.

²⁷ "I can guarantee this truth: Some people who are standing here will not die until they see the kingdom of God."

Moses and Elijah Appear With Jesus—*Matthew 17:1–8; Mark 9:2–13*

²⁸ About eight days after he had said this, Jesus took Peter, John, and James with him and went up a mountain to pray. ²⁹ While Jesus was praying, the appearance of his face changed, and his clothes became dazzling white. ³⁰ Suddenly, both Moses and Elijah were talking with him. ³¹ They appeared in heavenly glory and were discussing Jesus' approaching death and what he was about to fulfill in Jerusalem.

³² Peter and the men with him were sleeping soundly. When they woke up, they saw Jesus' glory and the two men standing with him. ³³ As Moses and Elijah were leaving him, Peter said to Jesus, "Teacher, it's good that we're here. Let's put up three tents—one for you, one for Moses, and one for Elijah." Peter didn't know what he was saying.

³⁴ While he was saying this, a cloud overshadowed them. They were frightened as they went into the cloud. ³⁵ A voice came out of

the cloud and said, "This is my Son, whom I have chosen. Listen to him!"

³⁶ After the voice had spoken, they saw that Jesus was alone. The disciples said nothing, and for some time they told no one about what they had seen.

Jesus Cures a Demon-Possessed Boy—
Matthew 17:14–20; Mark 9:14–29

³⁷ The next day, when they had come down from the mountain, a large crowd met Jesus. ³⁸ A man in the crowd shouted, "Teacher, I beg you to look at my son. He's my only child. ³⁹ Whenever a spirit takes control of him, he shrieks, goes into convulsions, and foams at the mouth. After a struggle, the spirit goes away, leaving the child worn out. ⁴⁰ I begged your disciples to force the spirit out of him, but they couldn't do it."

⁴¹ Jesus answered, "You unbelieving and corrupt generation! How long must I be with you and put up with you? Bring your son here!"

⁴² While he was coming ‚to Jesus‚, the demon knocked the boy to the ground and threw him into convulsions.

Jesus ordered the evil spirit to leave. He cured the boy and gave him back to his father. ⁴³ Everyone was amazed to see God's wonderful power.

The Son of Man Again Foretells His Betrayal—
Matthew 17:22–23; Mark 9:30–32

Everyone was amazed at all the things that Jesus was doing. So he said to his disciples, ⁴⁴ "Listen carefully to what I say. The Son of Man will be betrayed and handed over to people."

⁴⁵ They didn't know what he meant. The meaning was hidden from them so that they didn't understand it. Besides, they were afraid to ask him about what he had said.

Greatness in the Kingdom—Matthew 18:1–5; Mark 9:33–37

⁴⁶ A discussion started among them about who would be the greatest. ⁴⁷ Jesus knew what they were thinking. So he took a

little child and had him stand beside him. [48] Then he said to them, "Whoever welcomes this little child in my name welcomes me. Whoever welcomes me welcomes the one who sent me. The one who is least among all of you is the one who is greatest."

Using the Name of Jesus—Mark 9:38–41

[49] John replied, "Master, we saw someone forcing demons out of a person by using the power and authority of your name. We tried to stop him because he was not one of us."

[50] Jesus said to him, "Don't stop him! Whoever isn't against you is for you."

People From a Samaritan Village Reject Jesus

[51] The time was coming closer for Jesus to be taken to heaven. So he was determined to go to Jerusalem. [52] He sent messengers ahead of him. They went into a Samaritan village to arrange a place for him to stay. [53] But the people didn't welcome him, because he was on his way to Jerusalem. [54] James and John, his disciples, saw this. They asked, "Lord, do you want us to call down fire from heaven to burn them up?"

[55] But he turned and corrected them.[a] [56] So they went to another village.

What It Takes to Be a Disciple—Matthew 8:19–22

[57] As they were walking along the road, a man said to Jesus, "I'll follow you wherever you go."

[58] Jesus told him, "Foxes have holes, and birds have nests, but the Son of Man has nowhere to sleep."

[59] He told another man, "Follow me!"

But the man said, "Sir, first let me go to bury my father."

[60] But Jesus told him, "Let the dead bury their own dead. You must go everywhere and tell about the kingdom of God."

[a] 9:55 Some manuscripts and translations add " 'You don't know the kind of spirit that is influencing you. The Son of Man didn't come to destroy people's lives but to save them,' he said."

[61] Another said, "I'll follow you, sir, but first let me tell my family goodbye."

[62] Jesus said to him, "Whoever starts to plow and looks back is not fit for the kingdom of God."

Jesus Sends Disciples to Do Mission Work

10 [1] After this, the Lord appointed 70[a] other disciples to go ahead of him to every city and place that he intended to go. They were to travel in pairs.

[2] He told them, "The harvest is large, but the workers are few. So ask the Lord who gives this harvest to send workers to harvest his crops. [3] Go! I'm sending you out like lambs among wolves. [4] Don't carry a wallet, a traveling bag, or sandals, and don't stop to greet anyone on the way. [5] Whenever you go into a house, greet the family right away with the words, 'May there be peace in this house.' [6] If a peaceful person lives there, your greeting will be accepted. But if that's not the case, your greeting will be rejected. [7] Stay with the family that accepts you. Eat and drink whatever they offer you. After all, the worker deserves his pay. Do not move around from one house to another. [8] Whenever you go into a city and the people welcome you, eat whatever they serve you. [9] Heal the sick that are there, and tell the people, 'The kingdom of God is near you!'

[10] "But whenever you go into a city and people don't welcome you, leave. Announce in its streets, [11] 'We are wiping your city's dust from our feet in protest against you! But realize that the kingdom of God is near you!' [12] I can guarantee that judgment day will be easier for Sodom than for that city.

[13] "How horrible it will be for you, Chorazin! How horrible it will be for you, Bethsaida! If the miracles worked in your cities had been worked in Tyre and Sidon, they would have changed the way they thought and acted. Long ago they would have worn sackcloth and sat in ashes. [14] Judgment day will be better for Tyre and Sidon than for you. [15] And you, Capernaum, will you be lifted to heaven? No, you will go to hell!

a 10:1 Some manuscripts have "72."

¹⁶ "The person who hears you hears me, and the person who rejects you rejects me. The person who rejects me rejects the one who sent me."

¹⁷ The 70 disciples came back very happy. They said, "Lord, even demons obey us when we use the power and authority of your name!"

¹⁸ Jesus said to them, "I watched Satan fall from heaven like lightning. ¹⁹ I have given you the authority to trample snakes and scorpions and to destroy the enemy's power. Nothing will hurt you. ²⁰ However, don't be happy that evil spirits obey you. Be happy that your names are written in heaven."

²¹ In that hour the Holy Spirit filled Jesus with joy. Jesus said, "I praise you, Father, Lord of heaven and earth, for hiding these things from wise and intelligent people and revealing them to little children. Yes, Father, this is what pleased you.

²² "My Father has turned everything over to me. Only the Father knows who the Son is. And no one knows who the Father is except the Son and those to whom the Son is willing to reveal him."

²³ He turned to his disciples in private and said to them, "How blessed you are to see what you've seen. ²⁴ I can guarantee that many prophets and kings wanted to see and hear what you've seen and heard, but they didn't."

A Story About a Good Samaritan

²⁵ Then an expert in Moses' Teachings stood up to test Jesus. He asked, "Teacher, what must I do to inherit eternal life?"

²⁶ Jesus answered him, "What is written in Moses' Teachings? What do you read there?"

²⁷ He answered, " 'Love the Lord your God with all your heart, with all your soul, with all your strength, and with all your mind. And love your neighbor as you love yourself.' "

²⁸ Jesus told him, "You're right! Do this, and life will be yours."

²⁹ But the man wanted to justify his question. So he asked Jesus, "Who is my neighbor?"

³⁰ Jesus replied, "A man went from Jerusalem to Jericho. On the way robbers stripped him, beat him, and left him for dead.

³¹ "By chance, a priest was traveling along that road. When he saw the man, he went around him and continued on his way. ³² Then a Levite came to that place. When he saw the man, he, too, went around him and continued on his way.

³³ "But a Samaritan, as he was traveling along, came across the man. When the Samaritan saw him, he felt sorry for the man, ³⁴ went to him, and cleaned and bandaged his wounds. Then he put him on his own animal, brought him to an inn, and took care of him. ³⁵ The next day the Samaritan took out two silver coins and gave them to the innkeeper. He told the innkeeper, 'Take care of him. If you spend more than that, I'll pay you on my return trip.'

³⁶ "Of these three men, who do you think was a neighbor to the man who was attacked by robbers?"

³⁷ The expert said, "The one who was kind enough to help him." Jesus told him, "Go and imitate his example!"

Mary Listens to Jesus

³⁸ As they were traveling along, Jesus went into a village. A woman named Martha welcomed him into her home. ³⁹ She had a sister named Mary. Mary sat at the Lord's feet and listened to him talk.

⁴⁰ But Martha was upset about all the work she had to do. So she asked, "Lord, don't you care that my sister has left me to do the work all by myself? Tell her to help me."

⁴¹ The Lord answered her, "Martha, Martha! You worry and fuss about a lot of things. ⁴² There's only one thing you need.ᵇ Mary has made the right choice, and that one thing will not be taken away from her."

The Lord's Prayer—Matthew 6:9–13

11 ¹ Once Jesus was praying in a certain place. When he stopped praying, one of his disciples said to him, "Lord, teach us to pray as John taught his disciples."

² Jesus told them, "When you pray, say this:

ᵇ 10:42 Some manuscripts and translations read, "But of the few things ⌊worth worrying about⌋, there is only one thing you need."

Father,
> let your name be kept holy.
> Let your kingdom come.
3   Give us our bread day by day.
4   Forgive us as we forgive everyone else.
> Don't allow us to be tempted."

The Power of Prayer—*Matthew 7:7–11*

5 Jesus said to his disciples, "Suppose one of you has a friend. Suppose you go to him at midnight and say, 'Friend, let me borrow three loaves of bread. 6 A friend of mine on a trip has dropped in on me, and I don't have anything to serve him.' 7 Your friend might answer you from inside his house, 'Don't bother me! The door is already locked, and my children are in bed. I can't get up to give you anything.' 8 I can guarantee that although he doesn't want to get up to give you anything, he will get up and give you whatever you need because he is your friend and because you were so bold.

9 "So I tell you to ask, and you will receive. Search, and you will find. Knock, and the door will be opened for you. 10 Everyone who asks will receive. The one who searches will find, and for the person who knocks, the door will be opened.

11 "If your child asks you, his father, for a fish, would you give him a snake instead? 12 Or if your child asks you for an egg, would you give him a scorpion? 13 Even though you're evil, you know how to give good gifts to your children. So how much more will your Father in heaven give the Holy Spirit to those who ask him?"

Jesus Is Accused of Working With Beelzebul—
Matthew 12:22–32, 43–45; Mark 3:20–30

14 Jesus was forcing a demon out of a man. The demon had made the man unable to talk. When the demon had gone out, the man began to talk.

The people were amazed. 15 But some of them said, "He can force demons out of people only with the help of Beelzebul, the ruler of demons." **16** Others wanted to test Jesus and demanded that he show them some miraculous sign from heaven.

17 Since Jesus knew what they were thinking, he said to them, "Every kingdom divided against itself is ruined. A house divided against itself falls. **18** Now, if Satan is divided against himself, how can his kingdom last? I say this because you say Beelzebul helps me force demons out of people. **19** If I force demons out with the help of Beelzebul, who helps your followers force them out? That's why they will be your judges. **20** But if I force out demons with the help of God's power, then the kingdom of God has come to you.

21 "When a strong man, fully armed, guards his own mansion, his property is safe. **22** But a stronger man than he may attack him and defeat him. Then the stronger man will take away all the weapons in which the strong man trusted and will divide the loot.

23 "Whoever isn't with me is against me. Whoever doesn't gather with me scatters.

24 "When an evil spirit comes out of a person, it goes through dry places looking for a place to rest. But it doesn't find any. Then it says, 'I'll go back to the home I left.' **25** When it comes, it finds the house swept clean and in order. **26** Then the spirit goes and brings along seven other spirits more evil than itself. They enter and take up permanent residence there. In the end the condition of that person is worse than it was before."

The Sign of Jonah—*Matthew 12:38–42*

27 While Jesus was speaking, a woman in the crowd shouted, "How blessed is the mother who gave birth to you and the breasts that nursed you."

28 Jesus replied, "Rather, how blessed are those who hear and obey God's word."

29 As the people were gathering around him, Jesus said, "The people living today are evil. They look for a miraculous sign. But the only sign they will get is the sign of Jonah. **30** Just as Jonah became a miraculous sign to the people of Nineveh, so the Son

of Man will be a miraculous sign to the people living today.
[31] The queen from the south will stand up at the time of judgment
with the men who live today. She will condemn them, because
she came from the ends of the earth to hear Solomon's wisdom.
But look, someone greater than Solomon is here! [32] The men of
Nineveh will stand up at the time of judgment with the people living today. Since the men of Nineveh turned to God and changed
the way they thought and acted when Jonah spoke his message,
they will condemn the people living today. But look, someone
greater than Jonah is here!

Jesus Talks About Light

[33] "No one lights a lamp and hides it or puts it under a basket.
Instead, everyone who lights a lamp puts it on a lamp stand so that
those who come in will see its light.

[34] "Your eye is the lamp of your body. When your eye is
unclouded, your whole body is full of light. But when your eye is
evil, your body is full of darkness. [35] So be careful that the light
in you isn't darkness. [36] If your whole body is full of light and not
darkness, it will be as bright as a lamp shining on you."

Jesus Criticizes Some Jewish Leaders

[37] After Jesus spoke, a Pharisee invited him to have lunch at
his house. So Jesus accepted the invitation. [38] The Pharisee was
surprised to see that Jesus didn't wash before the meal.

[39] The Lord said to him, "You Pharisees clean the outside of
cups and dishes. But inside you are full of greed and evil. [40] You
fools! Didn't the one who made the outside make the inside too?
[41] Give what is inside as a gift to the poor, and then everything will
be clean[a] for you.

[42] "How horrible it will be for you Pharisees! You give ⌐God⌐
one-tenth of your mint, spices, and every garden herb. But you
have ignored justice and the love of God. You should have done
these things without ignoring the others.

[a] 11:41 "Clean" refers to anything that Moses' Teachings say is presentable to God.

⁴³ "How horrible it will be for you Pharisees! You love to sit in the front seats in the synagogues and to be greeted in the market-places. ⁴⁴ How horrible it will be for you! You are like unmarked graves. People walk on them without knowing what they are."

⁴⁵ One of the experts in Moses' Teachings said to him, "Teacher, when you talk this way, you insult us too."

⁴⁶ Jesus said, "How horrible it will be for you experts in Moses' Teachings! You burden people with loads that are hard to carry. But you won't lift a finger to carry any of these loads.

⁴⁷ "How horrible it will be for you! You build the monuments for the prophets. But it was your ancestors who murdered them. ⁴⁸ So you are witnesses and approve of what your ancestors did. They murdered the prophets for whom you build monuments. ⁴⁹ That's why the Wisdom of God said, 'I will send them prophets and apostles. They will murder some of those prophets and apostles and persecute others.' ⁵⁰ So the people living now will be charged with the murder of every prophet since the world was made. ⁵¹ This includes the murders from Abel to Zechariah, who was killed between the altar and the temple. Yes, I can guarantee this truth: The people living today will be held responsible for this.

⁵² "How horrible it will be for you experts in Moses' Teachings! You have taken away the key that unlocks knowledge. You haven't gained entrance into ˌknowledgeˌ yourselves, and you've kept out those who wanted to enter."

⁵³ When Jesus left, the scribes and the Pharisees held a terrible grudge against him. They questioned him about many things ⁵⁴ and watched him closely to trap him in something he might say.

Jesus Speaks to His Disciples

12 ¹ Meanwhile, thousands of people had gathered. They were so crowded that they stepped on each other. Jesus spoke to his disciples and said, "Watch out for the yeast of the Pharisees. I'm talking about their hypocrisy. ² Nothing has been covered that will not be exposed. Whatever is secret will be made known. ³ Whatever you have said in the dark will be heard in the daylight.

Whatever you have whispered in private rooms will be shouted from the housetops.

⁴ "My friends, I can guarantee that you don't need to be afraid of those who kill the body. After that they can't do anything more. ⁵ I'll show you the one you should be afraid of. Be afraid of the one who has the power to throw you into hell after killing you. I'm warning you to be afraid of him.

⁶ "Aren't five sparrows sold for two cents? God doesn't forget any of them. ⁷ Even every hair on your head has been counted. Don't be afraid! You are worth more than many sparrows. ⁸ I can guarantee that the Son of Man will acknowledge in front of God's angels every person who acknowledges him in front of others. ⁹ But God's angels will be told that I don't know those people who tell others that they don't know me. ¹⁰ Everyone who says something against the Son of Man will be forgiven. But the person who dishonors the Holy Spirit will not be forgiven.

¹¹ "When you are put on trial in synagogues or in front of rulers and authorities, don't worry about how you will defend yourselves or what you will say. ¹² At that time the Holy Spirit will teach you what you must say."

A Story About Material Possessions

¹³ Someone in the crowd said to him, "Teacher, tell my brother to give me my share of the inheritance that our father left us."

¹⁴ Jesus said to him, "Who appointed me to be your judge or to divide your inheritance?"

¹⁵ He told the people, "Be careful to guard yourselves from every kind of greed. Life is not about having a lot of material possessions."

¹⁶ Then he used this illustration. He said, "A rich man had land that produced good crops. ¹⁷ He thought, 'What should I do? I don't have enough room to store my crops.' ¹⁸ He said, 'I know what I'll do. I'll tear down my barns and build bigger ones so that I can store all my grain and goods in them. ¹⁹ Then I'll say to myself, "You've stored up a lot of good things for years to come. Take life easy, eat, drink, and enjoy yourself."'

²⁰ "But God said to him, 'You fool! I will demand your life from you tonight! Now who will get what you've accumulated?' ²¹ That's how it is when a person has material riches but is not rich in his relationship with God."

Stop Worrying—Matthew 6:25–34

²² Then Jesus said to his disciples, "So I tell you to stop worrying about what you will eat or wear. ²³ Life is more than food, and the body is more than clothes. ²⁴ Consider the crows. They don't plant or harvest. They don't even have a storeroom or a barn. Yet, God feeds them. You are worth much more than birds.

²⁵ "Can any of you add an hour to your life by worrying? ²⁶ If you can't do a small thing like that, why worry about other things? ²⁷ Consider how the flowers grow. They never work or spin yarn for clothes. But I say that not even Solomon in all his majesty was dressed like one of these flowers. ²⁸ That's the way God clothes the grass in the field. Today it's alive, and tomorrow it's thrown into an incinerator. So how much more will he clothe you people who have so little faith?

²⁹ "Don't concern yourself about what you will eat or drink, and quit worrying about these things. ³⁰ Everyone in the world is concerned about these things, but your Father knows you need them. ³¹ Rather, be concerned about his kingdom. Then these things will be provided for you. ³² Don't be afraid, little flock. Your Father is pleased to give you the kingdom.

³³ "Sell your material possessions, and give the money to the poor. Make yourselves wallets that don't wear out! Make a treasure for yourselves in heaven that never loses its value! In heaven thieves and moths can't get close enough to destroy your treasure. ³⁴ Your heart will be where your treasure is.

The Son of Man Will Return When You Least Expect Him

³⁵ "Be ready for action, and have your lamps burning. ³⁶ Be like servants waiting to open the door at their master's knock when he returns from a wedding. ³⁷ Blessed are those servants whom the

master finds awake when he comes. I can guarantee this truth: He will change his clothes, make them sit down at the table, and serve them. [38] They will be blessed if he comes in the middle of the night or toward morning and finds them awake.

[39] "Of course, you realize that if the homeowner had known at what hour the thief was coming, he would not have let him break into his house. [40] Be ready, because the Son of Man will return when you least expect him."

[41] Peter asked, "Lord, did you use this illustration just for us or for everyone?"

[42] The Lord asked, "Who, then, is the faithful, skilled manager that the master will put in charge of giving the other servants their share of food at the right time? [43] That servant will be blessed if his master finds him doing this job when he comes. [44] I can guarantee this truth: He will put that servant in charge of all his property. [45] On the other hand, that servant may think that his master is taking a long time to come home. The servant may begin to beat the other servants and to eat, drink, and get drunk. [46] His master will return at an unexpected time. Then his master will punish him severely and assign him a place with unfaithful people.

[47] "The servant who knew what his master wanted but didn't get ready to do it will receive a hard beating. [48] But the servant who didn't know ˌwhat his master wantedˌ and did things for which he deserved punishment will receive a light beating. A lot will be expected from everyone who has been given a lot. More will be demanded from everyone who has been entrusted with a lot.

Jesus Will Cause Conflict

[49] "I have come to throw fire on the earth. I wish that it had already started! [50] I have a baptism to go through, and I will suffer until it is over.

[51] "Do you think I came to bring peace to earth? No! I can guarantee that I came to bring nothing but division. [52] From now on a family of five will be divided. Three will be divided against

two and two against three. ⁵³ A father will be against his son and a son against his father. A mother will be against her daughter and a daughter against her mother. A mother-in-law will be against her daughter-in-law and a daughter-in-law against her mother-in-law."

Use Good Judgment

⁵⁴ Jesus said to the crowds, "When you see a cloud coming up in the west, you immediately say, 'There's going to be a rainstorm,' and it happens. ⁵⁵ When you see a south wind blowing, you say, 'It's going to be hot,' and that's what happens. ⁵⁶ You hypocrites! You can forecast the weather by judging the appearance of earth and sky. But for some reason you don't know how to judge the time in which you're living. ⁵⁷ So why don't you judge for yourselves what is right? ⁵⁸ For instance, when an opponent brings you to court in front of a ruler, do your best to settle with him before you get there. Otherwise, he will drag you in front of a judge. The judge will hand you over to an officer who will throw you into prison. ⁵⁹ I can guarantee that you won't get out until you pay every penny of your fine."

Jesus Tells People to Turn to God and Change the Way They Think and Act

13 ¹ At that time some people reported to Jesus about some Galileans whom Pilate had executed while they were sacrificing animals. ² Jesus replied to them, "Do you think that this happened to them because they were more sinful than other people from Galilee? ³ No! I can guarantee that they weren't. But if you don't turn to God and change the way you think and act, then you, too, will all die. ⁴ What about those 18 people who died when the tower at Siloam fell on them? Do you think that they were more sinful than other people living in Jerusalem? ⁵ No! I can guarantee that they weren't. But if you don't turn to God and change the way you think and act, then you, too, will all die."

A Story About a Fruitless Tree

6 Then Jesus used this illustration: "A man had a fig tree growing in his vineyard. He went to look for fruit on the tree but didn't find any. **7** He said to the gardener, 'For the last three years I've come to look for figs on this fig tree but haven't found any. Cut it down! Why should it use up ˌgoodˌ soil?'

8 "The gardener replied, 'Sir, let it stand for one more year. I'll dig around it and fertilize it. **9** Maybe next year it'll have figs. But if not, then cut it down.' "

Jesus Heals a Disabled Woman

10 Jesus was teaching in a synagogue on the day of worship. **11** A woman who was possessed by a spirit was there. The spirit had disabled her for 18 years. She was hunched over and couldn't stand up straight. **12** When Jesus saw her, he called her to come to him and said, "Woman, you are free from your disability." **13** He placed his hands on her, and she immediately stood up straight and praised God.

14 The synagogue leader was irritated with Jesus for healing on the day of worship. The leader told the crowd, "There are six days when work can be done. So come on one of those days to be healed. Don't come on the day of worship."

15 The Lord said, "You hypocrites! Don't each of you free your ox or donkey on the day of worship? Don't you then take it out of its stall to give it some water to drink? **16** Now, here is a descendant of Abraham. Satan has kept her in this condition for 18 years. Isn't it right to free her on the day of worship?"

17 As he said this, everyone who opposed him felt ashamed. But the entire crowd was happy about the miraculous things he was doing.

Stories About a Mustard Seed and Yeast—
Matthew 13:31–33; Mark 4:30–32

18 Jesus asked, "What is the kingdom of God like? What can I compare it to? **19** It's like a mustard seed that someone planted in a garden. It grew and became a tree, and the birds nested in its branches."

²⁰ He asked again, "What can I compare the kingdom of God to? ²¹ It's like yeast that a woman mixed into a large amount of flour until the yeast worked its way through all the dough."

The Narrow Door

²² Then Jesus traveled and taught in one city and village after another on his way to Jerusalem.

²³ Someone asked him, "Sir, are only a few people going to be saved?"

He answered, ²⁴ "Try hard to enter through the narrow door. I can guarantee that many will try to enter, but they won't succeed. ²⁵ After the homeowner gets up and closes the door, ⌊it's too late⌋. You can stand outside, knock at the door, and say, 'Sir, open the door for us!' But he will answer you, 'I don't know who you are.' ²⁶ Then you will say, 'We ate and drank with you, and you taught in our streets.' ²⁷ But he will tell you, 'I don't know who you are. Get away from me, all you evil people.' ²⁸ Then you will cry and be in extreme pain. That's what you'll do when you see Abraham, Isaac, Jacob, and all the prophets. They'll be in the kingdom of God, but you'll be thrown out. ²⁹ People will come from all over the world and will eat in the kingdom of God. ³⁰ Some who are last will be first, and some who are first will be last."

Jesus Warns Jerusalem

³¹ At that time some Pharisees told Jesus, "Get out of here, and go somewhere else! Herod wants to kill you."

³² Jesus said to them, "Tell that fox that I will force demons out of people and heal people today and tomorrow. I will finish my work on the third day. ³³ But I must be on my way today, tomorrow, and the next day. It's not possible for a prophet to die outside Jerusalem.

³⁴ "Jerusalem, Jerusalem, you kill the prophets and stone to death those sent to you! How often I wanted to gather your children together the way a hen gathers her chicks under her wings! But you were not willing! ³⁵ Your house will be abandoned. I can guarantee that you will not see me again until you say, 'Blessed is the one who comes in the name of the Lord!' "

Jesus Attends a Banquet

14 ¹ On a day of worship Jesus went to eat at the home of a prominent Pharisee. The guests were watching Jesus very closely.

² A man whose body was swollen with fluid was there. ³ Jesus reacted by asking the Pharisees and the experts in Moses' Teachings, "Is it right to heal on the day of worship or not?" ⁴ But they didn't say a thing.

So Jesus took hold of the man, healed him, and sent him away. ⁵ Jesus asked them, "If your son or your ox falls into a well on a day of worship, wouldn't you pull him out immediately?" ⁶ They couldn't argue with him about this.

⁷ Then Jesus noticed how the guests always chose the places of honor. So he used this illustration when he spoke to them: ⁸ "When someone invites you to a wedding, don't take the place of honor. Maybe someone more important than you was invited. ⁹ Then your host would say to you, 'Give this person your place.' Embarrassed, you would have to take the place of least honor. ¹⁰ So when you're invited, take the place of least honor. Then, when your host comes, he will tell you, 'Friend, move to a more honorable place.' Then all the other guests will see how you are honored. ¹¹ Those who honor themselves will be humbled, but people who humble themselves will be honored."

¹² Then he told the man who had invited him, "When you invite people for lunch or dinner, don't invite only your friends, family, other relatives, or rich neighbors. Otherwise, they will return the favor. ¹³ Instead, when you give a banquet, invite the poor, the handicapped, the lame, and the blind. ¹⁴ Then you will be blessed because they don't have any way to pay you back. You will be paid back when those who have God's approval come back to life."

¹⁵ One of those eating with him heard this. So he said to Jesus, "The person who will be at the banquet in the kingdom of God is blessed."

¹⁶ Jesus said to him, "A man gave a large banquet and invited many people. ¹⁷ When it was time for the banquet, he sent his servant to tell those who were invited, 'Come! Everything is ready now.'

¹⁸ "Everyone asked to be excused. The first said to him, 'I bought a field, and I need to see it. Please excuse me.' ¹⁹ Another said, 'I bought five pairs of oxen, and I'm on my way to see how well they plow. Please excuse me.' ²⁰ Still another said, 'I recently got married, and that's why I can't come.'

²¹ "The servant went back to report this to his master. Then the master of the house became angry. He told his servant, 'Run to every street and alley in the city! Bring back the poor, the handicapped, the blind, and the lame.'

²² "The servant said, 'Sir, what you've ordered has been done. But there is still room for more people.'

²³ "Then the master told his servant, 'Go to the roads and paths! Urge the people to come to my house. I want it to be full. ²⁴ I can guarantee that none of those invited earlier will taste any food at my banquet.' "

The Cost of Being a Disciple

²⁵ Large crowds were traveling with Jesus. He turned to them and said, ²⁶ "If people come to me and are not ready to abandon their fathers, mothers, wives, children, brothers, and sisters, as well as their own lives, they cannot be my disciples. ²⁷ So those who do not carry their crosses and follow me cannot be my disciples.

²⁸ "Suppose you want to build a tower. You would first sit down and figure out what it costs. Then you would see if you have enough money to finish it. ²⁹ Otherwise, if you lay a foundation and can't finish the building, everyone who watches will make fun of you. ³⁰ They'll say, 'This person started to build but couldn't finish the job.'

³¹ "Or suppose a king is going to war against another king. He would first sit down and think things through. Can he and his 10,000 soldiers fight against a king with 20,000 soldiers? ³² If he can't, he'll send ambassadors to ask for terms of peace while the

other king is still far away. ³³ In the same way, none of you can be my disciples unless you give up everything.

³⁴ "Salt is good. But if salt loses its taste, how will you restore its flavor? ³⁵ It's not any good for the ground or for the manure pile. People throw it away.

"Let the person who has ears listen!"

The Lost Sheep—Matthew 18:12–14

15 ¹ All the tax collectors and sinners came to listen to Jesus. ² But the Pharisees and the scribes complained, "This man welcomes sinners and eats with them."

³ Jesus spoke to them using this illustration: ⁴ "Suppose a man has 100 sheep and loses one of them. Doesn't he leave the 99 sheep grazing in the pasture and look for the lost sheep until he finds it? ⁵ When he finds it, he's happy. He puts that sheep on his shoulders and ⁶ goes home. Then he calls his friends and neighbors together and says to them, 'Let's celebrate! I've found my lost sheep!' ⁷ I can guarantee that there will be more happiness in heaven over one person who turns to God and changes the way he thinks and acts than over 99 people who already have turned to God and have his approval."

The Lost Coin

⁸ "Suppose a woman has ten coins and loses one. Doesn't she light a lamp, sweep the house, and look for the coin carefully until she finds it? ⁹ When she finds it, she calls her friends and neighbors together and says, 'Let's celebrate! I've found the coin that I lost.' ¹⁰ So I can guarantee that God's angels are happy about one person who turns to God and changes the way he thinks and acts."

The Lost Son

¹¹ Then Jesus said, "A man had two sons. ¹² The younger son said to his father, 'Father, give me my share of the property.' So the father divided his property between his two sons.

¹³ "After a few days, the younger son gathered his possessions and left for a country far away from home. There he wasted

everything he had on a wild lifestyle. [14] He had nothing left when a severe famine spread throughout that country. He had nothing to live on. [15] So he got a job from someone in that country and was sent to feed pigs in the fields. [16] No one in the country would give him any food, and he was so hungry that he would have eaten what the pigs were eating.

[17] "Finally, he came to his senses. He said, 'How many of my father's hired men have more food than they can eat, while I'm starving to death here? [18] I'll go at once to my father, and I'll say to him, "Father, I've sinned against heaven and you. [19] I don't deserve to be called your son anymore. Make me one of your hired men."'

[20] "So he went at once to his father. While he was still at a distance, his father saw him and felt sorry for him. He ran to his son, put his arms around him, and kissed him. [21] Then his son said to him, 'Father, I've sinned against heaven and you. I don't deserve to be called your son anymore.'[a]

[22] "The father said to his servants, 'Hurry! Bring out the best robe, and put it on him. Put a ring on his finger and sandals on his feet. [23] Bring the fattened calf, kill it, and let's celebrate with a feast. [24] My son was dead and has come back to life. He was lost but has been found.' Then they began to celebrate.

[25] "His older son was in the field. As he was coming back to the house, he heard music and dancing. [26] He called to one of the servants and asked what was happening.

[27] "The servant told him, 'Your brother has come home. So your father has killed the fattened calf to celebrate your brother's safe return.'

[28] "Then the older son became angry and wouldn't go into the house. His father came out and begged him to come in. [29] But he answered his father, 'All these years I've worked like a slave for you. I've never disobeyed one of your commands. Yet, you've never given me so much as a little goat for a celebration with my friends. [30] But this son of yours spent your money on prostitutes, and when he came home, you killed the fattened calf for him.'

---

[a] 15:21 Some manuscripts and translations add "Make me one of your hired hands."

³¹ "His father said to him, 'My child, you're always with me. Everything I have is yours. ³² But we have something to celebrate, something to be happy about. This brother of yours was dead but has come back to life. He was lost but has been found.' "

Jesus Speaks About Dishonesty

16 ¹ Then Jesus said to his disciples, "A rich man had a business manager. The manager was accused of wasting the rich man's property. ² So the rich man called for his manager and said to him, 'What's this I hear about you? Let me examine your books. It's obvious that you can't manage my property any longer.'

³ "The manager thought, 'What should I do? My master is taking my job away from me. I'm not strong enough to dig, and I'm ashamed to beg. ⁴ I know what I'll do so that people will welcome me into their homes when I've lost my job.'

⁵ "So the manager called for each one of his master's debtors. He said to the first, 'How much do you owe my master?'

⁶ "The debtor replied, 'Eight hundred gallons of olive oil.'

"The manager told him, 'Take my master's ledger. Quick! Sit down, and write "four hundred!" '

⁷ "Then he asked another debtor, 'How much do you owe?'

"The debtor replied, 'A thousand bushels of wheat.'

"The manager told him, 'Take the ledger, and write "eight hundred!" '

⁸ "The master praised the dishonest manager for being so clever. Worldly people are more clever than spiritually-minded people when it comes to dealing with others."

⁹ ⌊Jesus continued,⌋ "I'm telling you that although wealth is often used in dishonest ways, you should use it to make friends for yourselves. When life is over, you will be welcomed into an eternal home. ¹⁰ Whoever can be trusted with very little can also be trusted with a lot. Whoever is dishonest with very little is dishonest with a lot. ¹¹ Therefore, if you can't be trusted with wealth that is often used dishonestly, who will trust you with wealth that is real? ¹² If you can't be trusted with someone else's wealth, who will give you your own?

¹³ "A servant cannot serve two masters. He will hate the first master and love the second, or he will be devoted to the first and despise the second. You cannot serve God and wealth."

¹⁴ The Pharisees, who love money, heard all this and were making sarcastic remarks about him. ¹⁵ So Jesus said to them, "You try to justify your actions in front of people. But God knows what's in your hearts. What is important to humans is disgusting to God.

¹⁶ "Moses' Teachings and the Prophets were ⌞in force⌟ until the time of John. Since that time, people have been telling the Good News about the kingdom of God, and everyone is trying to force their way into it. ¹⁷ It is easier for the earth and the heavens to disappear than to drop a comma from Moses' Teachings.

¹⁸ "Any man who divorces his wife to marry another woman is committing adultery. The man who marries a woman divorced in this way is committing adultery.

A Rich Man and Lazarus

¹⁹ "There was a rich man who wore expensive clothes. Every day was like a party to him. ²⁰ There was also a beggar named Lazarus who was regularly brought to the gate of the rich man's house. ²¹ Lazarus would have eaten any scraps that fell from the rich man's table. Lazarus was covered with sores,ᵃ and dogs would lick them.

²² "One day the beggar died, and the angels carried him to be with Abraham. The rich man also died and was buried. ²³ He went to hell, where he was constantly tortured. As he looked up, in the distance he saw Abraham and Lazarus. ²⁴ He yelled, 'Father Abraham! Have mercy on me! Send Lazarus to dip the tip of his finger in water to cool off my tongue. I am suffering in this fire.'

²⁵ "Abraham replied, 'Remember, my child, that you had a life filled with good times, while Lazarus' life was filled with misery. Now he has peace here, while you suffer. ²⁶ Besides, a wide area separates us. People couldn't cross it in either direction even if they wanted to.'

ᵃ 16:21 The last sentence in verse 20 (in Greek) has been moved to verse 21 to express the complex Greek paragraph structure more clearly in English.

²⁷ "The rich man responded, 'Then I ask you, Father, to send Lazarus back to my father's home. ²⁸ I have five brothers. He can warn them so that they won't end up in this place of torture.'

²⁹ "Abraham replied, 'They have Moses' ˌTeachingsˌ and the Prophets. Your brothers should listen to them!'

³⁰ "The rich man replied, 'No, Father Abraham! If someone comes back to them from the dead, they will turn to God and change the way they think and act.'

³¹ "Abraham answered him, 'If they won't listen to Moses' ˌTeachingsˌ and the Prophets, they won't be persuaded even if someone comes back to life.'"

Causing Others to Lose Faith—Matthew 18:6–10; Mark 9:42–50

17 ¹ Jesus told his disciples, "Situations that cause people to lose their faith are certain to arise. But how horrible it will be for the person who causes someone to lose his faith! ² It would be best for that person to be thrown into the sea with a large stone hung around his neck than for him to cause one of these little ones to lose his faith. ³ So watch yourselves!

"If a believer sins, correct him. If he changes the way he thinks and acts, forgive him. ⁴ Even if he wrongs you seven times in one day and comes back to you seven times and says that he is sorry, forgive him."

The Apostles Ask For More Faith

⁵ Then the apostles said to the Lord, "Give us more faith."

⁶ The Lord said, "If you have faith the size of a mustard seed, you could say to this mulberry tree, 'Pull yourself up by the roots, and plant yourself in the sea!' and it would obey you.

⁷ "Suppose someone has a servant who is plowing fields or watching sheep. Does he tell his servant when he comes from the field, 'Have something to eat'? ⁸ No. Instead, he tells his servant, 'Get dinner ready for me! After you serve me my dinner, you can eat yours.' ⁹ He doesn't thank the servant for following orders. ¹⁰ That's the way it is with you. When you've done everything you're

ordered to do, say, 'We're worthless servants. We've only done our duty.' "

Ten Men With a Skin Disease Are Healed

[11] Jesus traveled along the border between Samaria and Galilee on his way to Jerusalem. [12] As he went into a village, ten men with a skin disease met him. They stood at a distance [13] and shouted, "Jesus, Teacher, have mercy on us!"

[14] When he saw them, he told them, "Show yourselves to the priests." As they went, they were made clean.[a] [15] When one of them saw that he was healed, he turned back and praised God in a loud voice. [16] He quickly bowed at Jesus' feet and thanked him. (The man was a Samaritan.)

[17] Jesus asked, "Weren't ten men made clean? Where are the other nine? [18] Only this foreigner came back to praise God."

[19] Jesus told the man, "Get up, and go home! Your faith has made you well."

The Pharisees Ask About the Kingdom of God

[20] The Pharisees asked Jesus when the kingdom of God would come.

He answered them, "People can't observe the coming of the kingdom of God. [21] They can't say, 'Here it is!' or 'There it is!' You see, the kingdom of God is within[b] you."

Jesus Teaches About the Time When He Will Come Again

[22] Jesus said to his disciples, "The time will come when you will long to see one of the days of the Son of Man, but you will not see it. [23] People will say, 'There he is!' or 'Here he is!' Don't run after those people. [24] The day of the Son of Man[c] will be like lightning that flashes from one end of the sky to the other. [25] But first he must suffer a lot and be rejected by the people of his day.

---

[a] 17:14 "Clean" refers to anything that Moses' Teachings say is presentable to God.
[b] 17:21 Or "among."   [c] 17:24 Some manuscripts and translations omit "The day of."

²⁶ "When the Son of Man comes again, the situation will be like the time of Noah. ²⁷ People were eating, drinking, and getting married until the day that Noah went into the ship. Then the flood destroyed all of them.

²⁸ "The situation will also be like the time of Lot. People were eating, drinking, buying and selling, planting and building. ²⁹ But on the day that Lot left Sodom, fire and sulfur rained from the sky and destroyed all of them. ³⁰ The day when the Son of Man is revealed will be like that.

³¹ "On that day those who are on the roof shouldn't come down to get their belongings out of their houses. Those who are in the field shouldn't turn back. ³² Remember Lot's wife! ³³ Those who try to save their lives will lose them, and those who lose their lives will save them.

³⁴ "I can guarantee that on that night if two people are in one bed, one will be taken and the other one will be left. ³⁵ Two women will be grinding grain together. One will be taken, and the other one will be left."ᵈ

³⁷ They asked him, "Where, Lord?"

Jesus told them, "Vultures will gather wherever there is a dead body."

God Will Help His People

18 ¹ Jesus used this illustration with his disciples to show them that they need to pray all the time and never give up. ² He said, "In a city there was a judge who didn't fear God or respect people. ³ In that city there was also a widow who kept coming to him and saying, 'Give me justice.'

⁴ "For a while the judge refused to do anything. But then he thought, 'This widow really annoys me. Although I don't fear God or respect people, ⁵ I'll have to give her justice. Otherwise, she'll keep coming to me until she wears me out.' "

ᵈ 17:35 Some manuscripts and translations add verse 36: "Two will be in a field. One will be taken, and the other will be left." See Matthew 24:40.

⁶ The Lord added, "Pay attention to what the dishonest judge thought. ⁷ Won't God give his chosen people justice when they cry out to him for help day and night? Is he slow to help them? ⁸ I can guarantee that he will give them justice quickly. But when the Son of Man comes, will he find faith on earth?"

A Pharisee and a Tax Collector

⁹ Jesus also used this illustration with some who were sure that God approved of them while they looked down on everyone else. ¹⁰ He said, "Two men went into the temple courtyard to pray. One was a Pharisee, and the other was a tax collector. ¹¹ The Pharisee stood up and prayed, 'God, I thank you that I'm not like other people! I'm not a robber or a dishonest person. I haven't committed adultery. I'm not even like this tax collector. ¹² I fast twice a week, and I give you a tenth of my entire income.'

¹³ "But the tax collector was standing at a distance. He wouldn't even look up to heaven. Instead, he became very upset, and he said, 'God, be merciful to me, a sinner!'

¹⁴ "I can guarantee that this tax collector went home with God's approval, but the Pharisee didn't. Everyone who honors himself will be humbled, but the person who humbles himself will be honored."

Jesus Blesses Children—Matthew 19:13–15; Mark 10:13–16

¹⁵ Some people brought infants to Jesus to have him hold them. When the disciples saw this, they told the people not to do that.

¹⁶ But Jesus called the infants to him and said, "Don't stop the children from coming to me! Children like these are part of the kingdom of God. ¹⁷ I can guarantee this truth: Whoever doesn't receive the kingdom of God as a little child receives it will never enter it."

Eternal Life in the Kingdom—Matthew 19:16–30; Mark 10:17–31

¹⁸ An official asked Jesus, "Good Teacher, what must I do to inherit eternal life?"

¹⁹ Jesus said to him, "Why do you call me good? No one is good except God. ²⁰ You know the commandments: Never commit

adultery. Never murder. Never steal. Never give false testimony. Honor your father and your mother."

²¹ The official replied, "I've obeyed all these commandments since I was a boy."

²² When Jesus heard this, he said to him, "You still need one thing. Sell everything you have. Distribute the money to the poor, and you will have treasure in heaven. Then follow me!"

²³ When the official heard this, he became sad, because he was very rich. ²⁴ Jesus watched him and said, "How hard it is for rich people to enter the kingdom of God! ²⁵ Indeed, it is easier for a camel to go through the eye of a needle than for a rich person to enter the kingdom of God."

²⁶ Those who heard him asked, "Who, then, can be saved?"

²⁷ Jesus said, "The things that are impossible for people to do are possible for God to do."

²⁸ Then Peter said, "We've left everything to follow you."

²⁹ Jesus said to them, "I can guarantee this truth: Anyone who gave up his home, wife, brothers, parents, or children because of the kingdom of God ³⁰ will certainly receive many times as much in this life and will receive eternal life in the world to come."

For the Third Time Jesus Foretells That He Will Die and Come Back to Life—Matthew 20:17–19; Mark 10:32–34

³¹ Jesus took the twelve apostles aside and said to them, "We're going to Jerusalem. Everything that the prophets wrote about the Son of Man will come true. ³² He will be handed over to foreigners. They will make fun of him, insult him, spit on him, ³³ whip him, and kill him. But on the third day he will come back to life."

³⁴ But they didn't understand any of this. What he said was a mystery to them, and they didn't know what he meant.

Jesus Gives Sight to a Blind Man—Matthew 20:29–34; Mark 10:46–52

³⁵ As Jesus came near Jericho, a blind man was sitting and begging by the road. ³⁶ When he heard the crowd going by, he tried to find out what was happening. ³⁷ The people told him that Jesus

from Nazareth was passing by. ³⁸ Then the blind man shouted, "Jesus, Son of David, have mercy on me!" ³⁹ The people at the front of the crowd told the blind man to be quiet. But he shouted even louder, "Son of David, have mercy on me!"

⁴⁰ Jesus stopped and ordered them to bring the man to him. When the man came near, Jesus asked him, ⁴¹ "What do you want me to do for you?"

The blind man said, "Lord, I want to see again."

⁴² Jesus told him, "Receive your sight! Your faith has made you well." ⁴³ Immediately, he could see again. He followed Jesus and praised God. All the people saw this, and they, too, praised God.

Zacchaeus Meets Jesus

19 ¹ Jesus was passing through Jericho. ² A man named Zacchaeus was there. He was the director of tax collectors, and he was rich. ³ He tried to see who Jesus was. But Zacchaeus was a small man, and he couldn't see Jesus because of the crowd. ⁴ So Zacchaeus ran ahead and climbed a fig tree to see Jesus, who was coming that way.

⁵ When Jesus came to the tree, he looked up and said, "Zacchaeus, come down! I must stay at your house today."

⁶ Zacchaeus came down and was glad to welcome Jesus into his home. ⁷ But the people who saw this began to express disapproval. They said, "He went to be the guest of a sinner."

⁸ ˏLater, at dinner,ˎ Zacchaeus stood up and said to the Lord, "Lord, I'll give half of my property to the poor. I'll pay four times as much as I owe to those I have cheated in any way."

⁹ Then Jesus said to Zacchaeus, "You and your family have been saved today. You've shown that you, too, are one of Abraham's descendants. ¹⁰ Indeed, the Son of Man has come to seek and to save people who are lost."

A Story About a King

¹¹ Jesus was getting closer to Jerusalem, and the people thought that the kingdom of God would appear suddenly. While Jesus

had the people's attention, he used this illustration. [12] He said, "A prince went to a distant country to be appointed king, and then he returned. [13] ⌞Before he left,⌟ he called ten of his servants and gave them ten coins. He said to his servants, 'Invest this money until I come back.'

[14] "The citizens of his own country hated him. They sent representatives to follow him and say ⌞to the person who was going to appoint him⌟, 'We don't want this man to be our king.'

[15] "After he was appointed king, he came back. Then he said, 'Call those servants to whom I gave money. I want to know how much each one has made by investing.'

[16] "The first servant said, 'Sir, the coin you gave me has earned ten times as much.'

[17] "The king said to him, 'Good job! You're a good servant. You proved that you could be trusted with a little money. Take charge of ten cities.'

[18] "The second servant said, 'The coin you gave me, sir, has made five times as much.'

[19] "The king said to this servant, 'You take charge of five cities.'

[20] "Then the other servant said, 'Sir, look! Here's your coin. I've kept it in a cloth for safekeeping because [21] I was afraid of you. You're a tough person to get along with. You take what isn't yours and harvest grain you haven't planted.'

[22] "The king said to him, 'I'll judge you by what you've said, you evil servant! You knew that I was a tough person to get along with. You knew that I take what isn't mine and harvest grain I haven't planted. [23] Then why didn't you put my money in the bank? When I came back, I could have collected it with interest.' [24] The king told his men, 'Take his coin away, and give it to the man who has ten.'

[25] "They replied, 'Sir, he already has ten coins.'

[26] " 'I can guarantee that everyone who has something will be given more. But everything will be taken away from those who don't have much. [27] Bring my enemies, who didn't want me to be their king. Kill them in front of me.' "

The King Comes to Jerusalem—
Matthew 21:1–11; Mark 11:1–11; John 12:12–19

²⁸ After Jesus had given this illustration, he continued on his way to Jerusalem.

²⁹ When he came near Bethphage and Bethany at the Mount of Olives (as it was called), Jesus sent two of his disciples ahead of him. ³⁰ He said to them, "Go into the village ahead of you. As you enter, you will find a young donkey tied there. No one has ever sat on it. Untie it, and bring it. ³¹ If anyone asks you why you are untying it, say that the Lord needs it."

³² The men Jesus sent found it as he had told them. ³³ While they were untying the young donkey, its owners asked them, "Why are you untying the donkey?"

³⁴ The disciples answered, "The Lord needs it."

³⁵ They brought the donkey to Jesus, put their coats on it, and helped Jesus onto it. ³⁶ As he was riding along, people spread their coats on the road. ³⁷ By this time he was coming near the place where the road went down the Mount of Olives. Then the whole crowd of disciples began to praise God for all the miracles they had seen. ³⁸ They shouted joyfully,

"Blessed is the king who comes in the name of the Lord!
Peace in heaven, and glory in the highest heaven."

³⁹ Some of the Pharisees in the crowd said to Jesus, "Teacher, tell your disciples to be quiet."

⁴⁰ Jesus replied, "I can guarantee that if they are quiet, the stones will cry out."

⁴¹ When he came closer and saw the city, he began to cry. ⁴² He said, "If you had only known today what would bring you peace! But now it is hidden, so you cannot see it. ⁴³ The time will come when enemy armies will build a wall to surround you and close you in on every side. ⁴⁴ They will level you to the ground and kill your people. One stone will not be left on top of another, because you didn't recognize the time when God came to help you."

Jesus Throws Out the Moneychangers—
Matthew 21:12–17; Mark 11:15–19

⁴⁵ Jesus went into the temple courtyard and began to throw out those who were selling things there. ⁴⁶ He said to them, "Scripture says, 'My house will be a house of prayer,' but you have turned it into a gathering place for thieves."

⁴⁷ Jesus taught in the temple courtyard every day. The chief priests, the scribes, and the leaders of the people looked for a way to kill him. ⁴⁸ But they could not find a way to do it, because all the people were eager to hear him.

Jesus' Authority Challenged—*Matthew 21:23–27; Mark 11:27–33*

20 ¹ One day Jesus was teaching the people in the temple courtyard and telling them the Good News. The chief priests, scribes, and leaders came up to him. ² They asked him, "Tell us, what gives you the right to do these things? Who told you that you could do this?"

³ Jesus answered them, "I, too, have a question for you. Tell me, ⁴ did John's right to baptize come from heaven or from humans?"

⁵ They talked about this among themselves. They said, "If we say, 'from heaven,' he will ask, 'Why didn't you believe him?' ⁶ But if we say, 'from humans,' everyone will stone us to death. They're convinced that John was a prophet." ⁷ So they answered that they didn't know who gave John the right to baptize.

⁸ Jesus told them, "Then I won't tell you why I have the right to do these things."

A Story About a Vineyard—*Matthew 21:33–46; Mark 12:1–12*

⁹ Then, using this illustration, Jesus spoke to the people: "A man planted a vineyard, leased it to vineyard workers, and went on a long trip.

¹⁰ "At the right time he sent a servant to the workers to obtain from them a share of the grapes from the vineyard. But the workers beat the servant and sent him back with nothing. ¹¹ So he sent a different servant. The workers beat him, treated him shamefully,

and sent him back with nothing. ¹² Then he sent a third servant. But they injured this one and threw him out ˻of the vineyard˼.

¹³ "Then the owner of the vineyard said, 'What should I do? I'll send my son, whom I love. They'll probably respect him.'

¹⁴ "When the workers saw him, they talked it over among themselves. They said, 'This is the heir. Let's kill him so that the inheritance will be ours.' ¹⁵ So they threw him out of the vineyard and killed him.

"What will the owner of the vineyard do to them? ¹⁶ He will destroy these workers and give the vineyard to others."

Those who heard him said, "That's unthinkable!"

¹⁷ Then Jesus looked straight at them and asked, "What, then, does this Scripture verse mean:

'The stone that the builders rejected
    has become the cornerstone'?

¹⁸ Everyone who falls on that stone will be broken. If that stone falls on anyone, it will crush that person."

¹⁹ The scribes and the chief priests wanted to arrest him right there, but they were afraid of the people. They knew that he had directed this illustration at them.

A Question About Taxes—Matthew 22:15–22; Mark 12:13–17

²⁰ So they watched for an opportunity to send out some spies. The spies were to act like sincere religious people. They wanted to catch him saying the wrong thing so that they could hand him over to the governor. ²¹ They asked him, "Teacher, we know that you're right in what you say and teach. Besides, you don't play favorites. Rather, you teach the way of God truthfully. ²² Is it right for us to pay taxes to the emperor or not?"

²³ He saw through their scheme, so he said to them, ²⁴ "Show me a coin. Whose face and name is this?"

They answered, "The emperor's."

²⁵ He said to them, "Well, then give the emperor what belongs to the emperor, and give God what belongs to God."

²⁶ They couldn't make him say anything wrong in front of the people. His answer surprised them, so they said no more.

The Dead Come Back to Life—*Matthew 22:23–33; Mark 12:18–27*

²⁷ Some Sadducees, who say that people will never come back to life, came to Jesus. They asked him, ²⁸ "Teacher, Moses wrote for us, 'If a married man dies and has no children, his brother should marry his widow and have children for his brother.' ²⁹ There were seven brothers. The first got married and died without having children. ³⁰ Then the second brother married the widow, ³¹ and so did the third. In the same way all seven brothers married the widow, died, and left no children. ³² Finally, the woman died. ³³ Now, when the dead come back to life, whose wife will she be? The seven brothers had married her."

³⁴ Jesus said to them, "In this world people get married. ³⁵ But people who are considered worthy to come back to life and live in the next world will neither marry ³⁶ nor die anymore. They are the same as the angels. They are God's children who have come back to life.

³⁷ "Even Moses showed in the passage about the bush that the dead come back to life. He says that the Lord is the God of Abraham, Isaac, and Jacob. ³⁸ He's not the God of the dead but of the living. In God's sight all people are living."

³⁹ Some scribes responded, "Teacher, that was well said." ⁴⁰ From that time on, no one dared to ask him another question.

How Can David's Son Be David's Lord?— *Matthew 22:41–46; Mark 12:35–37a*

⁴¹ Jesus said to them, "How can people say that the Messiah is David's son? ⁴² David says in the book of Psalms,

'The Lord said to my Lord,
    "Take the highest position in heaven
⁴³   until I make your enemies your footstool." '

⁴⁴ David calls him Lord. So how can he be his son?"

Jesus Disapproves of the Example Set By Scribes—
Matthew 23:1–12; Mark 12:37b–40

⁴⁵ While all the people were listening, Jesus said to the disciples, ⁴⁶ "Beware of the scribes! They like to walk around in long robes and love to be greeted in the marketplaces, to have the front seats in the synagogues and the places of honor at dinners. ⁴⁷ They rob widows by taking their houses and then say long prayers to make themselves look good. The scribes will receive the most severe punishment."

A Widow's Contribution—Mark 12:41–44

21 ¹ Looking up, Jesus saw people, especially the rich, dropping their gifts into the temple offering box. ² He noticed a poor widow drop in two small coins. ³ He said, "I can guarantee this truth: This poor widow has given more than all the others. ⁴ All of these people have given what they could spare. But she, in her poverty, has given everything she had to live on."

Jesus Teaches His Disciples—Matthew 24:1–35; Mark 13:1–31

⁵ Some ⌊of the disciples⌋ were talking about the temple complex. They noted that it was built with fine stones and decorated with beautiful gifts. So Jesus said, ⁶ "About these buildings that you see—the time will come when not one of these stones will be left on top of another. Each one will be torn down."

⁷ The disciples asked him, "Teacher, when will this happen? What will be the sign when all this will occur?"

⁸ Jesus said, "Be careful that you are not deceived. Many will come using my name. They will say, 'I am he!' and 'The time is near.' Don't follow them!

⁹ "When you hear of wars and revolutions, don't be terrified! These things must happen first, but the end will not come immediately."

¹⁰ Then Jesus continued, "Nation will fight against nation and kingdom against kingdom. ¹¹ There will be terrible earthquakes,

famines, and dreadful diseases in various places. Terrifying sights and miraculous signs will come from the sky.

¹² "Before all these things happen, people will arrest and persecute you. They will hand you over to their synagogues and put you into their prisons. They will drag you in front of kings and governors because of my name. ¹³ It will be your opportunity to testify to them. ¹⁴ So make up your minds not to worry beforehand how you will defend yourselves. ¹⁵ I will give you words and wisdom that none of your enemies will be able to oppose or prove wrong.

¹⁶ "Even parents, brothers, relatives, and friends will betray you and kill some of you. ¹⁷ Everyone will hate you because you are committed to me. ¹⁸ But not a hair on your head will be lost. ¹⁹ By your endurance you will save your life.

²⁰ "When you see armies camped around Jerusalem, realize that the time is near for it to be destroyed. ²¹ Then those of you in Judea should flee to the mountains. Those of you in Jerusalem should leave it. Those of you in the fields shouldn't go back into them. ²² This will be a time of vengeance. Everything that is written about it will come true.

²³ "How horrible it will be for women who are pregnant or who are nursing babies in those days. Indeed, the land will suffer very hard times, and its people will be punished. ²⁴ Swords will cut them down, and they will be carried off into all nations as prisoners. Nations will trample Jerusalem until the times allowed for the nations ₍to do this₎ are over.

²⁵ "Miraculous signs will occur in the sun, moon, and stars. The nations of the earth will be deeply troubled and confused because of the roaring and tossing of the sea. ²⁶ People will faint as they fearfully wait for what will happen to the world. Indeed, the powers of the universe will be shaken.

²⁷ "Then people will see the Son of Man coming in a cloud with power and great glory.

²⁸ "When these things begin to happen, stand with confidence! The time when you will be set free is near."

²⁹ Then Jesus used this story as an illustration. "Look at the fig tree or any other tree. ³⁰ As soon as leaves grow on them, you know without being told that summer is near. ³¹ In the same way, when you see these things happen, you know that the kingdom of God is near.

³² "I can guarantee this truth: This generation will not disappear until all this takes place. ³³ The earth and the heavens will disappear, but my words will never disappear.

No One Knows When the Earth and the Heavens Will Disappear

³⁴ "Make sure that you don't become drunk, hung over, and worried about life. Then that day could suddenly catch you by surprise ³⁵ like a trap that catches a bird. That day will surprise all people who live on the earth. ³⁶ Be alert at all times. Pray so that you have the power to escape everything that is about to happen and to stand in front of the Son of Man."

³⁷ During the day Jesus would teach in the temple courtyard. But at night he would go to the Mount of Olives (as it was called) and spend the night there. ³⁸ All of the people would get up early to hear him speak in the temple courtyard.

The Plot to Kill Jesus—
Matthew 26:1–5, 14–16; Mark 14:1–2, 10–11; John 11:45–57

22 ¹ The Festival of Unleavened Bread, called Passover, was near. ² The chief priests and the scribes were looking for some way to kill Jesus. However, they were afraid of the people.

³ Then Satan entered Judas Iscariot, one of the twelve apostles. ⁴ Judas went to the chief priests and the temple guards and discussed with them how he could betray Jesus. ⁵ They were pleased and agreed to give him some money. ⁶ So Judas promised to do it. He kept looking for an opportunity to betray Jesus to them when there was no crowd.

The Passover—Matthew 26:17–20; Mark 14:12–17

⁷ The day came during the Festival of Unleavened Bread when the Passover lamb had to be killed. ⁸ Jesus sent Peter and John and told them, "Go, prepare the Passover lamb for us to eat."

⁹ They asked him, "Where do you want us to prepare it?"

¹⁰ He told them, "Go into the city, and you will meet a man carrying a jug of water. Follow him into the house he enters. ¹¹ Tell the owner of the house that the teacher asks, 'Where is the room where I can eat the Passover meal with my disciples?' ¹² He will take you upstairs and show you a large furnished room. Get things ready there."

¹³ The disciples left. They found everything as Jesus had told them and prepared the Passover.

¹⁴ When it was time to eat the Passover meal, Jesus and the apostles were at the table. ¹⁵ Jesus said to them, "I've had a deep desire to eat this Passover with you before I suffer. ¹⁶ I can guarantee that I won't eat it again until it finds its fulfillment in the kingdom of God." ¹⁷ Then he took a cup and spoke a prayer of thanksgiving. He said, "Take this, and share it. ¹⁸ I can guarantee that from now on I won't drink this wine until the kingdom of God comes."

The Lord's Supper—Matthew 26:26–30; Mark 14:22–26

¹⁹ Then Jesus took bread and spoke a prayer of thanksgiving. He broke the bread, gave it to them, and said, "This is my body, which is given up for you. Do this to remember me."

²⁰ When supper was over, he did the same with the cup. He said, "This cup that is poured out for you is the new promise*a* made with my blood."

Jesus Knows Who Will Betray Him—Matthew 26:21–25; Mark 14:18–21; John 13:21–30

²¹ "The hand of the one who will betray me is with me on the table. ²² The Son of Man is going to die the way it has been planned for him. But how horrible it will be for that person who betrays him."

²³ So they began to discuss with each other who could do such a thing.

---

a 22:20 Or "testament," or "covenant."

An Argument About Greatness

²⁴ Then a quarrel broke out among the disciples. They argued about who should be considered the greatest.

²⁵ Jesus said to them, "The kings of nations have power over their people, and those in authority call themselves friends of the people. ²⁶ But you're not going to be that way! Rather, the greatest among you must be like the youngest, and your leader must be like a servant. ²⁷ Who's the greatest, the person who sits at the table or the servant? Isn't it really the person who sits at the table? But I'm among you as a servant.

²⁸ "You have stood by me in the troubles that have tested me. ²⁹ So as my Father has given me a kingdom, I'm giving it to you. ³⁰ You will eat and drink at my table in my kingdom. You will also sit on thrones and judge the twelve tribes of Israel."

Jesus Predicts Peter's Denial—
Matthew 26:31–35; Mark 14:27–31; John 13:36–38

³¹ ˌThen the Lord said,ˌ "Simon, Simon, listen! Satan has demanded to have you apostles for himself. He wants to separate you from me as a farmer separates wheat from husks. ³² But I have prayed for you, Simon, that your faith will not fail. So when you recover, strengthen the other disciples."

³³ But Peter said to him, "Lord, I'm ready to go to prison with you and to die with you."

³⁴ Jesus replied, "Peter, I can guarantee that the rooster won't crow tonight until you say three times that you don't know me."

³⁵ Then Jesus said to them, "When I sent you out without a wallet, traveling bag, or sandals, you didn't lack anything, did you?"

"Not a thing!" they answered.

³⁶ Then he said to them, "But now, the person who has a wallet and a traveling bag should take them along. The person who doesn't have a sword should sell his coat and buy one. ³⁷ I can guarantee that the Scripture passage which says, 'He was counted

---

ᵇ 22:44 Some manuscripts and translations omit verses 43 and 44.

with criminals,' must find its fulfillment in me. Indeed, whatever is written about me will come true."

38 The disciples said, "Lord, look! Here are two swords!"

Then Jesus said to them, "That's enough!"

Jesus Prays in the Garden of Gethsemane—
Matthew 26:36–46; Mark 14:32–42

39 Jesus went out ˌof the cityˌ to the Mount of Olives as he usually did. His disciples followed him. **40** When he arrived, he said to them, "Pray that you won't be tempted."

41 Then he withdrew from them about a stone's throw, knelt down, and prayed, **42** "Father, if it is your will, take this cup ˌof sufferingˌ away from me. However, your will must be done, not mine."

43 Then an angel from heaven appeared to him and gave him strength. **44** So he prayed very hard in anguish. His sweat became like drops of blood falling to the ground.[b]

45 When Jesus ended his prayer, he got up and went to the disciples. He found them asleep and overcome with sadness. **46** He said to them, "Why are you sleeping? Get up, and pray that you won't be tempted."

Jesus Is Arrested—Matthew 26:47–56; Mark 14:43–52; John 18:1–14

47 While he was still speaking to the disciples, a crowd arrived. The man called Judas, one of the twelve apostles, was leading them. He came close to Jesus to kiss him.

48 Jesus said to him, "Judas, do you intend to betray the Son of Man with a kiss?"

49 The men who were with Jesus saw what was going to happen. So they asked him, "Lord, should we use our swords to fight?"

50 One of the disciples cut off the right ear of the chief priest's servant.

51 But Jesus said, "Stop! That's enough of this." Then he touched the servant's ear and healed him.

52 Then Jesus said to the chief priests, temple guards, and leaders who had come for him, "Have you come out with swords and clubs as if I were a criminal? ⁵³ I was with you in the temple courtyard every day and you didn't try to arrest me. But this is your time, when darkness rules."

⁵⁴ So they arrested Jesus and led him away to the chief priest's house.

Peter Denies Jesus—
Matthew 26:69–75; Mark 14:66–72; John 18:15–18, 25–27

Peter followed at a distance.

⁵⁵ Some men had lit a fire in the middle of the courtyard. As they sat together, Peter sat among them. ⁵⁶ A female servant saw him as he sat facing the glow of the fire. She stared at him and said, "This man was with Jesus."

⁵⁷ But Peter denied it by saying, "I don't know him, woman."

⁵⁸ A little later someone else saw Peter and said, "You are one of them."

But Peter said, "Not me!"

⁵⁹ About an hour later another person insisted, "It's obvious that this man was with him. He's a Galilean!"

⁶⁰ But Peter said, "I don't know what you're talking about!"

Just then, while he was still speaking, a rooster crowed. ⁶¹ Then the Lord turned and looked directly at Peter. Peter remembered what the Lord had said: "Before a rooster crows today, you will say three times that you don't know me." ⁶² Then Peter went outside and cried bitterly.

The Trial in Front of the Jewish Council—
Matthew 26:57–68; Mark 14:53–65

⁶³ The men who were guarding Jesus made fun of him as they beat him. ⁶⁴ They blindfolded him and said to him, "Tell us who hit you." ⁶⁵ They also insulted him in many other ways.

⁶⁶ In the morning the council of the people's leaders, the chief priests and the scribes, gathered together. They brought Jesus in front of their highest court and asked him, ⁶⁷ "Tell us, are you the Messiah?"

Jesus said to them, "If I tell you, you won't believe me. [68] And if I ask you, you won't answer. [69] But from now on, the Son of Man will be in the highest position in heaven."

[70] Then all of them said, "So you're the Son of God?"

Jesus answered them, "You're right to say that I am."

[71] Then they said, "Why do we need any more testimony? We've heard him say it ourselves."

Pilate Questions Jesus—Matthew 27:11–14; Mark 15:1–5; John 18:28–38

23 [1] Then the entire assembly stood up and took him to Pilate. [2] They began to accuse Jesus by saying, "We found that he stirs up trouble among our people: He keeps them from paying taxes to the emperor, and he says that he is Christ, a king."

[3] Pilate asked him, "Are you the king of the Jews?"

"Yes, I am," Jesus answered.

[4] Pilate said to the chief priests and the crowd, "I can't find this man guilty of any crime."

Pilate Sends Jesus to Herod

[5] The priests and the crowd became more forceful. They said, "He stirs up the people throughout Judea with his teachings. He started in Galilee and has come here."

[6] When Pilate heard that, he asked if the man was from Galilee. [7] When Pilate found out that he was, he sent Jesus to Herod. Herod ruled Galilee and was in Jerusalem at that time.

[8] Herod was very pleased to see Jesus. For a long time he had wanted to see him. He had heard about Jesus and hoped to see him perform some kind of miracle. [9] Herod asked Jesus many questions, but Jesus wouldn't answer him. [10] Meanwhile, the chief priests and the scribes stood there and shouted their accusations against Jesus.

[11] Herod and his soldiers treated Jesus with contempt and made fun of him. They put a colorful robe on him and sent him back to Pilate. [12] So Herod and Pilate became friends that day. They had been enemies before this.

¹³ Then Pilate called together the chief priests, the rulers, and the people. ¹⁴ He told them, "You brought me this man as someone who turns the people against the government. I've questioned him in front of you and haven't found this man guilty of the crimes of which you accuse him. ¹⁵ Neither could Herod. So he sent this man back to us. This man hasn't done anything to deserve the death penalty. ¹⁶ So I'm going to have him whipped and set free."ᵃ

The Crowd Rejects Jesus—
Matthew 27:15–26; Mark 15:6–15; John 18:39–40

¹⁸ The whole crowd then shouted, "Take him away! Free Barabbas for us." ¹⁹ (Barabbas had been thrown into prison for his involvement in a riot that had taken place in the city and for murder.)

²⁰ But because Pilate wanted to free Jesus, he spoke to the people again.

²¹ They began yelling, "Crucify him! Crucify him!"

²² A third time Pilate spoke to them. He asked, "Why? What has he done wrong? I haven't found this man deserving of the death penalty. So I'm going to have him whipped and set free."

²³ But the crowd pressured Pilate. They shouted that Jesus had to be crucified, and they finally won. ²⁴ Pilate decided to give in to their demand. ²⁵ He freed Barabbas, who had been put in prison for rioting and murdering, because that's what they wanted. But he let them do what they wanted to Jesus.

Jesus Is Led Away to Be Crucified

²⁶ As the soldiers led Jesus away, they grabbed a man named Simon, who was from the city of Cyrene. Simon was coming into Jerusalem. They laid the cross on him and made him carry it behind Jesus.

²⁷ A large crowd followed Jesus. The women in the crowd cried and sang funeral songs for him. ²⁸ Jesus turned to them and

---

ᵃ 23:16 Some manuscripts and translations add verse 17: "At every Passover festival the governor had to set someone free for them."

said, "You women of Jerusalem, don't cry for me! Rather, cry for yourselves and your children! [29] The time is coming when people will say, 'Blessed are the women who couldn't get pregnant, who couldn't give birth, and who couldn't nurse a child.' [30] Then people will say to the mountains, 'Fall on us!' and to the hills, 'Cover us!' [31] If people do this to a green tree, what will happen to a dry one?"

[32] Two others, who were criminals, were led away to be executed with him.

The Crucifixion—Matthew 27:31–44; Mark 15:20–32; John 19:16b–24

[33] When they came to the place called The Skull, they crucified him. The criminals were also crucified, one on his right and the other on his left.

[34] Then Jesus said, "Father, forgive them. They don't know what they're doing."[b]

Meanwhile, the soldiers divided his clothes among themselves by throwing dice.

[35] The people stood there watching. But the rulers were making sarcastic remarks. They said, "He saved others. If he's the Messiah that God has chosen, let him save himself!" [36] The soldiers also made fun of him. They would go up to him, offer him some vinegar, [37] and say, "If you're the king of the Jews, save yourself!"

[38] A written notice was placed above him. It said, "This is the king of the Jews."

Criminals Talk to Jesus

[39] One of the criminals hanging there insulted Jesus by saying, "So you're really the Messiah, are you? Well, save yourself and us!"

[40] But the other criminal scolded him: "Don't you fear God at all? Can't you see that you're condemned in the same way that he is? [41] Our punishment is fair. We're getting what we deserve. But this man hasn't done anything wrong."

---

[b] 23:34 Some manuscripts and translations omit "Then . . . doing."

⁴² Then he said, "Jesus, remember me when you enter your kingdom."

⁴³ Jesus said to him, "I can guarantee this truth: Today you will be with me in paradise."

Jesus Dies on the Cross—
Matthew 27:45–56; Mark 15:33–41; John 19:28–30

⁴⁴ Around noon darkness came over the entire land and lasted until three in the afternoon. ⁴⁵ The sun had stopped shining. The curtain in the temple was split in two.

⁴⁶ Jesus cried out in a loud voice, "Father, into your hands I entrust my spirit." After he said this, he died.

⁴⁷ When an army officer saw what had happened, he praised God and said, "Certainly, this man was innocent!" ⁴⁸ Crowds had gathered to see the sight. But when all of them saw what had happened, they cried and returned to the city. ⁴⁹ All his friends, including the women who had followed him from Galilee, stood at a distance and watched everything.

Jesus Is Buried—Matthew 27:57–61; Mark 15:42–47; John 19:38–42

⁵⁰ There was a good man who had God's approval. His name was Joseph. He was a member of the Jewish council, ⁵¹ but he had not agreed with what they had done. He was from the Jewish city of Arimathea, and he was waiting for the kingdom of God.

⁵² He went to Pilate and asked for the body of Jesus. ⁵³ After he took it down from the cross, he wrapped it in linen. Then he laid the body in a tomb cut in rock, a tomb in which no one had ever been buried. ⁵⁴ It was Friday, and the day of worship was just beginning.

⁵⁵ The women who had come with Jesus from Galilee followed closely behind Joseph. They observed the tomb and how his body was laid in it. ⁵⁶ Then they went back to the city and prepared spices and perfumes. But on the day of worship they rested according to the commandment.

Jesus Comes Back to Life—
Matthew 28:1–10; Mark 16:1–8; John 20:1–10

24 [1] Very early on Sunday morning the women went to the tomb. They were carrying the spices that they had prepared. [2] They found that the stone had been rolled away from the tomb. [3] When they went in, they did not find the body of the Lord Jesus. [4] While they were puzzled about this, two men in clothes that were as bright as lightning suddenly stood beside them. [5] The women were terrified and bowed to the ground.

The men asked the women, "Why are you looking among the dead for the living one? [6] He's not here. He has been brought back to life! Remember what he told you while he was still in Galilee. [7] He said, 'The Son of Man must be handed over to sinful people, be crucified, and come back to life on the third day.' " [8] Then the women remembered what Jesus had told them.

[9] The women left the tomb and went back to the city. They told everything to the eleven apostles and all the others. [10] The women were Mary from Magdala, Joanna, and Mary (the mother of James). There were also other women with them. They told the apostles everything.

[11] The apostles thought that the women's story didn't make any sense, and they didn't believe them.

[12] But Peter got up and ran to the tomb. He bent down to look inside and saw only the strips of linen. Then he went away, wondering what had happened.

Jesus Appears to Disciples on a Road to Emmaus

[13] On the same day, two of Jesus' disciples were going to a village called Emmaus. It was about seven miles from Jerusalem. [14] They were talking to each other about everything that had happened.

[15] While they were talking, Jesus approached them and began walking with them. [16] Although they saw him, they didn't recognize him.

¹⁷ He asked them, "What are you discussing?"

They stopped and looked very sad. ¹⁸ One of them, Cleopas, replied, "Are you the only one in Jerusalem who doesn't know what has happened recently?"

¹⁹ "What happened?" he asked.

They said to him, "We were discussing what happened to Jesus from Nazareth. He was a powerful prophet in what he did and said in the sight of God and all the people. ²⁰ Our chief priests and rulers had him condemned to death and crucified. ²¹ We were hoping that he was the one who would free Israel. What's more, this is now the third day since everything happened. ²² Some of the women from our group startled us. They went to the tomb early this morning ²³ and didn't find his body. They told us that they had seen angels who said that he's alive. ²⁴ Some of our men went to the tomb and found it empty, as the women had said, but they didn't see him."

²⁵ Then Jesus said to them, "How foolish you are! You're so slow to believe everything the prophets said! ²⁶ Didn't the Messiah have to suffer these things and enter into his glory?" ²⁷ Then he began with Moses' Teachings and the Prophets to explain to them what was said about him throughout the Scriptures.

²⁸ When they came near the village where they were going, Jesus acted as if he were going farther. ²⁹ They urged him, "Stay with us! It's getting late, and the day is almost over." So he went to stay with them.

³⁰ While he was at the table with them, he took bread and blessed it. He broke the bread and gave it to them. ³¹ Then their eyes were opened, and they recognized him. But he vanished from their sight.

³² They said to each other, "Weren't we excited when he talked with us on the road and opened up the meaning of the Scriptures for us?"

³³ That same hour they went back to Jerusalem. They found the eleven apostles and those who were with them gathered together.

³⁴ They were saying, "The Lord has really come back to life and has appeared to Simon."

³⁵ Then the two disciples told what had happened on the road and how they had recognized Jesus when he broke the bread.

Jesus Appears to the Apostles—John 20:19–23

³⁶ While they were talking about what had happened, Jesus stood among them. He said to them, "Peace be with you!" ³⁷ They were terrified, and thought they were seeing a ghost.

³⁸ He asked them, "Why are you afraid? Why do you have doubts? ³⁹ Look at my hands and feet, and see that it's really me. Touch me, and see for yourselves. Ghosts don't have flesh and bones, but you can see that I do." ⁴⁰ As he said this, he showed them his hands and feet.

⁴¹ The disciples were overcome with joy and amazement because this seemed too good to be true. Then Jesus asked them, "Do you have anything to eat?" ⁴² They gave him a piece of broiled fish. ⁴³ He took it and ate it while they watched him.

⁴⁴ Then he said to them, "These are the words I spoke to you while I was still with you. I told you that everything written about me in Moses' Teachings, the Prophets, and the Psalms had to come true." ⁴⁵ Then he opened their minds to understand the Scriptures. ⁴⁶ He said to them, "Scripture says that the Messiah would suffer and that he would come back to life on the third day. ⁴⁷ Scripture also says that by the authority of Jesus people would be told to turn to God and change the way they think and act so that their sins will be forgiven. This would be told to people from all nations, beginning in the city of Jerusalem. ⁴⁸ You are witnesses to these things.

⁴⁹ "I'm sending you what my Father promised. Wait here in the city until you receive power from heaven."

⁵⁰ Then Jesus took them to a place near Bethany. There he raised his hands and blessed them. ⁵¹ While he was blessing them, he left them and was taken to heaven.

⁵²The disciples worshiped him and were overjoyed as they went back to Jerusalem. ⁵³They were always in the temple, where they praised God.

JOHN

The Word Becomes Human

1 ¹ In the beginning the Word already existed. The Word was with God, and the Word was God. ² He was already with God in the beginning.

³ Everything came into existence through him. Not one thing that exists was made without him.

⁴ He was the source of life, and that life was the light for humanity.

⁵ The light shines in the dark, and the dark has never extinguished it.ᵃ

⁶ God sent a man named John to be his messenger. ⁷ John came to declare the truth about the light so that everyone would become believers through his message. ⁸ John was not the light, but he came to declare the truth about the light.

⁹ The real light, which shines on everyone, was coming into the world. ¹⁰ He was in the world, and the world came into existence through him. Yet, the world didn't recognize him. ¹¹ He went to his own people, and his own people didn't accept him. ¹² However, he gave the right to become God's children to everyone who believed in him. ¹³ These people didn't become God's children in a physical way—from a human impulse or from a husband's desire ˌto have a childˌ. They were born from God.

¹⁴ The Word became human and lived among us. We saw his glory. It was the glory that the Father shares with his only Son, a glory full of kindnessᵇ and truth.

ᵃ 1:5 English equivalent difficult.   ᵇ 1:14 Or "grace."

¹⁵ (John declared the truth about him when he said loudly, "This is the person about whom I said, 'The one who comes after me was before me because he existed before I did.' ")

¹⁶ Each of us has received one gift after another because of all that the Word is. ¹⁷ The Teachings were given through Moses, but kindness and truth came into existence through Jesus Christ. ¹⁸ No one has ever seen God. God's only Son, the one who is closest to the Father's heart, has made him known.

John Prepares the Way—Matthew 3:1–12; Mark 1:1–8; Luke 3:1–18

¹⁹ This was John's answer when the Jews sent priests and Levites from Jerusalem to ask him, "Who are you?" ²⁰ John didn't refuse to answer. He told them clearly, "I'm not the Messiah."

²¹ They asked him, "Well, are you Elijah?"

John answered, "No, I'm not."

Then they asked, "Are you the prophet?"

John replied, "No."

²² So they asked him, "Who are you? Tell us so that we can take an answer back to those who sent us. What do you say about yourself?"

²³ John said, "I'm a voice crying out in the desert, 'Make the way for the Lord straight,' as the prophet Isaiah said."

²⁴ Some of those who had been sent were Pharisees. ²⁵ They asked John, "Why do you baptize if you're not the Messiah or Elijah or the prophet?"

²⁶ John answered them, "I baptize with water. Someone you don't know is standing among you. ²⁷ He's the one who comes after me. I am not worthy to untie his sandal strap."

²⁸ This happened in Bethany on the east side of the Jordan River, where John was baptizing.

John Identifies Jesus as the Lamb of God

²⁹ John saw Jesus coming toward him the next day and said, "Look! This is the Lamb of God who takes away the sin of the world. ³⁰ He is the one I spoke about when I said, 'A man who comes after me was before me because he existed before I did.'

³¹ I didn't know who he was. However, I came to baptize with water to show him to the people of Israel."

³² John said, "I saw the Spirit come down as a dove from heaven and stay on him. ³³ I didn't know who he was. But God, who sent me to baptize with water, had told me, 'When you see the Spirit come down and stay on someone, you'll know that person is the one who baptizes with the Holy Spirit.' ³⁴ I have seen this and have declared that this is the Son of God."

Calling of the First Disciples

³⁵ The next day John was standing with two of his disciples. ³⁶ John saw Jesus walk by. John said, "Look! This is the Lamb of God." ³⁷ When the two disciples heard John say this, they followed Jesus.

³⁸ Jesus turned around and saw them following him. He asked them, "What are you looking for?"

They said to him, "Rabbi" (which means "teacher"), "where are you staying?"

³⁹ Jesus told them, "Come, and you will see." So they went to see where he was staying and spent the rest of that day with him. It was about ten o'clock in the morning.

⁴⁰ Andrew, Simon Peter's brother, was one of the two disciples who heard John and followed Jesus. ⁴¹ Andrew at once found his brother Simon and told him, "We have found the Messiah" (which means "Christ"). ⁴² Andrew brought Simon to Jesus.

Jesus looked at Simon and said, "You are Simon, son of John. Your name will be Cephas" (which means "Peter").

⁴³ The next day Jesus wanted to go to Galilee. He found Philip and told him, "Follow me!" ⁴⁴ (Philip was from Bethsaida, the hometown of Andrew and Peter.)

⁴⁵ Philip found Nathanael and told him, "We have found the man whom Moses wrote about in his teachings and whom the prophets wrote about. He is Jesus, son of Joseph, from the city of Nazareth."

⁴⁶ Nathanael said to Philip, "Can anything good come from Nazareth?"

Philip told him, "Come and see!"

⁴⁷ Jesus saw Nathanael coming toward him and remarked, "Here is a true Israelite who is sincere."

⁴⁸ Nathanael asked Jesus, "How do you know anything about me?"

Jesus answered him, "I saw you under the fig tree before Philip called you."

⁴⁹ Nathanael said to Jesus, "Rabbi, you are the Son of God! You are the king of Israel!"

⁵⁰ Jesus replied, "You believe because I told you that I saw you under the fig tree. You will see greater things than that." ⁵¹ Jesus said to Nathanael, "I can guarantee this truth: You will see the sky open and God's angels going up and coming down to the Son of Man."

Jesus Changes Water Into Wine

2 ¹ Three days later a wedding took place in the city of Cana in Galilee. Jesus' mother was there. ² Jesus and his disciples had been invited too.

³ When the wine was gone, Jesus' mother said to him, "They're out of wine."

⁴ Jesus said to her, "Why did you come to me? My time has not yet come."

⁵ His mother told the servers, "Do whatever he tells you."

⁶ Six stone water jars were there. They were used for Jewish purification rituals. Each jar held 18 to 27 gallons.

⁷ Jesus told the servers, "Fill the jars with water." The servers filled the jars to the brim. ⁸ Jesus said to them, "Pour some, and take it to the person in charge." The servers did as they were told.

⁹ The person in charge tasted the water that had become wine. He didn't know where it had come from, although the servers who had poured the water knew. The person in charge called the groom ¹⁰ and said to him, "Everyone serves the best wine first. When people are drunk, the host serves cheap wine. But you have saved the best wine for now."

¹¹ Cana in Galilee was the place where Jesus began to perform miracles. He made his glory public there, and his disciples believed in him.

¹² After this, Jesus, his mother, brothers, and disciples went to the city of Capernaum and stayed there for a few days.

Jesus Throws Merchants and Moneychangers Out of the Temple Courtyard

¹³ The Jewish Passover was near, so Jesus went to Jerusalem. ¹⁴ He found those who were selling cattle, sheep, and pigeons in the temple courtyard. He also found moneychangers sitting there. ¹⁵ He made a whip from small ropes and threw everyone with their sheep and cattle out of the temple courtyard. He dumped the moneychangers' coins and knocked over their tables.

¹⁶ He told those who sold pigeons, "Pick up this stuff, and get it out of here! Stop making my Father's house a marketplace!"

¹⁷ His disciples remembered that Scripture said, "Devotion for your house will consume me."

¹⁸ The Jews reacted by asking Jesus, "What miracle can you show us to justify what you're doing?"

¹⁹ Jesus replied, "Tear down this temple, and I'll rebuild it in three days."

²⁰ The Jews said, "It took forty-six years to build this temple. Do you really think you're going to rebuild it in three days?"

²¹ But the temple Jesus spoke about was his own body. ²² After he came back to life, his disciples remembered that he had said this. So they believed the Scripture and this statement that Jesus had made.

²³ While Jesus was in Jerusalem at the Passover festival, many people believed in him because they saw the miracles that he performed. ²⁴ Jesus, however, was wary of these believers. He understood people ²⁵ and didn't need anyone to tell him about human nature. He knew what people were really like.

A Conversation With Nicodemus

3 ¹ Nicodemus was a Pharisee and a member of the Jewish council. ² He came to Jesus one night and said to him, "Rabbi, we know that God has sent you as a teacher. No one can perform the miracles you perform unless God is with him."

³ Jesus replied to Nicodemus, "I can guarantee this truth: No one can see the kingdom of God without being born from above."ᵃ

⁴ Nicodemus asked him, "How can anyone be born when he's an old man? He can't go back inside his mother a second time to be born, can he?"

⁵ Jesus answered Nicodemus, "I can guarantee this truth: No one can enter the kingdom of God without being born of water and the Spirit. ⁶ Flesh and blood give birth to flesh and blood, but the Spirit gives birth to things that are spiritual. ⁷ Don't be surprised when I tell you that all of you must be born from above. ⁸ The windᵇ blows wherever it pleases. You hear its sound, but you don't know where the wind comes from or where it's going. That's the way it is with everyone born of the Spirit."

⁹ Nicodemus replied, "How can that be?"

¹⁰ Jesus told Nicodemus, "You're a well-known teacher of Israel. Can't you understand this? ¹¹ I can guarantee this truth: We know what we're talking about, and we confirm what we've seen. Yet, you don't accept our message. ¹² If you don't believe me when I tell you about things on earth, how will you believe me when I tell you about things in heaven? ¹³ No one has gone to heaven except the Son of Man, who came from heaven.

¹⁴ "As Moses lifted up the snake ⌞on a pole⌟ in the desert, so the Son of Man must be lifted up. ¹⁵ Then everyone who believes in him will have eternal life."

¹⁶ God loved the world this way: He gave his only Son so that everyone who believes in him will not die but will have eternal life. ¹⁷ God sent his Son into the world, not to condemn the world, but to save the world. ¹⁸ Those who believe in him won't be condemned. But those who don't believe are already condemned because they don't believe in God's only Son.

¹⁹ This is why people are condemned: The light came into the world. Yet, people loved the dark rather than the light because

---

ᵃ 3:3 Or "born again."   ᵇ 3:8 The Greek word for *wind* is the same as the Greek word for *Spirit*.

their actions were evil. ²⁰ People who do what is wrong hate the light and don't come to the light. They don't want their actions to be exposed. ²¹ But people who do what is true come to the light so that the things they do for God may be clearly seen.

John the Baptizer Talks About Christ

²² Later, Jesus and his disciples went to the Judean countryside, where he spent some time with them and baptized people. ²³ John was baptizing in Aenon, near Salim. Water was plentiful there. (People came to John to be baptized, ²⁴ since John had not yet been put in prison.)

²⁵ Some of John's disciples had an argument with a Jew about purification ceremonies. ²⁶ So they went to John and asked him, "Rabbi, do you remember the man you spoke so favorably about when he was with you on the other side of the Jordan River? Well, he's baptizing, and everyone is going to him!"

²⁷ John answered, "People can't receive anything unless it has been given to them from heaven. ²⁸ You are witnesses that I said, 'I'm not the Messiah, but I've been sent ahead of him.'

²⁹ "The groom is the person to whom the bride belongs. The best man, who stands and listens to him, is overjoyed when the groom speaks. This is the joy that I feel. ³⁰ He must increase in importance, while I must decrease in importance.

³¹ "The person who comes from above is superior to everyone. I, a person from the earth, know nothing but what is on earth, and that's all I can talk about. The person who comes from heaven is superior to everyone ³² and tells what he has seen and heard. Yet, no one accepts what he says. ³³ I have accepted what that person said, and I have affirmed that God is truthful. ³⁴ The man whom God has sent speaks God's message. After all, God gives him the Spirit without limit. ³⁵ The Father loves his Son and has put everything in his power. ³⁶ Whoever believes in the Son has eternal life, but whoever rejects the Son will not see life. Instead, he will see God's constant anger."

A Samaritan Woman Meets Jesus at a Well

4 ¹ Jesus knew that the Pharisees had heard that he was making and baptizing more disciples than John. ² (Actually, Jesus was not baptizing people. His disciples were.) ³ So he left the Judean countryside and went back to Galilee.

⁴ Jesus had to go through Samaria. ⁵ He arrived at a city in Samaria called Sychar. Sychar was near the piece of land that Jacob had given to his son Joseph. ⁶ Jacob's Well was there. Jesus sat down by the well because he was tired from traveling. The time was about six o'clock in the evening.

⁷ A Samaritan woman went to get some water. Jesus said to her, "Give me a drink of water." ⁸ (His disciples had gone into the city to buy some food.)

⁹ The Samaritan woman asked him, "How can a Jewish man like you ask a Samaritan woman like me for a drink of water?" (Jews, of course, don't associate with Samaritans.)

¹⁰ Jesus replied to her, "If you only knew what God's gift is and who is asking you for a drink, you would have asked him for a drink. He would have given you living water."

¹¹ The woman said to him, "Sir, you don't have anything to use to get water, and the well is deep. So where are you going to get this living water? ¹² You're not more important than our ancestor Jacob, are you? He gave us this well. He and his sons and his animals drank water from it."

¹³ Jesus answered her, "Everyone who drinks this water will become thirsty again. ¹⁴ But those who drink the water that I will give them will never become thirsty again. In fact, the water I will give them will become in them a spring that gushes up to eternal life."

¹⁵ The woman told Jesus, "Sir, give me this water! Then I won't get thirsty or have to come here to get water."

¹⁶ Jesus told her, "Go to your husband, and bring him here."

¹⁷ The woman replied, "I don't have a husband."

Jesus told her, "You're right when you say that you don't have a husband. ¹⁸ You've had five husbands, and the man you have now isn't your husband. You've told the truth."

[19] The woman said to Jesus, "I see that you're a prophet! [20] Our ancestors worshiped on this mountain. But you Jews say that people must worship in Jerusalem."

[21] Jesus told her, "Believe me. A time is coming when you Samaritans won't be worshiping the Father on this mountain or in Jerusalem. [22] You don't know what you're worshiping. We Jews know what we're worshiping, because salvation comes from the Jews. [23] Indeed, the time is coming, and it is now here, when the true worshipers will worship the Father in spirit and truth. The Father is looking for people like that to worship him. [24] God is a spirit. Those who worship him must worship in spirit and truth."

[25] The woman said to him, "I know that the Messiah is coming. When he comes, he will tell us everything." (*Messiah* is the one called *Christ*.)

[26] Jesus told her, "I am he, and I am speaking to you now."

[27] At that time his disciples returned. They were surprised that he was talking to a woman. But none of them asked him, "What do you want from her?" or "Why are you talking to her?"

[28] Then the woman left her water jar and went back into the city. She told the people, [29] "Come with me, and meet a man who told me everything I've ever done. Could he be the Messiah?" [30] The people left the city and went to meet Jesus.

[31] Meanwhile, the disciples were urging him, "Rabbi, have something to eat."

[32] Jesus told them, "I have food to eat that you don't know about."

[33] The disciples asked each other, "Did someone bring him something to eat?"

[34] Jesus told them, "My food is to do what the one who sent me wants me to do and to finish the work he has given me.

[35] "Don't you say, 'In four more months the harvest will be here'? I'm telling you to look and see that the fields are ready to be harvested. [36] The person who harvests the crop is already getting paid. He is gathering grain for eternal life. So the person who plants the grain and the person who harvests it are happy together. [37] In this

respect the saying is true: 'One person plants, and another person harvests.' [38] I have sent you to harvest a crop you have not worked for. Other people have done the hard work, and you have followed them in their work."

[39] Many Samaritans in that city believed in Jesus because of the woman who said, "He told me everything I've ever done." [40] So when the Samaritans went to Jesus, they asked him to stay with them. He stayed in Samaria for two days. [41] Many more Samaritans believed because of what Jesus said. [42] They told the woman, "Our faith is no longer based on what you've said. We have heard him ourselves, and we know that he really is the savior of the world."

A Believing Official—Matthew 8:5–13; Luke 7:1–10

[43] After spending two days in Samaria, Jesus left for Galilee. [44] Jesus had said that a prophet is not honored in his own country. [45] But when Jesus arrived in Galilee, the people of Galilee welcomed him. They had seen everything he had done at the festival in Jerusalem, since they, too, had attended the festival.

[46] Jesus returned to the city of Cana in Galilee, where he had changed water into wine. A government official was in Cana. His son was sick in Capernaum. [47] The official heard that Jesus had returned from Judea to Galilee. So he went to Jesus and asked him to go to Capernaum with him to heal his son who was about to die.

[48] Jesus told the official, "If people don't see miracles and amazing things, they won't believe."

[49] The official said to him, "Sir, come with me before my little boy dies."

[50] Jesus told him, "Go home. Your son will live." The man believed what Jesus told him and left.

[51] While the official was on his way to Capernaum, his servants met him and told him that his boy was alive. [52] The official asked them at what time his son got better. His servants told him, "The fever left him yesterday evening at seven o'clock." [53] Then the boy's father realized that it was the same time that Jesus had told him, "Your son will live." So the official and his entire family became believers.

⁵⁴ This was the second miracle that Jesus performed after he had come back from Judea to Galilee.

Jesus Cures a Man at the Bethesda Pool

5 ¹ Later, Jesus went to Jerusalem for a Jewish festival. ² Near Sheep Gate in Jerusalem was a pool called *Bethesda* in Hebrew. It had five porches. ³ Under these porches a large number of sick people—people who were blind, lame, or paralyzed—used to lie.ᵃ ⁵ One man, who had been sick for 38 years, was lying there. ⁶ Jesus saw the man lying there and knew that he had been sick for a long time. So Jesus asked the man, "Would you like to get well?"

⁷ The sick man answered Jesus, "Sir, I don't have anyone to put me into the pool when the water is stirred. While I'm trying to get there, someone else steps into the pool ahead of me."

⁸ Jesus told the man, "Get up, pick up your cot, and walk." ⁹ The man immediately became well, picked up his cot, and walked.

That happened on a day of worship. ¹⁰ So the Jews told the man who had been healed, "This is a day of worship. You're not allowed to carry your cot today."

¹¹ The man replied, "The man who made me well told me to pick up my cot and walk."

¹² The Jews asked him, "Who is the man who told you to pick it up and walk?" ¹³ But the man who had been healed didn't know who Jesus was. (Jesus had withdrawn from the crowd.)

¹⁴ Later, Jesus met the man in the temple courtyard and told him, "You're well now. Stop sinning so that something worse doesn't happen to you."

¹⁵ The man went back to the Jews and told them that Jesus was the man who had made him well.

ᵃ 5:3 Some manuscripts and translations add verses 3b–4: "They would wait for the water to move. People believed that at a certain time an angel from the Lord would go into the pool and stir up the water. The first person who would step into the water after it was stirred up would be cured from whatever disease he had."

The Son Is Equal to the Father

16 The Jews began to persecute Jesus because he kept healing people on the day of worship. **17** Jesus replied to them, "My Father is working right now, and so am I."

18 His reply made the Jews more intent on killing him. Not only did he break the laws about the day of worship, but also he made himself equal to God when he said repeatedly that God was his Father.

19 Jesus said to the Jews, "I can guarantee this truth: The Son cannot do anything on his own. He can do only what he sees the Father doing. Indeed, the Son does exactly what the Father does. **20** The Father loves the Son and shows him everything he is doing. The Father will show him even greater things to do than these things so that you will be amazed. **21** In the same way that the Father brings back the dead and gives them life, the Son gives life to anyone he chooses.

22 "The Father doesn't judge anyone. He has entrusted judgment entirely to the Son **23** so that everyone will honor the Son as they honor the Father. Whoever doesn't honor the Son doesn't honor the Father who sent him. **24** I can guarantee this truth: Those who listen to what I say and believe in the one who sent me will have eternal life. They won't be judged because they have already passed from death to life.

25 "I can guarantee this truth: A time is coming (and is now here) when the dead will hear the voice of the Son of God and those who respond to it will live. **26** The Father is the source of life, and he has enabled the Son to be the source of life too.

27 "He has also given the Son authority to pass judgment because he is the Son of Man.[b] **28** Don't be surprised at what I've just said. A time is coming when all the dead will hear his voice, **29** and they will come out of their tombs. Those who have done good will come back to life and live. But those who have done evil will come back to life and will be judged. **30** I can't do anything on my own. As I listen ⌞to the Father⌟, I make my judgments. My

---

[b] 5:27 "Son of Man" is a name Jesus called himself to show that he was not only God's Son but also human.

judgments are right because I don't try to do what I want but what the one who sent me wants.

[31] "If I testify on my own behalf, what I say isn't true. [32] Someone else testifies on my behalf, and I know that what he says about me is true. [33] You sent people to John ⌊the Baptizer⌋, and he testified to the truth. [34] But I don't depend on human testimony. I'm telling you this to save you. [35] John was a lamp that gave off brilliant light. For a time you enjoyed the pleasure of his light. [36] But I have something that testifies more favorably on my behalf than John's testimony. The tasks that the Father gave me to carry out, these tasks which I perform, testify on my behalf. They prove that the Father has sent me. [37] The Father who sent me testifies on my behalf. You have never heard his voice, and you have never seen his form. [38] So you don't have the Father's message within you, because you don't believe in the person he has sent. [39] You study the Scriptures in detail because you think you have the source of eternal life in them. These Scriptures testify on my behalf. [40] Yet, you don't want to come to me to get ⌊eternal⌋ life.

[41] "I don't accept praise from humans. [42] But I know what kind of people you are. You don't have any love for God. [43] I have come with the authority my Father has given me, but you don't accept me. If someone else comes with his own authority, you will accept him. [44] How can you believe when you accept each other's praise and don't look for the praise that comes from the only God?

[45] "Don't think that I will accuse you in the presence of the Father. Moses, the one you trust, is already accusing you. [46] If you really believed Moses, you would believe me. Moses wrote about me. [47] If you don't believe what Moses wrote, how will you ever believe what I say?"

Jesus Feeds More Than Five Thousand—
Matthew 14:13–21; Mark 6:30–44; Luke 9:10–17

6 [1] Jesus later crossed to the other side of the Sea of Galilee (or the Sea of Tiberias). [2] A large crowd followed him because they saw the miracles that he performed for the sick. [3] Jesus went up a mountain and sat with his disciples. ⁴ The time for the Jewish Passover festival was near.

⁵ As Jesus saw a large crowd coming to him, he said to Philip, "Where can we buy bread for these people to eat?" ⁶ Jesus asked this question to test him. He already knew what he was going to do.

⁷ Philip answered, "We would need about a year's wages to buy enough bread for each of them to have a piece."

⁸ One of Jesus' disciples, Andrew, who was Simon Peter's brother, told him, ⁹ "A boy who has five loaves of barley bread and two small fish is here. But they won't go very far for so many people."

¹⁰ Jesus said, "Have the people sit down."

The people had plenty of grass to sit on. (There were about 5,000 men in the crowd.)

¹¹ Jesus took the loaves, gave thanks, and distributed them to the people who were sitting there. He did the same thing with the fish. All the people ate as much as they wanted.

¹² When the people were full, Jesus told his disciples, "Gather the leftover pieces so that nothing will be wasted." ¹³ The disciples gathered the leftover pieces of bread and filled twelve baskets.

¹⁴ When the people saw the miracle Jesus performed, they said, "This man is certainly the prophet who is to come into the world." ¹⁵ Jesus realized that the people intended to take him by force and make him king. So he returned to the mountain by himself.

Jesus Walks on the Sea—Matthew 14:22–33; Mark 6:45–52

¹⁶ When evening came, his disciples went to the sea. ¹⁷ They got into a boat and started to cross the sea to the city of Capernaum. By this time it was dark, and Jesus had not yet come to them. ¹⁸ A strong wind started to blow and stir up the sea.

¹⁹ After they had rowed three or four miles, they saw Jesus walking on the sea. He was coming near the boat, and they became terrified.

²⁰ Jesus told them, "It's me. Don't be afraid!"

²¹ So they were willing to help Jesus into the boat. Immediately, the boat reached the shore where they were going.

Jesus Is the Bread of Life

²² On the next day the people were still on the other side of the sea. They noticed that only one boat was there and that Jesus had not stepped into that boat with his disciples. The disciples had gone away without him. ²³ Other boats from Tiberias arrived near the place where they had eaten the bread after the Lord gave thanks. ²⁴ When the people saw that neither Jesus nor his disciples were there, they got into these boats and went to the city of Capernaum to look for Jesus. ²⁵ When they found him on the other side of the sea, they asked him, "Rabbi, when did you get here?"

²⁶ Jesus replied to them, "I can guarantee this truth: You're not looking for me because you saw miracles. You are looking for me because you ate as much of those loaves as you wanted. ²⁷ Don't work for food that spoils. Instead, work for the food that lasts into eternal life. This is the food the Son of Man will give you. After all, the Father has placed his seal of approval on him."

²⁸ The people asked Jesus, "What does God want us to do?"

²⁹ Jesus replied to them, "God wants to do something for you so that you believe in the one whom he has sent."

³⁰ The people asked him, "What miracle are you going to perform so that we can see it and believe in you? What are you going to do? ³¹ Our ancestors ate the manna in the desert. Scripture says, 'He gave them bread from heaven to eat.' "

³² Jesus said to them, "I can guarantee this truth: Moses didn't give you bread from heaven, but my Father gives you the true bread from heaven. ³³ God's bread is the man who comes from heaven and gives life to the world."

³⁴ They said to him, "Sir, give us this bread all the time."

³⁵ Jesus told them, "I am the bread of life. Whoever comes to me will never become hungry, and whoever believes in me will never become thirsty. ³⁶ I've told you that you have seen me. However, you don't believe in me. ³⁷ Everyone whom the Father gives me will come to me. I will never turn away anyone who comes to me. ³⁸ I haven't come from heaven to do what I want to do. I've come to do what the one who sent me wants me to do. ³⁹ The one who sent

me doesn't want me to lose any of those he gave me. He wants me to bring them back to life on the last day. [40] My Father wants all those who see the Son and believe in him to have eternal life. He wants me to bring them back to life on the last day."

[41] The Jews began to criticize Jesus for saying, "I am the bread that came from heaven." [42] They asked, "Isn't this man Jesus, Joseph's son? Don't we know his father and mother? How can he say now, 'I came from heaven'?"

[43] Jesus responded, "Stop criticizing me! [44] People cannot come to me unless the Father who sent me brings them to me. I will bring these people back to life on the last day. [45] The prophets wrote, 'God will teach everyone.' Those who do what they have learned from the Father come to me. [46] I'm saying that no one has seen the Father. Only the one who is from God has seen the Father. [47] I can guarantee this truth: Every believer has eternal life.

[48] "I am the bread of life. [49] Your ancestors ate the manna in the desert and died. [50] This is the bread that comes from heaven so that whoever eats it won't die. [51] I am the living bread that came from heaven. Whoever eats this bread will live forever. The bread I will give to bring life to the world is my flesh."

[52] The Jews began to quarrel with each other. They said, "How can this man give us his flesh to eat?"

[53] Jesus told them, "I can guarantee this truth: If you don't eat the flesh of the Son of Man and drink his blood, you don't have the source of life in you. [54] Those who eat my flesh and drink my blood have eternal life, and I will bring them back to life on the last day. [55] My flesh is true food, and my blood is true drink. [56] Those who eat my flesh and drink my blood live in me, and I live in them. [57] The Father who has life sent me, and I live because of the Father. So those who feed on me will live because of me. [58] This is the bread that came from heaven. It is not like the bread your ancestors ate. They eventually died. Those who eat this bread will live forever."

[59] Jesus said this while he was teaching in a synagogue in Capernaum. [60] When many of Jesus' disciples heard him, they said, "What he says is hard to accept. Who wants to listen to him anymore?"

⁶¹ Jesus was aware that his disciples were criticizing his message. So Jesus asked them, "Did what I say make you lose faith? ⁶² What if you see the Son of Man go where he was before? ⁶³ Life is spiritual. Your physical existence doesn't contribute to that life. The words that I have spoken to you are spiritual. They are life. ⁶⁴ But some of you don't believe." Jesus knew from the beginning those who wouldn't believe and the one who would betray him. ⁶⁵ So he added, "That is why I told you that people cannot come to me unless the Father provides the way."

⁶⁶ Jesus' speech made many of his disciples go back to the lives they had led before they followed Jesus. ⁶⁷ So Jesus asked the twelve apostles, "Do you want to leave me too?"

⁶⁸ Simon Peter answered Jesus, "Lord, to what person could we go? Your words give eternal life. ⁶⁹ Besides, we believe and know that you are the Holy One of God."

⁷⁰ Jesus replied, "I chose all twelve of you. Yet, one of you is a devil." ⁷¹ Jesus meant Judas, son of Simon Iscariot. Judas, who was one of the twelve apostles, would later betray Jesus.

Jesus Goes to the Festival of Booths

7 ¹ Jesus later traveled throughout Galilee. He didn't want to travel in Judea because Jews there wanted to kill him.

² The time for the Jewish Festival of Booths was near. ³ So Jesus' brothers told him, "Leave this place, and go to Judea so that your disciples can see the things that you're doing. ⁴ No one does things secretly when he wants to be known publicly. If you do these things, you should let the world see you." ⁵ Even his brothers didn't believe in him.

⁶ Jesus told them, "Now is not the right time for me to go. Any time is right for you. ⁷ The world cannot hate you, but it hates me because I say that what everyone does is evil. ⁸ Go to the festival. I'm not going to this festival right now. Now is not the right time for me to go."

⁹ After saying this, Jesus stayed in Galilee. ¹⁰ But after his brothers had gone to the festival, Jesus went. He didn't go publicly but secretly.

¹¹ The Jews were looking for Jesus in the crowd at the festival. They kept asking, "Where is that man?" ¹² The crowds argued about Jesus. Some people said, "He's a good man," while others said, "No he isn't. He deceives the people." ¹³ Yet, no one would talk openly about him because they were afraid of the Jews.

¹⁴ When the festival was half over, Jesus went to the temple courtyard and began to teach. ¹⁵ The Jews were surprised and asked, "How can this man be so educated when he hasn't gone to school?"

¹⁶ Jesus responded to them, "What I teach doesn't come from me but from the one who sent me. ¹⁷ Those who want to follow the will of God will know if what I teach is from God or if I teach my own thoughts. ¹⁸ Those who speak their own thoughts are looking for their own glory. But the man who wants to bring glory to the one who sent him is a true teacher and doesn't have dishonest motives. ¹⁹ Didn't Moses give you his teachings? Yet, none of you does what Moses taught you. So why do you want to kill me?"

²⁰ The crowd answered, "You're possessed by a demon! Who wants to kill you?"

²¹ Jesus answered them, "I performed one miracle, and all of you are surprised by it. ²² Moses gave you the teaching about circumcision (although it didn't come from Moses but from our ancestors). So you circumcise a male on a day of worship. ²³ If you circumcise a male on the day of worship to follow Moses' Teachings, why are you angry with me because I made a man entirely well on the day of worship? ²⁴ Stop judging by outward appearance! Instead, judge correctly."

²⁵ Some of the people who lived in Jerusalem said, "Isn't this the man they want to kill? ²⁶ But look at this! He's speaking in public, and no one is saying anything to him! Can it be that the rulers really know that this man is the Messiah? ²⁷ However, we know where this man comes from. When the Christ comes, no one will know where he is from."

²⁸ Then, while Jesus was teaching in the temple courtyard, he said loudly, "You know me, and you know where I come from. I didn't decide to come on my own. The one who sent me is true.

He's the one you don't know. ²⁹ I know him because I am from him and he sent me."

³⁰ The Jews tried to arrest him but couldn't because his time had not yet come.

³¹ However, many people in the crowd believed in him. They asked, "When the Messiah comes, will he perform more miracles than this man has?"

³² The Pharisees heard the crowd saying things like this about him. So the chief priests and the Pharisees sent temple guards to arrest Jesus.

³³ Jesus said, "I will still be with you for a little while. Then I'll go to the one who sent me. ³⁴ You will look for me, but you won't find me. You can't go where I'm going."

³⁵ The Jews said among themselves, "Where does this man intend to go so that we won't find him? Does he mean that he'll live with the Jews who are scattered among the Greeks and that he'll teach the Greeks? ³⁶ What does he mean when he says, 'You will look for me, but you won't find me,' and 'You can't go where I'm going'?"

³⁷ On the last and most important day of the festival, Jesus was standing ⌊in the temple courtyard⌋. He said loudly, "Whoever is thirsty must come to me to drink. ³⁸ As Scripture says, 'Streams of living water will flow from deep within the person who believes in me.' " ³⁹ Jesus said this about the Spirit, whom his believers would receive. The Spirit was not yet evident, as it would be after Jesus had been glorified.

⁴⁰ After some of the crowd heard Jesus say these words, they said, "This man is certainly the prophet." ⁴¹ Other people said, "This man is the Messiah." Still other people asked, "How can the Messiah come from Galilee? ⁴² Doesn't Scripture say that the Messiah will come from the descendants of David and from the village of Bethlehem, where David lived?" ⁴³ So the people were divided because of Jesus. ⁴⁴ Some of them wanted to arrest him, but they couldn't.

⁴⁵ When the temple guards returned, the chief priests and Pharisees asked them, "Why didn't you bring Jesus?"

[46] The temple guards answered, "No human has ever spoken like this man."

[47] The Pharisees asked the temple guards, "Have you been deceived too? [48] Has any ruler or any Pharisee believed in him? [49] This crowd is cursed because it doesn't know Moses' Teachings."

[50] One of those Pharisees was Nicodemus, who had previously visited Jesus. Nicodemus asked them, [51] "Do Moses' Teachings enable us to judge a person without first hearing that person's side of the story? We can't judge a person without finding out what that person has done."

[52] They asked Nicodemus, "Are you saying this because you're from Galilee? Study ˌthe Scripturesˌ, and you'll see that no prophet comes from Galilee."[a]

[53] Then each of them went home.

A Woman Caught in Adultery

8 [1] Jesus went to the Mount of Olives. [2] Early the next morning he returned to the temple courtyard. All the people went to him, so he sat down and began to teach them.

[3] The scribes and the Pharisees brought a woman who had been caught committing adultery. They made her stand in front of everyone [4] and asked Jesus, "Teacher, we caught this woman in the act of adultery. [5] In his teachings, Moses ordered us to stone women like this to death. What do you say?" [6] They asked this to test him. They wanted to find a reason to bring charges against him.

Jesus bent down and used his finger to write on the ground. [7] When they persisted in asking him questions, he straightened up and said, "The person who is sinless should be the first to throw a stone at her." [8] Then he bent down again and continued writing on the ground.

[9] One by one, beginning with the older men, the scribes and Pharisees left. Jesus was left alone with the woman. [10] Then Jesus

---

[a] 7:52 John 7:53–8:11 is not found in many manuscripts and some translations. Some manuscripts place these verses between 7:36 and 7:37. Other manuscripts place them between 7:44 and 7:45. Others place them after 21:25, and some place them between Luke 21:38 and 22:1.

straightened up and asked her, "Where did they go? Has anyone condemned you?"

¹¹ The woman answered, "No one, sir."

Jesus said, "I don't condemn you either. Go! From now on don't sin."

Jesus Speaks With the Pharisees About His Father

¹² Jesus spoke to the Pharisees again. He said, "I am the light of the world. Whoever follows me will have a life filled with light and will never live in the dark."

¹³ The Pharisees said to him, "You testify on your own behalf, so your testimony isn't true."

¹⁴ Jesus replied to them, "Even if I testify on my own behalf, my testimony is true because I know where I came from and where I'm going. However, you don't know where I came from or where I'm going. ¹⁵ You judge the way humans do. I don't judge anyone. ¹⁶ Even if I do judge, my judgment is valid because I don't make it on my own. I make my judgment with the Father who sent me. ¹⁷ Your own teachings say that the testimony of two people is true. ¹⁸ I testify on my own behalf, and so does the Father who sent me."

¹⁹ The Pharisees asked him, "Where is your father?"

Jesus replied, "You don't know me or my Father. If you knew me, you would also know my Father."

²⁰ Jesus spoke these words while he was teaching in the treasury area of the temple courtyard. No one arrested him, because his time had not yet come.

²¹ Jesus spoke to the Pharisees again. He said, "I'm going away, and you'll look for me. But you will die because of your sin. You can't go where I'm going."

²² Then the Jews asked, "Is he going to kill himself? Is that what he means when he says, 'You can't go where I'm going'?"

²³ Jesus said to them, "You're from below. I'm from above. You're from this world. I'm not from this world. ²⁴ For this reason I told you that you'll die because of your sins. If you don't believe that I am the one, you'll die because of your sins."

25 The Jews asked him, "Who did you say you are?"

Jesus told them, "I am who I said I was from the beginning. **26** I have a lot I could say about you and a lot I could condemn you for. But the one who sent me is true. So I tell the world exactly what he has told me." **27** (The Jews didn't know that he was talking to them about the Father.)

28 So Jesus told them, "When you have lifted up the Son of Man, then you'll know that I am the one and that I can't do anything on my own. Instead, I speak as the Father taught me. **29** Besides, the one who sent me is with me. He hasn't left me by myself. I always do what pleases him."

30 As Jesus was saying this, many people believed in him. **31** So Jesus said to those Jews who believed in him, "If you live by what I say, you are truly my disciples. **32** You will know the truth, and the truth will set you free."

33 They replied to Jesus, "We are Abraham's descendants, and we've never been anyone's slaves. So how can you say that we will be set free?"

34 Jesus answered them, "I can guarantee this truth: Whoever lives a sinful life is a slave to sin. **35** A slave doesn't live in the home forever, but a son does. **36** So if the Son sets you free, you will be absolutely free. **37** I know that you're Abraham's descendants. However, you want to kill me because you don't like what I'm saying. **38** What I'm saying is what I have seen in my Father's presence. But you do what you've heard from your father."

39 The Jews replied to Jesus, "Abraham is our father."

Jesus told them, "If you were Abraham's children, you would do what Abraham did. **40** I am a man who has told you the truth that I heard from God. But now you want to kill me. Abraham wouldn't have done that. **41** You're doing what your father does."

The Jews said to Jesus, "We're not illegitimate children. God is our only Father."

42 Jesus told them, "If God were your Father, you would love me. After all, I'm here, and I came from God. I didn't come on my own. Instead, God sent me. **43** Why don't you understand the language

I use? Is it because you can't understand the words I use? [44] You come from your father, the devil, and you desire to do what your father wants you to do. The devil was a murderer from the beginning. He has never been truthful. He doesn't know what the truth is. Whenever he tells a lie, he's doing what comes naturally to him. He's a liar and the father of lies. [45] So you don't believe me because I tell the truth. [46] Can any of you convict me of committing a sin? If I'm telling the truth, why don't you believe me? [47] The person who belongs to God understands what God says. You don't understand because you don't belong to God."

[48] The Jews replied to Jesus, "Aren't we right when we say that you're a Samaritan and that you're possessed by a demon?"

[49] Jesus answered, "I'm not possessed. I honor my Father, but you dishonor me. [50] I don't want my own glory. But there is someone who wants it, and he is the judge. [51] I can guarantee this truth: Whoever obeys what I say will never see death."

[52] The Jews told Jesus, "Now we know that you're possessed by a demon. Abraham died, and so did the prophets, but you say, 'Whoever does what I say will never taste death.' [53] Are you greater than our father Abraham, who died? The prophets have also died. Who do you think you are?"

[54] Jesus said, "If I bring glory to myself, my glory is nothing. My Father is the one who gives me glory, and you say that he is your God. [55] Yet, you haven't known him. However, I know him. If I would say that I didn't know him, I would be a liar like all of you. But I do know him, and I do what he says. [56] Your father Abraham was pleased to see that my day was coming. He saw it and was happy."

[57] The Jews said to Jesus, "You're not even fifty years old. How could you have seen Abraham?"

[58] Jesus told them, "I can guarantee this truth: Before Abraham was ever born, I am."

[59] Then some of the Jews picked up stones to throw at Jesus. However, Jesus was concealed, and he left the temple courtyard.

Jesus Gives Sight to a Blind Man

9 [1] As Jesus walked along, he saw a man who had been born blind. [2] His disciples asked him, "Rabbi, why was this man born blind? Did he or his parents sin?"

[3] Jesus answered, "Neither this man nor his parents sinned. Instead, he was born blind so that God could show what he can do for him. [4] We must do what the one who sent me wants us to do while it is day. The night when no one can do anything is coming. [5] As long as I'm in the world, I'm light for the world."

[6] After Jesus said this, he spit on the ground and mixed the spit with dirt. Then he smeared it on the man's eyes [7] and told him, "Wash it off in the pool of Siloam." (*Siloam* means "sent.") The blind man washed it off and returned. He was able to see.

[8] His neighbors and those who had previously seen him begging asked, "Isn't this the man who used to sit and beg?"

[9] Some of them said, "He's the one." Others said, "No, he isn't, but he looks like him." But the man himself said, "I am the one."

[10] So they asked him, "How did you receive your sight?"

[11] He replied, "The man people call Jesus mixed some spit with dirt, smeared it on my eyes, and told me, 'Go to Siloam, and wash it off.' So I went there, washed it off, and received my sight."

[12] They asked him, "Where is that man?"

The man answered, "I don't know."

[13] Some people brought the man who had been blind to the Pharisees. [14] The day when Jesus mixed the spit and dirt and gave the man sight was a day of worship. [15] So the Pharisees asked the man again how he received his sight.

The man told the Pharisees, "He put a mixture of spit and dirt on my eyes. I washed it off, and now I can see."

[16] Some of the Pharisees said, "The man who did this is not from God because he doesn't follow the traditions for the day of worship." Other Pharisees asked, "How can a man who is a sinner perform miracles like these?" So the Pharisees were divided in their opinions.

[17] They asked the man who had been born blind another question: "What do you say about the man who gave you sight?"

The man answered, "He's a prophet."

[18] Until they talked to the man's parents, the Jews didn't believe that the man had been blind and had been given sight. [19] They asked his parents, "Is this your son, the one you say was born blind? Why can he see now?"

[20] His parents replied, "We know that he's our son and that he was born blind. [21] But we don't know how he got his sight or who gave it to him. You'll have to ask him. He's old enough to answer for himself." [22] (His parents said this because they were afraid of the Jews. The Jews had already agreed to put anyone who acknowledged that Jesus was the Christ out of the synagogue. [23] That's why his parents said, "You'll have to ask him. He's old enough.")

[24] So once again the Jews called the man who had been blind. They told him, "Give glory to God. We know that this man who gave you sight is a sinner."

[25] The man responded, "I don't know if he's a sinner or not. But I do know one thing. I used to be blind, but now I can see."

[26] The Jews asked him, "What did he do to you? How did he give you sight?"

[27] The man replied, "I've already told you, but you didn't listen. Why do you want to hear the story again? Do you want to become his disciples too?"

[28] The Jews yelled at him, "You're his disciple, but we're Moses' disciples. [29] We know that God spoke to Moses, but we don't know where this man came from."

[30] The man replied to them, "That's amazing! You don't know where he's from. Yet, he gave me sight. [31] We know that God doesn't listen to sinners. Instead, he listens to people who are devout and who do what he wants. [32] Since the beginning of time, no one has ever heard of anyone giving sight to a person born blind. [33] If this man were not from God, he couldn't do anything like that."

[34] The Jews answered him, "You were born full of sin. Do you think you can teach us?" Then they threw him out ˌof the synagogue˳.

³⁵ Jesus heard that the Jews had thrown the man out ⌐of the synagogue⌐. So when Jesus found the man, he asked him, "Do you believe in the Son of Man?"

³⁶ The man replied, "Sir, tell me who he is so that I can believe in him."

³⁷ Jesus told him, "You've seen him. He is the person who is now talking with you."

³⁸ The man bowed in front of Jesus and said, "I believe, Lord."

³⁹ Then Jesus said, "I have come into this world to judge: Blind people will be given sight, and those who can see will become blind."

⁴⁰ Some Pharisees who were with Jesus heard this. So they asked him, "Do you think we're blind?"

⁴¹ Jesus told them, "If you were blind, you wouldn't be sinners. But now you say, 'We see,' so you continue to be sinners.

Jesus, the Good Shepherd

10 ¹ "I can guarantee this truth: The person who doesn't enter the sheep pen through the gate but climbs in somewhere else is a thief or a robber. ² But the one who enters through the gate is the shepherd. ³ The gatekeeper opens the gate for him, and the sheep respond to his voice. He calls his sheep by name and leads them out of the pen. ⁴ After he has brought out all his sheep, he walks ahead of them. The sheep follow him because they recognize his voice. ⁵ They won't follow a stranger. Instead, they will run away from a stranger because they don't recognize his voice." ⁶ Jesus used this illustration as he talked to the people, but they didn't understand what he meant.

⁷ Jesus emphasized, "I can guarantee this truth: I am the gate for the sheep. ⁸ All who came before I did were thieves or robbers. However, the sheep didn't respond to them. ⁹ I am the gate. Those who enter the sheep pen through me will be saved. They will go in and out of the sheep pen and find food. ¹⁰ A thief comes to steal, kill, and destroy. But I came so that my sheep will have life and so that they will have everything they need.

¹¹ "I am the good shepherd. The good shepherd gives his life for the sheep. ¹² A hired hand isn't a shepherd and doesn't own the

sheep. When he sees a wolf coming, he abandons the sheep and quickly runs away. So the wolf drags the sheep away and scatters the flock. ¹³ The hired hand is concerned about what he's going to get paid and not about the sheep.

¹⁴ "I am the good shepherd. I know my sheep as the Father knows me.ᵃ My sheep know me as I know the Father. ¹⁵ So I give my life for my sheep. ¹⁶ I also have other sheep that are not from this pen. I must lead them. They, too, will respond to my voice. So they will be one flock with one shepherd. ¹⁷ The Father loves me because I give my life in order to take it back again. ¹⁸ No one takes my life from me. I give my life of my own free will. I have the authority to give my life, and I have the authority to take my life back again. This is what my Father ordered me to do."

¹⁹ The Jews were divided because of what Jesus said. ²⁰ Many of them said, "He's possessed by a demon! He's crazy! Why do you listen to him?" ²¹ Others said, "No one talks like this if he's possessed by a demon. Can a demon give sight to the blind?"

The Jews Reject Jesus

²² The Festival of the Dedication of the Temple took place in Jerusalem during the winter. ²³ Jesus was walking on Solomon's porch in the temple courtyard.

²⁴ The Jews surrounded him. They asked him, "How long will you keep us in suspense? If you are the Messiah, tell us plainly."

²⁵ Jesus answered them, "I've told you, but you don't believe me. The things that I do in my Father's name testify on my behalf. ²⁶ However, you don't believe because you're not my sheep. ²⁷ My sheep respond to my voice, and I know who they are. They follow me, ²⁸ and I give them eternal life. They will never be lost, and no one will tear them away from me. ²⁹ My Father, who gave them to me, is greater than everyone else, and no one can tear them away from my Father. ³⁰ The Father and I are one."

ᵃ 10:14 The first part of verse 15 (in Greek) has been moved to verse 14 to express the complex Greek sentence structure more clearly in English.

³¹ The Jews had again brought some rocks to stone Jesus to death. ³² Jesus replied to them, "I've shown you many good things that come from the Father. For which of these good things do you want to stone me to death?"

³³ The Jews answered Jesus, "We're going to stone you to death, not for any good things you've done, but for dishonoring God. You claim to be God, although you're only a man."

³⁴ Jesus said to them, "Don't your Scriptures say, 'I said, "You are gods" '? ³⁵ The Scriptures cannot be discredited. So if God calls people gods (and they are the people to whom he gave the Scriptures), ³⁶ why do you say that I'm dishonoring God because I said, 'I'm the Son of God'? God set me apart for this holy purpose and has sent me into the world. ³⁷ If I'm not doing the things my Father does, don't believe me. ³⁸ But if I'm doing those things and you refuse to believe me, then at least believe the things that I'm doing. Then you will know and recognize that the Father is in me and that I am in the Father."

³⁹ The Jews tried to arrest Jesus again, but he got away from them. ⁴⁰ He went back across the Jordan River and stayed in the place where John first baptized people.

⁴¹ Many people went to Jesus. They said, "John didn't perform any miracles, but everything John said about this man is true." ⁴² Many people there believed in Jesus.

Jesus Brings Lazarus Back to Life

11 ¹ Lazarus, who lived in Bethany, the village where Mary and her sister Martha lived, was sick. ² (Mary was the woman who poured perfume on the Lord and wiped his feet with her hair. Her brother Lazarus was the one who was sick.)

³ So the sisters sent a messenger to tell Jesus, "Lord, your close friend is sick."

⁴ When Jesus heard the message, he said, "His sickness won't result in death. Instead, this sickness will bring glory to God so that the Son of God will receive glory through it."

⁵ Jesus loved Martha, her sister, and Lazarus. ⁶ Yet, when Jesus heard that Lazarus was sick, he stayed where he was for two more days.

⁷ Then, after the two days, Jesus said to his disciples, "Let's go back to Judea."

⁸ The disciples said to him, "Rabbi, not long ago the Jews wanted to stone you to death. Do you really want to go back there?"

⁹ Jesus answered, "Aren't there twelve hours of daylight? Those who walk during the day don't stumble, because they see the light of this world. ¹⁰ However, those who walk at night stumble because they have no light in themselves."

¹¹ After Jesus said this, he told his disciples, "Our friend Lazarus is sleeping, and I'm going to Bethany to wake him."

¹² His disciples said to him, "Lord, if he's sleeping, he'll get well."

¹³ Jesus meant that Lazarus was dead, but the disciples thought Jesus meant that Lazarus was only sleeping. ¹⁴ Then Jesus told them plainly, "Lazarus has died, ¹⁵ but I'm glad that I wasn't there so that you can grow in faith. Let's go to Lazarus."

¹⁶ Thomas, who was called Didymus, said to the rest of the disciples, "Let's go so that we, too, can die with Jesus."

¹⁷ When Jesus arrived, he found that Lazarus had been in the tomb for four days. ¹⁸ (Bethany was near Jerusalem, not quite two miles away.) ¹⁹ Many Jews had come to Martha and Mary to comfort them about their brother.

²⁰ When Martha heard that Jesus was coming, she went to meet him. Mary stayed at home. ²¹ Martha told Jesus, "Lord, if you had been here, my brother would not have died. ²² But even now I know that God will give you whatever you ask him."

²³ Jesus told Martha, "Your brother will come back to life."

²⁴ Martha answered Jesus, "I know that he'll come back to life on the last day, when everyone will come back to life."

²⁵ Jesus said to her, "I am the one who brings people back to life, and I am life itself. Those who believe in me will live even if they die. ²⁶ Everyone who lives and believes in me will never die. Do you believe that?"

²⁷ Martha said to him, "Yes, Lord, I believe that you are the Messiah, the Son of God, the one who was expected to come into the world."

²⁸ After Martha had said this, she went back home and whispered to her sister Mary, "The teacher is here, and he is calling for you."

²⁹ When Mary heard this, she got up quickly and went to Jesus. ³⁰ (Jesus had not yet come into the village but was still where Martha had met him.) ³¹ The Jews who were comforting Mary in the house saw her get up quickly and leave. So they followed her. They thought that she was going to the tomb to cry. ³² When Mary arrived where Jesus was and saw him, she knelt at his feet and said, "Lord, if you had been here, my brother would not have died."

³³ When Jesus saw her crying, and the Jews who were crying with her, he was deeply moved and troubled.

³⁴ So Jesus asked, "Where did you put Lazarus?"

They answered him, "Lord, come and see."

³⁵ Jesus cried. ³⁶ The Jews said, "See how much Jesus loved him." ³⁷ But some of the Jews asked, "Couldn't this man who gave a blind man sight keep Lazarus from dying?"

³⁸ Deeply moved again, Jesus went to the tomb. It was a cave with a stone covering the entrance. ³⁹ Jesus said, "Take the stone away."

Martha, the dead man's sister, told Jesus, "Lord, there must already be a stench. He's been dead for four days."

⁴⁰ Jesus said to her, "Didn't I tell you that if you believe, you would see God's glory?" ⁴¹ So the stone was moved away from the entrance of the tomb.

Jesus looked up and said, "Father, I thank you for hearing me. ⁴² I've known that you always hear me. However, I've said this so that the crowd standing around me will believe that you sent me." ⁴³ After Jesus had said this, he shouted as loudly as he could, "Lazarus, come out!"

⁴⁴ The dead man came out. Strips of cloth were wound around his feet and hands, and his face was wrapped with a handkerchief. Jesus told them, "Free Lazarus, and let him go."

The Jewish Council Plans to Kill Jesus

⁴⁵ Many Jews who had visited Mary and had seen what Jesus had done believed in him. ⁴⁶ But some of them went to the Pharisees and told them what Jesus had done. ⁴⁷ So the chief priests and the Pharisees called a meeting of the council. They asked, "What are we doing? This man is performing a lot of miracles. ⁴⁸ If we let him continue what he's doing, everyone will believe in him. Then the Romans will take away our position and our nation."

⁴⁹ One of them, Caiaphas, who was chief priest that year, told them, "You people don't know anything. ⁵⁰ You haven't even considered this: It is better for one man to die for the people than for the whole nation to be destroyed."

⁵¹ Caiaphas didn't say this on his own. As chief priest that year, he prophesied that Jesus would die for the Jewish nation. ⁵² He prophesied that Jesus wouldn't die merely for this nation, but that Jesus would die to bring God's scattered children together and make them one.

⁵³ From that day on, the Jewish council planned to kill Jesus. ⁵⁴ So Jesus no longer walked openly among the Jews. Instead, he left Bethany and went to the countryside near the desert, to a city called Ephraim, where he stayed with his disciples.

⁵⁵ The Jewish Passover was near. Many people came from the countryside to Jerusalem to purify themselves before the Passover. ⁵⁶ As they stood in the temple courtyard, they looked for Jesus and asked each other, "Do you think that he'll avoid coming to the festival?" ⁵⁷ (The chief priests and the Pharisees had given orders that whoever knew where Jesus was should tell them so that they could arrest him.)

Mary Prepares Jesus' Body for the Tomb—
Matthew 26:6–13; Mark 14:3–9

12 ¹ Six days before Passover, Jesus arrived in Bethany. Lazarus, whom Jesus had brought back to life, lived there. ² Dinner was prepared for Jesus in Bethany. Martha served the dinner, and Lazarus was one of the people eating with Jesus.

³ Mary took a bottle of very expensive perfume made from pure nard and poured it on Jesus' feet. Then she dried his feet with her hair. The fragrance of the perfume filled the house.

⁴ One of his disciples, Judas Iscariot, who was going to betray him, asked, ⁵ "Why wasn't this perfume sold for a high price and the money given to the poor?" ⁶ (Judas didn't say this because he cared about the poor but because he was a thief. He was in charge of the moneybag and carried the contributions.) ⁷ Jesus said to Judas, "Leave her alone! She has done this to prepare me for the day I will be placed in a tomb. ⁸ You will always have the poor with you, but you will not always have me with you."

⁹ A large crowd of Jews found out that Jesus was in Bethany. So they went there not only to see Jesus but also to see Lazarus, whom Jesus had brought back to life. ¹⁰ The chief priests planned to kill Lazarus too. ¹¹ Lazarus was the reason why many people were leaving the Jews and believing in Jesus.

The King Comes to Jerusalem—
Matthew 21:1–11; Mark 11:1–11; Luke 19:29–44

¹² On the next day the large crowd that had come to the Passover festival heard that Jesus was coming to Jerusalem. ¹³ So they took palm branches and went to meet him. They were shouting,

> "Hosanna!
>   Blessed is the one who comes in the name of the Lord,
>   the king of Israel!"

¹⁴ Jesus obtained a donkey and sat on it, as Scripture says:

> ¹⁵   "Don't be afraid, people of Zion!
>   Your king is coming.
>   He is riding on a donkey's colt."

¹⁶ At first Jesus' disciples didn't know what these prophecies meant. However, when Jesus was glorified, the disciples remembered that these prophecies had been written about him. The disciples remembered that they had taken part in fulfilling the prophecies.

¹⁷ The people who had been with Jesus when he called Lazarus from the tomb and brought him back to life reported what they had seen. ¹⁸ Because the crowd heard that Jesus had performed this miracle, they came to meet him.

¹⁹ The Pharisees said to each other, "This is getting us nowhere. Look! The whole world is following him!"

Some Greeks Ask to See Jesus

²⁰ Some Greeks were among those who came to worship during the Passover festival. ²¹ They went to Philip (who was from Bethsaida in Galilee) and told him, "Sir, we would like to meet Jesus." ²² Philip told Andrew, and they told Jesus.

²³ Jesus replied to them, "The time has come for the Son of Man to be glorified. ²⁴ I can guarantee this truth: A single grain of wheat doesn't produce anything unless it is planted in the ground and dies. If it dies, it will produce a lot of grain. ²⁵ Those who love their lives will destroy them, and those who hate their lives in this world will guard them for everlasting life. ²⁶ Those who serve me must follow me. My servants will be with me wherever I will be. If people serve me, the Father will honor them.

²⁷ "I am too deeply troubled now to know how to express my feelings. Should I say, 'Father, save me from this time ˻of suffering˼'? No! I came for this time of suffering. ²⁸ Father, give glory to your name."

A voice from heaven said, "I have given it glory, and I will give it glory again."

²⁹ The crowd standing there heard the voice and said that it had thundered. Others in the crowd said that an angel had talked to him. ³⁰ Jesus replied, "That voice wasn't for my benefit but for yours.

³¹ "This world is being judged now. The ruler of this world will be thrown out now. ³² When I have been lifted up from the earth, I will draw all people toward me." ³³ By saying this, he indicated how he was going to die.

³⁴ The crowd responded to him, "We have heard from the Scriptures that the Messiah will remain here forever. So how can

you say, 'The Son of Man must be lifted up from the earth'? Who is this 'Son of Man'?"

³⁵ Jesus answered the crowd, "The light will still be with you for a little while. Walk while you have light so that darkness won't defeat you. Those who walk in the dark don't know where they're going. ³⁶ While you have the light, believe in the light so that you will become people whose lives show the light."

After Jesus had said this, he was concealed as he left. ³⁷ Although they had seen Jesus perform so many miracles, they wouldn't believe in him. ³⁸ In this way the words of the prophet Isaiah came true:

> "Lord, who has believed our message?
> To whom has the Lord's power been revealed?"

³⁹ So the people couldn't believe because, as Isaiah also said,

> ⁴⁰ "God blinded them
> and made them close-minded
> so that their eyes don't see
> and their minds don't understand.
> And they never turn to me for healing!"

⁴¹ Isaiah said this because he had seen Jesus' glory and had spoken about him.

⁴² Many rulers believed in Jesus. However, they wouldn't admit it publicly because the Pharisees would have thrown them out of the synagogue. ⁴³ They were more concerned about what people thought of them than about what God thought of them.

⁴⁴ Then Jesus said loudly, "Whoever believes in me believes not only in me but also in the one who sent me. ⁴⁵ Whoever sees me sees the one who sent me. ⁴⁶ I am the light that has come into the world so that everyone who believes in me will not live in the dark. ⁴⁷ If anyone hears my words and doesn't follow them, I don't condemn them. I didn't come to condemn the world but to save the world. ⁴⁸ Those who reject me by not accepting what I say have a judge appointed for them. The words that I have spoken will judge

them on the last day. [49] I have not spoken on my own. Instead, the Father who sent me told me what I should say and how I should say it. [50] I know that what he commands is eternal life. Whatever I say is what the Father told me to say."

Jesus Washes the Disciples' Feet

13 [1] Before the Passover festival, Jesus knew that the time had come for him to leave this world and go back to the Father. Jesus loved his own who were in the world, and he loved them to the end.

[2] While supper was taking place, the devil had already put the idea of betraying Jesus into the mind of Judas, son of Simon Iscariot.

[3] The Father had put everything in Jesus' control. Jesus knew that. He also knew that he had come from God and was going back to God. [4] So he got up from the table, removed his outer clothes, took a towel, and tied it around his waist. [5] Then he poured water into a basin and began to wash the disciples' feet and dry them with the towel that he had tied around his waist.

[6] When Jesus came to Simon Peter, Peter asked him, "Lord, are you going to wash my feet?"

[7] Jesus answered Peter, "You don't know now what I'm doing. You will understand later."

[8] Peter told Jesus, "You will never wash my feet."

Jesus replied to Peter, "If I don't wash you, you don't belong to me."

[9] Simon Peter said to Jesus, "Lord, don't wash only my feet. Wash my hands and my head too!"

[10] Jesus told Peter, "People who have washed are completely clean. They need to have only their feet washed. All of you, except for one, are clean." [11] (Jesus knew who was going to betray him. That's why he said, "All of you, except for one, are clean.")

[12] After Jesus had washed their feet and put on his outer clothes, he took his place at the table again. Then he asked his disciples, "Do you understand what I've done for you? [13] You call me teacher and Lord, and you're right because that's what I am. [14] So if I, your Lord

and teacher, have washed your feet, you must wash each other's feet. **15** I've given you an example that you should follow. **16** I can guarantee this truth: Slaves are not superior to their owners, and messengers are not superior to the people who send them. **17** If you understand all of this, you are blessed whenever you follow my example.

18 "I'm not talking about all of you. I know the people I've chosen ⌊to be apostles⌋. However, I've made my choice so that Scripture will come true. It says, 'The one who eats my bread has turned against me.' **19** I'm telling you now before it happens. Then, when it happens, you will believe that I am the one.

20 "I can guarantee this truth: Whoever accepts me accepts the one who sent me."

Jesus Knows Who Will Betray Him—
Matthew 26:21–25; Mark 14:18–21; Luke 22:21–23

21 After saying this, Jesus was deeply troubled. He declared, "I can guarantee this truth: One of you is going to betray me!"

22 The disciples began looking at each other and wondering which one of them Jesus meant.

23 One disciple, the one whom Jesus loved, was near him at the table. **24** Simon Peter motioned to that disciple and said, "Ask Jesus whom he's talking about!"

25 Leaning close to Jesus, that disciple asked, "Lord, who is it?"

26 Jesus answered, "He's the one to whom I will give this piece of bread after I've dipped it in the sauce." So Jesus dipped the bread and gave it to Judas, son of Simon Iscariot.

27 Then, after Judas took the piece of bread, Satan entered him. So Jesus told him, "Hurry! Do what you have to do." **28** No one at the table knew why Jesus said this to him. **29** Judas had the money-bag. So some thought that Jesus was telling him to buy what they needed for the festival or to give something to the poor.

30 Judas took the piece of bread and immediately went outside. It was night.

31 When Judas was gone, Jesus said, "The Son of Man is now glorified, and because of him God is glorified. **32** If God is glori-

fied because of the Son of Man, God will glorify the Son of Man
because of himself, and he will glorify the Son of Man at once."

Jesus Predicts Peter's Denial—
Matthew 26:31–35; Mark 14:27–31; Luke 22:31–34

[33] Jesus said, "Dear children, I will still be with you for a little
while. I'm telling you what I told the Jews. You will look for me, but
you can't go where I'm going.

[34] "I'm giving you a new commandment: Love each other in the
same way that I have loved you. [35] Everyone will know that you are
my disciples because of your love for each other."

[36] Simon Peter asked him, "Lord, where are you going?"

Jesus answered him, "You can't follow me now to the place
where I'm going. However, you will follow me later."

[37] Peter said to Jesus, "Lord, why can't I follow you now? I'll give
my life for you."

[38] Jesus replied, "Will you give your life for me? I can guarantee
this truth: No rooster will crow until you say three times that you
don't know me.

Jesus Promises to Send the Holy Spirit

14 [1] "Don't be troubled. Believe in God, and believe in me. [2] My
Father's house has many rooms. If that were not true,
would I have told you that I'm going to prepare a place for you? [3] If
I go to prepare a place for you, I will come again. Then I will bring
you into my presence so that you will be where I am. [4] You know
the way to the place where I am going."

[5] Thomas said to him, "Lord, we don't know where you're going.
So how can we know the way?"

[6] Jesus answered him, "I am the way, the truth, and the life. No
one goes to the Father except through me. [7] If you have known
me, you will also know my Father. From now on you know him
‚through me‚ and have seen him ‚in me‚."

[8] Philip said to Jesus, "Lord, show us the Father, and that will
satisfy us."

⁹ Jesus replied, "I have been with all of you for a long time. Don't you know me yet, Philip? The person who has seen me has seen the Father. So how can you say, 'Show us the Father'? ¹⁰ Don't you believe that I am in the Father and the Father is in me? What I'm telling you doesn't come from me. The Father, who lives in me, does what he wants. ¹¹ Believe me when I say that I am in the Father and that the Father is in me. Otherwise, believe me because of the things I do.

¹² "I can guarantee this truth: Those who believe in me will do the things that I am doing. They will do even greater things because I am going to the Father. ¹³ I will do anything you ask ˌthe Fatherˌ in my name so that the Father will be given glory because of the Son. ¹⁴ If you ask me to do something, I will do it.

¹⁵ "If you love me, you will obey my commandments. ¹⁶ I will ask the Father, and he will give you another helper who will be with you forever. ¹⁷ That helper is the Spirit of Truth. The world cannot accept him, because it doesn't see or know him. You know him, because he lives with you and will be in you.

¹⁸ "I will not leave you all alone. I will come back to you. ¹⁹ In a little while the world will no longer see me, but you will see me. You will live because I live. ²⁰ On that day you will know that I am in my Father and that you are in me and that I am in you. ²¹ Whoever knows and obeys my commandments is the person who loves me. Those who love me will have my Father's love, and I, too, will love them and show myself to them."

²² Judas (not Iscariot) asked Jesus, "Lord, what has happened that you are going to reveal yourself to us and not to the world?"

²³ Jesus answered him, "Those who love me will do what I say. My Father will love them, and we will go to them and make our home with them. ²⁴ A person who doesn't love me doesn't do what I say. I don't make up what you hear me say. What I say comes from the Father who sent me.

²⁵ "I have told you this while I'm still with you. ²⁶ However, the helper, the Holy Spirit, whom the Father will send in my name, will teach you everything. He will remind you of everything that I have ever told you.

²⁷ "I'm leaving you peace. I'm giving you my peace. I don't give you the kind of peace that the world gives. So don't be troubled or cowardly. ²⁸ You heard me tell you, 'I'm going away, but I'm coming back to you.' If you loved me, you would be glad that I'm going to the Father, because the Father is greater than I am.

²⁹ "I'm telling you this now before it happens. When it does happen, you will believe. ³⁰ The ruler of this world has no power over me. But he's coming, so I won't talk with you much longer. ³¹ However, I want the world to know that I love the Father and that I am doing exactly what the Father has commanded me to do. Get up! We have to leave."

Jesus, the True Vine

15 ¹ ‚Then Jesus said,‚ "I am the true vine, and my Father takes care of the vineyard. ² He removes every one of my branches that doesn't produce fruit. He also prunes every branch that does produce fruit to make it produce more fruit.

³ "You are already clean^a because of what I have told you. ⁴ Live in me, and I will live in you. A branch cannot produce any fruit by itself. It has to stay attached to the vine. In the same way, you cannot produce fruit unless you live in me.

⁵ "I am the vine. You are the branches. Those who live in me while I live in them will produce a lot of fruit. But you can't produce anything without me. ⁶ Whoever doesn't live in me is thrown away like a branch and dries up. Branches like this are gathered, thrown into a fire, and burned. ⁷ If you live in me and what I say lives in you, then ask for anything you want, and it will be yours. ⁸ You give glory to my Father when you produce a lot of fruit and therefore show that you are my disciples.

⁹ "I have loved you the same way the Father has loved me. So live in my love. ¹⁰ If you obey my commandments, you will live in my love. I have obeyed my Father's commandments, and in that way I live in his love. ¹¹ I have told you this so that you will be as joyful as I am, and your joy will be complete. ¹² Love each other as I have loved you. This is what I'm commanding you to do. ¹³ The greatest

^a 15:3 "Clean" refers to anything that Moses' Teachings say is presentable to God.

love you can show is to give your life for your friends. ¹⁴ You are my friends if you obey my commandments. ¹⁵ I don't call you servants anymore, because a servant doesn't know what his master is doing. But I've called you friends because I've made known to you everything that I've heard from my Father. ¹⁶ You didn't choose me, but I chose you. I have appointed you to go, to produce fruit that will last, and to ask the Father in my name to give you whatever you ask for. ¹⁷ Love each other. This is what I'm commanding you to do.

¹⁸ "If the world hates you, realize that it hated me before it hated you. ¹⁹ If you had anything in common with the world, the world would love you as one of its own. But you don't have anything in common with the world. I chose you from the world, and that's why the world hates you. ²⁰ Remember what I told you: 'A servant isn't greater than his master.' If they persecuted me, they will also persecute you. If they did what I said, they will also do what you say. ²¹ Indeed, they will do all this to you because you are committed to me, since they don't know the one who sent me. ²² If I hadn't come and spoken to them, they wouldn't have any sin. But now they have no excuse for their sin. ²³ The person who hates me also hates my Father. ²⁴ If I hadn't done among them what no one else has done, they wouldn't have any sin. But now they have seen and hated both me and my Father. ²⁵ In this way what is written in their Scriptures has come true: 'They hate me for no reason.'

²⁶ "The helper whom I will send to you from the Father will come. This helper, the Spirit of Truth who comes from the Father, will declare the truth about me. ²⁷ You will declare the truth, too, because you have been with me from the beginning."

Sadness Will Turn to Joy

16 ¹ Jesus continued, "I have said these things to you so that you won't lose your faith. ² You will be thrown out of synagogues. Certainly, the time is coming when people who murder you will think that they are serving God. ³ They will do these things to you because they haven't known the Father or me. ⁴ But I've told you this so that when it happens you'll remember what I've told you. I didn't tell you this at first, because I was with you.

⁵ "Now I'm going to the one who sent me. Yet, none of you asks me where I'm going. ⁶ But because I've told you this, you're filled with sadness. ⁷ However, I am telling you the truth: It's good for you that I'm going away. If I don't go away, the helper won't come to you. But if I go, I will send him to you. ⁸ He will come to convict the world of sin, to show the world what has God's approval, and to convince the world that God judges it. ⁹ He will convict the world of sin, because people don't believe in me. ¹⁰ He will show the world what has God's approval, because I'm going to the Father and you won't see me anymore. ¹¹ He will convince the world that God judges it, because the ruler of this world has been judged.

¹² "I have a lot more to tell you, but that would be too much for you now. ¹³ When the Spirit of Truth comes, he will guide you into the full truth. He won't speak on his own. He will speak what he hears and will tell you about things to come. ¹⁴ He will give me glory, because he will tell you what I say. ¹⁵ Everything the Father says is also what I say. That is why I said, 'He will take what I say and tell it to you.'

¹⁶ "In a little while you won't see me anymore. Then in a little while you will see me again."

¹⁷ Some of his disciples said to each other, "What does he mean? He tells us that in a little while we won't see him. Then he tells us that in a little while we will see him again and that he's going to the Father." ¹⁸ So they were asking each other, "What does he mean when he says, 'In a little while'? We don't understand what he's talking about."

¹⁹ Jesus knew they wanted to ask him something. So he said to them, "Are you trying to figure out among yourselves what I meant when I said, 'In a little while you won't see me, and in a little while you will see me again'? ²⁰ I can guarantee this truth: You will cry because you are sad, but the world will be happy. You will feel pain, but your pain will turn to happiness. ²¹ A woman has pain when her time to give birth comes. But after the child is born, she doesn't remember the pain anymore because she's happy that a child has been brought into the world.

²² "Now you're in a painful situation. But I will see you again. Then you will be happy, and no one will take that happiness away

from you. ²³ When that day comes, you won't ask me any more questions. I can guarantee this truth: If you ask the Father for anything in my name, he will give it to you. ²⁴ So far you haven't asked for anything in my name. Ask and you will receive so that you can be completely happy.

²⁵ "I have used examples to illustrate these things. The time is coming when I won't use examples to speak to you. Rather, I will speak to you about the Father in plain words. ²⁶ When that day comes, you will ask for what you want in my name. I'm telling you that I won't have to ask the Father for you. ²⁷ The Father loves you because you have loved me and have believed that I came from God. ²⁸ I left the Father and came into the world. Again, as I've said, I'm going to leave the world and go back to the Father."

²⁹ His disciples said, "Now you're talking in plain words and not using examples. ³⁰ Now we know that you know everything. You don't need to wait for questions to be asked. Because of this, we believe that you have come from God."

³¹ Jesus replied to them, "Now you believe. ³² The time is coming, and is already here, when all of you will be scattered. Each of you will go your own way and leave me all alone. Yet, I'm not all alone, because the Father is with me. ³³ I've told you this so that my peace will be with you. In the world you'll have trouble. But cheer up! I have overcome the world."

Jesus Prays for Himself, His Disciples, and His Church

17 ¹ After saying this, Jesus looked up to heaven and said, "Father, the time is here. Give your Son glory so that your Son can give you glory. ² After all, you've given him authority over all humanity so that he can give eternal life to all those you gave to him. ³ This is eternal life: to know you, the only true God, and Jesus Christ, whom you sent. ⁴ On earth I have given you glory by finishing the work you gave me to do. ⁵ Now, Father, give me glory in your presence with the glory I had with you before the world existed.

⁶ "I made your name known to the people you gave me. They are from this world. They belonged to you, and you gave them to me. They did what you told them. ⁷ Now they know that everything you

gave me comes from you, [8] because I gave them the message that you gave me. They have accepted this message, and they know for sure that I came from you. They have believed that you sent me.

[9] "I pray for them. I'm not praying for the world but for those you gave me, because they are yours. [10] Everything I have is yours, and everything you have is mine. I have been given glory by the people you have given me. [11] I won't be in the world much longer, but they are in the world, and I'm coming back to you. Holy Father, keep them safe by the power of your name, the name that you gave me, so that their unity may be like ours. [12] While I was with them, I kept them safe by the power of your name, the name that you gave me. I watched over them, and none of them, except one person, became lost. So Scripture came true.

[13] "But now, ⌊Father,⌋ I'm coming back to you. I say these things while I'm still in the world so that they will have the same joy that I have. [14] I have given them your message. But the world has hated them because they don't belong to the world any more than I belong to the world. [15] I'm not asking you to take them out of the world but to protect them from the evil one. [16] They don't belong to the world any more than I belong to the world.

[17] "Use the truth to make them holy. Your words are truth. [18] I have sent them into the world the same way you sent me into the world. [19] I'm dedicating myself to this holy work I'm doing for them so that they, too, will use the truth to be holy.

[20] "I'm not praying only for them. I'm also praying for those who will believe in me through their message. [21] I pray that all of these people continue to have unity in the way that you, Father, are in me and I am in you. I pray that they may be united with us so that the world will believe that you have sent me. [22] I have given them the glory that you gave me. I did this so that they are united in the same way we are. [23] I am in them, and you are in me. So they are completely united. In this way the world knows that you have sent me and that you have loved them in the same way you have loved me.

[24] "Father, I want those you have given to me to be with me, to be where I am. I want them to see my glory, which you gave me because you loved me before the world was made. [25] Righteous

Father, the world didn't know you. Yet, I knew you, and these ⌜disciples⌝ have known that you sent me. [26] I have made your name known to them, and I will make it known so that the love you have for me will be in them and I will be in them."

Jesus Is Arrested—Matthew 26:47–56; Mark 14:43–52; Luke 22:47–54a

18 [1] After Jesus finished his prayer, he went with his disciples to the other side of the Kidron Valley. They entered the garden that was there.

[2] Judas, who betrayed him, knew the place because Jesus and his disciples often gathered there. [3] So Judas took a troop of soldiers and the guards from the chief priests and Pharisees and went to the garden. They were carrying lanterns, torches, and weapons.

[4] Jesus knew everything that was going to happen to him. So he went to meet them and asked, "Who are you looking for?"

[5] They answered him, "Jesus from Nazareth."

Jesus told them, "I am he."

Judas, who betrayed him, was standing with the crowd. [6] When Jesus told them, "I am he," the crowd backed away and fell to the ground.

[7] Jesus asked them again, "Who are you looking for?"

They said, "Jesus from Nazareth."

[8] Jesus replied, "I told you that I am he. So if you are looking for me, let these other men go." [9] In this way what Jesus had said came true: "I lost none of those you gave me."

[10] Simon Peter had a sword. He drew it, attacked the chief priest's servant, and cut off the servant's right ear. (The servant's name was Malchus.)

[11] Jesus told Peter, "Put your sword away. Shouldn't I drink the cup ⌜of suffering⌝ that my Father has given me?"

[12] Then the army officer and the Jewish guards arrested Jesus. They tied Jesus up [13] and took him first to Annas, the father-in-law of Caiaphas. Caiaphas, the chief priest that year, [14] was the person who had advised the Jews that it was better to have one man die for the people.

Peter Denies Jesus—*Matthew 26:69–75; Mark 14:66–72; Luke 22:54b–62*

[15] Simon Peter and another disciple followed Jesus. The other disciple was well-known to the chief priest. So that disciple went with Jesus into the chief priest's courtyard. [16] Peter, however, was standing outside the gate. The other disciple talked to the woman who was the gatekeeper and brought Peter into the courtyard.

[17] The gatekeeper asked Peter, "Aren't you one of this man's disciples too?"

Peter answered, "No, I'm not!"

[18] The servants and the guards were standing around a fire they had built and were warming themselves because it was cold. Peter was standing there, too, and warming himself with the others.

The Chief Priest Questions Jesus

[19] The chief priest questioned Jesus about his disciples and his teachings.

[20] Jesus answered him, "I have spoken publicly for everyone to hear. I have always taught in synagogues or in the temple courtyard, where all the Jews gather. I haven't said anything in secret. [21] Why do you question me? Question those who heard what I said to them. They know what I've said."

[22] When Jesus said this, one of the guards standing near Jesus slapped his face and said, "Is that how you answer the chief priest?"

[23] Jesus replied to him, "If I've said anything wrong, tell me what it was. But if I've told the truth, why do you hit me?"

[24] Annas sent Jesus to Caiaphas, the chief priest. Jesus was still tied up.

Peter Denies Jesus Again—
Matthew 26:69–75; Mark 14:66–72; Luke 22:54b–62

[25] Simon Peter continued to stand and warm himself by the fire. Some men asked him, "Aren't you, too, one of his disciples?"

Peter denied it by saying, "No, I'm not!"

[26] One of the chief priest's servants, a relative of the man whose ear Peter had cut off, asked him, "Didn't I see you with Jesus in the garden?"

[27] Peter again denied it, and just then a rooster crowed.

Pilate Questions Jesus—Matthew 27:11–14; Mark 15:1–5; Luke 23:1–4

²⁸ Early in the morning, Jesus was taken from Caiaphas' house to the governor's palace.

The Jews wouldn't go into the palace. They didn't want to become unclean,ᵃ since they wanted to eat the Passover. ²⁹ So Pilate came out to them and asked, "What accusation are you making against this man?"

³⁰ The Jews answered Pilate, "If he weren't a criminal, we wouldn't have handed him over to you."

³¹ Pilate told the Jews, "Take him, and try him by your law."

The Jews answered him, "We're not allowed to execute anyone." ³² In this way what Jesus had predicted about how he would die came true.

³³ Pilate went back into the palace, called for Jesus, and asked him, "Are you the king of the Jews?"

³⁴ Jesus replied, "Did you think of that yourself, or did others tell you about me?"

³⁵ Pilate answered, "Am I a Jew? Your own people and the chief priests handed you over to me. What have you done?"

³⁶ Jesus answered, "My kingdom doesn't belong to this world. If my kingdom belonged to this world, my followers would fight to keep me from being handed over to the Jews. My kingdom doesn't have its origin on earth."

³⁷ Pilate asked him, "So you are a king?"

Jesus replied, "You're correct in saying that I'm a king. I have been born and have come into the world for this reason: to testify to the truth. Everyone who belongs to the truth listens to me."

³⁸ Pilate said to him, "What is truth?"

After Pilate said this, he went out to the Jews again and told them, "I don't find this man guilty of anything. ³⁹ You have a custom that I should free one person for you at Passover. Would you like me to free the king of the Jews for you?"

⁴⁰ The Jews shouted again, "Don't free this man! Free Barabbas!" (Barabbas was a political revolutionary.)

ᵃ 18:28 "Unclean" refers to anything that Moses' Teachings say is not presentable to God.

The Soldiers Make Fun of Jesus—
Matthew 27:27–30; Mark 15:16–19

19 ¹ Then Pilate had Jesus taken away and whipped. ² The soldiers twisted some thorny branches into a crown, placed it on his head, and put a purple cape on him. ³ They went up to him, said, "Long live the king of the Jews!" and slapped his face.

The People Want Jesus Crucified

⁴ Pilate went outside again and told the Jews, "I'm bringing him out to you to let you know that I don't find this man guilty of anything." ⁵ Jesus went outside. He was wearing the crown of thorns and the purple cape. Pilate said to the Jews, "Look, here's the man!"

⁶ When the chief priests and the guards saw Jesus, they shouted, "Crucify him! Crucify him!"

Pilate told them, "You take him and crucify him. I don't find this man guilty of anything."

⁷ The Jews answered Pilate, "We have a law, and by that law he must die because he claimed to be the Son of God."

⁸ When Pilate heard them say that, he became more afraid than ever. ⁹ He went into the palace again and asked Jesus, "Where are you from?" But Jesus didn't answer him.

¹⁰ So Pilate said to Jesus, "Aren't you going to answer me? Don't you know that I have the authority to free you or to crucify you?"

¹¹ Jesus answered Pilate, "You wouldn't have any authority over me if it hadn't been given to you from above. That's why the man who handed me over to you is guilty of a greater sin."

¹² When Pilate heard what Jesus said, he wanted to free him. But the Jews shouted, "If you free this man, you're not a friend of the emperor. Anyone who claims to be a king is defying the emperor."

¹³ When Pilate heard what they said, he took Jesus outside and sat on the judge's seat in a place called Stone Pavement. (In Hebrew it is called *Gabbatha.*) ¹⁴ The time was about six o'clock in the morning on the Friday of the Passover festival.

Pilate said to the Jews, "Look, here's your king!"

¹⁵ Then the Jews shouted, "Kill him! Kill him! Crucify him!"

Pilate asked them, "Should I crucify your king?"

The chief priests responded, "The emperor is the only king we have!"

¹⁶ Then Pilate handed Jesus over to them to be crucified.

The Crucifixion—Matthew 27:31–44; Mark 15:20–32; Luke 23:26–38

So the soldiers took Jesus. ¹⁷ He carried his own cross and went out ˌof the cityˌ to a location called The Skull. (In Hebrew this place is called *Golgotha*.) ¹⁸ The soldiers crucified Jesus and two other men there. Jesus was in the middle.

¹⁹ Pilate wrote a notice and put it on the cross. The notice read, "Jesus from Nazareth, the king of the Jews." ²⁰ Many Jews read this notice, because the place where Jesus was crucified was near the city. The notice was written in Hebrew, Latin, and Greek.

²¹ The chief priests of the Jewish people told Pilate, "Don't write, 'The king of the Jews!' Instead, write, 'He said that he is the king of the Jews.' "

²² Pilate replied, "I have written what I've written."

²³ When the soldiers had crucified Jesus, they took his clothes and divided them four ways so that each soldier could have a share. His robe was left over. It didn't have a seam because it had been woven in one piece from top to bottom. ²⁴ The soldiers said to each other, "Let's not rip it apart. Let's throw dice to see who will get it." In this way the Scripture came true: "They divided my clothes among themselves. They threw dice for my clothing." So that's what the soldiers did.

²⁵ Jesus' mother, her sister, Mary (the wife of Clopas), and Mary from Magdala were standing beside Jesus' cross. ²⁶ Jesus saw his mother and the disciple whom he loved standing there. He said to his mother, "Look, here's your son!" ²⁷ Then he said to the disciple, "Look, here's your mother!"

From that time on she lived with that disciple in his home.

Jesus Dies on the Cross—
Matthew 27:45–56; Mark 15:33–41; Luke 23:44–49

²⁸ After this, when Jesus knew that everything had now been finished, he said, "I'm thirsty." He said this so that Scripture could finally be concluded.

²⁹ A jar filled with vinegar was there. So the soldiers put a sponge soaked in the vinegar on a hyssop stick and held it to his mouth.

³⁰ After Jesus had taken the vinegar, he said, "It is finished!"

Then he bowed his head and died.

³¹ Since it was Friday and the next day was an especially important day of worship, the Jews didn't want the bodies to stay on the crosses. So they asked Pilate to have the men's legs broken and their bodies removed. ³² The soldiers broke the legs of the first man and then of the other man who had been crucified with Jesus.

³³ When the soldiers came to Jesus and saw that he was already dead, they didn't break his legs. ³⁴ However, one of the soldiers stabbed Jesus' side with his spear, and blood and water immediately came out. ³⁵ The one who saw this is an eyewitness. What he says is true, and he knows that he is telling the truth so that you, too, will believe.

³⁶ This happened so that the Scripture would come true: "None of his bones will be broken." ³⁷ Another Scripture passage says, "They will look at the person whom they have stabbed."

Jesus Is Buried—
Matthew 27:57–61; Mark 15:42–47; Luke 23:50–56

³⁸ Later Joseph from the city of Arimathea asked Pilate to let him remove Jesus' body. (Joseph was a disciple of Jesus but secretly because he was afraid of the Jews). Pilate gave him permission to remove Jesus' body. So Joseph removed it. ³⁹ Nicodemus, the one who had first come to Jesus at night, went with Joseph and brought 75 pounds of a myrrh and aloe mixture.

⁴⁰ These two men took the body of Jesus and bound it with strips of linen. They laced the strips with spices. This was the Jewish custom for burial.

⁴¹ A garden was located in the place where Jesus was crucified. In that garden was a new tomb in which no one had yet been placed. ⁴² Joseph and Nicodemus put Jesus in that tomb, since that day was the Jewish day of preparation and since the tomb was nearby.

Jesus Comes Back to Life—Matthew 28:1–10; Mark 16:1–8; Luke 24:1–12

20 ¹ Early on Sunday morning, while it was still dark, Mary from Magdala went to the tomb. She saw that the stone had been removed from the tomb's entrance. ² So she ran to Simon Peter and the other disciple, whom Jesus loved. She told them, "They have removed the Lord from the tomb, and we don't know where they've put him."

³ So Peter and the other disciple headed for the tomb. ⁴ The two were running side by side, but the other disciple ran faster than Peter and came to the tomb first. ⁵ He bent over and looked inside the tomb. He saw the strips of linen lying there but didn't go inside.

⁶ Simon Peter arrived after him and went into the tomb. He saw the strips of linen lying there. ⁷ He also saw the cloth that had been on Jesus' head. It wasn't lying with the strips of linen but was rolled up separately. ⁸ Then the other disciple, who arrived at the tomb first, went inside. He saw and believed. ⁹ They didn't know yet what Scripture meant when it said that Jesus had to come back to life. ¹⁰ So the disciples went back home.

Jesus Appears to Mary From Magdala

¹¹ Mary, however, stood there and cried as she looked at the tomb. As she cried, she bent over and looked inside. ¹² She saw two angels in white clothes. They were sitting where the body of Jesus had been lying. One angel was where Jesus' head had been, and the other was where his feet had been. ¹³ The angels asked her why she was crying.

Mary told them, "They have removed my Lord, and I don't know where they've put him."

¹⁴ After she said this, she turned around and saw Jesus standing there. However, she didn't know that it was Jesus. ¹⁵ Jesus asked her, "Why are you crying? Who are you looking for?"

Mary thought it was the gardener speaking to her. So she said to him, "Sir, if you carried him away, tell me where you have put him, and I'll remove him."

¹⁶ Jesus said to her, "Mary!"

Mary turned around and said to him in Hebrew, "Rabboni!" (This word means "teacher.")

[17] Jesus told her, "Don't hold on to me. I have not yet gone to the Father. But go to my brothers and sisters and tell them, 'I am going to my Father and your Father, to my God and your God.' "

[18] Mary from Magdala went to the disciples and told them, "I have seen the Lord." She also told them what he had said to her.

Jesus Appears to the Disciples—
Luke 24:36–48

[19] That Sunday evening, the disciples were together behind locked doors because they were afraid of the Jews. Jesus stood among them and said to them, "Peace be with you!" [20] When he said this, he showed them his hands and his side. The disciples were glad to see the Lord.

[21] Jesus said to them again, "Peace be with you! As the Father has sent me, so I am sending you." [22] After he had said this, he breathed on the disciples and said, "Receive the Holy Spirit. [23] Whenever you forgive sins, they are forgiven. Whenever you don't forgive them, they are not forgiven."

Jesus Appears to Thomas

[24] Thomas, one of the twelve apostles, who was called Didymus, wasn't with them when Jesus came. [25] The other disciples told him, "We've seen the Lord."

Thomas told them, "I refuse to believe this unless I see the nail marks in his hands, put my fingers into them, and put my hand into his side."

[26] A week later Jesus' disciples were again in the house, and Thomas was with them. Even though the doors were locked, Jesus stood among them and said, "Peace be with you!" [27] Then Jesus said to Thomas, "Put your finger here, and look at my hands. Take your hand, and put it into my side. Stop doubting, and believe."

[28] Thomas responded to Jesus, "My Lord and my God!"

[29] Jesus said to Thomas, "You believe because you've seen me. Blessed are those who haven't seen me but believe."

³⁰ Jesus performed many other miracles that his disciples saw. Those miracles are not written in this book. ³¹ But these miracles have been written so that you will believe that Jesus is the Messiah, the Son of God, and so that you will have life by believing in him.

Jesus Appears to His Disciples Again

21 ¹ Later, by the Sea of Tiberias, Jesus showed himself again to the disciples. This is what happened. ² Simon Peter, Thomas (called Didymus), Nathanael from Cana in Galilee, Zebedee's sons, and two other disciples of Jesus were together. ³ Simon Peter said to the others, "I'm going fishing."

They told him, "We're going with you."

They went out in a boat but didn't catch a thing that night. ⁴ As the sun was rising, Jesus stood on the shore. The disciples didn't realize that it was Jesus.

⁵ Jesus asked them, "Friends, haven't you caught any fish?"

They answered him, "No, we haven't."

⁶ He told them, "Throw the net out on the right side of the boat, and you'll catch some." So they threw the net out and were unable to pull it in because so many fish were in it.

⁷ The disciple whom Jesus loved said to Peter, "It's the Lord." When Simon Peter heard that it was the Lord, he put back on the clothes that he had taken off and jumped into the sea. ⁸ The other disciples came with the boat and dragged the net full of fish. They weren't far from the shore, only about 100 yards.

⁹ When they went ashore, they saw a fire with a fish lying on the coals, and they saw a loaf of bread.

¹⁰ Jesus told them, "Bring some of the fish you've just caught." ¹¹ Simon Peter got into the boat and pulled the net ashore. Though the net was filled with 153 large fish, it was not torn.

¹² Jesus told them, "Come, have breakfast." None of the disciples dared to ask him who he was. They knew he was the Lord. ¹³ Jesus took the bread, gave it to them, and did the same with the fish.

¹⁴ This was the third time that Jesus showed himself to the disciples after he had come back to life.

Jesus Speaks With Peter

¹⁵ After they had eaten breakfast, Jesus asked Simon Peter, "Simon, son of John, do you love me more than the other disciples do?"

Peter answered him, "Yes, Lord, you know that I love you."

Jesus told him, "Feed my lambs."

¹⁶ Jesus asked him again, a second time, "Simon, son of John, do you love me?"

Peter answered him, "Yes, Lord, you know that I love you."

Jesus told him, "Take care of my sheep."

¹⁷ Jesus asked him a third time, "Simon, son of John, do you love me?"

Peter felt sad because Jesus had asked him a third time, "Do you love me?" So Peter said to him, "Lord, you know everything. You know that I love you."

Jesus told him, "Feed my sheep. ¹⁸ I can guarantee this truth: When you were young, you would get ready to go where you wanted. But when you're old, you will stretch out your hands, and someone else will get you ready to take you where you don't want to go." ¹⁹ Jesus said this to show by what kind of death Peter would bring glory to God. After saying this, Jesus told Peter, "Follow me!"

²⁰ Peter turned around and saw the disciple whom Jesus loved. That disciple was following them. He was the one who leaned against Jesus' chest at the supper and asked, "Lord, who is going to betray you?" ²¹ When Peter saw him, he asked Jesus, "Lord, what about him?"

²² Jesus said to Peter, "If I want him to live until I come again, how does that concern you? Follow me!" ²³ So a rumor that that disciple wouldn't die spread among Jesus' followers. But Jesus didn't say that he wouldn't die. What Jesus said was, "If I want him to live until I come again, how does that concern you?"

²⁴ This disciple was an eyewitness of these things and wrote them down. We know that what he says is true.

²⁵ Jesus also did many other things. If every one of them were written down, I suppose the world wouldn't have enough room for the books that would be written.

ACTS

Introduction

1 ¹ In my first book, Theophilus, I wrote about what Jesus began to do and teach. This included everything from the beginning ⌐of his life⌐ ² until the day he was taken to heaven. Before he was taken to heaven, he gave instructions through the Holy Spirit to the apostles, whom he had chosen.

Jesus Ascends to Heaven

³ After his death Jesus showed the apostles a lot of convincing evidence that he was alive. For 40 days he appeared to them and talked with them about the kingdom of God.

⁴ Once, while he was meeting with them, he ordered them not to leave Jerusalem but to wait there for what the Father had promised. Jesus said to them, "I've told you what the Father promises: ⁵ John baptized with water, but in a few days you will be baptized with the Holy Spirit."

⁶ So when the apostles came together, they asked him, "Lord, is this the time when you're going to restore the kingdom to Israel?"

⁷ Jesus told them, "You don't need to know about times or periods that the Father has determined by his own authority. ⁸ But you will receive power when the Holy Spirit comes to you. Then you will be my witnesses to testify about me in Jerusalem, throughout Judea and Samaria, and to the ends of the earth."

⁹ After he had said this, he was taken to heaven. A cloud hid him so that they could no longer see him.

¹⁰ They were staring into the sky as he departed. Suddenly, two men in white clothes stood near them. ¹¹ They asked, "Why are you men from Galilee standing here looking at the sky? Jesus, who

was taken from you to heaven, will come back in the same way that you saw him go to heaven."

A New Apostle Takes Judas' Place

[12] Then they returned to Jerusalem from the mountain called the Mount of Olives. It is near Jerusalem, about half a mile away.

[13] When they came into the city, Peter, John, James, Andrew, Philip, Thomas, Bartholomew, Matthew, James (son of Alphaeus), Simon the Zealot, and Judas (son of James) went to the second-story room where they were staying.

[14] The apostles had a single purpose as they devoted themselves to prayer. They were joined by some women, including Mary (the mother of Jesus), and they were joined by his brothers.

[15] At a time when about 120 disciples had gathered together, Peter got up and spoke to them.

He said, [16] "Brothers, what the Holy Spirit predicted through David in Scripture about Judas had to come true. Judas led the men to arrest Jesus. [17] He had been one of us and had been given an active role in this ministry. [18] With the money he received from the wrong he had done, he bought a piece of land where he fell headfirst to his death. His body split open, and all his internal organs came out. [19] Everyone living in Jerusalem knows about this. They even call that piece of land *Akeldama,* which means 'Field of Blood' in their dialect. [20] You've read in Psalms, 'Let his home be deserted, and let no one live there,' and 'Let someone else take his position.' "

"Therefore, someone must be added to our number to serve with us as a witness that Jesus came back to life. [21] He must be one of the men who accompanied Jesus with us the entire time that the Lord Jesus was among us. [22] This person must have been with us from the time that John was baptizing people to the day that Jesus was taken from us."[a]

---

[a] 1:22 Verses 21–22 have been rearranged to express the complex Greek sentence structure more clearly in English.

²³ The disciples determined that two men were qualified. These men were Joseph (who was called Barsabbas and was also known as Justus) and Matthias. ²⁴ Then they prayed, "Lord, you know everyone's thoughts. Show us which of these two you have chosen. ²⁵ Show us who is to take the place of Judas as an apostle, since Judas abandoned his position to go to the place where he belongs."

²⁶ They drew names to choose an apostle. Matthias was chosen and joined the eleven apostles.

The Believers Are Filled With the Holy Spirit

2 ¹ When Pentecost, the fiftieth day after Passover, came, all the believers were together in one place. ² Suddenly, a sound like a violently blowing wind came from the sky and filled the whole house where they were staying. ³ Tongues that looked like fire appeared to them. The tongues arranged themselves so that one came to rest on each believer. ⁴ All the believers were filled with the Holy Spirit and began to speak in other languages as the Spirit gave them the ability to speak.

⁵ Devout Jewish men from every nation were living in Jerusalem. ⁶ They gathered when they heard the wind. Each person was startled to recognize his own dialect when the disciples spoke.

⁷ Stunned and amazed, the people in the crowd said, "All of these men who are speaking are Galileans. ⁸ Why do we hear them speaking in our native dialects? ⁹ We're Parthians, Medes, and Elamites. We're people from Mesopotamia, Judea, Cappadocia, Pontus, the province of Asia, ¹⁰ Phrygia, Pamphylia, Egypt, and the country near Cyrene in Libya. We're Jewish people, converts to Judaism, and visitors from Rome, ¹¹ Crete, and Arabia. We hear these men in our own languages as they tell about the miracles that God has done."

¹² All of these devout men were stunned and puzzled. They asked each other, "What can this mean?" ¹³ Others said jokingly, "They're drunk on sweet wine."

Peter Talks to the Crowd

¹⁴ Then Peter stood up with the eleven apostles. In a loud voice he said to them, "Men of Judea and everyone living in Jerusalem!

You must understand this, so pay attention to what I say. [15] These men are not drunk as you suppose. It's only nine in the morning. [16] Rather, this is what the prophet Joel spoke about:

[17] 'In the last days, God says,
      I will pour my Spirit on everyone.
         Your sons and daughters will speak
            what God has revealed.
         Your young men will see visions.
         Your old men will dream dreams.
[18]   In those days
         I will pour my Spirit on my servants, on both men
            and women.
         They will speak what God has revealed.
[19]   I will work miracles in the sky and give signs
            on the earth:
         blood, fire, and clouds of smoke.
[20]   The sun will become dark,
            and the moon will become as red as blood
            before the terrifying day of the Lord comes.
[21]   Then whoever calls on the name of the Lord
         will be saved.'

[22] "Men of Israel, listen to what I say: Jesus from Nazareth was a man whom God brought to your attention. You know that through this man God worked miracles, did amazing things, and gave signs. [23] By using men who don't acknowledge Moses' Teachings, you crucified Jesus, who was given over ⌞to death⌟ by a plan that God had determined in advance. [24] But God raised him from death to life and destroyed the pains of death, because death had no power to hold him. [25] This is what David meant when he said about Jesus:

      'I always see the Lord in front of me.
         I cannot be moved because he is by my side.
[26]   That is why my heart is glad and my tongue rejoices.
         My body also rests securely

27   because you do not abandon my soul to the grave
            or allow your holy one to decay.
28   You make the path of life known to me.
            In your presence there is complete joy.'

29 "Brothers, I can tell you confidently that our ancestor David died and was buried and that his tomb is here to this day. 30 David was a prophet and knew that God had promised with an oath that he would place one of David's descendants on his throne. 31 David knew that the Messiah would come back to life, and he spoke about that before it ever happened. He said that the Messiah wouldn't be left in the grave and that his body wouldn't decay.

32 "God brought this man Jesus back to life. We are all witnesses to that. 33 God used his power to give Jesus the highest position. Jesus has also received and has poured out the Holy Spirit as the Father had promised, and this is what you're seeing and hearing. 34 David didn't go up to heaven, but he said,

            'The Lord said to my Lord,
                "Take my highest position of power
35   until I put your enemies under your control." '

36 "All the people of Israel should know beyond a doubt that God made Jesus, whom you crucified, both Lord and Christ."

37 When the people heard this, they were deeply upset. They asked Peter and the other apostles, "Brothers, what should we do?"

38 Peter answered them, "All of you must turn to God and change the way you think and act, and each of you must be baptized in the name of Jesus Christ so that your sins will be forgiven. Then you will receive the Holy Spirit as a gift. 39 This promise belongs to you and to your children and to everyone who is far away. It belongs to everyone who worships the Lord our God."

40 Peter said much more to warn them. He urged, "Save yourselves from this corrupt generation." 41 Those who accepted what Peter said were baptized. That day about 3,000 people were added to the group.

Life as a Christian

⁴² The disciples were devoted to the teachings of the apostles, to fellowship, to the breaking of bread, and to prayer. ⁴³ A feeling of fear came over everyone as many amazing things and miraculous signs happened through the apostles. ⁴⁴ All the believers kept meeting together, and they shared everything with each other. ⁴⁵ From time to time, they sold their property and other possessions and distributed the money to anyone who needed it. ⁴⁶ The believers had a single purpose and went to the temple every day. They were joyful and humble as they ate at each other's homes and shared their food. ⁴⁷ At the same time, they praised God and had the good will of all the people. Every day the Lord saved people, and they were added to the group.

A Lame Man Is Healed

3 ¹ Peter and John were going to the temple courtyard for the three o'clock prayer. ² At the same time, a man who had been lame from birth was being carried by some men. Every day these men would put the lame man at a gate in the temple courtyard. The gate was called Beautiful Gate. There he would beg for handouts from people going into the courtyard. ³ When the man saw that Peter and John were about to go into the courtyard, he asked them for a handout.

⁴ Peter and John stared at him. "Look at us!" Peter said. ⁵ So the man watched them closely. He expected to receive something from them. ⁶ However, Peter said to him, "I don't have any money, but I'll give you what I do have. Through the power of Jesus Christ from Nazareth, walk!" ⁷ Peter took hold of the man's right hand and began to help him up. Immediately, the man's feet and ankles became strong. ⁸ Springing to his feet, he stood up and started to walk. He went with Peter and John into the temple courtyard. The man was walking, jumping, and praising God.

⁹ All the people saw him walking and praising God. ¹⁰ They knew that he was the man who used to sit and beg at the temple's Beautiful Gate. The people were amazed and stunned to see what

had happened to him. [11] They were excited, and everyone ran to see them at the place called Solomon's Porch. The man wouldn't let go of Peter and John.

[12] When Peter saw this, he said to the people, "Men of Israel, why are you amazed about this man? Why are you staring at us as though we have made him walk by our own power or godly life? [13] The God of our ancestors Abraham, Isaac, and Jacob has glorified his servant Jesus. You handed Jesus over to Pilate. You rejected him in Pilate's presence, even though Pilate had decided to let him go free. [14] You rejected the man who was holy and innocent. You asked to have a murderer given to you, [15] and you killed the source of life. But God brought him back to life, and we are witnesses to that. [16] We believe in the one named Jesus. Through his power alone this man, whom you know, was healed, as all of you saw.

[17] "And now, brothers, I know that like your rulers you didn't know what you were doing. [18] But in this way God made the sufferings of his Messiah come true. God had predicted these sufferings through all the prophets. [19] So change the way you think and act, and turn ⌞to God⌟ to have your sins removed. [20] Then times will come when the Lord will refresh you. He will send you Jesus, whom he has appointed to be the Christ. [21] Heaven must receive Jesus until the time when everything will be restored as God promised through his holy prophets long ago.

[22] "Moses said, 'The Lord your God will send you a prophet, an Israelite like me. Listen to everything he tells you. [23] Those who won't listen to that prophet will be excluded from the people.' [24] Samuel and all the prophets who followed him spoke about these days. [25] You are the descendants of the prophets and the heirs of the promise[a] that God made to our ancestors when he said to Abraham, 'Through your descendant all people on earth will be blessed.' [26] God has brought his servant back to life and has sent him to you first. God did this to bless you by turning every one of you from your evil ways."

---

[a] 3:25 Or "covenant."

Peter and John's Trial in Front of the Jewish Council

4 ¹Some priests, the officer in charge of the temple guards, and some Sadducees approached Peter and John while they were speaking to the people. ²These religious authorities were greatly annoyed. Peter and John were teaching the people and spreading the message that the dead will come back to life through Jesus. ³ So the temple guards arrested them. Since it was already evening, they put Peter and John in jail until the next day.

⁴But many of those who had heard the message became believers, so the number of men who believed grew to about 5,000.

⁵ The next day the Jewish rulers, leaders, and scribes met in Jerusalem. ⁶ The chief priest Annas, Caiaphas, John, Alexander, and the rest of the chief priest's family were present. ⁷ They made Peter and John stand in front of them and then asked, "By what power or in whose name did you do this?"

⁸ Then Peter, because he was filled with the Holy Spirit, said to them, "Rulers and leaders of the people, ⁹ today you are cross-examining us about the good we did for a crippled man. You want to know how he was made well. ¹⁰ You and all the people of Israel must understand that this man stands in your presence with a healthy body because of the power of Jesus Christ from Nazareth. You crucified Jesus Christ, but God has brought him back to life. ¹¹ He is the stone that the builders rejected, the stone that has become the cornerstone. ¹² No one else can save us. Indeed, we can be saved only by the power of the one named Jesus and not by any other person."

¹³After they found out that Peter and John had no education or special training, they were surprised to see how boldly they spoke. They realized that these men had been with Jesus. ¹⁴ When they saw the man who was healed standing with Peter and John, they couldn't say anything against the two apostles. ¹⁵ So they ordered Peter and John to leave the council room and began to discuss the matter among themselves. ¹⁶ They said, "What should we do to these men? Clearly, they've performed a miracle that everyone in Jerusalem knows about. We can't deny that. ¹⁷ So let's threaten

them. Let's tell them that they must never speak to anyone about the one named Jesus. Then the news about the miracle that they have performed will not spread any further among the people."

¹⁸ They called Peter and John and ordered them never to teach about Jesus or even mention his name.

¹⁹ Peter and John answered them, "Decide for yourselves whether God wants people to listen to you rather than to him. ²⁰ We cannot stop talking about what we've seen and heard."

²¹ The authorities threatened them even more and then let them go. Since all the people were praising God for what had happened, the authorities couldn't find any way to punish Peter and John. ²² (The man who was healed by this miracle was over 40 years old.)

The Apostles Pray for God's Help

²³ When Peter and John were released, they went to the other apostles and told them everything the chief priests and leaders had said. ²⁴ When the apostles heard this, they were united and loudly prayed to God, "Master, you made the sky, the land, the sea, and everything in them. ²⁵ You said through the Holy Spirit, who spoke through your servant David (our ancestor),

> 'Why do the nations act arrogantly?
> Why do their people devise useless plots?
> ²⁶   Kings take their stand.
>   Rulers make plans together
>   against the Lord and against his Messiah.'

²⁷ "In this city Herod and Pontius Pilate made plans together with non-Jewish people and the people of Israel. They made their plans against your holy servant Jesus, whom you anointed. ²⁸ Through your will and power, they did everything that you had already decided should be done.

²⁹ "Lord, pay attention to their threats now, and allow us to speak your word boldly. ³⁰ Show your power by healing, performing miracles, and doing amazing things through the power and the name of your holy servant Jesus."

[31] When the apostles had finished praying, their meeting place shook. All of them were filled with the Holy Spirit and continued to speak the word of God boldly.

The Believers Share Their Property

[32] The whole group of believers lived in harmony. No one called any of his possessions his own. Instead, they shared everything.

[33] With great power the apostles continued to testify that the Lord Jesus had come back to life. ˌGod'sˌ abundant good will[a] was with all of them. [34] None of them needed anything. From time to time, people sold land or houses and brought the money [35] to the apostles. Then the money was distributed to anyone who needed it.

[36] Joseph, a descendant of Levi, had been born on the island of Cyprus. The apostles called him Barnabas, which means "a person who encourages." [37] He had some land. He sold it and turned the money over to the apostles.

Ananias and Sapphira

5 [1] A man named Ananias and his wife Sapphira sold some property. [2] They agreed to hold back some of the money ˌthey had pledgedˌ and turned only part of it over to the apostles.

[3] Peter asked, "Ananias, why did you let Satan fill you with the idea that you could deceive the Holy Spirit? You've held back some of the money you received for the land. [4] While you had the land, it was your own. After it was sold, you could have done as you pleased with the money. So how could you do a thing like this? You didn't lie to people but to God!"

[5] When Ananias heard Peter say this, he dropped dead. Everyone who heard about his death was terrified. [6] Some young men got up, wrapped his body in a sheet, carried him outside, and buried him.

[7] About three hours later Ananias' wife arrived. She didn't know what had happened. [8] So Peter asked her, "Tell me, did you sell the land for that price?"

---

[a] 4:33 Or "grace."

She answered, "Yes, that was the price."

⁹ Then Peter said to her, "How could you and your husband agree to test the Lord's Spirit? Those who buried your husband are standing at the door, and they will carry you outside for burial."

¹⁰ Immediately, she dropped dead in front of Peter. When the young men came back, they found Sapphira dead. So they carried her outside and buried her next to her husband. ¹¹ The whole church and everyone else who heard about what had happened were terrified.

The Apostles Perform Many Miracles

¹² The people saw the apostles perform many miracles and do amazing things. The believers had a common faith in Jesus as they met on Solomon's Porch. ¹³ None of the other people dared to join them, although everyone spoke highly of them. ¹⁴ More men and women than ever began to believe in the Lord. ¹⁵ As a result, people carried their sick into the streets. They placed them on stretchers and cots so that at least Peter's shadow might fall on some sick people as he went by. ¹⁶ Crowds from the cities around Jerusalem would gather. They would bring their sick and those who were troubled by evil spirits, and each person was cured.

The Apostles' Trial in Front of the Jewish Council

¹⁷ The chief priest and the whole party of the Sadducees who were with him were extremely jealous. So they took action ¹⁸ by arresting the apostles and putting them in the city jail. ¹⁹ But at night an angel from the Lord opened the doors to their cell and led them out of the prison. ²⁰ The angel told them, "Stand in the temple courtyard, and tell the people everything about life ⌊in Christ⌋."

²¹ Early in the morning, after they had listened to the angel, the apostles went into the temple courtyard and began to teach.

The chief priest and those who were with him called together the Jewish council, that is, all the leaders of Israel. They also sent men to the prison to get the apostles. ²² When the temple guards arrived at the prison, they didn't find the apostles. The guards came back and reported, **23** "We found the prison securely locked and the guards standing at the doors. However, when we opened the doors, we found no one inside." **24** When the officer of the temple guards and the chief priests heard this, they were puzzled about what could have happened.

25 Then someone told them, "The men you put in prison are standing in the temple courtyard. They're teaching the people."

26 Then the officer of the temple guards went with some of his men to bring back the apostles without using force. After all, the officer and his guards were afraid that the people would stone them to death for using force. **27** When they brought back the apostles, they made them stand in front of the council. The chief priest questioned them. **28** He said, "We gave you strict orders not to mention Jesus' name when you teach. Yet, you've filled Jerusalem with your teachings. You want to take revenge on us for putting that man to death."

29 Peter and the other apostles answered, "We must obey God rather than people. **30** You murdered Jesus by hanging him on a cross. But the God of our ancestors brought him back to life. **31** God used his power to give Jesus the highest position as leader and savior. He did this to lead the people of Israel to him, to change the way they think and act, and to forgive their sins. **32** We are witnesses to these things, and so is the Holy Spirit, whom God has given to those who obey him."

33 When the men on the council heard this, they became furious and wanted to execute the apostles. **34** But a Pharisee named Gamaliel stood up. He was a highly respected expert in Moses' Teachings. He ordered that the apostles should be taken outside for a little while.

35 Then he said to the council, "Men of Israel, consider carefully what you do with these men. **36** Some time ago Theudas appeared. He claimed that he was important, and about four hundred men joined him. He was killed, and all his followers were scattered. The whole movement was a failure.

37 "After that man, at the time of the census, Judas from Galilee appeared and led people in a revolt. He, too, died, and all his followers were scattered.

[38] "We should keep away from these men for now. We should leave them alone. I can guarantee that if the plan they put into action is of human origin, it will fail. [39] However, if it's from God, you won't be able to stop them. You may even discover that you're fighting against God."

[40] The council took his advice. They called the apostles, beat them, ordered them not to speak about the one named Jesus, and let them go.

[41] The apostles left the council room. They were happy to have been considered worthy to suffer dishonor for speaking about Jesus. [42] Every day in the temple courtyard and from house to house, they refused to stop teaching and telling the Good News that Jesus is the Messiah.

The Disciples Choose Seven Men to Help the Apostles

6 [1] At that time, as the number of disciples grew, Greek-speaking Jews complained about the Hebrew-speaking Jews. The Greek-speaking Jews claimed that the widows among them were neglected every day when food and other assistance was distributed.

[2] The twelve apostles called all the disciples together and told them, "It's not right for us to give up God's word in order to distribute food. [3] So, brothers and sisters, choose seven men whom the people know are spiritually wise. We will put them in charge of this problem. [4] However, we will devote ourselves to praying and to serving in ways that are related to the word."

[5] The suggestion pleased the whole group. So they chose Stephen, who was a man full of faith and the Holy Spirit, and they chose Philip, Prochorus, Nicanor, Timon, Parmenas, and Nicolaus, who had converted to Judaism in the city of Antioch. [6] The disciples had these men stand in front of the apostles, who prayed and placed their hands on these seven men.

[7] The word of God continued to spread, and the number of disciples in Jerusalem grew very large. A large number of priests accepted the faith.

Stephen Is Arrested

8 Stephen was a man filled with God's favor[a] and power. He did amazing things and performed miracles. **9** ⌊One day⌋ some men from the cities of Cyrene and Alexandria and the provinces of Cilicia and Asia started an argument with Stephen. They belonged to a synagogue called Freedmen's Synagogue. **10** They couldn't argue with Stephen because he spoke with the wisdom that the Spirit had given him. **11** Then they bribed some men to lie.

These men said, "We heard him slander Moses and God." **12** The liars stirred up trouble among the people, the leaders, and the scribes. So they went to Stephen, took him by force, and brought him in front of the Jewish council. **13** Some witnesses stood up and lied about Stephen. They said, "This man never stops saying bad things about the holy place and Moses' Teachings. **14** We heard him say that Jesus from Nazareth will destroy the temple and change the customs that Moses gave us."

15 Everyone who sat in the council stared at him and saw that his face looked like an angel's face.

Stephen Speaks in His Own Defense

7 **1** Then the chief priest asked Stephen, "Is this true?"
2 Stephen answered, "Brothers and fathers, listen to me. The God who reveals his glory appeared to our ancestor Abraham in Mesopotamia. This happened before Abraham lived in Haran. **3** God told him, 'Leave your land and your relatives. Go to the land that I will show you.'

4 "Then Abraham left the country of Chaldea and lived in the city of Haran. After his father died, God made him move from there to this land where we now live.

5 "Yet, God didn't give Abraham anything in this land to call his own, not even a place to rest his feet. But God promised to give this land to him and to his descendants, even though Abraham didn't have a child. **6** God told Abraham that his descendants would be for-

---

a 6:8 Or "grace."

eigners living in another country and that the people there would make them slaves and mistreat them for 400 years. [7] God also told him, 'I will punish the people whom they will serve. After that, they will leave that country and worship me here.'

[8] "God gave Abraham circumcision to confirm his promise.[a] So when Abraham's son Isaac was born, Abraham circumcised him on the eighth day. Isaac did the same to his son Jacob, and Jacob did the same to his twelve sons (the ancestors of our tribes).

[9] "Jacob's sons were jealous of their brother Joseph. They sold him into slavery, and he was taken to Egypt. But God was with Joseph [10] and rescued him from all his suffering. When Joseph stood in the presence of Pharaoh (the king of Egypt), God gave Joseph divine favor[b] and wisdom so that he became ruler of Egypt and of Pharaoh's whole palace. [11] Then a famine throughout Egypt and Canaan brought a lot of suffering. Our ancestors couldn't find any food. [12] When Jacob heard that Egypt had food, he sent our ancestors there. That was their first trip. [13] On the second trip, Joseph told his brothers who he was, and Pharaoh learned about Joseph's family. [14] Joseph sent for his father Jacob and his relatives, 75 people in all. [15] So Jacob went to Egypt, and he and our ancestors died there. [16] They were taken to Shechem for burial in the tomb that Abraham purchased in Shechem from Hamor's sons.

[17] "When the time that God had promised to Abraham had almost come, the number of our people in Egypt had grown very large. [18] Then a different king, who knew nothing about Joseph, began to rule in Egypt. [19] This king was shrewd in the way he took advantage of our people. He mistreated our ancestors. He made them abandon their newborn babies outdoors, where they would die.

[20] "At that time Moses was born, and he was a very beautiful child. His parents took care of him for three months. [21] When Moses was abandoned outdoors, Pharaoh's daughter adopted him and raised him as her son. [22] So Moses was educated in all the wisdom of the Egyptians and became a great man in what he

---

[a] 7:8 Or "covenant."   [b] 7:10 Or "grace."

said and did. **23** When he was 40 years old, he decided to visit his own people, the Israelites. **24** When he saw an Israelite man being treated unfairly by an Egyptian, he defended the Israelite. He took revenge by killing the Egyptian. **25** Moses thought his own people would understand that God was going to use him to give them freedom. But they didn't understand. **26** The next day Moses saw two Israelites fighting, and he tried to make peace between them. He said to them, 'Men, you are brothers. Why are you treating each other unfairly?'

27 "But one of the men pushed Moses aside. He asked Moses, 'Who made you our ruler and judge? **28** Do you want to kill me as you killed the Egyptian yesterday?' **29** After he said that, Moses quickly left Egypt and lived in Midian as a foreigner. In Midian he fathered two sons.

30 "Forty years later, a messenger appeared to him in the flames of a burning bush in the desert of Mount Sinai. **31** Moses was surprised when he saw this. As he went closer to look at the bush, the voice of the Lord said to him, **32** 'I am the God of your ancestors—the God of Abraham, Isaac, and Jacob.' Moses began to tremble and didn't dare to look at the bush. **33** The Lord told him, 'Take off your sandals. The place where you're standing is holy ground. **34** I've seen how my people are mistreated in Egypt. I've heard their groaning and have come to rescue them. So now I'm sending you to Egypt.'

35 "This is the Moses whom the Israelites rejected by saying, 'Who made you our ruler and judge?' This is the one God sent to free them and to rule them with the help of the messenger who appeared to him in the bush. **36** This is the man who led our ancestors out of Egypt. He is the person who did amazing things and worked miracles in Egypt, at the Red Sea, and in the desert for 40 years. **37** This is the same Moses who told the Israelites, 'God will send you a prophet, an Israelite like me.' **38** This is the Moses who was in the assembly in the desert. Our ancestors and the messenger who spoke to him on Mount Sinai were there with him. Moses received life-giving messages to give to us, **39** but our ancestors were not willing to obey him. Instead, they pushed him aside, and in their hearts they turned back to Egypt. ⁴⁰ They told Aaron, 'We don't know what has happened to this Moses, who led us out of Egypt. So make gods who will lead us.' ⁴¹ That was the time they made a calf. They offered a sacrifice to that false god and delighted in what they had made.

⁴² "So God turned away from them and let them worship the sun, moon, and stars. This is written in the book of the prophets: 'Did you bring me sacrifices and grain offerings in the desert for 40 years, nation of Israel? ⁴³ You carried along the shrine of Moloch, the star of the god Rephan, and the statues you made for yourselves to worship. I will send you into exile beyond the city of Babylon.'

⁴⁴ "In the desert our ancestors had the tent of God's promise. Moses built this tent exactly as God had told him. He used the model he had seen. ⁴⁵ After our ancestors received the tent, they brought it into this land. They did this with Joshua's help when they took possession of the land from the nations that God forced out of our ancestors' way. This tent remained here until the time of David, ⁴⁶ who won God's favor. David asked that he might provide a permanent place for the family of Jacob.ᶜ ⁴⁷ But Solomon was the one who built a house for God.

⁴⁸ "However, the Most High doesn't live in a house built by humans, as the prophet says:

⁴⁹   'The Lord says,
       "Heaven is my throne.
       The earth is my footstool.
          What kind of house are you going to build for me?
          Where will I rest?
⁵⁰   Didn't I make all these things?" '

⁵¹ "How stubborn can you be? How can you be so heartless and disobedient? You're just like your ancestors. They always opposed the Holy Spirit, and so do you! ⁵² Was there ever a prophet your ancestors didn't persecute? They killed those who predicted that a man with God's approval would come. You have now become the

---

ᶜ 7:46 Some manuscripts and translations read "God of Jacob."

people who betrayed and murdered that man. ⁵³You are the people who received Moses' Teachings, which were put into effect by angels. But you haven't obeyed those teachings."

Stephen Is Executed

⁵⁴As council members listened to Stephen, they became noticeably furious. ⁵⁵But Stephen was full of the Holy Spirit. He looked into heaven, saw God's glory, and Jesus in the position of authority that God gives. ⁵⁶So Stephen said, "Look, I see heaven opened and the Son of Man in the position of authority that God has given him!"

⁵⁷But the council members shouted and refused to listen. Then they rushed at Stephen with one purpose in mind, ⁵⁸and after they had thrown him out of the city, they began to stone him to death. The witnesses left their coats with a young man named Saul.

⁵⁹While council members were executing Stephen, he called out, "Lord Jesus, welcome my spirit." ⁶⁰Then he knelt down and shouted, "Lord, don't hold this sin against them." After he had said this, he died.

8 ¹Saul approved of putting Stephen to death.

On that day widespread persecution broke out against the church in Jerusalem. Most believers, except the apostles, were scattered throughout Judea and Samaria.

²Devout men buried Stephen as they mourned loudly for him.

³Saul tried to destroy the church. He dragged men and women out of one home after another and threw them into prison.

Some Samaritans Become Believers

⁴The believers who were scattered went from place to place, where they spread the word. ⁵Philip went to the city of Samaria and told people about the Messiah. ⁶The crowds paid close attention to what Philip said. They listened to him and saw the miracles that he performed. ⁷Evil spirits screamed as they came out of the many people they had possessed. Many paralyzed and lame people were cured. ⁸As a result, that city was extremely happy.

⁹A man named Simon lived in that city. He amazed the people of Samaria with his practice of magic. He claimed that he was

great. ¹⁰ Everyone from children to adults paid attention to him. They said, "This man is the power of God, and that power is called great." ¹¹ They paid attention to Simon because he had amazed them for a long time with his practice of magic. ¹² However, when Philip spread the Good News about the kingdom of God and the one named Jesus Christ, men and women believed him and were baptized. ¹³ Even Simon believed, and after he was baptized, he became devoted to Philip. Simon was amazed to see the miracles and impressive things that were happening.

¹⁴ When the apostles in Jerusalem heard that the Samaritans had accepted the word of God, they sent Peter and John to them. ¹⁵ Peter and John went to Samaria and prayed that the Samaritans would receive the Holy Spirit. ¹⁶ (Before this the Holy Spirit had not come to any of the Samaritans. They had only been baptized in the name of the Lord Jesus.) ¹⁷ Then Peter and John placed their hands on them, and the Samaritans received the Holy Spirit.

¹⁸ Simon saw that the Spirit was given to the Samaritans when the apostles placed their hands on them. So he offered Peter and John money ¹⁹ and said, "Give me this power so that anyone I place my hands on will receive the Holy Spirit."

²⁰ Peter told Simon, "May your money be destroyed with you because you thought you could buy God's gift. ²¹ You won't have any share in this because God can see how twisted your thinking is. ²² So change your wicked thoughts, and ask the Lord if he will forgive you for thinking like this. ²³ I can see that you are bitter with jealousy and wrapped up in your evil ways."

²⁴ Simon answered, "Pray to the Lord for me that none of the things you said will happen to me."

²⁵ After they had boldly spoken about the message of the Lord, they spread the Good News in many Samaritan villages on their way back to Jerusalem.

Philip Tells an Ethiopian About Jesus

²⁶ An angel from the Lord said to Philip, "Get up, and take the desert road that goes south from Jerusalem to Gaza." ²⁷ So Philip went.

An Ethiopian man who had come to Jerusalem to worship was on his way home. The man was a eunuch, a high-ranking official in charge of all the treasures of Queen Candace of Ethiopia. [28] As the official rode along in his carriage, he was reading the prophet Isaiah out loud.

[29] The Spirit said to Philip, "Go to that carriage, and stay close to it." [30] Philip ran to the carriage and could hear the official reading the prophet Isaiah out loud. Philip asked him, "Do you understand what you're reading?"

[31] The official answered, "How can I understand unless someone guides me?" So he invited Philip to sit with him in his carriage. [32] This was the part of the Scriptures that the official was reading:

"He was led like a lamb to the slaughter.
He was like a sheep that is silent
when its wool is cut off.
He didn't open his mouth.
[33] When he humbled himself,
he was not judged fairly.
Who from his generation
will talk about his life on earth being cut short?"

[34] The official said to Philip, "I would like to know who the prophet is talking about. Is he talking about himself or someone else?" [35] Then Philip spoke. Starting with that passage, Philip told the official the Good News about Jesus.

[36] As they were going along the road, they came to some water. The official said to Philip, "Look, there's some water. What can keep me from being baptized?"[a] [38] The official ordered the carriage to stop. He and Philip stepped into the water, and Philip baptized him. [39] When they had stepped out of the water, the Spirit of the Lord suddenly took Philip away. The official joyfully continued on his way and didn't see Philip again.

[a] 8:36 Some manuscripts and translations add verse 37: "Philip said to the official, 'If you believe with all your heart, you can be baptized.' The official answered, 'I believe Jesus Christ is the Son of God.'"

⁴⁰ Philip found himself in the city of Azotus. He traveled through all the cities and spread the Good News until he came to the city of Caesarea.

Saul Becomes a Follower of Jesus

9 ¹ Saul kept threatening to murder the Lord's disciples. He went to the chief priest ² and asked him to write letters of authorization to the synagogue leaders in the city of Damascus. Saul wanted to arrest any man or woman who followed the way ⌊of Christ⌋ and imprison them in Jerusalem.

³ As Saul was coming near the city of Damascus, a light from heaven suddenly flashed around him. ⁴ He fell to the ground and heard a voice say to him, "Saul! Saul! Why are you persecuting me?"

⁵ Saul asked, "Who are you, sir?"

The person replied, "I'm Jesus, the one you're persecuting. ⁶ Get up! Go into the city, and you'll be told what you should do."

⁷ Meanwhile, the men traveling with him were speechless. They heard the voice but didn't see anyone.

⁸ Saul was helped up from the ground. When he opened his eyes, he was blind. So his companions led him into Damascus. ⁹ For three days he couldn't see and didn't eat or drink.

¹⁰ A disciple named Ananias lived in the city of Damascus. The Lord said to him in a vision, "Ananias!"

Ananias answered, "Yes, Lord."

¹¹ The Lord told him, "Get up! Go to Judas' house on Straight Street, and ask for a man named Saul from the city of Tarsus. He's praying. ¹² In a vision he has seen a man named Ananias place his hands on him to restore his sight."

¹³ Ananias replied, "Lord, I've heard a lot of people tell about the many evil things this man has done to your people in Jerusalem. ¹⁴ Saul has come here to Damascus with authority from the chief priests to put anyone who calls on your name in prison."

¹⁵ The Lord told Ananias, "Go! I've chosen this man to bring my name to nations, to kings, and to the people of Israel. ¹⁶ I'll show him how much he has to suffer for the sake of my name."

¹⁷ Ananias left and entered Judas' house. After he placed his hands on Saul, Ananias said, "Brother Saul, the Lord Jesus, who appeared to you on your way to Damascus, sent me to you. He wants you to see again and to be filled with the Holy Spirit."

¹⁸ Immediately, something like fish scales fell from Saul's eyes, and he could see again. Then Saul stood up and was baptized. ¹⁹ After he had something to eat, his strength came back to him.

Saul was with the disciples in the city of Damascus for several days. ²⁰ He immediately began to spread the word in their synagogues that Jesus was the Son of God. ²¹ Everyone who heard him was amazed. They asked, "Isn't this the man who destroyed those who worshiped the one named Jesus in Jerusalem? Didn't he come here to take these worshipers as prisoners to the chief priests ‚in Jerusalem‚?"

²² Saul grew more powerful, and he confused the Jews living in Damascus by proving that Jesus was the Messiah. ²³ Later the Jews planned to murder Saul, ²⁴ but Saul was told about their plot. They were watching the city gates day and night in order to murder him. ²⁵ However, Saul's disciples lowered him in a large basket through an opening in the wall one night.

²⁶ After Saul arrived in Jerusalem, he tried to join the disciples. But everyone was afraid of him. They wouldn't believe that he was a disciple.

²⁷ Then Barnabas took an interest in Saul and brought him to the apostles. Barnabas told the apostles how Saul had seen the Lord on the road and that the Lord had spoken to him. Barnabas also told them how boldly Saul had spoken about the one named Jesus in the city of Damascus. ²⁸ Then Saul went throughout Jerusalem with the disciples. He spoke boldly with the power and authority of the Lord.

²⁹ He talked and argued with Greek-speaking Jews, but they tried to murder him. ³⁰ As soon as the disciples found out about this, they took Saul to Caesarea and sent him to Tarsus.

³¹ Then the church throughout Judea, Galilee, and Samaria had peace. The number of people increased as people lived in the fear of the Lord and the comfort of the Holy Spirit.

Peter Heals Aeneas

32 When Peter was going around to all of God's people, he came to those who lived in the city of Lydda. **33** In Lydda Peter found a man named Aeneas who was paralyzed and confined to a cot for eight years.

34 Peter said to him, "Aeneas, Jesus Christ makes you well. Get up, and pick up your cot." Aeneas immediately got up.

35 Everyone who lived in the city of Lydda and the coastal region of Sharon saw what had happened to Aeneas and turned to the Lord in faith.

Peter Brings Tabitha Back to Life

36 A disciple named Tabitha lived in the city of Joppa. Her Greek name was Dorcas. She always helped people and gave things to the poor. **37** She became sick and died. Her body was prepared for burial and was laid in an upstairs room.

38 Lydda is near the city of Joppa. When the disciples heard that Peter was in Lydda, they sent two men to him. They begged Peter, "Hurry to Joppa! We need your help!"

39 So Peter went with them. When he arrived, he was taken upstairs. All the widows stood around him. They were crying and showing Peter the articles of clothing that Dorcas had made while she was still with them.

40 Peter made everyone leave the room.

He knelt and prayed. Then he turned toward the body and said, "Tabitha, get up!"

Tabitha opened her eyes, saw Peter, and sat up. **41** Peter took her hand and helped her stand up. After he called the believers, especially the widows, he presented Tabitha to them. She was alive.

42 The news about this spread throughout the city of Joppa, and as a result, many people believed in the Lord.

43 Peter stayed in Joppa for a number of days with Simon, a leatherworker.

Cornelius Has a Vision

10 [1] A man named Cornelius lived in the city of Caesarea. He was a Roman army officer in the Italian Regiment. [2] He and everyone in his home were devout and respected God. Cornelius gave many gifts to poor Jewish people and always prayed to God.

[3] One day, about three in the afternoon, he had a vision. He clearly saw an angel from God come to him and say, "Cornelius!"

[4] He stared at the angel and was terrified. Cornelius asked the angel, "What do you want, sir?"

The angel answered him, "God is aware of your prayers and your gifts to the poor, and he has remembered you. [5] Send messengers now to the city of Joppa, and summon a man whose name is Simon Peter. [6] He is a guest of Simon, a leatherworker, whose house is by the sea."

[7] After saying this, the angel left. Cornelius called two of his household servants and a devout soldier, one of those who served him regularly. [8] Cornelius explained everything to them and sent them to Joppa.

Peter Has a Vision

[9] Around noon the next day, while Cornelius' men were on their way and coming close to Joppa, Peter went on the roof to pray. [10] He became hungry and wanted to eat. While the food was being prepared, he fell into a trance. [11] He saw the sky open and something like a large linen sheet being lowered by its four corners to the ground. [12] In the sheet were all kinds of four-footed animals, reptiles, and birds.

[13] A voice told him, "Get up, Peter! Kill these animals, and eat them."

[14] Peter answered, "I can't do that, Lord! I've never eaten anything that is impure or unclean."[a]

[15] A voice spoke to him a second time, "Don't say that the things which God has made clean[b] are impure."

---

[a] 10:14 "Unclean" refers to anything that Moses' Teachings say is not presentable to God.
[b] 10:15 "Clean" refers to anything that Moses' Teachings say is presentable to God.

¹⁶ This happened three times. Then the sheet was quickly taken into the sky.

¹⁷ While Peter was puzzled by the meaning of the vision, the men sent by Cornelius found Simon's house and went to the gate. ¹⁸ They asked if Simon Peter was staying there. ¹⁹ Peter was still thinking about the vision when the Spirit said to him, "Three men are looking for you. ²⁰ Get up, and go downstairs. Don't hesitate to go with these men. I have sent them."

²¹ So Peter went to the men. He said, "I'm the man you're looking for. Why are you here?"

²² The men replied, "Cornelius, a Roman army officer, sent us. He's a man who has God's approval and who respects God. Also, the Jewish people respect him. A holy angel told him to summon you to his home to hear what you have to say."

²³ Peter asked the men to come into the house and had them stay overnight.

Peter Speaks With Cornelius

The next day Peter left with them. Some disciples from Joppa went along. ²⁴ The following day they arrived in Caesarea. Cornelius was expecting them and had called his relatives and close friends together.

²⁵ When Peter was about to enter Cornelius' house, Cornelius met him, bowed down, and worshiped Peter. ²⁶ But Peter made him get up. He told him, "Stand up! I'm only a man."

²⁷ As Peter talked, he entered Cornelius' house and found that many people had gathered. ²⁸ He said to them, "You understand how wrong it is for a Jewish man to associate or visit with anyone of another race. But God has shown me that I should no longer call anyone impure or unclean. ²⁹ That is why I didn't object to coming here when you sent for me. I want to know why you sent for me."

³⁰ Cornelius answered, "Four days ago I was praying at home. It was at this same time, three o'clock in the afternoon. Suddenly, a man dressed in radiant clothes stood in front of me. ³¹ He said to me, 'Cornelius, God has heard your prayer and has remembered your

gifts to the poor. [32] So send messengers to Joppa, and summon a man whose name is Simon Peter. He's a guest in the home of Simon, a leatherworker who lives by the sea.' [33] So I sent for you immediately. Thank you for coming. All of us are here now in the presence of God to listen to everything the Lord has ordered you to say."

[34] Then Peter said, "Now I understand that God doesn't play favorites. [35] Rather, whoever respects God and does what is right is acceptable to him in any nation. [36] God sent his word to the people of Israel and brought them the Good News of peace through Jesus Christ. This Jesus Christ is everyone's Lord. [37] You know what happened throughout Judea. Everything began in Galilee after John spread the news about baptism. [38] You know that God anointed Jesus from Nazareth with the Holy Spirit and with power. Jesus went everywhere and did good things, such as healing everyone who was under the devil's power. Jesus did these things because God was with him. [39] We can testify to everything Jesus did in the land of the Jews and in Jerusalem. People hung him on a cross and killed him, [40] but God brought him back to life on the third day. God didn't show him [41] to all the people. He showed Jesus to witnesses, apostles he had already chosen. We apostles are those men who ate and drank with Jesus after he came back to life. [42] He ordered us to warn the people, 'God has appointed Jesus to judge the living and the dead.' [43] In addition, all the prophets testify that people who believe in the one named Jesus receive forgiveness for their sins through him."

[44] While Peter was still speaking, the Holy Spirit came to everyone who heard his message. [45] All the believers who were circumcised and who had come with Peter were amazed that the gift of the Holy Spirit had been poured on people who were not Jewish. [46] They heard these non-Jewish people speaking in other languages and praising God.

Then Peter said, [47] "No one can refuse to baptize these people with water. They have received the Holy Spirit in the same way that we did." [48] So Peter ordered that they should be baptized in the name of Jesus Christ.

Then they asked Peter to stay with them for several days.

Peter Reports That Non-Jewish People Can Belong to the Church

11 [1] The apostles and the believers throughout Judea heard that people who were not Jewish had accepted God's word. [2] However, when Peter went to Jerusalem, the believers who insisted on circumcision began to argue with him. [3] They said, "You went to visit men who were uncircumcised, and you even ate with them."

[4] Then Peter began to explain to them point by point what had happened. He said, [5] "I was praying in the city of Joppa when I fell into a trance. I saw something like a large linen sheet being lowered by its four corners from the sky. The sheet came near me. [6] I looked into the sheet very closely and saw tame animals, wild animals, reptiles, and birds. [7] I also heard a voice telling me, 'Get up, Peter! Kill these animals, and eat them.'

[8] "But I answered, 'I can't do that, Lord! I've never put anything impure or unclean[a] into my mouth.'

[9] "A voice spoke from heaven a second time, 'Don't say that the things which God has made clean[b] are impure.' [10] This happened three times. Then everything was pulled back into the sky again.

[11] "At that moment three men arrived at the house where we were staying. They had been sent from Caesarea to find me. [12] The Spirit told me to go with them without any hesitation. Six believers from Joppa went with me, and we visited Cornelius' home.

[13] "He told us that he had seen an angel standing in his home. The angel told him, 'Send messengers to Joppa, and summon a man whose name is Simon Peter. [14] He will give you a message that will save you and everyone in your home.'

[15] "When I began to speak, the Holy Spirit came to these people. This was the same thing that happened to us in the beginning. [16] I remembered that the Lord had said, 'John baptized with water, but you will be baptized by the Holy Spirit.' [17] When they believed, God gave them the same gift that he gave us when we believed in the Lord Jesus Christ. So who was I to interfere with God?"

---

[a] 11:8 "Unclean" refers to anything that Moses' Teachings say is not presentable to God.
[b] 11:9 "Clean" refers to anything that Moses' Teachings say is presentable to God.

[18] When the others heard this, they had no further objections. They praised God by saying, "Then God has also led people who are not Jewish to turn to him so that they can change the way they think and act and have eternal life."

The New Church in Antioch

[19] Some of the believers who were scattered by the trouble that broke out following Stephen's death went as far as Phoenicia, Cyprus, and the city of Antioch. They spoke God's word only to Jewish people. [20] But other believers, who were from Cyprus and Cyrene, arrived in Antioch. They started to spread the Good News about the Lord Jesus to Greeks. [21] The Lord's power was with his followers, and a large number of people believed and turned to the Lord.

[22] After the news about Antioch reached the church in Jerusalem, Barnabas was sent to Antioch. [23] When he arrived there, he was pleased to see what God had done for them out of kindness.[c] So he encouraged all the people to remain solidly committed to the Lord. [24] Barnabas was a dependable man, and he was full of the Holy Spirit and faith. A large crowd believed in the Lord.

[25] Then Barnabas left Antioch to go to the city of Tarsus to look for Saul. [26] After finding Saul, Barnabas brought him back to Antioch. Barnabas and Saul met with the church in Antioch for a whole year and taught a large group of people. The disciples were called Christians for the first time in the city of Antioch.

[27] At that time some prophets came from Jerusalem to the city of Antioch. [28] One of them was named Agabus. Through the Spirit Agabus predicted that a severe famine would affect the entire world. This happened while Claudius was emperor. [29] All the disciples in Antioch decided to contribute whatever they could afford to help the believers living in Judea. [30] The disciples did this and sent their contribution with Barnabas and Saul to the leaders in Jerusalem.

---

c 11:23 Or "grace."

An Angel Frees Peter From Prison

12 ¹ About that time King Herod devoted his attention to mistreating certain members of the church. ² He had James, the brother of John, executed. ³ When he saw how this pleased the Jews, he arrested Peter too. This happened during the days of Unleavened Bread. ⁴ After capturing Peter, Herod had him thrown into prison with sixteen soldiers in squads of four to guard him. Herod wanted to bring Peter to trial in front of the people after Passover. ⁵ So Peter was kept in prison, but the church was praying very hard to God for him.

⁶ The night before Herod was going to bring Peter to trial, Peter was sleeping between two soldiers. His hands were bound with two chains, and guards were in front of the door. They were watching the prison.

⁷ Suddenly, an angel from the Lord stood near Peter, and his cell was filled with light. The angel nudged Peter's side, woke him up, and said, "Hurry! Get up!" At that moment the chains fell from Peter's hands.

⁸ The angel told him, "Put your shoes on, and get ready to go!" Peter did this. Then the angel told him, "Put your coat on, and follow me."

⁹ Peter followed the angel out of the cell. He didn't realize that what the angel was doing was actually happening. He thought he was seeing a vision. ¹⁰ They passed the first and second guardposts and came to the iron gate that led into the city. This gate opened by itself for them, so they went outside and up the street. The angel suddenly left Peter.

¹¹ When Peter came to his senses, he said, "Now I'm sure that the Lord sent his angel to rescue me from Herod and from everything the Jewish people are expecting to happen to me."

¹² When Peter realized what had happened, he went to the home of Mary, the mother of John Mark. Many people had gathered at her home and were praying. ¹³ Peter knocked on the door of the entryway, and a servant named Rhoda came to answer.

¹⁴ When she recognized Peter's voice, she was so happy that instead of opening the door, she ran back inside and reported, "Peter is standing at the door!"

¹⁵ The people told her, "You're crazy!" But she insisted that Peter was at the door. They said, "It has to be his angel."

¹⁶ But Peter kept knocking. When they opened the door, they were shocked to see him. ¹⁷ Peter motioned with his hand to quiet them down and told them how the Lord had taken him out of prison. He added, "Tell James and the other believers about this." Then he left and went somewhere else.

¹⁸ In the morning the soldiers were in an uproar over what had happened to Peter. ¹⁹ Herod searched for Peter but couldn't find him. So he questioned the guards and gave orders to have them executed.

Herod's Death

Then Herod left Judea and went to Caesarea, where he stayed for a while.

²⁰ Herod was very angry with the people of Tyre and Sidon. They were going to meet with Herod. They had agreed on what they wanted to do: They enlisted the help of Blastus to ask Herod for terms of peace. This was because their cities depended on Herod for their food supply. (Blastus was in charge of the king's living quarters.)

²¹ The appointed day came. Herod, wearing his royal clothes, sat on his throne and began making a speech to them. ²² The people started shouting, "The voice of a god and not of a man!"

²³ Immediately, an angel from the Lord killed Herod for not giving glory to God. Herod was eaten by maggots, and he died.

²⁴ But God's word continued to spread and win many followers.

Barnabas and Saul Travel to Cyprus

²⁵ After Barnabas and Saul delivered the contribution ⌐to the leaders in Jerusalem⌐, they returned ⌐to Antioch⌐ from Jerusalem. They brought John Mark with them.

13 ¹ Barnabas, Simeon (called the Black), Lucius (from Cyrene), Manaen (a close friend of Herod since childhood), and Saul were prophets and teachers in the church in Antioch.

² While they were worshiping the Lord and fasting, the Holy Spirit said, "Set Barnabas and Saul apart for me. I want them to do the work for which I called them." ³ After fasting and praying, Simeon, Lucius, and Manaen placed their hands on Barnabas and Saul, and released them ˌfrom their work in Antiochˌ.

⁴ After Barnabas and Saul were sent by the Holy Spirit, they went to the city of Seleucia and from there sailed to the island of Cyprus. ⁵ Arriving in the city of Salamis, they began to spread God's word in the synagogues. John Mark had gone along to help them. ⁶ They went through the whole island as far as the city of Paphos.

In Paphos they met a Jewish man named Barjesus. He was an astrologer who claimed to be a prophet. ⁷ He was associated with an intelligent man, Sergius Paulus, who was the governor of the island. The governor sent for Barnabas and Saul because he wanted to hear the word of God. ⁸ Elymas, whose name means *astrologer,* opposed them and tried to distort the meaning of the faith so that the governor wouldn't believe.

⁹ But Saul, also known as Paul, was filled with the Holy Spirit. He stared at Elymas ¹⁰ and said, "You are full of dirty tricks and schemes, you son of the devil! You hate everything that has God's approval. Quit trying to distort the truth about the way the Lord wants people to live. ¹¹ The Lord is against you now. For a while you will be blind, unable to see the light of day."

Suddenly, Elymas couldn't see a thing. He tried to find people to lead him. ¹² When the governor saw what had happened, he believed. The Lord's teachings amazed him.

Paul and Barnabas Go to Antioch Near Pisidia

¹³ Paul and his men took a ship from Paphos and arrived in Perga, a city in Pamphylia. John Mark deserted them there and went back to Jerusalem. ¹⁴ Paul and Barnabas left Perga and

arrived in Antioch, a city near Pisidia. On the day of worship they went into the synagogue and sat down.

[15] After reading from Moses' Teachings and the Prophets, the synagogue leaders sent ˌa messageˌ to Paul and Barnabas. The message said, "Brothers, if you have any words of encouragement for the people, feel free to speak."

[16] Then Paul stood up, motioned with his hand, and said, "Men of Israel and converts to Judaism, listen to me. [17] The God of the people of Israel chose our ancestors and made them a strong nation while they lived as foreigners in Egypt. He used his powerful arm to bring them out of Egypt, [18] and he put up with them for about forty years in the desert. [19] Then he destroyed seven nations in Canaan and gave their land to his people as an inheritance. [20] He did all this in about four hundred and fifty years.

"After that he gave his people judges until the time of the prophet Samuel.

[21] "Then the people demanded a king, so God gave them Saul, son of Kish, from the tribe of Benjamin. After forty years [22] God removed Saul and made David their king. God spoke favorably about David. He said, 'I have found that David, son of Jesse, is a man after my own heart. He will do everything I want him to do.'

[23] "God had the Savior, Jesus, come to Israel from David's descendants, as he had promised. [24] Before Jesus began his ministry, John ˌthe Baptizerˌ told everyone in Israel about the baptism of repentance.[a] [25] When John was finishing his work, he said, 'Who do you think I am? I'm not the person you're looking for. He will come later. I'm not even good enough to untie his sandals.'

[26] "Brothers—descendants of Abraham and converts to Judaism—the message that God saves people was sent to us. [27] The people who live in Jerusalem and their rulers didn't know who Jesus was. They didn't understand the prophets' messages, which are read every day of worship. So they condemned Jesus and fulfilled what the prophets had said. [28] Although they couldn't find any

---

[a] 13:24 "Repentance" is turning to God with a complete change in the way a person thinks and acts.

good reason to kill him, they asked Pilate to have him executed. [29] When they had finished doing everything that was written about him, they took him down from the cross and placed him in a tomb. [30] But God brought him back to life, [31] and for many days he appeared to those who had come with him to Jerusalem from Galilee. These people are now witnesses and are testifying to the Jewish people about him. [32] We are telling you the Good News: What God promised our ancestors has happened. [33] God has fulfilled the promise for us, their descendants, by bringing Jesus back to life. This is what Scripture says in the second psalm:

> 'You are my Son.
> Today I have become your Father.'

[34] "God stated that he brought Jesus back to life and that Jesus' body never decayed. He said, 'I will give you the enduring love promised to David.' [35] Another psalm says, 'You will not allow your holy one to decay.' [36] After doing God's will by serving the people of his time, David died. He was laid to rest with his ancestors, but his body decayed. [37] However, the man God brought back to life had a body that didn't decay.

[38] "So, brothers, I'm telling you that through Jesus your sins can be forgiven. Sins kept you from receiving God's approval through Moses' Teachings. [39] However, everyone who believes in Jesus receives God's approval.

[40] "Be careful, or what the prophets said may happen to you.

> [41]   'Look, you mockers!
>   Be amazed and die!
>   I am going to do something in your days
>   that you would not believe even if it were reported
>   to you!' "

[42] As Paul and Barnabas were leaving the synagogue, the people invited them to speak on the same subject the next day of worship. [43] When the meeting of the synagogue broke up, many Jews and converts to Judaism followed Paul and Barnabas. Paul and

Barnabas talked with them and were persuading them to continue trusting God's good will.[b]

⁴⁴ On the next day of worship, almost the whole city gathered to hear the Lord's word. ⁴⁵ When the Jews saw the crowds, they became very jealous. They used insulting language to contradict whatever Paul said.

⁴⁶ Paul and Barnabas told them boldly, "We had to speak the word of God to you first. Since you reject the word and consider yourselves unworthy of everlasting life, we are now going to turn to people of other nations. ⁴⁷ The Lord gave us the following order:

'I have made you a light for the nations
    so that you would save people all over the world.' "

⁴⁸ The people who were not Jews were pleased with what they heard and praised the Lord's word. Everyone who had been prepared for everlasting life believed. ⁴⁹ The word of the Lord spread throughout the whole region. ⁵⁰ But Jews stirred up devout women of high social standing and the officials of the city. These people started to persecute Paul and Barnabas and threw them out of their territory.

⁵¹ In protest against these people, Paul and Barnabas shook the dust off their feet and went to the city of Iconium. ⁵² Meanwhile, the disciples ͺin Antiochͺ continued to be full of joy and the Holy Spirit.

Paul and Barnabas in Iconium

14 ¹ The same thing happened in the city of Iconium. Paul and Barnabas went into the synagogue and spoke in such a way that a large crowd of Jews and Greeks believed. ² But the Jews who refused to believe stirred up some people who were not Jewish and poisoned their minds against the believers. ³ Paul and Barnabas stayed in the city of Iconium for a long time. They spoke boldly about the Lord, who confirmed their message about his good will[a] by having them perform miracles and do amazing

---

b 13:43 Or "grace."   *a* 14:3 Or "grace."

things. ⁴ But the people of Iconium were divided. Some were for the Jews, while others were for the apostles.

⁵ In the meantime, Paul and Barnabas found out that the non-Jewish people and the Jewish people with their rulers planned to attack them and stone them to death. ⁶ So they escaped to Lystra and Derbe, cities of Lycaonia, and to the surrounding territory. ⁷ They spread the Good News there.

Paul and Barnabas in Lystra

⁸ A man who was born lame was in Lystra. He was always sitting because he had never been able to walk. ⁹ He listened to what Paul was saying. Paul observed him closely and saw that the man believed he could be made well. ¹⁰ So Paul said in a loud voice, "Stand up." The man jumped up and began to walk.

¹¹ The crowds who saw what Paul had done shouted in the Lycaonian language, "The gods have come to us, and they look human." ¹² They addressed Barnabas as Zeus and Paul as Hermes because Paul did most of the talking. ¹³ Zeus' temple was at the entrance to the city. The priest of the god Zeus brought bulls with flowery wreaths around their necks to the temple gates. The priest and the crowd wanted to offer a sacrifice ˌto Paul and Barnabasˌ.

¹⁴ When the apostles Barnabas and Paul heard what was happening, they were very upset. They rushed into the crowd ¹⁵ and said, "Men, what are you doing? We're human beings like you. We're spreading the Good News to you to turn you away from these worthless gods to the living God. The living God made the sky, the land, the sea, and everything in them. ¹⁶ In the past God allowed all people to live as they pleased. ¹⁷ Yet, by doing good, he has given evidence of his existence. He gives you rain from heaven and crops in their seasons. He fills you with food and your lives with happiness." ¹⁸ Although Paul and Barnabas said these things, they hardly kept the crowd from sacrificing to them.

¹⁹ However, Jews from the cities of Antioch and Iconium arrived in Lystra and won the people over. They tried to stone Paul to death and dragged him out of the city when they thought that he was dead.

[20] But when the disciples gathered around him, he got up and went back into the city.

Paul and Barnabas Return to Antioch in Syria

The next day Paul and Barnabas left for the city of Derbe. [21] They spread the Good News in that city and won many disciples. Then they went back to the cities of Lystra, Iconium, and Antioch (which is in Pisidia). [22] They strengthened the disciples in these cities and encouraged the disciples to remain faithful. Paul and Barnabas told them, "We must suffer a lot to enter the kingdom of God." [23] They had the disciples in each church choose spiritual leaders,[b] and with prayer and fasting they entrusted the leaders to the Lord in whom they believed.

[24] After they had gone through Pisidia, they went to Pamphylia. [25] They spoke the message in the city of Perga and went to the city of Attalia. [26] From Attalia they took a boat and headed home to the city of Antioch ˪in Syria˩. (In Antioch they had been entrusted to God's care[c] for the work they had now finished.) [27] When they arrived, they called the members of the church together. They reported everything God had done through them, especially that he had given people who were not Jewish the opportunity to believe. [28] They stayed for a long time with these disciples.

Controversy About Moses' Teachings

15 [1] Some men came from Judea and started to teach believers that people can't be saved unless they are circumcised as Moses' Teachings require. [2] Paul and Barnabas had a fierce dispute with these men. So Paul and Barnabas and some of the others were sent to Jerusalem to see the apostles and spiritual leaders[a] about this claim.

[3] The church sent Paul and Barnabas ˪to Jerusalem˩. As they were going through Phoenicia and Samaria, they told the whole story of how non-Jewish people were turning to God. This story brought great joy to all the believers.

[b] 14:23 Or "pastors," or "elders."   [c] 14:26 Or "grace."   [a] 15:2 Or "pastors," or "elders."

⁴ The church in Jerusalem, the apostles, and the spiritual leaders welcomed Paul and Barnabas when they arrived. Paul and Barnabas reported everything that God had done through them. ⁵ But some believers from the party of the Pharisees stood up and said, "People who are not Jewish must be circumcised and ordered to follow Moses' Teachings."

⁶ The apostles and spiritual leaders met to consider this statement. ⁷ After a lot of debating, Peter stood up and said to them, "Brothers, you know what happened some time ago. God chose me so that people who aren't Jewish could hear the Good News and believe. ⁸ God, who knows everyone's thoughts, showed that he approved of people who aren't Jewish by giving them the Holy Spirit as he gave the Holy Spirit to us. ⁹ God doesn't discriminate between Jewish and non-Jewish people. He has cleansed non-Jewish people through faith as he has cleansed us Jews. ¹⁰ So why are you testing God? You're putting a burden on the disciples, a burden neither our ancestors nor we can carry. ¹¹ We certainly believe that the Lord Jesus saves us the same way that he saves them—through his kindness."*ᵇ*

¹² The whole crowd was silent. They listened to Barnabas and Paul tell about all the miracles and amazing things that God had done through them among non-Jewish people.

¹³ After they finished speaking, James responded, "Brothers, listen to me. ¹⁴ Simon has explained how God first showed his concern by taking from non-Jewish people those who would honor his name. ¹⁵ This agrees with what the prophets said. Scripture says,

16   'Afterwards, I will return.
          I will set up David's fallen tent again.
          I will restore its ruined places again.
          I will set it up again
17   so that the survivors and all the people
                  who aren't Jewish

ᵇ 15:11 Or "grace."

over whom my name is spoken,
    may search for the Lord, declares the Lord.
¹⁸ He is the one who will do these things that have always
    been known!'

¹⁹ "So I've decided that we shouldn't trouble non-Jewish people who are turning to God. ²⁰ Instead, we should write a letter telling them to keep away from things polluted by false gods, from sexual sins, from eating the meat of strangled animals, and from eating bloody meat. ²¹ After all, Moses' words have been spread to every city for generations. His teachings are read in synagogues on every day of worship."

²² Then the apostles, the spiritual leaders, and the whole church decided to choose some of their men to send with Paul and Barnabas to the city of Antioch. They chose Judas (called Barsabbas) and Silas, who were leaders among the believers. ²³ They wrote this letter for them to deliver:

From the apostles and the spiritual leaders, your brothers.
To their non-Jewish brothers and sisters in Antioch, Syria,
    and Cilicia.
Dear brothers and sisters,

²⁴ We have heard that some individuals who came from us have confused you with statements that disturb you. We did not authorize these men ⌊to speak⌋. ²⁵ So we have come to a unanimous decision that we should choose men and send them to you with our dear Barnabas and Paul. ²⁶ Barnabas and Paul have dedicated their lives to our Lord, the one named Jesus Christ. ²⁷ We have sent Judas and Silas to report to you on our decision. ²⁸ The Holy Spirit and we have agreed not to place any additional burdens on you. Do only what is necessary ²⁹ by keeping away from food sacrificed to false gods, from eating bloody meat, from eating the meat of strangled animals, and from sexual sins. If you avoid these things, you will be doing what's right.
Farewell!

³⁰ So the men were sent on their way and arrived in the city of Antioch. They gathered the congregation together and delivered the letter. ³¹ When the people read the letter, they were pleased with the encouragement it brought them. ³² Judas and Silas, who were also prophets, spoke a long time to encourage and strengthen the believers.

³³ After Judas and Silas had stayed in Antioch for some time, the congregation sent them back to Jerusalem with friendly greetings to those who had sent them.ᶜ ³⁵ Paul and Barnabas stayed in Antioch. They and many others taught people about the Lord's word and spread the Good News.

Paul and Barnabas Disagree

³⁶ After a while Paul said to Barnabas, "Let's go back to every city where we spread the Lord's word. We'll visit the believers to see how they're doing."

³⁷ Barnabas wanted to take John Mark along. ³⁸ However, Paul didn't think it was right to take a person like him along. John Mark had deserted them in Pamphylia and had not gone with them to work. ³⁹ Paul and Barnabas disagreed so sharply that they parted ways. Barnabas took Mark with him and sailed to the island of Cyprus. ⁴⁰ Paul chose Silas and left after the believers entrusted him to the Lord's care.ᵈ

⁴¹ Paul went through the provinces of Syria and Cilicia and strengthened the churches.

Timothy Joins Paul in Lystra

16 ¹ Paul arrived in the city of Derbe and then went to Lystra, where a disciple named Timothy lived. Timothy's mother was a Jewish believer, but his father was Greek. ² The believers in Lystra and Iconium spoke well of Timothy. ³ Paul wanted Timothy to go with him. So he circumcised him because of the Jews who lived in those places and because he knew that Timothy's father was Greek.

ᶜ 15:33 Some manuscripts and translations add verse 34: "But Silas decided to stay there, and Judas went back to Jerusalem alone."   ᵈ 15:40 Or "grace."

⁴ As they went through the cities, they told people about the decisions that the apostles and spiritual leaders[a] in Jerusalem had made for the people. ⁵ So the churches were strengthened in the faith and grew in numbers every day.

Paul Has a Vision

⁶ Paul and Silas went through the regions of Phrygia and Galatia because the Holy Spirit kept them from speaking the word in the province of Asia. ⁷ They went to the province of Mysia and tried to enter Bithynia, but the Spirit of Jesus wouldn't allow this. ⁸ So they passed by Mysia and went to the city of Troas.

⁹ During the night Paul had a vision of a man from Macedonia. The man urged Paul, "Come to Macedonia to help us."

¹⁰ As soon as Paul had seen the vision, we immediately looked for a way to go to Macedonia. We concluded that God had called us to tell the people of Macedonia about the Good News.

Paul and Silas in Philippi

¹¹ So we took a ship from Troas and sailed straight to the island of Samothrace. The next day we sailed to the city of Neapolis, ¹² and from there we went to the city of Philippi. Philippi is a leading city in that part of Macedonia, and it is a Roman colony. We were in this city for a number of days.

¹³ On the day of worship we went out of the city to a place along the river where we thought Jewish people gathered for prayer. We sat down and began talking to the women who had gathered there. ¹⁴ A woman named Lydia was present. She was a convert to Judaism from the city of Thyatira and sold purple dye for a living. She was listening because the Lord made her willing to pay attention to what Paul said. ¹⁵ When Lydia and her family were baptized, she invited us to stay at her home. She said, "If you're convinced that I believe in the Lord, then stay at my home." She insisted. So we did.

¹⁶ One day when we were going to the place of prayer, a female servant met us. She was possessed by an evil spirit that told for-

a 16:4 Or "pastors," or "elders."

tunes. She made a lot of money for her owners by telling fortunes.
[17] She used to follow Paul and shout, "These men are servants of the Most High God. They're telling you how you can be saved." [18] She kept doing this for many days. Paul became annoyed, turned to the evil spirit, and said, "I command you in the name of Jesus Christ to come out of her!"

As Paul said this, the evil spirit left her. [19] When her owners realized that their hope of making money was gone, they grabbed Paul and Silas and dragged them to the authorities in the public square. [20] In front of the Roman officials, they said, "These men are stirring up a lot of trouble in our city. They're Jews, [21] and they're advocating customs that we can't accept or practice as Roman citizens."

[22] The crowd joined in the attack against Paul and Silas. Then the officials tore the clothes off Paul and Silas and ordered ˌthe guardsˌ to beat them with sticks. [23] After they had hit Paul and Silas many times, they threw them in jail and ordered the jailer to keep them under tight security. [24] So the jailer followed these orders and put Paul and Silas into solitary confinement with their feet in leg irons.

[25] Around midnight Paul and Silas were praying and singing hymns of praise to God. The other prisoners were listening to them. [26] Suddenly, a violent earthquake shook the foundations of the jail. All the doors immediately flew open, and all the prisoners' chains came loose.

[27] The jailer woke up and saw the prison doors open. Thinking the prisoners had escaped, he drew his sword and was about to kill himself. [28] But Paul shouted as loudly as he could, "Don't hurt yourself! We're all here!"

[29] The jailer asked for torches and rushed into the jail. He was trembling as he knelt in front of Paul and Silas. [30] Then he took Paul and Silas outside and asked, "Sirs, what do I have to do to be saved?"

[31] They answered, "Believe in the Lord Jesus, and you and your family will be saved." [32] They spoke the Lord's word to the jailer and everyone in his home.

[33] At that hour of the night, the jailer washed Paul and Silas' wounds. The jailer and his entire family were baptized immediately. [34] He took Paul and Silas upstairs into his home and gave them something to eat. He and his family were thrilled to be believers in God.

[35] In the morning the Roman officials sent guards who told the jailer, "You can release those men now."

[36] The jailer reported this order to Paul by saying, "The officials have sent word to release you. So you can leave peacefully now."

[37] But Paul told the guards, "Roman officials have had us beaten publicly without a trial and have thrown us in jail, even though we're Roman citizens. Now are they going to throw us out secretly? There's no way they're going to get away with that! Have them escort us out!"

[38] The guards reported to the officials what Paul had said. When the Roman officials heard that Paul and Silas were Roman citizens, they were afraid. [39] So the officials went to the jail and apologized to Paul and Silas. As the officials escorted Paul and Silas out of the jail, they asked them to leave the city.

[40] After Paul and Silas left the jail, they went to Lydia's house. They met with the believers, encouraged them, and then left.

Paul and Silas in Thessalonica

17 [1] Paul and Silas traveled through the cities of Amphipolis and Apollonia and came to the city of Thessalonica, where there was a synagogue. [2] As usual, Paul went into the synagogue. On three consecutive days of worship, he had discussions about Scripture with the synagogue members. [3] He explained and showed them that the Messiah had to suffer, die, and come back to life, and that Jesus, the person he talked about, was this Messiah.

[4] Some of the Jews were persuaded to join Paul and Silas, especially a large group of Greeks who had converted to Judaism and the wives of many prominent men.

[5] Then the Jews became jealous. They took some low-class characters who hung around the public square, formed a mob,

and started a riot in the city. They attacked Jason's home and searched it for Paul and Silas in order to bring them out to the crowd. ⁶ When they didn't find Paul and Silas, they dragged Jason and some other believers in front of the city officials. They shouted, "Those men who have made trouble all over the world are now here in Thessalonica, ⁷ and Jason has welcomed them as his guests. All of them oppose the emperor's decrees by saying that there is another king, whose name is Jesus."

⁸ The crowd and the officials were upset when they heard this. ⁹ But after they had made Jason and the others post bond, they let them go.

¹⁰ Immediately when night came, the believers sent Paul and Silas to the city of Berea.

Paul and Silas in Berea

When Paul and Silas arrived in the city of Berea, they entered the synagogue. ¹¹ The people of Berea were more open-minded than the people of Thessalonica. They were very willing to receive God's message, and every day they carefully examined the Scriptures to see if what Paul said was true. ¹² Many of them became believers, and quite a number of them were prominent Greek men and women.

¹³ But when the Jews in Thessalonica found out that Paul was also spreading God's word in Berea, they went there to upset and confuse the people. ¹⁴ The believers immediately sent Paul to the seacoast, but Silas and Timothy stayed in Berea.

Paul in Athens

¹⁵ The men who escorted Paul took him all the way to the city of Athens. When the men left Athens, they took instructions back to Silas and Timothy to join Paul as soon as possible.

¹⁶ While Paul was waiting for Silas and Timothy in Athens, he saw that the city had statues of false gods everywhere. This upset him. ¹⁷ He held discussions in the synagogue with Jews and converts to Judaism. He also held discussions every day in the public

square with anyone who happened to be there. ¹⁸ Some Epicurean and Stoic philosophers had discussions with him. Some asked, "What is this babbling fool trying to say?" Others said, "He seems to be speaking about foreign gods." The philosophers said these things because Paul was telling the Good News about Jesus and saying that people would come back to life.

¹⁹ Then they brought Paul to the city court, the Areopagus, and asked, "Could you tell us these new ideas that you're teaching? ²⁰ Some of the things you say sound strange to us. So we would like to know what they mean."

²¹ Everyone who lived in Athens looked for opportunities to tell or hear something new and unusual.

²² Paul stood in the middle of the court and said, "Men of Athens, I see that you are very religious. ²³ As I was going through your city and looking closely at the objects you worship, I noticed an altar with this written on it: 'To an unknown god.' I'm telling you about the unknown god you worship. ²⁴ The God who made the universe and everything in it is the Lord of heaven and earth. He doesn't live in shrines made by humans, ²⁵ and he isn't served by humans as if he needed anything. He gives everyone life, breath, and everything they have. ²⁶ From one man he has made every nation of humanity to live all over the earth. He has given them the seasons of the year and the boundaries within which to live. ²⁷ He has done this so that they would look for God, somehow reach for him, and find him. In fact, he is never far from any one of us. ²⁸ Certainly, we live, move, and exist because of him. As some of your poets have said, 'We are God's children.' ²⁹ So if we are God's children, we shouldn't think that the divine being is like an image made from gold, silver, or stone, an image that is the product of human imagination and skill.

³⁰ "God overlooked the times when people didn't know any better. But now he commands everyone everywhere to turn to him and change the way they think and act. ³¹ He has set a day when he is going to judge the world with justice, and he will use a man he has appointed to do this. God has given proof to everyone that he will do this by bringing that man back to life."

³² When the people of the court heard that a person had come back to life, some began joking about it, while others said, "We'll hear you talk about this some other time."

³³ With this response, Paul left the court. ³⁴ Some men joined him and became believers. With them were Dionysius, who was a member of the court, and a woman named Damaris, and some other people.

Paul in Corinth

18 ¹ After this, Paul left Athens and went to the city of Corinth. ² In Corinth he met a Jewish man named Aquila and his wife Priscilla. Aquila had been born in Pontus, and they had recently come from Italy because Claudius had ordered all Jews to leave Rome. Paul went to visit them, ³ and because they made tents for a living as he did, he stayed with them and they worked together.

⁴ On every day of worship, Paul would discuss ˍScriptureˌ in the synagogue. He tried to win over Jews and Greeks who had converted to Judaism. ⁵ But when Silas and Timothy arrived from Macedonia, Paul devoted all his time to teaching the word of God. He assured the Jews that Jesus is the Messiah. ⁶ But they opposed him and insulted him. So Paul shook the dust from his clothes and told them, "You're responsible for your own death. I'm innocent. From now on I'm going to people who are not Jewish."

⁷ Then he left the synagogue and went to the home of a man named Titius Justus, who was a convert to Judaism. His house was next door to the synagogue. ⁸ The synagogue leader Crispus and his whole family believed in the Lord. Many Corinthians who heard Paul believed and were baptized.

⁹ One night the Lord said to Paul in a vision, "Don't be afraid to speak out! Don't be silent! ¹⁰ I'm with you. No one will attack you or harm you. I have many people in this city."

¹¹ Paul lived in Corinth for a year and a half and taught the word of God to them.

¹² While Gallio was governor of Greece, the Jews had one thought in mind. They attacked Paul and brought him to court.

¹³ They said, "This man is persuading people to worship God in ways that are against Moses' Teachings."

¹⁴ Paul was about to answer when Gallio said to the Jews, "If there were some kind of misdemeanor or crime involved, reason would demand that I put up with you Jews. ¹⁵ But since you're disputing words, names, and your own teachings, you'll have to take care of that yourselves. I don't want to be a judge who gets involved in those things." ¹⁶ So Gallio had them forced out of his court.

¹⁷ Then all ˏthe governor's officersˎ took Sosthenes, the synagogue leader, and beat him in front of the court. But Gallio couldn't have cared less.

Paul's Return Trip to Antioch

¹⁸ After staying in Corinth quite a while longer, Paul left ˏfor Ephesusˎ. Priscilla and Aquila went with him. In the city of Cenchrea, Aquila had his hair cut, since he had taken a vow. From Cenchrea they took a boat headed for Syria ¹⁹ and arrived in the city of Ephesus, where Paul left Priscilla and Aquila. Paul went into the synagogue and had a discussion with the Jews. ²⁰ The Jews asked him to stay longer, but he refused. ²¹ As he left, he told them, "I'll come back to visit you if God wants me to."

Paul took a boat from Ephesus ²² and arrived in the city of Caesarea. He went ˏto Jerusalemˎ, greeted the church, and went back to the city of Antioch.

²³ After spending some time in Antioch, Paul went through the regions of Galatia and Phrygia, where he strengthened ˏthe faith ofˎ all the disciples.

Apollos Tells Others About Jesus

²⁴ A Jew named Apollos, who had been born in Alexandria, arrived in the city of Ephesus. He was an eloquent speaker and knew how to use the Scriptures in a powerful way. ²⁵ He had been instructed in the Lord's way and spoke enthusiastically. He accurately taught about Jesus but knew only about the baptism John performed. ²⁶ He began to speak boldly in the synagogue. When

Priscilla and Aquila heard him, they took him ⌐home⌐ with them and explained God's way to him more accurately.

²⁷ When Apollos wanted to travel to Greece, the believers ⌐in Ephesus⌐ encouraged him. They wrote to the disciples in Greece to tell them to welcome him. When he arrived in Greece, God's kindness[a] enabled him to help the believers a great deal. ²⁸ In public Apollos helped them by clearly showing from the Scriptures that Jesus is the Messiah and that the Jews were wrong.

Paul in Ephesus

19 ¹ While Apollos was in Corinth, Paul traveled through the interior provinces to get to the city of Ephesus. He met some disciples in Ephesus ² and asked them, "Did you receive the Holy Spirit when you became believers?"

They answered him, "No, we've never even heard of the Holy Spirit."

³ Paul asked them, "What kind of baptism did you have?"

They answered, "John's baptism."

⁴ Paul said, "John's baptism was a baptism of repentance.[a] John told people to believe in Jesus, who was coming later."

⁵ After they heard this, they were baptized in the name of the Lord Jesus. ⁶ When Paul placed his hands on them, the Holy Spirit came to them, and they began to talk in other languages and to speak what God had revealed. ⁷ About twelve men were in the group.

⁸ For three months Paul would go into the synagogue and speak boldly. He had discussions with people to convince them about the kingdom of God. ⁹ But when some people became stubborn, refused to believe, and had nothing good to say in front of the crowd about the way ⌐of Christ⌐, he left them. He took his disciples and held daily discussions in the lecture hall of Tyrannus. ¹⁰ This continued for two years so that all the Jews and Greeks who lived in the province of Asia heard the word of the Lord.

---

[a] 18:27 Or "grace."   [a] 19:4 "Repentance" is turning to God with a complete change in the way a person thinks and acts.

[11] God worked unusual miracles through Paul. [12] People would take handkerchiefs and aprons that had touched Paul's skin to those who were sick. Their sicknesses would be cured, and evil spirits would leave them.

[13] Some Jews used to travel from place to place and force evil spirits out of people. They tried to use the name of the Lord Jesus to force evil spirits out of those who were possessed. These Jews would say, "I order you ˌto come outˌ in the name of Jesus, whom Paul talks about." [14] Seven sons of Sceva, a Jewish chief priest, were doing this.

[15] But the evil spirit answered them, "I know Jesus, and I'm acquainted with Paul, but who are you?" [16] Then the man possessed by the evil spirit attacked them. He beat them up so badly that they ran out of that house naked and wounded.

[17] All the Jews and Greeks living in the city of Ephesus heard about this. All of them were filled with awe for the name of the Lord Jesus and began to speak very highly about it. [18] Many believers openly admitted their involvement with magical spells and told all the details. [19] Many of those who were involved in the occult gathered their books and burned them in front of everyone. They added up the cost of these books and found that they were worth 50,000 silver coins. [20] In this powerful way the word of the Lord was spreading and gaining strength.

[21] After all these things had happened, Paul decided to go to Jerusalem by traveling through Macedonia and Greece. He said, "After I have been there, I must see Rome." [22] So he sent two of his helpers, Timothy and Erastus, to Macedonia, while he stayed longer in the province of Asia.

A Riot in Ephesus

[23] During that time a serious disturbance concerning the way ˌof Christˌ broke out in the city of Ephesus.

[24] Demetrius, a silversmith, was in the business of making silver models of the temple of Artemis. His business brought a huge profit for the men who worked for him. [25] He called a meeting of his workers and others who did similar work. Demetrius

said, "Men, you know that we're earning a good income from this business, [26] and you see and hear what this man Paul has done. He has won over a large crowd that follows him not only in Ephesus but also throughout the province of Asia. He tells people that gods made by humans are not gods. [27] There's a danger that people will discredit our line of work, and there's a danger that people will think that the temple of the great goddess Artemis is nothing. Then she whom all Asia and the rest of the world worship will be robbed of her glory."

[28] When Demetrius' workers and the others heard this, they became furious and began shouting, "Artemis of the Ephesians is great!" [29] The confusion spread throughout the city, and the people had one thought in mind as they rushed into the theater. They grabbed Gaius and Aristarchus, the Macedonians who traveled with Paul, and they dragged the two men into the theater with them.

[30] Paul wanted to go into the crowd, but his disciples wouldn't let him. [31] Even some officials who were from the province of Asia and who were Paul's friends sent messengers to urge him not to risk going into the theater.

[32] Some people shouted one thing while others shouted something else. The crowd was confused. Most of the people didn't even know why they had come together. [33] Some people concluded that Alexander was the cause, so the Jews pushed him to the front. Alexander motioned with his hand to quiet the people because he wanted to defend himself in front of them. [34] But when they recognized that Alexander was a Jew, everyone started to shout in unison, "Artemis of the Ephesians is great!" They kept doing this for about two hours.

[35] The city clerk finally quieted the crowd. Then he said, "Citizens of Ephesus, everyone knows that this city of the Ephesians is the keeper of the temple of the great Artemis. Everyone knows that Ephesus is the keeper of the statue that fell down from Zeus. [36] No one can deny this. So you have to be quiet and not do anything foolish. [37] The men you brought here don't rob temples or insult our goddess. [38] If Demetrius and the men who work for him have a

legal complaint against anyone, we have special days and officials
to hold court. That's where they should bring charges against
each other. [39] If you want anything else, you must settle the matter in a legal assembly. [40] At this moment we run the risk of being
accused of rioting today for no reason. We won't be able to explain
this mob." [41] After saying this, he dismissed the assembly.[b]

20 [1] When the uproar was over, Paul sent for the disciples,
encouraged them, said goodbye, and left for Macedonia. [2] He
went through that region and spoke many words of encouragement
to the people. Then he went to Greece [3] and stayed there for three
months.

Paul in Troas

When Paul was going to board a ship for Syria, he found
out that the Jews were plotting to kill him. So he decided to go
back through Macedonia. [4] Sopater (son of Pyrrhus) from Berea,
Aristarchus and Secundus from Thessalonica, Gaius from Derbe,
Timothy, and Tychicus and Trophimus from the province of Asia
accompanied Paul. [5] All these men went ahead and were waiting for us in Troas. [6] After the Festival of Unleavened Bread, we
boarded a ship at Philippi. Five days later we joined them in Troas
and stayed there for seven days.

[7] On Sunday we met to break bread. Paul was discussing
⌐Scripture⌐ with the people. Since he intended to leave the next
day, he kept talking until midnight. [8] (Many lamps were lit in the
upstairs room where we were meeting.)

[9] A young man named Eutychus was sitting in a window. As
Paul was talking on and on, Eutychus was gradually falling asleep.
Finally, overcome by sleep, he fell from the third story and was
dead when they picked him up. [10] Paul went to him, took him into
his arms, and said, "Don't worry! He's alive!" [11] Then Eutychus
went upstairs again, broke the bread, and ate. Paul talked with the
people for a long time, until sunrise, and then left.

---

[b] 19:41 Acts 19:41 in English Bibles is Acts 19:40b in the Greek Bible.

¹² The people took the boy home. They were greatly relieved that he was alive.

Paul's Trip to Miletus

¹³ We went ahead to the ship and sailed for the city of Assos. At Assos, we were going to pick up Paul. He had made these arrangements, since he had planned to walk overland to Assos. ¹⁴ When Paul met us in Assos, we took him on board and went to the city of Mitylene. ¹⁵ We sailed from there. On the following day we approached the island of Chios. The next day we went by the island of Samos, and on the next day we arrived at the city of Miletus. ¹⁶ Paul had decided to sail past Ephesus to avoid spending time in the province of Asia. He was in a hurry to get to Jerusalem for the day of Pentecost, if that was possible.

Paul Meets With the Spiritual Leaders From Ephesus

¹⁷ From Miletus Paul sent messengers to the city of Ephesus and called the spiritual leaders[a] of the church to meet with him ˌin Miletusˌ. ¹⁸ When they were with him, he said to them, "You know how I spent all my time with you from the first day I arrived in the province of Asia. ¹⁹ I humbly served the Lord, often with tears in my eyes. I served the Lord during the difficult times I went through when the Jews plotted against me. ²⁰ I didn't avoid telling you anything that would help you, and I didn't avoid teaching you publicly and from house to house. ²¹ I warned Jews and Greeks to change the way they think and act and to believe in our Lord Jesus.

²² "I am determined to go to Jerusalem now. I don't know what will happen to me there. ²³ However, the Holy Spirit warns me in every city that imprisonment and suffering are waiting for me. ²⁴ But I don't place any value on my own life. I want to finish the race I'm running. I want to carry out the mission I received from the Lord Jesus—the mission of testifying to the Good News of God's kindness.[b]

²⁵ "Now I know that none of you whom I told about the kingdom ˌof Godˌ will see me again. ²⁶ Therefore, I declare to you today that I am not responsible for the ˌspiritualˌ death of any of you.

---

[a] 20:17 Or "pastors," or "elders."   [b] 20:24 Or "grace."

²⁷ I didn't avoid telling you the whole plan of God. ²⁸ Pay attention to yourselves and to the entire flock in which the Holy Spirit has placed you as bishops*c* to be shepherds for God's church which he acquired with his own blood. ²⁹ I know that fierce wolves will come to you after I leave, and they won't spare the flock. ³⁰ Some of your own men will come forward and say things that distort the truth. They will do this to lure disciples into following them. ³¹ So be alert! Remember that I instructed each of you for three years, day and night, at times with tears in my eyes.

³² "I am now entrusting you to God and to his message that tells how kind he is. That message can help you grow and can give you the inheritance that is shared by all of God's holy people.

³³ "I never wanted anyone's silver, gold, or clothes. ³⁴ You know that I worked to support myself and those who were with me. ³⁵ I have given you an example that by working hard like this we should help the weak. We should remember the words that the Lord Jesus said, 'Giving gifts is more satisfying than receiving them.' "

³⁶ When Paul had finished speaking, he knelt down and prayed with all of them. ³⁷ Everyone cried a lot as they put their arms around Paul and kissed him. ³⁸ The thought of not seeing Paul again hurt them most of all. Then they took Paul to the ship.

Paul in Tyre

21 ¹ When we finally left them, we sailed straight to the island of Cos. The next day we sailed to the island of Rhodes and from there to the city of Patara. ² In Patara, we found a ship that was going to Phoenicia, so we went aboard and sailed away. ³ We could see the island of Cyprus as we passed it on our left and sailed to Syria. We landed at the city of Tyre, where the ship was to unload its cargo.

⁴ In Tyre we searched for the disciples. After we found them, we stayed there for seven days. The Spirit had the disciples tell Paul not to go to Jerusalem. ⁵ When our time was up, we started on our way. All of them with their wives and children accompanied us

---

c 20:28 English equivalent difficult.

out of the city. We knelt on the beach, prayed, [6] and said goodbye to each other. Then we went aboard the ship, and the disciples went back home.

Paul in Caesarea

[7] Our sea travel ended when we sailed from Tyre to the city of Ptolemais. We greeted the believers in Ptolemais and spent the day with them. [8] The next day we went to Philip's home in Caesarea and stayed with him. He was a missionary and one of the seven men who helped the apostles. [9] Philip had four unmarried daughters who had the ability to speak what God had revealed.

[10] After we had been there for a number of days, a prophet named Agabus arrived from Judea. [11] During his visit he took Paul's belt and tied his own feet and hands with it. Then he said, "The Holy Spirit says, 'This is how the Jews in Jerusalem will tie up the man who owns this belt. Then they will hand him over to people who are not Jewish.' "

[12] When we heard this, we and the believers who lived there begged Paul not to go to Jerusalem.

[13] Then Paul replied, "Why are you crying like this and breaking my heart? I'm ready not only to be tied up in Jerusalem but also to die there for the sake of the Lord, the one named Jesus."

[14] When Paul could not be persuaded, we dropped the issue and said, "May the Lord's will be done."

Paul in Jerusalem

[15] After that, we got ready to go to Jerusalem. [16] Some of the disciples from Caesarea went with us. They took us to Mnason's home, where we would be staying. Mnason was from the island of Cyprus and was one of the first disciples. [17] When we arrived in Jerusalem, the believers welcomed us warmly.

[18] The next day Paul went with us to visit James. All the spiritual leaders[a] were present. [19] After greeting them, Paul related everything God had done through his work with non-Jewish people.

---

[a] 21:18 Or "pastors," or "elders."

²⁰ When the spiritual leaders heard about everything, they praised God. They said to Paul, "You see, brother, how many thousands of Jews are now believers, and all of them are deeply committed to Moses' Teachings. ²¹ But they have been told that you teach all the Jews living among non-Jewish people to abandon Moses. They claim that you tell them not to circumcise their children or follow Jewish customs. ²² What should we do about this? They will certainly hear that you're in town. ²³ So follow our advice. We have four men who have made a vow to God. ²⁴ Take these men, go through the purification ceremony with them, and pay the expenses to shave their heads. Then everyone will know that what they've been told about you isn't true. Instead, they'll see that you carefully follow Moses' Teachings.

²⁵ "⌊To clarify this matter,⌋ we have written non-Jewish believers a letter with our decision. We told them that they should not eat food sacrificed to false gods, bloody meat, or the meat of strangled animals. They also should not commit sexual sins."

²⁶ The next day, Paul took the men and went through the purification ceremony with them. Then he went into the temple courtyard to announce the time when the purification would be over and the sacrifice would be offered for each of them.

²⁷ When the seven days were almost over, the Jews from the province of Asia saw Paul in the temple courtyard. They stirred up the whole crowd and grabbed Paul. ²⁸ Then they began shouting, "Men of Israel, help! This is the man who teaches everyone everywhere to turn against the Jewish people, Moses' Teachings, and this temple. He has even brought Greeks into the temple courtyard and has made this holy place unclean."ᵇ ²⁹ They had seen Trophimus from Ephesus with him in the city earlier and thought Paul had taken him into the temple courtyard.

³⁰ The whole city was in chaos, and a mob formed. The mob grabbed Paul and dragged him out of the temple courtyard. The courtyard doors were immediately shut.

ᵇ 21:28 "Unclean" refers to anything that Moses' Teachings say is not presentable to God.

³¹ As the people were trying to kill Paul, the officer in charge of the Roman soldiers received a report that all Jerusalem was rioting. ³² Immediately, he took some soldiers and officers and charged the crowd. When the crowd saw the officer and the soldiers, they stopped beating Paul. ³³ Then the officer went to Paul, grabbed him, and ordered him to be tied up with two chains.

The officer asked who Paul was and what he had done. ³⁴ Some of the crowd shouted one thing, while others shouted something else. The officer couldn't get any facts because of the noise and confusion, so he ordered Paul to be taken into the barracks. ³⁵ When Paul came to the stairs of the barracks, the crowd was so violent that the soldiers had to carry him. ³⁶ The mob was behind them shouting, "Kill him!"

Paul Speaks in His Own Defense

³⁷ As the soldiers were about to take Paul into the barracks, he asked the officer, "May I say something to you?"

The officer replied to Paul, "Can you speak Greek? ³⁸ Aren't you the Egyptian who started a revolution not long ago and led four thousand terrorists into the desert?"

³⁹ Paul answered, "I'm a Jew, a citizen from the well-known city of Tarsus in Cilicia. I'm asking you to let me talk to the people."

⁴⁰ The officer gave Paul permission to speak. So Paul stood on the stairs of the barracks and motioned with his hand for the people to be quiet. When the mob was silent, Paul spoke to them in the Hebrew language.

22 ¹ "Brothers and fathers, listen as I now present my case to you." ² When the mob heard him speak to them in Hebrew, they became even more quiet. Then Paul continued, ³ "I'm a Jew. I was born and raised in the city of Tarsus in Cilicia and received my education from Gamaliel here in Jerusalem. My education was in the strict rules handed down by our ancestors. I was as devoted to God as all of you are today. ⁴ I persecuted people who followed the way ˏof Christˎ: I tied up men and women and put them into prison until they were executed. ⁵ The chief priest and the entire council of our leaders can prove that I did this. In fact, they even gave me let-

ters to take to the Jewish community in the city of Damascus. I was
going there to tie up believers and bring them back to Jerusalem to
punish them.

⁶ "But as I was on my way and approaching the city of Damascus
about noon, a bright light from heaven suddenly flashed around
me. ⁷ I fell to the ground and heard a voice asking me, 'Saul! Saul!
Why are you persecuting me?'

⁸ "I answered, 'Who are you, sir?'

"The person told me, 'I'm Jesus from Nazareth, the one you're
persecuting.'

⁹ "The men who were with me saw the light but didn't understand what the person who was speaking to me said.

¹⁰ "Then I asked, 'What do you want me to do, Lord?'

"The Lord told me, 'Get up! Go into the city of Damascus, and
you'll be told everything I've arranged for you to do.'

¹¹ "I was blind because the light had been so bright. So the men
who were with me led me into the city of Damascus.

¹² "A man named Ananias lived in Damascus. He was a devout
person who followed Moses' Teachings. All the Jews living in
Damascus spoke highly of him. ¹³ He came to me, stood beside
me, and said, 'Brother Saul, receive your sight!' At that moment
my sight came back and I could see Ananias.

¹⁴ "Ananias said, 'The God of our ancestors has chosen you to
know his will, to see the one who has God's approval, and to hear
him speak to you. ¹⁵ You will be his witness and will tell everyone
what you have seen and heard. ¹⁶ What are you waiting for now?
Get up! Be baptized, and have your sins washed away as you call
on his name.'

¹⁷ "After that, I returned to Jerusalem. While I was praying in
the temple courtyard, I fell into a trance ¹⁸ and saw the Lord. He
told me, 'Hurry! Get out of Jerusalem immediately. The people
here won't accept your testimony about me.'

¹⁹ "I said, 'Lord, people here know that I went from synagogue
to synagogue to imprison and whip those who believe in you.
²⁰ When Stephen, who witnessed about you, was being killed, I was

standing there. I approved of his death and guarded the coats of those who were murdering him.'

²¹ "But the Lord told me, 'Go! I'll send you on a mission. You'll go far away to people who aren't Jewish.' "

²² Up to that point the mob listened. Then they began to shout, "Kill him! The world doesn't need a man like this. He shouldn't have been allowed to live this long!"

²³ The mob was yelling, taking off their coats, and throwing dirt into the air. ²⁴ So the officer ordered the soldiers to take Paul into the barracks and told them to question Paul as they whipped him. The officer wanted to find out why the people were yelling at Paul like this. ²⁵ But when the soldiers had Paul stretch out ˌto tie him to the whipping postˌ with the straps, Paul asked the sergeant who was standing there, "Is it legal for you to whip a Roman citizen who hasn't had a trial?"

²⁶ When the sergeant heard this, he reported it to his commanding officer. The sergeant asked him, "What are you doing? This man is a Roman citizen."

²⁷ The officer went to Paul and asked him, "Tell me, are you a Roman citizen?"

Paul answered, "Yes."

²⁸ The officer replied, "I paid a lot of money to become a Roman citizen."

Paul replied, "But I was born a Roman citizen."

²⁹ Immediately, the soldiers who were going to question Paul stepped away from him. The officer was afraid when he found out that he had tied up a Roman citizen.

Paul in Front of the Jewish Council

³⁰ The officer wanted to find out exactly what accusation the Jews had against Paul. So the officer released Paul the next day and ordered the chief priests and the entire Jewish council to meet. Then the officer brought Paul and had him stand in front of them.

23 ¹ Paul stared at the Jewish council and said, "Brothers, my relationship with God has always given me a perfectly clear conscience."

² The chief priest Ananias ordered the men standing near Paul to strike him on the mouth. ³ Then Paul said to him, "God will strike you, you hypocrite! You sit there and judge me by Moses' Teachings and yet you break those teachings by ordering these men to strike me!"

⁴ The men standing near Paul said to him, "You're insulting God's chief priest!"

⁵ Paul answered, "Brothers, I didn't know that he is the chief priest. After all, Scripture says, 'Don't speak evil about a ruler of your people.' "

⁶ When Paul saw that some of them were Sadducees and others were Pharisees, he shouted in the council, "Brothers, I'm a Pharisee and a descendant of Pharisees. I'm on trial because I expect that the dead will come back to life."

⁷ After Paul said that, the Pharisees and Sadducees began to quarrel, and the men in the meeting were divided. ⁸ (The Sadducees say that the dead won't come back to life and that angels and spirits don't exist. The Pharisees believe in all these things.) ⁹ The shouting became very loud. Some of the scribes were Pharisees who argued their position forcefully. They said, "We don't find anything wrong with this man. Maybe a spirit or an angel actually spoke to him!"

¹⁰ The quarrel was becoming violent, and the officer was afraid that they would tear Paul to pieces. So the officer ordered his soldiers to drag Paul back to the barracks.

¹¹ The Lord stood near Paul the next night and said to him, "Don't lose your courage! You've told the truth about me in Jerusalem. Now you must tell the truth about me in Rome."

Some Jews Plot to Kill Paul

¹² In the morning the Jews formed a conspiracy. They asked God to curse them if they ate or drank anything before they had killed Paul. ¹³ More than forty men took part in this plot.

¹⁴ They went to the chief priests and leaders ˪of the people˺ and said, "We've asked God to curse us if we taste any food before we've killed Paul. ¹⁵ Here's our plan: You and the council must go

to the Roman officer on the pretext that you need more information from Paul. You have to make it look as though you want to get more accurate information about him. We'll be ready to kill him before he gets to you."

¹⁶ But Paul's nephew heard about the ambush. He entered the barracks and told Paul. ¹⁷ Then Paul called one of the sergeants and told him, "Take this young man to the officer. He has something to tell him."

¹⁸ The sergeant took the young man to the officer and said, "The prisoner Paul called me. He asked me to bring this young man to you because he has something to tell you."

¹⁹ The officer took the young man by the arm, went where they could be alone, and asked him, "What do you have to tell me?"

²⁰ The young man answered, "The Jews have planned to ask you to bring Paul to the Jewish council tomorrow. They're going to make it look as though they want more accurate information about him. ²¹ Don't let them persuade you to do this. More than forty of them are planning to ambush him. They have asked God to curse them if they eat or drink anything before they have murdered him. They are ready now and are expecting you to promise ₗthat you will bring Paulₗ."

²² The officer dismissed the young man and ordered him not to tell this information to anyone else.

²³ Then the officer summoned two of his sergeants and told them, "I want 200 infantrymen, 70 soldiers on horseback, and 200 soldiers with spears. Have them ready to go to Caesarea at nine o'clock tonight. ²⁴ Provide an animal for Paul to ride, and take him safely to Governor Felix." ²⁵ The officer wrote a letter to the governor with the following message:

²⁶ Claudius Lysias sends greetings to Your Excellency, Governor Felix:

²⁷ The Jews had seized this man and were going to murder him. When I found out that he was a Roman citizen, I went with my soldiers to rescue him. ²⁸ I wanted to know what

they had against him. So I took him to their Jewish council [29] and found their accusations had to do with disputes about Jewish teachings. He wasn't accused of anything for which he deserved to die or to be put into prison. [30] Since I was informed that there was a plot against this man, I immediately sent him to you. I have also ordered his accusers to state their case against him in front of you.

[31] So the infantrymen did as they had been ordered. They took Paul to the city of Antipatris during the night. [32] They returned to their barracks the next day and let the soldiers on horseback travel with Paul. [33] When the soldiers arrived in the city of Caesarea with Paul, they delivered the letter to the governor and handed Paul over to him.

[34] After the governor had read the letter, he asked Paul which province he was from. When he found out that Paul was from the province of Cilicia, [35] he said, "I'll hear your case when your accusers arrive." Then the governor gave orders to keep Paul under guard in Herod's palace.

Paul Presents His Case to Felix

24 [1] Five days later the chief priest Ananias went to the city of Caesarea with some leaders of the people and an attorney named Tertullus. They reported to the governor their charges against Paul.

[2] When Paul had been summoned, Tertullus began to accuse him. He said to Felix, "Your Excellency, through your wise leadership we have lasting peace and reforms that benefit the people. [3] We appreciate what you've done in every way and in every place, and we want to thank you very much. [4] I don't want to keep you too long. Please listen to us. We will be brief. [5] We have found this man to be a troublemaker. He starts quarrels among all Jews throughout the world. He's a ringleader of the Nazarene sect. [6] He also entered the temple courtyard in a way that violates our tradition. So we arrested him.[a] [8] When you cross-examine him, you'll be able to find out from him that our accusations are true."

⁹ The Jews supported Tertullus' accusations and asserted that everything Tertullus said was true.

¹⁰ The governor motioned for Paul to speak. Paul responded, "I know that you have been a judge over this nation for many years. So I'm pleased to present my case to you. ¹¹ You can verify for yourself that I went to Jerusalem to worship no more than twelve days ago. ¹² No one found me having a discussion with anyone in the temple courtyard or stirring up a crowd in the synagogues throughout the city. ¹³ These people cannot even prove their accusations to you. ¹⁴ But I'll admit to you that I'm a follower of the way ˌof Christˌ, which they call a sect. This means that I serve our ancestors' God and believe everything written in Moses' Teachings and the Prophets. ¹⁵ I hope for the same thing my accusers do, that people with God's approval and those without it will come back to life. ¹⁶ With this belief I always do my best to have a clear conscience in the sight of God and people. ¹⁷ After many years I have come back to my people and brought gifts for the poor and offerings ˌfor Godˌ. ¹⁸ My accusers found me in the temple courtyard doing these things after I had gone through the purification ceremony. No crowd or noisy mob was present. ¹⁹ But some Jews from the province of Asia were there. They should be here in front of you to accuse me if they have anything against me. ²⁰ Otherwise, these men who are accusing me should tell what I was charged with when I stood in front of their council. ²¹ They could accuse me of only one thing. As I stood among them, I shouted, 'I'm being tried in front of you because ˌI believe thatˌ the dead will come back to life.' "

²² Felix knew the way ˌof Christˌ rather well, so he adjourned the trial. He told them, "When the officer Lysias arrives, I'll decide your case." ²³ Felix ordered the sergeant to guard Paul but to let him have some freedom and to let his friends take care of his needs.

²⁴ Some days later Felix arrived with his wife Drusilla, who was Jewish. He sent for Paul and listened to him talk about faith in Christ Jesus. ²⁵ As Paul discussed the subjects of God's approval, self-control, and the coming judgment, Felix became afraid and said, "That's enough for now. You can go. When I find time, I'll

send for you again." [26] At the same time, Felix was hoping that Paul would give him some money. For that reason, Felix would send for Paul rather often to have friendly conversations with him.

[27] Two years passed. Then Porcius Festus took Felix's place. (Since Felix wanted to do the Jews a favor, he left Paul in prison.)

Paul Makes an Appeal

25 [1] Three days after Festus took over his duties in the province of Judea, he went from the city of Caesarea to Jerusalem. [2] The chief priests and the other important Jewish leaders informed Festus about their charges against Paul. They were urging [3] Festus to do them the favor of having Paul brought to Jerusalem. The Jews had a plan to ambush and kill Paul as he traveled to Jerusalem.

[4] Festus replied that he would be returning to Caesarea soon and would keep Paul there. [5] He told them, "Have your authorities come to Caesarea with me and accuse him there if the man has done something wrong."

[6] Festus stayed in Jerusalem for eight or ten days at the most and then returned to Caesarea. The next day Festus took his place in court and summoned Paul.

[7] When Paul entered the room, the Jews who had come from Jerusalem surrounded him. They made a lot of serious accusations that they couldn't prove. [8] Paul defended himself by saying, "I haven't broken any Jewish law or done anything against the temple or the emperor."

[9] But Festus wanted to do the Jews a favor. So he asked Paul, "Are you willing to go to Jerusalem to be tried there on these charges with me as your judge?"

[10] Paul said, "I am standing in the emperor's court where I must be tried. I haven't done anything wrong to the Jews, as you know very well. [11] If I am guilty and have done something wrong for which I deserve the death penalty, I don't reject the idea of dying.

---

[a] 24:6 Some manuscripts and translations add verses 6b–8a: "We wanted to try him under our law. But the officer Lysias used force to take him from us. He ordered his accusers to come in front of you."

But if their accusations are untrue, no one can hand me over to them as a favor. I appeal my case to the emperor!"

¹² Festus discussed the appeal with his advisers and then replied to Paul, "You have appealed your case to the emperor, so you'll go to the emperor!"

King Agrippa Meets Paul

¹³ Later King Agrippa and Bernice came to the city of Caesarea to welcome Festus. ¹⁴ Since they were staying there for a number of days, Festus told the king about Paul's case.

Festus said, "Felix left a man here in prison. ¹⁵ When I went to Jerusalem, the chief priests and the Jewish leaders brought me some information about him and asked me to condemn him.

¹⁶ "I replied to them, 'That's not the Roman way of doing things. A person can't be sentenced as a favor. Before he is sentenced, he must face his accusers and have a chance to defend himself against their accusation.'

¹⁷ "So the Jewish leaders came to Caesarea with me. The next day I immediately convened court and summoned the man. ¹⁸ When his accusers stood up, they didn't accuse him of the crimes I was expecting. ¹⁹ They were disputing with him about their own religion and about some man named Jesus who had died. But Paul claimed that Jesus is alive. ²⁰ Their debate about these things left me puzzled. So I asked Paul if he would like to go to Jerusalem to have his case heard there. ²¹ But Paul appealed his case. He asked to be held in prison and to have His Majesty the Emperor decide his case. So I ordered him to be held in prison until I could send him to the emperor."

²² Agrippa told Festus, "I would like to hear the man."

Festus replied, "You'll hear him tomorrow."

²³ The next day Agrippa and Bernice entered the auditorium with a lot of fanfare. Roman army officers and the most important men of the city entered the auditorium with them. Festus gave the order, and Paul was brought into the auditorium.

²⁴ Then Festus said, "King Agrippa and everyone who is present with us! All the Jews in Jerusalem and Caesarea have talked to me

about this man you see in front of you. They shout that he must not be allowed to live any longer. ²⁵ However, I don't think that he has done anything to deserve the death penalty. But since he made an appeal to His Majesty the Emperor, I have decided to send him to Rome. ²⁶ But I don't have anything reliable to write our emperor about him. So I have brought him to all of you, and especially to you, King Agrippa. Then I'll have something to write after he is cross-examined. ²⁷ I find it ridiculous to send a prisoner to Rome when I can't specify any charges against him."

26 ¹ Agrippa said to Paul, "You're free to speak for yourself." Paul acknowledged King Agrippa and then began his defense. ² "King Agrippa, I think I'm fortunate today to stand in front of you and defend myself against every charge that the Jews brought against me. ³ I say this since you are especially familiar with every custom and controversy in Judaism. So I ask you to listen patiently to me.

⁴ "All the Jews know how I lived the earliest days of my youth with my own people and in Jerusalem. ⁵ They've known me for a long time and can testify, if they're willing, that I followed the strictest party of our religion. They know that I lived my life as a Pharisee.

⁶ "I'm on trial now because I expect God to keep the promise that he made to our ancestors. ⁷ Our twelve tribes expect this promise to be kept as they worship with intense devotion day and night. Your Majesty, the Jews are making accusations against me because I expect God to keep his promise. ⁸ Why do all of you refuse to believe that God can bring dead people back to life?

⁹ "I used to think that I had to do a lot of things to oppose the one named Jesus of Nazareth. ¹⁰ That is what I did in Jerusalem. By the authority I received from the chief priests, I locked many Christians in prison. I voted to have them killed every time a vote was taken. ¹¹ I even went to each synagogue, punished believers, and forced them to curse ˻the name of Jesus˼. In my furious rage against them, I hunted them down in cities outside ˻Jerusalem˼.

¹² "I was carrying out these activities when I went to the city of Damascus. I had the power and authority of the chief priests. ¹³ Your

Majesty, at noon, while I was traveling, I saw a light that was brighter than the sun. The light came from the sky and shined around me and those who were with me. [14] All of us fell to the ground, and I heard a voice asking me in Hebrew, 'Saul, Saul! Why are you persecuting me? It's hard for ˌa mortal likeˌ you to resist God.'

[15] "I asked, 'Who are you, sir?'

"The Lord answered, 'I am Jesus, the one you're persecuting. [16] Stand up! I have appeared to you for a reason. I'm appointing you to be a servant and witness of what you have seen and of what I will show you. [17] I will rescue you from the Jewish people and from the non-Jewish people to whom I am sending you. [18] You will open their eyes and turn them from darkness to light and from Satan's control to God's. Then they will receive forgiveness for their sins and a share among God's people who are made holy by believing in me.'

[19] "At that point I did not disobey the vision I saw from heaven, King Agrippa. [20] Instead, I spread the message that I first told to the ˌJewishˌ people in Damascus and Jerusalem and throughout the whole country of Judea. I spread the same message to non-Jewish people. Both groups were expected to change the way they thought and acted and to turn to God. I told them to do things that prove they had changed their lives. [21] For this reason the Jews took me prisoner in the temple courtyard and tried to murder me.

[22] "God has been helping me to this day so that I can stand and testify to important and unimportant people. I tell them only what the prophets and Moses said would happen. [23] They said that the Messiah would suffer and be the first to come back to life and would spread light to Jewish and non-Jewish people."

[24] As Paul was defending himself in this way, Festus shouted, "Paul, you're crazy! Too much education is driving you crazy!"

[25] Paul replied, "I'm not crazy, Your Excellency Festus. What I'm saying is true and sane. [26] I can easily speak to a king who knows about these things. I'm sure that none of these things has escaped his attention. None of this was done secretly. [27] King Agrippa, do you believe the prophets? I know you believe them!"

[28] Agrippa said to Paul, "Do you think you can quickly persuade me to become a Christian?"

²⁹ Paul replied, "I wish to God that you and everyone listening to me today would quickly and completely become as I am (except for being a prisoner)."

³⁰ The king, the governor, Bernice, and the people who were sitting with them got up. ³¹ As they were leaving, they said to each other, "This man isn't doing anything for which he deserves to die or be put in prison."

³² Agrippa told Festus, "This man could have been set free if he hadn't appealed his case to the emperor."

Paul Sails for Rome

27 ¹ When it was decided that we should sail to Italy, Paul and some other prisoners were turned over to an army officer. His name was Julius, and he belonged to the emperor's division. ² We set sail on a ship from the city of Adramyttium. The ship was going to stop at ports on the coast of the province of Asia. Aristarchus, a Macedonian from the city of Thessalonica, went with us.

³ The next day we arrived at the city of Sidon. Julius treated Paul kindly and allowed him to visit his friends and receive any care he needed. ⁴ Leaving Sidon, we sailed on the northern side of the island of Cyprus because we were traveling against the wind. ⁵ We sailed along the coast of the provinces of Cilicia and Pamphylia and arrived at the city of Myra in the province of Lycia. ⁶ In Myra the officer found a ship from Alexandria that was on its way to Italy and put us on it. ⁷ We were sailing slowly for a number of days. Our difficulties began along the coast of the city of Cnidus because the wind would not let us go further. So at Cape Salmone, we started to sail for the south side of the island of Crete. ⁸ We had difficulty sailing along the shore of Crete. We finally came to a port called Fair Harbors. The port was near the city of Lasea.

⁹ We had lost so much time that the day of fasting had already past. Sailing was now dangerous, so Paul advised them, ¹⁰ "Men, we're going to face a disaster and heavy losses on this voyage. This disaster will cause damage to the cargo and the ship, and it will affect our lives." ¹¹ However, the officer was persuaded by what the pilot and the owner of the ship said and not by what Paul

said. ¹² Since the harbor was not a good place to spend the winter, most of the men decided to sail from there. They hoped to reach the city of Phoenix somehow and spend the winter there. (Phoenix is a harbor that faces the southwest and northwest winds and is located on the island of Crete.)

¹³ When a gentle breeze began to blow from the south, the men thought their plan would work. They raised the anchor and sailed close to the shore of Crete.

¹⁴ Soon a powerful wind (called a northeaster) blew from the island. ¹⁵ The wind carried the ship away, and we couldn't sail against the wind. We couldn't do anything, so we were carried along by the wind. ¹⁶ As we drifted to the sheltered side of a small island called Cauda, we barely got control of the ship's lifeboat. ¹⁷ The men pulled it up on deck. Then they passed ropes under the ship to reinforce it. Fearing that they would hit the large sandbank off the shores of Libya, they lowered the sail and were carried along by the wind. ¹⁸ We continued to be tossed so violently by the storm that the next day the men began to throw the cargo overboard. ¹⁹ On the third day they threw the ship's equipment overboard. ²⁰ For a number of days we couldn't see the sun or the stars. The storm wouldn't let up. It was so severe that we finally began to lose any hope of coming out of it alive.

²¹ Since hardly anyone wanted to eat, Paul stood among them and said, "Men, you should have followed my advice not to sail from Crete. You would have avoided this disaster and loss. ²² Now I advise you to have courage. No one will lose his life. Only the ship will be destroyed. ²³ I know this because an angel from the God to whom I belong and whom I serve stood by me last night. ²⁴ The angel told me, 'Don't be afraid, Paul! You must present your case to the emperor. God has granted safety to everyone who is sailing with you.' ²⁵ So have courage, men! I trust God that everything will turn out as he told me. ²⁶ However, we will run aground on some island."

The Shipwreck

²⁷ On the fourteenth night we were still drifting through the Mediterranean Sea. About midnight the sailors suspected that we

were approaching land. [28] So they threw a line with a weight on it into the water. It sank 120 feet. They waited a little while and did the same thing again. This time the line sank 90 feet. [29] Fearing we might hit rocks, they dropped four anchors from the back of the ship and prayed for morning to come.

[30] The sailors tried to escape from the ship. They let the lifeboat down into the sea and pretended they were going to lay out the anchors from the front of the ship. [31] Paul told the officer and the soldiers, "If these sailors don't stay on the ship, you have no hope of staying alive." [32] Then the soldiers cut the ropes that held the lifeboat and let it drift away.

[33] Just before daybreak Paul was encouraging everyone to have something to eat. "This is the fourteenth day you have waited and have had nothing to eat. [34] So I'm encouraging you to eat something. Eating will help you survive, since not a hair from anyone's head will be lost." [35] After Paul said this, he took some bread, thanked God in front of everyone, broke it, and began to eat. [36] Everyone was encouraged and had something to eat. [37] (There were 276 of us on the ship.) [38] After the people had eaten all they wanted, they lightened the ship by dumping the wheat into the sea.

[39] In the morning they couldn't recognize the land, but they could see a bay with a beach. So they decided to try to run the ship ashore. [40] They cut the anchors free and left them in the sea. At the same time they untied the ropes that held the steering oars. Then they raised the top sail to catch the wind and steered the ship to the shore. [41] They struck a sandbar in the water and ran the ship aground. The front of the ship stuck and couldn't be moved, while the back of the ship was broken to pieces by the force of the waves.

[42] The soldiers had a plan to kill the prisoners to keep them from swimming away and escaping. [43] However, the officer wanted to save Paul, so he stopped the soldiers from carrying out their plan. He ordered those who could swim to jump overboard first and swim ashore. [44] Then he ordered the rest to follow on planks or some other pieces ˻of wood˼ from the ship. In this way everyone got to shore safely.

Paul on the Island of Malta

28 ¹ When we were safely on shore, we found out that the island was called Malta. ² The people who lived on the island were unusually kind to us. They made a fire and welcomed all of us around it because of the rain and the cold.

³ Paul gathered a bundle of brushwood and put it on the fire. The heat forced a poisonous snake out of the brushwood. The snake bit Paul's hand and wouldn't let go. ⁴ When the people who lived on the island saw the snake hanging from his hand, they said to each other, "This man must be a murderer! He may have escaped from the sea, but justice won't let him live."

⁵ Paul shook the snake into the fire and wasn't harmed. ⁶ The people were waiting for him to swell up or suddenly drop dead. But after they had waited a long time and saw nothing unusual happen to him, they changed their minds and said he was a god.

⁷ A man named Publius, who was the governor of the island, had property around the area. He welcomed us and treated us kindly, and for three days we were his guests. ⁸ His father happened to be sick in bed. He was suffering from fever and dysentery. Paul went to him, prayed, placed his hands on him, and made him well.

⁹ After that had happened, other sick people on the island went to Paul and were made well. ¹⁰ They showed respect for us in many ways, and when we were going to set sail, they put whatever we needed on board.

Paul Sails From Malta to Rome

¹¹ After three months we sailed on an Alexandrian ship that had spent the winter at the island. The ship had the gods Castor and Pollux carved on its front. ¹² We stopped at the city of Syracuse and stayed there for three days. ¹³ We sailed from Syracuse and arrived at the city of Rhegium. The next day a south wind began to blow, and two days later we arrived at the city of Puteoli. ¹⁴ In Puteoli we discovered some believers who begged us to spend a week with them.

¹⁵ Believers in Rome heard that we were coming, so they came as far as the cities of Appius' Market and Three Taverns to meet

us. When Paul saw them, he thanked God and felt encouraged. So
we finally arrived in the city of Rome.*[a] **16** After our arrival, Paul was
allowed to live by himself, but he had a soldier who guarded him.

Paul in Rome

17 After three days Paul invited the most influential Jews in
Rome to meet with him. When they assembled, he said to them,
"Brothers, I haven't done anything against the Jewish people or
violated the customs handed down by our ancestors. Yet, I'm a
prisoner from Jerusalem, and I've been handed over to the Roman
authorities. **18** The Roman authorities cross-examined me and
wanted to let me go because I was accused of nothing for which
I deserved to die. **19** But when the Jews objected, I was forced to
appeal my case to the emperor. That doesn't mean I have any
charges to bring against my own people. **20** That's why I asked to
see you and speak with you. I'm wearing these chains because of
what Israel hopes for."

21 The Jewish leaders told Paul, "We haven't received any letters from Judea about you, and no Jewish person who has come
to Rome has reported or mentioned anything bad about you.
22 However, we would like to hear what you think. We know that
everywhere people are talking against this sect."

23 On a designated day a larger number of influential Jews
⌊than expected⌋ went to the place where Paul was staying. From
morning until evening, Paul was explaining the kingdom of God
to them. He was trying to convince them about Jesus from Moses'
Teachings and the Prophets. **24** Some of them were convinced by
what he said, but others continued to disbelieve.

25 The Jews, unable to agree among themselves, left after Paul
had quoted this particular passage to them: "How well the Holy
Spirit spoke to your ancestors through the prophet Isaiah! **26** The
Spirit said: 'Go to these people and say,

---

*[a] 28:15 The last sentence in verse 14 has been placed in verse 15 to express the
complex Greek sentence structure more clearly in English.

"You will hear clearly but never understand.
You will see clearly but never comprehend.
27   These people have become close-minded
         and hard of hearing.
             They have shut their eyes
             so that their eyes never see.
         Their ears never hear.
         Their minds never understand.
         And they never turn to me for healing." '

28 "You need to know that God has sent his salvation to people who are not Jews. They will listen."[b]

30 Paul rented a place to live for two full years and welcomed everyone who came to him. **31** He spread the message about God's kingdom and taught very boldly about the Lord Jesus Christ. No one stopped him.

---

[b] 28:28 Some manuscripts and translations add verse 29: "After Paul said this, the Jews left. They argued intensely among themselves."

ROMANS

Greeting

1 ¹ From Paul, a servant of Jesus Christ, called to be an apostle and appointed to spread the Good News of God.

² (God had already promised this Good News through his prophets in the Holy Scriptures. ³ This Good News is about his Son, our Lord Jesus Christ.*a* In his human nature he was a descendant of David. ⁴ In his spiritual, holy nature he was declared the Son of God. This was shown in a powerful way when he came back to life. ⁵ Through him we have received God's kindness*b* and the privilege of being apostles who bring people from every nation to the obedience that is associated with faith. This is for the honor of his name. ⁶ You are among those who have been called to belong to Jesus Christ.)

⁷ To everyone in Rome whom God loves and has called to be his holy people.

Good will*b* and peace from God our Father and the Lord Jesus Christ are yours!

Paul's Prayer and Desire to Visit Rome

⁸ First, I thank my God through Jesus Christ for every one of you because the news of your faith is spreading throughout the whole world. ⁹ I serve God by spreading the Good News about his Son. God is my witness that I always mention you ¹⁰ every time I pray. I ask that somehow God will now at last make it possible for me to visit you. ¹¹ I long to see you to share a spiritual blessing with you so that you will be strengthened. ¹² What I mean is that we may be encouraged by each other's faith.

---

a 1:3 "Our Lord Jesus Christ" from verse 4 (in Greek) has been placed in verse 3 to express the complex Greek sentence structure more clearly in English.   *b* 1:5, 7 Or "grace."

¹³ I want you to know, brothers and sisters, that I often planned to visit you. However, until now I have been kept from doing so. What I want is to enjoy some of the results of working among you as I have also enjoyed the results of working among the rest of the nations. ¹⁴ I have an obligation to those who are civilized and those who aren't, to those who are wise and those who aren't. ¹⁵ That's why I'm eager to tell you who live in Rome the Good News also.

¹⁶ I'm not ashamed of the Good News. It is God's power to save everyone who believes, Jews first and Greeks as well. ¹⁷ God's approval is revealed in this Good News. This approval begins and ends with faith as Scripture says, "The person who has God's approval will live by faith."

God's Anger Against Sinful Humanity

¹⁸ God's anger is revealed from heaven against every ungodly and immoral thing people do as they try to suppress the truth by their immoral living. ¹⁹ What can be known about God is clear to them because he has made it clear to them. ²⁰ From the creation of the world, God's invisible qualities, his eternal power and divine nature, have been clearly observed in what he made. As a result, people have no excuse. ²¹ They knew God but did not praise and thank him for being God. Instead, their thoughts were pointless, and their misguided minds were plunged into darkness. ²² While claiming to be wise, they became fools. ²³ They exchanged the glory of the immortal God for statues that looked like mortal humans, birds, animals, and snakes.

²⁴ For this reason God allowed their lusts to control them. As a result, they dishonor their bodies by sexual perversion with each other. ²⁵ These people have exchanged God's truth for a lie. So they have become ungodly and serve what is created rather than the Creator, who is blessed forever. Amen!

²⁶ For this reason God allowed their shameful passions to control them. Their women have exchanged natural sexual relations for unnatural ones. ²⁷ Likewise, their men have given up natural sexual relations with women and burn with lust for each other.

Men commit indecent acts with men, so they experience among themselves the punishment they deserve for their perversion. [28] And because they thought it was worthless to acknowledge God, God allowed their own immoral minds to control them. So they do these indecent things. [29] Their lives are filled with all kinds of sexual sins, wickedness, and greed. They are mean. They are filled with envy, murder, quarreling, deceit, and viciousness. They are gossips, [30] slanderers, haters of God, haughty, arrogant, and boastful. They think up new ways to be cruel. They don't obey their parents, [31] don't have any sense, don't keep promises, and don't show love to their own families or mercy to others. [32] Although they know God's judgment that those who do such things deserve to die, they not only do these things but also approve of others who do them.

God Will Judge Everyone

2 [1] No matter who you are, if you judge anyone, you have no excuse. When you judge another person, you condemn yourself, since you, the judge, do the same things. [2] We know that God's judgment is right when he condemns people for doing these things. [3] When you judge people for doing these things but then do them yourself, do you think you will escape God's judgment? [4] Do you have contempt for God, who is very kind to you, puts up with you, and deals patiently with you? Don't you realize that it is God's kindness that is trying to lead you to him and change the way you think and act?

[5] Since you are stubborn and don't want to change the way you think and act, you are adding to the anger that God will have against you on that day when God vents his anger. At that time God will reveal that his decisions are fair. [6] He will pay all people back for what they have done. [7] He will give everlasting life to those who search for glory, honor, and immortality by persisting in doing what is good. But he will bring [8] anger and fury on those who, in selfish pride, refuse to believe the truth and who follow what is wrong. [9] There will be suffering and distress for every person who does

evil, for Jews first and Greeks as well. [10] But there will be glory, honor, and peace for every person who does what is good, for Jews first and Greeks as well. [11] God does not play favorites.

[12] Here's the reason: Whoever sins without having laws from God will still be condemned to destruction. And whoever has laws from God and sins will still be judged by them. [13] People who merely listen to laws from God don't have God's approval. Rather, people who do what those laws demand will have God's approval.

God Will Judge People Who Are Not Jewish

[14] For example, whenever non-Jews who don't have laws from God do by nature the things that Moses' Teachings contain, they are a law to themselves even though they don't have any laws from God. [15] They show that some requirements found in Moses' Teachings are written in their hearts. Their consciences speak to them. Their thoughts accuse them on one occasion and defend them on another. [16] This happens as they face the day when God, through Christ Jesus, will judge people's secret thoughts. He will use the Good News that I am spreading to make that judgment.

God Will Judge Jewish People

[17] You call yourself a Jew, rely on the laws in Moses' Teachings, brag about your God, [18] know what he wants, and distinguish right from wrong because you have been taught Moses' Teachings. [19] You are confident that you are a guide for the blind, a light to those in the dark, [20] an instructor of ignorant people, and a teacher of children because you have the full content of knowledge and truth in Moses' Teachings. [21] As you teach others, are you failing to teach yourself? As you preach against stealing, are you stealing? [22] As you tell others not to commit adultery, are you committing adultery? As you treat idols with disgust, are you robbing temples? [23] As you brag about the laws in Moses' Teachings, are you dishonoring God by ignoring Moses' Teachings? [24] As Scripture says, "God's name is cursed among the nations because of you."

[25] For example, circumcision is valuable if you follow Moses' laws. If you don't follow those laws, your circumcision amounts to

uncircumcision. ²⁶ So if a man does what Moses' Teachings demand, won't he be considered circumcised even if he is uncircumcised? ²⁷ The uncircumcised man who carries out what Moses' Teachings say will condemn you for not following them. He will condemn you in spite of the fact that you are circumcised and have Moses' Teachings in writing. ²⁸ A person is not a Jew because of his appearance, nor is circumcision a matter of how the body looks. ²⁹ Rather, a person is a Jew inwardly, and circumcision is something that happens in a person's heart. Circumcision is spiritual, not just a written rule. That person's praise will come from God, not from people.

Everyone Is a Sinner

3 ¹ Is there any advantage, then, in being a Jew? Or is there any value in being circumcised? ² There are all kinds of advantages. First of all, God entrusted them with his word.

³ What if some of them were unfaithful? Can their unfaithfulness cancel God's faithfulness? ⁴ That would be unthinkable! God is honest, and everyone else is a liar, as Scripture says,

> "So you hand down justice when you speak,
>   and you win your case in court."

⁵ But if what we do wrong shows that God is fair, what should we say? Is God unfair when he vents his anger on us? (I'm arguing the way humans would.) ⁶ That's unthinkable! Otherwise, how would God be able to judge the world? ⁷ If my lie increases the glory that God receives by showing that God is truthful, why am I still judged as a sinner? ⁸ Or can we say, "Let's do evil so that good will come from it"? Some slander us and claim that this is what we say. They are condemned, and that's what they deserve.

⁹ What, then, is the situation? Do we have any advantage? Not at all. We have already accused everyone (both Jews and Greeks) of being under the power of sin, ¹⁰ as Scripture says,

> "Not one person has God's approval.
> ¹¹   No one understands.
>   No one searches for God.

¹²   Everyone has turned away.
           Together they have become rotten to the core.
           No one does anything good,
               not even one person.
¹³   Their throats are open graves.
           Their tongues practice deception.
           Their lips hide the venom of poisonous snakes.
¹⁴   Their mouths are full of curses and bitter resentment.
¹⁵   They run quickly to murder people.
¹⁶   There is ruin and suffering wherever they go.
¹⁷   They have not learned to live in peace.
¹⁸   They are not terrified of God."

¹⁹ We know that whatever is in Moses' Teachings applies to everyone under their influence, and no one can say a thing. The whole world is brought under the judgment of God. ²⁰ Not one person can have God's approval by following Moses' Teachings. Moses' Teachings show what sin is.

God Gives Us His Approval as a Gift

²¹ Now, the way to receive God's approval has been made plain in a way other than Moses' Teachings. Moses' Teachings and the Prophets tell us this. ²² Everyone who believes has God's approval through faith in Jesus Christ.

There is no difference between people. ²³ Because all people have sinned, they have fallen short of God's glory. ²⁴ They receive God's approval freely by an act of his kindnessᵃ through the price Christ Jesus paid to set us free ˌfrom sinˌ. ²⁵ God showed that Christ is the throne of mercy where God's approval is given through faith in Christ's blood. In his patience God waited to deal with sins committed in the past. ²⁶ He waited so that he could display his approval at the present time. This shows that he is a God of justice, a God who approves of people who believe in Jesus.

ᵃ 3:24 Or "grace."

²⁷ So, do we have anything to brag about? Bragging has been eliminated. On what basis was it eliminated? On the basis of our own efforts? No, indeed! Rather, it is eliminated on the basis of faith. ²⁸ We conclude that a person has God's approval by faith, not by his own efforts.

²⁹ Is God only the God of the Jews? Isn't he also the God of people who are not Jewish? Certainly, he is, ³⁰ since it is the same God who approves circumcised people by faith and uncircumcised people through this same faith.

³¹ Are we abolishing Moses' Teachings by this faith? That's unthinkable! Rather, we are supporting Moses' Teachings.

We Have God's Approval by Faith

4 ¹ What can we say that we have discovered about our ancestor Abraham? ² If Abraham had God's approval because of something he did, he would have had a reason to brag. But he could not brag to God about it. ³ What does Scripture say? "Abraham believed God, and that faith was regarded by God to be his approval of Abraham."

⁴ When people work, their pay is not regarded as a gift but something they have earned. ⁵ However, when people don't work but believe God, the one who approves ungodly people, their faith is regarded as God's approval. ⁶ David says the same thing about those who are blessed: God approves of people without their earning it. David said,

⁷ "Blessed are those whose disobedience is forgiven
and whose sins are pardoned.
⁸ Blessed is the person
whom the Lord no longer considers sinful."

⁹ Are only the circumcised people blessed, or are uncircumcised people blessed as well? We say, "Abraham's faith was regarded as God's approval of him." ¹⁰ How was his faith regarded as God's approval? Was he circumcised or was he uncircumcised at that time? He had not been circumcised. ¹¹ Abraham's faith was regarded as

God's approval while he was still uncircumcised. The mark of circumcision is the seal of that approval. Therefore, he is the father of every believer who is not circumcised, and their faith, too, is regarded as God's approval of them. [12] He is also the father of those who not only are circumcised but also are following in the footsteps of his faith. Our father Abraham had that faith before he was circumcised.

[13] So it was not by obeying Moses' Teachings that Abraham or his descendants received the promise that he would inherit the world. Rather, it was through God's approval of his faith. [14] If those who obey Moses' Teachings are the heirs, then faith is useless and the promise is worthless. [15] The laws in Moses' Teachings bring about anger. But where laws don't exist, they can't be broken. [16] Therefore, the promise is based on faith so that it can be a gift.[a] Consequently, the promise is guaranteed for every descendant, not only for those who are descendants by obeying Moses' Teachings but also for those who are descendants by believing as Abraham did. He is the father of all of us, [17] as Scripture says: "I have made you a father of many things."

Abraham believed when he stood in the presence of the God who gives life to dead people and calls into existence nations that don't even exist. [18] When there was nothing left to hope for, Abraham still hoped and believed. As a result, he became a father of many nations, as he had been told: "That is how many descendants you will have." [19] Abraham didn't weaken. Through faith he regarded the facts: His body was already as good as dead now that he was about a hundred years old, and Sarah was unable to have children. [20] He didn't doubt God's promise out of a lack of faith. Instead, giving honor to God ˌfor the promiseˌ, he became strong because of faith [21] and was absolutely confident that God would do what he promised. [22] That is why his faith was regarded as God's approval of him.

[23] But the words "his faith was regarded as God's approval of him" were written not only for him [24] but also for us. Our faith

---

[a] 4:16 Or "grace."

will be regarded as God's approval of us who believe in the one who brought Jesus, our Lord, back to life. [25] Jesus, our Lord, was handed over to death because of our failures and was brought back to life so that we could receive God's approval.

We Are at Peace With God Because of Jesus

5 [1] Now that we have God's approval by faith, we have peace with God because of what our Lord Jesus Christ has done. [2] Through Christ we can approach God[a] and stand in his favor.[b] So we brag because of our confidence that we will receive glory from God. [3] But that's not all. We also brag when we are suffering. We know that suffering creates endurance, [4] endurance creates character, and character creates confidence. [5] We're not ashamed to have this confidence, because God's love has been poured into our hearts by the Holy Spirit, who has been given to us.

[6] Look at it this way: At the right time, while we were still helpless, Christ died for ungodly people. [7] Finding someone who would die for a godly person is rare. Maybe someone would have the courage to die for a good person. [8] Christ died for us while we were still sinners. This demonstrates God's love for us.

[9] Since Christ's blood has now given us God's approval, we are even more certain that Christ will save us from God's anger. [10] If the death of his Son restored our relationship with God while we were still his enemies, we are even more certain that, because of this restored relationship, the life of his Son will save us. [11] In addition, our Lord Jesus Christ lets us continue to brag about God. After all, it is through Christ that we now have this restored relationship with God.

A Comparison Between Adam and Christ

[12] Sin came into the world through one person, and death came through sin. So death spread to everyone, because everyone sinned. [13] Sin was in the world before there were any laws. But

---

[a] 5:2 Some manuscripts read "we can approach God through faith."
[b] 5:2, 15 Or "grace."

no record of sin can be kept when there are no laws. [14] Yet, death ruled from the time of Adam to the time of Moses, even over those who did not sin in the same way Adam did when he disobeyed. Adam is an image of the one who would come.

[15] There is no comparison between ˌGod'sˌ gift and ˌAdam'sˌ failure. If humanity died as the result of one person's failure, it is certainly true that God's kindness[b] and the gift given through the kindness of one person, Jesus Christ, have been showered on humanity.

[16] There is also no comparison between ˌGod'sˌ gift and the one who sinned. The verdict which followed one person's failure condemned everyone. But, even after many failures, the gift brought God's approval. [17] It is certain that death ruled because of one person's failure. It's even more certain that those who receive God's overflowing kindness and the gift of his approval will rule in life because of one person, Jesus Christ.

[18] Therefore, everyone was condemned through one failure, and everyone received God's life-giving approval through one verdict. [19] Clearly, through one person's disobedience humanity became sinful, and through one person's obedience humanity will receive God's approval. [20] Laws were added to increase the failure. But where sin increased, God's kindness increased even more. [21] As sin ruled by bringing death, God's kindness would rule by bringing us his approval. This results in our living forever because of Jesus Christ our Lord.

No Longer Slaves to Sin, but God's Servants

6 [1] What should we say then? Should we continue to sin so that God's kindness[a] will increase? [2] That's unthinkable! As far as sin is concerned, we have died. So how can we still live under sin's influence?

[3] Don't you know that all of us who were baptized into Christ Jesus were baptized into his death? [4] When we were baptized into his death, we were placed into the tomb with him. As Christ

[a] 6:1 Or "grace."

was brought back from death to life by the glorious power of the Father, so we, too, should live a new kind of life. ⁵ If we've become united with him in a death like his, certainly we will also be united with him when we come back to life as he did. ⁶ We know that the person we used to be was crucified with him to put an end to sin in our bodies. Because of this we are no longer slaves to sin. ⁷ The person who has died has been freed from sin.

⁸ If we have died with Christ, we believe that we will also live with him. ⁹ We know that Christ, who was brought back to life, will never die again. Death no longer has any power over him. ¹⁰ When he died, he died once and for all to sin's power. But now he lives, and he lives for God. ¹¹ So consider yourselves dead to sin's power but living for God in the power Christ Jesus gives you.

¹² Therefore, never let sin rule your physical body so that you obey its desires. ¹³ Never offer any part of your body to sin's power. No part of your body should ever be used to do any ungodly thing. Instead, offer yourselves to God as people who have come back from death and are now alive. Offer all the parts of your body to God. Use them to do everything that God approves of. ¹⁴ Certainly, sin shouldn't have power over you because you're not controlled by laws, but by God's favor.ᵇ

¹⁵ Then what is the implication? Should we sin because we are not controlled by laws but by God's favor? That's unthinkable! ¹⁶ Don't you know that if you offer to be someone's slave, you must obey that master? Either your master is sin, or your master is obedience. Letting sin be your master leads to death. Letting obedience be your master leads to God's approval. ¹⁷ You were slaves to sin. But I thank God that you have become wholeheartedly obedient to the teachings which you were given. ¹⁸ Freed from sin, you were made slaves who do what God approves of.

¹⁹ I'm speaking in a human way because of the weakness of your corrupt nature. Clearly, you once offered all the parts of your body as slaves to sexual perversion and disobedience. This led you to live disobedient lives. Now, in the same way, offer all the parts of

ᵇ 6:14 Or "grace."

your body as slaves that do what God approves of. This leads you to live holy lives. ²⁰ When you were slaves to sin, you were free from doing what God approves of.

²¹ What did you gain by doing those things? You're ashamed of what you used to do because it ended in death. ²² Now you have been freed from sin and have become God's slaves. This results in a holy life and, finally, in everlasting life. ²³ The payment for sin is death, but the gift that God freely gives is everlasting life found in Christ Jesus our Lord.

7 ¹ Don't you realize, brothers and sisters, that laws have power over people only as long as they are alive? (I'm speaking to people who are familiar with Moses' Teachings.) ² For example, a married woman is bound by law to her husband as long as he is alive. But if her husband dies, that marriage law is no longer in effect for her. ³ So if she marries another man while her husband is still alive, she will be called an adulterer. But if her husband dies, she is free from this law, so she is not committing adultery if she marries another man.

⁴ In the same way, brothers and sisters, you have died to the laws in Moses' Teachings through Christ's body. You belong to someone else, the one who was brought back to life.

As a result, we can do what God wants. ⁵ While we were living under the influence of our corrupt nature, sinful passions were at work throughout our bodies. Stirred up by Moses' laws, our sinful passions did things that result in death. ⁶ But now we have died to those laws that bound us. God has broken their effect on us so that we are serving in a new spiritual way, not in an old way dictated by written words.

Moses' Laws Show What Sin Is

⁷ What should we say, then? Are Moses' laws sinful? That's unthinkable! In fact, I wouldn't have recognized sin if those laws hadn't shown it to me. For example, I wouldn't have known that some desires are sinful if Moses' Teachings hadn't said, "Never have wrong desires." ⁸ But sin took the opportunity provided by this com-

mandment and made me have all kinds of wrong desires. Clearly, without laws sin is dead. [9] At one time I was alive without any laws. But when this commandment came, sin became alive [10] and I died. I found that the commandment which was intended to bring me life actually brought me death. [11] Sin, taking the opportunity provided by this commandment, deceived me and then killed me.

[12] So Moses' Teachings are holy, and the commandment is holy, right, and good. [13] Now, did something good cause my death? That's unthinkable! Rather, my death was caused by sin so that sin would be recognized for what it is. Through a commandment sin became more sinful than ever.

God's Standards Are at War With Sin's Standards

[14] I know that God's standards are spiritual, but I have a corrupt nature, sold as a slave to sin. [15] I don't realize what I'm doing. I don't do what I want to do. Instead, I do what I hate. [16] I don't do what I want to do, but I agree that God's standards are good. [17] So I am no longer the one who is doing the things I hate, but sin that lives in me is doing them.

[18] I know that nothing good lives in me; that is, nothing good lives in my corrupt nature. Although I have the desire to do what is right, I don't do it. [19] I don't do the good I want to do. Instead, I do the evil that I don't want to do. [20] Now, when I do what I don't want to do, I am no longer the one who is doing it. Sin that lives in me is doing it.

[21] So I've discovered this truth: Evil is present with me even when I want to do what God's standards say is good. [22] I take pleasure in God's standards in my inner being. [23] However, I see a different standard ⌊at work⌋ throughout my body. It is at war with the standards my mind sets and tries to take me captive to sin's standards which still exist throughout my body. [24] What a miserable person I am! Who will rescue me from my dying body? [25] I thank God that our Lord Jesus Christ rescues me! So I am obedient to God's standards with my mind, but I am obedient to sin's standards with my corrupt nature.

God's Spirit Makes Us His Children

8 [1] So those who are believers in Christ Jesus can no longer be condemned. [2] The standards of the Spirit, who gives life through Christ Jesus, have set you free from the standards of sin and death. [3] It is impossible to do what God's standards demand because of the weakness our human nature has. But God sent his Son to have a human nature as sinners have and to pay for sin. That way God condemned sin in our corrupt nature. [4] Therefore, we, who do not live by our corrupt nature but by our spiritual nature, are able to meet God's standards.

[5] Those who live by the corrupt nature have the corrupt nature's attitude. But those who live by the spiritual nature have the spiritual nature's attitude. [6] The corrupt nature's attitude leads to death. But the spiritual nature's attitude leads to life and peace. [7] This is so because the corrupt nature has a hostile attitude toward God. It refuses to place itself under the authority of God's standards because it can't. [8] Those who are under the control of the corrupt nature can't please God. [9] But if God's Spirit lives in you, you are under the control of your spiritual nature, not your corrupt nature.

Whoever doesn't have the Spirit of Christ doesn't belong to him. [10] However, if Christ lives in you, your bodies are dead because of sin, but your spirits are alive because you have God's approval. [11] Does the Spirit of the one who brought Jesus back to life live in you? Then the one who brought Christ back to life will also make your mortal bodies alive by his Spirit who lives in you.

[12] So, brothers and sisters, we have no obligation to live the way our corrupt nature wants us to live. [13] If you live by your corrupt nature, you are going to die. But if you use your spiritual nature to put to death the evil activities of the body, you will live. [14] Certainly, all who are guided by God's Spirit are God's children. [15] You haven't received the spirit of slaves that leads you into fear again. Instead, you have received the spirit of God's adopted children by which we call out, "Abba![a] Father!" [16] The Spirit himself testifies with our spirit that we are God's children. [17] If we are his children,

[a] 8:15 *Abba* is Aramaic for "father.".

we are also God's heirs. If we share in Christ's suffering in order to share his glory, we are heirs together with him.

God's Spirit Helps Us

[18] I consider our present sufferings insignificant compared to the glory that will soon be revealed to us. [19] All creation is eagerly waiting for God to reveal who his children are. [20] Creation was subjected to frustration but not by its own choice. The one who subjected it to frustration did so in the hope [21] that it would also be set free from slavery to decay in order to share the glorious freedom that the children of God will have. [22] We know that all creation has been groaning with the pains of childbirth up to the present time.

[23] However, not only creation groans. We, who have the Spirit as the first of God's gifts, also groan inwardly. We groan as we eagerly wait for our adoption, the freeing of our bodies ˎfrom sinˏ. [24] We were saved with this hope in mind. If we hope for something we already see, it's not really hope. Who hopes for what can be seen? [25] But if we hope for what we don't see, we eagerly wait for it with perseverance.

[26] At the same time the Spirit also helps us in our weakness, because we don't know how to pray for what we need. But the Spirit intercedes along with our groans that cannot be expressed in words. [27] The one who searches our hearts knows what the Spirit has in mind. The Spirit intercedes for God's people the way God wants him to.

Nothing Can Separate Us From God's Love

[28] We know that all things work together for the good of those who love God—those whom he has called according to his plan. [29] This is true because he already knew his people and had already appointed them to have the same form as the image of his Son. Therefore, his Son is the firstborn among many children. [30] He also called those whom he had already appointed. He approved of those whom he had called, and he gave glory to those whom he had approved of.

[31] What can we say about all of this? If God is for us, who can be against us? [32] God didn't spare his own Son but handed him

over ˌto deathˌ for all of us. So he will also give us everything along with him. [33] Who will accuse those whom God has chosen? God has approved of them. [34] Who will condemn them? Christ has died, and more importantly, he was brought back to life. Christ has the highest position in heaven. Christ also intercedes for us. [35] What will separate us from the love Christ has for us? Can trouble, distress, persecution, hunger, nakedness, danger, or violent death separate us from his love? [36] As Scripture says:

> "We are being killed all day long because of you.
> We are thought of as sheep to be slaughtered."

[37] The one who loves us gives us an overwhelming victory in all these difficulties. [38] I am convinced that nothing can ever separate us from God's love which Christ Jesus our Lord shows us.[b] We can't be separated by death or life, by angels or rulers, by anything in the present or anything in the future, by forces [39] or powers in the world above or in the world below, or by anything else in creation.

Paul's Concern for the Jewish People

9 [1] As a Christian, I'm telling you the truth. I'm not lying. The Holy Spirit, along with my own thoughts, supports me in this. [2] I have deep sorrow and endless heartache. [3] I wish I could be condemned and cut off from Christ for the sake of others who, like me, are Jewish by birth. [4] They are Israelites, God's adopted children. They have the Lord's glory, the pledges,[a] Moses' Teachings, the true worship, and the promises. [5] The Messiah is descended from their ancestors according to his human nature. The Messiah is God over everything, forever blessed. Amen.

[6] Now it is not as though God's word has failed. Clearly, not everyone descended from Israel is part of Israel [7] or a descendant of Abraham. However, ˌas Scripture says,ˌ "Through Isaac your descendants will carry on your name." [8] This means that children born by natural descent ˌfrom Abrahamˌ are not necessarily God's

---

[b] 8:38 The last part of verse 39 (in Greek) has been moved to verse 38 to express the complex Greek sentence structure more clearly in English.   [a] 9:4 Or "covenants."

children. Instead, children born by the promise are considered Abraham's descendants.

⁹ For example, this is what the promise said, "I will come back at the right time, and Sarah will have a son." ¹⁰ The same thing happened to Rebekah. Rebekah became pregnant by our ancestor Isaac. ¹¹ Before the children had been born or had done anything good or bad, Rebekah was told that the older child would serve the younger one. This was said to Rebekah so that God's plan would remain a matter of his choice, ¹² a choice based on God's call and not on anything people do.*ᵇ* ¹³ The Scriptures say, "I loved Jacob, but I hated Esau."

¹⁴ What can we say—that God is unfair? That's unthinkable! ¹⁵ For example, God said to Moses, "I will be kind to anyone I want to. I will be merciful to anyone I want to." ¹⁶ Therefore, God's choice does not depend on a person's desire or effort, but on God's mercy.

¹⁷ For example, Scripture says to Pharaoh, "I put you here for this reason: to demonstrate my power through you and to spread my name throughout the earth." ¹⁸ Therefore, if God wants to be kind to anyone, he will be. If he wants to make someone stubborn, he will.

¹⁹ You may ask me, "Why does God still find fault with anyone? Who can resist whatever God wants to do?"

²⁰ Who do you think you are to talk back to God like that? Can an object that was made say to its maker, "Why did you make me like this?" ²¹ A potter has the right to do whatever he wants with his clay. He can make something for a special occasion or something for everyday use from the same lump of clay.

²² If God wants to demonstrate his anger and reveal his power, he can do it. But can't he be extremely patient with people who are objects of his anger because they are headed for destruction? ²³ Can't God also reveal the riches of his glory to people who are objects of his mercy and who he had already prepared for glory? ²⁴ This is what God did for us whom he called—whether we are Jews or not.

ᵇ 9:12 The last part of verse 12 (in Greek) has been placed in verse 11 to express the complex Greek sentence structure more clearly in English.

God Chose People Who Are Not Jewish

25 As God says in Hosea:

"Those who are not my people
  I will call my people.
Those who are not loved
  I will call my loved ones.
26 Wherever they were told,
  'You are not my people,'
    they will be called children of the living God."

27 Isaiah also says about Israel:

"Although the descendants of Israel are
  as numerous as the grains of sand on the seashore,
    only a few will be saved.
28 The Lord will carry out his sentence on the land,
  completely and decisively."

29 This is what Isaiah predicted:

"If the Lord of Armies hadn't left us some descendants,
  we would have been like Sodom and Gomorrah."

30 So what can we say? We can say that non-Jewish people who were not trying to gain God's approval won his approval, an approval based on faith. **31** The people of Israel tried to gain God's approval by obeying Moses' Teachings, but they did not reach their goal. **32** Why? They didn't rely on faith to gain God's approval, but they relied on their own efforts. They stumbled over the rock that trips people. **33** As Scripture says,

"I am placing a rock in Zion that people trip over,
  a large rock that people find offensive.
Whoever believes in him will not be ashamed."

If You Believe You Will Be Saved

10 **1** Brothers and sisters, my heart's desire and prayer to God on behalf of the Jewish people is that they would be saved.

[2] I can assure you that they are deeply devoted to God, but they are misguided. [3] They don't understand ˌhow to receiveˌ God's approval. So they try to set up their own way to get it, and they have not accepted God's way for receiving his approval. [4] Christ is the fulfillment of Moses' Teachings so that everyone who has faith may receive God's approval.

[5] Moses writes about receiving God's approval by following his laws. He says, "The person who obeys laws will live because of the laws he obeys." [6] However, Scripture says about God's approval which is based on faith, "Don't ask yourself who will go up to heaven," (that is, to bring Christ down). [7] "Don't ask who will go down into the depths," (that is, to bring Christ back from the dead). [8] However, what else does it say? "This message is near you. It's in your mouth and in your heart." This is the message of faith that we spread. [9] If you declare that Jesus is Lord, and believe that God brought him back to life, you will be saved. [10] By believing you receive God's approval, and by declaring your faith you are saved. [11] Scripture says, "Whoever believes in him will not be ashamed."

[12] There is no difference between Jews and Greeks. They all have the same Lord, who gives his riches to everyone who calls on him. [13] So then, "Whoever calls on the name of the Lord will be saved."

[14] But how can people call on him if they have not believed in him? How can they believe in him if they have not heard his message? How can they hear if no one tells ˌthe Good Newsˌ? [15] How can people tell the Good News if no one sends them? As Scripture says, "How beautiful are the feet of the messengers who announce the Good News." [16] But not everyone has believed the Good News.

Isaiah asks, "Lord, who has believed our message?" [17] So faith comes from hearing the message, and the message that is heard is what Christ spoke.

[18] But I ask, "Didn't they hear that message?" Certainly they did! "The voice of the messengers has gone out into the whole world and their words to the ends of the earth."

[19] Again I ask, "Didn't Israel understand ˌthat messageˌ?" Moses was the first to say, "I will make you jealous of people who

are not a nation. I will make you angry about a nation that doesn't understand." [20] Isaiah said very boldly, "I was found by those who weren't looking for me. I was revealed to those who weren't asking for me." [21] Then Isaiah said about Israel, "All day long I have stretched out my hands to disobedient and rebellious people."

God's Continuing Love for Jewish People

11 [1] So I ask, "Has God rejected his people Israel?" That's unthinkable! Consider this. I'm an Israelite myself, a descendant of Abraham from the tribe of Benjamin. [2] God has not rejected his people whom he knew long ago. Don't you know what Elijah says in the Scripture passage when he complains to God about Israel? He says, [3] "Lord, they've killed your prophets and torn down your altars. I'm the only one left, and they're trying to take my life." [4] But what was God's reply? God said, "I've kept 7,000 people for myself who have not knelt to worship Baal." [5] So, as there were then, there are now a few left that God has chosen by his kindness.[a] [6] If they were chosen by God's kindness, they weren't chosen because of anything they did. Otherwise, God's kindness wouldn't be kindness.

[7] So what does all this mean? It means that Israel has never achieved what it has been striving for. However, those whom God has chosen have achieved it. The minds of the rest of Israel were closed, [8] as Scripture says,

> "To this day God has given them a spirit of deep sleep.
>   Their eyes don't see,
>   and their ears don't hear!"

[9] And David says,

> "Let the table set for them become a trap and a net,
>   a snare and a punishment for them.
> [10]   Let their vision become clouded so that they cannot see.
>   Let them carry back-breaking burdens forever."

---

[a] 11:5 Or "grace."

11 So I ask, "Has Israel stumbled so badly that it can't get up again?" That's unthinkable! By Israel's failure, salvation has come to people who are not Jewish to make the Jewish people jealous. **12** The fall of the Jewish people made the world spiritually rich. Their failure made people who are not Jewish spiritually rich. So the inclusion of Jewish people will make the world even richer.

13 Now, I speak to you who are not Jewish. As long as I am an apostle sent to people who are not Jewish, I bring honor to my ministry. **14** Perhaps I can make my people jealous and save some of them. **15** If Israel's rejection means that the world has been brought back to God, what does Israel's acceptance mean? It means that Israel has come back to life.

16 If the first handful of dough is holy, the whole batch of dough is holy. If the root is holy, the branches are holy. **17** But some of the olive branches have been broken off, and you, a wild olive branch, have been grafted in their place. You get your nourishment from the roots of the olive tree. **18** So don't brag about being better than the other branches. If you brag, remember that you don't support the root, the root supports you. **19** "Well," you say, "Branches were cut off so that I could be grafted onto the tree." **20** That's right! They were broken off because they didn't believe, but you remain on the tree because you do believe. Don't feel arrogant, but be afraid. **21** If God didn't spare the natural branches, he won't spare you, either. **22** Look at how kind and how severe God can be. He is severe to those who fell, but kind to you if you continue to hold on to his kindness. Otherwise, you, too, will be cut off ˌfrom the treeˌ.

23 If Jewish people do not continue in their unbelief, they will be grafted onto the tree again, because God is able to do that. **24** In spite of the fact that you have been cut from a wild olive tree, you have been grafted onto a cultivated one. So wouldn't it be easier for these natural branches to be grafted onto the olive tree they belong to?

25 Brothers and sisters, I want you to understand this mystery so that you won't become arrogant. The minds of some Israelites have become closed until all of God's non-Jewish people are included. **26** In this way Israel as a whole will be saved, as Scripture says,

"The Savior will come from Zion.
    He will remove godlessness from Jacob.
[27] My promise[b] to them will be fulfilled
    when I take away their sins."

[28] The Good News made the Jewish people enemies because of you. But by God's choice they are loved because of their ancestors. [29] God never changes his mind when he gives gifts or when he calls someone. [30] In the past, you disobeyed God. But now God has been merciful to you because of the disobedience of the Jewish people. [31] In the same way, the Jewish people have also disobeyed so that God may be merciful to them as he was to you. [32] God has placed all people into the prison of their own disobedience so that he could be merciful to all people.

[33]   God's riches, wisdom, and knowledge are so deep
       that it is impossible to explain his decisions
       or to understand his ways.
[34]   "Who knows how the Lord thinks?
       Who can become his adviser?"
[35]   Who gave the Lord something
       which the Lord must pay back?
[36]   Everything is from him and by him and for him.
       Glory belongs to him forever! Amen!

Dedicate Your Lives to God

12 [1] Brothers and sisters, in view of all we have just shared about God's compassion, I encourage you to offer your bodies as living sacrifices, dedicated to God and pleasing to him. This kind of worship is appropriate for you. [2] Don't become like the people of this world. Instead, change the way you think. Then you will always be able to determine what God really wants—what is good, pleasing, and perfect.

[3] Because of the kindness[a] that God has shown me, I ask you not to think of yourselves more highly than you should. Instead, your

b 11:27 Or "covenant."

thoughts should lead you to use good judgment based on what God has given each of you as believers. [4] Our bodies have many parts, but these parts don't all do the same thing. [5] In the same way, even though we are many individuals, Christ makes us one body and individuals who are connected to each other. [6] God in his kindness gave each of us different gifts. If your gift is speaking God's word, make sure what you say agrees with the Christian faith. [7] If your gift is serving, then devote yourself to serving. If it is teaching, devote yourself to teaching. [8] If it is encouraging others, devote yourself to giving encouragement. If it is sharing, be generous. If it is leadership, lead enthusiastically. If it is helping people in need, help them cheerfully.

[9] Love sincerely. Hate evil. Hold on to what is good. [10] Be devoted to each other like a loving family. Excel in showing respect for each other. [11] Don't be lazy in showing your devotion. Use your energy to serve the Lord. [12] Be happy in your confidence, be patient in trouble, and pray continually. [13] Share what you have with God's people who are in need. Be hospitable.

[14] Bless those who persecute you. Bless them, and don't curse them. [15] Be happy with those who are happy. Be sad with those who are sad. [16] Live in harmony with each other. Don't be arrogant, but be friendly to humble people. Don't think that you are smarter than you really are.

[17] Don't pay people back with evil for the evil they do to you. Focus your thoughts on those things that are considered noble. [18] As much as it is possible, live in peace with everyone. [19] Don't take revenge, dear friends. Instead, let God's anger take care of it. After all, Scripture says, "I alone have the right to take revenge. I will pay back, says the Lord." [20] But,

> "If your enemy is hungry, feed him.
> If he is thirsty, give him a drink.
> If you do this, you will make him feel guilty
> and ashamed."

[21] Don't let evil conquer you, but conquer evil with good.

---

a 12:3 Or "grace."

Obey the Government

13 [1] Every person should obey the government in power. No government would exist if it hadn't been established by God. The governments which exist have been put in place by God. [2] Therefore, whoever resists the government opposes what God has established. Those who resist will bring punishment on themselves.

[3] People who do what is right don't have to be afraid of the government. But people who do what is wrong should be afraid of it. Would you like to live without being afraid of the government? Do what is right, and it will praise you. [4] The government is God's servant working for your good.

But if you do what is wrong, you should be afraid. The government has the right to carry out the death sentence. It is God's servant, an avenger to execute God's anger on anyone who does what is wrong. [5] Therefore, it is necessary for you to obey, not only because you're afraid of God's anger but also because of your own conscience.

[6] That is also why you pay your taxes. People in the government are God's servants while they do the work he has given them. [7] Pay everyone whatever you owe them. If you owe taxes, pay them. If you owe tolls, pay them. If you owe someone respect, respect that person. If you owe someone honor, honor that person.

Love One Another

[8] Pay your debts as they come due. However, one debt you can never finish paying is the debt of love that you owe each other. The one who loves another person has fulfilled Moses' Teachings. [9] The commandments, "Never commit adultery; never murder; never steal; never have wrong desires," and every other commandment are summed up in this statement: "Love your neighbor as you love yourself." [10] Love never does anything that is harmful to a neighbor. Therefore, love fulfills Moses' Teachings.

[11] You know the times ˻in which we are living˼. It's time for you to wake up. Our salvation is nearer now than when we first became believers. [12] The night is almost over, and the day is near. So we

should get rid of the things that belong to the dark and take up the weapons that belong to the light. ¹³ We should live decently, as people who live in the light of day. Wild parties, drunkenness, sexual immorality, promiscuity, rivalry, and jealousy cannot be part of our lives. ¹⁴ Instead, live like the Lord Jesus Christ did, and forget about satisfying the desires of your sinful nature.

How to Treat Christians Who Are Weak in Faith

14 ¹ Welcome people who are weak in faith, but don't get into an argument over differences of opinion. ² Some people believe that they can eat all kinds of food. Other people with weak faith believe that they can eat only vegetables. ³ People who eat all foods should not despise people who eat only vegetables. In the same way, the vegetarians should not criticize people who eat all foods, because God has accepted those people. ⁴ Who are you to criticize someone else's servant? The Lord will determine whether his servant has been successful. The servant will be successful because the Lord makes him successful.

⁵ One person decides that one day is holier than another. Another person decides that all days are the same. Every person must make his own decision. ⁶ When people observe a special day, they observe it to honor the Lord. When people eat all kinds of foods, they honor the Lord as they eat, since they give thanks to God. Vegetarians also honor the Lord when they eat, and they, too, give thanks to God. ⁷ It's clear that we don't live to honor ourselves, and we don't die to honor ourselves. ⁸ If we live, we honor the Lord, and if we die, we honor the Lord. So whether we live or die, we belong to the Lord. ⁹ For this reason Christ died and came back to life so that he would be the Lord of both the living and the dead.

¹⁰ Why do you criticize or despise other Christians? Everyone will stand in front of God to be judged. ¹¹ Scripture says,

> "As certainly as I live, says the Lord,
>   everyone will worship me,
>   and everyone will praise God."

¹² All of us will have to give an account of ourselves to God.

¹³ So let's stop criticizing each other. Instead, you should decide never to do anything that would make other Christians have doubts or lose their faith.

¹⁴ The Lord Jesus has given me the knowledge and conviction that no food is unacceptable in and of itself. But it is unacceptable to a person who thinks it is. ¹⁵ So if what you eat hurts another Christian, you are no longer living by love. Don't destroy anyone by what you eat. Christ died for that person. ¹⁶ Don't allow anyone to say that what you consider good is evil.

¹⁷ God's kingdom does not consist of what a person eats or drinks. Rather, God's kingdom consists of God's approval and peace, as well as the joy that the Holy Spirit gives. ¹⁸ The person who serves Christ with this in mind is pleasing to God and respected by people.

¹⁹ So let's pursue those things which bring peace and which are good for each other. ²⁰ Don't ruin God's work because of what you eat. All food is acceptable, but it's wrong for a person to eat something if it causes someone else to have doubts. ²¹ The right thing to do is to avoid eating meat, drinking wine, or doing anything else that causes another Christian to have doubts. ²² So whatever you believe about these things, keep it between yourself and God. The person who does what he knows is right shouldn't feel guilty. He is blessed. ²³ But if a person has doubts and still eats, he is condemned because he didn't act in faith. Anything that is not done in faith is sin.

15 ¹ So those of us who have a strong ˏfaithˏ must be patient with the weaknesses of those whose ˏfaithˏ is not so strong. We must not think only of ourselves. ² We should all be concerned about our neighbor and the good things that will build his faith. ³ Christ did not think only of himself. Rather, as Scripture says, "The insults of those who insult you have fallen on me."

God Gives Us Unity

⁴ Everything written long ago was written to teach us so that we would have confidence through the endurance and encourage-

ment which the Scriptures give us. ⁵ May God, who gives you this endurance and encouragement, allow you to live in harmony with each other by following the example of Christ Jesus. ⁶ Then, having the same goal, you will praise the God and Father of our Lord Jesus Christ.

⁷ Therefore, accept each other in the same way that Christ accepted you. He did this to bring glory to God. ⁸ Let me explain. Christ became a servant for the Jewish people to reveal God's truth. As a result, he fulfilled God's promise to the ancestors of the Jewish people. ⁹ People who are not Jewish praise God for his mercy as well. This is what the Scriptures say,

> "That is why I will give thanks to you among the nations
>   and I will sing praises to your name."

¹⁰ And Scripture says again,

> "You nations, be happy together with his people!"

¹¹ And again,

> "Praise the Lord, all you nations!
>   Praise him, all you people of the world!"

¹² Again, Isaiah says,

> "There will be a root from Jesse.
>   He will rise to rule the nations,
>   and he will give the nations hope."

¹³ May God, the source of hope, fill you with joy and peace through your faith in him. Then you will overflow with hope by the power of the Holy Spirit.

Paul's Desire to Tell the Good News to the World

¹⁴ I'm convinced, brothers and sisters, that you, too, are filled with goodness. I'm also convinced that you have all the knowledge you need and that you are able to instruct each other. ¹⁵ However, I've written you a letter, parts of which are rather bold, as a reminder to

you. I'm doing this because God gave me the gift [16] to be a servant of Christ Jesus to people who are not Jewish. I serve as a priest by spreading the Good News of God. I do this in order that I might bring the nations to God as an acceptable offering, made holy by the Holy Spirit. [17] So Christ Jesus gives me the right to brag about what I'm doing for God. [18] I'm bold enough to tell you only what Christ has done through me to bring people who are not Jewish to obedience. By what I have said and done, [19] by the power of miraculous and amazing signs, and by the power of God's Spirit, I have finished spreading the Good News about Christ from Jerusalem to Illyricum. [20] My goal was to spread the Good News where the name of Christ was not known. I didn't want to build on a foundation which others had laid. [21] As Scripture says,

"Those who were never told about him will see,
    and those who never heard will understand."

[22] This is what has so often kept me from visiting you. [23] But now I have no new opportunities for work in this region. For many years I have wanted to visit you. [24] Now I am on my way to Spain, so I hope to see you when I come your way. After I have enjoyed your company for a while, I hope that you will support my trip to Spain.

[25] Right now I'm going to Jerusalem to bring help to the Christians there. [26] Because the believers in Macedonia and Greece owe a debt to the Christians in Jerusalem, they have decided to take up a collection for the poor among the Christians in Jerusalem. [27] These Macedonians and Greeks have shared the spiritual wealth of the Christians in Jerusalem. So they are obligated to use their earthly wealth to help them.

[28] When the collection is completed and I have officially turned the money over to the Christians in Jerusalem, I will visit you on my way to Spain. [29] I know that when I come to you I will bring the full blessing of Christ.

[30] Brothers and sisters, I encourage you through our Lord Jesus Christ and by the love that the Spirit creates, to join me in my struggle. Pray to God for me [31] that I will be rescued from those people

in Judea who refuse to believe. Pray that God's people in Jerusalem will accept the help I bring. [32] Also pray that by the will of God I may come to you with joy and be refreshed when I am with you.

[33] May the God of peace be with you all. Amen.

Farewell

16 [1] With this letter I'm introducing Phoebe to you. She is our sister in the Christian faith and a deacon[a] of the church in the city of Cenchrea. [2] Give her a Christian welcome that shows you are God's holy people. Provide her with anything she may need, because she has provided help to many people, including me.

[3] Greet Prisca and Aquila, my coworkers in the service of Christ Jesus. [4] They risked their lives to save me. I'm thankful to them and so are all the churches among the nations. [5] Also greet the church that meets in their house.

Greet my dear friend Epaenetus. He was the first person in the province of Asia to become a believer in Christ.

[6] Greet Mary, who has worked very hard for you.

[7] Greet Andronicus and Junia, who are Jewish by birth like me. They are prisoners like me and are prominent among the apostles. They also were Christians before I was.

[8] Greet Ampliatus my dear friend in the service of the Lord.

[9] Greet Urbanus our coworker in the service of Christ, and my dear friend Stachys.

[10] Greet Apelles, a true Christian.

Greet those who belong to the family of Aristobulus.

[11] Greet Herodion, who is Jewish by birth like me.

Greet those Christians who belong to the family of Narcissus.

[12] Greet Tryphaena and Tryphosa, who have worked hard for the Lord.

Greet dear Persis, who has worked very hard for the Lord.

[13] Greet Rufus, that outstanding Christian, and his mother, who has been a mother to me too.

---

[a] 16:1 English equivalent difficult.

¹⁴ Greet Asyncritus, Phlegon, Hermes, Patrobas, Hermas, and the brothers and sisters who are with them.

¹⁵ Greet Philologus and Julia, Nereus, and his sister, and Olympas, and all God's people who are with them.

¹⁶ Greet each other with a holy kiss.

All the churches of Christ greet you.

¹⁷ Brothers and sisters, I urge you to watch out for those people who create divisions and who make others fall away ˌfrom the Christian faithˌ by teaching doctrine that is not the same as you have learned. Stay away from them. ¹⁸ People like these are not serving Christ our Lord. They are serving their own desires. By their smooth talk and flattering words they deceive unsuspecting people.

¹⁹ Everyone has heard about your obedience and this makes me happy for you. I want you to do what is good and to avoid what is evil. ²⁰ The God of peace will quickly crush Satan under your feet. May the good will[b] of our Lord Jesus be with you!

²¹ Timothy my coworker greets you; so do Lucius, Jason, and Sosipater, who are Jewish by birth like me.

²² I, Tertius, who wrote this letter, send you Christian greetings.

²³ Gaius greets you. He is host to me and the whole church.

Erastus, the city treasurer, greets you.

Quartus, our brother in the Christian faith, greets you.[c]

²⁵ God can strengthen you by the Good News and the message I tell about Jesus Christ. He can strengthen you by revealing the mystery that was kept in silence for a very long time ²⁶ but now is publicly known. The everlasting God ordered that what the prophets wrote must be shown to the people of every nation to bring them to the obedience that is associated with faith. ²⁷ God alone is wise. Glory belongs to him through Jesus Christ forever! Amen.

---

[b] 16:20 Or "grace."   [c] 16:23 Some manuscripts and translations add verse 24: "May the good will of our Lord Jesus Christ be with all of you. Amen."

1 CORINTHIANS

Greeting

1 ¹ From Paul, called to be an apostle of Christ Jesus by the will of God, and from Sosthenes, our brother in the Christian faith.

² To God's church that was made holy by Christ Jesus and called to be God's holy people in the city of Corinth and to people everywhere who call on the name of our Lord Jesus Christ.

³ Good will*a* and peace from God our Father and the Lord Jesus Christ are yours!

⁴ I always thank God for you because Christ Jesus has shown you God's good will. ⁵ Through Christ Jesus you have become rich in every way—in speech and knowledge of every kind. ⁶ Our message about Christ has been verified among you. ⁷ Therefore, you don't lack any gift as you wait eagerly for our Lord Jesus Christ to be revealed. ⁸ He will continue to give you strength until the end so that no one can accuse you of anything on the day of our Lord Jesus Christ. ⁹ God faithfully keeps his promises. He called you to be partners with his Son Jesus Christ our Lord.

God's Wisdom Is Better Than the World's Wisdom

¹⁰ Brothers and sisters, I encourage all of you in the name of our Lord Jesus Christ to agree with each other and not to split into opposing groups. I want you to be united in your understanding and opinions. ¹¹ Brothers and sisters, some people from Chloe's family have made it clear to me that you are quarreling among yourselves. ¹² This is what I mean: Each of you is saying, "I follow Paul," or "I follow Apollos," or "I follow Cephas,"*b* or "I follow Christ." ¹³ Has

---

a 1:3 Or "Grace."   *b* 1:12 Cephas is the Aramaic name for the Apostle Peter.

Christ been divided? Was Paul crucified for you? Were you baptized in Paul's name? [14] I thank God that[c] I didn't baptize any of you except Crispus and Gaius [15] so that no one can say you were baptized in my name. [16] I also baptized Stephanas and his family. Beyond that, I'm not sure whether I baptized anyone else. [17] Christ didn't send me to baptize. Instead, he sent me to spread the Good News. I didn't use intellectual arguments. That would have made the cross of Christ lose its meaning.

[18] The message about the cross is nonsense to those who are being destroyed, but it is God's power to us who are being saved. [19] Scripture says,

"I will destroy the wisdom of the wise.
I will reject the intelligence of intelligent people."

[20] Where is the wise person? Where is the scholar? Where is the persuasive speaker of our time? Hasn't God turned the wisdom of the world into nonsense? [21] The world with its wisdom was unable to recognize God in terms of his own wisdom. So God decided to use the nonsense of the Good News we speak to save those who believe. [22] Jews ask for miraculous signs, and Greeks look for wisdom, [23] but our message is that Christ was crucified. This offends Jewish people and makes no sense to people who are not Jewish. [24] But to those Jews and Greeks who are called, he is Christ, God's power and God's wisdom. [25] God's nonsense is wiser than human wisdom, and God's weakness is stronger than human strength.

[26] Brothers and sisters, consider what you were when God called you to be Christians. Not many of you were wise from a human point of view. You were not in powerful positions or in the upper social classes. [27] But God chose what the world considers nonsense to put wise people to shame. God chose what the world considers weak to put what is strong to shame. [28] God chose what the world considers ordinary and what it despises—what it considers to be nothing—in order to destroy what it considers to be

---

c 1:14 A few of the older manuscripts read "I am thankful that."

something. [29] As a result, no one can brag in God's presence. [30] You are partners with Christ Jesus because of God. Jesus has become our wisdom sent from God, our righteousness, our holiness, and our ransom from sin. [31] As Scripture says, "Whoever brags must brag about what the Lord has done."

2 [1] Brothers and sisters, when I came to you, I didn't speak about God's mystery[a] as if it were some kind of brilliant message or wisdom. [2] While I was with you, I decided to deal with only one subject—Jesus Christ, who was crucified. [3] When I came to you, I was weak. I was afraid and very nervous. [4] I didn't speak my message with persuasive intellectual arguments. I spoke my message with a show of spiritual power [5] so that your faith would not be based on human wisdom but on God's power.

[6] However, we do use wisdom to speak to those who are mature. It is a wisdom that doesn't belong to this world or to the rulers of this world who are in power today and gone tomorrow. [7] We speak about the mystery of God's wisdom. It is a wisdom that has been hidden, which God had planned for our glory before the world began. [8] Not one of the rulers of this world has known it. If they had, they wouldn't have crucified the Lord of glory. [9] But as Scripture says:

> "No eye has seen,
> no ear has heard,
> and no mind has imagined
> the things that God has prepared
> for those who love him."

[10] God has revealed those things to us by his Spirit. The Spirit searches everything, especially the deep things of God. [11] After all, who knows everything about a person except that person's own spirit? In the same way, no one has known everything about God except God's Spirit. [12] Now, we didn't receive the spirit that belongs to the world. Instead, we received the Spirit who comes from God so that we could know the things which God has freely given us.

[a] 2:1 Some manuscripts and translations read "testimony."

¹³ We don't speak about these things using teachings that are based on intellectual arguments like people do. Instead, we use the Spirit's teachings. We explain spiritual things to those who have the Spirit.*ᵇ*

¹⁴ A person who isn't spiritual doesn't accept the teachings of God's Spirit. He thinks they're nonsense. He can't understand them because a person must be spiritual to evaluate them. ¹⁵ Spiritual people evaluate everything but are subject to no one's evaluation.

¹⁶   "Who has known the mind of the Lord
         so that he can teach him?"

However, we have the mind of Christ.

You Belong to Christ

3 ¹ Brothers and sisters, I couldn't talk to you as spiritual people but as people still influenced by your corrupt nature. You were infants in your faith in Christ. ² I gave you milk to drink. I didn't give you solid food because you weren't ready for it. Even now you aren't ready for it ³ because you're still influenced by your corrupt nature.

When you are jealous and quarrel among yourselves, aren't you influenced by your corrupt nature and living by human standards? ⁴ When some of you say, "I follow Paul" and others say, "I follow Apollos," aren't you acting like ˌsinfulˌ humans? ⁵ Who is Apollos? Who is Paul? They are servants who helped you come to faith. Each did what the Lord gave him to do. ⁶ I planted, and Apollos watered, but God made it grow. ⁷ So neither the one who plants nor the one who waters is important because ˌonlyˌ God makes it grow. ⁸ The one who plants and the one who waters have the same goal, and each will receive a reward for his own work. ⁹ We are God's coworkers. You are God's field.

You are God's building. ¹⁰ As a skilled and experienced builder, I used the gift*ᵃ* that God gave me to lay the foundation ˌfor that buildingˌ. However, someone else is building on it. Each person must be careful how he builds on it. ¹¹ After all, no one can lay any

ᵇ 2:13 Or "We explain spiritual things in spiritual words."

other foundation than the one that is already laid, and that foundation is Jesus Christ. ¹² People may build on this foundation with gold, silver, precious stones, wood, hay, or straw. ¹³ The day will make what each one does clearly visible because fire will reveal it. That fire will determine what kind of work each person has done. ¹⁴ If what a person has built survives, he will receive a reward. ¹⁵ If his work is burned up, he will suffer ⌊the loss⌋. However, he will be saved, though it will be like going through a fire.

¹⁶ Don't you know that you are God's temple and that God's Spirit lives in you? ¹⁷ If anyone destroys God's temple, God will destroy him because God's temple is holy. You are that holy temple!

¹⁸ Don't deceive yourselves. If any of you think you are wise in the ways of this world, you should give up that wisdom in order to become really wise. ¹⁹ The wisdom of this world is nonsense in God's sight. That's why Scripture says, "God catches the wise in their cleverness." ²⁰ Again Scripture says, "The Lord knows that the thoughts of the wise are pointless."

²¹ So don't brag about people. Everything belongs to you. ²² Whether it is Paul, Apollos, Cephas, the world, life or death, present or future things, everything belongs to you. ²³ You belong to Christ, and Christ belongs to God.

The Work of the Apostles

4 ¹ People should think of us as servants of Christ and managers who are entrusted with God's mysteries. ² Managers are required to be trustworthy.

³ It means very little to me that you or any human court should cross-examine me. I don't even ask myself questions. ⁴ I have a clear conscience, but that doesn't mean I have God's approval. It is the Lord who cross-examines me. ⁵ Therefore, don't judge anything before the appointed time. Wait until the Lord comes. He will also bring to light what is hidden in the dark and reveal people's motives. Then each person will receive praise from God.

ᵃ 3:10 Or "grace."

⁶ Brothers and sisters, I have applied this to Apollos and myself for your sake. You should learn from us not to go beyond what is written in Scripture. Then you won't arrogantly place one of us in opposition to the other.

⁷ Who says that you are any better than other people? What do you have that wasn't given to you? If you were given what you have, why are you bragging as if it weren't a gift?

⁸ You already have what you want! You've already become rich! You've become kings without us! I wish you really were kings so that we could be kings with you.

⁹ As I see it, God has placed us apostles last in line, like people condemned to die. We have become a spectacle for people and angels to look at. ¹⁰ We have given up our wisdom for Christ, but you have insight because of Christ. We are weak, but you are strong. You are honored, but we are dishonored. ¹¹ To this moment, we are hungry, thirsty, poorly dressed, roughly treated, and homeless. ¹² We wear ourselves out doing physical labor. When people verbally abuse us, we bless them. When people persecute us, we endure it. ¹³ When our reputations are attacked, we remain courteous. Right now we have become garbage in the eyes of the world and trash in the sight of all people.

¹⁴ I'm not writing this to make you feel ashamed but to instruct you as my dear children. ¹⁵ You may have countless Christian guardians, but you don't have many ˎspiritualˎ fathers. I became your father in the Christian life by telling you the Good News about Christ Jesus. ¹⁶ So I encourage you to imitate me. ¹⁷ That's why I've sent Timothy to you to help you remember my Christian way of life as I teach it everywhere in every church. Timothy is my dear child, and he faithfully does the Lord's work.

¹⁸ Some of you have become arrogant because you think I won't pay you a visit. ¹⁹ If it's the Lord's will, I'll visit you soon. Then I'll know what these arrogant people are saying and what power they have. ²⁰ God's kingdom is not just talk, it is power.

²¹ When I come to visit you, would you prefer that I punish you or show you love and a gentle spirit?

How to Treat Christians Who Live Like Non-Christians

5 [1] Your own members are aware that there is sexual sin going on among them. This kind of sin is not even heard of among unbelievers—a man is actually married to his father's wife. [2] You're being arrogant when you should have been more upset about this. If you had been upset, the man who did this would have been removed from among you. [3] Although I'm not physically present with you, I am with you in spirit. I have already judged the man who did this as though I were present with you. [4] When you have gathered together, I am with you in spirit. Then, in the name of our Lord Jesus, and with his power, [5] hand such a person over to Satan to destroy his corrupt nature so that his spiritual nature may be saved on the day of the Lord.

[6] It's not good for you to brag. Don't you know that a little yeast spreads through the whole batch of dough? [7] Remove the old yeast ˪of sin˼ so that you may be a new batch of dough, since you don't actually have the yeast ˪of sin˼.

Christ, our Passover lamb, has been sacrificed. [8] So we must not celebrate our festival with the old yeast ˪of sin˼ or with the yeast of vice and wickedness. Instead, we must celebrate it with the bread of purity and truth that has no yeast.

[9] In my letter to you I told you not to associate with people who continue to commit sexual sins. [10] I didn't tell you that you could not have any contact with unbelievers who commit sexual sins, are greedy, are dishonest, or worship false gods. If that were the case, you would have to leave this world. [11] Now, what I meant was that you should not associate with people who call themselves brothers or sisters in the Christian faith but live in sexual sin, are greedy, worship false gods, use abusive language, get drunk, or are dishonest. Don't eat with such people.

[12] After all, do I have any business judging those who are outside ˪the Christian faith˼? Isn't it your business to judge those who are inside? [13] God will judge those who are outside. Remove that wicked man from among you.

Settling Disagreements Between Christians

6 ¹ When one of you has a complaint against another, how dare you go to court to settle the matter in front of wicked people. Why don't you settle it in front of God's holy people? ² Don't you know that God's people will judge the world? So if you're going to judge the world, aren't you capable of judging insignificant cases? ³ Don't you know that we will judge angels, not to mention things in this life? ⁴ When you have cases dealing with this life, why do you allow people whom the church has a low opinion of to be your judges? ⁵ You should be ashamed of yourselves! Don't you have at least one wise person who is able to settle disagreements between believers? ⁶ Instead, one believer goes to court against another believer, and this happens in front of unbelievers.

⁷ You are already totally defeated because you have lawsuits against each other. Why don't you accept the fact that you have been wronged? Why don't you accept that you have been cheated? ⁸ Instead, you do wrong and cheat, and you do this to other believers.

⁹ Don't you know that wicked people won't inherit the kingdom of God? Stop deceiving yourselves! People who continue to commit sexual sins, who worship false gods, those who commit adultery, homosexuals, ¹⁰ or thieves, those who are greedy or drunk, who use abusive language, or who rob people will not inherit the kingdom of God. ¹¹ That's what some of you were! But you have been washed and made holy, and you have received God's approval in the name of the Lord Jesus Christ and in the Spirit of our God.

Stay Away From Sexual Sins

¹² Someone may say, "I'm allowed to do anything," but not everything is helpful. I'm allowed to do anything, but I won't allow anything to gain control over my life. ¹³ Food is for the stomach, and the stomach is for food, but God will put an end to both of them. However, the body is not for sexual sin but for the Lord, and the Lord is for the body. ¹⁴ God raised the Lord, and by his power God will also raise us.

¹⁵ Don't you realize that your bodies are parts of Christ's body? Should I take the parts of Christ's body and make them parts of a prostitute's body? That's unthinkable! ¹⁶ Don't you realize that the person who unites himself with a prostitute becomes one body with her? God says, "The two will be one." ¹⁷ However, the person who unites himself with the Lord becomes one spirit with him.

¹⁸ Stay away from sexual sins. Other sins that people commit don't affect their bodies the same way sexual sins do. People who sin sexually sin against their own bodies. ¹⁹ Don't you know that your body is a temple that belongs to the Holy Spirit? The Holy Spirit, whom you received from God, lives in you. You don't belong to yourselves. ²⁰ You were bought for a price. So bring glory to God in the way you use your body.

Advice About Marriage

7 ¹ Now, concerning the things that you wrote about: It's good for men not to get married. ² But in order to avoid sexual sins, each man should have his own wife, and each woman should have her own husband.

³ Husbands and wives should satisfy each other's ⌐sexual⌐ needs. ⁴ A wife doesn't have authority over her own body, but her husband does. In the same way, a husband doesn't have authority over his own body, but his wife does.

⁵ Don't withhold yourselves from each other unless you agree to do so for a set time to devote yourselves to prayer. Then you should get back together so that Satan doesn't use your lack of self-control to tempt you. ⁶ What I have just said is not meant as a command but as a suggestion. ⁷ I would like everyone to be like me. However, each person has a special gift from God, and these gifts vary from person to person.

⁸ I say to those who are not married, especially to widows: It is good for you to stay single like me. ⁹ However, if you cannot control your desires, you should get married. It is better for you to marry than to burn ⌐with sexual desire⌐.

¹⁰ I pass this command along (not really I, but the Lord): A wife shouldn't leave her husband. ¹¹ If she does, she should stay single or make up with her husband. Likewise, a husband should not divorce his wife.

¹² I (not the Lord) say to the rest of you: If any Christian man is married to a woman who is an unbeliever, and she is willing to live with him, he should not divorce her. ¹³ If any Christian woman is married to a man who is an unbeliever, and he is willing to live with her, she should not divorce her husband. ¹⁴ Actually, the unbelieving husband is made holy because of his wife, and an unbelieving wife is made holy because of her husband. Otherwise, their children would be unacceptable ⌊to God⌋, but now they are acceptable to him. ¹⁵ But if the unbelieving partners leave, let them go. Under these circumstances a Christian man or Christian woman is not bound ⌊by a marriage vow⌋. God has called you to live in peace. ¹⁶ How do you as a wife know whether you will save your husband? How do you as a husband know whether you will save your wife?

¹⁷ Everyone should live the life that the Lord gave him when God called him. This is the guideline I use in every church.

¹⁸ Any man who was already circumcised when he was called to be a Christian shouldn't undo his circumcision. Any man who was uncircumcised when he was called to be a Christian shouldn't get circumcised. ¹⁹ Circumcision is nothing, and the lack of it is nothing. But keeping what God commands is everything. ²⁰ All people should stay as they were when they were called. ²¹ Were you a slave when you were called? That shouldn't bother you. However, if you have a chance to become free, take it. ²² If the Lord called you when you were a slave, you are the Lord's free person. In the same way, if you were free when you were called, you are Christ's slave. ²³ You were bought for a price. Don't become anyone's slaves. ²⁴ Brothers and sisters, you should remain in whatever circumstances you were in when God called you. God is with you in those circumstances.

²⁵ Concerning virgins: Even though I don't have any command from the Lord, I'll give you my opinion. I'm a person to whom the Lord has shown mercy, so I can be trusted. ²⁶ Because of the present

crisis I believe it is good for people to remain as they are. ²⁷ Do you have a wife? Don't seek a divorce. Are you divorced from your wife? Don't look for another one. ²⁸ But if you do get married, you have not sinned. If a virgin gets married, she has not sinned. However, these people will have trouble, and I would like to spare them from that.

²⁹ This is what I mean, brothers and sisters: The time has been shortened. While it lasts, those who are married should live as though they were not. ³⁰ Those who have eyes filled with tears should live as though they have no sorrow. Those who are happy should live as though there was nothing to be happy about. Those who buy something should live as though they didn't own it. ³¹ Those who use the things in this world should do so but not depend on them. It is clear that this world in its present form is passing away.

³² So I don't want you to have any concerns. An unmarried man is concerned about the things of the Lord, ˌthat is,˩ about how he can please the Lord. ³³ But the married man is concerned about earthly things, ˌthat is,˩ about how he can please his wife. ³⁴ His attention is divided.

An unmarried woman or a virgin is concerned about the Lord's things so that she may be holy in body and in spirit. But the married woman is concerned about earthly things, ˌthat is,˩ about how she can please her husband. ³⁵ I'm saying this for your benefit, not to restrict you. I'm showing you how to live a noble life of devotion to the Lord without being distracted by other things.

³⁶ No father would want to do the wrong thing when his virgin daughter is old enough to get married. If she wants to get married, he isn't sinning by letting her get married. ³⁷ However, a father may have come to a decision about his daughter. If his decision is to keep her ˌat home˩ because she doesn't want to get married, that's fine. ³⁸ So it's fine for a father to give his daughter in marriage, but the father who doesn't give his daughter in marriage does even better.

³⁹ A married woman must remain with her husband as long as he lives. If her husband dies, she is free to marry anyone she wishes, but only if the man is a Christian.ᵃ ⁴⁰ However, she will be more blessed if she stays as she is. That is my opinion, and I think that I, too, have God's Spirit.

Advice About Food Offered to False Gods

8 ¹Now, concerning food offered to false gods: We know that we all have knowledge. Knowledge makes people arrogant, but love builds them up. ²Those who think they know something still have a lot to learn. ³But if they love God, they are known by God.

⁴Now about eating food that was offered to false gods: We know that the false gods in this world don't really exist and that no god exists except the one God. ⁵People may say that there are gods in heaven and on earth—many gods and many lords, as they would call them. ⁶But for us,

> "There is only one God, the Father.
>   Everything came from him, and we live for him.
> There is only one Lord, Jesus Christ.
>   Everything came into being through him,
>   and we live because of him."

⁷But not everyone knows this. Some people are so used to worshiping false gods that they believe they are eating food offered to a false god. So they feel guilty because their conscience is weak.

⁸Food will not affect our relationship with God. We are no worse off if we eat ⌊that food⌋ and no better off if we don't. ⁹But be careful that by using your freedom you don't somehow make a believer who is weak in faith fall into sin. ¹⁰For example, suppose someone with a weak conscience sees you, who have this knowledge, eating in the temple of a false god. Won't you be encouraging that person to eat food offered to a false god? ¹¹In that case, your knowledge is ruining a believer whose faith is weak, a believer for whom Christ died. ¹²When you sin against other believers in this way and harm their weak consciences, you are sinning against Christ.

¹³Therefore, if eating food ⌊offered to false gods⌋ causes other believers to lose their faith, I will never eat that kind of food so that I won't make other believers lose their faith.

---

a 7:39 Or "only as the Lord guides her."

Paul's Right to Be Paid for His Work as an Apostle

9 [1] Don't you agree that I'm a free man? Don't you agree that I'm an apostle? Haven't I seen Jesus our Lord? Aren't you the result of my work for the Lord? [2] If I'm not an apostle to other people, at least I'm an apostle to you. You are the seal which proves that I am the Lord's apostle. [3] This is how I defend myself to those who cross-examine me. [4] Don't we have the right to eat and drink? [5] Don't we have the right to take our wives along with us like the other apostles, the Lord's brothers, and Cephas[a] do? [6] Or is it only Barnabas and I who don't have any rights, except to find work to support ourselves?

[7] Does a soldier ever serve in the army at his own expense? Does anyone plant a vineyard and not eat the grapes? Does anyone take care of a flock and not drink milk from the sheep? [8] Am I merely stating some human rule? Don't Moses' Teachings say the same thing? [9] Moses' Teachings say, "Never muzzle an ox when it is threshing[b] grain." God's concern isn't for oxen. [10] Isn't he speaking entirely for our benefit? This was written for our benefit so that the person who plows or threshes should expect to receive a share of the crop. [11] If we have planted the spiritual seed that has been of benefit to you, is it too much if we receive part of the harvest from your earthly goods? [12] If others have the right to expect this from you, don't we deserve even more? But we haven't used our rights. Instead, we would put up with anything in order not to hinder the Good News of Christ in any way.

[13] Don't you realize that those who work at the temple get their food from the temple? Don't those who help at the altar get a share of what is on the altar? [14] In the same way, the Lord has commanded that those who spread the Good News should earn their living from the Good News.

[15] I haven't used any of these rights, and I haven't written this in order to use them now. I would rather die than have anyone turn my bragging into meaningless words. [16] If I spread the Good

[a] 9:5 Cephas is the Aramaic name for the Apostle Peter.   [b] 9:9 Threshing is the process of beating stalks to separate them from the grain.

News, I have nothing to brag about because I have an obligation to do this. How horrible it will be for me if I don't spread the Good News! **17** If I spread the Good News willingly, I'll have a reward. But if I spread the Good News unwillingly, I'm ˌonlyˌ doing what I've been entrusted to do.

18 So what is my reward? It is to spread the Good News free of charge. In that way I won't use the rights that belong to those who spread the Good News.

Paul's Work as an Apostle

19 Although I'm free from all people, I have made myself a slave for all people to win more of them. **20** I became Jewish for Jewish people. I became subject to Moses' Teachings for those who are subject to those laws. I did this to win them even though I'm not subject to Moses' Teachings. **21** I became like a person who does not have Moses' Teachings for those who don't have those teachings. I did this to win them even though I have God's teachings. I'm really subject to Christ's teachings. **22** I became like a person weak in faith to win those who are weak in faith. I have become everything to everyone in order to save at least some of them. **23** I do all this for the sake of the Good News in order to share what it offers.

24 Don't you realize that everyone who runs in a race runs to win, but only one runner gets the prize? Run like them, so that you can win. **25** Everyone who enters an athletic contest goes into strict training. They do it to win a temporary crown, but we do it to win one that will be permanent. **26** So I run—but not without a clear goal ahead of me. So I box—but not as if I were just shadow boxing. **27** Rather, I toughen my body with punches and make it my slave so that I will not be disqualified after I have spread the Good News to others.

Learn From What Happened in the Time of Moses

10 **1** I want you to know, brothers and sisters, that all our ancestors ˌwho left Egyptˌ were under the cloud, and they all went through the sea. **2** They were all united with Moses by baptism in the cloud and in the sea. **3** All of them ate the same spiritual food, [4] and all of them drank the same spiritual drink. They drank from the spiritual rock that went with them, and that rock was Christ. [5] Yet, God was not pleased with most of them, so their dead bodies were scattered over the desert.

[6] These things have become examples for us so that we won't desire what is evil, as they did. [7] So don't worship false gods as some of them did, as Scripture says, "The people sat down to a feast which turned into an orgy." [8] We shouldn't sin sexually as some of them did. Twenty-three thousand of them died on one day. [9] We shouldn't put the Lord[a] to the test as some of them did. They were killed by snakes. [10] Don't complain as some of them did. The angel of death destroyed them. [11] These things happened to make them an example for others. These things were written down as a warning for us who are living in the closing days of history. [12] So, people who think they are standing firmly should be careful that they don't fall.

[13] There isn't any temptation that you have experienced which is unusual for humans. God, who faithfully keeps his promises, will not allow you to be tempted beyond your power to resist. But when you are tempted, he will also give you the ability to endure the temptation as your way of escape.

Stay Away From Worshiping False Gods

[14] Therefore, my dear friends, get as far away from the worship of false gods as you can.

[15] I'm talking to intelligent people. Judge for yourselves what I'm saying. [16] When we bless the cup of blessing aren't we sharing in the blood of Christ? When we break the bread aren't we sharing in the body of Christ? [17] Because there is one loaf, we are one body, although we are many individuals. All of us share one loaf.

[18] Look at the people of Israel from a human point of view. Don't those who eat the sacrifices share what is on the altar? [19] Do I mean that an offering made to a false god is anything, or that a false god itself is anything? [20] Hardly! What I am saying is that these

---

[a] 10:9 Some manuscripts and translations; other manuscripts and translations "Christ."

sacrifices which people make are made to demons and not to God. I don't want you to be partners with demons. ²¹ You cannot drink the Lord's cup and the cup of demons. You cannot participate at the table of the Lord and at the table of demons. ²² Are we trying to make the Lord jealous? Are we stronger than he is?

²³ Someone may say, "I'm allowed to do anything," but not everything is helpful. I'm allowed to do anything, but not everything encourages growth. ²⁴ People should be concerned about others and not just about themselves. ²⁵ Eat anything that is sold in the market without letting your conscience trouble you. ²⁶ Certainly, "The earth is the Lord's and everything it contains is his." ²⁷ If an unbeliever invites you ˌto his house for dinnerˌ, and you wish to go, eat anything he serves you without letting your conscience trouble you. ²⁸ However, if someone says to you, "This was sacrificed to a god," don't eat it because of the one who informed you and because of conscience. ²⁹ I'm not talking about your conscience but the other person's conscience. Why should my freedom be judged by someone else's conscience? ³⁰ If I give thanks to God for the food I eat, why am I condemned for that? ³¹ So, whether you eat or drink, or whatever you do, do everything to the glory of God. ³² Don't cause others to stumble, whether they are Jewish, Greek, or members of God's church. ³³ I try to please everyone in every way. I don't think about what would be good for me but about what would be good for many people so that they might be saved.

11

¹ Imitate me as I imitate Christ.

Advice About Worship

² I praise you for always thinking about me and for carefully following the traditions that I handed down to you.

³ However, I want you to realize that Christ has authority over every man, a husband has authority over his wife, and God has authority over Christ. ⁴ Every man who covers his head when he prays or speaks what God has revealed dishonors the one who has authority over him. ⁵ Every woman who prays or speaks what God

has revealed and has her head uncovered while she speaks dishonors the one who has authority over her. She is like the woman who has her head shaved. **⁶** So if a woman doesn't cover her head, she should cut off her hair. If it's a disgrace for a woman to cut off her hair or shave her head, she should cover her head. **⁷** A man should not cover his head. He is God's image and glory. The woman, however, is man's glory. **⁸** Clearly, man wasn't made from woman but woman from man. **⁹** Man wasn't created for woman but woman for man. **¹⁰** Therefore, a woman should wear something on her head to show she is under ˌsomeone'sˌ authority, out of respect for the angels.

¹¹ Yet, as believers in the Lord, women couldn't exist without men and men couldn't exist without women. **¹²** As a woman came into existence from a man, so men come into existence by women, but everything comes from God.

¹³ Judge your own situation. Is it proper for a woman to pray to God with her head uncovered? **¹⁴** Doesn't nature itself teach you that it is disgraceful for a man to have long hair? **¹⁵** Doesn't it teach you that it is a woman's pride to wear her hair long? Her hair is given to her in place of a covering. **¹⁶** If anyone wants to argue about this ˌthey can't, becauseˌ we don't have any custom like this—nor do any of the churches of God.

¹⁷ I have no praise for you as I instruct you in the following matter: When you gather, it results in more harm than good. **¹⁸** In the first place, I hear that when you gather as a church you split up into opposing groups. I believe some of what I hear. **¹⁹** Factions have to exist in order to make it clear who the genuine believers among you are.

²⁰ When you gather in the same place, you can't possibly be eating the Lord's Supper. **²¹** Each of you eats his own supper ˌwithout waiting for each otherˌ. So one person goes hungry and another gets drunk. **²²** Don't you have homes in which to eat and drink? Do you despise God's church and embarrass people who don't have anything to eat? What can I say to you? Should I praise you? I won't praise you for this. **²³** After all, I passed on to you what I had received from the Lord.

On the night he was betrayed, the Lord Jesus took bread [24] and spoke a prayer of thanksgiving. He broke the bread and said, "This is my body, which is given for you. Do this to remember me." [25] When supper was over, he did the same with the cup. He said, "This cup is the new promise[a] made with my blood. Every time you drink from it, do it to remember me." [26] Every time you eat this bread and drink from this cup, you tell about the Lord's death until he comes.

[27] Therefore, whoever eats the bread or drinks from the Lord's cup in an improper way will be held responsible for the Lord's body and blood. [28] With this in mind, individuals must determine whether what they are doing is proper when they eat the bread and drink from the cup. [29] Anyone who eats and drinks is eating and drinking a judgment against himself when he doesn't recognize the Lord's body.

[30] This is the reason why many of you are weak and sick and quite a number ˻of you˼ have died. [31] If we were judging ourselves correctly, we would not be judged. [32] But when the Lord judges us, he disciplines us so that we won't be condemned along with the rest of the world.

[33] Therefore, brothers and sisters, when you gather to eat, wait for each other. [34] Whoever is hungry should eat at home so that you don't have a gathering that brings judgment on you.

I will give directions concerning the other matters when I come.

Spiritual Gifts

12 [1] Brothers and sisters, I don't want there to be any misunderstanding concerning spiritual gifts. [2] You know that when you were unbelievers, every time you were led to worship false gods you were worshiping gods who couldn't even speak. [3] So I want you to know that no one speaking by God's Spirit says, "Jesus is cursed." No one can say, "Jesus is Lord," except by the Holy Spirit.

[4] There are different spiritual gifts, but the same Spirit gives them. [5] There are different ways of serving, and yet the same Lord

---

[a] 11:25 Or "testament," or "covenant."

is served. ⁶ There are different types of work to do, but the same God produces every gift in every person.

⁷ The evidence of the Spirit's presence is given to each person for the common good of everyone. ⁸ The Spirit gives one person the ability to speak with wisdom. The same Spirit gives another person the ability to speak with knowledge. ⁹ To another person the same Spirit gives ˌcourageousˌ faith. To another person the same Spirit gives the ability to heal. ¹⁰ Another can work miracles. Another can speak what God has revealed. Another can tell the difference between spirits. Another can speak in different kinds of languages. Another can interpret languages. ¹¹ There is only one Spirit who does all these things by giving what God wants to give to each person.

¹² For example, the body is one unit and yet has many parts. As all the parts form one body, so it is with Christ. ¹³ By one Spirit we were all baptized into one body. Whether we are Jewish or Greek, slave or free, God gave all of us one Spirit to drink.

¹⁴ As you know, the human body is not made up of only one part, but of many parts. ¹⁵ Suppose a foot says, "I'm not a hand, so I'm not part of the body!" Would that mean it's no longer part of the body? ¹⁶ Or suppose an ear says, "I'm not an eye, so I'm not a part of the body!" Would that mean it's no longer part of the body? ¹⁷ If the whole body were an eye, how could it hear? If the whole body were an ear, how could it smell? ¹⁸ So God put each and every part of the body together as he wanted it. ¹⁹ How could it be a body if it only had one part? ²⁰ So there are many parts but one body.

²¹ An eye can't say to a hand, "I don't need you!" Or again, the head can't say to the feet, "I don't need you!" ²² The opposite is true. The parts of the body that we think are weaker are the ones we really need. ²³ The parts of the body that we think are less honorable are the ones we give special honor. So our unpresentable parts are made more presentable. ²⁴ However, our presentable parts don't need this kind of treatment. God has put the body together and given special honor to the part that doesn't have it. ²⁵ God's purpose was that the body should not be divided but rather that all of its parts should feel the same concern for each other. ²⁶ If one part of

the body suffers, all the other parts share its suffering. If one part is praised, all the others share in its happiness.

[27] You are Christ's body and each of you is an individual part of it. [28] In the church God has appointed first apostles, next prophets, third teachers, then those who perform miracles, then those who have the gift of healing, then those who help others, those who are managers, and those who can speak in a number of languages. [29] Not all believers are apostles, are they? Are all of them prophets? Do all of them teach? Do all of them perform miracles [30] or have gifts of healing? Can all of them speak in other languages or interpret languages?

[31] You ͵only͵ want the better gifts, but I will show you the best thing to do.[a]

Love

13 [1] I may speak in the languages of humans and of angels. But if I don't have love, I am a loud gong or a clashing cymbal. [2] I may have the gift to speak what God has revealed, and I may understand all mysteries and have all knowledge. I may even have enough faith to move mountains. But if I don't have love, I am nothing. [3] I may even give away all that I have and give up my body to be burned.[a] But if I don't have love, none of these things will help me.

[4] Love is patient. Love is kind. Love isn't jealous. It doesn't sing its own praises. It isn't arrogant. [5] It isn't rude. It doesn't think about itself. It isn't irritable. It doesn't keep track of wrongs. [6] It isn't happy when injustice is done, but it is happy with the truth. [7] Love never stops being patient, never stops believing, never stops hoping, never gives up.

[8] Love never comes to an end. There is the gift of speaking what God has revealed, but it will no longer be used. There is the gift of speaking in other languages, but it will stop by itself. There is the gift of knowledge, but it will no longer be used. [9] Our knowledge is incomplete and our ability to speak what God has revealed is incom-

---

[a] 12:31 Or "Desire the better gifts, and I will show you the best thing to do."
[a] 13:3 Some manuscripts read "give up my body so that I may brag."

plete. [10] But when what is complete comes, then what is incomplete will no longer be used. [11] When I was a child, I spoke like a child, thought like a child, and reasoned like a child. When I became an adult, I no longer used childish ways. [12] Now we see a blurred image in a mirror. Then we will see very clearly. Now my knowledge is incomplete. Then I will have complete knowledge as God has complete knowledge of me.

[13] So these three things remain: faith, hope, and love. But the best one of these is love.

Speak in Ways That Can Be Understood

14 [1] Pursue love, and desire spiritual gifts, but especially the gift of speaking what God has revealed. [2] When a person speaks in another language, he doesn't speak to people but to God. No one understands him. His spirit is speaking mysteries. [3] But when a person speaks what God has revealed, he speaks to people to help them grow, to encourage them, and to comfort them. [4] When a person speaks in another language, he helps himself grow. But when a person speaks what God has revealed, he helps the church grow. [5] I wish that all of you could speak in other languages, but especially that you could speak what God has revealed. The person who speaks what God has revealed is more important than the person who speaks in other languages. This is true unless he can interpret what he says to help the church grow. [6] Brothers and sisters, it wouldn't do you any good if I came to you speaking in other languages, unless I explained revelation, knowledge, prophecy, or doctrine to you.

[7] Musical instruments like the flute or harp produce sounds. If there is no difference in the notes, how can a person tell what tune is being played? [8] For example, if the trumpet doesn't sound a clear call, who will get ready for battle? [9] In the same way, if you don't speak in a way that can be understood, how will anyone know what you're saying? You will be talking into thin air.

[10] No matter how many different languages there are in the world, not one of them is without meaning. [11] If I don't know what

a language means, I will be a foreigner to the person who speaks it and that person will be a foreigner to me. ¹² In the same way, since you're eager to have spiritual gifts, try to excel in them so that you help the church grow. ¹³ So the person who speaks in another language should pray for an interpretation of what he says.

¹⁴ If I pray in another language, my spirit prays, but my mind is not productive. ¹⁵ So what does this mean? It means that I will pray with my spirit, and I will pray with my mind. I will sing psalms with my spirit, and I will sing psalms with my mind. ¹⁶ Otherwise, if you praise God only with your spirit, how can outsiders say "Amen!" to your prayer of thanksgiving? They don't know what you're saying. ¹⁷ Your prayer of thanksgiving may be very good, but it doesn't help other people grow. ¹⁸ I thank God that I speak in other languages more than any of you. ¹⁹ Yet, in order to teach others in church, I would rather say five words that can be understood than ten thousand words in another language.

²⁰ Brothers and sisters, don't think like children. When it comes to evil, be like babies, but think like mature people. ²¹ God's word says,

> "Through people who speak foreign languages
>   and through the mouths of foreigners
>   I will speak to these people,
>   but even then they will not listen to me,
>   says the Lord."

²² So the gift of speaking in other languages is a sign for unbelievers, not for believers. The gift of speaking what God had revealed is a sign for believers, not for unbelievers. ²³ Suppose the whole congregation gathers in the same place and you speak in other languages. When outsiders or unbelievers come in, won't they say that you're out of your mind? ²⁴ Now suppose you speak what God has revealed. When unbelievers or outsiders come in you will show them where they are wrong and convince them that they are sinners. ²⁵ The secrets in their hearts will become known, and in this way they will quickly bow with their faces touching the ground, worship God, and confess that God is truly among you.

Maintain Order in Your Worship Services

²⁶ So what does this mean, brothers and sisters? When you gather, each person has a psalm, doctrine, revelation, another language, or an interpretation. Everything must be done to help each other grow. ²⁷ If people speak in other languages, only two or three at the most should speak. They should do it one at a time, and someone must interpret what each person says. ²⁸ But if an interpreter isn't present, those people should remain silent in church. They should only speak to themselves and to God.

²⁹ Two or three people should speak what God has revealed. Everyone else should decide whether what each person said is right or wrong. ³⁰ If God reveals something to another person who is seated, the first speaker should be silent. ³¹ All of you can take your turns speaking what God has revealed. In that way, everyone will learn and be encouraged. ³² People who speak what God has revealed must control themselves. ³³ God is not a God of disorder but a God of peace.

As in all the churches of God's holy people, ³⁴ the women must keep silent. They don't have the right to speak. They must take their place as Moses' Teachings say. ³⁵ If they want to know anything they should ask their husbands at home. It's shameful for a woman to speak in church. ³⁶ Did God's word originate with you? Are you the only ones it has reached?

³⁷ Whoever thinks that he speaks for God or that he is spiritually gifted must acknowledge that what I write to you is what the Lord commands. ³⁸ But whoever ignores what I write should be ignored.

³⁹ So, brothers and sisters, desire to speak what God has revealed, and don't keep anyone from speaking in other languages. ⁴⁰ Everything must be done in a proper and orderly way.

Jesus Came Back to Life

15 ¹ Brothers and sisters, I'm making known to you the Good News which I already told you, which you received, and on which your faith is based. ² In addition, you are saved by this Good News if you hold on to the doctrine I taught you, unless you

believed it without thinking it over. ³ I passed on to you the most important points of doctrine that I had received:

Christ died to take away our sins as the Scriptures predicted.

⁴ He was placed in a tomb.

He was brought back to life on the third day as the Scriptures predicted.

⁵ He appeared to Cephas.ᵃ Next he appeared to the twelve apostles. ⁶ Then he appeared to more than 500 believers at one time. (Most of these people are still living, but some have died.) ⁷ Next he appeared to James. Then he appeared to all the apostles. ⁸ Last of all, he also appeared to me.

I'm like an aborted fetus ͺwho was given lifeͺ. ⁹ I'm the least of the apostles. I'm not even fit to be called an apostle because I persecuted God's church. ¹⁰ But God's kindnessᵇ made me what I am, and that kindness was not wasted on me. Instead, I worked harder than all the others. It was not I who did it, but God's kindness was with me. ¹¹ So, whether it was I or someone else, this is the message we brought you, and this is what you believed.

We Will Come Back to Life

¹² If we have told you that Christ has been brought back to life, how can some of you say that coming back from the dead is impossible? ¹³ If the dead can't be brought back to life, then Christ hasn't come back to life. ¹⁴ If Christ hasn't come back to life, our message has no meaning and your faith also has no meaning. ¹⁵ In addition, we are obviously witnesses who lied about God because we testified that he brought Christ back to life. But if it's true that the dead don't come back to life, then God didn't bring Christ back to life. ¹⁶ Certainly, if the dead don't come back to life, then Christ hasn't come back to life either. ¹⁷ If Christ hasn't come back to life, your faith is worthless and sin still has you in its power. ¹⁸ Then those who have died as believers in Christ no longer exist. ¹⁹ If Christ is our hope in this life only, we deserve more pity than any other people.

ᵃ 15:5 Cephas is the Aramaic name for the Apostle Peter.   ᵇ 15:10 Or "grace."

²⁰ But now Christ has come back from the dead. He is the very first person of those who have died to come back to life. ²¹ Since a man brought death, a man also brought life back from death. ²² As everyone dies because of Adam, so also everyone will be made alive because of Christ. ²³ This will happen to each person in his own turn. Christ is the first, then at his coming, those who belong to him ˌwill be made aliveˌ. ²⁴ Then the end will come. Christ will hand over the kingdom to God the Father as he destroys every ruler, authority, and power.

²⁵ Christ must rule until God has put every enemy under his control. ²⁶ The last enemy he will destroy is death. ²⁷ Clearly, God has put everything under Christ's authority. When God says that everything has been put under Christ's authority, this clearly excludes God, since God has put everything under Christ's authority. ²⁸ But when God puts everything under Christ's authority, the Son will put himself under God's authority, since God had put everything under the Son's authority. Then God will be in control of everything.

²⁹ However, people are baptized because the dead ˌwill come back to lifeˌ. What will they do? If the dead can't come back to life, why do people get baptized as if they can ˌcome back to lifeˌ?

³⁰ Why are we constantly putting ourselves in danger? ³¹ Brothers and sisters, I swear to you on my pride in you which Christ Jesus our Lord has given me: I face death every day. ³² If I have fought with wild animals in Ephesus, what have I gained according to the way people look at things? If the dead are not raised, "Let's eat and drink because tomorrow we're going to die!" ³³ Don't let anyone deceive you. Associating with bad people will ruin decent people. ³⁴ Come back to the right point of view, and stop sinning. Some people don't know anything about God. You should be ashamed of yourselves.

We Will Have Bodies That Will Not Decay

³⁵ But someone will ask, "How do the dead come back to life? With what kind of body will they come back?"

³⁶ You fool! The seed you plant doesn't come to life unless it dies first. **³⁷** What you plant, whether it's wheat or something else, is only a seed. It doesn't have the form that the plant will have. **³⁸** God gives the plant the form he wants it to have. Each kind of seed grows into its own form. **³⁹** Not all flesh is the same. Humans have one kind of flesh, animals have another, birds have another, and fish have still another. **⁴⁰** There are heavenly bodies and earthly bodies. Heavenly bodies don't all have the same splendor, neither do earthly bodies. **⁴¹** The sun has one kind of splendor, the moon has another kind of splendor, and the stars have still another kind of splendor. Even one star differs in splendor from another star.

⁴² That is how it will be when the dead come back to life. When the body is planted, it decays. When it comes back to life, it cannot decay. **⁴³** When the body is planted, it doesn't have any splendor and is weak. When it comes back to life, it has splendor and is strong. **⁴⁴** It is planted as a physical body. It comes back to life as a spiritual body. As there is a physical body, so there is also a spiritual body.

⁴⁵ This is what Scripture says: "The first man, Adam, became a living being." The last Adam became a life-giving spirit. **⁴⁶** The spiritual does not come first, but the physical and then the spiritual. **⁴⁷** The first man was made from the dust of the earth. He came from the earth. The second man came from heaven. **⁴⁸** The people on earth are like the man who was made from the dust of the earth. The people in heaven are like the man who came from heaven. **⁴⁹** As we have worn the likeness of the man who was made from the dust of the earth, we will also wear the likeness of the man who came from heaven. **⁵⁰** Brothers and sisters, this is what I mean: Flesh and blood cannot inherit the kingdom of God. What decays cannot inherit what doesn't decay.

⁵¹ I'm telling you a mystery. Not all of us will die, but we will all be changed. **⁵²** It will happen in an instant, in a split second at the sound of the last trumpet. Indeed, that trumpet will sound, and then the dead will come back to life. They will be changed so that they can live forever. **⁵³** This body that decays must be changed into a body that cannot decay. This mortal body must be changed

into a body that will live forever. [54] When this body that decays
is changed into a body that cannot decay, and this mortal body
is changed into a body that will live forever, then the teaching of
Scripture will come true:

> "Death is turned into victory!
> [55]   Death, where is your victory?
>   Death, where is your sting?"

[56] Sin gives death its sting, and God's standards give sin its
power. [57] Thank God that he gives us the victory through our Lord
Jesus Christ.

[58] So, then, brothers and sisters, don't let anyone move you off
the foundation ⌊of your faith⌋. Always excel in the work you do for
the Lord. You know that the hard work you do for the Lord is not
pointless.

The Collection for the People in Jerusalem

16 [1] Now, concerning the money to be collected for God's
people ⌊in Jerusalem⌋: I want you to do as I directed the
churches in Galatia. [2] Every Sunday each of you should set aside
some of your money and save it. Then money won't have to be
collected when I come. [3] When I come, I will give letters of intro-
duction to the people whom you choose. You can send your gift to
Jerusalem with them. [4] If I think it's worthwhile for me to go, they
can go with me.

Paul's Plans

[5] After I go through the province of Macedonia, I'll visit you. (I
will be going through Macedonia.) [6] I'll probably stay with you. I
might even spend the winter. Then you can give me your support
as I travel, wherever I decide to go. [7] Right now all I could do is visit
you briefly, but if the Lord lets me, I hope to spend some time with
you. [8] I will be staying here in Ephesus until Pentecost. [9] I have a
great opportunity to do effective work here, although there are
many people who oppose me.

News About Timothy, Apollos, and Others

[10] If Timothy comes, make sure that he doesn't have anything to be afraid of while he is with you. He's doing the Lord's work as I am, [11] so no one should treat him with contempt. Without quarreling, give him your support for his trip so that he may come to me. I'm expecting him to arrive with the other Christians.

[12] Concerning Apollos, our brother in the Christian faith: I tried hard to get him to visit you with the other Christians. He didn't want to at this time. However, he will visit you when he has an opportunity.

[13] Be alert. Be firm in the Christian faith. Be courageous and strong. [14] Do everything with love.

[15] You know that the family of Stephanas was the first family to be won ˌfor Christˌ in Greece. This family has devoted itself to serving God's people. So I encourage you, brothers and sisters, [16] to follow the example of people like these and anyone else who shares their labor and hard work. [17] I am glad that Stephanas, Fortunatus, and Achaicus came here. They have made up for your absence. [18] They have comforted me, and they have comforted you. Therefore, show people like these your appreciation.

Greetings

[19] The churches in the province of Asia greet you. Aquila and Prisca and the church that meets in their house send their warmest Christian greetings. [20] All the brothers and sisters ˌhereˌ greet you. Greet each other with a holy kiss. [21] I, Paul, am writing this greeting with my own hand.

[22] If anyone doesn't love the Lord, let him be cursed! Our Lord, come!

[23] May the good will[a] of the Lord Jesus be with you. [24] Through Christ Jesus my love is with all of you.

---

[a] 16:23 Or "grace."

2 CORINTHIANS

Greeting

1 ¹ From Paul, an apostle of Christ Jesus by the will of God, and from Timothy our brother.

To God's church in the city of Corinth and to all God's holy people everywhere in Greece.

² Good will[a] and peace from God our Father and the Lord Jesus Christ are yours!

God Comforts Paul and the Corinthians

³ Praise the God and Father of our Lord Jesus Christ! He is the Father who is compassionate and the God who gives comfort. ⁴ He comforts us whenever we suffer. That is why whenever other people suffer, we are able to comfort them by using the same comfort we have received from God. ⁵ Because Christ suffered so much for us, we can receive so much comfort from him. ⁶ Besides, if we suffer, it brings you comfort and salvation. If we are comforted, we can effectively comfort you when you endure the same sufferings that we endure. ⁷ We have confidence in you. We know that as you share our sufferings, you also share our comfort.

God Rescued Paul When He Was Suffering

⁸ Brothers and sisters, we don't want you to be ignorant about the suffering we experienced in the province of Asia. It was so extreme that it was beyond our ability to endure. We even wondered if we could go on living. ⁹ In fact, we still feel as if we're under a death sentence. But we suffered so that we would stop

a 1:2 Or "grace."

trusting ourselves and learn to trust God, who brings the dead back to life. [10] He has rescued us from a terrible death, and he will rescue us in the future. We are confident that he will continue to rescue us, [11] since you are also joining to help us when you pray for us. Then many people will thank God for the favor he will show us because many people prayed for us.

Paul's Reason for Being Proud

[12] We are proud that our conscience is clear. We are proud of the way that we have lived in this world. We have lived with a God-given holiness[b] and sincerity, especially toward you. It was not by human wisdom that we have lived but by God's kindness.[c] [13] We are only writing you what you already knew before you read this. I hope you will understand this as long as you live, [14] even though you now understand it only partially. We are your reason to be proud, as you will be our reason to be proud on the day of our Lord Jesus.

Why Paul Changed His Plans

[15] Confident of this, I had previously wanted to visit you so that you could benefit twice. [16] My plans had been to go from the city of Corinth to the province of Macedonia. Then from Macedonia I had planned to return to you again in Corinth and have you support my trip to Judea.

[17] You don't think that I made these plans lightly, do you? Do you think that when I make plans, I make them in a sinful way? Why would I say that something is true when it isn't? [18] You can depend on God. Our message to you isn't false; it's true. [19] God's Son, Jesus Christ, whom I, Silvanus, and Timothy told you about, was true not false. Because of him our message was always true. [20] Certainly, Christ made God's many promises come true. For that reason, because of our message, people also honor God by saying, "Amen!"

---

[b] 1:12 Or "grace."   [c] 1:12 Some manuscripts and translations read "God-given openness."

²¹ God establishes us, together with you, in a relationship with Christ. He has also anointed us. ²² In addition, he has put his seal ⌞of ownership⌟ on us and has given us the Spirit as his guarantee.

²³ I appeal to God as a witness on my behalf, that I stayed away from Corinth because I wanted to spare you. ²⁴ It isn't that we want to have control over your Christian faith. Rather, we want to work with you so that you will be happy. Certainly, you are firmly established in the Christian faith.

2 ¹ I decided not to visit you again while I was distressed. ² After all, if I had made you uncomfortable, how could you have cheered me up when you were uncomfortable?

³ This is the very reason I wrote to you. I didn't want to visit you and be distressed by those who should make me happy. I'm confident about all of you that whatever makes me happy also makes you happy.

⁴ I was deeply troubled and anguished. In fact, I had tears in my eyes when I wrote to you. I didn't write to make you uncomfortable but to let you know how much I love you.

Forgive the Person Who Sinned

⁵ If someone caused distress, I'm not the one really affected. To some extent—although I don't want to emphasize this too much—it has affected all of you. ⁶ The majority of you have imposed a severe enough punishment on that person. ⁷ So now forgive and comfort him. Such distress could overwhelm someone like that if he's not forgiven and comforted. ⁸ That is why I urge you to assure him that you love him. ⁹ I had also written to you to test you. I wanted to see if you would be obedient in every way.

¹⁰ If you forgive someone, so do I. Indeed, what I have forgiven, if I have forgiven anything, I did in the presence of Christ for your benefit. ¹¹ I don't want Satan to outwit us. After all, we are not ignorant about Satan's scheming.

Paul's Mission as Christ's Spokesman

¹² When I went to the city of Troas, the Lord gave me an opportunity to spread the Good News about Christ. ¹³ But I didn't have

any peace of mind, because I couldn't find Titus, our brother, there. So I said goodbye to the people in Troas and went to the province of Macedonia.

¹⁴ But I thank God, who always leads us in victory because of Christ. Wherever we go, God uses us to make clear what it means to know Christ. It's like a fragrance that fills the air. ¹⁵ To God we are the aroma of Christ among those who are saved and among those who are dying. ¹⁶ To some people we are a deadly fragrance, while to others we are a life-giving fragrance.

Who is qualified to tell about Christ? ¹⁷ At least we don't go around selling an impure word of God like many others. The opposite is true. As Christ's spokesmen and in God's presence, we speak the pure message that comes from God.

The Ministry That Comes From Christ Is Greater Than Moses' Ministry

3 ¹ Do we have to show you our qualifications again? Do we, like some people, need letters that recommend us to you or letters from you that recommend us to others? ² You're our letter of recommendation written in our hearts that everyone knows and reads. ³ It's clear that you are Christ's letter, written as a result of our ministry. You are a letter written not with ink but with the Spirit of the living God, a letter written not on tablets of stone but on tablets of human hearts.

⁴ Christ gives us confidence about you in God's presence. ⁵ By ourselves we are not qualified in any way to claim that we can do anything. Rather, God makes us qualified. ⁶ He has also qualified us to be ministers of a new promise,ᵃ a spiritual promise, not a written one. Clearly, what was written brings death, but the Spirit brings life.

⁷ The ministry that brought death was inscribed on stone. Yet, it came with such glory that the people of Israel couldn't look at Moses' face. His face was shining with glory, even though that glory was fading. ⁸ Won't the ministry that brings the Spirit have

ᵃ 3:6 Or "covenant."

even more glory? [9] If the ministry that brings punishment has glory, then the ministry that brings God's approval has an overwhelming glory. [10] In fact, the ministry that brings punishment lost its glory because of the superior glory of the other ministry. [11] If that former ministry faded away despite its glory, how much more does that ministry which remains continue to be glorious?

[12] Since we have confidence ⌊in the new promise⌋, we speak very boldly. [13] We are not like Moses. He kept covering his face with a veil. He didn't want the people of Israel to see the glory fading away. [14] However, their minds became closed. In fact, to this day the same veil is still there when they read the Old Testament. It isn't removed, because only Christ can remove it. [15] Yet, even today, when they read the books of Moses, a veil covers their minds. [16] But whenever a person turns to the Lord, the veil is taken away.

[17] This Lord is the Spirit. Wherever the Lord's Spirit is, there is freedom. [18] As all of us reflect the Lord's glory with faces that are not covered with veils, we are being changed into his image with ever-increasing glory. This comes from the Lord, who is the Spirit.

Paul Is Never Discouraged

4 [1] We don't become discouraged, since God has given us this ministry through his mercy. [2] Instead, we have refused to use secret and shameful ways. We don't use tricks, and we don't distort God's word. As God watches, we clearly reveal the truth to everyone. This is our ⌊letter of⌋ recommendation.

[3] So if the Good News that we tell others is covered with a veil, it is hidden from those who are dying. [4] The god of this world has blinded the minds of those who don't believe. As a result, they don't see the light of the Good News about Christ's glory. It is Christ who is God's image.

[5] Our message is not about ourselves. It is about Jesus Christ as the Lord. We are your servants for his sake. [6] We are his servants because the same God who said that light should shine out of darkness has given us light. For that reason we bring to light the knowledge about God's glory which shines from Christ's face.

[7] Our bodies are made of clay, yet we have the treasure of the Good News in them. This shows that the superior power of this treasure belongs to God and doesn't come from us. [8] In every way we're troubled, but we aren't crushed by our troubles. We're frustrated, but we don't give up. [9] We're persecuted, but we're not abandoned. We're captured, but we're not killed. [10] We always carry around the death of Jesus in our bodies so that the life of Jesus is also shown in our bodies. [11] While we are alive, we are constantly handed over to death for Jesus' sake so that the life of Jesus is also shown in our mortal nature. [12] Death is at work in us, but life is at work in you.

[13] The following is written, "I believed; therefore, I spoke." We have that same spirit of faith. We also believe; therefore, we also speak. [14] We know that the one who brought the Lord Jesus back to life will also bring us back to life through Jesus. He will present us to God together with you.

[15] All this is for your sake so that, as God's kindness[a] overflows in the lives of many people, it will produce even more thanksgiving to the glory of God. [16] That is why we are not discouraged. Though outwardly we are wearing out, inwardly we are renewed day by day. [17] Our suffering is light and temporary and is producing for us an eternal glory that is greater than anything we can imagine. [18] We don't look for things that can be seen but for things that can't be seen. Things that can be seen are only temporary. But things that can't be seen last forever.

Faith Guides Our Lives

5 [1] We know that if the life we live here on earth is ever taken down like a tent, we still have a building from God. It is an eternal house in heaven that isn't made by human hands. [2] In our present tent-like existence we sigh, since we long to put on the house we will have in heaven. [3] After we have put it on,[a] we won't be naked. [4] While we are in this tent, we sigh. We feel distressed because we don't want to take off the tent, but we do want to put on

---

[a] 4:15 Or "grace."   [a] 5:3 Some manuscripts and translations read "taken it off."

the eternal house. Then ⌞eternal⌟ life will put an end to our mortal
existence. 5 God has prepared us for this and has given us his Spirit
to guarantee it.

6 So we are always confident. We know that as long as we are
living in these bodies, we are living away from the Lord. 7 Indeed,
our lives are guided by faith, not by sight. 8 We are confident
and prefer to live away from this body and to live with the Lord.
9 Whether we live in the body or move out of it, our goal is to be
pleasing to him. 10 All of us must appear in front of Christ's judgment seat. Then all people will receive what they deserve for the
good or evil they have done while living in their bodies.

Christ's Love Guides Us

11 As people who know what it means to fear the Lord, we try
to persuade others. God already knows what we are, and I hope
that you also know what we are. 12 We are not trying to show you
our qualifications again, but we are giving you an opportunity to
be proud of us. Then you can answer those who are proud of their
appearance rather than their character. 13 So if we were crazy, it
was for God. If we are sane, it is for you. 14 Clearly, Christ's love
guides us. We are convinced of the fact that one man has died for
all people. Therefore, all people have died. 15 He died for all people
so that those who live should no longer live for themselves but for
the man who died and was brought back to life for them.

16 So from now on we don't think of anyone from a human point
of view. If we did think of Christ from a human point of view, we
don't anymore. 17 Whoever is a believer in Christ is a new creation.
The old way of living has disappeared. A new way of living has
come into existence. 18 God has done all this. He has restored our
relationship with him through Christ, and has given us this ministry of restoring relationships. 19 In other words, God was using
Christ to restore his relationship with humanity. He didn't hold
people's faults against them, and he has given us this message of
restored relationships to tell others. 20 Therefore, we are Christ's

representatives, and through us God is calling you. We beg you on behalf of Christ to become reunited with God. [21] God had Christ, who was sinless, take our sin so that we might receive God's approval through him.

6 [1] Since we are God's coworkers, we urge you not to let God's kindness[a] be wasted on you. [2] God says,

> "At the right time I heard you.
> On the day of salvation I helped you."

Listen, now is God's acceptable time! Now is the day of salvation!

Our Lives Demonstrate That We Are God's Servants

[3] We don't give people any opportunity to find fault with how we serve. [4] Instead, our lives demonstrate that we are God's servants. We have endured many things: suffering, distress, anxiety, [5] beatings, imprisonments, riots, hard work, sleepless nights, and lack of food. [6] ⌊People can see⌋ our purity, knowledge, patience, kindness, the Holy Spirit's presence ⌊in our lives⌋, our sincere love, [7] truthfulness, and the presence of God's power. We demonstrate that we are God's servants [8] as we are praised and dishonored, as we are slandered and honored, and as we use what is right to attack what is wrong and to defend the truth.[b] We are treated as dishonest although we are honest, [9] as unknown although we are well-known, as dying although, as you see, we go on living. We are punished, but we are not killed. [10] People think we are sad although we're always glad, that we're beggars although we make many people spiritually rich, that we have nothing although we possess everything.

[11] We have been very open in speaking to you Corinthians. We have a place for you in our hearts. [12] We haven't cut you off. Your own emotions have cut you off ⌊from us⌋. [13] I'm talking to you as I would talk to children. Treat us the same way we've treated you. Make a place for us in your hearts too.

---

a 6:1 Or "grace."   *b* 6:8 The last part of verse 7 (in Greek) has been moved to verse 8 to express the complex Greek sentence structure more clearly in English.

Christians and Their Relationships With Unbelievers

¹⁴ Stop forming inappropriate relationships with unbelievers. Can right and wrong be partners? Can light have anything in common with darkness? ¹⁵ Can Christ agree with the devil? Can a believer share life with an unbeliever? ¹⁶ Can God's temple contain false gods? Clearly, we are the temple of the living God. As God said,

> "I will live and walk among them.
> I will be their God,
>   and they will be my people."

¹⁷ The Lord says, "Get away from unbelievers.
>   Separate yourselves from them.
>   Have nothing to do with anything unclean.*c*
>   Then I will welcome you."

¹⁸ The Lord Almighty says, "I will be your Father,
>   and you will be my sons and daughters."

7 ¹ Since we have these promises, dear friends, we need to cleanse ourselves from everything that contaminates body and spirit and live a holy life in the fear of God.

Paul Was Comforted by What the Corinthians Did

² Open your hearts to us. We haven't treated anyone unjustly, ruined anyone, or cheated anyone. ³ I'm not saying this to condemn you. I've already told you that you are in our hearts so that we will live and die together. ⁴ I have great confidence in you, and I have a lot of reasons to be proud of you. Even as we suffer, I'm encouraged and feel very happy.

⁵ Ever since we arrived in the province of Macedonia, we've had no rest. Instead, we suffer in a number of ways. Outwardly we have conflicts, and inwardly we have fears. ⁶ Yet God, who comforts those who are dejected, comforted us when Titus arrived. ⁷ We were comforted not only by his arrival but also by learning about the comfort he had received while he was with you. He told us how

---

c 6:17 "Unclean" refers to anything that Moses' Teachings say is not presentable to God.

you wanted to see me, how sorry you are for what you've done, and how concerned you are about me. This made me even happier.

[8] If my letter made you uncomfortable, I'm not sorry. But since my letter did make you uncomfortable for a while, I was sorry. [9] But I'm happy now, not because I made you uncomfortable, but because the distress I caused you has led you to change the way you think and act. You were distressed in a godly way, so we haven't done you any harm. [10] In fact, to be distressed in a godly way causes people to change the way they think and act and leads them to be saved. No one can regret that. But the distress that the world causes brings only death.

[11] When you became distressed in a godly way, look at how much devotion it caused you to have. You were ready to clear yourselves of the charges against you. You were disgusted with the wrong that had been done. You were afraid. You wanted to see us. You wanted to show your concern for us. You were ready to punish the wrong that had been done. In every way you have demonstrated that you are people who are innocent in this matter. [12] So, when I wrote to you, I didn't write because of the man who did the wrong or the man who was hurt by it. Rather, I wrote because I wanted you to show your devotion to us in God's sight. [13] This is what has comforted us.

In addition to being comforted, we were especially pleased to see how happy Titus was. All of you had put his mind at ease. [14] I didn't have to be ashamed of anything I had said to him when I bragged about you. Since everything we told you was true, our bragging to Titus has also proved to be true. [15] His deepest feelings go out to you even more as he remembers how obedient all of you were, and how you welcomed him with fear and trembling. [16] I'm pleased that I can be confident about you in every way.

The Collection for Christians in Jerusalem

8 [1] Brothers and sisters, we want you to know how God showed his kindness[a] to the churches in the province of Macedonia.

---

[a] 8:1 Or "grace."

² While they were being severely tested by suffering, their overflowing joy, along with their extreme poverty, has made them even more generous. ³ I assure you that by their own free will they have given all they could, even more than they could afford. ⁴ They made an appeal to us, begging us to let them participate in the ministry of God's kindness to his holy people ⌊in Jerusalem⌋. ⁵ They did more than we had expected. First, they gave themselves to the Lord and to us, since this was God's will. ⁶ This led us to urge Titus to finish his work of God's kindness among you in the same way as he had already started it.

⁷ Indeed, the more your faith, your ability to speak, your knowledge, your dedication, and your love for us increase, the more we want you to participate in this work of God's kindness.

⁸ I'm not commanding you, but I'm testing how genuine your love is by pointing out the dedication of others. ⁹ You know about the kindness of our Lord Jesus Christ. He was rich, yet for your sake he became poor in order to make you rich through his poverty.

¹⁰ I'm giving you my opinion because it will be helpful to you. Last year you were not only willing ⌊to take a collection⌋ but had already started to do it. ¹¹ So finish what you began to do. Then your willingness will be matched by what you accomplish ¹² with whatever contributions you have. Since you are willing to do this, ⌊remember⌋ that people are accepted if they give what they are able to give. God doesn't ask for what they don't have.

¹³ I don't mean that others should have relief while you have hardship. Rather, it's a matter of striking a balance. ¹⁴ At the present time, your surplus fills their need so that their surplus may fill your need. In this way things balance out. ¹⁵ This is what Scripture says: "Those who had gathered a lot didn't have too much, and those who gathered a little didn't have too little."

¹⁶ I thank God for making Titus as dedicated to you as I am. ¹⁷ He accepted my request and eagerly went to visit you by his own free will.

[18] With him we have sent our Christian brother whom all the churches praise for the way he tells the Good News. [19] More than that, the churches elected him to travel with us and bring this gift of God's kindness. We are administering it in a way that brings glory to the Lord and shows that we are doing it willingly. [20] We don't want anyone to find fault with the way we are administering this generous gift. [21] We intend to do what is right, not only in the sight of the Lord, but also in the sight of people.

[22] We have also sent with them our Christian brother whom we have often tested in many ways and found to be a dedicated worker. We find that he is much more dedicated now than ever because he has so much confidence in you.

[23] If any questions are raised, remember that Titus is my partner and coworker to help you. The other men are representatives of the churches and bring glory to Christ. [24] So give these men a demonstration of your love. Show their congregations that we were right to be proud of you.

The Reason to Give to the Christians in Jerusalem

9 [1] I don't need to write anything further to you about helping the Christians ˌin Jerusalemˌ. [2] I know how willing you are to help, and I brag about you to the believers in the province of Macedonia. I tell them, "The people of Greece have been ready ˌto send their collectionˌ since last year," and your enthusiasm has moved most of them ˌto actˌ. [3] I've sent my coworkers so that when we brag that you're ready, we can back it up. [4] Otherwise, if any Macedonians come with me, they might find out that you're not ready after all. This would embarrass us for feeling so confident as much as it would embarrass you. [5] So I thought that I should encourage our coworkers to visit you before I do and make arrangements for this gift that you had already promised to give. Then it will be the blessing it was intended to be, and it won't be something you're forced to do.

[6] Remember this: The farmer who plants a few seeds will have a very small harvest. But the farmer who plants because he has

received God's blessings will receive a harvest of God's blessings in return. [7] Each of you should give whatever you have decided. You shouldn't be sorry that you gave or feel forced to give, since God loves a cheerful giver. [8] Besides, God will give you his constantly overflowing kindness.[a] Then, when you always have everything you need, you can do more and more good things. [9] Scripture says,

> "The righteous person gives freely to the poor.
>   His righteousness continues forever."

[10] God gives seed to the farmer and food to those who need to eat. God will also give you seed and multiply it. In your lives he will increase the things you do that have his approval. [11] God will make you rich enough so that you can always be generous. Your generosity will produce thanksgiving to God because of us. [12] What you do to serve others not only provides for the needs of God's people, but also produces more and more prayers of thanksgiving to God. [13] You will honor God through this genuine act of service because of your commitment to spread the Good News of Christ and because of your generosity in sharing with them and everyone else. [14] With deep affection they will pray for you because of the extreme kindness that God has shown you. [15] I thank God for his gift that words cannot describe.

Paul's Authority to Speak Forcefully

10 [1] I, Paul, make my appeal to you with the gentleness and kindness of Christ. I'm the one who is humble when I'm with you but forceful toward you when I'm not with you. [2] I beg you that when I am with you I won't have to deal forcefully with you. I expect I will have to because some people think that we are only guided by human motives. [3] Of course we are human, but we don't fight like humans. [4] The weapons we use in our fight are not made by humans. Rather, they are powerful weapons from God. With them we destroy people's defenses, that is, their arguments [5] and all their intellectual arrogance that oppose the knowledge of

---

[a] 9:8 Or "grace."

God. We take every thought captive so that it is obedient to Christ. [6] We are ready to punish every act of disobedience when you have become completely obedient.

[7] Look at the plain facts! If anyone is confident he belongs to Christ, he should take note that we also belong to Christ. [8] So, if I brag a little too much about the authority which the Lord gave us, I'm not ashamed. The Lord gave us this authority to help you, not to hurt you.

[9] I don't want you to think that I'm trying to frighten you with my letters. [10] I know that someone is saying that my letters are powerful and strong, but that I'm a weakling and a terrible speaker. [11] The person who is saying those things should take note of this fact: When we are with you we will do the things that we wrote about in our letters when we weren't with you.

Paul's Reason for Bragging

[12] We wouldn't put ourselves in the same class with or compare ourselves to those who are bold enough to make their own recommendations. Certainly, when they measure themselves by themselves and compare themselves to themselves, they show how foolish they are.

[13] How can we brag about things that no one can evaluate? Instead, we will only brag about what God has given us to do— coming to ˏthe city of Corinthˏ where you live. [14] It's not as though we hadn't already been to Corinth. We're not overstating the facts. The fact is that we were the first to arrive in Corinth with the Good News about Christ. [15] How can we brag about things done by others that can't be evaluated?

We have confidence that as your faith grows, you will think enough of us to give us the help we need to carry out our assignment— [16] spreading the Good News in the regions far beyond you. We won't brag about things already accomplished by someone else.

[17] "Whoever brags should brag about what the Lord has done." [18] It isn't the person who makes his own recommendation who receives approval, but the person whom the Lord recommends.

Paul Contrasts Himself With False Apostles

11 ¹ I want you to put up with a little foolishness from me. I'm sure that you will. ² I'm as protective of you as God is. After all, you're a virgin whom I promised in marriage to one man—Christ. ³ However, I'm afraid that as the snake deceived Eve by its tricks, so your minds may somehow be lured away from your sincere and pure devotion to Christ. ⁴ When someone comes to you telling about another Jesus whom we didn't tell you about, you're willing to put up with it. When you receive a spirit that is different from the Spirit you received earlier, you're also willing to put up with that. When someone tells you good news that is different from the Good News you already accepted, you're willing to put up with that too.

⁵ I don't think I'm inferior in any way to your super-apostles. ⁶ Even though I'm not good with words, I know what I'm talking about. Timothy and I have made this clear to you in every possible way.

⁷ Did I commit a sin when I humbled myself by telling you the Good News of God free of charge so that you could become important? ⁸ I robbed other churches by taking pay from them to serve you. ⁹ When I was with you and needed something, I didn't bother any of you for help. My friends from the province of Macedonia supplied everything I needed. I kept myself from being a financial burden to you in any way, and I will continue to do that.

¹⁰ As surely as I have Christ's truth, my bragging will not be silenced anywhere in Greece. ¹¹ Why? Because I don't love you? God knows that I do love you. ¹² But I'll go on doing what I'm doing. This will take away the opportunity of those people who want to brag because they think they're like us. ¹³ People who brag like this are false apostles. They are dishonest workers, since they disguise themselves as Christ's apostles. ¹⁴ And no wonder, even Satan disguises himself as an angel of light. ¹⁵ So it's not surprising if his servants also disguise themselves as servants who have God's approval. In the end they will get what they deserve.

More Reasons for Paul to Brag

[16] Again I say that no one should think that I'm a fool. But if you do, then take me for a fool so that I can also brag a little. [17] What I say as I start bragging is foolishness. It's not something I would say if I were speaking for the Lord. [18] Since it's common for people to brag, I'll do it too. [19] You're wise, so you'll gladly put up with fools. [20] When someone makes you slaves, consumes your wealth, seizes your property, orders you around, or slaps your faces, you put up with it. [21] I'm ashamed to admit it, but Timothy and I don't have the strength to do those things to you.

Whatever other people dare to brag about, I, like a fool, can also brag about. [22] Are they Hebrews? So am I. Are they Israelites? So am I. Are they Abraham's descendants? So am I. [23] Are they Christ's servants? It's insane to say it, but I'm a far better one. I've done much more work, been in prison many more times, been beaten more severely, and have faced death more often. [24] Five times the Jewish leaders had me beaten with 39 lashes; [25] three times Roman officials had me beaten with clubs. Once people tried to stone me to death; three times I was shipwrecked, and I drifted on the sea for a night and a day. [26] Because I've traveled a lot, I've faced dangers from raging rivers, from robbers, from my own people, and from other people. I've faced dangers in the city, in the open country, on the sea, and from believers who turned out to be false friends. [27] Because I've had to work so hard, I've often gone without sleep, been hungry and thirsty, and gone without food and without proper clothes during cold weather. [28] Besides these external matters, I have the daily pressure of my anxiety about all the churches. [29] When anyone is weak, I'm weak too. When anyone is caught in a trap, I'm also harmed.

[30] If I must brag, I will brag about the things that show how weak I am. [31] The God and Father of the Lord Jesus, who is praised forever, knows that I'm not lying. [32] The governor under King Aretas put guards around the city of Damascus to catch me. [33] So I was let down in a basket through an opening in the wall and escaped from him.

Paul's Visions and Revelations From the Lord

12 [1] I must brag, although it doesn't do any good. I'll go on to visions and revelations from the Lord. [2] I know a follower of Christ who was snatched away to the third heaven fourteen years ago. I don't know whether this happened to him physically or spiritually. Only God knows. [3] I know that this person [4] was snatched away to paradise where he heard things that can't be expressed in words, things that humans cannot put into words. I don't know whether this happened to him physically or spiritually. Only God knows.[a] [5] I'll brag about this person, but I won't brag about myself unless it's about my weaknesses.

[6] If I ever wanted to brag, I wouldn't be a fool. Instead, I would be telling the truth. But I'm going to spare you so that no one may think more of me than what he sees or hears about me, [7] especially because of the excessive number of revelations that I've had.

Therefore, to keep me from becoming conceited, I am forced to deal with a recurring problem. That problem, Satan's messenger, torments me to keep me from being conceited. [8] I begged the Lord three times to take it away from me. [9] But he told me: "My kindness[b] is all you need. My power is strongest when you are weak." So I will brag even more about my weaknesses in order that Christ's power will live in me. [10] Therefore, I accept weakness, mistreatment, hardship, persecution, and difficulties suffered for Christ. It's clear that when I'm weak, I'm strong.

Paul Was Not a Burden to the Corinthians

[11] I have become a fool. You forced me to be one. You should have recommended me to others. Even if I'm nothing, I wasn't inferior in any way to your super-apostles. [12] While I was among you I patiently did the signs, wonders, and miracles which prove that I'm an apostle. [13] How were you treated worse than the other

---

[a] 12:4 The last two sentences of verse 3 (in Greek) have been moved to verse 4 to express the complex Greek sentence structure more clearly in English.
[b] 12:9 Or "grace."

churches, except that I didn't bother you for help? Forgive me for this wrong!

¹⁴ I'm ready to visit you for a third time, and I won't bother you for help. I don't want your possessions. Instead, I want you. Children shouldn't have to provide for their parents, but parents should provide for their children. ¹⁵ I will be very glad to spend whatever I have. I'll even give myself for you. Do you love me less because I love you so much?

¹⁶ You agree, then, that I haven't been a burden to you. Was I a clever person who trapped you by some trick? ¹⁷ Did I take advantage of you through any of the men I sent you? ¹⁸ I encouraged Titus to visit you, and I sent my friend with him. Did Titus take advantage of you? Didn't we have the same motives and do things the same way?

¹⁹ Have you been thinking all along that we're trying to defend ourselves to you? We speak as Christ's people in God's sight. Everything we do, dear friends, is for your benefit.

Paul's Concern About the Corinthians' Way of Life

²⁰ I'm afraid that I may come and find you different from what I want you to be, and that you may find me different from what you want me to be. I'm afraid that there may be rivalry, jealousy, hot tempers, selfish ambition, slander, gossip, arrogance, and disorderly conduct. ²¹ I'm afraid that when I come to you again, my God may humble me. I may have to grieve over many who formerly led sinful lives and have not changed the way they think and act about the perversion, sexual sins, and promiscuity in which they have been involved.

Paul Tells the Corinthians to Prepare for His Visit

13 ¹ This is the third time that I'll be visiting you. Every accusation must be verified by two or three witnesses. ² I already warned you when I was with you the second time, and even though I'm not there now, I'm warning you again. When I visit you again, I won't spare you. That goes for all those who formerly led sinful lives as well as for all the others. ³ Since you want proof that Christ is speaking through me, that's what you'll get. Christ isn't weak in dealing with you. Instead, he makes his power felt among you. ⁴ He was weak when he was crucified, but by God's power he lives. We are weak with him, but by God's power we will live for you with his help.

⁵ Examine yourselves to see whether you are still in the Christian faith. Test yourselves! Don't you recognize that you are people in whom Jesus Christ lives? Could it be that you're failing the test? ⁶ I hope that you will realize that we haven't failed the test. ⁷ We pray to God that you won't do anything wrong. It's not that we want to prove that we've passed the test. Rather, we want you to do whatever is right, even if we seem to have failed. ⁸ We can't do anything against the truth but only to help the truth. ⁹ We're glad when we are weak and you are strong. We are also praying for your improvement.

¹⁰ That's why I'm writing this letter while I'm not with you. When I am with you I don't want to be harsh by using the authority that the Lord gave me. The Lord gave us this authority to help you, not to hurt you.

Farewell

¹¹ With that, brothers and sisters, I must say goodbye. Make sure that you improve. Accept my encouragement. Share the same attitude and live in peace. The God of love and peace will be with you. ¹² Greet one another with a holy kiss. All of God's holy people greet you.ᵃ

¹³ May the Lord Jesus Christ's good will,ᵇ God's love, and the Holy Spirit's presence be with all of you!

ᵃ 13:12 Some English Bibles count the last sentence of verse 12 as verse 13. Verse 13 is then counted as verse 14.   ᵇ 13:13 Or "grace."

GALATIANS

Greeting

1 ¹ From Paul—an apostle ⌐chosen¬ not by any group or individual but by Jesus Christ and God the Father who brought him back to life— ² and all the believers who are with me.

To the churches in Galatia.

³ Good will[a] and peace are yours from God the Father and our Lord Jesus Christ! ⁴ In order to free us from this present evil world, Christ took the punishment for our sins, because that was what our God and Father wanted. ⁵ Glory belongs to our God and Father forever! Amen.

Follow the Good News We Gave You

⁶ I'm surprised that you're so quickly deserting Christ, who called you in his kindness,[a] to follow a different kind of good news. ⁷ But what some people are calling good news is not really good news at all. They are confusing you. They want to distort the Good News about Christ. ⁸ Whoever tells you good news that is different from the Good News we gave you should be condemned to hell, even if he is one of us or an angel from heaven. ⁹ I'm now telling you again what we've told you in the past: If anyone tells you good news that is different from the Good News you received, that person should be condemned to hell.

¹⁰ Am I saying this now to win the approval of people or God? Am I trying to please people? If I were still trying to please people, I would not be Christ's servant.

---

[a] 1:3, 6 Or "Grace."

Jesus Alone Gave Paul the Good News He Spreads

¹¹ I want you to know, brothers and sisters, that the Good News I have spread is not a human message. ¹² I didn't receive it from any person. I wasn't taught it, but Jesus Christ revealed it to me.

¹³ You heard about the way I once lived when I followed the Jewish religion. You heard how I violently persecuted God's church and tried to destroy it. ¹⁴ You also heard how I was far ahead of other Jews in my age group in following the Jewish religion. I had become that fanatical for the traditions of my ancestors.

¹⁵ But God, who appointed me before I was born and who called me by his kindness, was pleased ¹⁶ to show me his Son. He did this so that I would tell people who are not Jewish that his Son is the Good News. When this happened, I didn't talk it over with any other person. ¹⁷ I didn't even go to Jerusalem to see those who were apostles before I was. Instead, I went to Arabia and then came back to Damascus.

¹⁸ Then, three years later I went to Jerusalem to become personally acquainted with Cephas.^b I stayed with him for fifteen days. ¹⁹ I didn't see any other apostle. I only saw James, the Lord's brother. ²⁰ (God is my witness that what I'm writing is not a lie.)

²¹ Then I went to the regions of Syria and Cilicia. ²² The churches of Christ in Judea didn't know me personally. ²³ The only thing they had heard was this: "The man who persecuted us is now spreading the faith that he once tried to destroy." ²⁴ So they praised God for what had happened to me.

Paul Was Accepted as an Apostle by the Leaders in Jerusalem

2 ¹ Then 14 years later I went to Jerusalem again with Barnabas. I also took Titus along. ² I went in response to a revelation ⌊from God⌋. I showed them the way I spread the Good News among people who are not Jewish. I did this in a private meeting with those recognized as important people to see whether all my efforts had been wasted.

---

^b 1:18 Cephas is the Aramaic name for the apostle Peter.

³ Titus was with me, and although he is Greek, no one forced him to be circumcised.

⁴ False Christians were brought in. They slipped in as spies to learn about the freedom Christ Jesus gives us. They hoped to find a way to control us. ⁵ But we did not give in to them for a moment, so that the truth of the Good News would always be yours.

⁶ Those who were recognized as important people didn't add a single thing to my message. (What sort of people they were makes no difference to me, since God doesn't play favorites.) ⁷ In fact, they saw that I had been entrusted with telling the Good News to people who are not circumcised as Peter had been entrusted to tell it to those who are circumcised. ⁸ The one who made Peter an apostle to Jewish people also made me an apostle to people who are not Jewish. ⁹ James, Cephas, and John (who were recognized as the most important people) acknowledged that God had given me this special gift.ᵃ So they shook hands with Barnabas and me, agreeing to be our partners. It was understood that we would work among the people who are not Jewish and they would work among Jewish people. ¹⁰ The only thing they asked us to do was to remember the poor, the very thing which I was eager to do.

Paul Shows How Cephas Was Wrong

¹¹ When Cephas came to Antioch, I had to openly oppose him because he was completely wrong. ¹² He ate with people who were not Jewish until some men James had sent ⌞from Jerusalem⌟ arrived. Then Cephas drew back and would not associate with people who were not Jewish. He was afraid of those who insisted that circumcision was necessary. ¹³ The other Jewish Christians also joined him in this hypocrisy. Even Barnabas was swept along with them.

¹⁴ But I saw that they were not properly following the truth of the Good News. So I told Cephas in front of everyone, "You're Jewish, but you live like a person who is not Jewish. So how can you insist that people who are not Jewish must live like Jews?"

ᵃ 2:9 Or "had given me grace."

¹⁵ We are Jewish by birth, not sinners from other nations. ¹⁶ Yet, we know that people don't receive God's approval because of their own efforts to live according to a set of standards, but only by believing in Jesus Christ. So we also believed in Jesus Christ in order to receive God's approval by faith in Christ and not because of our own efforts. People won't receive God's approval because of their own efforts to live according to a set of standards.

¹⁷ If we, the same people who are searching for God's approval in Christ, are still sinners, does that mean that Christ encourages us to sin? That's unthinkable! ¹⁸ If I rebuild something that I've torn down, I admit that I was wrong to tear it down. ¹⁹ When I tried to obey the law's standards, those laws killed me. As a result, I live in a relationship with God. I have been crucified with Christ. ²⁰ I no longer live, but Christ lives in me. The life I now live I live by believing in God's Son, who loved me and took the punishment for my sins. ²¹ I don't reject God's kindness.ᵇ If we receive God's approval by obeying laws, then Christ's death was pointless.

God Approves of Those Who Believe

3 ¹ You stupid people of Galatia! Who put you under an evil spell? Wasn't Christ Jesus' crucifixion clearly described to you? ² I want to learn only one thing from you. Did you receive the Spirit by your own efforts to live according to a set of standards or by believing what you heard? ³ Are you that stupid? Did you begin in a spiritual way only to end up doing things in a human way? ⁴ Did you suffer so much for nothing? ₍I doubt₎ that it was for nothing! ⁵ Does God supply you with the Spirit and work miracles among you through your own efforts or through believing what you heard?

⁶ Abraham serves as an example. He believed God, and that faith was regarded by God to be his approval of Abraham. ⁷ You must understand that people who have faith are Abraham's descendants. ⁸ Scripture saw ahead of time that God would give his approval to non-Jewish people who have faith. So Scripture announced the

ᵇ 2:21 Or "grace."

Good News to Abraham ahead of time when it said, "Through you all the people of the world will be blessed." [9] So people who believe are blessed together with Abraham, the man of faith.

[10] Certainly, there is a curse on all who rely on their own efforts to live according to a set of standards because Scripture says, "Whoever doesn't obey everything that is written in Moses' Teachings is cursed." [11] No one receives God's approval by obeying the law's standards since, "The person who has God's approval will live by faith." [12] Laws have nothing to do with faith, but, "Whoever obeys laws will live because of the laws he obeys."

[13] Christ paid the price to free us from the curse that God's laws bring by becoming cursed instead of us. Scripture says, "Everyone who is hung on a tree is cursed." [14] ⌊Christ paid the price⌋ so that the blessing promised to Abraham would come to all the people of the world through Jesus Christ and we would receive the promised Spirit through faith.

The Relationship Between Law and Promise

[15] Brothers and sisters, let me use an example from everyday life. No one can cancel a person's will or add conditions to it once that will is put into effect. [16] The promises were spoken to Abraham and to his descendant. Scripture doesn't say, "descendants," referring to many, but "your descendant," referring to one. That descendant is Christ. [17] This is what I mean: The laws ⌊given to Moses⌋ 430 years after God had already put his promise ⌊to Abraham⌋ into effect didn't cancel the promise ⌊to Abraham⌋. [18] If we have to gain the inheritance by following those laws, then it no longer comes to us because of the promise. However, God freely gave the inheritance to Abraham through a promise.

[19] What, then, is the purpose of the laws given to Moses? They were added to identify what wrongdoing is. Moses' laws did this until the descendant to whom the promise was given came.[a] It was put into effect through angels, using a mediator. [20] A mediator

---

[a] 3:19 Or "Moses' laws did this until the descendant referred to in the promise [to Abraham] came."

is not used when there is only one person involved, and God has acted on his own.

²¹ Does this mean, then, that the laws given to Moses contradict God's promises? That's unthinkable! If those laws could give us life, then certainly we would receive God's approval because we obeyed them. ²² But Scripture states that the whole world is controlled by the power of sin. Therefore, a promise based on faith in Jesus Christ could be given to those who believe.

²³ We were kept under control by Moses' laws until this faith came. We were under their control until this faith which was about to come would be revealed.

²⁴ Before Christ came, Moses' laws served as our guardian. Christ came so that we could receive God's approval by faith. ²⁵ But now that this faith has come, we are no longer under the control of a guardian. ²⁶ You are all God's children by believing in Christ Jesus. ²⁷ Clearly, all of you who were baptized in Christ's name have clothed yourselves with Christ. ²⁸ There are neither Jews nor Greeks, slaves nor free people, males nor females. You are all the same in Christ Jesus. ²⁹ If you belong to Christ, then you are Abraham's descendants and heirs, as God promised.

You Are God's Children

4 ¹ Let me explain further. As long as an heir is a child, he is no better off than a slave, even though he owns everything. ² He is placed under the control of guardians and trustees until the time set by his father. ³ It was the same way with us. When we were children, we were slaves to the principles of this world. ⁴ But when the right time came, God sent his Son ⌐into the world⌐. A woman gave birth to him, and he came under the control of God's laws.

⁵ God sent him to pay for the freedom of those who were controlled by these laws so that we would be adopted as his children.

⁶ Because you are God's children, God has sent the Spirit of his Son into us to call out, "Abba!ᵃ Father!" ⁷ So you are no longer

---

ᵃ 4:6 Abba is Aramaic for "father."

slaves but God's children. Since you are God's children, God has also made you heirs.

[8] When you didn't know God, you were slaves to things which are really not gods at all. [9] But now you know God, or rather, God knows you. So how can you turn back again to the powerless and bankrupt principles of this world? Why do you want to become their slaves all over again? [10] You religiously observe days, months, seasons, and years! [11] I'm afraid for you. Maybe the hard work I spent on you has been wasted.

What Happened to Your Positive Attitude?

[12] Brothers and sisters, I beg you to become like me. After all, I became like you were.

You didn't do anything wrong to me. [13] You know that the first time I brought you the Good News I was ill. [14] Even though my illness was difficult for you, you didn't despise or reject me. Instead, you welcomed me as if I were God's messenger[b] or Christ Jesus himself. [15] What happened to your positive attitude? It's a fact that if it had been possible, you would have torn out your eyes and given them to me. [16] Can it be that I have become your enemy for telling you the truth?

[17] These people ⌊who distort the Good News⌋ are devoted to you, but not in a good way. They don't want you to associate with me so that you will be devoted only to them. [18] (Devotion to a good cause is always good, even when I'm not with you.)

[19] My children, I am suffering birth pains for you again until Christ is formed in you. [20] I wish I were with you right now so that I could change the tone of my voice. I'm completely puzzled by what you've done!

You Are Children of the Promise

[21] Those who want to be controlled by Moses' laws should tell me something. Are you really listening to what Moses' Teachings say?

---

[b] 4:14 Or "an angel of God."

²² Scripture says that Abraham had two sons, one by a woman who was a slave and the other by a free woman. ²³ Now, the son of the slave woman was conceived in a natural way, but the son of the free woman was conceived through a promise ⌊made to Abraham⌋.

²⁴ I'm going to use these historical events as an illustration. The women illustrate two arrangements.ᶜ The one woman, Hagar, is the arrangement made on Mount Sinai. Her children are born into slavery. ²⁵ Hagar is Mount Sinai in Arabia. She is like Jerusalem today because she and her children are slaves. ²⁶ But the Jerusalem that is above is free, and she is our mother. ²⁷ Scripture says:

> "Rejoice, women who cannot get pregnant,
>   who cannot give birth to any children!
> Break into shouting, those who feel no pains of childbirth!
>   Because the deserted woman will have more children
>   than the woman who has a husband."

²⁸ Now you, brothers and sisters, are children of the promise like Isaac.

²⁹ Furthermore, at that time the son who was conceived in a natural way persecuted the son conceived in a spiritual way. That's exactly what's happening now. ³⁰ But what does Scripture say? "Get rid of the slave woman and her son, because the son of the slave woman must never share the inheritance with the son of the free woman." ³¹ Brothers and sisters, we are not children of a slave woman but of the free woman.

Live in the Freedom That Christ Gives You

5 ¹ Christ has freed us so that we may enjoy the benefits of freedom. Therefore, be firm ⌊in this freedom⌋, and don't become slaves again.

² I, Paul, can guarantee that if you allow yourselves to be circumcised, Christ will be of no benefit to you. ³ Again, I insist that everyone who allows himself to be circumcised must realize that

---

ᶜ 4:24 Or "covenants."

he obligates himself to do everything Moses' Teachings demand. [4] Those of you who try to earn God's approval by obeying his laws have been cut off from Christ. You have fallen out of God's favor.[a] [5] However, in our spiritual nature, faith causes us to wait eagerly for the confidence that comes with God's approval. [6] As far as our relationship to Christ Jesus is concerned, it doesn't matter whether we are circumcised or not. But what matters is a faith that expresses itself through love.

[7] You were doing so well. Who stopped you from being influenced by the truth? [8] The arguments of the person who is influencing you do not come from the one who is calling you. [9] A little yeast spreads through the whole batch of dough. [10] The Lord gives me confidence that you will not disagree with this. However, the one who is confusing you will suffer God's judgment regardless of who he is. [11] Brothers and sisters, if I am still preaching that circumcision is necessary, why am I still being persecuted? In that case the cross wouldn't be offensive anymore. [12] I wish those troublemakers would castrate themselves.

[13] You were indeed called to be free, brothers and sisters. Don't turn this freedom into an excuse for your corrupt nature to express itself. Rather, serve each other through love. [14] All of Moses' Teachings are summarized in a single statement, "Love your neighbor as you love yourself." [15] But if you criticize and attack each other, be careful that you don't destroy each other.

[16] Let me explain further. Live your life as your spiritual nature directs you. Then you will never follow through on what your corrupt nature wants. [17] What your corrupt nature wants is contrary to what your spiritual nature wants, and what your spiritual nature wants is contrary to what your corrupt nature wants. They are opposed to each other. As a result, you don't always do what you intend to do. [18] If your spiritual nature is your guide, you are not subject to Moses' laws.

---

[a] 5:4 Or "grace."

[19] Now, the effects of the corrupt nature are obvious: illicit sex, perversion, promiscuity, [20] idolatry, drug use, hatred, rivalry, jealousy, angry outbursts, selfish ambition, conflict, factions, [21] envy, drunkenness, wild partying, and similar things. I've told you in the past and I'm telling you again that people who do these kinds of things will not inherit the kingdom of God.

[22] But the spiritual nature produces love, joy, peace, patience, kindness, goodness, faithfulness, [23] gentleness, and self-control. There are no laws against things like that. [24] Those who belong to Christ Jesus have crucified their corrupt nature along with its passions and desires. [25] If we live by our spiritual nature, then our lives need to conform to our spiritual nature. [26] We can't allow ourselves to act arrogantly and to provoke or envy each other.

Help Carry Each Other's Burdens

6 [1] Brothers and sisters, if a person gets trapped by wrongdoing, those of you who are spiritual should help that person turn away from doing wrong. Do it in a gentle way. At the same time watch yourself so that you also are not tempted. [2] Help carry each other's burdens. In this way you will follow Christ's teachings. [3] So if any one of you thinks you're important when you're really not, you're only fooling yourself. [4] Each of you must examine your own actions. Then you can be proud of your own accomplishments without comparing yourself to others. [5] Assume your own responsibility.

We Will Harvest What We Plant

[6] The person who is taught God's word should share all good things with his teacher. [7] Make no mistake about this: You can never make a fool out of God. Whatever you plant is what you'll harvest. [8] If you plant in ⸢the soil of⸣ your corrupt nature, you will harvest destruction. But if you plant in ⸢the soil of⸣ your spiritual nature, you will harvest everlasting life. [9] We can't allow ourselves to get tired of living the right way. Certainly, each of us will receive ⸢everlasting life⸣ at the proper time, if we don't give up. [10] Whenever we have the opportunity, we have to do what is good for everyone, especially for the family of believers.

Paul Summarizes His Teachings About Circumcision

[11] Look at how large the letters ⌊in these words⌋ are because I'm writing this myself.

[12] These people who want to make a big deal out of a physical thing are trying to force you to be circumcised. Their only aim is to avoid persecution because of the cross of Christ. [13] It's clear that not even those who had themselves circumcised did this to follow Jewish laws. Yet, they want you to be circumcised so that they can brag about what was done to your body. [14] But it's unthinkable that I could ever brag about anything except the cross of our Lord Jesus Christ. By his cross my relationship to the world and its relationship to me have been crucified. [15] Certainly, it doesn't matter whether a person is circumcised or not. Rather, what matters is being a new creation. [16] Peace and mercy will come to rest on all those who conform to this principle. They are the Israel of God.[a]

[17] From now on, don't make any trouble for me! After all, I carry the scars of Jesus on my body.

[18] May the good will[b] of our Lord Jesus Christ be with your spirit, brothers and sisters! Amen.

---

[a] 6:16 Or "Peace and mercy will come to rest on them and on the Israel of God."
[b] 6:18 Or "grace."

EPHESIANS

Greeting

1 ¹ From Paul, an apostle of Christ Jesus by God's will. To God's holy and faithful people who are united with Christ in the city of Ephesus.*

² Good will* and peace from God our Father and the Lord Jesus Christ are yours!

God Chose Us Through Christ

³ Praise the God and Father of our Lord Jesus Christ! Through Christ, God has blessed us with every spiritual blessing that heaven has to offer. ⁴ Before the creation of the world, he chose us through Christ to be holy and perfect in his presence. ⁵ Because of his love he had already decided to adopt us through Jesus Christ. He freely chose to do this ⁶ so that the kindness* he had given us in his dear Son would be praised and given glory.

⁷ Through the blood of his Son, we are set free from our sins. God forgives our failures because of his overflowing kindness.

⁸ He poured out his kindness by giving us every kind of wisdom and insight ⁹ when he revealed the mystery of his plan to us. He had decided to do this through Christ. ¹⁰ He planned to bring all of history to its goal in Christ. Then Christ would be the head of everything in heaven and on earth. ¹¹ God also decided ahead of time to choose us through Christ according to his plan, which makes everything work the way he intends. ¹² He planned all of this so that we who had already focused our hope on Christ would praise him and give him glory.

---

a 1:1 Some early manuscripts omit "in the city of Ephesus."   *b* 1:2, 6 Or "Grace."

¹³ You heard and believed the message of truth, the Good News that he has saved you. In him you were sealed with the Holy Spirit whom he promised. ¹⁴ This Holy Spirit is the guarantee that we will receive our inheritance. We have this guarantee until we are set free to belong to him. God receives praise and glory for this.

Paul's Prayer for the Ephesians

¹⁵ I, too, have heard about your faith in the Lord Jesus and your love for all of God's people. For this reason ¹⁶ I never stop thanking God for you. I always remember you in my prayers. ¹⁷ I pray that the glorious Father, the God of our Lord Jesus Christ, would give you a spirit of wisdom and revelation as you come to know Christ better. ¹⁸ Then you will have deeper insight. You will know the confidence that he calls you to have and the glorious wealth that God's people will inherit. ¹⁹ You will also know the unlimited greatness of his power as it works with might and strength for us, the believers. ²⁰ He worked with that same power in Christ when he brought him back to life and gave him the highest position in heaven. ²¹ He is far above all rulers, authorities, powers, lords, and all other names that can be named, not only in this present world but also in the world to come. ²² God has put everything under the control of Christ. He has made Christ the head of everything for the good of the church. ²³ The church is Christ's body and completes him as he fills everything in every way.

God Saved Us Because of His Great Love for Us

2 ¹ You were once dead because of your failures and sins. ² You followed the ways of this present world and its spiritual ruler. This ruler continues to work in people who refuse to obey God.

³ All of us once lived among these people, and followed the desires of our corrupt nature. We did what our corrupt desires and thoughts wanted us to do. So, because of our nature, we deserved God's anger just like everyone else.

[4] But God is rich in mercy because of his great love for us. [5] We were dead because of our failures, but he made us alive together with Christ. (It is God's kindness[a] that saved you.) [6] God has brought us back to life together with Christ Jesus and has given us a position in heaven with him. [7] He did this through Christ Jesus out of his generosity to us in order to show his extremely rich kindness in the world to come. [8] God saved you through faith as an act of kindness. You had nothing to do with it. Being saved is a gift from God. [9] It's not the result of anything you've done, so no one can brag about it. [10] God has made us what we are. He has created us in Christ Jesus to live lives filled with good works that he has prepared for us to do.

God Has United Jewish and Non-Jewish People

[11] Remember that once you were not Jewish physically. Those who called themselves "the circumcised" because of what they had done to their bodies called you "the uncircumcised." [12] Also, at that time you were without Christ. You were excluded from citizenship in Israel, and the pledges[b] ⌊God made in his⌋ promise were foreign to you. You had no hope and were in the world without God.

[13] But now through Christ Jesus you, who were once far away, have been brought near by the blood of Christ. [14] So he is our peace. In his body he has made Jewish and non-Jewish people one by breaking down the wall of hostility that kept them apart. [15] He brought an end to the commandments and demands found in Moses' Teachings so that he could take Jewish and non-Jewish people and create one new humanity in himself. So he made peace. [16] He also brought them back to God in one body by his cross, on which he killed the hostility. [17] He came with the Good News of peace for you who were far away and for those who were near. [18] So Jewish and non-Jewish people can go to the Father in one Spirit.

[19] That is why you are no longer foreigners and outsiders but citizens together with God's people and members of God's family.

---

[a] 2:5 Or "grace."   [b] 2:12 Or "covenants."

[20] You are built on the foundation of the apostles and prophets. Christ Jesus himself is the cornerstone. [21] In him all the parts of the building fit together and grow into a holy temple in the Lord. [22] Through him you, also, are being built in the Spirit together with others into a place where God lives.

Paul's Work of Spreading the Good News

3 [1] This is the reason I, Paul, am the prisoner of Christ Jesus[a] for those of you who are not Jewish.

[2] Certainly, you have heard how God gave me the responsibility of bringing his kindness[b] to you. [3] You have heard that he let me know this mystery through a revelation. I've already written to you about this briefly. [4] When you read this, you'll see that I understand the mystery about Christ. [5] In the past, this mystery was not known by people as it is now. The Spirit has now revealed it to his holy apostles and prophets. [6] This mystery is the Good News that people who are not Jewish have the same inheritance as Jewish people do. They belong to the same body and share the same promise that God made in Christ Jesus. [7] I became a servant of this Good News through God's kindness freely given to me when his power worked ⌊in me⌋.

[8] I am the least of all God's people. Yet, God showed me his kindness by allowing me to spread the Good News of the immeasurable wealth of Christ to people who are not Jewish. [9] He allowed me to explain the way this mystery works. God, who created all things, kept it hidden in the past. [10] He did this so that now, through the church, he could let the rulers and authorities in heaven know his infinite wisdom. [11] This was God's plan for all of history which he carried out through Christ Jesus our Lord. [12] We can go to God with bold confidence through faith in Christ. [13] So then, I ask you not to become discouraged by the troubles I suffer for you. In fact, my troubles bring you glory.

---

[a] 3:1 Some manuscripts omit "Jesus."   [b] 3:2 Or "grace."

Paul Prays That God Would Strengthen Christians

14 This is the reason I kneel in the presence of the Father **15** from whom all the family in heaven and on earth receives its name. **16** I'm asking God to give you a gift from the wealth of his glory. I pray that he would give you inner strength and power through his Spirit.

17 Then Christ will live in you through faith. I also pray that love may be the ground into which you sink your roots and on which you have your foundation. **18** This way, with all of God's people you will be able to understand how wide, long, high, and deep his love is. **19** You will know Christ's love, which goes far beyond any knowledge. I am praying this so that you may be completely filled with God.

20 Glory belongs to God, whose power is at work in us. By this power he can do infinitely more than we can ask or imagine.

21 Glory belongs to God in the church and in Christ Jesus for all time and eternity! Amen.

Christ's Gifts to the Church

4 **1** I, a prisoner in the Lord, encourage you to live the kind of life which proves that God has called you. **2** Be humble and gentle in every way. Be patient with each other and lovingly accept each other. **3** Through the peace that ties you together, do your best to maintain the unity that the Spirit gives. **4** There is one body and one Spirit. In the same way you were called to share one hope. **5** There is one Lord, one faith, one baptism, **6** one God and Father of all, who is over everything, through everything, and in everything.

7 God's favor*a* has been given to each of us. It was measured out to us by Christ who gave it. **8** That's why the Scriptures say:

> "When he went to the highest place,
> he took captive those who had captured us
> and gave gifts to people."

9 Now what does it mean that he went up except that he also had gone down to the lowest parts of the earth? **10** The one who

---

a 4:7 Or "grace."

had gone down also went up above all the heavens so that he fills everything.

¹¹ He also gave apostles, prophets, missionaries, as well as pastors and teachers as gifts ˌto his churchˌ. ¹² Their purpose is to prepare God's people to serve and to build up the body of Christ.

¹³ This is to continue until all of us are united in our faith and in our knowledge about God's Son, until we become mature, until we measure up to Christ, who is the standard. ¹⁴ Then we will no longer be little children, tossed and carried about by all kinds of teachings that change like the wind. We will no longer be influenced by people who use cunning and clever strategies to lead us astray. ¹⁵ Instead, as we lovingly speak the truth, we will grow up completely in our relationship to Christ, who is the head. ¹⁶ He makes the whole body fit together and unites it through the support of every joint. As each and every part does its job, he makes the body grow so that it builds itself up in love.

Live as God's People

¹⁷ So I tell you and encourage you in the Lord's name not to live any longer like other people in the world. Their minds are set on worthless things. ¹⁸ They can't understand because they are in the dark. They are excluded from the life that God approves of because of their ignorance and stubbornness. ¹⁹ Since they no longer have any sense of shame, they have become promiscuous. They practice every kind of sexual perversion with a constant desire for more.

²⁰ But that is not what you learned from Christ's teachings.

²¹ You have certainly heard his message and have been taught his ways. The truth is in Jesus. ²² You were taught to change the way you were living. The person you used to be will ruin you through desires that deceive you. ²³ However, you were taught to have a new attitude. ²⁴ You were also taught to become a new person created to be like God, truly righteous and holy.

²⁵ So then, get rid of lies. Speak the truth to each other, because we are all members of the same body.

²⁶ Be angry without sinning. Don't go to bed angry. ²⁷ Don't give the devil any opportunity ˌto workˌ.

²⁸ Thieves must quit stealing and, instead, they must work hard. They should do something good with their hands so that they'll have something to share with those in need.

²⁹ Don't say anything that would hurt ˌanother personˌ. Instead, speak only what is good so that you can give help wherever it is needed. That way, what you say will help those who hear you.

³⁰ Don't give God's Holy Spirit any reason to be upset with you. He has put his seal on you for the day you will be set free ˌfrom the world of sinˌ.

³¹ Get rid of your bitterness, hot tempers, anger, loud quarreling, cursing, and hatred. ³² Be kind to each other, sympathetic, forgiving each other as God has forgiven you through Christ.

Imitate God

5 ¹ Imitate God, since you are the children he loves. ² Live in love as Christ also loved us. He gave his life for us as an offering and sacrifice, a soothing aroma to God.

³ Don't let sexual sin, perversion of any kind, or greed even be mentioned among you. This is not appropriate behavior for God's holy people. ⁴ It's not right that dirty stories, foolish talk, or obscene jokes should be mentioned among you either. Instead, give thanks ˌto Godˌ. ⁵ You know very well that no person who is involved in sexual sin, perversion, or greed (which means worshiping wealth) can have any inheritance in the kingdom of Christ and of God. ⁶ Don't let anyone deceive you with meaningless words. It is because of sins like these that God's anger comes to those who refuse to obey him. ⁷ Don't be partners with them.

⁸ Once you lived in the dark, but now the Lord has filled you with light. Live as children who have light. ⁹ Light produces everything that is good, that has God's approval, and that is true. ¹⁰ Determine which things please the Lord. ¹¹ Have nothing to do with the useless works that darkness produces. Instead, expose them for what they are. ¹² It is shameful to talk about what some people do in secret.

[13] Light exposes the true character of everything [14] because light makes everything easy to see. That's why it says:

"Wake up, sleeper!
    Rise from the dead,
        and Christ will shine on you."[a]

[15] So then, be very careful how you live. Don't live like foolish people but like wise people. [16] Make the most of your opportunities because these are evil days. [17] So don't be foolish, but understand what the Lord wants. [18] Don't get drunk on wine, which leads to wild living. Instead, be filled with the Spirit[b] [19] by reciting psalms, hymns, and spiritual songs for your own good. Sing and make music to the Lord with your hearts. [20] Always thank God the Father for everything in the name of our Lord Jesus Christ.

Advice to Wives and Husbands

[21] Place yourselves under each other's authority out of respect for Christ.

[22] Wives, place yourselves under your husbands' authority as you have placed yourselves under the Lord's authority.[c] [23] The husband is the head of his wife as Christ is the head of the church. It is his body, and he is its Savior. [24] As the church is under Christ's authority, so wives are under their husbands' authority in everything.

[25] Husbands, love your wives as Christ loved the church and gave his life for it. [26] He did this to make the church holy by cleansing it, washing it using water along with spoken words. [27] Then he could present it to himself as a glorious church, without any kind of stain or wrinkle—holy and without faults. [28] So husbands must love their wives as they love their own bodies. A man who loves his wife loves himself. [29] No one ever hated his own body. Instead, he feeds and takes care of it, as Christ takes care of the church. [30] We are parts of his body. [31] That's why a man will leave his father and mother and be united with his wife, and the two will be one. [32] This is a great

[a] 5:14 Or "and you will shine with Christ's light."   [b] 5:18 Or "in [your] spirit."
[c] 5:22 English equivalent difficult.

mystery. (I'm talking about Christ's relationship to the church.)
[33] But every husband must love his wife as he loves himself, and
wives should respect their husbands.

Advice to Children and Parents

6 [1] Children, obey your parents because you are Christians.[a]
This is the right thing to do. [2] "Honor your father and mother
[3] that everything may go well for you, and you may have a long life
on earth." This is an important commandment with a promise.[b]

[4] Fathers, don't make your children bitter about life. Instead,
bring them up in Christian discipline and instruction.

Advice to Slaves and Masters

[5] Slaves, obey your earthly masters with proper respect. Be as
sincere as you are when you obey Christ. [6] Don't obey them only
while you're being watched, as if you merely wanted to please
people. But obey like slaves who belong to Christ, who have a deep
desire to do what God wants them to do. [7] Serve eagerly as if you
were serving your heavenly master and not merely serving human
masters. [8] You know that your heavenly master will reward all of us
for whatever good we do, whether we're slaves or free people.

[9] Masters, treat your slaves with respect. Don't threaten a slave.
You know that there is one master in heaven who has authority
over both of you, and he doesn't play favorites.

Put On All the Armor That God Supplies

[10] Finally, receive your power from the Lord and from his mighty
strength. [11] Put on all the armor that God supplies. In this way
you can take a stand against the devil's strategies. [12] This is not a
wrestling match against a human opponent. We are wrestling with
rulers, authorities, the powers who govern this world of darkness,
and spiritual forces that control evil in the heavenly world.

---

[a] 6:1 Some manuscripts and translations omit "because you are Christians."
[b] 6:3 The first part of verse 2 (in Greek) has been placed at the end of verse 3 to
express the complex Greek sentence structure more clearly in English.

¹³ For this reason, take up all the armor that God supplies. Then you will be able to take a stand during these evil days.ᶜ Once you have overcome all obstacles, you will be able to stand your ground. ¹⁴ So then, take your stand! Fasten truth around your waist like a belt. Put on God's approval as your breastplate. ¹⁵ Put on your shoes so that you are ready to spread the Good News that gives peace. ¹⁶ In addition to all these, take the Christian faith as your shield. With it you can put out all the flaming arrows of the evil one. ¹⁷ Also take salvation as your helmet and the word of God as the sword that the Spirit supplies.

¹⁸ Pray in the Spiritᵈ in every situation. Use every kind of prayer and request there is. For the same reason be alert. Use every kind of effort and make every kind of request for all of God's people.

¹⁹ Also pray that God will give me the right words to say. Then I will speak boldly when I reveal the mystery of the Good News.

²⁰ Because I have already been doing this as Christ's representative, I am in prison. So pray that I speak about this Good News as boldly as I have to.

Greetings From Paul

²¹ I'm sending Tychicus to you. He is our dear brother and a faithful deaconᵉ in the Lord's work. He will tell you everything that is happening to me so that you will know how I'm getting along.

²² That's why I'm sending him to you so that you may know how we're doing and that he may encourage you.

²³ May God the Father and the Lord Jesus Christ give our brothers and sisters peace and love along with faith. ²⁴ His favorᶠ is with everyone who has an undying love for our Lord Jesus Christ.

ᶜ 6:13 Or "when the evil day comes."   ᵈ 6:18 Or "in [your] spirit."
ᵉ 6:21 English equivalent difficult.   ᶠ 6:24 Or "grace."

PHILIPPIANS

Greeting

1 ¹ From Paul and Timothy, servants of Christ Jesus.
To God's people in the city of Philippi and their bishops[a] and
deacons[a]—to everyone who is united with Christ Jesus.
² Good will[b] and peace from God our Father and the Lord Jesus
Christ are yours!

Paul's Prayer for the Philippians

³ I thank my God for all the memories I have of you. ⁴ Every time
I pray for all of you, I do it with joy. ⁵ I can do this because of the part-
nership we've had with you in the Good News from the first day ˼you
believed˻ until now. ⁶ I'm convinced that God, who began this good
work in you, will carry it through to completion on the day of Christ
Jesus. ⁷ You have a special place in my heart. So it's right for me to
think this way about all of you. All of you are my partners. Together
we share God's favor,[b] whether I'm in prison or defending and con-
firming the truth of the Good News. ⁸ God is my witness that, with all
the compassion of Christ Jesus, I long ˼to see˻ every one of you.

⁹ I pray that your love will keep on growing because of your
knowledge and insight. ¹⁰ That way you will be able to determine
what is best and be pure and blameless until the day of Christ.
¹¹ Jesus Christ will fill your lives with everything that God's
approval produces. Your lives will then bring glory and praise to
God.

---

^a 1:1 English equivalent difficult.   ^b 1:2, 7 Or "Grace."

Nothing Matters Except That People Are Told About Christ

[12] I want you to know, brothers and sisters, that what happened to me has helped to spread the Good News. [13] As a result, it has become clear to all the soldiers who guard the emperor and to everyone else that I am in prison because of Christ. [14] So through my being in prison, the Lord has given most of our brothers and sisters confidence to speak God's word more boldly and fearlessly than ever.

[15] Some people tell the message about Christ because of their jealousy and envy. Others tell the message about him because of their good will. [16] Those who tell the message about Christ out of love know that God has put me here to defend the Good News. [17] But the others are insincere. They tell the message about Christ out of selfish ambition in order to stir up trouble for me while I'm in prison. [18] But what does it matter? Nothing matters except that, in one way or another, people are told the message about Christ, whether with honest or dishonest motives, and I'm happy about that.

Paul Honors Christ Whether He Lives or Dies

Yes, I will continue to be happy [19] for another reason. I know that I will be set free through your prayers and through the help that comes from the Spirit of Jesus Christ. [20] I eagerly expect and hope that I will have nothing to be ashamed of. I will speak very boldly and honor Christ in my body, now as always, whether I live or die. [21] Christ means everything to me in this life, and when I die I'll have even more. [22] If I continue to live in this life, my work will produce more results. I don't know which I would prefer. [23] I find it hard to choose between the two. I would like to leave this life and be with Christ. That's by far the better choice. [24] But for your sake it's better that I remain in this life. [25] Since I'm convinced of this, I know that I will continue to live and be with all of you. This will help you to grow and be joyful in your faith. [26] So by coming to you again, I want to give you even more reason to have pride in Christ Jesus with me.

Fighting for the Faith

27 Live as citizens who reflect the Good News about Christ. Then, whether I come to see you or whether I stay away, I'll hear all about you. I'll hear that you are firmly united in spirit, united in fighting for the faith that the Good News brings. **28** So don't let your opponents intimidate you in any way. This is God's way of showing them that they will be destroyed and that you will be saved. **29** God has given you the privilege not only to believe in Christ but also to suffer for him. **30** You are involved in the same struggle that you saw me having. Now you hear that I'm still involved in it.

Have the Same Attitude as Christ

2 **1** So then, as Christians, do you have any encouragement? Do you have any comfort from love? Do you have any spiritual relationships? Do you have any sympathy and compassion? **2** Then fill me with joy by having the same attitude and the same love, living in harmony, and keeping one purpose in mind. **3** Don't act out of selfish ambition or be conceited. Instead, humbly think of others as being better than yourselves. **4** Don't be concerned only about your own interests, but also be concerned about the interests of others. **5** Have the same attitude that Christ Jesus had.

6   Although he was in the form of God and equal with God,
           he did not take advantage of this equality.
7   Instead, he emptied himself by taking on the form
               of a servant,
           by becoming like other humans,
           by having a human appearance.
8   He humbled himself by becoming obedient
               to the point of death,
           death on a cross.
9   This is why God has given him an exceptional honor—
           the name honored above all other names—
10   so that at the name of Jesus everyone in heaven,
               on earth,

and in the world below will kneel
[11]   and confess that Jesus Christ is Lord
to the glory of God the Father.

[12] My dear friends, you have always obeyed, not only when I was with you but even more now that I'm absent. In the same way continue to work out your salvation with fear and trembling. [13] It is God who produces in you the desires and actions that please him.

[14] Do everything without complaining or arguing. [15] Then you will be blameless and innocent. You will be God's children without any faults among people who are crooked and corrupt. You will shine like stars among them in the world [16] as you hold firmly to the word of life. Then I can brag on the day of Christ that my effort was not wasted and that my work produced results. [17] My life is being poured out as a part of the sacrifice and service ⌊I offer to God⌋ for your faith. Yet, I am filled with joy, and I share that joy with all of you. [18] For this same reason you also should be filled with joy and share that joy with me.

Paul Will Send Timothy and Epaphroditus

[19] I hope that the Lord Jesus will allow me to send Timothy to you soon so that I can receive some encouraging news about you. [20] I don't have anyone else like Timothy. He takes a genuine interest in your welfare. [21] Everyone else looks after his own interests, not after those of Jesus Christ. [22] But you know what kind of person Timothy proved to be. Like a father and son we worked hard together to spread the Good News. [23] I hope to send him as soon as I see how things are going to turn out for me. [24] But the Lord gives me confidence that I will come ⌊to visit you⌋ soon.

[25] I feel that I must send Epaphroditus—my brother, coworker, and fellow soldier—back to you. You sent him as your personal representative to help me in my need. [26] He has been longing to see all of you and is troubled because you heard that he was sick. [27] Indeed, he was so sick that he almost died. But God had mercy not only on him but also on me and kept me from having one sorrow on top of another. [28] So I'm especially eager to send him to you.

In this way you will have the joy of seeing him again and I will feel relieved. [29] Give him a joyful Christian welcome. Make sure you honor people like Epaphroditus highly. [30] He risked his life and almost died for the work of Christ in order to make up for the help you couldn't give me.

Run Straight Toward the Goal

3 [1] Now then, brothers and sisters, be joyful in the Lord. It's no trouble for me to write the same things to you, and it's for your safety. [2] Beware of dogs! Beware of those who do evil things. Beware of those who insist on circumcision. [3] We are the ˎtrueˎ circumcised people ˎof Godˎ because we serve God's Spirit and take pride in Christ Jesus. We don't place any confidence in physical things, [4] although I could have confidence in my physical qualifications. If anyone else thinks that he can trust in something physical, I can claim even more. [5] I was circumcised on the eighth day. I'm a descendant of Israel. I'm from the tribe of Benjamin. I'm a pureblooded Hebrew. When it comes to living up to standards, I was a Pharisee. [6] When it comes to being enthusiastic, I was a persecutor of the church. When it comes to winning God's approval by keeping Jewish laws, I was perfect.

[7] These things that I once considered valuable, I now consider worthless for Christ. [8] It's far more than that! I consider everything else worthless because I'm much better off knowing Christ Jesus my Lord. It's because of him that I think of everything as worthless. I threw it all away in order to gain Christ [9] and to have a relationship with him. This means that I didn't receive God's approval by obeying his laws. The opposite is true! I have God's approval through faith in Christ. This is the approval that comes from God and is based on faith [10] that knows Christ. Faith knows the power that his coming back to life gives and what it means to share his suffering. In this way I'm becoming like him in his death, [11] with the confidence that I'll come back to life from the dead.

[12] It's not that I've already reached the goal or have already completed the course. But I run to win that which Jesus Christ has

already won for me. [13] Brothers and sisters, I can't consider myself a winner yet. This is what I do: I don't look back, I lengthen my stride, and [14] I run straight toward the goal to win the prize that God's heavenly call offers in Christ Jesus.

[15] Whoever has a mature faith should think this way. And if you think differently, God will show you how to think. [16] However, we should be guided by what we have learned so far.

Imitate Me

[17] Brothers and sisters, imitate me, and pay attention to those who live by the example we have given you. [18] I have often told you, and now tell you with tears in my eyes, that many live as the enemies of the cross of Christ. [19] In the end they will be destroyed. Their own emotions are their god, and they take pride in the shameful things they do. Their minds are set on worldly things. [20] We, however, are citizens of heaven. We look forward to the Lord Jesus Christ coming from heaven as our Savior. [21] Through his power to bring everything under his authority, he will change our humble bodies and make them like his glorified body.

Paul's Advice

4 [1] So, brothers and sisters, I love you and miss you. You are my joy and my crown. Therefore, dear friends, keep your relationship with the Lord firm!

[2] I encourage both Euodia and Syntyche to have the attitude the Lord wants them to have. [3] Yes, I also ask you, Syzugus, my true partner, to help these women. They fought beside me to spread the Good News along with Clement and the rest of my coworkers, whose names are in the Book of Life.

Always Be Joyful

[4] Always be joyful in the Lord! I'll say it again: Be joyful! [5] Let everyone know how considerate you are. The Lord is near. [6] Never worry about anything. But in every situation let God know what you need in prayers and requests while giving thanks. [7] Then God's

peace, which goes beyond anything we can imagine, will guard your thoughts and emotions through Christ Jesus.

[8] Finally, brothers and sisters, keep your thoughts on whatever is right or deserves praise: things that are true, honorable, fair, pure, acceptable, or commendable. [9] Practice what you've learned and received from me, what you heard and saw me do. Then the God who gives this peace will be with you.

Thanks for Your Gifts

[10] The Lord has filled me with joy because you again showed interest in me. You were interested but did not have an opportunity to show it. [11] I'm not saying this because I'm in any need. I've learned to be content in whatever situation I'm in. [12] I know how to live in poverty or prosperity. No matter what the situation, I've learned the secret of how to live when I'm full or when I'm hungry, when I have too much or when I have too little. [13] I can do everything through Christ who strengthens me. [14] Nevertheless, it was kind of you to share my troubles.

[15] You Philippians also know that in the early days, when I left the province of Macedonia to spread the Good News, you were the only church to share your money with me. You gave me what I needed, and you received what I gave you. [16] Even while I was in Thessalonica, you provided for my needs twice. [17] It's not that I'm looking for a gift. The opposite is true. I'm looking for your resources to increase. [18] You have paid me in full, and I have more than enough. Now that Epaphroditus has brought me your gifts, you have filled my needs. Your gifts are a soothing aroma, a sacrifice that God accepts and with which he is pleased. [19] My God will richly fill your every need in a glorious way through Christ Jesus. [20] Glory belongs to our God and Father forever! Amen.

[21] Greet everyone who believes in Christ Jesus. The brothers and sisters who are with me send greetings to you. [22] All God's people here, especially those in the emperor's palace, greet you. [23] May the good will[a] of our Lord Jesus Christ be with you.

---

[a] 4:23 Or "grace."

COLOSSIANS

Greeting

1 ¹ From Paul, an apostle of Christ Jesus by God's will, and from our brother Timothy.

² To God's holy and faithful people, our brothers and sisters who are united with Christ in the city of Colossae.

Good will[a] and peace from God our Father are yours!

Paul's Prayer for the Colossians

³ We always thank God, the Father of our Lord Jesus Christ, in our prayers for you. ⁴ We thank God because we have heard about your faith in Christ Jesus and your love for all of God's people. ⁵ You have these because of the hope which is kept safe for you in heaven. Some time ago you heard about this hope in the Good News which is the message of truth. ⁶ This Good News is present with you now. It is producing results and spreading all over the world as it did among you from the first day you heard it. At that time you came to know what God's kindness[a] truly means. ⁷ You learned about this Good News from Epaphras, our dear fellow servant. He is taking your place here as a trustworthy deacon[b] for Christ ⁸ and has told us about the love that the Spirit has given you.

⁹ For this reason we have not stopped praying for you since the day we heard about you. We ask ⌊God⌋ to fill you with the knowledge of his will through every kind of spiritual wisdom and insight. ¹⁰ We ask this so that you will live the kind of lives that prove you belong to the Lord. Then you will want to please him in every way as you grow in producing every kind of good work by this knowl-

---

[a] 1:2, 6 Or "Grace." [b] 1:7 English equivalent difficult.

edge about God. **11** We ask him to strengthen you by his glorious might with all the power you need to patiently endure everything with joy. **12** You will also thank the Father, who has made you able to share the light, which is what God's people inherit.

What God Has Done Through Christ

13 God has rescued us from the power of darkness and has brought us into the kingdom of his Son, whom he loves. **14** His Son paid the price to free us, which means that our sins are forgiven.

> **15** He is the image of the invisible God,
> the firstborn of all creation.
> **16** He created all things in heaven and on earth,
> visible and invisible.
> Whether they are kings or lords,
> rulers or powers—
> everything has been created through him
> and for him.
> **17** He existed before everything
> and holds everything together.
> **18** He is also the head of the church, which is his body.
> He is the beginning,
> the first to come back to life
> so that he would have first place in everything.

19 God was pleased to have all of himself live in Christ. **20** God was also pleased to bring everything on earth and in heaven back to himself through Christ. He did this by making peace through Christ's blood sacrificed on the cross.

21 Once you were separated from God. The evil things you did showed your hostile attitude. **22** But now Christ has brought you back to God by dying in his physical body. He did this so that you could come into God's presence without sin, fault, or blame. **23** This is on the condition that you continue in faith without being moved from the solid foundation of the hope that the Good News contains.

You've heard this Good News of which I, Paul, became a servant. It has been spread throughout all creation under heaven.

Paul Describes His Work

[24] I am happy to suffer for you now. In my body I am completing whatever remains of Christ's sufferings. I am doing this on behalf of his body, the church. [25] I became a servant of the church when God gave me the work of telling you his entire message. [26] In the past God hid this mystery, but now he has revealed it to his people. [27] God wanted his people throughout the world to know the glorious riches of this mystery—which is Christ living in you, giving you the hope of glory.

[28] We spread the message about Christ as we instruct and teach everyone with all the wisdom there is. We want to present everyone as mature Christian people. [29] I work hard and struggle to do this while his mighty power works in me.

2 [1] I want you to know how hard I work for you, for the people of Laodicea, and for people I have never met. [2] Because they are united in love, I work so that they may be encouraged by all the riches that come from a complete understanding of Christ. He is the mystery of God. [3] God has hidden all the treasures of wisdom and knowledge in Christ. [4] I say this so that no one will mislead you with arguments that merely sound good. [5] Although I'm absent from you physically, I'm with you in spirit. I'm happy to see how orderly you are and how firm your faith in Christ is.

[6] You received Christ Jesus the Lord, so continue to live as Christ's people. [7] Sink your roots in him and build on him. Be strengthened by the faith that you were taught, and overflow with thanksgiving.

Beware of Requirements Invented by Humans

[8] Be careful not to let anyone rob you ˌof this faithˌ through a shallow and misleading philosophy. Such a person follows human traditions and the world's way of doing things rather than following Christ.

⁹ All of God lives in Christ's body, ¹⁰ and God has made you complete in Christ. Christ is in charge of every ruler and authority. ¹¹ In him you were also circumcised. It was not a circumcision performed by human hands. But it was a removal of the corrupt nature in the circumcision performed by Christ. ¹² This happened when you were placed in the tomb with Christ through baptism. In baptism you were also brought back to life with Christ through faith in the power of God,ᵃ who brought him back to life.

¹³ You were once dead because of your failures and your uncircumcised corrupt nature. But God made you alive with Christ when he forgave all our failures. ¹⁴ He did this by erasing the charges that were brought against us by the written laws God had established. He took the charges away by nailing them to the cross. ¹⁵ He stripped the rulers and authorities ˎof their powerˎ and made a public spectacle of them as he celebrated his victory in Christ.

¹⁶ Therefore, let no one judge you because of what you eat or drink or about the observance of annual holy days, New Moon Festivals, or weekly worship days. ¹⁷ These are a shadow of the things to come, but the body ˎthat casts the shadowˎ belongs to Christ.

¹⁸ Let no one who delights in ˎfalseˎ humility and the worship of angels tell you that you don't deserve a prize. Such a person, whose sinful mind fills him with arrogance, gives endless details of the visions he has seen. ¹⁹ He doesn't hold on to ˎChrist,ˎ the head. Christ makes the whole body grow as God wants it to, through support and unity given by the joints and ligaments.

²⁰ If you have died with Christ to the world's way of doing things, why do you let others tell you how to live? It's as though you were still under the world's influence. ²¹ People will tell you, "Don't handle this! Don't taste or touch that!" ²² All of these things deal with objects that are only used up anyway. ²³ These things look like wisdom with their self-imposed worship, ˎfalseˎ humility, and harsh treatment of the body. But they have no value for holding back the constant desires of your corrupt nature.

ᵃ 2:12 Or "through faith produced by God."

Live as God's People

3 [1] Since you were brought back to life with Christ, focus on the things that are above—where Christ holds the highest position. [2] Keep your mind on things above, not on worldly things. [3] You have died, and your life is hidden with Christ in God. [4] Christ is your life. When he appears, then you, too, will appear with him in glory.

[5] Therefore, put to death whatever is worldly in you: your sexual sin, perversion, passion, lust, and greed (which is the same thing as worshiping wealth). [6] It is because of these sins that God's anger comes on those who refuse to obey him.[a] [7] You used to live that kind of sinful life. [8] Also get rid of your anger, hot tempers, hatred, cursing, obscene language, and all similar sins. [9] Don't lie to each other. You've gotten rid of the person you used to be and the life you used to live, [10] and you've become a new person. This new person is continually renewed in knowledge to be like its Creator. [11] Where this happens, there is no Greek or Jew, circumcised or uncircumcised, barbarian, uncivilized person, slave, or free person. Instead, Christ is everything and in everything.

[12] As holy people whom God has chosen and loved, be sympathetic, kind, humble, gentle, and patient. [13] Put up with each other, and forgive each other if anyone has a complaint. Forgive as the Lord forgave you. [14] Above all, be loving. This ties everything together perfectly. [15] Also, let Christ's peace control you. God has called you into this peace by bringing you into one body. Be thankful. [16] Let Christ's word with all its wisdom and richness live in you. Use psalms, hymns, and spiritual songs to teach and instruct yourselves about ˻God's˼ kindness.[b] Sing to God in your hearts. [17] Everything you say or do should be done in the name of the Lord Jesus, giving thanks to God the Father through him.

---

[a] 3:6 Some manuscripts and translations omit "on those who refuse to obey him."
[b] 3:16 Or "grace."

Advice for Wives and Husbands, Parents and Children,
Slaves and Masters

[18] Wives, place yourselves under your husbands' authority.[c]
This is appropriate behavior for the Lord's people. [19] Husbands,
love your wives, and don't be harsh with them.

[20] Children, always obey your parents. This is pleasing to the
Lord. [21] Fathers, don't make your children resentful, or they will
become discouraged.

[22] Slaves, always obey your earthly masters. Don't obey them
only while you're being watched, as if you merely wanted to please
people. Be sincere in your motives out of respect for your real
master. [23] Whatever you do, do it wholeheartedly as though you
were working for your real master and not merely for humans.
[24] You know that your real master will give you an inheritance as
your reward. It is Christ, your real master, whom you are serving.
[25] The person who does wrong will be paid back for the wrong he
has done. God does not play favorites.

4 [1] Masters, be just and fair to your slaves because you know
that you also have a master in heaven.

Advice for All Christians

[2] Keep praying. Pay attention when you offer prayers of
thanksgiving. [3] At the same time also pray for us. Pray that God
will give us an opportunity to speak the word so that we may tell
the mystery about Christ. It is because of this mystery that I am a
prisoner. [4] Pray that I may make this mystery as clear as possible.
This is what I have to do.

[5] Be wise in the way you act toward those who are outside ˌthe
Christian faithˌ. Make the most of your opportunities.

[6] Everything you say should be kind and well thought out so
that you know how to answer everyone.

---

[c] 3:18 English equivalent difficult.

Greetings From Paul and His Coworkers

⁷ I'm sending Tychicus to you. He is our dear brother, trustworthy deacon,[a] and partner in the Lord's work. He will tell you everything that is happening to me. ⁸ I'm sending him to you so that you may know how we are doing and so that he may encourage you. ⁹ I'm sending Onesimus with him. Onesimus is from your city and is our faithful and dear brother. They will tell you about everything that's happening here.

¹⁰ Aristarchus, who is a prisoner like me, sends greetings. So does Mark, the cousin of Barnabas. You have received instructions about Mark. If he comes to you, welcome him. ¹¹ Jesus, called Justus, also greets you. They are the only converts from the Jewish religion who are working with me for God's kingdom. They have provided me with comfort. ¹² Epaphras, a servant of Christ Jesus from your city, greets you. He always prays intensely for you. He prays that you will continue to be mature and completely convinced of everything that God wants. ¹³ I assure you that he works hard for you and the people in Laodicea and Hierapolis. ¹⁴ My dear friend Luke, the physician, and Demas greet you. ¹⁵ Greet our brothers and sisters in Laodicea, especially Nympha and the church that meets in her house.

¹⁶ After you have read this letter, read it in the church at Laodicea. Make sure that you also read the letter from Laodicea.

¹⁷ Tell Archippus to complete all the work that he started as the Lord's servant.

¹⁸ I, Paul, am writing this greeting with my own hand. Remember that I'm a prisoner. God's good will[b] be with you.

---

^a 4:7 English equivalent difficult.   ^b 4:18 Or "grace."

1 THESSALONIANS

Greeting

1 ¹ From Paul, Silas, and Timothy.

To the church at Thessalonica united with God the Father and the Lord Jesus Christ.

Good will*a* and peace are yours!

Paul's Prayer for the Thessalonians

² We always thank God for all of you as we remember you in our prayers. ³ In the presence of our God and Father, we never forget that your faith is active, your love is working hard, and your confidence in our Lord Jesus Christ is enduring. ⁴ Brothers and sisters, we never forget this because we know that God loves you and has chosen you. ⁵ We know this because the Good News we brought came to you not only with words but also with power, with the Holy Spirit, and with complete certainty. In the same way you know what kind of people we were while we were with you and the good things we did for you.

⁶ You imitated us and the Lord. In spite of a lot of suffering, you welcomed God's word with the kind of joy that the Holy Spirit gives. ⁷ This way, you became a model for all the believers in the province of Macedonia and Greece. ⁸ From you the Lord's word has spread out not only through the province of Macedonia and Greece but also to people everywhere who have heard about your faith in God. We don't need to say a thing about it. ⁹ They talk about how you welcomed us when we arrived. They even report how you turned away from false gods to serve the real, living God

---

a 1:1 Or "Grace."

¹⁰ and to wait for his Son to come from heaven. His Son is Jesus, whom he brought back to life. Jesus is the one who rescues us from ˌGod'sˌ coming anger.

Paul Remembers When He Was With the Thessalonians

2 ¹ You know, brothers and sisters, that our time with you was not wasted. ² As you know, we suffered rough and insulting treatment in Philippi. But our God gave us the courage to tell you his Good News in spite of strong opposition.

³ When we encouraged you, we didn't use unethical schemes, corrupt practices, or deception. ⁴ Rather, we are always spreading the Good News. God trusts us to do this because we passed his test. We don't try to please people but God, who tests our motives. ⁵ As you know, we never used flattery or schemes to make money. God is our witness! ⁶ We didn't seek praise from people, from you or from anyone else, ⁷ although as apostles of Christ we had the right to do this.

Instead, we were gentle when we were with you, like a mother taking care of her children. ⁸ We felt so strongly about you that we were determined to share with you not only the Good News of God but also our lives. That's how dear you were to us! ⁹ You remember, brothers and sisters, our work and what we did to earn a living. We worked night and day so that we could bring you the Good News of God without being a burden to any of you. ¹⁰ You and God are witnesses of how pure, honest, and blameless we were in our dealings with you believers. ¹¹ You know very well that we treated each of you the way a father treats his children. We comforted you and encouraged you. Yet, we insisted that ¹² you should live in a way that proves you belong to the God who calls you into his kingdom and glory.

Paul Remembers How the Thessalonians Received the Word of God

¹³ Here is another reason why we never stop thanking God: When you received God's word from us, you realized it wasn't the word of humans. Instead, you accepted it for what it really is—the word of God. This word is at work in you believers.

¹⁴ You, brothers and sisters, were like the churches of God in Judea that are united with Christ Jesus. You suffered the same persecutions from the people of your own country as those churches did from the Jews ¹⁵ who killed the Lord Jesus and the prophets and who have persecuted us severely. They are displeasing to God. They are enemies of the whole human race ¹⁶ because they try to keep us from telling people who are not Jewish how they can be saved. The result is that those Jews always commit as many sins as possible. So at last they are receiving ˻God's˼ anger.

¹⁷ Brothers and sisters, we have been separated from you for a little while. Although we may not be able to see you, you're always in our thoughts. We have made every possible effort to fulfill our desire to see you. ¹⁸ We wanted to visit you. I, Paul, wanted to visit you twice already, but Satan made that impossible.

¹⁹ Who is our hope, joy, or prize that we can brag about in the presence of our Lord Jesus when he comes? Isn't it you? ²⁰ You are our glory and joy!

Timothy's Report to Paul

3 ¹ We thought it best to remain in Athens by ourselves. But, because we couldn't wait any longer ˻for news about you˼, ² we sent our brother Timothy to you. He serves God by spreading the Good News about Christ. His mission was to strengthen and encourage you in your faith ³ so that these troubles don't disturb any of you. You know that we're destined to suffer persecution. ⁴ In fact, when we were with you, we told you ahead of time that we were going to suffer persecution. And as you know, that's what happened. ⁵ But when I couldn't wait any longer, I sent ˻Timothy˼ to find out about your faith. I wanted to see whether the tempter had in some way tempted you, making our work meaningless.

⁶ But Timothy has just now come back to us from you and has told us the good news about your faith and love. He also told us that you always have fond memories of us and want to see us, as we want to see you. ⁷ So brothers and sisters, your faith has encouraged us in

all our distress and trouble. [8] Now we can go on living as long as you keep your relationship with the Lord firm.

[9] We can never thank God enough for all the joy you give us as we rejoice in God's presence. [10] We pray very hard night and day that we may see you again so that we can supply whatever you still need for your faith. [11] We pray that God our Father and the Lord Jesus will guide us to you. [12] We also pray that the Lord will greatly increase your love for each other and for everyone else, just as we love you. [13] Then he will strengthen you to be holy. Then you will be blameless in the presence of our God and Father when our Lord Jesus comes with all God's holy people.

Instructions on the Way Christians Should Live

4 [1] Now then, brothers and sisters, because of the Lord Jesus we ask and encourage you to excel in living a God-pleasing life even more than you already do. Do this the way we taught you. [2] You know what orders we gave you through the Lord Jesus. [3] It is God's will that you keep away from sexual sin as a mark of your devotion to him. [4] Each of you should know that finding a husband or wife for yourself is to be done in a holy and honorable way, [5] not in the passionate, lustful way of people who don't know God. [6] No one should take advantage of or exploit other believers that way. The Lord is the one who punishes people for all these things. We've already told you and warned you about this. [7] God didn't call us to be sexually immoral but to be holy. [8] Therefore, whoever rejects this ⌞order⌟ is not rejecting human authority but God, who gives you his Holy Spirit.

[9] You don't need anyone to write to you about the way Christians should love each other. God has taught you to love each other. [10] In fact, you are showing love to all the Christians throughout the province of Macedonia. We encourage you as believers to excel in love even more. [11] Also, make it your goal to live quietly, do your work, and earn your own living, as we ordered you. [12] Then your way of life will win respect from those outside ⌞the

church„, and you won't have to depend on anyone else for what you need.

Comfort About Christians Who Have Died

¹³ Brothers and sisters, we don't want you to be ignorant about those who have died. We don't want you to grieve like other people who have no hope. ¹⁴ We believe that Jesus died and came back to life. We also believe that, through Jesus, God will bring back those who have died. They will come back with Jesus. ¹⁵ We are telling you what the Lord taught. We who are still alive when the Lord comes will not go „into his kingdom„ ahead of those who have already died. ¹⁶ The Lord will come from heaven with a command, with the voice of the archangel, and with the trumpet „call„ of God. First, the dead who believed in Christ will come back to life. ¹⁷ Then, together with them, we who are still alive will be taken in the clouds to meet the Lord in the air. In this way we will always be with the Lord. ¹⁸ So then, comfort each other with these words!

Be Ready for the Day of the Lord

5 ¹ Brothers and sisters, you don't need anyone to write to you about times and dates. ² You know very well that the day of the Lord will come like a thief in the night. ³ When people say, "Everything is safe and sound!" destruction will suddenly strike them. It will be as sudden as labor pains come to a pregnant woman. They won't be able to escape. ⁴ But, brothers and sisters, you don't live in the dark. That day won't take you by surprise as a thief would. ⁵ You belong to the day and the light not to the night and the dark. ⁶ Therefore, we must not fall asleep like other people, but we must stay awake and be sober. ⁷ People who sleep, sleep at night; people who get drunk, get drunk at night. ⁸ Since we belong to the day, we must be sober. We must put on faith and love as a breastplate and the hope of salvation as a helmet. ⁹ It was not God's intention that we experience his anger but that we obtain salvation through our Lord Jesus Christ. ¹⁰ He died for us so that, whether we are awake in this life or asleep in death, we will live together

with him. [11] Therefore, encourage each other and strengthen one another as you are doing.

Paul Encourages the Thessalonians

[12] Brothers and sisters, we ask you to show your appreciation for those leaders who work among you and instruct you. [13] We ask you to love them and think very highly of them because of the work they are doing. Live in peace with each other.

[14] We encourage you, brothers and sisters, to instruct those who are not living right, cheer up those who are discouraged, help the weak, and be patient with everyone. [15] Make sure that no one ever pays back one wrong with another wrong. Instead, always try to do what is good for each other and everyone else.

[16] Always be joyful. [17] Never stop praying. [18] Whatever happens, give thanks, because it is God's will in Christ Jesus that you do this.

[19] Don't put out the Spirit's fire. [20] Don't despise what God has revealed. [21] Instead, test everything. Hold on to what is good. [22] Keep away from every kind of evil.

Farewell

[23] May the God who gives peace make you holy in every way. May he keep your whole being—spirit, soul, and body—blameless when our Lord Jesus Christ comes. [24] The one who calls you is faithful, and he will do this.

[25] Brothers and sisters, pray for us.

[26] Greet all the brothers and sisters with a holy kiss.

[27] In the Lord's name, I order you to read this letter to all the brothers and sisters.

[28] The good will[a] of our Lord Jesus Christ be with you.

---

[a] 5:28 Or "grace."

2 THESSALONIANS

Greeting

1 [1] From Paul, Silas, and Timothy.

To the church at Thessalonica united with God our Father and the Lord Jesus Christ.

[2] Good will[a] and peace from God our Father and the Lord Jesus Christ are yours!

Paul's Prayer for the Thessalonians

[3] We always have to thank God for you, brothers and sisters. It's right to do this because your faith is showing remarkable growth and your love for each other is increasing. [4] That's why we brag in God's churches about your endurance and faith in all the persecutions and suffering you are experiencing. [5] Your suffering proves that God's judgment is right and that you are considered worthy of his kingdom.

[6] Certainly, it is right for God to give suffering to those who cause you to suffer. [7] It is also right for God to give all of us relief from our suffering. He will do this when the Lord Jesus is revealed, ⌐coming¬ from heaven with his mighty angels in a blazing fire. [8] He will take revenge on those who refuse to acknowledge God and on those who refuse to respond to the Good News about our Lord Jesus. [9] They will pay the penalty by being destroyed forever, by being separated from the Lord's presence and from his glorious power. [10] ⌐This will happen¬ on that day when he comes to be honored among all his holy people and admired by all who have

---

a 1:2 Or "Grace."

believed in him. This includes you because you believed the testimony we gave you.

[11] With this in mind, we always pray that our God will make you worthy of his call. We also pray that through ˌhisˌ power he will help you accomplish every good desire and help you do everything your faith produces. [12] That way the name of our Lord Jesus will be honored among you. Then, because of the good will of Jesus Christ, our God and Lord, you will be honored by him.

Don't Be Deceived About the Day of the Lord

2 [1] Brothers and sisters, we have this request to make of you about our Lord Jesus Christ's coming and our gathering to meet him. [2] Don't get upset right away or alarmed when someone claims that we said through some spirit, conversation, or letter that the day of the Lord has already come. [3] Don't let anyone deceive you about this in any way. ˌThat day cannot come unlessˌ a revolt takes place first, and the man of sin, the man of destruction, is revealed. [4] He opposes every so-called god or anything that is worshiped and places himself above them, sitting in God's temple and claiming to be God.

[5] Don't you remember that I told you about these things when I was still with you? [6] You know what it is that now holds him back, so that he will be revealed when his time comes. [7] The mystery of this sin is already at work. But it cannot work effectively until the person now holding it back gets out of the way. [8] Then the man of sin will be revealed and the Lord Jesus will destroy him by what he says. When the Lord Jesus comes, his appearance will put an end to this man.

[9] The man of sin will come with the power of Satan. He will use every kind of power, including miraculous and wonderful signs. But they will be lies. [10] He will use everything that God disapproves of to deceive those who are dying, those who refused to love the truth that would save them. [11] That's why God will send them a powerful delusion so that they will believe a lie. [12] Then everyone who did not believe the truth, but was delighted with what God disapproves of, will be condemned.

Paul Encourages the Thessalonians

¹³ We always have to thank God for you, brothers and sisters. You are loved by the Lord and we thank God that in the beginning he chose you to be saved through a life of spiritual devotion and faith in the truth. ¹⁴ With this in mind he called you by the Good News which we told you so that you would obtain the glory of our Lord Jesus Christ.

¹⁵ Then, brothers and sisters, firmly hold on to the traditions we taught you either when we spoke to you or in our letter.

¹⁶ God our Father loved us and by his kindness*a* gave us everlasting encouragement and good hope. Together with our Lord Jesus Christ, ¹⁷ may he encourage and strengthen you to do and say everything that is good.

Paul's Final Instructions for the Thessalonians

3 ¹ Finally, brothers and sisters, pray that we spread the Lord's word rapidly and that it will be honored the way it was among you. ² Also pray that we may be rescued from worthless and evil people, since not everyone shares our faith. ³ But the Lord is faithful and will strengthen you and protect you against the evil one.

⁴ The Lord gives us confidence that you are doing and will continue to do what we ordered you to do. ⁵ May the Lord direct your lives as you show God's love and Christ's endurance.

⁶ Brothers and sisters, in the name of our Lord Jesus Christ we order you not to associate with any believer who doesn't live a disciplined life and doesn't follow the tradition you received from us. ⁷ You know what you must do to imitate us. We lived a disciplined life among you. ⁸ We didn't eat anyone's food without paying for it. Instead, we worked hard and struggled night and day in order not to be a burden to any of you. ⁹ It's not as though we didn't have a right to receive support. Rather, we wanted to set an example for you to follow. ¹⁰ While we were with you, we gave you the order: "Whoever doesn't want to work shouldn't be allowed to eat."

a 2:16 Or "grace."

[11] We hear that some of you are not living disciplined lives. You're not working, so you go around interfering in other people's lives. [12] We order and encourage such people by the Lord Jesus Christ to pay attention to their own work so they can support themselves. [13] Brothers and sisters, we can't allow ourselves to get tired of doing what is right.

[14] It may be that some people will not listen to what we say in this letter. Take note of them and don't associate with them so that they will feel ashamed. [15] Yet, don't treat them like enemies, but instruct them like brothers and sisters.

Farewell

[16] May the Lord of peace give you his peace at all times and in every way. The Lord be with all of you.

[17] I, Paul, am writing this greeting with my own hand. In every letter that I send, this is proof that I wrote it.

[18] The good will[a] of our Lord Jesus Christ be with all of you.

---

[a] 3:18 Or "grace."

1 TIMOTHY

Greeting

1 ¹ From Paul, an apostle of Christ Jesus by the command of God our Savior and Christ Jesus our confidence.

² To Timothy, a genuine child in faith.

Good will,ᵃ mercy, and peace from God the Father and Christ Jesus our Lord are yours!

A Warning About False Teachers

³ When I was going to the province of Macedonia, I encouraged you to stay in the city of Ephesus. That way you could order certain people to stop teaching false doctrine ⁴ and occupying themselves with myths and endless genealogies. These myths and genealogies raise a lot of questions rather than promoting God's plan, which centers in faith.

⁵ My goal in giving you this order is for love to flow from a pure heart, from a clear conscience, and from a sincere faith. ⁶ Some people have left these qualities behind and have turned to useless discussions. ⁷ They want to be experts in Moses' Teachings. However, they don't understand what they're talking about or the things about which they speak so confidently.

⁸ We know that Moses' Teachings are good if they are used as they were intended to be used. ⁹ For example, a person must realize that laws are not intended for people who have God's approval. Laws are intended for lawbreakers and rebels, for ungodly people and sinners, for those who think nothing is holy or sacred, for those who kill their fathers, their mothers, or other people. ¹⁰ Laws

ᵃ 1:2 Or "Grace."

are intended for people involved in sexual sins, for homosexuals, for kidnappers, for liars, for those who lie when they take an oath, and for whatever else is against accurate teachings. [11] Moses' Teachings were intended to be used in agreement with the Good News that contains the glory of the blessed God. I was entrusted with that Good News.

God's Mercy to Paul

[12] I thank Christ Jesus our Lord that he has trusted me and has appointed me to do his work with the strength he has given me. [13] In the past I cursed him, persecuted him, and acted arrogantly toward him. However, I was treated with mercy because I acted ignorantly in my unbelief. [14] Our Lord was very kind[b] to me. Through his kindness he brought me to faith and gave me the love that Christ Jesus shows people.

[15] This is a statement that can be trusted and deserves complete acceptance: Christ Jesus came into the world to save sinners, and I am the foremost sinner. [16] However, I was treated with mercy so that Christ Jesus could use me, the foremost sinner, to demonstrate his patience. This patience serves as an example for those who would believe in him and live forever. [17] Worship and glory belong forever to the eternal king, the immortal, invisible, and only God. Amen.

Guidelines for the Church

[18] Timothy, my child, I'm giving you this order about the prophecies that are still coming to you: Use these prophecies in faith and with a clear conscience to fight this noble war. [19] Some have refused to let their faith guide their conscience and their faith has been destroyed like a wrecked ship.[c] [20] Among these people are Hymenaeus and Alexander, whom I have handed over to Satan in order to teach them not to dishonor God.

2 [1] First of all, I encourage you to make petitions, prayers, intercessions, and prayers of thanks for all people, [2] for rulers, and

---

[b] 1:14 Or "gracious."   [c] 1:19 Verses 18 and 19 have been rearranged to express the complex Greek sentence structure more clearly in English.

for everyone who has authority over us. Pray for these people so that we can have a quiet and peaceful life always lived in a godly and reverent way. [3] This is good and pleases God our Savior. [4] He wants all people to be saved and to learn the truth. [5] There is one God. There is also one mediator between God and humans—a human, Christ Jesus. [6] He sacrificed himself for all people to free them from their sins.

This message is valid for every era. [7] I was appointed to spread this Good News and to be an apostle to teach people who are not Jewish about faith and truth. I'm telling you the truth. I'm not lying.

[8] I want men to offer prayers everywhere. They should raise their hands in prayer after putting aside their anger and any quarrels they have with anyone.

[9] I want women to show their beauty by dressing in appropriate clothes that are modest and respectable. Their beauty will be shown by what they do,[a] not by their hair styles or the gold jewelry, pearls, or expensive clothes they wear. [10] This is what is proper for women who claim to have reverence for God.

[11] A woman must learn in silence, in keeping with her position. [12] I don't allow a woman to teach or to have authority over a man. Instead, she should be quiet. [13] After all, Adam was formed first, then Eve. [14] Besides that, Adam was not deceived. It was the woman who was deceived and sinned. [15] However, she ˻and all women˼ will be saved through the birth of the child,[b] if they lead respectable lives in faith, love, and holiness.

Guidelines for Leaders in the Church

3 [1] This is a statement that can be trusted: If anyone sets his heart on being a bishop,[a] he desires something excellent. [2] A bishop must have a good reputation. He must have only one wife,

---

[a] 2:9 The first part of verse 10 (in Greek) has been moved to verse 9 to express the complex Greek sentence structure more clearly in English.   [b] 2:15 Taken to refer to Jesus. Or "will be saved by having children," or "will be kept safe as they have children."   [a] 3:1 English equivalent difficult.

be sober, use good judgment, be respectable, be hospitable, and be able to teach. ³ He must not drink excessively or be a violent person, but he must be gentle. He must not be quarrelsome or love money. ⁴ He must manage his own family well. His children should respectfully obey him. ⁵ (If a man doesn't know how to manage his own family, how can he take care of God's church?) ⁶ He must not be a new Christian, or he might become arrogant like the devil and be condemned. ⁷ People who are not Christians must speak well of him, or he might become the victim of disgraceful insults that the devil sets as traps for him.

⁸ Deacons*ᵇ* must also be of good character. They must not be two-faced or addicted to alcohol. They must not use shameful ways to make money. ⁹ They must have clear consciences about possessing the mystery of the Christian faith. ¹⁰ First, a person must be evaluated. Then, if he has a good reputation, he may become a deacon.

¹¹ Their wives must also be of good character. They must not be gossips, but they must control their tempers and be trustworthy in every way.

¹² A deacon must have only one wife. Deacons must manage their children and their families well. ¹³ Those deacons who serve well gain an excellent reputation and will have confidence as a result of their faith in Christ Jesus.

¹⁴ I hope to visit you soon. However, I'm writing this to you ¹⁵ in case I'm delayed. I want you to know how people who are members of God's family must live. God's family is the church of the living God, the pillar and foundation of the truth.

¹⁶ The mystery that gives us our reverence for God is acknowledged to be great:

He*ᶜ* appeared in his human nature,
    was approved by the Spirit,
    was seen by angels,
    was announced throughout the nations,

ᵇ 3:8 English equivalent difficult.   *ᶜ* 3:16 Some manuscripts read "God."

was believed in the world,
and was taken to heaven in glory.

A Prophecy About the Last Times

4 [1] The Spirit says clearly that in later times some believers will desert the Christian faith. They will follow spirits that deceive, and they will believe the teachings of demons. [2] These people will speak lies disguised as truth. Their consciences have been scarred as if branded by a red-hot iron. [3] They will try to stop others from getting married and from eating certain foods. God created food to be received with prayers of thanks by those who believe and know the truth. [4] Everything God created is good. Nothing should be rejected if it is received with prayers of thanks. [5] The word of God and prayer set it apart as holy.

Guidelines for Serving Christ

[6] You are a good servant of Christ Jesus when you point these things out to our brothers and sisters. Then you will be nourished by the words of the Christian faith and the excellent teachings which you have followed closely. [7] Don't have anything to do with godless myths that old women like to tell. Rather, train yourself to live a godly life. [8] Training the body helps a little, but godly living helps in every way. Godly living has the promise of life now and in the world to come. [9] This is a statement that can be trusted and deserves complete acceptance. [10] Certainly, we work hard and struggle to live a godly life, because we place our confidence in the living God. He is the Savior of all people, especially of those who believe.

[11] Insist on these things and teach them. [12] Don't let anyone look down on you for being young. Instead, make your speech, behavior, love, faith, and purity an example for other believers. [13] Until I get there, concentrate on reading ⸢Scripture⸥ in worship, giving encouraging messages, and teaching people. [14] Don't neglect the gift which you received through prophecy when the spiritual leaders[a] placed

---

[a] 4:14 Or "pastors," or "elders."

their hands on you ⌊to ordain you⌋. ¹⁵ Practice these things. Devote your life to them so that everyone can see your progress. ¹⁶ Focus on your life and your teaching. Continue to do what I've told you. If you do this, you will save yourself and those who hear you.

Guidelines for Dealing With Other Christians

5 ¹ Never use harsh words when you correct an older man, but talk to him as if he were your father. Talk to younger men as if they were your brothers, ² older women as if they were your mothers, and younger women as if they were your sisters, while keeping yourself morally pure.

³ Honor widows who have no families. ⁴ The children or grandchildren of a widow must first learn to respect their own family by repaying their parents. This is pleasing in God's sight.

⁵ A widow who has no family has placed her confidence in God by praying and asking for his help night and day. ⁶ But the widow who lives for pleasure is dead although she is still alive. ⁷ Insist on these things so that widows will have good reputations. ⁸ If anyone doesn't take care of his own relatives, especially his immediate family, he has denied the Christian faith and is worse than an unbeliever.

⁹ Any widow who had only one husband and is at least 60 years old should be put on your list ⌊of widows⌋. ¹⁰ People should tell about the good things she has done: raising children, being hospitable, taking care of believers' needs, helping the suffering, or always doing good things.

¹¹ Don't include younger widows ⌊on your list⌋. Whenever their natural desires become stronger than their devotion to Christ, they'll want to marry. ¹² They condemn themselves by rejecting the Christian faith, the faith they first accepted. ¹³ At the same time, they learn to go around from house to house since they have nothing else to do. Not only this, but they also gossip and get involved in other people's business, saying things they shouldn't say.

¹⁴ So I want younger widows to marry, have children, manage their homes, and not give the enemy any chance to ridicule them.

[15] Some of them have already turned away to follow Satan. [16] If any woman is a believer and has relatives who are widows, she should help them. In this way the church is not burdened and can help widows who have no families.

[17] Give double honor to spiritual leaders[a] who handle their duties well. This is especially true if they work hard at teaching the word ˎof Godˎ. [18] After all, Scripture says, "Never muzzle an ox when it is threshing[b] grain," and "The worker deserves his pay."

[19] Don't pay attention to an accusation against a spiritual leader unless it is supported by two or three witnesses. [20] Reprimand those leaders who sin. Do it in front of everyone so that the other leaders will also be afraid.

[21] I solemnly call on you in the sight of God, Christ Jesus, and the chosen angels to be impartial when you follow what I've told you. Never play favorites.

[22] Don't be in a hurry to place your hands on anyone ˎto ordain himˎ. Don't participate in the sins of others. Keep yourself morally pure.

[23] Stop drinking only water. Instead, drink a little wine for your stomach because you are frequently sick.

[24] The sins of some people are obvious, going ahead of them to judgment. The sins of others follow them there. [25] In the same way, the good things that people do are obvious, and those that aren't obvious can't remain hidden.

6 [1] All slaves who believe must give complete respect to their own masters. In this way no one will speak evil of God's name and what we teach. [2] Slaves whose masters also believe should respect their masters even though their masters are also believers. As a result, believers who are slaves should serve their masters even better because those who receive the benefit of their work are believers whom they love.

---

[a] 5:17 Or "pastors," or "elders."   [b] 5:18 Threshing is the process of beating stalks to separate them from the grain.

Guidelines for Living a Godly Life

Teach and encourage people to do these things. ³ Whoever teaches false doctrine and doesn't agree with the accurate words of our Lord Jesus Christ and godly teachings ⁴ is a conceited person. He shows that he doesn't understand anything. Rather, he has an unhealthy desire to argue and quarrel about words. This produces jealousy, rivalry, cursing, suspicion, ⁵ and conflict between people whose corrupt minds have been robbed of the truth. They think that a godly life is a way to make a profit.

⁶ A godly life brings huge profits to people who are content with what they have. ⁷ We didn't bring anything into the world, and we can't take anything out of it. ⁸ As long as we have food and clothes, we should be satisfied.

⁹ But people who want to get rich keep falling into temptation. They are trapped by many stupid and harmful desires which drown them in destruction and ruin. ¹⁰ Certainly, the love of money is the root of all kinds of evil. Some people who have set their hearts on getting rich have wandered away from the Christian faith and have caused themselves a lot of grief.

¹¹ But you, man of God, must avoid these things. Pursue what God approves of: a godly life, faith, love, endurance, and gentleness. ¹² Fight the good fight for the Christian faith. Take hold of everlasting life to which you were called and about which you made a good testimony in front of many witnesses.

¹³ In the sight of God, who gives life to everything, and in the sight of Christ Jesus, who gave a good testimony in front of Pontius Pilate, ¹⁴ I insist that, until our Lord Jesus Christ appears, you obey this command completely. Then you cannot be blamed for doing anything wrong. ¹⁵ At the right time God will make this known. God is the blessed and only ruler. He is the King of kings and Lord of lords. ¹⁶ He is the only one who cannot die. He lives in light that no one can come near. No one has seen him, nor can they see him. Honor and power belong to him forever! Amen.

¹⁷ Tell those who have the riches of this world not to be arrogant and not to place their confidence in anything as uncertain as riches. Instead, they should place their confidence in God who richly provides us with everything to enjoy. ¹⁸ Tell them to do good, to do a lot of good things, to be generous, and to share. ¹⁹ By doing this they store up a treasure for themselves which is a good foundation for the future. In this way they take hold of what life really is.

²⁰ Timothy, guard the Good News which has been entrusted to you. Turn away from pointless discussions and the claims of false knowledge that people use to oppose ⌊the Christian faith⌋. ²¹ Although some claim to have knowledge, they have abandoned the faith.

God's good will*ᵃ* be with all of you.

ᵃ 6:21 Or "grace."

2 TIMOTHY

Greeting

1 ¹ From Paul, an apostle of Christ Jesus by God's will—a will that contains Christ Jesus' promise of life.

² To Timothy, my dear child.

Good will,[a] mercy, and peace from God the Father and Christ Jesus our Lord.

³ I constantly remember you in my prayers night and day when I thank God, whom I serve with a clear conscience as my ancestors did. ⁴ I remember your tears and want to see you so that I can be filled with happiness. ⁵ I'm reminded of how sincere your faith is. That faith first lived in your grandmother Lois and your mother Eunice. I'm convinced that it also lives in you.

Paul's Advice for Timothy

⁶ You received a gift from God when I placed my hands on you ⌞to ordain you⌟. Now I'm reminding you to fan that gift into flames. ⁷ God didn't give us a cowardly spirit but a spirit of power, love, and good judgment. ⁸ So never be ashamed to tell others about our Lord or be ashamed of me, his prisoner. Instead, by God's power, join me in suffering for the sake of the Good News. ⁹ God saved us and called us to be holy, not because of what we had done, but because of his own plan and kindness.[a] Before the world began, God planned that Christ Jesus would show us God's kindness. ¹⁰ Now with the coming of our Savior Christ Jesus, he has revealed it. Christ has destroyed death, and through the Good News he has

---

[a] 1:2, 9 Or "Grace."

brought eternal life into full view. [11] I was appointed to be a messenger of this Good News, an apostle, and a teacher.

[12] For this reason I suffer as I do. However, I'm not ashamed. I know whom I trust. I'm convinced that he is able to protect what he had entrusted to me until that day.

[13] With faith and love for Christ Jesus, consider what you heard me say to be the pattern of accurate teachings. [14] With the help of the Holy Spirit who lives in us, protect the Good News that has been entrusted to you.

News About Paul's Coworkers

[15] You know that everyone in the province of Asia has deserted me, including Phygelus and Hermogenes.

[16] May the Lord be merciful to the family of Onesiphorus. He often took care of my needs and wasn't ashamed that I was a prisoner. [17] When he arrived in Rome, he searched hard for me and found me. [18] May the Lord grant that Onesiphorus finds mercy when that day comes. You know very well that he did everything possible to help me in Ephesus.

Remain Focused on Jesus

2 [1] My child, find your source of strength in the kindness[a] of Christ Jesus. [2] You've heard my message, and it's been confirmed by many witnesses. Entrust this message to faithful individuals who will be competent to teach others.

[3] Join me in suffering like a good soldier of Christ Jesus. [4] Whoever serves in the military doesn't get mixed up in nonmilitary activities. This pleases his commanding officer. [5] Whoever enters an athletic competition wins the prize only when playing by the rules. [6] A hard-working farmer should have the first share of the crops. [7] Understand what I'm saying. The Lord will help you understand all these things.

[8] Always think about Jesus Christ. He was brought back to life and is a descendant of David. This is the Good News that I tell oth-

a 2:1 Or "Grace."

ers. [9] I'm suffering disgrace for spreading this Good News. I have even been put into prison like a criminal. However, God's word is not imprisoned. [10] For that reason, I endure everything for the sake of those who have been chosen so that they, too, may receive salvation from Christ Jesus with glory that lasts forever. [11] This is a statement that can be trusted:

> If we have died with him, we will live with him.
> [12] If we endure, we will rule with him.
> If we disown him, he will disown us.
> [13] If we are unfaithful, he remains faithful
>   because he cannot be untrue to himself.

[14] Remind believers about these things, and warn them in the sight of God not to quarrel over words. Quarreling doesn't do any good but only destroys those who are listening.

[15] Do your best to present yourself to God as a tried-and-true worker who isn't ashamed to teach the word of truth correctly. [16] Avoid pointless discussions. People who ˌpay attention to these pointless discussionsˌ will become more ungodly, [17] and what they say will spread like cancer. Hymenaeus and Philetus are like that. [18] They have abandoned the truth. They are destroying the faith of others by saying that people who have died have already come back to life.

[19] In spite of all that, God's ˌpeopleˌ have a solid foundation. These words are engraved on it: "The Lord knows those who belong to him," and "Whoever worships the Lord must give up doing wrong."

[20] In a large house there are not only objects made of gold and silver, but also those made of wood and clay. Some objects are honored when they are used; others aren't. [21] Those who stop associating with dishonorable people will be honored. They will be set apart for the master's use, prepared to do good things.

[22] Stay away from lusts which tempt young people. Pursue what has God's approval. Pursue faith, love, and peace together

with those who worship the Lord with a pure heart. ²³ Don't have anything to do with foolish and stupid arguments. You know they cause quarrels. ²⁴ A servant of the Lord must not quarrel. Instead, he must be kind to everyone. He must be a good teacher. He must be willing to suffer wrong. ²⁵ He must be gentle in correcting those who oppose the Good News. Maybe God will allow them to change the way they think and act and lead them to know the truth. ²⁶ Then they might come back to their senses and God will free them from the devil's snare so that they can do his will.

Watch Out for Sinful People

3 ¹ You must understand this: In the last days there will be violent periods of time. ² People will be selfish and love money. They will brag, be arrogant, and use abusive language. They will curse their parents, show no gratitude, have no respect for what is holy, ³ and lack normal affection for their families. They will refuse to make peace with anyone. They will be slanderous, lack self-control, be brutal, and have no love for what is good. ⁴ They will be traitors. They will be reckless and conceited. They will love pleasure rather than God. ⁵ They will appear to have a godly life, but they will not let its power change them. Stay away from such people.

⁶ Some of these men go into homes and mislead weak-minded women who are burdened with sins and led by all kinds of desires. ⁷ These women are always studying but are never able to recognize the truth.

⁸ As Jannes and Jambres opposed Moses, so these men oppose the truth. Their minds are corrupt, and the faith they teach is counterfeit. ⁹ Certainly, they won't get very far. Like the stupidity of Jannes and Jambres, their stupidity will be plain to everyone.

Teach the Truth

¹⁰ But you know all about my teachings, my way of life, my purpose, my faith, my patience, my love, and my endurance. ¹¹ You also know about the kind of persecutions and sufferings which happened to me in the cities of Antioch, Iconium, and Lystra. I

endured those persecutions, and the Lord rescued me from all of them. [12] Those who try to live a godly life because they believe in Christ Jesus will be persecuted. [13] But evil people and phony preachers will go from bad to worse as they mislead people and are themselves misled.

[14] However, continue in what you have learned and found to be true. You know who your teachers were. [15] From infancy you have known the Holy Scriptures. They have the power to give you wisdom so that you can be saved through faith in Christ Jesus. [16] Every Scripture passage is inspired by God. All of them are useful for teaching, pointing out errors, correcting people, and training them for a life that has God's approval. [17] They equip God's servants so that they are completely prepared to do good things.

Continue to Do Your Work

4 [1] I solemnly call on you in the presence of God and Christ Jesus, who is going to judge those who are living and those who are dead. I do this because Christ Jesus will come to rule ⌊the world⌋. [2] Be ready to spread the word whether or not the time is right. Point out errors, warn people, and encourage them. Be very patient when you teach.

[3] A time will come when people will not listen to accurate teachings. Instead, they will follow their own desires and surround themselves with teachers who tell them what they want to hear. [4] People will refuse to listen to the truth and turn to myths.

[5] But you must keep a clear head in everything. Endure suffering. Do the work of a missionary. Devote yourself completely to your work.

[6] My life is coming to an end, and it is now time for me to be poured out as a sacrifice to God. [7] I have fought the good fight. I have completed the race. I have kept the faith. [8] The prize that shows I have God's approval is now waiting for me. The Lord, who is a fair judge, will give me that prize on that day. He will give it not only to me but also to everyone who is eagerly waiting for him to come again.

Paul's Final Instructions to Timothy

9 Hurry to visit me soon. **10** Demas has abandoned me. He fell in love with this present world and went to the city of Thessalonica. Crescens went to the province of Galatia, and Titus went to the province of Dalmatia. **11** Only Luke is with me. Get Mark and bring him with you. He is useful to me in my work. **12** I'm sending Tychicus to the city of Ephesus as my representative.

13 When you come, bring the warm coat I left with Carpus in the city of Troas. Also bring the scrolls and especially the parchments.[a]

14 Alexander the metalworker did me a great deal of harm. The Lord will pay him back for what he did. **15** Watch out for him. He violently opposed what we said. **16** At my first hearing no one stood up in my defense. Everyone abandoned me. I pray that it won't be held against them. **17** However, the Lord stood by me and gave me strength so that I could finish spreading the Good News for all the nations to hear. I was snatched out of a lion's mouth. **18** The Lord will rescue me from all harm and will take me safely to his heavenly kingdom. Glory belongs to him forever! Amen.

Final Greetings

19 Give my greetings to Prisca and Aquila and the family of Onesiphorus. **20** Erastus stayed in the city of Corinth and I left Trophimus in the city of Miletus because he was sick. **21** Hurry to visit me before winter comes. Eubulus, Pudens, Linus, Claudia and all the brothers and sisters send you greetings.

22 The Lord be with you. His good will[b] be with all of you.

---

a 4:13 Parchments are writing materials made from animal skins.   *b* 4:22 Or "grace."

TITUS

Greeting

1 ¹From Paul, a servant of God and an apostle of Jesus Christ. I was sent to lead God's chosen people to faith and to the knowledge of the truth that leads to a godly life. ² My message is based on the confidence of eternal life. God, who never lies, promised this eternal life before the world began. ³ God has revealed this in every era by spreading his word. I was entrusted with this word by the command of God our Savior.

⁴ To Titus, a genuine child in the faith we share.

Good will*a* and peace from God the Father and from Christ Jesus our Savior are yours!

Guidelines for Leaders in the Church

⁵ I left you in Crete to do what still needed to be done—appointing spiritual leaders*b* in every city as I directed you. ⁶ A spiritual leader must have a good reputation. He must have only one wife and have children who are believers. His children shouldn't be known for having wild lifestyles or being rebellious. ⁷ Because a bishop*c* is a supervisor appointed by God, he must have a good reputation. He must not be a stubborn or irritable person. He must not drink too much or be a violent person. He must not use shameful ways to make money. ⁸ Instead, he must be hospitable, love what is good, use good judgment, be fair and moral, and have self-control. ⁹ He must be devoted to the trustworthy message we

---

a 1:4 Or "Grace."   *b* 1:5 Or "pastors," or "elders."   *c* 1:7 English equivalent difficult.

teach. Then he can use these accurate teachings to encourage people and correct those who oppose the word.

Correct Whoever Teaches What Is Wrong

¹⁰ There are many believers, especially converts from Judaism, who are rebellious. They speak nonsense and deceive people. ¹¹ They must be silenced because they are ruining whole families by teaching what they shouldn't teach. This is the shameful way they make money.

¹² Even one of their own prophets said, "Cretans are always liars, savage animals, and lazy gluttons." ¹³ That statement is true. For this reason, sharply correct believers so that they continue to have faith that is alive and well. ¹⁴ They shouldn't pay attention to Jewish myths or commands given by people who are always rejecting the truth. ¹⁵ Everything is clean*d* to those who are clean. But nothing is clean to corrupt unbelievers. Indeed, their minds and their consciences are corrupted. ¹⁶ They claim to know God, but they deny him by what they do. They are detestable, disobedient, and unfit to do anything good.

Guidelines for Christian Living

2 ¹ Tell believers to live the kind of life that goes along with accurate teachings. ² Tell older men to be sober. Tell them to be men of good character, to use good judgment, and to be well-grounded in faith, love, and endurance.

³ Tell older women to live their lives in a way that shows they are dedicated to God. Tell them not to be gossips or addicted to alcohol, but to be examples of virtue. ⁴ In this way they will teach young women to show love to their husbands and children, ⁵ to use good judgment, and to be morally pure. Also, tell them to teach young women to be homemakers, to be kind, and to place themselves under their husbands' authority. Then no one can speak evil of God's word.

---

d 1:15 "Clean" refers to anything that Moses' Teachings say is presentable to God.

⁶ Encourage young men to use good judgment. ⁷ Always set an example by doing good things. When you teach, be an example of moral purity and dignity. ⁸ Speak an accurate message that cannot be condemned. Then those who oppose us will be ashamed because they cannot say anything bad about us.

⁹ Tell slaves who are believers to place themselves under their masters' authority in everything they do. Tell them to please their masters, not to argue with them ¹⁰ or steal from them. Instead, tell slaves to show their masters how good and completely loyal they can be. Then they will show the beauty of the teachings about God our Savior in everything they do.

¹¹ After all, God's saving kindness*a* has appeared for the benefit of all people. ¹² It trains us to avoid ungodly lives filled with worldly desires so that we can live self-controlled, moral, and godly lives in this present world. ¹³ At the same time we can expect what we hope for—the appearance of the glory of our great God and Savior, Jesus Christ. ¹⁴ He gave himself for us to set us free from every sin and to cleanse us so that we can be his special people who are enthusiastic about doing good things.

¹⁵ Tell these things to the believers. Encourage and correct them, using your full authority. Don't let anyone ignore you.

3 ¹ Remind believers to willingly place themselves under the authority of government officials. Believers should obey them and be ready to help them with every good thing they do. ² Believers shouldn't curse anyone or be quarrelsome, but they should be gentle and show courtesy to everyone.

What God Did for Us

³ Indeed, we, too, were once stupid, disobedient, and misled. We were slaves to many kinds of lusts and pleasures. We were mean and jealous. We were hated, and we hated each other.

⁴ However, when God our Savior made his kindness and love for humanity appear, ⁵ he saved us, but not because of anything we had

a 2:11 Or "Grace."

done to gain his approval. Instead, because of his mercy he saved us through the washing in which the Holy Spirit gives us new birth and renewal. ⁶ God poured a generous amount of the Spirit on us through Jesus Christ our Savior. ⁷ As a result, God in his kindness*a* has given us his approval and we have become heirs who have the confidence that we have everlasting life. ⁸ This is a statement that can be trusted. I want you to insist on these things so that those who believe in God can concentrate on setting an example by doing good things. This is good and helps other people.

Advice for Titus

⁹ Avoid foolish controversies, arguments about genealogies, quarrels, and fights about Moses' Teachings. This is useless and worthless. ¹⁰ Have nothing to do with people who continue to teach false doctrine after you have warned them once or twice. ¹¹ You know that people like this are corrupt. They are sinners condemned by their own actions.

Farewell

¹² When I send Artemas or Tychicus to you, hurry to visit me in the city of Nicopolis. I have decided to spend the winter there. ¹³ Give Zenas the lawyer and Apollos your best support for their trip so that they will have everything they need.

¹⁴ Our people should also learn how to set an example by doing good things when urgent needs arise so that they can live productive lives.

¹⁵ Everyone with me sends you greetings. Greet our faithful friends.

⌊God's⌋ good will*a* be with all of you.

---

a 3:7, 15 Or "grace."

PHILEMON

Greeting

¹ From Paul, who is a prisoner for Christ Jesus, and our brother Timothy.

To our dear coworker Philemon, ² our sister Apphia, our fellow soldier Archippus, and the church that meets in your house.

³ Good will[a] and peace from God our Father and the Lord Jesus Christ are yours!

Paul's Prayer for Philemon

⁴ ⌊Philemon,⌋ I always thank my God when I mention you in my prayers because ⁵ I hear about your faithfulness to the Lord Jesus and your love for all of God's people. ⁶ As you share the faith you have in common with others, I pray that you may come to have a complete knowledge of every blessing we have in Christ. ⁷ Your love ⌊for God's people⌋ gives me a lot of joy and encouragement. You, brother, have comforted God's people.

Paul's Advice About Onesimus

⁸ Christ makes me bold enough to order you to do the right thing. ⁹ However, I would prefer to make an appeal on the basis of love. I, Paul, as an old man and now a prisoner for Christ Jesus, ¹⁰ appeal to you for my child Onesimus [Useful]. I became his spiritual father here in prison. ¹¹ Once he was useless to you, but now he is very useful to both of us.

---

^a 3 Or "Grace."

¹² I am sending him back to you. This is like sending you a part of myself. ¹³ I wanted to keep him here with me. Then he could have served me in your place while I am in prison for spreading the Good News. ¹⁴ Yet, I didn't want to do anything without your consent. I want you to do this favor for me out of your own free will without feeling forced to do it.

¹⁵ Maybe Onesimus was gone for a while so that you could have him back forever— ¹⁶ no longer as a slave but better than a slave—as a dear brother. He is especially dear to me, but even more so to you, both as a person and as a Christian.

¹⁷ If you think of me as your partner, welcome him as you would welcome me. ¹⁸ If he wronged you in any way or owes you anything, charge it to me. ¹⁹ I, Paul, promise to pay it back. I'm writing this with my own hand. I won't even mention that you owe me your life. ²⁰ So, because we're brothers in the Lord, do something for me. Give me some comfort because of Christ. ²¹ I am confident as I write to you that you will do this. And I know that you will do even more than I ask.

²² One more thing—have a guest room ready for me. I hope that, because of your prayers, God will give me back to you.

Greetings From Paul's Coworkers

²³ Epaphras, who is a prisoner because of Christ Jesus like I am, ²⁴ and my coworkers Mark, Aristarchus, Demas, and Luke send you greetings.

²⁵ The good will of our Lord Jesus Christ be yours.

HEBREWS

God Has Spoken to Us Through His Son

1 [1] In the past God spoke to our ancestors at many different times and in many different ways through the prophets. [2] In these last days he has spoken to us through his Son. God made his Son responsible for everything. His Son is the one through whom God made the universe. [3] His Son is the reflection of God's glory and the exact likeness of God's being. He holds everything together through his powerful words. After he had cleansed people from their sins, he received the highest position, the one next to the Father in heaven.

God's Son Is Superior to the Angels

[4] The Son has become greater than the angels since he has been given a name that is superior to theirs. [5] God never said to any of his angels,

> "You are my Son.
> Today I have become your Father."

And God never said to any of his angels,

> "I will be his Father,
> and he will be my Son."

[6] When God was about to send his firstborn Son into the world, he said,

> "All of God's angels must worship him."

[7] God said about the angels,

"He makes his messengers winds.
He makes his servants flames of fire."

⁸ But God said about his Son,

"Your throne, O God, is forever and ever.
    The scepter in your kingdom is a scepter for justice.
⁹   You have loved what is right and hated what is wrong.
        That is why God, your God,
            anointed you, rather than your companions,
                with the oil of joy."

¹⁰ God also said,

"Lord, in the beginning you laid the foundation of the earth.
    With your own hands you made the heavens.
¹¹   They will come to an end, but you will live forever.
        They will all wear out like clothes.
¹²   They will be taken off like a coat.
            You will change them like clothes.
                But you remain the same,
                    and your life will never end."

¹³ But God never said to any of the angels,

"Sit in the highest position in heaven
    until I make your enemies your footstool."

¹⁴ What are all the angels? They are spirits sent to serve those
who are going to receive salvation.

Everything Is Under Jesus' Control

2 ¹ For this reason we must pay closer attention to what we have
heard. Then we won't drift away ˌfrom the truthˌ. ² After all, the
message that the angels brought was reliable, and every violation
and act of disobedience was properly punished. ³ So how will we
escape punishment if we reject the important message, the message
that God saved us? First, the Lord told this saving message. Then

those who heard him confirmed that message. ⁴ God verified what they said through miraculous signs, amazing things, other powerful acts, and with other gifts from the Holy Spirit as he wanted.

⁵ He didn't put the world that will come (about which we are talking) under the angels' control. ⁶ Instead, someone has declared this somewhere in Scripture:

> "What is a mortal that you should remember him,
>   or the Son of Man*a* that you take care of him?
> ⁷ You made him a little lower than the angels.
>   You crowned him with glory and honor.
> ⁸ You put everything under his control."

When God put everything under his Son's control, nothing was left out.

However, at the present time we still don't see everything under his Son's control. ⁹ Jesus was made a little lower than the angels, but we see him crowned with glory and honor because he suffered death. Through God's kindness*b* he died on behalf of everyone. ¹⁰ God is the one for whom and through whom everything exists. Therefore, while God was bringing many sons and daughters to glory, it was the right time to bring Jesus, the source of their salvation, to the end of his work through suffering.

Jesus Became One of Us to Help Us

¹¹ Jesus, who makes people holy, and all those who are made holy have the same Father. That is why Jesus isn't ashamed to call them brothers and sisters. ¹² He says,

> "I will tell my people about your name.
>   I will praise you within the congregation."

¹³ In addition, Jesus says,

> "I will trust him."

---

a 2:6 "Son of Man" is a name for Jesus. It shows that he was not only God's Son but also human. Some believe "son of man" here refers to humans in general.
b 2:9 Or "grace."

And Jesus says,

> "I am here with the sons and daughters God has given me."

14 Since all of these sons and daughters have flesh and blood, Jesus took on flesh and blood to be like them. He did this so that by dying he would destroy the one who had power over death (that is, the devil). **15** In this way he would free those who were slaves all their lives because they were afraid of dying. **16** So Jesus helps Abraham's descendants rather than helping angels. **17** Therefore, he had to become like his brothers and sisters so that he could be merciful. He became like them so that he could serve as a faithful chief priest in God's presence and make peace with God for their sins. **18** Because Jesus experienced temptation when he suffered, he is able to help others when they are tempted.

Christ Is Superior to Moses

3 **1** Brothers and sisters, you are holy partners in a heavenly calling. So look carefully at Jesus, the apostle and chief priest about whom we make our declaration of faith. **2** Jesus is faithful to God, who appointed him, in the same way that Moses was faithful when he served in God's house. **3** Jesus deserves more praise than Moses in the same way that the builder of a house is praised more than the house. **4** After all, every house has a builder, but the builder of everything is God.

5 Moses was a faithful servant in God's household. He told ˌthe peopleˌ what God would say in the future. **6** But Christ is a faithful son in charge of God's household. We are his household if we continue to have courage and to be proud of the confidence we have.

7 As the Holy Spirit says,

> "If you hear God speak today, don't be stubborn.
> **8**   Don't be stubborn like those who rebelled
>   and tested me in the desert.
> **9**   That is where your ancestors tested me,
> **10**   although they had seen what I had done
>   for 40 years.

That is why I was angry with those people. So I said,

'Their hearts continue to stray,

and they have not learned my ways.'

¹¹ So I angrily took a solemn oath

that they would never enter my place of rest."

¹² Be careful, brothers and sisters, that none of you ever develop a wicked, unbelieving heart that turns away from the living God. ¹³ Encourage each other every day while you have the opportunity. If you do this, none of you will be deceived by sin and become stubborn. ¹⁴ After all, we will remain Christ's partners only if we continue to hold on to our original confidence until the end.

¹⁵ Scripture says,

"If you hear God speak today, don't be stubborn.

Don't be stubborn like those who rebelled."

¹⁶ Who heard God and rebelled? All those whom Moses led out of Egypt rebelled. ¹⁷ With whom was God angry for 40 years? He was angry with those who sinned and died in the desert. ¹⁸ Who did God swear would never enter his place of rest? He was talking about those who didn't obey him. ¹⁹ So we see that they couldn't enter his place of rest because they didn't believe.

We Will Enter God's Place of Rest

4 ¹ God's promise that we may enter his place of rest still stands. We are afraid that some of you think you won't enter his place of rest. ² We have heard the same Good News that your ancestors heard. But the message didn't help those who heard it in the past because they didn't believe.

³ We who believe are entering that place of rest. As God said, "So I angrily took a solemn oath that they would never enter my place of rest." God said this even though he had finished his work when he created the world. ⁴ Somewhere in Scripture God has said this about the seventh day: "On the seventh day God rested from all his work."

[5] God also said in the same passage, "They will never enter my place of rest." [6] However, some people enter that place of rest. Those who heard the Good News in the past did not enter God's place of rest because they did not obey God. [7] So God set another day. That day is today. Many years after ˌyour ancestors failed to enter that place of restˌ God spoke about it through David in the passage already quoted: "If you hear God speak today, don't be stubborn." [8] If Joshua had given the people rest, God would not have spoken about another day. [9] Therefore, a time of rest and worship exists for God's people. [10] Those who entered his place of rest also rested from their work as God did from his.

[11] So we must make every effort to enter that place of rest. Then no one will be lost by following the example of those who refused to obey.

[12] God's word is living and active. It is sharper than any two-edged sword and cuts as deep as the place where soul and spirit meet, the place where joints and marrow meet. God's word judges a person's thoughts and intentions. [13] No creature can hide from God. Everything is uncovered and exposed for him to see. We must answer to him.

Christ Is Superior to Other Chief Priests

[14] We need to hold on to our declaration of faith: We have a superior chief priest who has gone through the heavens. That person is Jesus, the Son of God. [15] We have a chief priest who is able to sympathize with our weaknesses. He was tempted in every way that we are, but he didn't sin. [16] So we can go confidently to the throne of God's kindness[a] to receive mercy and find kindness, which will help us at the right time.

5 [1] Every chief priest is chosen from humans to represent them in front of God, that is, to offer gifts and sacrifices for sin. [2] The chief priest can be gentle with people who are ignorant and easily deceived, because he also has weaknesses. [3] Because he has

---

[a] 4:16 Or "grace."

weaknesses, he has to offer sacrifices for his own sins in the same
way that he does for the sins of his people.

⁴ No one takes this honor for himself. Instead, God calls him
as he called Aaron. ⁵ So Christ did not take the glory of being a
chief priest for himself. Instead, the glory was given to him by
God, who said,

> "You are my Son.
>   Today I have become your Father."

⁶ In another place in Scripture, God said,

> "You are a priest forever,
>   in the way Melchizedek was a priest."

⁷ During his life on earth, Jesus prayed to God, who could save
him from death. He prayed and pleaded with loud crying and
tears, and he was heard because of his devotion to God. ⁸ Although
Jesus was the Son ˌof Godˌ, he learned to be obedient through his
sufferings. ⁹ After he had finished his work, he became the source
of eternal salvation for everyone who obeys him. ¹⁰ God appointed
him chief priest in the way Melchizedek was a priest.

You Need Someone to Teach You

¹¹ We have a lot to explain about this. But since you have
become too lazy to pay attention, explaining it to you is hard. ¹² By
now you should be teachers. Instead, you still need someone to
teach you the elementary truths of God's word. You need milk, not
solid food. ¹³ All those who live on milk lack the experience to talk
about what is right. They are still babies. ¹⁴ However, solid food is
for mature people, whose minds are trained by practice to know
the difference between good and evil.

6 ¹ With this in mind, we should stop going over the elementary
truths about Christ and move on to topics for more mature
people. We shouldn't repeat the basics about turning away from
the useless things we did and the basics about faith in God. ² We
shouldn't repeat the basic teachings about such things as baptisms,

setting people apart for holy tasks, dead people coming back to life, and eternal judgment. ³ If God permits, we will do this.

⁴ Some people once had God's light. They experienced the heavenly gift and shared in the Holy Spirit. ⁵ They experienced the goodness of God's word and the powers of the world to come. ⁶ Yet, they have deserted ˍChristˍ. They are crucifying the Son of God again and publicly disgracing him. Therefore, they cannot be led a second time to God.

⁷ God blesses the earth. So rain often falls on it, and it produces useful crops for farmers. ⁸ However, if the earth produces thorns and thistles, it is worthless and in danger of being cursed. In the end it will be burned.

God Will Not Forget You

⁹ Dear friends, even though we say these things, we are still convinced that better things are in store for you and that they will save you. ¹⁰ God is fair. He won't forget what you've done or the love you've shown for him. You helped his holy people, and you continue to help them. ¹¹ We want each of you to prove that you're working hard so that you will remain confident until the end. ¹² Then, instead of being lazy, you will imitate those who are receiving the promises through faith and patience.

¹³ God made a promise to Abraham. Since he had no one greater on whom to base his oath, he based it on himself. ¹⁴ He said, "I will certainly bless you and give you many descendants." ¹⁵ So Abraham received what God promised because he waited patiently for it.

¹⁶ When people take oaths, they base their oaths on someone greater than themselves. Their oaths guarantee what they say and end all arguments. ¹⁷ God wouldn't change his plan. He wanted to make this perfectly clear to those who would receive his promise, so he took an oath. ¹⁸ God did this so that we would be encouraged. God cannot lie when he takes an oath or makes a promise. These two things can never be changed. Those of us who have taken refuge in him hold on to the confidence we have been given. ¹⁹ We

have this confidence as a sure and strong anchor for our lives. This confidence goes into the ˌholyˌ place behind the curtain [20] where Jesus went before us on our behalf. He has become the chief priest forever in the way Melchizedek was a priest.

Christ Is Superior to Melchizedek

7 [1] Melchizedek was king of Salem and priest of the Most High God. He met Abraham and blessed him when Abraham was returning from defeating the kings. [2] Abraham gave Melchizedek a tenth of everything he had captured.

In the first place, Melchizedek's name means king of righteousness. He is also called king of Salem (which means king of peace). [3] No one knows anything about Melchizedek's father, mother, or ancestors. No one knows when he was born or when he died. Like the Son of God, Melchizedek continues to be a priest forever.

[4] You can see how important Melchizedek was. Abraham gave him a tenth of what he had captured, even though Abraham was the father of the chosen people. [5] Moses' Teachings say that members of the tribe of Levi who become priests must receive a tenth of everything from the people. The priests collect it from their own people, Abraham's descendants. [6] Although Melchizedek was not from the tribe of Levi, he received a tenth of everything from Abraham. Then Melchizedek blessed Abraham, who had God's promises. [7] No one can deny that the more important person blesses the less important person.

[8] Priests receive a tenth of everything, but they die. Melchizedek received a tenth of everything, but we are told that he lives. [9] We could even say that when Abraham gave Melchizedek a tenth of everything, Levi was giving a tenth of everything. Levi gave, although later his descendants would receive a tenth of everything. [10] Even though Levi had not yet been born, he was in the body of Abraham when Melchizedek met him.

[11] The people established the Levitical priesthood based on instructions they received. If the work of the Levitical priests had been perfect, we wouldn't need to speak about another kind of

priest. However, we speak about another kind of priest, a priest like Melchizedek, not a Levitical priest like Aaron.

¹² When a different kind of priesthood is established, the regulations for those priests are different. ¹³ The priest whom we are talking about was a member of a different tribe. No one from that tribe ever served as a priest at the altar. ¹⁴ Everyone knows that our Lord came from the tribe of Judah. Moses never said anything about priests coming from that tribe. ¹⁵ The regulations were different. This became clear when a different priest who is like Melchizedek appeared. ¹⁶ That person is a priest, not because he met human requirements, but because he has power that comes from a life that cannot be destroyed. ¹⁷ The Scriptures say the following about him: "You are a priest forever, in the way Melchizedek was a priest." ¹⁸ The former requirements are rejected because they are weak and useless. ¹⁹ Moses' Teachings couldn't accomplish everything that God required. But we have something else that gives us greater confidence and allows us to approach God.

²⁰ None of this happened without an oath. The men from the tribe of Levi may have become priests without an oath, ²¹ but Jesus became a priest when God took an oath. God said about him, "The Lord has taken an oath and will not change his mind. You are a priest forever." ²² In this way Jesus has become the guarantee of a better promise.[a]

²³ There was a long succession of priests because when a priest died he could no longer serve. ²⁴ But Jesus lives forever, so he serves as a priest forever. ²⁵ That is why he is always able to save those who come to God through him. He can do this because he always lives and intercedes for them.

²⁶ We need a chief priest who is holy, innocent, pure, set apart from sinners, and who has the highest position in heaven. ²⁷ We need a priest who doesn't have to bring daily sacrifices as those chief priests did. First they brought sacrifices for their own sins, and then they brought sacrifices for the sins of the people. Jesus

---

[a] 7:22; 8:6 Or "covenant."

brought the sacrifice for the sins of the people once and for all when he sacrificed himself. [28] Moses' Teachings designated mortals as chief priests even though they had weaknesses. But God's promise, which came after Moses' Teachings, designated the Son who forever accomplished everything that God required.

Jesus' Priestly Work Is Superior to Other Priests' Work

8 [1] The main point we want to make is this: We do have this kind of chief priest. This chief priest has received the highest position, the throne of majesty in heaven. [2] He serves as priest of the holy place and of the true tent set up by the Lord and not by any human.

[3] Every chief priest is appointed to offer gifts and sacrifices. Therefore, this chief priest had to offer something. [4] If he were on earth, he would not even be a priest. On earth ⸢other⸣ priests offer gifts by following the instructions that Moses gave. [5] They serve at a place that is a pattern, a shadow, of what is in heaven. When Moses was about to make the tent, God warned him, "Be sure to make everything based on the plan I showed you on the mountain."

[6] Jesus has been given a priestly work that is superior to the Levitical priests' work. He also brings a better promise[a] from God that is based on better guarantees. [7] If nothing had been wrong with the first promise, no one would look for another one. [8] But God found something wrong with his people and said to them,

> "The days are coming, says the Lord, when I will make a new promise to Israel and Judah. [9] It will not be like the promise that I made to their ancestors when I took them by the hand and brought them out of Egypt. They rejected that promise, so I ignored them, says the Lord. [10] But this is the promise that I will make to Israel after those days, says the Lord: I will put my teachings inside them, and I will write those teachings on their hearts. I will be their God, and they will be my people. [11] No longer will each person teach his neighbors or his relatives by saying, 'Know the Lord.' All of

them from the least important to the most important will all know me [12] because I will forgive their wickedness and I will no longer hold their sins against them."

[13] God made this new promise and showed that the first promise was outdated. What is outdated and aging will soon disappear.

Christ Offered a Superior Sacrifice

9 [1] The first promise had rules for the priests' service. It also had a holy place on earth. [2] A tent was set up. The first part of this tent was called the holy place. The lamp stand, the table, and the bread of the presence were in this part of the tent. [3] Behind the second curtain was the part of the tent called the most holy place. [4] It contained the gold incense burner and the ark of the Lord's promise. The ark was completely covered with gold. In the ark were the gold jar filled with manna, Aaron's staff that had blossomed, and the tablets on which the promise[a] was written. [5] Above the ark were the angels[b] of glory ⸢with their wings⸣ overshadowing the throne of mercy. (Discussing these things in detail isn't possible now.)

[6] That is how these two parts of the tent were set up. The priests always went into the first part of the tent to perform their duties. [7] But only the chief priest went into the second part of the tent. Once a year he entered and brought blood that he offered for himself and for the things that the people did wrong unintentionally. [8] The Holy Spirit used this to show that the way into the most holy place was not open while the tent was still in use.

[9] The first part of the tent is an example for the present time. The gifts and sacrifices that were brought there could not give the worshiper a clear conscience. [10] These gifts and sacrifices were meant to be food, drink, and items used in various purification ceremonies. These ceremonies were required for the body until God would establish a new way of doing things.

---

[a] 9:4 Or "covenant."   [b] 9:5 Or "cherubim."

¹¹ But Christ came as a chief priest of the good things that are now here. Christ went through a better, more perfect tent that was not made by human hands and that is not part of this created world. ¹² He used his own blood, not the blood of goats and bulls, for the sacrifice. He went into the most holy place and offered this sacrifice once and for all to free us forever.

¹³ The blood of goats and bulls and the ashes of cows sprinkled on unclean*c* people made their bodies holy and clean. ¹⁴ The blood of Christ, who had no defect, does even more. Through the eternal Spirit he offered himself to God and cleansed our consciences from the useless things we had done. Now we can serve the living God.

¹⁵ Because Christ offered himself to God, he is able to bring a new promise from God. Through his death he paid the price to set people free from the sins they committed under the first promise. He did this so that those who are called can be guaranteed an inheritance that will last forever.

¹⁶ In order for a will to take effect, it must be shown that the one who made it has died. ¹⁷ A will is used only after a person is dead because it goes into effect only when a person dies.

¹⁸ That is why even the first promise was made with blood. ¹⁹ As Moses' Teachings tell us, Moses told all the people every commandment. Then he took the blood of calves and goats together with some water, red yarn, and hyssop and sprinkled the scroll and all the people. ²⁰ He said, "Here is the blood that seals the promise God has made to you." ²¹ In the same way, Moses sprinkled blood on the tent and on everything used in worship. ²² As Moses' Teachings tell us, blood was used to cleanse almost everything, because if no blood is shed, no sins can be forgiven.

²³ The copies of the things in heaven had to be cleansed by these sacrifices. But the heavenly things themselves had to be cleansed by better sacrifices. ²⁴ Christ didn't go into a holy place made by human hands. He didn't go into a model of the real thing. Instead, he went into heaven to appear in God's presence on our behalf. ²⁵ Every year

---

c 9:13 "Unclean" refers to anything that Moses' Teachings say is not presentable to God.

the chief priest went into the holy place to make a sacrifice with blood that isn't his own. However, Christ didn't go into heaven to sacrifice himself again and again. ²⁶ Otherwise, he would have had to suffer many times since the world was created. But now, at the end of the ages, he has appeared once to remove sin by his sacrifice. ²⁷ People die once, and after that they are judged. ²⁸ Likewise, Christ was sacrificed once to take away the sins of humanity, and after that he will appear a second time. This time he will not deal with sin, but he will save those who eagerly wait for him.

We Can Enter the Most Holy Place Because of Christ's Superior Work

10 ¹ Moses' Teachings with their yearly cycle of sacrifices are only a shadow of the good things in the future. They aren't an exact likeness of those things. They can never make those who worship perfect. ² If these sacrifices could have made the worshipers perfect, the sacrifices would have stopped long ago. Those who worship would have been cleansed once and for all. Their consciences would have been free from sin. ³ Instead, this yearly cycle of sacrifices reminded people of their sins. ⁴ (The blood of bulls and goats cannot take away sins.)

⁵ For this reason, when Christ came into the world, he said,

"'You did not want sacrifices and offerings,
    but you prepared a body for me.
⁶   You did not approve of burnt offerings and sacrifices
        for sin.'
⁷   Then I said, 'I have come!
        (It is written about me in the scroll of the book.)
        I have come to do what you want, my God.'"

⁸ In this passage Christ first said, "You did not want sacrifices, offerings, burnt offerings, and sacrifices for sin. You did not approve of them." (These are the sacrifices that Moses' Teachings require people to offer.) ⁹ Then Christ says, "I have come to do what you want." He did away with sacrifices in order to establish the obedi-

ence that God wants. [10] We have been set apart as holy because Jesus Christ did what God wanted him to do by sacrificing his body once and for all.

[11] Every day each priest performed his religious duty. He offered the same type of sacrifice again and again. Yet, these sacrifices could never take away sins. [12] However, this chief priest made one sacrifice for sins, and this sacrifice lasts forever. Then he received the highest position in heaven. [13] Since that time, he has been waiting for his enemies to be made his footstool. [14] With one sacrifice he accomplished the work of setting them apart for God forever.

[15] The Holy Spirit tells us the same thing: [16] "This is the promise[a] that I will make to them after those days, says the Lord: 'I will put my teachings in their hearts and write them in their minds.' "

[17] Then he adds, "I will no longer hold their sins and their disobedience against them."

[18] When sins are forgiven, there is no longer any need to sacrifice for sins.

[19] Brothers and sisters, because of the blood of Jesus we can now confidently go into the holy place. [20] Jesus has opened a new and living way for us to go through the curtain. (The curtain is his own body.) [21] We have a superior priest in charge of God's house. [22] We have been sprinkled ˎwith his bloodˌ to free us from a guilty conscience, and our bodies have been washed with clean water. So we must continue to come ˎto himˌ with a sincere heart and strong faith. [23] We must continue to hold firmly to our declaration of faith. The one who made the promise is faithful.

Encourage Each Other

[24] We must also consider how to encourage each other to show love and to do good things. [25] We should not stop gathering together with other believers, as some of you are doing. Instead, we must continue to encourage each other even more as we see the day of the Lord coming.

---

a 10:16 Or "covenant."

²⁶ If we go on sinning after we have learned the truth, no sacrifice can take away our sins. ²⁷ All that is left is a terrifying wait for judgment and a raging fire that will consume God's enemies. ²⁸ If two or three witnesses accused someone of rejecting Moses' Teachings, that person was shown no mercy as he was executed. ²⁹ What do you think a person who shows no respect for the Son of God deserves? That person looks at the blood of the promise (the blood that made him holy) as no different from other people's blood, and he insults the Spirit that God gave us out of his kindness.ᵇ He deserves a much worse punishment. ³⁰ We know the God who said,

> "I alone have the right to take revenge.
>   I will pay back."

God also said,

> "The Lord will judge his people."

³¹ Falling into the hands of the living God is a terrifying thing.

³² Remember the past, when you first learned the truth. You endured a lot of hardship and pain. ³³ At times you were publicly insulted and mistreated. At times you associated with people who were treated this way. ³⁴ You suffered with prisoners. You were cheerful even though your possessions were stolen, since you know that you have a better and more permanent possession.ᶜ

³⁵ So don't lose your confidence. It will bring you a great reward. ³⁶ You need endurance so that after you have done what God wants you to do, you can receive what he has promised.

³⁷   "Yet, the one who is coming will come soon.
>   He will not delay.
³⁸   The person who has God's approval will live by faith.
>   But if he turns back, I will not be pleased with him."

³⁹ We don't belong with those who turn back and are destroyed. Instead, we belong with those who have faith and are saved.

ᵇ 10:29 Or "grace."   ᶜ 10:34 Some manuscripts and translations add "in heaven."

Faith Directed People's Lives

11 ¹ Faith assures us of things we expect and convinces us of the existence of things we cannot see. ² God accepted our ancestors because of their faith.

³ Faith convinces us that God created the world through his word. This means what can be seen was made by something that could not be seen.

⁴ Faith led Abel to offer God a better sacrifice than Cain's sacrifice. Through his faith Abel received God's approval, since God accepted his sacrifices. Through his faith Abel still speaks, even though he is dead.

⁵ Faith enabled Enoch to be taken instead of dying. No one could find him, because God had taken him. Scripture states that before Enoch was taken, God was pleased with him. ⁶ No one can please God without faith. Whoever goes to God must believe that God exists and that he rewards those who seek him.

⁷ Faith led Noah to listen when God warned him about the things in the future that he could not see. He obeyed God and built a ship to save his family. Through faith Noah condemned the world and received God's approval that comes through faith.

⁸ Faith led Abraham to obey when God called him to go to a place that he would receive as an inheritance. Abraham left his own country without knowing where he was going.

⁹ Faith led Abraham to live as a foreigner in the country that God had promised him. He lived in tents, as did Isaac and Jacob, who received the same promise from God. ¹⁰ Abraham was waiting for the city that God had designed and built, the city with permanent foundations.

¹¹ Faith enabled Abraham to become a father, even though he was old and Sarah had never been able to have children. Abraham trusted that God would keep his promise. ¹² Abraham was as good as dead. Yet, from this man came descendants as numerous as the stars in the sky and as countless as the grains of sand on the seashore.

¹³ All these people died having faith. They didn't receive the things that God had promised them, but they saw these things

coming in the distant future and rejoiced. They acknowledged that they were living as strangers with no permanent home on earth. [14] Those who say such things make it clear that they are looking for their own country. [15] If they had been thinking about the country that they had left, they could have found a way to go back. [16] Instead, these men were longing for a better country—a heavenly country. That is why God is not ashamed to be called their God. He has prepared a city for them.

[17] When God tested Abraham, faith led him to offer his son Isaac. Abraham, the one who received the promises from God, was willing to offer his only son as a sacrifice. [18] God had said to him, "Through Isaac your descendants will carry on your name." [19] Abraham believed that God could bring Isaac back from the dead. Abraham did receive Isaac back from the dead in a figurative sense.

[20] Faith led Isaac to bless Jacob and Esau.

[21] While Jacob was dying, faith led him to bless each of Joseph's sons. He leaned on the top of his staff and worshiped God.

[22] While Joseph was dying, faith led him to speak about the Israelites leaving Egypt and give them instructions about burying his bones.

[23] Faith led Moses' parents to hide him for three months after he was born. They did this because they saw that Moses was a beautiful baby and they were not afraid to disobey the king's order.

[24] When Moses grew up, faith led him to refuse to be known as a son of Pharaoh's daughter. [25] He chose to suffer with God's people rather than to enjoy the pleasures of sin for a little while. [26] He thought that being insulted for Christ would be better than having the treasures of Egypt. He was looking ahead to his reward.

[27] Faith led Moses to leave Egypt without being afraid of the king's anger. Moses didn't give up but continued as if he could actually see the invisible God.

[28] Faith led Moses to establish the Passover and spread the blood ˎon the doorposts˼ so that the destroying angel would not kill the firstborn sons.

²⁹ Faith caused the people to go through the Red Sea as if it were dry land. The Egyptians also tried this, but they drowned.

³⁰ Faith caused the walls of Jericho to fall after the Israelites marched around them for seven days.

³¹ Faith led the prostitute Rahab to welcome the spies as friends. She was not killed with those who refused to obey God.

³² What more should I say? I don't have enough time to tell you about Gideon, Barak, Samson, Jephthah, David, Samuel, and the prophets. ³³ Through faith they conquered kingdoms, did what God approved, and received what God had promised. They shut the mouths of lions, ³⁴ put out raging fires, and escaped death. They found strength when they were weak. They were powerful in battle and defeated other armies. ³⁵ Women received their loved ones back from the dead. Other believers were brutally tortured but refused to be released so that they might gain eternal life. ³⁶ Some were made fun of and whipped, and some were chained and put in prison. ³⁷ Some were stoned to death, sawed in half, and killed with swords. Some wore the skins of sheep and goats. Some were poor, abused, and mistreated. ³⁸ The world didn't deserve these good people. Some wandered around in deserts and mountains and lived in caves and holes in the ground.

³⁹ All these people were known for their faith, but none of them received what God had promised. ⁴⁰ God planned to give us something very special so that we would gain eternal life with them.

Faith Directs Our Lives

12 ¹ Since we are surrounded by so many examples ⌞of faith⌟, we must get rid of everything that slows us down, especially sin that distracts us. We must run the race that lies ahead of us and never give up. ² We must focus on Jesus, the source and goal of our faith. He saw the joy ahead of him, so he endured death on the cross and ignored the disgrace it brought him. Then he received the highest position in heaven, the one next to the throne of God. ³ Think about Jesus, who endured opposition from sinners, so that you don't become tired and give up.

⁴ You struggle against sin, but your struggles haven't killed you. ⁵ You have forgotten the encouraging words that God speaks to you as his children:

> "My child, pay attention when the Lord disciplines you.
>   Don't give up when he corrects you.
> ⁶   The Lord disciplines everyone he loves.
>   He severely disciplines everyone he accepts as his child."

⁷ Endure your discipline. God corrects you as a father corrects his children. All children are disciplined by their fathers. ⁸ If you aren't disciplined like the other children, you aren't part of the family. ⁹ On earth we have fathers who disciplined us, and we respect them. Shouldn't we place ourselves under the authority of God, the father of spirits, so that we will live? ¹⁰ For a short time our fathers disciplined us as they thought best. Yet, God disciplines us for our own good so that we can become holy like him. ¹¹ We don't enjoy being disciplined. It always seems to cause more pain than joy. But later on, those who learn from that discipline have peace that comes from doing what is right.

¹² Strengthen your tired arms and weak knees. ¹³ Keep walking along straight paths so that your injured leg won't get worse. Instead, let it heal.

¹⁴ Try to live peacefully with everyone, and try to live holy lives, because if you don't, you will not see the Lord. ¹⁵ Make sure that everyone has kindness[a] from God so that bitterness doesn't take root and grow up to cause trouble that corrupts many of you. ¹⁶ Make sure that no one commits sexual sin or is as concerned about earthly things as Esau was. He sold his rights as the first-born son for a single meal. ¹⁷ You know that afterwards, when he wanted to receive the blessing that the firstborn son was to receive, he was rejected. Even though he begged and cried for the blessing, he couldn't do anything to change what had happened.

---

[a] 12:15 Or "grace."

[18] You have not come to something that you can feel, to a blazing fire, to darkness, to gloom, to a storm, [19] to a trumpet's blast, and to a voice. When your ancestors heard that voice, they begged not to hear it say another word. [20] They couldn't obey the command that was given, "If even an animal touches the mountain, it must be stoned to death." [21] The sight was so terrifying that even Moses said he was trembling and afraid.

[22] Instead, you have come to Mount Zion, to the city of the living God, to the heavenly Jerusalem. You have come to tens of thousands of angels joyfully gathered together [23] and to the assembly of God's firstborn children (whose names are written in heaven). You have come to a judge (the God of all people) and to the spirits of people who have God's approval and have gained eternal life. [24] You have come to Jesus, who brings the new promise[b] from God, and to the sprinkled blood that speaks a better message than Abel's.

[25] Be careful that you do not refuse to listen when God speaks. Your ancestors didn't escape when they refused to listen to God, who warned them on earth. We certainly won't escape if we turn away from God, who warns us from heaven. [26] When God spoke to your ancestors, his voice shook the earth. But now he has promised, "Once more I will shake not only the earth but also the sky."

[27] The words *once more* show clearly that God will change what he has made. These are the things that can be shaken. Then only the things that cannot be shaken will remain. [28] Therefore, we must be thankful that we have a kingdom that cannot be shaken. Because we are thankful, we must serve God with fear and awe in a way that pleases him. [29] After all, our God is a destructive fire.

13 [1] Continue to love each other. [2] Don't forget to show hospitality to believers you don't know. By doing this some believers have shown hospitality to angels without being aware of it. [3] Remember those in prison as if you were in prison with them. Remember those who are mistreated as if you were being mistreated.

---

[b] 12:24 Or "covenant."

⁴ Marriage is honorable in every way, so husbands and wives should be faithful to each other. God will judge those who commit sexual sins, especially those who commit adultery.

⁵ Don't love money. Be happy with what you have because God has said, "I will never abandon you or leave you." ⁶ So we can confidently say,

> "The Lord is my helper.
>   I will not be afraid.
>   What can mortals do to me?"

⁷ Remember your leaders who have spoken God's word to you. Think about how their lives turned out, and imitate their faith.

⁸ Jesus Christ is the same yesterday, today, and forever.

⁹ Don't get carried away by all kinds of unfamiliar teachings. Gaining inner strength from God's kindness*a* is good for us. This strength does not come from following rules about food, rules that don't help those who follow them. ¹⁰ Those who serve at the tent have no right to eat what is sacrificed at our altar.

¹¹ The chief priest brings the blood of animals into the holy place as an offering for sin. But the bodies of those animals were burned outside the Israelite camp. ¹² That is why Jesus suffered outside the gates of Jerusalem. He suffered to make the people holy with his own blood. ¹³ So we must go to him outside the camp and endure the insults he endured. ¹⁴ We don't have a permanent city here on earth, but we are looking for the city that we will have in the future. ¹⁵ Through Jesus we should always bring God a sacrifice of praise, that is, words that acknowledge him. ¹⁶ Don't forget to do good things for others and to share what you have with them. These are the kinds of sacrifices that please God.

¹⁷ Obey your leaders, and accept their authority. They take care of you because they are responsible for you. Obey them so that they may do this work joyfully and not complain about you. (Causing them to complain would not be to your advantage.)

---

a 13:9 Or "grace."

¹⁸ Pray for us. We are sure that our consciences are clear because we want to live honorably in every way. ¹⁹ I especially ask for your prayers so that I may come back to you soon.

²⁰ The God of peace brought the great shepherd of the sheep, our Lord Jesus, back to life through the blood of an eternal promise.^b ²¹ May this God of peace prepare you to do every good thing he wants. May he work in us through Jesus Christ to do what is pleasing to him. Glory belongs to Jesus Christ forever. Amen.

Farewell

²² I urge you, brothers and sisters, to listen patiently to my encouraging words. I have written you a short letter. ²³ You know that Timothy, our brother, has been freed. If he comes here soon, both of us will visit you.

²⁴ Greet all your leaders and all God's holy people. Those who are with us from Italy greet you.

²⁵ May God's good will^c be with all of you!

---

^b 13:20 Or "covenant."   ^c 13:25 Or "grace."

JAMES

Greeting

1 ¹ From James, a servant of God and of the Lord Jesus Christ. To God's faithful people*a* who have been scattered. Greetings.

When You Are Tested, Turn to God

² My brothers and sisters, be very happy when you are tested in different ways. ³ You know that such testing of your faith produces endurance. ⁴ Endure until your testing is over. Then you will be mature and complete, and you won't need anything.

⁵ If any of you needs wisdom to know what you should do, you should ask God, and he will give it to you. God is generous to everyone and doesn't find fault with them. ⁶ When you ask for something, don't have any doubts. A person who has doubts is like a wave that is blown by the wind and tossed by the sea. ⁷ A person who has doubts shouldn't expect to receive anything from the Lord. ⁸ A person who has doubts is thinking about two different things at the same time and can't make up his mind about anything.

⁹ Humble believers should be proud because being humble makes them important. ¹⁰ Rich believers should be proud because being rich should make them humble. Rich people will wither like flowers. ¹¹ The sun rises with its scorching heat and dries up plants. The flowers drop off, and the beauty is gone. The same thing will happen to rich people. While they are busy, they will die.

¹² Blessed are those who endure when they are tested. When they pass the test, they will receive the crown of life that God has

a 1:1 Or "to the twelve tribes."

promised to those who love him. ¹³ When someone is tempted, he shouldn't say that God is tempting him. God can't be tempted by evil, and God doesn't tempt anyone. ¹⁴ Everyone is tempted by his own desires as they lure him away and trap him. ¹⁵ Then desire becomes pregnant and gives birth to sin. When sin grows up, it gives birth to death.

¹⁶ My dear brothers and sisters, don't be fooled. ¹⁷ Every good present and every perfect gift comes from above, from the Father who made the sun, moon, and stars. The Father doesn't change like the shifting shadows produced by the sun and the moon.

¹⁸ God decided to give us life through the word of truth to make us his most important creatures.

¹⁹ Remember this, my dear brothers and sisters: Everyone should be quick to listen, slow to speak, and should not get angry easily. ²⁰ An angry person doesn't do what God approves of. ²¹ So get rid of all immoral behavior and all the wicked things you do. Humbly accept the word that God has placed in you. This word can save you.

²² Do what God's word says. Don't merely listen to it, or you will fool yourselves. ²³ If someone listens to God's word but doesn't do what it says, he is like a person who looks at his face in a mirror, ²⁴ studies his features, goes away, and immediately forgets what he looks like. ²⁵ However, the person who continues to study God's perfect teachings that make people free and who remains committed to them will be blessed. People like that don't merely listen and forget; they actually do what God's teachings say.

²⁶ If a person thinks that he is religious but can't control his tongue, he is fooling himself. That person's religion is worthless. ²⁷ Pure, unstained religion, according to God our Father, is to take care of orphans and widows when they suffer and to remain uncorrupted by this world.

Don't Favor Rich People Over Poor People

2 ¹ My brothers and sisters, practice your faith in our glorious Lord Jesus Christ by not favoring one person over another. ² For

example, two men come to your worship service. One man is wearing gold rings and fine clothes; the other man, who is poor, is wearing shabby clothes. ³ Suppose you give special attention to the man wearing fine clothes and say to him, "Please have a seat." But you say to the poor man, "Stand over there," or "Sit on the floor at my feet." ⁴ Aren't you discriminating against people and using a corrupt standard to make judgments?

⁵ Listen, my dear brothers and sisters! Didn't God choose poor people in the world to become rich in faith and to receive the kingdom that he promised to those who love him? ⁶ Yet, you show no respect to poor people. Don't rich people oppress you and drag you into court? ⁷ Don't they curse the good name ˌof Jesusˌ, the name that was used to bless you?

⁸ You are doing right if you obey this law from the highest authority: "Love your neighbor as you love yourself." ⁹ If you favor one person over another, you're sinning, and this law convicts you of being disobedient. ¹⁰ If someone obeys all of God's laws except one, that person is guilty of breaking all of them. ¹¹ After all, the one who said, "Never commit adultery," is the same one who said, "Never murder." If you do not commit adultery but you murder, you become a person who disobeys God's laws.

¹² Talk and act as people who are going to be judged by laws that bring freedom. ¹³ No mercy will be shown to those who show no mercy to others. Mercy triumphs over judgment.

We Show Our Faith by What We Do

¹⁴ My brothers and sisters, what good does it do if someone claims to have faith but doesn't do any good things? Can this kind of faith save him? ¹⁵ Suppose a believer, whether a man or a woman, needs clothes or food ¹⁶ and one of you tells that person, "God be with you! Stay warm, and make sure you eat enough." If you don't provide for that person's physical needs, what good does it do? ¹⁷ In the same way, faith by itself is dead if it doesn't cause you to do any good things.

¹⁸ Another person might say, "You have faith, but I do good things." Show me your faith apart from the good things you do. I will show you my faith by the good things I do. ¹⁹ You believe that there is one God. That's fine! The demons also believe that, and they tremble with fear.

²⁰ You fool! Do you have to be shown that faith which does nothing is useless? ²¹ Didn't our ancestor Abraham receive God's approval as a result of what he did when he offered his son Isaac as a sacrifice on the altar? ²² You see that Abraham's faith and what he did worked together. His faith was shown to be genuine by what he did. ²³ The Scripture passage came true. It says, "Abraham believed God, and that faith was regarded by God to be his approval of Abraham." So Abraham was called God's friend. ²⁴ You see that a person receives God's approval because of what he does, not only because of what he believes. ²⁵ The same is true of the prostitute Rahab who welcomed the spies and sent them away on another road. She received God's approval because of what she did.

²⁶ A body that doesn't breathe[a] is dead. In the same way faith that does nothing is dead.

Speak Wisely

3 ¹ Brothers and sisters, not many of you should become teachers. You know that we who teach will be judged more severely.

² All of us make a lot of mistakes. If someone doesn't make any mistakes when he speaks, he would be perfect. He would be able to control everything he does. ³ We put bits in the mouths of horses to make them obey us, and we have control over everything they do. ⁴ The same thing is true for ships. They are very big and are driven by strong winds. Yet, by using small rudders, pilots steer ships wherever they want them to go. ⁵ In the same way the tongue is a small part of the body, but it can brag about doing important things.

---

[a] 2:26 Or "A body without a spirit."

A large forest can be set on fire by a little flame. ⁶ The tongue is that kind of flame. It is a world of evil among the parts of our bodies, and it completely contaminates our bodies. The tongue sets our lives on fire, and is itself set on fire from hell. ⁷ People have tamed all kinds of animals, birds, reptiles, and sea creatures. ⁸ Yet, no one can tame the tongue. It is an uncontrollable evil filled with deadly poison.

⁹ With our tongues we praise our Lord and Father. Yet, with the same tongues we curse people, who were created in God's likeness. ¹⁰ Praise and curses come from the same mouth. My brothers and sisters, this should not happen! ¹¹ Do clean and polluted water flow out of the same spring? ¹² My brothers and sisters, can a fig tree produce olives? Can a grapevine produce figs? In the same way, a pool of salt water can't produce fresh water.

Live Wisely

¹³ Do any of you have wisdom and insight? Show this by living the right way with the humility that comes from wisdom. ¹⁴ But if you are bitterly jealous and filled with self-centered ambition, don't brag. Don't say that you are wise when it isn't true. ¹⁵ That kind of wisdom doesn't come from above. It belongs to this world. It is self-centered and demonic. ¹⁶ Wherever there is jealousy and rivalry, there is disorder and every kind of evil.

¹⁷ However, the wisdom that comes from above is first of all pure. Then it is peaceful, gentle, obedient, filled with mercy and good deeds, impartial, and sincere. ¹⁸ A harvest that has God's approval comes from the peace planted by peacemakers.

Stop Fighting With Each Other

4 ¹ What causes fights and quarrels among you? Aren't they caused by the selfish desires that fight to control you? ² You want what you don't have, so you commit murder. You're determined to have things, but you can't get what you want. You quarrel and fight. You don't have the things you want, because you don't pray for them. ³ When you pray for things, you don't get them because you want them for the wrong reason—for your own pleasure.

⁴ You unfaithful people! Don't you know that love for this ˌevilˌ world is hatred toward God? Whoever wants to be a friend of this world is an enemy of God. ⁵ Do you think this passage means nothing? It says, "The Spirit that lives in us wants us to be his own." ⁶ But God shows us even more kindness.ᵃ Scripture says,

> "God opposes arrogant people,
>   but he is kind to humble people."

⁷ So place yourselves under God's authority. Resist the devil, and he will run away from you. ⁸ Come close to God, and he will come close to you. Clean up your lives, you sinners, and clear your minds, you doubters. ⁹ Be miserable, mourn, and cry. Turn your laughter into mourning and your joy into gloom. ¹⁰ Humble yourselves in the Lord's presence. Then he will give you a high position.

Stop Slandering Each Other

¹¹ Brothers and sisters, stop slandering each other. Those who slander and judge other believers slander and judge God's teachings. If you judge God's teachings, you are no longer following them. Instead, you are judging them. ¹² There is only one teacher and judge. He is able to save or destroy you. So who are you to judge your neighbor?

Don't Brag About Your Plans for the Future

¹³ Pay attention to this! You're saying, "Today or tomorrow we will go into some city, stay there a year, conduct business, and make money." ¹⁴ You don't know what will happen tomorrow. What is life? You are a mist that is seen for a moment and then disappears. ¹⁵ Instead, you should say, "If the Lord wants us to, we will live and carry out our plans." ¹⁶ However, you brag because you're arrogant. All such bragging is evil.

¹⁷ Whoever knows what is right but doesn't do it is sinning.

ᵃ 4:6 Or "grace."

Advice to Rich People

5 ¹ Pay attention to this if you're rich. Cry and moan about the misery that is coming to you. ² Your riches have decayed, and your clothes have been eaten by moths. ³ Your gold and silver are corroded, and their corrosion will be used as evidence against you. Like fire, it will destroy your body.

You have stored up riches in these last days. ⁴ The wages you refused to pay the people who harvested your fields shout ˌto God˳ against you. The Lord of Armies has heard the cries of those who gather the crops. ⁵ You have lived in luxury and pleasure here on earth. You have fattened yourselves for the day of slaughter. ⁶ You have condemned and murdered people who have God's approval, even though they didn't resist you.

Be Patient

⁷ Brothers and sisters, be patient until the Lord comes again. See how farmers wait for their precious crops to grow. They wait patiently for fall and spring rains. ⁸ You, too, must be patient. Don't give up hope. The Lord will soon be here. ⁹ Brothers and sisters, stop complaining about each other, or you will be condemned. Realize that the judge is standing at the door.

¹⁰ Brothers and sisters, follow the example of the prophets who spoke in the name of the Lord. They were patient when they suffered unjustly. ¹¹ We consider those who endure to be blessed. You have heard about Job's endurance. You saw that the Lord ended Job's suffering because the Lord is compassionate and merciful.

Don't Take Oaths

¹² Above all things, my brothers and sisters, do not take an oath on anything in heaven or on earth. Do not take any oath. If you mean yes, say yes. If you mean no, say no. Do this so that you won't be condemned.

Prayer Is Powerful

¹³ If any of you are having trouble, pray. If you are happy, sing psalms. ¹⁴ If you are sick, call for the church leaders. Have them pray for you and anoint you with olive oil[a] in the name of the Lord. ¹⁵ (Prayers offered in faith will save those who are sick, and the Lord will cure them.) If you have sinned, you will be forgiven. ¹⁶ So admit your sins to each other, and pray for each other so that you will be healed.

Prayers offered by those who have God's approval are effective. ¹⁷ Elijah was human like us. Yet, when he prayed that it wouldn't rain, no rain fell on the ground for three-and-a-half years. ¹⁸ Then he prayed again. It rained, and the ground produced crops.

Help Those Who Have Wandered Away From the Truth

¹⁹ My brothers and sisters, if one of you wanders from the truth, someone can bring that person back. ²⁰ Realize that whoever brings a sinner back from the error of his ways will save him from death, and many sins will be forgiven.

---

a 5:14 People in ancient times used olive oil for healing.

1 PETER

Greeting

1 ¹ From Peter, an apostle of Jesus Christ.
To God's chosen people who are temporary residents ⌊in the
world⌋ and are scattered throughout the provinces of
Pontus, Galatia, Cappadocia, Asia, and Bithynia. ² God the
Father knew you long ago and chose you to live holy lives
with the Spirit's help so that you are obedient to Jesus
Christ and are sprinkled with his blood.
May good will[a] and peace fill your lives!

Faith in Christ Brings You Joy

³ Praise the God and Father of our Lord Jesus Christ! God has
given us a new birth because of his great mercy. We have been
born into a new life that has a confidence which is alive because
Jesus Christ has come back to life. ⁴ We have been born into a new
life which has an inheritance that can't be destroyed or corrupted
and can't fade away. That inheritance is kept in heaven for you,
⁵ since you are guarded by God's power through faith for a salvation that is ready to be revealed at the end of time.

⁶ You are extremely happy about these things, even though
you have to suffer different kinds of trouble for a little while now.
⁷ The purpose of these troubles is to test your faith as fire tests
how genuine gold is. Your faith is more precious than gold, and by
passing the test, it gives praise, glory, and honor to God. This will
happen when Jesus Christ appears again.

---

a 1:2 Or "grace."

⁸ Although you have never seen Christ, you love him. You don't see him now, but you believe in him. You are extremely happy with joy and praise that can hardly be expressed in words ⁹ as you obtain the salvation that is the goal of your faith.

¹⁰ The prophets carefully researched and investigated this salvation. Long ago they spoke about God's kindness*b* that would come to you. ¹¹ So they tried to find out what time or situation the Spirit of Christ kept referring to whenever he predicted Christ's sufferings and the glory that would follow. ¹² God revealed to the prophets that the things they had spoken were not for their own benefit but for yours. What the prophets had spoken, the Holy Spirit, who was sent from heaven, has now made known to you by those who spread the Good News among you. These are things that even the angels want to look into.

Live Holy Lives

¹³ Therefore, your minds must be clear and ready for action. Place your confidence completely in what God's kindness will bring you when Jesus Christ appears again. ¹⁴ Because you are children who obey God, don't live the kind of lives you once lived. Once you lived to satisfy your desires because you didn't know any better. ¹⁵ But because the God who called you is holy you must be holy in every aspect of your life. ¹⁶ Scripture says, "Be holy, because I am holy." ¹⁷ So if you call God your Father, live your time as temporary residents on earth in fear. He is the God who judges all people by what they have done, and he doesn't play favorites. ¹⁸ Realize that you weren't set free from the worthless life handed down to you from your ancestors by a payment of silver or gold which can be destroyed. ¹⁹ Rather, the payment that freed you was the precious blood of Christ, the lamb with no defects or imperfections. ²⁰ He is the lamb who was known long ago before the world existed, but for your good he became publicly known in the last period of time. ²¹ Through him you believe in God who

b 1:10 Or "grace."

brought Christ back to life and gave him glory. So your faith and confidence are in God.

Love Each Other

[22] Love each other with a warm love that comes from the heart. After all, you have purified yourselves by obeying the truth. As a result you have a sincere love for each other. [23] You have been born again, not from a seed that can be destroyed, but through God's everlasting word that can't be destroyed. That's why ͵Scripture says͵,

[24]   "All people are like grass,
           and all their beauty is like a flower of the field.
         The grass dries up and the flower drops off,
[25]   but the word of the Lord lasts forever."

This word is the Good News that was told to you.

Live as God's Chosen People

2 [1] So get rid of every kind of evil, every kind of deception, hypocrisy, jealousy, and every kind of slander. [2] Desire God's pure word as newborn babies desire milk. Then you will grow in your salvation. [3] Certainly you have tasted that the Lord is good!

[4] You are coming to Christ, the living stone who was rejected by humans but was chosen as precious by God. [5] You come to him as living stones, a spiritual house that is being built into a holy priesthood. So offer spiritual sacrifices that God accepts through Jesus Christ. [6] That is why Scripture says,

        "I am laying a chosen and precious cornerstone in Zion,
           and the person who believes in him
              will never be ashamed."

[7] This honor belongs to those who believe. But to those who don't believe:

        "The stone that the builders rejected
           has become the cornerstone,

⁸   a stone that people trip over,
            a large rock that people find offensive."

The people tripped over the word because they refused to believe
it. Therefore, this is how they ended up.

⁹ However, you are chosen people, a royal priesthood, a holy
nation, people who belong to God. You were chosen to tell about
the excellent qualities of God, who called you out of darkness into
his marvelous light. ¹⁰ Once you were not God's people, but now
you are. Once you were not shown mercy, but now you have been
shown mercy.

¹¹ Dear friends, since you are foreigners and temporary residents
‚in the world‚, I'm encouraging you to keep away from the desires
of your corrupt nature. These desires constantly attack you. ¹² Live
decent lives among unbelievers. Then, although they ridicule you
as if you were doing wrong while they are watching you do good
things, they will praise God on the day he comes to help you.

Respect the Authority of Others

¹³ Place yourselves under the authority of human governments to
please the Lord. Obey the emperor. He holds the highest position
of authority. ¹⁴ Also obey governors. They are people the emperor
has sent to punish those who do wrong and to praise those who do
right. ¹⁵ God wants you to silence the ignorance of foolish people
by doing what is right. ¹⁶ Live as free people, but don't hide behind
your freedom when you do evil. Instead, use your freedom to serve
God. ¹⁷ Honor everyone. Love your brothers and sisters in the faith.
Fear God. Honor the emperor.

¹⁸ Slaves, place yourselves under the authority of your owners
and show them complete respect. Obey not only those owners who
are good and kind, but also those who are unfair. ¹⁹ God is pleased if
a person is aware of him while enduring the pains of unjust suffering. ²⁰ What credit do you deserve if you endure a beating for doing
something wrong? But if you endure suffering for doing something
good, God is pleased with you.

²¹ God called you to endure suffering because Christ suffered for you. He left you an example so that you could follow in his footsteps. ²² Christ never committed any sin. He never spoke deceitfully. ²³ Christ never verbally abused those who verbally abused him. When he suffered, he didn't make any threats but left everything to the one who judges fairly. ²⁴ Christ carried our sins in his body on the cross so that freed from our sins, we could live a life that has God's approval. His wounds have healed you. ²⁵ You were like lost sheep. Now you have come back to the shepherd and bishop*ᵃ* of your lives.

3 ¹ Wives, in a similar way, place yourselves under your husbands' authority. Some husbands may not obey God's word. Their wives could win these men [for Christ] by the way they live without saying anything. ² Their husbands would see how pure and reverent their lives are.

³ Wives must not let their beauty be something external. Beauty doesn't come from hairstyles, gold jewelry, or clothes. ⁴ Rather, beauty is something internal that can't be destroyed. Beauty expresses itself in a gentle and quiet attitude which God considers precious. ⁵ After all, this is how holy women who had confidence in God expressed their beauty in the past. They placed themselves under their husbands' authority ⁶ as Sarah did. Sarah obeyed Abraham and spoke to him respectfully. You became Sarah's daughters by not letting anything make you afraid to do good.

⁷ Husbands, in a similar way, live with your wives with understanding since they are weaker than you are. Honor your wives as those who share God's life-giving kindness*ᵃ* so that nothing will interfere with your prayers.

Dedicate Your Lives to Jesus

⁸ Finally, everyone must live in harmony, be sympathetic, love each other, have compassion, and be humble. ⁹ Don't pay people back with evil for the evil they do to you, or ridicule those who

---

ᵃ 2:25 English equivalent difficult.   *ᵃ* 3:7 Or "grace."

ridicule you. Instead, bless them, because you were called to inherit a blessing.

10 "People who want to live a full life and enjoy good days
         must keep their tongues from saying evil things,
             and their lips from speaking deceitful things.
11 They must turn away from evil and do good.
         They must seek peace and pursue it.
12 The Lord's eyes are on those who do what he approves.
         His ears hear their prayer.
         The Lord confronts those who do evil."

13 Who will harm you if you are devoted to doing what is good? 14 But even if you suffer for doing what God approves, you are blessed. Don't be afraid of those who want to harm you. Don't get upset. 15 But dedicate your lives to Christ as Lord. Always be ready to defend your confidence ⌊in God⌋ when anyone asks you to explain it. However, make your defense with gentleness and respect. 16 Keep your conscience clear. Then those who treat the good Christian life you live with contempt will feel ashamed that they have ridiculed you. 17 After all, if it is God's will, it's better to suffer for doing good than for doing wrong.

18 This is true because Christ suffered for our sins once. He was an innocent person, but he suffered for guilty people so that he could bring you to God. His body was put to death, but he was brought to life through his spirit. 19 In it he also went to proclaim his victory to the spirits kept in prison. 20 They are like those who disobeyed long ago in the days of Noah when God waited patiently while Noah built the ship. In this ship a few people—eight in all—were saved by water. 21 Baptism, which is like that water, now saves you. Baptism doesn't save by removing dirt from the body. Rather, baptism is a request to God for a clear conscience. It saves you through Jesus Christ, who came back from death to life. 22 Christ has gone to heaven where he has the highest position that God gives. Angels, rulers, and powers have been placed under his authority.

4 ¹ Since Christ has suffered physically, take the same attitude that he had. (A person who has suffered physically no longer sins.) ² That way you won't be guided by sinful human desires as you live the rest of your lives on earth. Instead, you will be guided by what God wants you to do. ³ You spent enough time in the past doing what unbelievers like to do. You were promiscuous, had sinful desires, got drunk, went to wild parties, and took part in the forbidden worship of false gods. ⁴ Unbelievers insult you now because they are surprised that you no longer join them in the same excesses of wild living. ⁵ They will give an account to the one who is ready to judge the living and the dead. ⁶ After all, the Good News was told to people like that, although they are now dead. It was told to them so that they could be judged like humans in their earthly lives and live like God in their spiritual lives.

⁷ The end of everything is near. Therefore, practice self-control, and keep your minds clear so that you can pray. ⁸ Above all, love each other warmly, because love covers many sins. ⁹ Welcome each other as guests without complaining. ¹⁰ Each of you as a good manager must use the gift that God has given you to serve others. ¹¹ Whoever speaks must speak God's words. Whoever serves must serve with the strength God supplies so that in every way God receives glory through Jesus Christ. Glory and power belong to Jesus Christ forever and ever! Amen.

Share Christ's Sufferings

¹² Dear friends, don't be surprised by the fiery troubles that are coming in order to test you. Don't feel as though something strange is happening to you, ¹³ but be happy as you share Christ's sufferings. Then you will also be full of joy when he appears again in his glory. ¹⁴ If you are insulted because of the name of Christ, you are blessed because the Spirit of glory—the Spirit of God—is resting on you.

¹⁵ If you suffer, you shouldn't suffer for being a murderer, thief, criminal, or troublemaker. ¹⁶ If you suffer for being a Christian,

don't feel ashamed, but praise God for being called that name.
[17] The time has come for the judgment to begin, and it will begin
with God's family. If it starts with us, what will be the end for those
who refuse to obey the Good News of God? [18] If it's hard for the
person who has God's approval to be saved, what will happen to
the godless sinner? [19] Those who suffer because that is God's will
for them must entrust themselves to a faithful creator and continue to do what is good.

Instructions for Spiritual Leaders

5 [1] I appeal to your spiritual leaders.[a] I make this appeal as a
spiritual leader who also witnessed Christ's sufferings and will
share in the glory that will be revealed. [2] Be shepherds over the
flock God has entrusted to you. Watch over it as God does: Don't
do this because you have to, but because you want to. Don't do it
out of greed, but out of a desire to serve. [3] Don't be rulers over the
people entrusted to you, but be examples for the flock to follow.
[4] Then, when the chief shepherd appears, you will receive the
crown of glory that will never fade away.

Instructions for Christians

[5] Young people, in a similar way, place yourselves under the
authority of spiritual leaders.

Furthermore, all of you must serve each other with humility,
because God opposes the arrogant but favors the humble. [6] Be
humbled by God's power so that when the right time comes he
will honor you.

[7] Turn all your anxiety over to God because he cares for you.
[8] Keep your mind clear, and be alert. Your opponent the devil is
prowling around like a roaring lion as he looks for someone to
devour. [9] Be firm in the faith and resist him, knowing that other
believers throughout the world are going through the same kind of
suffering. [10] God, who shows you his kindness[b] and who has called
you through Christ Jesus to his eternal glory, will restore you,

[a] 5:1 Or "pastors," or "elders."   [b] 5:10 Or "grace"

strengthen you, make you strong, and support you as you suffer for a little while. [11] Power belongs to him forever. Amen.

Farewell

[12] I've written this short letter to you and I'm sending it by Silvanus, whom I regard as a faithful brother. I've written to encourage you and to testify that this is God's genuine good will.[c] Remain firmly established in it!

[13] Your sister church in Babylon, chosen by God, and my son Mark send you greetings. [14] Greet each other with a kiss of love. Peace to all of you who are in Christ.

---

[c] 5:12 Or "grace."

2 PETER

Greeting

1 ¹ From Simon Peter, a servant and apostle of Jesus Christ.
To those who have obtained a faith that is as valuable as ours,
a faith based on the approval that comes from our God and
Savior, Jesus Christ.
² May good will[a] and peace fill your lives through your knowledge about Jesus, our God and Lord!

God's Power Gives Us the Ability to Live Godly Lives

³ God's divine power has given us everything we need for life
and for godliness. This power was given to us through knowledge of the one who called us by his own glory and integrity.
⁴ Through his glory and integrity he has given us his promises that
are of the highest value. Through these promises you will share
in the divine nature because you have escaped the corruption that
sinful desires cause in the world.

⁵ Because of this, make every effort to add integrity to your
faith; and to integrity add knowledge; ⁶ to knowledge add self-
control; to self-control add endurance; to endurance add godliness;
⁷ to godliness add Christian affection; and to Christian affection
add love. ⁸ If you have these qualities and they are increasing, it
demonstrates that your knowledge about our Lord Jesus Christ is
living and productive. ⁹ If these qualities aren't present in your life,
you're shortsighted and have forgotten that you were cleansed
from your past sins. ¹⁰ Therefore, brothers and sisters, use more
effort to make God's calling and choosing of you secure.

---

a 1:2 Or "grace."

If you keep doing this, you will never fall away. [11] Then you will also be given the wealth of entering into the eternal kingdom of our Lord and Savior Jesus Christ.

[12] Therefore, I will always remind you about these qualities, although you already know about them and are well-grounded in the truth that you now have. [13] As long as I'm still alive, I think it's right to refresh your memory. [14] I know that I will die soon. Our Lord Jesus Christ has made that clear to me. [15] So I will make every effort to see that you remember these things after I die.

Pay Attention to God's Words

[16] When we apostles told you about the powerful coming of our Lord Jesus Christ, we didn't base our message on clever myths that we made up. Rather, we witnessed his majesty with our own eyes. [17] For example, we were eyewitnesses when he received honor and glory from God the Father and when the voice of our majestic God spoke these words to him: "This is my Son, whom I love and in whom I delight." [18] We heard that voice speak to him from heaven when we were with him on the holy mountain. [19] So we regard the words of the prophets as confirmed beyond all doubt. You're doing well by paying attention to their words. Continue to pay attention as you would to a light that shines in a dark place as you wait for day to come and the morning star to rise in your hearts. [20] First, you must understand this: No prophecy in Scripture is a matter of one's own interpretation. [21] No prophecy ever originated from humans. Instead, it was given by the Holy Spirit as humans spoke under God's direction.

Warnings About False Teachers

2 [1] False prophets were among God's people ˌin the pastˌ, as false teachers will be among you. They will secretly bring in their own destructive teachings. They will deny the Lord, who has bought them, and they will bring themselves swift destruction. [2] Many people will follow them in their sexual freedom and will cause others to dishonor the way of truth. [3] In their greed they will use good-

sounding arguments to exploit you. The verdict against them from long ago is still in force, and their destruction is not asleep.

⁴ God didn't spare angels who sinned. He threw them into hell, where he has secured them with chains of darkness and is holding them for judgment.

⁵ God didn't spare the ancient world either. He brought the flood on the world of ungodly people, but he protected Noah and seven other people. Noah was his messenger who told people about the kind of life that has God's approval.

⁶ God condemned the cities of Sodom and Gomorrah and destroyed them by burning them to ashes. He made those cities an example to ungodly people of what is going to happen to them. ⁷ Yet, God rescued Lot, a man who had his approval. Lot was distressed by the lifestyle of people who had no principles and lived in sexual freedom. ⁸ Although he was a man who had God's approval, he lived among the people of Sodom and Gomorrah. Each day was like torture to him as he saw and heard the immoral things that people did.

⁹ Since the Lord did all this, he knows how to rescue godly people when they are tested. He also knows how to hold immoral people for punishment on the day of judgment. ¹⁰ This is especially true of those who follow their corrupt nature along the path of impure desires and who despise the Lord's authority.

These false teachers are bold and arrogant. They aren't afraid to insult the ˌLord'sˌ glory. ¹¹ Angels, who have more strength and power than these teachers, don't bring an insulting judgment against them from the Lord. ¹² These false teachers insult what they don't understand. They are like animals, which are creatures of instinct that are born to be caught and killed. So they will be destroyed like animals ¹³ and lose what their wrongdoing earned them.

These false teachers are stains and blemishes. They take pleasure in holding wild parties in broad daylight. They especially enjoy deceiving you while they eat with you. ¹⁴ They're always looking for an adulterous woman. They can't stop looking for sin as they seduce people who aren't sure of what they believe. Their minds are focused on their greed. They are cursed.

¹⁵ These false teachers have left the straight path and wandered off to follow the path of Balaam, son of Beor. Balaam loved what his wrongdoing earned him. ¹⁶ But he was convicted for his evil. A donkey, which normally can't talk, spoke with a human voice and wouldn't allow the prophet to continue his insanity.

¹⁷ These false teachers are dried-up springs. They are a mist blown around by a storm. Gloomy darkness has been kept for them. ¹⁸ They arrogantly use nonsense to seduce people by appealing to their sexual desires, especially to sexual freedom. They seduce people who have just escaped from those who live in error. ¹⁹ They promise these people freedom, but they themselves are slaves to corruption. A person is a slave to whatever he gives in to.

²⁰ People can know our Lord and Savior Jesus Christ and escape the world's filth. But if they get involved in this filth again and give in to it, they are worse off than they were before. ²¹ It would have been better for them never to have known the way of life that God approves of than to know it and turn their backs on the holy life God told them to live. ²² These proverbs have come true for them: "A dog goes back to its vomit," and "A sow that has been washed goes back to roll around in the mud."

Be Ready for the Day of the Lord

3 ¹ Dear friends, this is the second letter I'm writing to you. In both letters I'm trying to refresh your memory. ² I want you to remember the words spoken in the past by the holy prophets and what the Lord and Savior commanded you through your apostles.

³ First, you must understand this: In the last days people who follow their own desires will appear. These disrespectful people will ridicule ˌGod's promiseˌ ⁴ by saying, "What's happened to his promise to return? Ever since our ancestors died, everything continues as it did from the beginning of the world."

⁵ They are deliberately ignoring one fact: Because of God's word, heaven and earth existed a long time ago. The earth ˌappearedˌ out of water and was kept alive by water. ⁶ Water also flooded and destroyed that world. ⁷ By God's word, the present

heaven and earth are designated to be burned. They are being kept until the day ungodly people will be judged and destroyed.

⁸ Dear friends, don't ignore this fact: One day with the Lord is like a thousand years, and a thousand years are like one day. ⁹ The Lord isn't slow to do what he promised, as some people think. Rather, he is patient for your sake. He doesn't want to destroy anyone but wants all people to have an opportunity to turn to him and change the way they think and act.

¹⁰ The day of the Lord will come like a thief. On that day heaven will pass away with a roaring sound. Everything that makes up the universe will burn and be destroyed. The earth and everything that people have done on it will be exposed.ª

¹¹ All these things will be destroyed in this way. So think of the kind of holy and godly lives you must live ¹² as you look forward to the day of God and eagerly wait for it to come. When that day comes, heaven will be on fire and will be destroyed. Everything that makes up the universe will burn and melt. ¹³ But we look forward to what God has promised—a new heaven and a new earth—a place where everything that has God's approval lives.

¹⁴ Therefore, dear friends, with this to look forward to, make every effort to have him find you at peace, without ˌspiritualˌ stains or blemishes. ¹⁵ Think of our Lord's patience as an opportunity ˌfor usˌ to be saved. This is what our dear brother Paul wrote to you about, using the wisdom God gave him. ¹⁶ He talks about this subject in all his letters. Some things in his letters are hard to understand. Ignorant people and people who aren't sure of what they believe distort what Paul says in his letters the same way they distort the rest of the Scriptures. These people will be destroyed.

¹⁷ Dear friends, you already know these things. So be on your guard not to be carried away by the deception of people who have no principles. Then you won't fall from your firm position. ¹⁸ But grow in the good willᵇ and knowledge of our Lord and Savior Jesus Christ. Glory belongs to him now and for that eternal day! Amen.

ª 3:10 Some manuscripts and translations read "will be burned up."   ᵇ 3:18 Or "grace."

1 JOHN

John's Reason for Writing

1 ¹ The Word of life existed from the beginning. We have heard it. We have seen it. We observed and touched it. ² This life was revealed to us. We have seen it, and we testify about it. We are reporting to you about this eternal life that was in the presence of the Father and was revealed to us. ³ This is the life we have seen and heard. We are reporting about it to you also so that you, too, can have a relationship with us. Our relationship is with the Father and with his Son Jesus Christ. ⁴ We are writing this so that we can be completely filled with joy.

Through Jesus We Have a Relationship With God

⁵ This is the message we heard from Christ and are reporting to you: God is light, and there isn't any darkness in him. ⁶ If we say, "We have a relationship with God" and yet live in the dark, we're lying. We aren't being truthful.

⁷ But if we live in the light in the same way that God is in the light, we have a relationship with each other. And the blood of his Son Jesus cleanses us from every sin. ⁸ If we say, "We aren't sinful" we are deceiving ourselves, and the truth is not in us. ⁹ God is faithful and reliable. If we confess our sins, he forgives them and cleanses us from everything we've done wrong. ¹⁰ If we say, "We have never sinned," we turn God into a liar and his Word is not in us.

2 ¹ My dear children, I'm writing this to you so that you will not sin. Yet, if anyone does sin, we have Jesus Christ, who has God's full approval. He speaks on our behalf when we come into the presence of the Father. ² He is the payment for our sins, and not only for our sins, but also for the sins of the whole world.

Those Who Know Christ Obey His Commandments

³ We are sure that we know Christ if we obey his commandments. ⁴ The person who says, "I know him," but doesn't obey his commandments is a liar. The truth isn't in that person. ⁵ But whoever obeys what Christ says is the kind of person in whom God's love is perfected. That's how we know we are in Christ. ⁶ Those who say that they live in him must live the same way he lived.

⁷ Dear friends, it's not as though I'm writing to give you a new commandment. Rather, I'm giving you an old commandment that you've had from the beginning. It's the old commandment you've already heard. ⁸ On the other hand, I'm writing to give you a new commandment. It's a truth that exists in Christ and in you: The darkness is fading, and the true light is already shining.

⁹ Those who say that they are in the light but hate other believers are still in the dark. ¹⁰ Those who love other believers live in the light. Nothing will destroy the faith of those who live in the light. ¹¹ Those who hate other believers are in the dark and live in the dark. They don't know where they're going, because they can't see in the dark.

Don't Love the World

¹² I'm writing to you, dear children, because your sins are forgiven through Christ.

¹³ I'm writing to you, fathers, because you know Christ who has existed from the beginning.

I'm writing to you, young people, because you have won the victory over the evil one.

¹⁴ I've written to you, children, because you know the Father.

I've written to you, fathers, because you know Christ, who has existed from the beginning.

I've written to you, young people, because you are strong and God's word lives in you. You have won the victory over the evil one.

¹⁵ Don't love the world and what it offers. Those who love the world don't have the Father's love in them. ¹⁶ Not everything that

the world offers—physical gratification, greed, and extravagant lifestyles—comes from the Father. It comes from the world, and [17] the world and its evil desires are passing away. But the person who does what God wants lives forever.

Live in Christ

[18] Children, it's the end of time. You've heard that an antichrist is coming. Certainly, many antichrists are already here. That's how we know it's the end of time. [19] They left us. However, they were never really part of us. If they had been, they would have stayed with us. But by leaving they made it clear that none of them were part of us.

[20] The Holy One has anointed you, so all of you have knowledge. [21] I'm writing to you because you know the truth, not because you don't know the truth. You know that no lie ever comes from the truth.

[22] Who is a liar? Who else but the person who rejects Jesus as the Messiah? The person who rejects the Father and the Son is an antichrist. [23] Everyone who rejects the Son doesn't have the Father either. The person who acknowledges the Son also has the Father. [24] Make sure that the message you heard from the beginning lives in you. If that message lives in you, you will also live in the Son and in the Father. [25] Christ has given us the promise of eternal life.

[26] I'm writing to you about those who are trying to deceive you. [27] The anointing you received from Christ lives in you. You don't need anyone to teach you something else. Instead, Christ's anointing teaches you about everything. His anointing is true and contains no lie. So live in Christ as he taught you to do.

We Are God's Children

[28] Now, dear children, live in Christ. Then, when he appears we will have confidence, and when he comes we won't turn from him in shame. [29] If you know that Christ has God's approval, you also know that everyone who does what God approves of has been born from God.

3 [1] Consider this: The Father has given us his love. He loves us so much that we are actually called God's dear children. And that's what we are. For this reason the world doesn't recognize us, and it didn't recognize him either. ² Dear friends, now we are God's children. What we will be isn't completely clear yet. We do know that when Christ appears we will be like him because we will see him as he is. ³ So all people who have this confidence in Christ keep themselves pure, as Christ is pure.

⁴ Those who live sinful lives are disobeying God. Sin is disobedience. ⁵ You know that Christ appeared in order to take away our sins. He isn't sinful. ⁶ Those who live in Christ don't go on sinning. Those who go on sinning haven't seen or known Christ.

⁷ Dear children, don't let anyone deceive you. Whoever does what God approves of has God's approval as Christ has God's approval. ⁸ The person who lives a sinful life belongs to the devil, because the devil has been committing sin since the beginning. The reason that the Son of God appeared was to destroy what the devil does. ⁹ Those who have been born from God don't live sinful lives. What God has said lives in them, and they can't live sinful lives. They have been born from God. ¹⁰ This is the way God's children are distinguished from the devil's children. Everyone who doesn't do what is right or love other believers isn't God's child.

Love One Another

¹¹ The message that you have heard from the beginning is to love each other. ¹² Don't be like Cain. He was a child of the evil one and murdered his brother. And why did Cain murder his brother? Because the things Cain did were evil and the things his brother did had God's approval. ¹³ Brothers and sisters, don't be surprised if the world hates you.

¹⁴ We know that we have passed from death to life, because we love other believers. The person who doesn't grow in love remains in death. ¹⁵ Everyone who hates another believer is a murderer, and you know that a murderer doesn't have eternal life.

¹⁶ We understand what love is when we realize that Christ gave his life for us. That means we must give our lives for other believers. ¹⁷ Now, suppose a person has enough to live on and notices another believer in need. How can God's love be in that person if he doesn't bother to help the other believer? ¹⁸ Dear children,

we must show love through actions that are sincere, not through empty words.

¹⁹ This is how we will know that we belong to the truth and how we will be reassured in his presence. ²⁰ Whenever our conscience condemns us, we will be reassured that God is greater than our conscience and knows everything. ²¹ Dear friends, if our conscience doesn't condemn us, we can boldly look to God ²² and receive from him anything we ask. We receive it because we obey his commandments and do what pleases him. ²³ This is his commandment: to believe in his Son, the one named Jesus Christ, and to love each other as he commanded us. ²⁴ Those who obey Christ's commandments live in God, and God lives in them. We know that he lives in us because he has given us the Spirit.

Test People Who Say They Have God's Spirit

4 ¹ Dear friends, don't believe all people who say that they have the Spirit. Instead, test them. See whether the spirit they have is from God, because there are many false prophets in the world. ² This is how you can recognize God's Spirit: Every person who declares that Jesus Christ has come as a human has the Spirit that is from God. ³ But every person who doesn't declare that Jesus Christ has come as a human has a spirit that isn't from God. This is the spirit of the antichrist that you have heard is coming. That spirit is already in the world.

⁴ Dear children, you belong to God. So you have won the victory over these people, because the one who is in you is greater than the one who is in the world. ⁵ These people belong to the world. That's why they speak the thoughts of the world, and the world listens to them. ⁶ We belong to God. The person who knows God listens to us. Whoever doesn't belong to God doesn't listen to us. That's how we can tell the Spirit of truth from the spirit of lies.

God's Love Lives in His People

⁷ Dear friends, we must love each other because love comes from God. Everyone who loves has been born from God and knows God. ⁸ The person who doesn't love doesn't know God,

because God is love. [9] God has shown us his love by sending his only Son into the world so that we could have life through him. [10] This is love: not that we have loved God, but that he loved us and sent his Son to be the payment for our sins. [11] Dear friends, if this is the way God loved us, we must also love each other. [12] No one has ever seen God. If we love each other, God lives in us, and his love is perfected in us. [13] We know that we live in him and he lives in us because he has given us his Spirit.

[14] We have seen and testify to the fact that the Father sent his Son as the Savior of the world. [15] God lives in those who declare that Jesus is the Son of God, and they live in God. [16] We have known and believed that God loves us. God is love. Those who live in God's love live in God, and God lives in them.

[17] God's love has reached its goal in us. So we look ahead with confidence to the day of judgment. While we are in this world, we are exactly like him ₍with regard to love₎. [18] No fear exists where his love is. Rather, perfect love gets rid of fear, because fear involves punishment. The person who lives in fear doesn't have perfect love.

[19] We love because God loved us first. [20] Whoever says, "I love God," but hates another believer is a liar. People who don't love other believers, whom they have seen, can't love God, whom they have not seen. [21] Christ has given us this commandment: The person who loves God must also love other believers.

Those Who Believe in Jesus Are God's Children

5 [1] Everyone who believes that Jesus is the Messiah has been born from God. Everyone who loves the Father also loves his children. [2] We know that we love God's children when we love God by obeying his commandments. [3] To love God means that we obey his commandments. Obeying his commandments isn't difficult [4] because everyone who has been born from God has won the victory over the world. Our faith is what wins the victory over the world. [5] Who wins the victory over the world? Isn't it the person who believes that Jesus is the Son of God?

[6] This Son of God is Jesus Christ, who came by water and blood. He didn't come with water only, but with water and with

blood. The Spirit is the one who verifies this, because the Spirit is the truth. [7] There are three witnesses:[a] [8] the Spirit, the water, and the blood. These three witnesses agree.

[9] We accept human testimony. God's testimony is greater because it is the testimony that he has given about his Son. [10] Those who believe in the Son of God have the testimony of God in them. Those who don't believe God have made God a liar. They haven't believed the testimony that God has given about his Son.

[11] This is the testimony: God has given us eternal life, and this life is found in his Son. [12] The person who has the Son has this life. The person who doesn't have the Son of God doesn't have this life.

Conclusion

[13] I've written this to those who believe in the Son of God so that they will know that they have eternal life.

[14] We are confident that God listens to us if we ask for anything that has his approval. [15] We know that he listens to our requests. So we know that we already have what we ask him for.

[16] If you see another believer committing a sin that doesn't lead to death, you should pray that God would give that person life. This is true for those who commit sins that don't lead to death. There is a sin that leads to death. I'm not telling you to pray about that. [17] Every kind of wrongdoing is sin, yet there are sins that don't lead to death.

[18] We know that those who have been born from God don't go on sinning. Rather, the Son of God protects them, and the evil one can't harm them.

[19] We know that we are from God, and that the whole world is under the control of the evil one.

[20] We know that the Son of God has come and has given us understanding so that we know the real God. We are in the one who is real, his Son Jesus Christ. This Jesus Christ is the real God and eternal life.

[21] Dear children, guard yourselves from false gods.

---

[a] 5:7 Four very late manuscripts add verses 7b–8a: "in heaven: the Father, the Word, and the Holy Spirit. These three witnesses agree. And there are three witnesses on earth:"

2 JOHN

Greeting

¹ From the church leader.ᵃ

To the chosen lady and her children, whom I love because we share the truth. I'm not the only one who loves you. Everyone who knows the truth also loves you. ² We love you because of the truth which lives in us and will be with us forever.

³ Good will,ᵇ mercy, and peace will be with us. They come from God the Father and from Jesus Christ, who in truth and love is the Father's Son.

Living in the Truth

⁴ I was very happy to find some of your children living in the truth as the Father has commanded us. ⁵ Dear lady, I'm now requesting that we continue to love each other. It's not as though I'm writing to give you a new commandment. Rather, from the beginning we were commanded to love each other. ⁶ Love means that we live by doing what he commands. We were commanded to live in love, and you have heard this from the beginning.

Reject Teachers Who Don't Teach What Christ Taught

⁷ Many people who deceive others have gone into the world. They refuse to declare that Jesus Christ came in flesh and blood. This is the mark of a deceiver and an antichrist. ⁸ Be careful that you don't destroy what we've worked for, but that you receive your full reward.

ᵃ 1 Or "pastor," or "elder."   ᵇ 3 Or "Grace."

[9] Everyone who doesn't continue to teach what Christ taught doesn't have God. The person who continues to teach what Christ taught has both the Father and the Son. [10] If anyone comes to you and doesn't bring these teachings, don't take him into your home or even greet him. [11] Whoever greets him shares the evil things he's doing.

Farewell

[12] I have a lot to write to you. I would prefer not to write a letter. Instead, I hope to visit and talk things over with you personally. Then we will be completely filled with joy.

[13] The children of your chosen sister greet you.

3 JOHN

Greeting

¹ From the church leader.[a]

To my dear friend Gaius, whom I love because we share the truth.

Encouragement for Gaius

² Dear friend, I know that you are spiritually well. I pray that you're doing well in every other way and that you're healthy. ³ I was very happy when some believers came and told us that you are living according to the truth. ⁴ Nothing makes me happier than to hear that my children are living according to the truth.

⁵ Dear friend, you are showing your faith in whatever you do for other believers, especially when they're your guests. ⁶ These believers have told the congregation about your love. You will do well to support them on their trip in a way that proves you belong to God. ⁷ After all, they went on their trip to serve the one named Christ, and they didn't accept any help from the people to whom they went. ⁸ We must support believers who go on trips like this so that we can work together with them in spreading the truth.

Criticism of Diotrephes

⁹ I wrote a letter to the congregation. But Diotrephes, who loves to be in charge, won't accept us. ¹⁰ For this reason, when I come I will bring up what he's doing. He's not satisfied with saying malicious things about us. He also refuses to accept the believers ₍we send₎ as guests. He even tries to stop others who

---

[a] 1 Or "pastor," or "elder."

want to accept them and attempts to throw those people out of the congregation.

Praise for Demetrius

[11] Dear friend, never imitate evil, but imitate good. The person who does good is from God. The person who does evil has never seen God.

[12] Everyone, including the truth itself, says good things about Demetrius. We also say good things about him, and you know that what we say is true.

Farewell

[13] I have a lot to write to you. However, I would rather not write. [14] I hope to visit you very soon. Then we can talk things over personally.

[15] Peace be with you! Your friends here send you their greetings. Greet each of our friends by name.

JUDE

Greeting

¹ From Jude, a servant of Jesus Christ and brother of James.

To those who have been called, who are loved by God the Father, and who are kept safe for Jesus Christ.

² May mercy, peace, and love fill your lives!

Warnings About False Teachers

³ Dear friends, I had intended to write to you about the salvation we share. But something has come up. It demands that I write to you and encourage you to continue your fight for the Christian faith that was entrusted to God's holy people once for all time.

⁴ Some people have slipped in among you unnoticed. Not long ago they were condemned in writing for the following reason: They are people to whom God means nothing. They use God's kindness*a* as an excuse for sexual freedom and deny our only Master and Lord, Jesus Christ.

⁵ I want to remind you about what you already know: The Lord once saved his people from Egypt. But on another occasion he destroyed those who didn't believe. ⁶ He held angels for judgment on the great day. They were held in darkness, bound by eternal chains. These are the angels who didn't keep their position of authority but abandoned their assigned place. ⁷ What happened to Sodom and Gomorrah and the cities near them is an example for us of the punishment of eternal fire. The people of these cities suffered the same fate that God's people and the angels did, because they committed sexual sins and engaged in homosexual activities.

---

a 4 Or "grace."

⁸ Yet, in a similar way, the people who slipped in among you are dreamers. They contaminate their bodies with sin, reject the Lord's authority, and insult his glory. ⁹ When the archangel Michael argued with the devil, they were arguing over the body of Moses. But Michael didn't dare to hand down a judgment against the devil. Instead, Michael said, "May the Lord reprimand you!"

¹⁰ Whatever these people don't understand, they insult. Like animals, which are creatures of instinct, they use whatever they know to destroy themselves. ¹¹ How horrible it will be for them! They have followed the path of Cain. They have rushed into Balaam's error to make a profit. They have rebelled like Korah and destroyed themselves.

¹² These people are a disgrace at the special meals you share with other believers. They eat with you and don't feel ashamed. They are shepherds who care ⌊only⌋ for themselves. They are dry clouds blown around by the winds. They are withered, uprooted trees without any fruit. As a result, they have died twice. ¹³ Their shame is like the foam on the wild waves of the sea. They are wandering stars for whom gloomy darkness is kept forever.

¹⁴ Furthermore, Enoch, from the seventh generation after Adam, prophesied about them. He said, "The Lord has come with countless thousands of his holy angels. ¹⁵ He has come to judge all these people. He has come to convict all these ungodly sinners for all the ungodly things they have done and all the harsh things they have said about him."

¹⁶ These people complain, find fault, follow their own desires, say arrogant things, and flatter people in order to take advantage of them.

¹⁷ Dear friends, remember what the apostles of our Lord Jesus Christ told you to expect: ¹⁸ "In the last times people who ridicule ⌊God⌋ will appear. They will follow their own ungodly desires." ¹⁹ These are the people who cause divisions. They are concerned about physical things, not spiritual things.

Final Advice

20 Dear friends, use your most holy faith to grow. Pray with the Holy Spirit's help. **21** Remain in God's love as you look for the mercy of our Lord Jesus Christ to give you eternal life.

22 Show mercy to those who have doubts. **23** Save others by snatching them from the fire ⌊of hell⌋. Show mercy to others, even though you are afraid that you might be stained by their sinful lives.

24 God can guard you so that you don't fall and so that you can be full of joy as you stand in his glorious presence without fault. **25** Before time began, now, and for eternity glory, majesty, power, and authority belong to the only God, our Savior, through Jesus Christ our Lord. Amen.

REVELATION

The Revelation of Jesus Christ to the Seven Churches

1 ¹ This is the revelation of Jesus Christ. God gave it to him to show his servants the things that must happen soon. He sent this revelation through his angel to his servant John. ² John testified about what he saw: God's word and the testimony about Jesus Christ. ³ Blessed is the one who reads, as well as those who hear the words of this prophecy and pay attention to what is written in it because the time is near.

⁴ From John to the seven churches in the province of Asia. Good will*a* and peace to you from the one who is, the one who was, and the one who is coming, from the seven spirits who are in front of his throne, ⁵ and from Jesus Christ, the witness, the trustworthy one, the first to come back to life, and the ruler over the kings of the earth. Glory and power forever and ever*b* belong to the one who loves us and has freed us from our sins by his blood ⁶ and has made us a kingdom, priests for God his Father. Amen.

⁷   Look! He is coming in the clouds.
        Every eye will see him,
            even those who pierced him.
        Every tribe on earth will mourn because of him.
        This is true. Amen.

⁸ "I am the A and the Z,"*c* says the Lord God, the one who is, the one who was, and the one who is coming, the Almighty.

---

a 1:4 Or "Grace."   *b* 1:5 The last part of verse 6 (in Greek) has been moved to verse 5 to express the complex Greek sentence structure more clearly in English.
c 1:8 Or "the Alpha and the Omega."

[9] I am John, your brother. I share your suffering, ruling, and endurance because of Jesus. I was ₍exiled₎ on the island of Patmos because of God's word and the testimony about Jesus. [10] I came under the Spirit's power on the Lord's day. I heard a loud voice behind me like a trumpet, [11] saying, "Write on a scroll what you see, and send it to the seven churches: Ephesus, Smyrna, Pergamum, Thyatira, Sardis, Philadelphia, and Laodicea."

[12] I turned toward the voice which was talking to me, and when I turned, I saw seven gold lamp stands. [13] There was someone like the Son of Man among the lamp stands. He was wearing a robe that reached his feet. He wore a gold belt around his waist. [14] His head and his hair were white like wool—like snow. His eyes were like flames of fire. [15] His feet were like glowing bronze refined in a furnace. His voice was like the sound of raging waters. [16] In his right hand he held seven stars, and out of his mouth came a sharp, two-edged sword. His face was like the sun when it shines in all its brightness.

[17] When I saw him, I fell down at his feet like a dead man. Then he laid his right hand on me and said, "Don't be afraid! I am the first and the last, [18] the living one. I was dead, but now I am alive forever. I have the keys of death and hell. [19] Therefore, write down what you have seen, what is, and what is going to happen after these things. [20] The hidden meaning of the seven stars that you saw in my right hand and the seven gold lamp stands is this: The seven stars are the messengers of the seven churches, and the seven lamp stands are the seven churches.

A Letter to the Church in Ephesus

2 [1] "To the messenger of the church in Ephesus, write:

The one who holds the seven stars in his right hand, the one who walks among the seven gold lamp stands, says: [2] I know what you have done—how hard you have worked and how you have endured. I also know that you cannot tolerate wicked people. You have tested those who call themselves apostles but are not apostles. You have discovered that they are liars. [3] You have endured, suffered trouble because of my name, and have not grown weary. ⁴ However, I have this against you: The love you had at first is gone. ⁵ Remember how far you have fallen. Return to me and change the way you think and act, and do what you did at first. I will come to you and take your lamp stand from its place if you don't change. ⁶ But you have this in your favor—you hate what the Nicolaitans are doing. I also hate what they're doing.

⁷ "Let the person who has ears listen to what the Spirit says to the churches. I will give the privilege of eating from the tree of life, which stands in the paradise of God, to everyone who wins the victory.

A Letter to the Church in Smyrna

⁸ "To the messenger of the church in Smyrna, write:

The first and the last, who was dead and became alive, says: ⁹ I know how you are suffering, how poor you are—but you are rich. I also know that those who claim to be Jews slander you. They are the synagogue of Satan. ¹⁰ Don't be afraid of what you are going to suffer. The devil is going to throw some of you into prison so that you may be tested. Your suffering will go on for ten days. Be faithful until death, and I will give you the crown of life.

¹¹ Let the person who has ears listen to what the Spirit says to the churches. Everyone who wins the victory will never be hurt by the second death.

A Letter to the Church in Pergamum

¹² "To the messenger of the church in Pergamum, write:

The one who holds the sharp two-edged sword says: ¹³ I know where you live. Satan's throne is there. You hold on to my name and have not denied your belief in me, even in the days of Antipas. He was my faithful witness who was killed in your presence, where Satan lives. ¹⁴ But I have a few things against you: You have among you those who follow what Balaam taught Balak. Balak trapped the people of Israel by ⌊encouraging⌋ them to eat food sacrificed to idols and to sin sexually. [15] You also have some who follow what the Nicolaitans teach. [16] So return to me and change the way you think and act, or I will come to you quickly and wage war against them with the sword from my mouth.

[17] Let the person who has ears listen to what the Spirit says to the churches. I will give some of the hidden manna to everyone who wins the victory. I will also give each person a white stone with a new name written on it, a name that is known only to the person who receives it.

A Letter to the Church in Thyatira

[18] "To the messenger of the church in Thyatira, write:

The Son of God, whose eyes are like flames of fire and whose feet are like glowing bronze, says: [19] I know what you do. I know your love, faith, service, and endurance. I also know that what you are doing now is greater than what you did at first. [20] But I have something against you: You tolerate that woman Jezebel, who calls herself a prophet. She teaches and misleads my servants to sin sexually and to eat food sacrificed to idols. [21] I gave her time to turn to me and change the way she thinks and acts, but she refuses to turn away from her sexual sins. [22] Watch me! I'm going to throw her into a sickbed. Those who commit sexual sins with her will also suffer a lot, unless they turn away from what she is doing. [23] I will kill her children. Then all the churches will know that I am the one who searches hearts and minds. I will reward each of you for what you have done. [24] But the rest of you in Thyatira—all who don't hold on to Jezebel's teaching, who haven't learned what are called the deep things of Satan—I won't burden you with anything else. [25] Just hold on to what you have until I come.

[26] I have received authority from my Father.[a] I will give authority over the nations to everyone who wins the victory and continues to do what I want until the end. [27] Those people will

---

[a] 2:26 The first part of verse 28 (in Greek) has been moved to the beginning of verse 26 to express the complex Greek sentence structure more clearly in English.

rule the nations with iron scepters and shatter them like pottery. [28] I will also give them the morning star. [29] Let the person who has ears listen to what the Spirit says to the churches.

A Letter to the Church in Sardis

3 [1] "To the messenger of the church in Sardis, write:

The one who has God's seven spirits and the seven stars says: I know what you have done. You are known for being alive, but you are dead. [2] Be alert, and strengthen the things that are left which are about to die. I have found that what you are doing has not been completed in the sight of my God. [3] So remember what you received and heard. Obey, and change the way you think and act. If you're not alert, I'll come like a thief. You don't know when I will come. [4] But you have a few people in Sardis who have kept their clothes clean. They will walk with me in white clothes because they deserve it.

[5] Everyone who wins the victory this way will wear white clothes. I will never erase their names from the Book of Life. I will acknowledge them in the presence of my Father and his angels. [6] Let the person who has ears listen to what the Spirit says to the churches.

A Letter to the Church in Philadelphia

[7] "To the messenger of the church in Philadelphia, write:

The one who is holy, who is true, who has the key of David, who opens ˌa doorˌ that no one can shut, and who shuts ˌa doorˌ that no one can open, says: [8] I know what you have done. See, I have opened a door in front of you that no one can shut. You only have a little strength, but you have paid attention to my word and have not denied my name. [9] I will make those who are in Satan's synagogue come and bow at your feet and realize that I have loved you. They claim that they are Jewish, but they are lying. [10] Because you have obeyed my command to endure, I will keep you safe during the time of testing which is coming to the whole world to test those living on earth. [11] I am coming soon! Hold on to what you have so that no one takes your crown.

[12] I will make everyone who wins the victory a pillar in the temple of my God. They will never leave it again. I will write on them the name of my God, the name of the city of my God (the New Jerusalem coming down out of heaven from my God), and my new name. [13] Let the person who has ears listen to what the Spirit says to the churches.

A Letter to the Church in Laodicea

[14] "To the messenger of the church in Laodicea, write:

The amen, the witness who is faithful and true, the source of God's creation, says: [15] I know what you have done, that you are neither cold nor hot. I wish you were cold or hot. [16] But since you are lukewarm and not hot or cold, I'm going to spit you out of my mouth. [17] You say, 'I'm rich. I'm wealthy. I don't need anything.' Yet, you do not realize that you are miserable, pitiful, poor, blind, and naked. [18] I advise you: Buy gold purified in fire from me so that you may be rich. Buy white clothes from me. Wear them so that you may keep your shameful, naked body from showing. Buy ointment to put on your eyes so that you may see. [19] I correct and discipline everyone I love. Take this seriously, and change the way you think and act. [20] Look, I'm standing at the door and knocking. If anyone listens to my voice and opens the door, I'll come in and we'll eat together.

[21] I will allow everyone who wins the victory to sit with me on my throne, as I have won the victory and have sat down with my Father on his throne. [22] Let the person who has ears listen to what the Spirit says to the churches."

A Vision of God's Throne in Heaven

4 [1] After these things I saw a door standing open in heaven. I heard the first voice like a trumpet speaking to me. It said, "Come up here, and I will show you what must happen after this."

² Instantly, I came under the Spirit's power. I saw a throne in heaven, and someone was sitting on it. ³ The one sitting there looked like gray quartz and red quartz. There was a rainbow around the throne which looked like an emerald.

⁴ Around that throne were 24 other thrones, and on these thrones sat 24 leaders wearing white clothes. They had gold crowns on their heads. ⁵ Lightning, noise, and thunder came from the throne. Seven flaming torches were burning in front of the throne. These are the seven spirits of God.

⁶ In front of the throne, there was something like a sea of glass as clear as crystal. In the center near the throne and around the throne were four living creatures covered with eyes in front and in back. ⁷ The first living creature was like a lion, the second was like a young bull, the third had a face like a human, and the fourth was like a flying eagle. ⁸ Each of the four living creatures had six wings and were covered with eyes, inside and out. Without stopping day or night they were singing,

> "Holy, holy, holy is the Lord God Almighty,
>   who was, who is, and who is coming."

⁹ Whenever the living creatures give glory, honor, and thanks to the one who sits on the throne, to the one who lives forever and ever, ¹⁰ the 24 leaders bow in front of the one who sits on the throne and worship the one who lives forever and ever. They place their crowns in front of the throne and say,

¹¹   "Our Lord and God, you deserve to receive glory, honor,
            and power because you created everything.
        Everything came into existence and was created because
            of your will."

The Lamb Takes the Scroll That Has Seven Seals

5 ¹ I saw a scroll in the right hand of the one who sits on the throne. It had writing both on the inside and on the outside. It was sealed with seven seals. ² I saw a powerful angel calling out

in a loud voice, "Who deserves to open the scroll and break the seals on it?" ³ No one in heaven, on earth, or under the earth could open the scroll or look inside it. ⁴ I cried bitterly because no one was found who deserved to open the scroll or look inside it.

⁵ Then one of the leaders said to me, "Stop crying! The Lion from the tribe of Judah, the Root of David, has won the victory. He can open the scroll and the seven seals on it."

⁶ I saw a lamb standing in the center near the throne with the four living creatures and the leaders. The lamb looked like he had been slaughtered. He had seven horns and seven eyes, which are the seven spirits of God sent all over the world. ⁷ He took the scroll from the right hand of the one who sits on the throne.

⁸ When the lamb had taken the scroll, the four living creatures and the 24 leaders bowed in front of him. Each held a harp and a gold bowl full of incense, the prayers of God's holy people. ⁹ Then they sang a new song,

> "You deserve to take the scroll and open the seals on it,
>   because you were slaughtered.
> You bought people with your blood to be God's own.
>   They are from every tribe, language, people, and nation.
> 10 You made them a kingdom and priests for our God.
>   They will rule as kings on the earth."

¹¹ Then I heard the voices of many angels, the four living creatures, and the leaders surrounding the throne. They numbered ten thousand times ten thousand and thousands times thousands. ¹² In a loud voice they were singing,

> "The lamb who was slain deserves to receive
>   power, wealth, wisdom, strength, honor, glory,
>   and praise."

¹³ I heard every creature in heaven, on earth, under the earth, and on the sea. Every creature in those places was singing,

> "To the one who sits on the throne and to the lamb
>   be praise, honor, glory, and power forever and ever."

¹⁴ The four living creatures said, "Amen!" Then the leaders bowed and worshiped.

The Lamb Opens the First Six Seals

6 ¹ I watched as the lamb opened the first of the seven seals. I heard one of the four living creatures say with a voice like thunder, "Go!" ² Then I looked, and there was a white horse, and its rider had a bow. He was given a crown and rode off as a warrior to win battles.

³ When the lamb opened the second seal, I heard the second living creature say, "Go!" ⁴ A second horse went out. It was fiery red. Its rider was given the power to take peace away from the earth and to make people slaughter one another. So he was given a large sword.

⁵ When the lamb opened the third seal, I heard the third living creature say, "Go!" I looked, and there was a black horse, and its rider held a scale. ⁶ I heard what sounded like a voice from among the four living creatures, saying, "A quart of wheat for a day's pay or three quarts of barley for a day's pay. But do not damage the olive oil and the wine."

⁷ When the lamb opened the fourth seal, I heard the voice of the fourth living creature say, "Go!" ⁸ I looked, and there was a pale horse, and its rider's name was Death. Hell followed him. They were given power over one-fourth of the earth to kill people using wars, famines, plagues, and the wild animals on the earth.

⁹ When the lamb opened the fifth seal, I saw under the altar the souls of those who had been slaughtered because of God's word and the testimony they had given about him. ¹⁰ They cried out in a loud voice, "Holy and true Master, how long before you judge and take revenge on those living on earth who shed our blood?" ¹¹ Each of the souls was given a white robe. They were told to rest a little longer until all their coworkers, the other Christians, would be killed as they had been killed.

¹² I watched as the lamb opened the sixth seal. A powerful earthquake struck. The sun turned as black as sackcloth made of hair.

The full moon turned as red as blood. [13] The stars fell from the sky to the earth like figs dropping from a fig tree when it is shaken by a strong wind. [14] The sky vanished like a scroll being rolled up. Every mountain and island was moved from its place. [15] Then the kings of the earth, the important people, the generals, the rich, the powerful, and all the slaves and free people hid themselves in caves and among the rocks in the mountains. [16] They said to the mountains and rocks, "Fall on us, and hide us from the face of the one who sits on the throne and from the anger of the lamb, [17] because the frightening day of their anger has come, and who is able to endure it?"

144,000 People Are Sealed

7 [1] After this I saw four angels standing at the four corners of the earth. They were holding back the four winds of the earth to keep them from blowing on the land, the sea, or any tree. [2] I saw another angel coming from the east with the seal of the living God. He cried out in a loud voice to the four angels who had been allowed to harm the land and sea, [3] "Don't harm the land, the sea, or the trees until we have put the seal on the foreheads of the servants of our God."

[4] I heard how many were sealed: 144,000. Those who were sealed were from every tribe of the people of Israel:

[5]   12,000 from the tribe of Judah were sealed,
       12,000 from the tribe of Reuben,
       12,000 from the tribe of Gad,
[6]   12,000 from the tribe of Asher,
       12,000 from the tribe of Naphtali,
       12,000 from the tribe of Manasseh,
[7]   12,000 from the tribe of Simeon,
       12,000 from the tribe of Levi,
       12,000 from the tribe of Issachar,
[8]   12,000 from the tribe of Zebulun,
       12,000 from the tribe of Joseph,
       12,000 from the tribe of Benjamin were sealed.

God's People Around His Throne in Heaven

⁹ After these things I saw a large crowd from every nation, tribe, people, and language. No one was able to count how many people there were. They were standing in front of the throne and the lamb. They were wearing white robes, holding palm branches in their hands, ¹⁰ and crying out in a loud voice, "Salvation belongs to our God, who sits on the throne, and to the lamb!"

¹¹ All the angels stood around the throne with the leaders and the four living creatures. They bowed in front of the throne with their faces touching the ground, worshiped God, ¹² and said,

> "Amen! Praise, glory, wisdom, thanks, honor, power,
>   and strength
> be to our God forever and ever! Amen!"

¹³ One of the leaders asked me, "Who are these people wearing white robes, and where did they come from?"

¹⁴ I answered him, "Sir, you know."

Then he told me,

> "These are the people who are coming out
>   of the terrible suffering.
> They have washed their robes
>   and made them white in the blood of the lamb.
> ¹⁵   That is why they are in front of the throne of God.
>   They serve him day and night in his temple.
>   The one who sits on the throne will spread his tent
>   over them.
> ¹⁶   They will never be hungry or thirsty again.
>   Neither the sun nor any burning heat
>   will ever overcome them.
> ¹⁷   The lamb in the center near the throne will be
>   their shepherd.
>   He will lead them to springs filled with the water of life,
>   and God will wipe every tear from their eyes."

The Lamb Opens the Seventh Seal

8 ¹ When he opened the seventh seal, there was silence in heaven for about half an hour.

Seven Angels With Seven Trumpets

² Then I saw the seven angels who stand in God's presence, and they were given seven trumpets. ³ Another angel came with a gold incense burner and stood at the altar. He was given a lot of incense to offer on the gold altar in front of the throne. He offered it with the prayers of all of God's people. ⁴ The smoke from the incense went up from the angel's hand to God along with the prayers of God's people. ⁵ The angel took the incense burner, filled it with fire from the altar, and threw it on the earth. Then there was thunder, noise, lightning, and an earthquake.

⁶ The seven angels who had the seven trumpets got ready to blow them.

The First Four Angels Blow Their Trumpets

⁷ When the first angel blew his trumpet, hail and fire were mixed with blood, and were thrown on the earth. One-third of the earth was burned up, one-third of the trees were burned up, and all the green grass was burned up.

⁸ When the second angel blew his trumpet, something like a huge mountain burning with fire was thrown into the sea. One-third of the sea turned into blood, ⁹ one-third of the creatures that were living in the sea died, and one-third of the ships were destroyed.

¹⁰ When the third angel blew his trumpet, a huge star flaming like a torch fell from the sky. It fell on one-third of the rivers and on the springs. ¹¹ That star was named Wormwood. One-third of the water turned into wormwood, and many people died from this water because it had turned bitter.

¹² When the fourth angel blew his trumpet, one-third of the sun, one-third of the moon, and one-third of the stars were struck so that one-third of them turned dark. There was no light for one-third of the day and one-third of the night.

¹³ I saw an eagle flying overhead, and I heard it say in a loud voice, "Catastrophe, catastrophe, catastrophe for those living on earth, because of the remaining trumpet blasts which the three angels are about to blow."

The Fifth and Sixth Angels Blow Their Trumpets

9 ¹ When the fifth angel blew his trumpet, I saw a star that had fallen to earth from the sky. The star was given the key to the shaft of the bottomless pit. ² It opened the shaft of the bottomless pit, and smoke came out of the shaft like the smoke from a large furnace. The smoke darkened the sun and the air. ³ Locusts came out of the smoke onto the earth, and they were given power like the power of earthly scorpions. ⁴ They were told not to harm any grass, green plant, or tree on the earth. They could harm only the people who do not have the seal of God on their foreheads. ⁵ They were not allowed to kill them. They were only allowed to torture them for five months. Their torture was like the pain of a scorpion's sting. ⁶ At that time people will look for death and never find it. They will long to die, but death will escape them.

⁷ The locusts looked like horses prepared for battle. They seemed to have crowns that looked like gold on their heads. Their faces were like human faces. ⁸ They had hair like women's hair and teeth like lions' teeth. ⁹ They had breastplates like iron. The noise from their wings was like the roar of chariots with many horses rushing into battle. ¹⁰ They had tails and stingers like scorpions. They had the power to hurt people with their tails for five months. ¹¹ The king who ruled them was the angel from the bottomless pit. In Hebrew he is called Abaddon, and in Greek he is called Apollyon.

¹² The first catastrophe is over. After these things there are two more catastrophes yet to come.

¹³ When the sixth angel blew his trumpet, I heard a voice from the four horns of the gold altar in front of God. ¹⁴ The voice said to the sixth angel who had the trumpet, "Release the four angels who are held at the great Euphrates River." ¹⁵ The four angels who were ready for that hour, day, month, and year were released to

kill one-third of humanity. ¹⁶ The soldiers on horses numbered 20,000 times 10,000. I heard how many there were.

¹⁷ In the vision that I had, the horses and their riders looked like this: The riders had breastplates that were fiery red, pale blue, and yellow. The horses had heads like lions. Fire, smoke, and sulfur came out of their mouths. ¹⁸ These three plagues—the fire, smoke, and sulfur which came out of their mouths—killed one-third of humanity. ¹⁹ The power of these horses is in their mouths and their tails. (Their tails have heads like snakes which they use to hurt people.)

²⁰ The people who survived these plagues still did not turn to me and change the way they were thinking and acting. If they had, they would have stopped worshiping demons and idols made of gold, silver, bronze, stone, and wood, which cannot see, hear, or walk. ²¹ They did not turn away from committing murder, practicing witchcraft, sinning sexually, or stealing.

John Eats a Small Scroll

10 ¹ I saw another powerful angel come down from heaven. He was dressed in a cloud, and there was a rainbow over his head. His face was like the sun, and his feet were like columns of fire. ² He held a small, opened scroll in his hand. He set his right foot on the sea and his left on the land. ³ Then he shouted in a loud voice as a lion roars. When he shouted, the seven thunders spoke with voices of their own. ⁴ When the seven thunders spoke, I was going to write it down. I heard a voice from heaven say, "Seal up what the seven thunders have said, and don't write it down."

⁵ The angel whom I saw standing on the sea and on the land raised his right hand to heaven. ⁶ He swore an oath by the one who lives forever and ever, who created heaven and everything in it, the earth and everything in it, and the sea and everything in it. He said, "There will be no more delay. ⁷ In the days when the seventh angel is ready to blow his trumpet, the mystery of God will be completed, as he had made this Good News known to his servants, the prophets." ⁸ The voice which I had heard from heaven spoke to me again. It said, "Take the opened scroll from

the hand of the angel who is standing on the sea and on the land."
⁹ I went to the angel and asked him to give me the small scroll. He said to me, "Take it and eat it. It will be bitter in your stomach, but it will be as sweet as honey in your mouth."

¹⁰ I took the small scroll from the angel's hand and ate it. It was as sweet as honey in my mouth, but when I had eaten it, it was bitter in my stomach. ¹¹ The seven thunders told me, "Again you must speak what God has revealed in front of many people, nations, languages, and kings."

God's Two Witnesses

11 ¹ Then I was given a stick like a measuring stick. I was told, "Stand up and measure the temple of God and the altar. Count those who worship there. ² But do not measure the temple courtyard. Leave that out, because it is given to the nations, and they will trample the holy city for 42 months. ³ I will allow my two witnesses who wear sackcloth to speak what God has revealed. They will speak for 1,260 days."

⁴ These witnesses are the two olive trees and the two lamp stands standing in the presence of the Lord of the earth. ⁵ If anyone wants to hurt them, fire comes out of the witnesses' mouths and burns up their enemies. If anyone wants to hurt them, he must be killed the same way. ⁶ These witnesses have authority to shut the sky in order to keep rain from falling during the time they speak what God has revealed. They have authority to turn water into blood and to strike the earth with any plague as often as they want.

⁷ When the witnesses finish their testimony, the beast which comes from the bottomless pit will fight them, conquer them, and kill them. ⁸ Their dead bodies will lie on the street of the important city where their Lord was crucified. The spiritual names of that city are Sodom and Egypt. ⁹ For 32 days some members of the people, tribes, languages, and nations will look at the witnesses' dead bodies and will not allow anyone to bury them. ¹⁰ Those living on earth will gloat over the witnesses' death. They will celebrate

and send gifts to each other because these two prophets had tormented those living on earth.

¹¹ After 32 days the breath of life from God entered the two witnesses, and they stood on their feet. Great fear fell on those who watched them. ¹² The witnesses heard a loud voice from heaven calling to them, "Come up here." They went up to heaven in a cloud, and their enemies watched them. ¹³ At that moment a powerful earthquake struck. One-tenth of the city collapsed, 7,000 people were killed by the earthquake, and the rest were terrified. They gave glory to the God of heaven.

¹⁴ The second catastrophe is over. The third catastrophe will soon be here.

¹⁵ When the seventh angel blew his trumpet, there were loud voices in heaven, saying,

> "The kingdom of the world has become
>   the kingdom of our Lord and of his Messiah,
>   and he will rule as king forever and ever."

¹⁶ Then the 24 leaders, who were sitting on their thrones in God's presence, immediately bowed, worshiped God, ¹⁷ and said,

> "We give thanks to you, Lord God Almighty,
>   who is and who was,
>   because you have taken your great power
>   and have begun ruling as king.
> ¹⁸   The nations were angry, but your anger has come.
>   The time has come for the dead to be judged:
>   to reward your servants, the prophets,
>   your holy people,
>   and those who fear your name,
>   no matter if they are important or unimportant,
>   and to destroy those who destroy the earth."

¹⁹ God's temple in heaven was opened, and the ark of his promise was seen inside his temple. There was lightning, noise, thunder, an earthquake, and heavy hail.

Two Signs

12 ¹ A spectacular sign appeared in the sky: There was a woman who was dressed in the sun, who had the moon under her feet and a crown of 12 stars on her head. ² She was pregnant. She cried out from labor pains and the agony of giving birth.

³ Another sign appeared in the sky: a huge fiery red serpent with seven heads, ten horns, and seven crowns on its heads. ⁴ Its tail swept away one-third of the stars in the sky and threw them down to earth. The serpent stood in front of the woman who was going to give birth so that it could devour her child when it was born. ⁵ She gave birth to a son, a boy, who is to rule all the nations with an iron scepter. Her child was snatched away and taken to God and to his throne. ⁶ Then the woman fled into the wilderness where God had prepared a place for her so that she might be taken care of for 1,260 days.

⁷ Then a war broke out in heaven. Michael and his angels had to fight a war with the serpent. The serpent and its angels fought. ⁸ But it was not strong enough, and there was no longer any place for them in heaven. ⁹ The huge serpent was thrown down. That ancient snake, named Devil and Satan, the deceiver of the whole world, was thrown down to earth. Its angels were thrown down with it.

¹⁰ Then I heard a loud voice in heaven, saying,

> "Now the salvation, power, kingdom of our God,
>   and the authority of his Messiah have come.
> The one accusing our brothers and sisters,
>   the one accusing them day and night in the presence
>   of our God,
>   has been thrown out.
> ¹¹   They won the victory over him because of the blood
>   of the lamb
>   and the word of their testimony.
> They didn't love their life so much that they refused
>   to give it up.
> ¹²   Be glad for this reason, heavens and those who live in them.

> How horrible it is for the earth and the sea
>   because the Devil has come down to them
>   with fierce anger,
>   knowing that he has little time left."

[13] When the serpent saw that it had been thrown down to earth, it persecuted the woman who had given birth to the boy. [14] The woman was given the two wings of the large eagle in order to fly away from the snake to her place in the wilderness, where she could be taken care of for a time, times, and half a time. [15] The snake's mouth poured out a river of water behind the woman in order to sweep her away. [16] The earth helped the woman by opening its mouth and swallowing the river which had poured out of the serpent's mouth. [17] The serpent became angry with the woman. So it went away to fight with her other children, the ones who keep God's commands and hold on to the testimony of Jesus.

[18] The serpent stood on the sandy shore of the sea.[a]

The Beast From the Sea

13 [1] I saw a beast coming out of the sea. It had ten horns, seven heads, and ten crowns on its horns. There were insulting names on its heads. [2] The beast that I saw was like a leopard. Its feet were like bear's feet. Its mouth was like a lion's mouth. The serpent gave its power, kingdom, and far-reaching authority to the beast. [3] One of the beast's heads looked like it had a fatal wound, but its fatal wound was healed.

All the people of the world were amazed and followed the beast. [4] They worshiped the serpent because it had given authority to the beast. They also worshiped the beast and said, "Who is like the beast? Who can fight a war with it?" [5] The beast was allowed to speak arrogant and insulting things. It was given authority to act for 42 months. [6] It opened its mouth to insult God, to insult his name and his tent—those who are living in heaven. [7] It was allowed to wage war against God's holy people and to conquer them. It was also given

---

[a] 12:18 Some translations include this verse at the beginning of 13:1.

authority over every tribe, people, language, and nation. [8] Everyone living on earth will worship it, everyone whose name is not written in the Book of Life. That book belongs to the lamb who was slaughtered before the creation of the world.

[9] If anyone has ears, let him listen:

[10] If anyone is taken prisoner, he must go to prison.
  If anyone is killed with a sword, with a sword
    he must be killed.

In this situation God's holy people need endurance and confidence.

The Beast From the Earth

[11] I saw another beast come from the earth, and it had two horns like a lamb. It talked like a serpent. [12] The second beast uses all the authority of the first beast in its presence. The second beast makes the earth and those living on it worship the first beast, whose fatal wound was healed. [13] The second beast performs spectacular signs. It even makes fire come down from heaven to earth in front of people. [14] It deceives those living on earth with the signs that it is allowed to do in front of the ˌfirstˌ beast. It tells those living on earth to make a statue for the beast who was wounded by a sword and yet lived.

[15] The second beast was allowed to put breath into the statue of the ˌfirstˌ beast. Then the statue of the ˌfirstˌ beast could talk and put to death whoever would not worship it. [16] The second beast forces all people—important and unimportant people, rich and poor people, free people and slaves—to be branded on their right hands or on their foreheads. [17] It does this so that no one may buy or sell unless he has the brand, which is the beast's name or the number of its name.

[18] In this situation wisdom is needed. Let the person who has insight figure out the number of the beast, because it is a human number.[a] The beast's number is 666.

---

[a] 13:18 Or "it is the number of a human."

The New Song on Mount Zion

14 ¹I looked, and the lamb was standing on Mount Zion. There were 144,000 people with him who had his name and his Father's name written on their foreheads. ²Then I heard a sound from heaven like the noise of raging water and the noise of loud thunder. The sound I heard was like the music played by harpists. ³They were singing a new song in front of the throne, the four living creatures, and the leaders. Only the 144,000 people who had been bought on earth could learn the song.

⁴These 144,000 virgins are pure. They follow the lamb wherever he goes. They were bought from among humanity as the first ones offered to God and to the lamb. ⁵They've never told a lie. They are blameless.

The Harvest of the Earth

⁶I saw another angel flying overhead with the everlasting Good News to spread to those who live on earth—to every nation, tribe, language, and people. ⁷The angel said in a loud voice, "Fear God and give him glory, because the time has come for him to judge. Worship the one who made heaven and earth, the sea and springs."

⁸Another angel, a second one, followed him, and said, "Fallen! Babylon the Great has fallen! She has made all the nations drink the wine of her passionate sexual sins."

⁹Another angel, a third one, followed them, and said in a loud voice, "Whoever worships the beast or its statue, whoever is branded on his forehead or his hand, ¹⁰will drink the wine of God's fury, which has been poured unmixed into the cup of God's anger. Then he will be tortured by fiery sulfur in the presence of the holy angels and the lamb. ¹¹The smoke from their torture will go up forever and ever. There will be no rest day or night for those who worship the beast or its statue, or for anyone branded with its name." ¹²In this situation God's holy people, who obey his commands and keep their faith in Jesus, need endurance.

¹³I heard a voice from heaven saying, "Write this: From now on those who die believing in the Lord are blessed."

"Yes," says the Spirit. "Let them rest from their hard work. What they have done goes with them."

[14] Then I looked, and there was a white cloud, and on the cloud sat someone who was like the Son of Man. He had a gold crown on his head and a sharp sickle in his hand. [15] Another angel came out of the temple. He cried out in a loud voice to the one who sat on the cloud, "Swing your sickle, and gather the harvest. The time has come to gather it, because the harvest on the earth is overripe."

[16] The one who sat on the cloud swung his sickle over the earth, and the harvesting of the earth was completed.

[17] Another angel came out of the temple in heaven. He, too, had a sharp sickle. [18] Yet another angel came from the altar with authority over fire. This angel called out in a loud voice to the angel with the sharp sickle, "Swing your sickle, and gather the bunches of grapes from the vine of the earth, because those grapes are ripe." [19] The angel swung his sickle on the earth and gathered the grapes from the vine of the earth. He threw them into the winepress of God's anger. [20] The grapes were trampled in the winepress outside the city. Blood flowed out of the winepress as high as a horse's bridle for 1,600 stadia.[a]

Seven Angels With Seven Plagues

15 [1] I saw another sign in heaven. It was spectacular and amazing. There were seven angels with the last seven plagues which are the final expression of God's anger.

[2] Then I saw what looked like a sea of glass mixed with fire. Those who had won the victory over the beast, its statue, and the number of its name were standing on the glassy sea. They were holding God's harps [3] and singing the song of God's servant Moses and the song of the lamb. They sang,

"The things you do are spectacular and amazing,
    Lord God Almighty.
The way you do them is fair and true, King of the Nations.

---

[a] 14:20 One stadion is equivalent to 607 feet.

⁴   Lord, who won't fear and praise your name?
    You are the only holy one,
        and all the nations will come to worship you
            because they know about your fair judgments."

⁵ After these things I looked, and I saw that the temple of the tent containing the words of God's promise was open in heaven. ⁶ The seven angels with the seven plagues came out of the temple wearing clean, shining linen with gold belts around their waists. ⁷ One of the four living creatures gave seven gold bowls full of the anger of God, who lives forever and ever, to the seven angels. ⁸ The temple was filled with smoke from the glory of God and his power. No one could enter the temple until the seven plagues of the seven angels came to an end.

The Seven Angels Pour Out Their Bowls

16 ¹ I heard a loud voice from the temple saying to the seven angels, "Pour the seven bowls of God's anger over the earth."

² The first angel poured his bowl over the earth. Horrible, painful sores appeared on the people who had the brand of the beast and worshiped its statue.

³ The second angel poured his bowl over the sea. The sea turned into blood like the blood of a dead man, and every living thing in the sea died.

⁴ The third angel poured his bowl over the rivers and the springs. They turned into blood. ⁵ Then I heard the angel of the water say,

    "You are fair.
    You are the one who is and the one who was, the holy one,
        because you have judged these things.
⁶   You have given them blood to drink
    because they have poured out
        the blood of God's people and prophets.
        This is what they deserve."

[7] Then I heard the altar answer,

"Yes, Lord God Almighty, your judgments are true and fair."

[8] The fourth angel poured his bowl on the sun. The sun was allowed to burn people with fire. [9] They were severely burned. They cursed the name of God, who has the authority over these plagues. They would not change the way they think and act and give him glory.

[10] The fifth angel poured his bowl on the throne of the beast. Its kingdom turned dark. People gnawed on their tongues in anguish [11] and cursed the God of heaven for their pains and their sores. However, they would not stop what they were doing.

[12] The sixth angel poured his bowl on the great Euphrates River. The water in the river dried up to make a road for the kings from the east. [13] Then I saw three evil spirits like frogs come out of the mouths of the serpent, the beast, and the false prophet. [14] They are spirits of demons that do miracles. These spirits go to the kings of the whole world and gather them for the war on the frightening day of God Almighty.

[15] "See, I am coming like a thief. Blessed is the one who remains alert and doesn't lose his clothes. He will not have to go naked and let others see his shame."

[16] The spirits gathered the kings at the place which is called Armageddon in Hebrew.

[17] The seventh angel poured his bowl into the air. A loud voice came from the throne in the temple, and said, "It has happened!" [18] There was lightning, noise, thunder, and a powerful earthquake. There has never been such a powerful earthquake since humans have been on earth. [19] The important city split into three parts, and the cities of the nations fell. God remembered to give Babylon the Great the cup of wine from his fierce anger. [20] Every island vanished, and the mountains could no longer be seen. [21] Large, heavy hailstones fell from the sky on people. The people cursed God because the plague of hail was such a terrible plague.

Babylon the Great

17 [1] One of the seven angels who held the seven bowls came and said to me, "Come, I will show you the judgment of that notorious prostitute who sits on raging waters. [2] The kings of the earth had sex with her, and those living on earth became drunk on the wine of her sexual sins." [3] Then the angel carried me by his power into the wilderness.

I saw a woman sitting on a bright red beast covered with insulting names. It had seven heads and ten horns. [4] The woman wore purple clothes, bright red clothes, gold jewelry, gems, and pearls. In her hand she was holding a gold cup filled with detestable and evil things from her sexual sins. [5] A name was written on her forehead. The name was Mystery: Babylon the Great, the Mother of Prostitutes and Detestable Things of the Earth. [6] I saw that the woman was drunk with the blood of God's holy people and of those who testify about Jesus. I was very surprised when I saw her.

[7] The angel asked me, "Why are you surprised? I will tell you the mystery of the woman and the beast with the seven heads and the ten horns that carries her.

[8] "You saw the beast which once was, is no longer, and will come from the bottomless pit and go to its destruction. Those living on earth, whose names were not written in the Book of Life when the world was created, will be surprised when they see the beast because it was, is no longer, and will come again.

[9] "In this situation a wise mind is needed. The seven heads are seven mountains on which the woman is sitting. [10] They are also seven kings. Five of them have fallen, one is ruling now, and the other has not yet come. When he comes, he must remain for a little while. [11] The beast that was and is no longer is the eighth king. It belongs with the seven kings and goes to its destruction.

[12] "The ten horns that you saw are ten kings who have not yet started to rule. They will receive authority to rule as kings with the beast for one hour. [13] They have one purpose—to give their power

and authority to the beast. ¹⁴ They will go to war against the lamb. The lamb will conquer them because he is Lord of lords and King of kings. Those who are called, chosen, and faithful are with him."

¹⁵ The angel also said to me, "The waters you saw, on which the prostitute is sitting, are people, crowds, nations, and languages. ¹⁶ The ten horns and the beast you saw will hate the prostitute. They will leave her abandoned and naked. They will eat her flesh and burn her up in a fire. ¹⁷ God has made them do what he wants them to do. So they will give their kingdom to the beast until God's words are carried out. ¹⁸ The woman you saw is the important city which dominates the kings of the earth."

Babylon's Fall

18 ¹ After these things I saw another angel come from heaven. He had tremendous power, and his glory lit up the earth. ² He cried out in a powerful voice, "Fallen! Babylon the Great has fallen! She has become a home for demons. She is a prison for every evil spirit, every unclean^a bird, and every unclean and hated beast. ³ All the nations fell because of the wine of her sexual sins. The kings of the earth had sex with her. Her luxurious wealth has made the merchants of the earth rich."

⁴ I heard another voice from heaven saying, "Come out of Babylon, my people, so that you do not participate in her sins and suffer from any of her plagues. ⁵ Her sins are piled as high as heaven, and God has remembered her crimes. ⁶ Do to her what she has done. Give her twice as much as she gave. Serve her a drink in her own cup twice as large as the drink she served others. ⁷ She gave herself glory and luxury. Now give her just as much torture and misery. She says to herself, 'I'm a queen on a throne, not a widow. I'll never be miserable.' ⁸ For this reason her plagues of death, misery, and starvation will come in a single day. She will be burned up in a fire, because the Lord God, who judges her, is powerful.

⁹ "The kings of the earth who had sex with her and lived in luxury with her will cry and mourn over her when they see the

---

^a 18:2 "Unclean" refers to anything that Moses' Teachings say is not presentable to God.

smoke rise from her raging fire. [10] Frightened by her torture, they will stand far away and say,

> 'How horrible, how horrible it is for that important city,
>> the powerful city Babylon!
> In one moment judgment has come to it!'

[11] "The merchants of the earth cry and mourn over her, because no one buys their cargo anymore. [12] No one buys their cargo of gold, silver, gems, pearls, fine linen, purple cloth, silk, bright red cloth, all kinds of citron wood, articles made of ivory and very costly wood, bronze, iron, marble, [13] cinnamon, spices, incense, perfume, frankincense, wine, olive oil, flour, wheat, cattle, sheep, horses, wagons, slaves (that is, humans).

[14]   'The fruit you craved is gone.
>> All your luxuries and your splendor have disappeared.
>> No one will ever find them again.'

[15] "Frightened by her torture, the merchants who had become rich by selling these things will stand far away. They will cry and mourn, [16] saying,

> 'How horrible, how horrible for that important city
>> which was wearing fine linen, purple clothes,
>>> bright red clothes, gold jewelry, gems, and pearls.
[17]   In one moment all this wealth has been destroyed!'

Every ship's captain, everyone who traveled by ship, sailors, and everyone who made their living from the sea stood far away. [18] When they saw the smoke rise from her raging fire, they repeatedly cried out, 'Was there ever a city as important as this?' [19] Then they threw dust on their heads and shouted while crying and mourning,

> 'How horrible, how horrible for that important city.
>> Everyone who had a ship at sea
>>> grew rich because of that city's high prices.
> In one moment it has been destroyed!'

²⁰ "Gloat over it, heaven, God's people, apostles, and prophets.
God has condemned it for you."

²¹ Then a powerful angel picked up a stone that was like a large
millstone. He threw it into the sea and said,

"The important city Babylon will be thrown down with
the same force.
It will never be found again.
²² The sound of harpists, musicians, flutists, and trumpeters
will never be heard in it again.
Skilled craftsman
will never be found in it again.
The sound of a millstone
will never be heard in it again.
²³ Light from lamps
will never shine in it again.
Voices of brides and grooms
will never be heard in it again.
Its merchants were the important people of the world,
because all the nations were deceived by its witchcraft.

²⁴ "The blood of prophets, God's people, and everyone who had
been murdered on earth was found in it."

The Lamb's Wedding

19 ¹ After these things I heard what sounded like the loud
noise from a large crowd in heaven, saying,

"Hallelujah!
Salvation, glory, and power belong to our God.
² His judgments are true and fair.
He has condemned the notorious prostitute
who corrupted the world with her sexual sins.
He has taken revenge on her for the blood
of his servants."

³ A second time they said, "Hallelujah! The smoke goes up from her forever and ever." ⁴ The 24 leaders and the 4 living creatures bowed and worshiped God, who was sitting on the throne. They said, "Amen! Hallelujah!" ⁵ A voice came from the throne. It said, "Praise our God, all who serve and fear him, no matter who you are."

⁶ I heard what sounded like the noise from a large crowd, like the noise of raging waters, like the noise of loud thunder, saying,

"Hallelujah! The Lord our God, the Almighty,
has become king.

⁷   Let us rejoice, be happy, and give him glory
because it's time for the marriage of the lamb.
His bride has made herself ready.

⁸   She has been given the privilege of wearing
dazzling, pure linen."

This fine linen represents the things that God's holy people do that have his approval.

⁹ Then the angel said to me, "Write this: 'Blessed are those who are invited to the lamb's wedding banquet.'" He also told me, "These are the true words of God." ¹⁰ I bowed at his feet to worship him. But he told me, "Don't do that! I am your coworker and a coworker of the Christians who hold on to the testimony of Jesus. Worship God, because the testimony of Jesus is the spirit of prophecy!"

The Great Banquet of God

¹¹ I saw heaven standing open. There was a white horse, and its rider is named Faithful and True. With integrity he judges and wages war. ¹² His eyes are flames of fire. On his head are many crowns. He has a name written on him, but only he knows what it is. ¹³ He wears clothes dipped in blood, and his name is the Word of God.

¹⁴ The armies of heaven, wearing pure, white linen, follow him on white horses. ¹⁵ A sharp sword comes out of his mouth to defeat the nations. He will rule them with an iron scepter and tread the winepress of the fierce anger of God Almighty. ¹⁶ On his clothes

and his thigh he has a name written: King of kings and Lord of lords.

¹⁷ I saw an angel standing in the sun. He cried out in a loud voice to all the birds flying overhead, "Come! Gather for the great banquet of God. ¹⁸ Eat the flesh of kings, generals, warriors, horses and their riders, and all free people and slaves, both important or insignificant people."

¹⁹ I saw the beast, the kings of the earth, and their armies gathered to wage war against the rider on the horse and his army. ²⁰ The beast and the false prophet who had done miracles for the beast were captured. By these miracles the false prophet had deceived those who had the brand of the beast and worshiped its statue. Both of them were thrown alive into the fiery lake of burning sulfur. ²¹ The rider on the horse killed the rest with the sword that came out of his mouth. All the birds gorged themselves on the flesh of those who had been killed.

An Angel Overpowers the Devil

20 ¹ I saw an angel coming down from heaven, holding the key to the bottomless pit and a large chain in his hand. ² He overpowered the serpent, that ancient snake, named Devil and Satan. The angel chained up the serpent for 1,000 years. ³ He threw it into the bottomless pit. The angel shut and sealed the pit over the serpent to keep it from deceiving the nations anymore until the 1,000 years were over. After that it must be set free for a little while.

⁴ I saw thrones, and those who sat on them were allowed to judge. Then I saw the souls of those whose heads had been cut off because of their testimony about Jesus and because of the word of God. They had not worshiped the beast or its statue and were not branded on their foreheads or hands. They lived and ruled with Christ for 1,000 years. ⁵ The rest of the dead did not live until the 1,000 years ended.

This is the first time that people come back to life. ⁶ Blessed and holy are those who are included the first time that people come back to life. The second death has no power over them. They will continue to be priests of God and Christ. They will rule with him for 1,000 years.

The Final Judgment

⁷ When 1,000 years are over, Satan will be freed from his prison. ⁸ He will go out to deceive Gog and Magog, the nations in the four corners of the earth, and gather them for war. They will be as numerous as the grains of sand on the seashore. ⁹ I saw that they spread over the broad expanse of the earth and surrounded the camp of God's holy people and the beloved city. Fire came from heaven and burned them up. ¹⁰ The devil, who deceived them, was thrown into the fiery lake of sulfur, where the beast and the false prophet were also thrown. They will be tortured day and night forever and ever.

¹¹ I saw a large, white throne and the one who was sitting on it. The earth and the sky fled from his presence, but no place was found for them. ¹² I saw the dead, both important and unimportant people, standing in front of the throne. Books were opened, including the Book of Life. The dead were judged on the basis of what they had done, as recorded in the books. ¹³ The sea gave up its dead. Death and hell gave up their dead. People were judged based on what they had done. ¹⁴ Death and hell were thrown into the fiery lake. (The fiery lake is the second death.) ¹⁵ Those whose names were not found in the Book of Life were thrown into the fiery lake.

A New Heaven and a New Earth

21 ¹ I saw a new heaven and a new earth, because the first heaven and earth had disappeared, and the sea was gone. ² Then I saw the holy city, New Jerusalem, coming down from God out of heaven, dressed like a bride ready for her husband. ³ I heard a loud voice from the throne say, "God lives with humans! God will make his home with them, and they will be his people. God himself will be with them and be their God. ⁴ He will wipe every tear from their eyes. There won't be any more death. There won't be any grief, crying, or pain, because the first things have disappeared."

⁵ The one sitting on the throne said, "I am making everything new." He said, "Write this: 'These words are faithful and true.' " ⁶ He said to me, "It has happened! I am the A and the Z,ᵃ the beginning and the end. I will give a drink from the fountain filled with the water of life to anyone who is thirsty. It won't cost anything. ⁷ Everyone who wins the victory will inherit these things. I will be their God, and they will be my children. ⁸ But cowardly, unfaithful, and detestable people, murderers, sexual sinners, sorcerers, idolaters, and all liars will find themselves in the fiery lake of burning sulfur. This is the second death."

A New Jerusalem

⁹ One of the seven angels who had the seven bowls full of the last seven plagues came to me and said, "Come! I will show you the bride, the wife of the lamb." ¹⁰ He carried me by his power away to a large, high mountain. He showed me the holy city, Jerusalem, coming down from God out of heaven. ¹¹ It had the glory of God. Its light was like a valuable gem, like gray quartz, as clear as crystal. ¹² It had a large, high wall with 12 gates. Twelve angels were at the gates. The names of the 12 tribes of Israel were written on the gates. ¹³ There were three gates on the east, three gates on the north, three gates on the south, and three gates on the west. ¹⁴ The wall of the city had 12 foundations. The 12 names of the 12 apostles of the lamb were written on them.

¹⁵ The angel who was talking to me had a gold measuring stick to measure the city, its gates, and its wall. ¹⁶ The city was square. It was as wide as it was long. He measured the city with the stick. It was 12,000 stadiaᵇ long. Its length, width, and height were the same. ¹⁷ He measured its wall. According to human measurement, which the angel was using, it was 144 cubits.ᶜ ¹⁸ Its wall was made of gray quartz. The city was made of pure gold, as clear as glass. ¹⁹ The foundations of the city wall were beautifully decorated with all kinds of gems: The first foundation was gray quartz, the second

---

ᵃ 21:6 Or "the Alpha and the Omega."   ᵇ 21:16 One stadion is equivalent to 607 feet.
ᶜ 21:17 One cubit is equivalent to 21 inches.

sapphire, the third agate, the fourth emerald, [20] the fifth onyx, the sixth red quartz, the seventh yellow quartz, the eighth beryl, the ninth topaz, the tenth green quartz, the eleventh jacinth, and the twelfth amethyst. [21] The 12 gates were 12 pearls. Each gate was made of one pearl. The street of the city was made of pure gold, as clear as glass.

[22] I did not see any temple in it, because the Lord God Almighty and the lamb are its temple. [23] The city doesn't need any sun or moon to give it light because the glory of God gave it light. The lamb was its lamp. [24] The nations will walk in its light, and the kings of the earth will bring their glory into it. [25] Its gates will be open all day. They will never close because there won't be any night there. [26] They will bring the glory and wealth of the nations into the holy city. [27] Nothing unclean,[d] no one who does anything detestable, and no liars will ever enter it. Only those whose names are written in the lamb's Book of Life will enter it.

22 [1] The angel showed me a river filled with the water of life, as clear as crystal. It was flowing from the throne of God and the lamb. [2] Between the street of the city and the river there was a tree of life visible from both sides. It produced 12 kinds of fruit. Each month had its own fruit. The leaves of the tree will heal the nations. [3] There will no longer be any curse. The throne of God and the lamb will be in the city. His servants will worship him [4] and see his face. His name will be on their foreheads. [5] There will be no more night, and they will not need any light from lamps or the sun because the Lord God will shine on them. They will rule as kings forever and ever.

Jesus Says: I'm Coming Soon

[6] He said to me, "These words are trustworthy and true. The Lord God of the spirits of the prophets has sent his angel to show his servants the things that must happen soon. [7] I'm coming soon! Blessed is the one who follows the words of the prophecy in this book."

---

[d] 21:27 "Unclean" refers to anything that Moses' Teachings say is not presentable to God.

[8] I, John, heard and saw these things. When I had heard and seen them, I bowed to worship at the feet of the angel who had been showing me these things. [9] He told me, "Don't do that! I am your coworker. I work with other Christians, the prophets, and those who follow the words in this book. Worship God!"

[10] Then the angel said to me, "Don't seal up the words of the prophecy in this book because the time is near. [11] Let those who don't have God's approval go without it, and let filthy people continue to be filthy. Let those who have God's approval continue to have it, and let holy people continue to be holy."

[12] "I'm coming soon! I will bring my reward with me to pay all people based on what they have done. [13] I am the A and the Z,[a] the first and the last, the beginning and the end.

[14] "Blessed are those who wash their robes so that they may have the right to the tree of life and may go through the gates into the city. [15] Outside are dogs, sorcerers, sexual sinners, murderers, idolaters, and all who lie in what they say and what they do.

[16] "I, Jesus, have sent my angel to give this testimony to you for the churches. I am the root and descendant of David. I am the bright morning star."

[17] The Spirit and the bride say, "Come!" Let those who hear this say, "Come!" Let those who are thirsty come! Let those who want the water of life take it as a gift.

[18] I warn everyone who hears the words of the prophecy in this book: If anyone adds anything to this, God will strike him with the plagues that are written in this book. [19] If anyone takes away any words from this book of prophecy, God will take away his portion of the tree of life and the holy city that are described in this book.

[20] The one who is testifying to these things says, "Yes, I'm coming soon!"

Amen! Come, Lord Jesus!

[21] The good will[b] of the Lord Jesus be with all of you. Amen!

---

[a] 22:13 Or "the Alpha and the Omega."   [b] 22:21 Or "grace."

About the Translation

GOD'S WORD® *Is New*

The twentieth century produced more Bible translations than any other. This includes English as well as foreign language translations. *GOD'S WORD*, produced by God's Word to the Nations, fills a need that has remained unmet by English Bibles: to communicate in clear, natural English to God's people today without compromising the Bible's saving, life-changing message. This translation is an exceptional literary work that consciously combines scholarly fidelity with natural English.

Traditionally, the Scriptures have been translated into English by teams of Bible scholars serving part-time. This translation employed full-time Bible scholars and full-time English editorial reviewers. *GOD'S WORD* is the first English Bible in which English reviewers have been actively involved with scholars at every stage of the translation process.

Because of the involvement of English reviewers, *GOD'S WORD* looks and reads like contemporary English literature. It uses natural grammar, follows standard punctuation and capitalization rules, and is printed in a single column. Because of the involvement of scholars, *GOD'S WORD* is an accurate, trustworthy translation.

GOD'S WORD Is for Everyone

One of the goals of *GOD'S WORD* is to communicate the saving, life-changing Good News about Jesus. *GOD'S WORD* is intended to be read by those who are well-versed in Scripture as well as first-time Bible readers, Christians as well as non-Christians, adults as well as children.

God's Word Is a Translation

Of course, the Word of God didn't originally come to us in the English language. Since many people have wanted to read the Scriptures in their own language, scholars have found it necessary to translate the Bible from the original Hebrew, Aramaic, and Greek texts. Like many Bibles published before it, God's Word has been translated directly from those original languages. Unlike Bibles before it, however, the translation theory used to produce God's Word is different because the theory and practice of translation has advanced through the years.

The oldest theory of translation is form-equivalent translation (often inaccurately called literal translation). In this type of translation, the translator chooses one of a limited number of meanings assigned to each Hebrew, Aramaic, or Greek word. The translator fills in the words that belong in the sentence but follows the word arrangement and grammar that is characteristic of the original language. Such a translation is often viewed as accurate. However, it can result in awkward, misleading, incomprehensible, or even amusing sentences. For instance, a form-equivalent translation of 1 Samuel 9:2 could read: "From his shoulders upward Saul was taller than any of the people." In English this implies that Saul had a misshapen head and neck. Translations using this theory have made the Bible more difficult to read and understand in English than it was in the original languages.

A newer theory of translation is function-equivalent translation (often inaccurately called paraphrasing). In this type of translation, the translator tries to make the English function the same way the original language functioned for the original readers. However, in trying to make the translation easy to read, the translator can omit concepts from the original text that don't seem to have corresponding modern English equivalents. Such a translation can produce a readable text, but that text can convey the wrong meaning or not enough meaning. Furthermore, function-equivalent translations attempt to make some books readable on levels at which they were not intended. For instance, Song of Songs was not written for children. Paul's letter to the Ephesians is very sophisticated and not intended for novices.

The theory followed by God's Word to the Nations is closest natural equivalent translation. The first consideration for the translators of GOD'S WORD was to find equivalent English ways of expressing the meaning of the original Hebrew, Aramaic, or Greek text. This procedure ensures that the translation is faithful to the meaning intended by the original writer. The next consideration was readability. The meaning is expressed in natural English by using common English punctuation, capitalization, grammar, and word choice. The third consideration was to choose the natural equivalent that most closely reflects the style of the Hebrew, Aramaic, or Greek text. This translation theory is designed to avoid the awkwardness and inaccuracy associated with form-equivalent translation, and it avoids the loss of meaning and oversimplification associated with function-equivalent translation.

Features of GOD'S WORD

Layout
The features that distinguish GOD'S WORD from other Bible translations are designed to aid readers. The most obvious of these is the open, single-column format. This invites readers

into the page. The single column takes the Bible out of the reference book category and presents it as the literary work that God intended it to be.

In prose GOD'S WORD looks like other works of literature. It contains frequent paragraphing. Whenever a different speaker's words are quoted, a new paragraph begins. Lists, genealogies, and long prayers are formatted to help readers recognize the thought pattern of the text. The prose style of GOD'S WORD favors concise, clear sentences. While avoiding very long, complicated sentences, which characterize many English Bible translations, GOD'S WORD strives to vary the word arrangement in a natural way. Doing this brings the Scriptures to life.

Poetry in GOD'S WORD is instantly recognized by its format. The single-column format enables readers to recognize parallel thoughts in parallel lines of poetry. In a single-column, across-the-page layout, a variety of indentations are possible. The mission society's translators have used indentation to indicate the relationship of one line to others in the same context. This enables a person reading the Bible in English to appreciate the Bible's poetry in much the same way a person reading the Bible in the original languages of Hebrew, Aramaic, or Greek would appreciate it.

Punctuation, Capitalization

In English, meaning is conveyed not only by words but also by punctuation. However, no punctuation existed in ancient Hebrew and Greek writing, and words were used where English grammar would prefer punctuation marks. GOD'S WORD strives to use standard English punctuation wherever possible. At times this means that a punctuation mark or paragraph break represents the meaning that could only be expressed in words in Hebrew or Greek.

Italics are also used as they would be in other printed English texts: for foreign words or to indicate that a word is used as a word. (GOD'S WORD never uses italics to indicate emphasis.)

Wherever possible, GOD'S WORD has supplied information in headings or half-brackets to identify the speaker in quoted material. To minimize the confusion produced by quotations within quotations, quotation marks are used sparingly. For instance, they are not used after formulaic statements such as "This is what the LORD says:…"

Contractions can fit comfortably into many English sentences. Certainly, "Don't you care that we're going to die" is less stiff than, "Do you not care that we are going to die?" GOD'S WORD achieves a warmer style by using contractions where appropriate. However, uncontracted words are used in contexts that require special emphasis.

GOD'S WORD capitalizes the first letter in proper nouns and sentences and all the letters in the word LORD when it represents Yahweh, the name of God in the Old Testament. Some religious literature chooses to capitalize pronouns that refer to the deity. As in the original languages, GOD'S WORD does not capitalize any pronouns (unless they begin sentences). In some cases scholars are uncertain whether pronouns in the original texts refer to God or someone else. In these cases the presence of capitalized pronouns would be misleading. However, when the Hebrew or Greek pronouns are not ambiguous, but an English pronoun would be, GOD'S WORD uses the appropriate proper noun in its place.

Gender References

The Scriptures contain many passages that apply to all people. Therefore, *GOD'S WORD* strives to use gender-neutral language in these passages so that all readers will apply these passages to themselves. For example, traditionally, Psalm 1:1 has been translated, "Blessed is the man who does not follow the advice of the wicked..." As a result, many readers will understand this verse to mean that only adult males, not women or children, can receive a blessing. However, in *GOD'S WORD* the first Psalm begins "Blessed is the person who does not follow the advice of the wicked..."

However, if a passage focuses upon an individual, *GOD'S WORD* does not use plural nouns and pronouns to avoid the gender-specific pronouns *he, him,* and *his.* In these cases the translators considered the text's focus upon an individual more important than an artificial use of plural pronouns. In addition, gender-specific language is preserved in passages that apply specifically to men or specifically to women.

Word Choice

Many Bible translations contain theological terms that have little, if any, meaning for most nontheologically-trained readers. *GOD'S WORD* avoids using these terms and substitutes words that carry the same meaning in common English. In some cases traditional theological words are contained in footnotes the first time they occur in a chapter. Examples of these theological terms include *covenant, grace, justify, repent,* and *righteousness.*

While all these features make *GOD'S WORD* a uniquely readable and understandable Bible, the ultimate goal of the mission society is to bring the readers of *GOD'S WORD* into a new or closer relationship with Jesus. The translation team and support staff of God's Word to the Nations pray that your reading of *GOD'S WORD* makes the words of our great God and Savior, as revealed through his prophets and apostles, come to life for you.

For more details on the translation process and the unique features that enable *GOD'S WORD* to accurately and clearly communicate God's saving, life-changing message, contact God's Word to the Nations or Green Key Books.

Notes on the Text of *GOD'S WORD*

Brackets

Proper names or foreign words whose meaning is significant for understanding a particular Bible passage are translated in brackets ([ ]) following the name or phrase. When reading aloud a bracketed word may be treated as "that is."

Half-brackets (⌞ ⌟) enclose words that the translation team supplied because the context contains meaning that is not explicitly stated in the original language.

Footnotes

Five types of footnotes are used in *GOD'S WORD*:

1. Explanatory footnotes clarify historical, cultural, and geographical details from the ancient world to make the text more understandable to modern readers. These footnotes also identify word play in Hebrew or Greek that would otherwise be lost to the English reader.
2. Alternate translation footnotes offer other plausible translations. They are introduced by the word *or.*
3. Footnotes that state "English equivalent difficult" mark passages where a Hebrew or Greek expression cannot be adequately translated into modern English without resorting to a long, inappropriate paraphrase.

565

4. Footnotes that state "Hebrew meaning uncertain" or "Greek meaning uncertain" mark passages where scholars are not sure what a Hebrew or Greek expression means.

5. Textual footnotes are included wherever *GOD'S WORD* translates the meaning of some text other than the Masoretic Text printed in *Biblia Hebraica Stuttgartensia* or its footnotes (Old Testament) or the Greek text printed in the twenty-seventh edition of *Novum Testamentum Graece* (New Testament).

Terms Used In Footnotes

Aramaic	one of the languages of the Old Testament, related to Hebrew
Dead Sea Scrolls	one or more of the Qumran manuscripts
Egyptian	one or more of the ancient translations of the Bible into the ancient Egyptian or Ethiopic languages
Greek	in the Old Testament: one or more of the ancient Greek translations of the Old Testament; in the New Testament: the Greek language, the language of the New Testament
Hebrew	the primary language of the Old Testament
Latin	one or more of the ancient Latin translations of the Bible
Masoretic Text	the traditional Hebrew text of the Old Testament
manuscript	an ancient, handwritten copy of a text
Samaritan Pentateuch	Samaritan Hebrew version of the first five books of the Bible
Syriac	the ancient Syriac translation of the Bible
Targum	one of the ancient Aramaic translations of the Old Testament